The Globalization Reader

Fifth Edition

Edited by

Frank J. Lechner
and John Boli

This fifth edition first published 2015
Editorial material and organization © 2015 John Wiley & Sons, Ltd
Edition history: Blackwell Publishers Ltd (1e, 2000), Blackwell Publishing Ltd (2e, 2004 and 3e, 2008),
John Wiley & Sons, Ltd (4e, 2012)

Registered Office
John Wiley & Sons, Ltd, The Atrium, Southern Gate, Chichester, West Sussex, PO19 8SQ, UK

Editorial Offices
350 Main Street, Malden, MA 02148-5020, USA
9600 Garsington Road, Oxford, OX4 2DQ, UK
The Atrium, Southern Gate, Chichester, West Sussex, PO19 8SQ, UK

For details of our global editorial offices, for customer services, and for information about how to apply for
permission to reuse the copyright material in this book please see our website at www.wiley.com/wiley-blackwell.

The right of Frank J. Lechner and John Boli to be identified as the authors of the editorial material in this work has
been asserted in accordance with the UK Copyright, Designs and Patents Act 1988.

Library of Congress Cataloging-in-Publication Data

The globalization reader / edited by Frank J. Lechner and John Boli. – Fifth Edition.
    pages cm
  Includes bibliographical references and index.
  ISBN 978-1-118-73355-4 (pbk.)
1. International economic relations.   2. International economic relations–Social aspects.   3. International
economic integration.   4. Globalization.   5. Anti-globalization movement.   I. Lechner, Frank J.,
editor.   II. Boli, John, 1948– editor.
  HF1359.G59 2015
  337–dc23
                                          2014030307

A catalogue record for this book is available from the British Library.

Cover image: Photo © Ed Honowitz / Getty Images

Set in 11/13pt Dante by SPi Publisher Services, Pondicherry, India

Printed in Singapore by C.O.S. Printers Pte Ltd

3   2015

Contents

Preface to the Fifth Edition

In this fifth edition of *The Globalization Reader*, we retain several features of the previous editions:

- *Purpose:* Our goal is to provide a variety of perspectives on different dimensions of globalization, thus conveying its importance and complexity.
- *Structure:* Like its predecessors, this book is organized into sections covering many aspects of globalization, from theoretical to experiential, and from economic to cultural.
- *Issues:* The *Reader* illustrates many issues related to globalization, including trends in global inequality, the specter of greater cultural homogeneity, and the movement for global justice.
- *Selections:* As in the fourth edition, we draw from several disciplines to offer a diverse sample of high-quality, readable scholarly work on globalization.

To reflect new developments and to make the *Reader* even more useful and engaging, we have also made some changes:

- *Introductions:* We have updated several editorial introductions.
- *New section:* We have added a new section on globalization and identity, covering aspects of individual and collective identity with examples ranging geographically from Nepal to Senegal.
- *Revised sections:* We have enhanced various sections as follows:
    - A new item offering a critical perspective in the section on debating globalization
    - A new item on neoliberalism in the section on explanations of globalization
    - New items on food, health, and tourism, covering Jamaica, Dubai, Haiti, and Japan, in the section on global experience
    - New items on inequality, poverty, and the economic crisis in the section on economic globalization

- o New items on women's rights in Iran, the trade in "blood diamonds," and microfinance and development in the section on civil society
  - o A new item on global warming in the section on the environment
  - o A new item on the global justice movement in the section on that topic.
- *A wider range of voices:* The selections represent both established and younger scholars with diverse backgrounds, and new items add authors from Australia, Belgium, India, the Netherlands, and Switzerland.

As always, we hope this updated edition will help both new and returning readers make better sense of globalization.

Frank Lechner and John Boli

General Introduction

Globalization means different things to different people. To a Korean Pentecostal missionary, it means new opportunities to spread the faith and convert lost souls abroad. To a Dominican immigrant in the United States, it means growing new roots while staying deeply involved in the home village. To an Indian television viewer, it means sampling a variety of new shows, some adapted from foreign formats. To a Chinese apparel worker, it means a chance to escape rural poverty by cutting threads off designer jeans. To an American shoe company executive, it means managing a far-flung supply chain to get products to stores. To a Filipino global justice advocate, it means rules of the global game that favor the rich North over the poor South. For all their diversity, these examples have something in common. They indicate some of the many ways in which more people become more closely connected across larger distances, and grow more aware of their connections as well. "Globalization" captures that process. Of course, new connections entail new risks, as the economic crisis that started in 2007 brought home to many people, when the troubles of Americans unable to pay their mortgages cascaded across the world economy. As the pull-back in trade and investment during that episode showed, connections can be broken, our shared awareness can be put to the test; globalization does not march forward along a smooth path. Caveats aside, however, the record of global change since World War II is quite striking: more people and places have become more interdependent and have organized their new connections in more intricate ways. For all the fault lines it still displays, a new global society, not just a world economy, has been growing all around us. How to guide its growth, how to make it work for most, and how to understand the process are key challenges of the years to come. As a way to help meet those challenges, the selections compiled in this *Reader* aim to describe and explain the course of globalization and the shape of its outcomes.

The Globalization Reader, Fifth Edition. Edited by Frank J. Lechner and John Boli.
Editorial material and organization © 2015 John Wiley & Sons, Ltd.
Published 2015 by John Wiley & Sons, Ltd.

What does globalization involve? Globalization refers to the processes by which more people across large distances become connected in more and different ways. They can become connected very simply by doing or experiencing the same sort of thing. For example, Japanese cuisine "globalizes" when more people on different continents enjoy the taste of sushi. Since the nineteenth century soccer has become globalized as players and fans in many countries took an interest in the game. Though many people lack access to good medicine, parents the world over routinely decide to immunize their children against major diseases. These are instances of diffusion: ways of thinking, acting, or feeling spread widely. Such diffusion increased greatly in recent decades as the infrastructure for communication and transportation improved dramatically, connecting groups, institutions, and countries in new ways. The spread of sushi involved not just a shared consumer experience; it also made many American fishermen dependent on a Japanese market as tuna caught off the US coast is sold and shipped overseas. In soccer, the professional prospects of great players from South America depend on the demand from European teams. The health of many children depends on breakthroughs in distant laboratories and an intricate global system for dispensing medication; at the same time, the movement of people around the globe also exposes people to new health risks. For good and ill, such links make more people more interdependent. These links are molded into new organizational forms as regional institutions go global or new ones take shape on the world stage. For example, international law governs who can fish in coastal waters, and the World Trade Organization handles disputes between members, including the United States and Japan. FIFA is an international nongovernmental organization that sets the rules of soccer and organizes major tournaments such as the World Cup. The World Health Organization, as well as more informal networks of professionals and volunteers, organizes campaigns to address major health threats.

Such institutions, which have emerged in many areas of human activity, reflect increasingly common knowledge and awareness. Eating sushi, watching the World Cup, and getting a hepatitis B shot involve elements of world culture – the meaning of sushi, the application of the offside rule, or the reason for immunization are known to consumers, fans, and patients regardless of their location. Even if they do not know the larger structures, their everyday life is nevertheless embedded in a world culture that transcends their village, town, or country, and that becomes part of individual and collective identities. As people become more intricately connected to many others across large distances – not all people to the same extent, of course – the world is becoming a "single place." Globalization thus involves growing diffusion, expanding interdependence, more transnational institutions, and an emerging world culture and consciousness – all aspects of the connectedness at the heart of globalization, all elements of the world society globalization is creating.

Is globalization new? Many scholars point to sixteenth-century Europe as the original source of globalization. After all, the Europeans established worldwide trade connections on their own terms, brought their culture to different regions by settling vast areas, and defined the ways in which different peoples were to interact with each other. Economically and culturally, the modern world system already existed nearly five centuries ago. Others point to the late nineteenth century as a period of intense globalization, when millions migrated, trade greatly expanded, and new norms and organizations came to govern international conduct. At the beginning of the twentieth century, such scholars would stress, the movement of people, goods, and finance across national borders was at least as free and significant as it is today.

We agree that globalization has been happening for a long time, a point illustrated in a selection in Part III. We also agree that specific features of world society have their roots in earlier periods. We add, however, that the second half of the twentieth century was a significant period of globalization in its own right. World War II gave globalization a new impetus. Obscured by Cold War divisions, the transformation of world society in the past six decades – in terms of linkages, institutions, and culture and consciousness – was nevertheless profound. This *Reader* includes selections from scholars skeptical of this claim, but it also illustrates by many examples that globalization has entered a new phase.

Is globalization driven by the expanding market? The pursuit of economic opportunity has long sent merchants around the globe, and powerful states have supported their profit-seeking activities. Capitalism knows no bounds, as Marx noted more than a century ago. Marx expected the European economy to become a truly global system, and in many ways it has. In recent years, the integration of financial markets has added a new kind of interdependence. To us, this does not mean that globalization is first and foremost an economic project. While an economic system operating along capitalist lines now encompasses most regions of the world, and economic motives always have been important in creating global linkages, globalization takes place in many spheres for many reasons. The economy may be a driving force in creating global change in some periods, but its effects depend on what happens outside of world markets. To understand the world economy, then, one also needs to understand world society. Accordingly, this *Reader* presents a comprehensive picture of globalization, covering economic, political, cultural, and experiential dimensions.

Does globalization make the world more homogeneous? This question would seem to answer itself: If certain activities or institutions become global, they must displace existing, locally variable activities and institutions. If there are more global linkages, global institutions, and global values, presumably this means that more people will have more in common. To many critics of globalization, this seemingly neutral description is nefarious. Globalization is the work of the West, they argue. Markets set Western rules for economic activity; one kind of Western state has taken hold around the world; by controlling information flows, Western media companies shape global consciousness; the popular culture of "McWorld" is of mostly Western origin. Globalization thus entails cultural imperialism.

We agree that some things become more similar around the world as globalization proceeds. There is only one World Trade Organization and it enforces one set of trade rules; there is only one kind of bureaucratic state that societies can legitimately adopt. But we do not think this leads to a homogeneous world, for three reasons. First, general rules and models are interpreted in light of local circumstances. Thus, regions respond to similar economic constraints in different ways; countries still have great leeway in structuring their own policies; the same television program means different things to different audiences; McDonald's adapts its menu and marketing to local tastes. Second, growing similarity provokes reactions. Advocates for many cultures seek to protect their heritage or assert their identity. Witness the efforts of fundamentalists to reinstate what they consider orthodoxy, the actions of indigenous peoples to claim their right to cultural survival, and the attempt of Asian leaders to put forth a distinctive Asian model of human rights. Third, cultural and political differences have themselves become globally valid. The notion that people and countries are entitled to their particularity or distinctiveness is itself part of global culture. The tension between homogeneity and heterogeneity is integral to globalization, and this *Reader* illustrates it in several ways.

Does globalization determine local events? In recent years, Afghan girls returned to school after the United States defeated the Taliban regime; a war crimes tribunal in The Hague handed down convictions for atrocities committed during the war in Bosnia; African countries struggled to achieve progress as parts of their educated classes succumbed to AIDS; and melting glaciers raised concern about the impact of global warming. Around the world, local events bear the imprint of global processes. It would be easy to infer that local autonomy and local tradition must fall by the wayside, but globalization is not a one-way street. To be sure, local and global events become more and more intertwined, as illustrated by the way a global "war on terror" enhances the educational opportunities of some Muslim women, by the role of global institutions in dealing with the aftermath of major regional conflicts, by the domestic reverberations of a global epidemic, and by the way global climate change alters the habitat of specific groups. But the local feeds into the global as well. Both their own desires and the Taliban's failures helped to change the fortunes of Afghan women; the Bosnian war provoked the innovative establishment of a war crimes tribunal to vindicate global principles; domestic hesitations and constraints contribute to the spread of HIV/AIDS in many countries; global warming results from the release of greenhouse gases in specific manufacturing centers and high-consumption countries. Yet, even if globalization does not necessarily "determine" local events, there is no escaping it. As world society integrates, individuals become conscious of being enveloped in global networks, subject to global forces, governed by global rules. Some of our selections concretely illustrate this local–global connection.

Is globalization harmful? Implicit in the questions we have raised is a widespread sense that globalization may be harmful to the well-being of individuals, countries, and cultures. If the market is the driving force in globalization, many fear, it is bound to exacerbate inequality by creating winners and losers. If globalization makes the world more homogeneous, others fear, many cultures are in trouble. Loss of local autonomy may mean that more people will be vulnerable to economic swings, environmental degradation, and epidemics. For these and other reasons, globalization has become an extremely contentious process. Indeed, the debate about the merits and direction of globalization is itself an important component of global culture. As we already indicated above, we are skeptical of the most sweeping critiques of globalization. But our purpose in this *Reader* is not to offer definitive judgments; the subject is too complex for a clear-cut assessment in any case. Rather, we present a variety of perspectives that convey the thrust of actual debates and ongoing research so that readers can understand the varied consequences of globalization and make their own informed judgments.

What does globalization mean? Activists use the term in denouncing global injustice. Politicians invoke it to explain the problems they face. Academics employ it to describe important trends. Even within these various groups, people disagree. As mentioned, globalization has different meanings for different groups. Not surprisingly, this often provokes complaints that the concept is too fuzzy. However, we detect two common meanings. The simple definition we gave above captures one of these: globalization is the set of processes by which more people become connected in more and different ways across ever-greater distances. A more academic version of this idea is to equate globalization with "deterritorialization," the process through which the constraints of physical space lose their hold on social relations. This is a generic definition since it captures a wide variety of possible relations. When viewers in India enjoy reality shows that originate in Europe, or when Americans buy baby products made in China, or when Iran plays against Angola in the World Cup, these are all instances of generic globalization. Used in this way, the concept is analytically clear and applicable in many contexts. It does not favor a particular theory or call for a particular judgment.

A second kind of definition is more specific. It identifies globalization with the process by which capitalism expands across the globe as powerful economic actors seek profit in global markets and impose their rules everywhere, a process often labeled "neoliberalism" (as illustrated in a selection in Part II). Though sometimes invoked by defenders of globalization, this is a critical definition that usually serves to challenge the process it tries to capture. Through this lens, generic globalization looks a little different: the export of TV show formats as cultural commodities is driven by media producers in core markets, Chinese workers making baby products are exploited as nodes in a global commodity chain, and the World Cup has turned into a marketing event for multinational shoe companies and an audition for players seeking professional advancement. This lens filters out much of what the generic view includes but also sharpens the focus, in a way that especially suits contemporary critics of capitalist market society.

The Globalization Reader aims to convey the complexity, importance, and contentiousness of globalization. This is an exciting time in social science scholarship, as many creative minds try to discern the outlines of a new era. The *Reader* includes some of their best work. But making sense of globalization is not just a task for scholars and students. It is a public concern. We hope this *Reader* will assist a diverse audience in understanding the patterns and problems of globalization, which is likely to remain a dominant concern of the twenty-first century.

Note on Selections

1. Footnotes, citations, and sources of quoted passages have been excised. Omitted text is indicated by "[. . .]".

Part I
Debating Globalization

Introduction

When the Cold War drew to a close in the late 1980s, some in the West proclaimed the "end of history": from now on, there would be no more deep conflicts about how to organize societies, no more ideological divisions in the world. In the "new world order" heralded by the American president at the time, George H. W. Bush, countries would cooperate peacefully as participants in one worldwide market, pursuing their interests while sharing commitments to basic human values. These triumphant responses to the new global situation heartily embraced economic liberalization and the prosperity and democratization it supposedly entailed. As global trade and investment expanded, more and more people could share in the bounty of a growing economy. Economic and political interdependence would create shared interests that would help prevent destructive conflict and foster support for common values. As vehicles of globalization, international organizations could represent these common values for the benefit of humanity. Globalization, in this rosy scenario, created both wealth and solidarity. The spread of market-oriented policies, democratic polities, and individual rights promised to promote the well-being of billions of people.

This influential perspective on globalization has been challenged by critics who see globalization as a juggernaut of untrammeled capitalism. They fear a world ruled by profit-seeking global corporations. They see economic interdependence making countries more vulnerable to the destructive impact of market shifts. The social fabric – the ties among people all across the globe – is strained when winners in the global game become disconnected from losers. "By allowing market values to become all-important," said George Soros, himself a significant player in world financial markets, in 1998, "we actually narrow the space for moral judgment and undermine public morality . . .. Globalization has increased this aberration, because it has actually reduced the power of individual states to determine their destiny."[1] The process, other critics add, is

The Globalization Reader, Fifth Edition. Edited by Frank J. Lechner and John Boli.
Editorial material and organization © 2015 John Wiley & Sons, Ltd.
Published 2015 by John Wiley & Sons, Ltd.

lopsided because it imposes the political and cultural standards of one region in the world – namely, the West – on all other regions. Globalization is Westernization by another name. It undermines the cultural integrity of other cultures and is therefore repressive, exploitative, and harmful to most people in most places.

Our selections in this part illustrate the major positions in the global debate about the merits and direction of globalization. John Micklethwait and Adrian Wooldridge, journalists at *The Economist*, represent the positive view of globalization by arguing that it not only produces greater economic efficiency and prosperity but also extends the "idea of liberty." Globalization opens up societies and reduces the "tyranny of place." In a more globalized world, more people can freely exercise their talents, decide where they want to live, and fashion their own identities. Like Micklethwait and Wooldridge, Amartya Sen, winner of the Nobel Memorial Prize in Economics, recognizes the potential benefits of global integration. Briefly illustrating worldwide contributions to the process, he refutes the idea that it is a "new Western curse." Yet he agrees with critics of globalization that it is profoundly unjust in its consequences. To him, however, the central question is not whether to use the global market economy, but how to create institutions that can lead to a more equitable distribution of its benefits.

In the next selection, Dutch professor of communications Cees J. Hamelink reviews many different aspects of globalization and the corresponding disputes that have arisen regarding its substance and significance. Using a discursive approach pitting "supporters" and "sceptics" of the concept against one another, he provides a useful framework for developing an informed understanding of globalization's dimensions and complexities but does not try to resolve the many controversies surrounding the concept.

The selection by Benjamin R. Barber, an American political scientist, questions the impact of economic globalization. He espies an increasingly homogeneous "McWorld" in which American-inspired popular culture overwhelms all others and societies lose the capacity to govern themselves democratically. He emphasizes that McWorld evokes a defense of indigenous national or religious traditions around the world, producing a variety of movements he captures with the label "Jihad." Pushing Barber's ideas still further, Samuel P. Huntington, another American scholar, argues that the defense of distinct cultural values is not merely reactive; rather, he points out, the globe is now divided into several civilizations with often irreconcilable worldviews. Resisting incorporation into one world society, these civilizations struggle with one another in profound conflicts that ultimately will reduce the influence of the West.

The critics thus share a fear of the unrestrained capitalist system. Some lament its imperial obliteration of cultural distinctions and advocate preserving or reviving traditional cultural distinctions. Others are more concerned about the impact on solidarity within societies and advocate stronger self-governance in democratic states. Still others worry most about the economic, political, and cultural divisions that result from globalization and advocate the cosmopolitan pursuit of a unified but just world. Such critical views of globalization themselves affect the course of the process. The increasingly deliberate efforts from many quarters to define the proper shape of world society also contribute significantly to its formation, an issue to which we return in the last section of this book. At the very least, the debate expresses a common global consciousness, though not, of course, a global consensus.

Note

1. Quoted in Timothy O'Brien, "He's seen the enemy: It looks like him," *New York Times*, December 6, 1998.

1

The Hidden Promise
Liberty Renewed

John Micklethwait and Adrian Wooldridge

[…] Karl Marx's tomb in Highgate Cemetery is a sorry place. The sculpture of his great bearded head is sometimes soiled with pigeon droppings; the army of celebrated intellectuals and communist dignitaries that used to come to pay its respects to the master has dwindled into a tiny band of eccentrics. In one way, this is a pity. As a prophet of socialism, Marx may be kaput; but as a prophet of "the universal interdependence of nations," as he called globalization, he can still seem startlingly relevant.

For all his hatred of the Victorian bourgeoisie, Marx could not conceal his admiration for its ability to turn the world into a single marketplace. Some of this admiration was mere schadenfreude, to be sure, born of his belief that in creating a global working class the bourgeoisie was also creating its very own grave diggers; but a surprising amount of this respect was genuine, like a prizefighter's respect for his muscle-bound opponent. In less than a hundred years, Marx argued, the bourgeoisie had "accomplished wonders far surpassing Egyptian pyramids, Roman aqueducts and Gothic cathedrals"; had conducted "expeditions that put in the shade all former exoduses of nations and crusades"; and had "created more massive and more colossal productive forces" than all preceding generations put together. In achieving all this, it had begun to transform an agglomeration of warring nations and petty principalities into a global marketplace.

Marx was at his most expansive on globalization in *The Communist Manifesto*, which he cowrote with Friedrich Engels, a factory owner turned revolutionary,

Original publication details: John Micklethwait and Adrian Wooldridge, *A Future Perfect: The Essentials of Globalization*. New York: Crown Business, 2000. pp. 332–42. Reproduced with permission from Random House Group.

The Globalization Reader, Fifth Edition. Edited by Frank J. Lechner and John Boli.

and published in 1848, a year in which ancien régimes were tottering throughout Europe.

> The need of a constantly expanding market for its products chases the bourgeoisie over the entire surface of the globe. It must nestle everywhere, settle everywhere, establish connections everywhere.
>
> The bourgeoisie has through its exploitation of the world market given a cosmopolitan character to production and consumption in every country. … In place of the old wants, satisfied by the production of the country, we find new wants, requiring for their satisfaction the products of distant land and climes. In place of the old local and national seclusion and self-sufficiency, we have intercourse in every direction, universal interdependence of nations.

Even Marx's final resting place is, to some extent, a vindication of this great insight. Opposite him in Highgate lies William Nassar Kennedy, a colonel of the Winnipeg Rifles who was "called home" in 1885 while returning to Canada from Egypt, where he was in command of the Nile Voyageurs. A little further down there is John MacKinlay and his wife, Caroline Louisa, "late of Bombay." Highgate Cemetery is strewn with the graves of Victorian soldiers, bureaucrats, and merchants who devoted their lives to turning the world into a single market.

What would Marx make of the world today? Imagine for a moment that the prayers of the faithful were answered and the great man awoke from his slumber. Having climbed out of his mausoleum, dusted himself off, and taken a frustrated sniff at the bottle of scotch, what would Marx find? There would, of course, be the shock of discovering that, on all the big issues, he had been proved hopelessly wrong. It was communism that succumbed to its own internal contradictions and capitalism that swept all before it. But he might at least console himself with the thought that his description of globalization remains as sharp today as it was 150 years ago.

Wandering down Highgate Hill, Marx would discover the Bank of Cyprus (which services the three hundred thousand Cypriots that live in London), several curry houses (now England's most popular sort of eatery), and a Restaurante do Brazil. He might be less surprised to find a large Irish community. But the sign inviting him to watch "Irish Sports Live," thanks to a pub's satellite-television linkup, might intrigue him. On the skyline, he would soon spot the twin towers of Canary Wharf, built by Canadian developers with money borrowed from Japanese banks and now occupied mostly by American investment banks.

Marx would hear Asian voices and see white schoolchildren proudly wearing T-shirts with pictures of black English soccer stars. Multicultural London (which is now home to thirty-three ethnic communities, each with a population of more than ten thousand) might well exhilarate a man who was called "the Moor" by his own children because of his dark complexion. He could stop at almost any newsstand and pick up a copy of the *Frankfurter Allgemeine Zeitung* that would be no more than a day old. Nearly swept off his feet by a passing Rolls-Royce, he might be more surprised to discover that the vehicle, like the rest of Britain's car industry, was now owned by a German company.

If Marx were to venture back to his old haunts in Soho, he would find a cluster of video-production companies and advertising agencies that sells its services to the world. If he climbed up to Hampstead Heath, the Marx family's favorite picnic spot, he might be surprised to discover that the neighborhood's most expensive house is now owned by an Indian, Lakshmi Mittal, who has built up one of the world's biggest steel companies. London is home to around a quarter of Europe's five hundred biggest companies. Its financial-services industry alone employs directly or indirectly 850,000 people, more than the population of the city of Frankfurt.

Yet even as Marx marveled at these new creations of the bourgeoisie and perhaps applauded its meritocratic dynamism, it is hard to believe that some of the old revolutionary fires would not burn anew. Poverty of the grinding sort that inspired Engels to write *The Condition of the Working Class in England* (1845) might have disappeared; the rigid class system of the Victorians might have evaporated: Marx might even have been slightly shocked by the absence of domestic servants. But the founder of communism would have no trouble tracking down inequality and sensing that it was on the increase.

Barely ten miles separate elegant Chelsea (where ironically enough the Marx family lived when they first came to London, before being evicted for not paying the rent) from the crumbling wasteland of Newham, but they seem like two different countries. In one, you might be forgiven for thinking that the biggest problem is the availability of residential parking permits; in the other, two thirds of the sixteen-year-olds fail their basic high-school exams, and the mortality rate for people under twenty-five is 50 percent above the national average. As he studied the newspaper and looked at the pictures on the flashing television screens of, say, Somalia or even parts of Los Angeles, Marx might well see globalization as a process that is only just beginning – a job half done. Once again, he might consider, the world is hurtling toward a "crisis of capitalism" – not unlike the last one that his own theories did so much to make ruinous.

The Priority of Liberty

This, then, is the beginning of the future, perfect or not, that we have tried to describe in this book. The fact that it has much in common with the world of yesterday (and especially the world of a century ago) is not surprising. History condemns us to repeat ourselves, though not necessarily to repeat all our mistakes.

… we have tried to build a measured defense of globalization. Yes, it does increase inequality, but it does not create a winner-take-all society, and the winners hugely outnumber the losers. Yes, it leaves some people behind, but it helps millions more to leap ahead. Yes, it can make bad government worse, but the onus should be on crafting better government, not blaming globalization. Yes, it curtails some of the power of nation-states, but they remain the fundamental unit of modern politics. Globalization is not destroying geography, merely enhancing it.

In most cases, the bulwarks of our defense have been economic. The simple fact is that globalization makes us richer – or makes enough of us richer to make the whole process worthwhile. Globalization clearly benefits producers by giving them greater choice over their raw materials, production techniques, and human talent, not to mention over the markets where they sell their goods. Equally clearly, globalization benefits consumers by providing them with better goods at better prices. Globalization increases efficiency and thus prosperity.

These economic arguments need to be made, and with far more eloquence, by our leaders. Too many politicians take the Clintonesque tack of defending the easy bits of globalization – typically, the successes of their own country's exports – and shying away from talking about the benefits that flow, say, from imports or foreign takeovers of "their" companies. This is not only economically illiterate but dangerous, because it allows myths to emerge, such as the idea that globalization is a zero-sum game. But there is also a broader need to wrench globalization from all the dry talk of markets penetrated, currencies depreciated, and GDPs accelerated and to place the process in its proper political context: as an extension of the idea of liberty and as a chance to renew the fundamental rights of the individual. [...]

The Open Society

Globalization redresses this balance in two ways. The most obvious is that it puts limits on the power of government. This advantage is most obvious in commerce. Free trade makes it easier for businesspeople to escape from interfering officials by moving their money and operations abroad. As we have pointed out, companies seldom want to flee, but the very fact that they might acts as a brake on those officials. The sullen fury of a Bangalore bureaucrat staring at the satellite dishes that allow "his" software companies to export their products without his grasping fingers interfering would delight Mill (even though he worked for the often more extortionate East India Company). More important still, free trade allows ordinary people to buy products from companies who make the best of their kind rather than from those that enjoy cozy relationships with governments. Similarly, they can put their retirement money in pension funds that are not tied to schemes of national aggrandizement.

Governments are not retreating from this easily. They can still slap controls on the flow of capital (as Malaysia did in the wake of the Asian crisis) or even on the flow of information. (Singapore employs a staff of censors whose job is to surf the Internet ceaselessly looking for objectionable information to block.) But the world is nevertheless a lot freer today than it was just a few decades ago, before globalization got into high gear. In 1966, for example, the British Labour government imposed a travel allowance that virtually confined Britons to their own country except for two weeks' worth of penny-pinching foreign vacation. Today, any politician who suggested such a restriction would be carted off to an asylum.

Indeed, the recent history of globalization can be written as a story, albeit an uneven story, of spreading a political culture that is based on individual liberty to areas that have been longing to embrace it for years. The last dozen years of the twentieth century saw not only the spectacular death of the biggest alternative to liberal democracy, totalitarian communism, but also the slow death of other collectivist models. Around the world, countries have abandoned attempts to plan their way to prosperity. Even the Asian crisis, in its own awful way, has made it more difficult for the continent's authoritarians to boast that they had discovered a nondemocratic way to generate growth.

Many on the left would argue that globalization has merely involved a change of master. Globalization may have liberated us from the onus of having to get our television programs – or our health care and pensions – from our governments, but it has forced us to get the same things from giant companies that are just as remote and even less accountable. The gentleman in Whitehall has been replaced by the knucklehead in the boardroom or, if you work in the Académie Française, by the illiterate in Hollywood.

This suspicion is healthy and should be encouraged. But so far the evidence is that it is misplaced. Of course, businesses will try to control markets, but that does not mean that they will be able to. As we have seen, one of the wonders of global capitalism is its capacity to hurl challenges at incumbent champions. Most of the forces of globalization – particularly the availability of capital and technology – favor small companies. In parts of Europe and Asia, commercial oligarchies are clinging to power, but only because governments collude with them. There is nothing global about, say, the importance of *guanxi* in Asia – quite the opposite. By the same token, the Department of Justice campaign to restrain Microsoft's power, no matter how misguided, has a legitimately global aim of trying to open up a market.

In fact, many of the most vengeful howls directed at globalization come from self-interested business elites who are being forced to surrender to consumer choice. Globalization does not mean homogenization. People want to consume books, movies, even potato chips, that reflect their own identities, and those identities remain primarily national. When politicians complain that globalization is changing society, they are correct, but they seldom bother to ask whose society it is. When society is defined by a fairly compact national economy, an elite has a chance of co-opting it. But when society is an open-ended international system, it becomes increasingly difficult for any elite to identify their values with the common good.

The Individual's Prayer

Restricting overmighty states and elites is all very well, but globalization increases the basic freedom of individuals as well. We have already talked about the tyranny of place: Most people's lots in life are determined by where they were born, something illiberal regimes everywhere have done their best to reinforce. As Leszek Kolakawski, a Polish intellectual, points out, one of the defining features of communist regimes is their refusal to allow people to move from city to city without official permission; they even made short journeys difficult, providing few road signs or decent street maps. Even today, the lives of half the world's population are bounded by local villages, and local markets.

Travel and migration have long provided a fraction of the world's population with freedom from the tyranny of place. The printing press and the television have allowed others a more imaginary form of escape. Globalization is now making these freedoms more pervasive. The impact of the Internet, particularly as it goes wireless, will also be dramatic. The World Wide Web allows people to gain access to information anywhere at any time. And it allows them to do so in a way that undermines local elites and expensive middlemen. People will never escape the pull of geography entirely, as the tendency of business to cluster in particular places shows. But those clusters only survive if they work with the grain of globalization. And the penalty for being born a long way from those clusters is diminishing. Remember the Bangladeshi farmers using their cell phones to check the proper prices for their produce rather than having to accept the diktats of local grain merchants.

The more these ties weaken, the more people can exercise what used to be called God-given talents. Again, businesspeople are the most obvious beneficiaries: If you have a good idea and the entrepreneurial vim to pursue it, you can take it anywhere you want. If, like Michael Skok of AlphaBlox, you think that your business belongs in Silicon Valley, not the Thames valley, you can take it there. But there are also more spiritual, artistic reasons to believe that globalization is a good thing. The thousands of Miltons who remain "mute and inglorious" in their villages often begin to sing only after they move to the "mansion houses of liberty" that are the world's great cities. Bustling centers of trade from fifteenth-century Venice to twentieth-century New York have usually been centers of creativity, too. Even if your God-given talents are more prosaic, it is becoming ever easier to study abroad, and, thanks again to the Internet, you will soon be able to do so (more or less) without leaving home.

Somewhere behind the freedom to exercise our talents lies the most fundamental freedom of all: the freedom to define our own identities. This can sound like the moan of a petulant teenager, but it is at the heart of what is becoming one of the main debates of our time, between liberals and the growing band of communitarians. (To the extent that "the third way" means anything at all, its adherents are probably on the side of the communitarians.) Communitarians, as their name suggests, worry about the effect of things like globalization on communities. John Gray, one of globalization's most searching critics, has argued that human beings' "deepest need is a home, a network of common practices and inherited traditions that confers on them the blessings of a settled identity."

There can be no doubt that people need a home and a network. But does this home have to be the one they were born in? And does this network have to be the one provided by their ancestors? People also have a drive to better themselves, to extend their identities, to cross traditional boundaries, and to try out new experiences. John Gray himself happily abandoned the Newcastle working class into which he was born for the metropolitan intelligentsia. One of the many benefits of globalization is that it increases the number of people who can exercise Gray's privilege of fashioning his own identity.

This is not to say that conservative and communitarian worries about individualism run wild are empty. In the same breath that he praised America's faith in individualism, Tocqueville warned of the danger that each man may be "shut up in the solitude of his own heart." One of the great risks of globalization is that it fosters anomie – the normlessness that comes from having your ties with the rest of society weakened. Anybody who spends long periods of time on business trips knows the loneliness of the long-distance traveler. Ex-pats complain that their children grow up not knowing their grandparents. The most common complaint among Internet addicts is that they end up feeling (rather like the compulsive masturbators of Victorian medical treatises) isolated, lonely, and depressed.

All too true. Yet the issue that separates liberals from communitarians is not the desirability of human ties but the question of coercion. For liberals, the best communities are the spontaneous creations of free individuals rather than the products of bossy politicians, and one of the many cases for globalization is that it lets a million of these spontaneous communities bloom. The smaller the world becomes, the more communities are defined by common interests and outlooks rather than by the mere accident of physical proximity.

The idea of spontaneous communities will hardly placate globalization's harshest critics. For some people, the idea that individuals take precedence over society is nothing more than Western cultural imperialism. Wee Kim Wee, the former president of Singapore, argues that "placing society above the self" is one of his country's "core values." It is all very well for the egomaniacs of Manhattan and Los Angeles to abandon their gods in pursuit of self-fulfillment. But everybody else knows that such selfishness leads inexorably to the wasteland.

Yet the yearning for freedom is no more peculiar to the West than the yearning for prosperity. Other parts of the world have been quieter on the subject not because their peoples are wedded to collectivism but because their rulers have been less fussy about the methods they have used to hold onto power. Singaporeans bitterly resent the fact that their government gives them a superb education but then proceeds to treat them like children. The students who were brutally crushed at Tiananmen Square constructed replicas of the Statue of Liberty.

An Empire without End

Look around the world, and it is not hard to find examples of people for whom this message may seem a little empty. What does Reginaldo Gobetti care about the freedom to create his own identity; he just wants a job. Our argument is not that globalization is delivering the liberal dream, with billions of people gradually becoming the wired (or wireless) equivalent of Jefferson's yeoman farmers. Our argument is merely that globalization is delivering enough of that dream to make it worth pressing forward and to make it worth defending on more than just narrow economic grounds.

In fact, the two arguments should run in tandem. Globalization is helping to give birth to an economy that is closer to the classic theoretical model of capitalism, under which rational individuals pursue their interests in the light of perfect information, relatively free from government and geographical obstacles. It is also helping to create a society that is closer to the model that liberal political theorists once imagined, in which power lies increasingly in the hands of individuals rather than governments, and in which people are free, within reasonable bounds, to pursue the good life wherever they find it.

It would be nice if we could end on that optimistic, perhaps even slightly utopian, note. Yet we have also stressed the importance of vigilance and the need for not just politicians but also those who have prospered from globalization – particularly the cosmocrats – to help those who have done less well.

The trouble is that the devil has all the best tunes. One reason why globalization's enemies are so much more persuasive than its friends is that they are more visible: The victims are usually concentrated in particular places, whereas its beneficiaries are spread out all over the place. But supporters have also done a lousy job of making their case. We have already lamented the shortage of Peels and Rockefellers. But consider once again whether any modern leader would stand up and argue that "by encouraging freedom of intercourse between the nations of the world we are promoting the separate welfare of each and are fulfilling the beneficent designs of an all-seeing Creator" or invite his audience to celebrate "commerce, the happy instrument of promoting civilization, of abating national jealousies and prejudices and of encouraging the maintenance of general peace by every consideration as well as every obligation of Christian duty." […]

2

How to Judge Globalism

Amartya Sen

Globalization is often seen as global Westernization. On this point, there is substantial agreement among many proponents and opponents. Those who take an upbeat view of globalization see it as a marvelous contribution of Western civilization to the world. There is a nicely stylized history in which the great developments happened in Europe: First came the Renaissance, then the Enlightenment and the Industrial Revolution, and these led to a massive increase in living standards in the West. And now the great achievements of the West are spreading to the world. In this view, globalization is not only good, it is also a gift from the West to the world. The champions of this reading of history tend to feel upset not just because this great benefaction is seen as a curse but also because it is undervalued and castigated by an ungrateful world.

From the opposite perspective, Western dominance – sometimes seen as a continuation of Western imperialism – is the devil of the piece. In this view, contemporary capitalism, driven and led by greedy and grabby Western countries in Europe and North America, has established rules of trade and business relations that do not serve the interests of the poorer people in the world. The celebration of various non-Western identities – defined by religion (as in Islamic fundamentalism), region (as in the championing of Asian values), or culture (as in the glorification of Confucian ethics) – can add fuel to the fire of confrontation with the West.

Is globalization really a new Western curse? It is, in fact, neither new nor necessarily Western; and it is not a curse. Over thousands of years, globalization has contributed to the progress of the world through travel, trade, migration, spread of

Original publication details: Amartya Sen, "How to Judge Globalism," in *The American Prospect*, 13, 1, January 1, 2002. Reproduced with permission from A. Sen.

cultural influences, and dissemination of knowledge and understanding (including that of science and technology). These global interrelations have often been very productive in the advancement of different countries. They have not necessarily taken the form of increased Western influence. Indeed, the active agents of globalization have often been located far from the West.

To illustrate, consider the world at the beginning of the last millennium rather than at its end. Around 1000 AD, global reach of science, technology, and mathematics was changing the nature of the old world, but the dissemination then was, to a great extent, in the opposite direction of what we see today. The high technology in the world of 1000 AD included paper, the printing press, the crossbow, gunpowder, the iron-chain suspension bridge, the kite, the magnetic compass, the wheelbarrow, and the rotary fan. A millennium ago, these items were used extensively in China – and were practically unknown elsewhere. Globalization spread them across the world, including Europe.

A similar movement occurred in the Eastern influence on Western mathematics. The decimal system emerged and became well developed in India between the second and sixth centuries; it was used by Arab mathematicians soon thereafter. These mathematical innovations reached Europe mainly in the last quarter of the tenth century and began having an impact in the early years of the last millennium, playing an important part in the scientific revolution that helped to transform Europe. The agents of globalization are neither European nor exclusively Western, nor are they necessarily linked to Western dominance. Indeed, Europe would have been a lot poorer – economically, culturally, and scientifically – had it resisted the globalization of mathematics, science, and technology at that time. And today, the same principle applies, though in the reverse direction (from West to East). To reject the globalization of science and technology because it represents Western influence and imperialism would not only amount to overlooking global contributions – drawn from many different parts of the world – that lie solidly behind so-called Western science and technology, but would also be quite a daft practical decision, given the extent to which the whole world can benefit from the process. [...]

Global Interdependences and Movements

The misdiagnosis that globalization of ideas and practices has to be resisted because it entails dreaded Westernization has played quite a regressive part in the colonial and postcolonial world. This assumption incites parochial tendencies and undermines the possibility of objectivity in science and knowledge. It is not only counterproductive in itself; given the global interactions throughout history, it can also cause non-Western societies to shoot themselves in the foot – even in their precious cultural foot.

Consider the resistance in India to the use of Western ideas and concepts in science and mathematics. In the nineteenth century, this debate fitted into a broader controversy about Western education versus indigenous Indian education. The "Westernizers," such as the redoubtable Thomas Babington Macaulay, saw no merit whatsoever in Indian tradition. "I have never found one among them [advocates of Indian tradition] who could deny that a single shelf of a good European library was worth the whole native literature of India and Arabia," he declared. Partly in retaliation, the advocates of native education resisted Western imports altogether. Both sides, however, accepted too readily the foundational dichotomy between two disparate civilizations.

European mathematics, with its use of such concepts as sine, was viewed as a purely "Western" import into India. In fact, the fifth-century Indian mathematician Aryabhata had discussed the concept of sine in his classic work on astronomy and mathematics in 499 AD, calling it by its Sanskrit name, *jya-ardha* (literally, "half-chord"). This word, first shortened to *jya* in Sanskrit, eventually became the Arabic *jiba* and, later, *jaib*, which means "a cove or a bay." In his history of mathematics, Howard Eves explains that around 1150 AD, Gherardo of Cremona, in his translations from the Arabic, rendered *jaib* as the Latin *sinus*, the corresponding word for a cove or a bay. And this is the source of the modern word *sine*. The concept had traveled full circle – from India, and then back.

To see globalization as merely Western imperialism of ideas and beliefs (as the rhetoric often suggests) would be a serious and costly error, in the same way that any European resistance to Eastern influence would have been at the beginning of the last millennium. Of course, there are issues related to globalization that do connect with imperialism (the history of conquests, colonialism, and alien rule remains relevant today in many ways), and a postcolonial understanding of the world has its merits. But it would be a great mistake to see globalization primarily as a feature of imperialism. It is much bigger – much greater – than that.

The issue of the distribution of economic gains and losses from globalization remains an entirely separate question, and it must be addressed as a further – and extremely relevant – issue. There is extensive evidence that the global economy has brought prosperity to many different areas of the globe. Pervasive poverty dominated the world a few centuries ago; there were only a few rare pockets of affluence. In overcoming that penury, extensive economic interrelations and modern technology have been and remain influential. What has happened in Europe, America, Japan, and East Asia has important messages for all other regions, and we cannot go very far into understanding the nature of globalization today without first acknowledging the positive fruits of global economic contacts.

Indeed, we cannot reverse the economic predicament of the poor across the world by withholding from them the great advantages of contemporary technology, the well-established efficiency of international trade and exchange, and the social as well as economic merits of living in an open society. Rather, the main issue is how to make good use of the remarkable benefits of economic intercourse and technological progress in a way that pays adequate attention to the interests of the deprived and the underdog. That is, I would argue, the constructive question that emerges from the so-called antiglobalization movements.

Are the Poor Getting Poorer?

The principal challenge relates to inequality – international as well as intranational. The troubling inequalities include disparities in affluence and also gross asymmetries in political, social, and economic opportunities and power.

A crucial question concerns the sharing of the potential gains from globalization – between rich and poor countries and among different groups within a country. It is not sufficient to understand that the poor of the world need globalization as much as the rich do; it is also important to make sure that they actually get what they need. This may require extensive institutional reform, even as globalization is defended.

There is also a need for more clarity in formulating the distributional questions. For example, it is often argued that the rich are getting richer and the poor poorer. But this is by no means uniformly so, even though there are cases in which this has happened. Much depends on the region or the group chosen and what indicators of economic prosperity are used. But the attempt to base the castigation of economic globalization on this rather thin ice produces a peculiarly fragile critique.

On the other side, the apologists of globalization point to their belief that the poor who participate in trade and exchange are mostly getting richer. Ergo – the argument runs – globalization is not unfair to the poor; they too benefit. If the central relevance of this question is accepted, then the whole debate turns on determining which side is correct in this empirical dispute. But is this the right battleground in the first place? I would argue that it is not.

Global Justice and the Bargaining Problem

Even if the poor were to get just a little richer, this would not necessarily imply that the poor were getting a fair share of the potentially vast benefits of global economic interrelations. It is not adequate to ask whether international inequality is getting marginally larger or smaller. In order to rebel against the appalling poverty and the staggering inequalities that characterize the contemporary world – or to protest against the unfair sharing of benefits of global cooperation – it is not necessary to show that the massive inequality or distributional unfairness is also getting marginally larger. This is a separate issue altogether.

When there are gains from cooperation, there can be many possible arrangements. As the game theorist and mathematician John Nash discussed more than half a century ago (in "The Bargaining Problem," published in *Econometrica* in 1950, which was cited, among other writings, by the Royal Swedish Academy of Sciences when Nash was awarded the Nobel Prize in economics), the central issue in general is not whether a particular arrangement is better for everyone than no cooperation at all would be, but whether that is a fair division of the benefits. One cannot rebut the criticism that a distributional arrangement is unfair simply by noting that all the parties are better off than they would be in the absence of cooperation; the real exercise is the choice *between* these alternatives. […]

Likewise, one cannot rebut the charge that the global system is unfair by showing that even the poor gain something from global contacts and are not necessarily made poorer. That answer may or may not be wrong, but the question certainly is. The critical issue is not whether the poor are getting marginally poorer or richer. Nor is it whether they are better off than they would be had they excluded themselves from globalized interactions.

Again, the real issue is the distribution of globalization's benefits. Indeed, this is why many of the antiglobalization protesters, who seek a better deal for the under-dogs of the world economy, are not – contrary to their own rhetoric and to the views attributed to them by others – really "antiglobalization." It is also why there is no real contradiction in the fact that the so-called antiglobalization protests have become among the most globalized events in the contemporary world.

Altering Global Arrangements

However, can those less-well-off groups get a better deal from globalized economic and social relations without dispensing with the market economy itself? They certainly can. The use of the market economy is consistent with many different ownership patterns, resource availabilities, social opportunities, and rules of operation (such as patent laws and antitrust regulations). And depending on these conditions, the market economy would generate different prices, terms of trade, income distribution, and, more generally, diverse overall outcomes. The arrangements for social security and other public interventions can make further modifications to the outcomes of the market processes, and together they can yield varying levels of inequality and poverty.

The central question is not whether to use the market economy. That shallow question is easy to answer, because it is hard to achieve economic prosperity without making extensive use of the opportunities of exchange and specialization that market relations offer. Even though the operation of a given market economy can be significantly defective, there is no way of dispensing with the institution of markets in general as a powerful engine of economic progress.

But this recognition does not end the discussion about globalized market relations. The market economy does not work by itself in global relations – indeed, it cannot operate alone even within a given country. It is not only the case that a market-inclusive system can generate very distinct results depending on various enabling conditions (such as how physical resources are distributed, how human resources are developed, what rules of business relations prevail, what social-security arrangements are in place, and so on). These enabling conditions themselves depend critically on economic, social, and political institutions that operate nationally and globally.

The crucial role of the markets does not make the other institutions insignificant, even in terms of the results that the market economy can produce. As has been amply established in empirical studies, market outcomes are massively influenced by public policies in education, epidemiology, land reform, microcredit facilities, appropriate legal protections, et cetera; and in each of these fields, there is work to be done through public action that can radically alter the outcome of local and global economic relations.

Institutions and Inequality

Globalization has much to offer; but even as we defend it, we must also, without any contradiction, see the legitimacy of many questions that the antiglobalization protesters ask. There may be a misdiagnosis about where the main problems lie (they do not lie in globalization, as such), but the ethical and human concerns that yield these questions call for serious reassessments of the adequacy of the national and global institutional arrangements that characterize the contemporary world and shape globalized economic and social relations.

Global capitalism is much more concerned with expanding the domain of market relations than with, say, establishing democracy, expanding elementary education, or enhancing the social opportunities of society's underdogs. Since globalization of markets is, on its own, a very inadequate approach to world prosperity, there is a need to go beyond the priorities that find expression in the chosen focus of global capitalism. As George Soros has pointed out, international business concerns often have a strong preference for working in orderly and highly organized autocracies rather than in activist and less-regimented democracies, and this can be a regressive influence on equitable development. Further, multinational firms can exert their influence on the priorities of public expenditure in less secure third-world countries by giving preference to the safety and convenience of the managerial classes and of privileged workers over the removal of widespread illiteracy, medical deprivation, and other adversities of the poor. These possibilities do not, of course, impose any insurmountable barrier to development, but it is important to make sure that the surmountable barriers are actually surmounted. [...]

Fair Sharing of Global Opportunities

To conclude, the confounding of globalization with Westernization is not only ahistorical, it also distracts attention from the many potential benefits of global integration. Globalization is a historical process that has offered an abundance of opportunities and rewards in the past and continues to do so today. The very existence of potentially large benefits makes the question of fairness in sharing the benefits of globalization so critically important.

The central issue of contention is not globalization itself, nor is it the use of the market as an institution, but the inequity in the overall balance of institutional arrangements – which produces very unequal sharing of the benefits of globalization. The question is not just whether the poor, too, gain something from globalization, but whether they get a fair share and a fair opportunity. There is an urgent need for reforming institutional arrangements – in addition to national ones – in order to overcome both the errors of omission and those of commission that tend to give the poor across the world such limited opportunities. Globalization deserves a reasoned defense, but it also needs reform.

3

The Elusive Concept
of Globalisation

Cees J. Hamelink

[…]

In order to explore the meaning of the globalisation concept, it is worth distinguishing between its use as an analytical tool and as a political programme.

Globalisation: The Analytical Tool

The concept of globalisation is used to describe and interpret contemporary social processes. In this application, it has both supporters and sceptics.

- Supporters argue that since the 1980s (with the deregulatory policies of Ronald Reagan and Margaret Thatcher and the demise of communism) more and more people around the globe have been living in, or are indirectly affected by, free-market economies. Capitalism has spread from covering some 20 per cent of the world population in the 1970s to some 90 per cent in the 1990s. Large numbers of people have become integrated into the global capitalist economy.

  Sceptics respond that this is superficially true, but claim that the "global economy" is in fact the economy of just a few rich countries, in particular those belonging to the Organisation for Economic Co-operation and Development (OECD). They point out that if the world were a global village of one hundred residents, only six would be Americans. Yet these six would have half the village's entire income, with the other ninety-four existing on the other half.

Original publication details: Cees J. Hamelink, "The Elusive Concept of Globalisation," in *Global Dialogue* 1, 1, Summer 1999. pp. 1–9. Reproduced with permission from C. J. Hamelink.

- Supporters argue that today there is more global trading than ever before. Sweeping reductions in the cost of air travel and shipping have facilitated a phenomenal expansion of crossborder trading. In the process, not only has the volume of trade increased enormously, but its character has also changed considerably. Firms are under strong pressure to take a global approach to their sales (e.g., through global brandnames and global advertising), thereby reinforcing the globalisation of markets.

  Sceptics protest that most world trading is not global, but takes place within geographical regions. Moreover, the volume of international trading by the industrialised countries has not increased dramatically since the early twentieth century. In fact, some sceptics even present trade figures which indicate that the world economy of the nineteenth century was far more internationalised than today's so-called global economy. Sceptics also note that the contribution of developing countries to international exports decreased from 30 per cent in 1950 to 20 per cent in 1990. Moreover, the share of the least developed countries in world trade decreased from 0.6 per cent in the 1970s to less than 0.3 per cent in the 1990s.

- Supporters point to the growth of global financial markets and explain that this began in the 1970s with the rapid proliferation of offshore financial markets and the global circulation of vast amounts of money outside the jurisdiction of national authorities. They conclude that today there is unprecedented global financial mobility.

  Sceptics agree, but say these capital flows refer mainly to one type of capital: short-term speculative investments, not productive capital. Financial mobility remains very limited where productive investments are concerned and the rapid money poses serious risks to Third World economies.

- Another argument cited by supporters is the increased global mobility of people: there are more refugees and there is more migrant labour around the globe. But the sceptics reply that most people stay at home, most refugees stay in their own region, and most labour is not mobile.

- Supporters refer to the global nature of the world's leading corporations. They say that the multinational corporation of the 1970s is obsolete. A new type of global company is emerging that does business around the globe, carries out research and product development in many different sites and has shareholders from all over the world.

  However, sceptics say that most internationally operating companies largely retain national management as well as local research and development sites and investments. They argue that of the hundred largest companies in the world, not one can seriously be called "global".

- For supporters, globalisation as a social process refers to the intensification of global consciousness. Sceptics reply that while on the surface there is a CNN-type global solidarity, the world is really more a collection of many local villages than a single global village. People may know the US president better than they do their neighbours, but in the end they will take sides with the parochial interests of their own tribe. Although more people may have become more cosmopolitan than ever before, this does not yet create a collectively shared cosmopolitan consciousness.

- Supporters argue that growing economic interdependence leads to social interdependence. Sceptics reply that this thesis lacks empirical confirmation. While there may be some evidence of global solidarity, there are equal or even more indications that people across the world do not feel part of a global family. Whereas supporters like to assert that current social processes are inevitably leading to global integration, sceptics believe that the same forces propelling these processes may equally lead to disintegration. Sceptics wonder why the supporters completely ignore the fact that the world is very starkly divided and fractured on many counts. They point to the highly visible fissures in the growing economic disparities between both the North and the South and between different social groups within most countries. According to their analysis, greater interdependence does not necessarily merge nations into larger units, as the supporters seem to assume. The sceptics take the rather more reserved position that since interdependencies are often asymmetrical, a growing number of global transactions are as likely to create more competition and conflict as they are to create more co-operation.

- Supporters believe the intensification of contacts around the world creates more global cohesion. But sceptics think this may also lead to more cultural competition:

    The cultures themselves have been thrown into conflict, as communities in their struggle for political rights and recognition have drawn upon their cultural resources – music, literature, the arts and crafts, dress, food and so on – to make their mark in the wider political arena, regionally and internationally, and continue to do so by the use of comparative statistics, prestige projects, tourism and the like. These are veritable "cultural wars", which underline the polycentric nature of our interdependent world.

    Globalisation means both integration and polarisation. It promotes both social movements that fight for the respect of human rights and social movements that further racism, ethnic divisions and fundamentalism.

- Supporters maintain that global consciousness is fostered by the growing density of communication flows around the world. The growth of globe-spanning communication networks (TV chains and data networks) cannot be denied and their importance should not be underestimated.

    Sceptics may agree with this and yet point out that there is at present an enormous disparity in access to these flows and networks. How "global" is global communication, they ask, when by early 1997 some 62 per cent of the world's main telephone lines were installed in just twenty-three affluent countries accounting for only 15 per cent of the world's population? How "global" is global communication when more than 950 million households (65 per cent of the world total) had no telephone in 1997? Or when Internet host computers are distributed in such a way that the United States (51.5 per cent), European Union countries (23 per cent), Canada (6.1 per cent) and Japan (5.2 per cent) constituted 85.8 per cent of the world's total in 1997?

- Supporters say globalisation describes what happens to consumer markets worldwide. As the 1998 United Nations Development Programme report claims, "globalisation, the integration of trade, investment and financial markets, has also integrated the consumer market." The opening of markets for consumer goods, mass production, mass consumption and advertising has both economic and social dimensions. The latter involve the alleged fact that "people all over the world are becoming part of an integrated global consumer market with the same products and advertisements". As a result they begin to share the same standards of the "good life".

Against this, the sceptics say that this global integration is very unequally distributed around the world. The increasing visibility of consumer goods is not the same as their availability: "While the global elite are consumers in an integrated market, many others are marginalised out of the global consumption network." On the global consumer market most people are merely gawking. As markets open worldwide and more advertising for consumer products arrives, there develops an explosive disparity between visibility and availability. In the global shopping mall the world spent in 1998 some US$24 trillion in consumer expenditures. Over 80 per cent of this was spent by 20 per cent of the world's population.

Supporters and sceptics thus disagree about the appropriateness of globalisation as an analytical tool. They are also divided on the question of whether the driving force of contemporary social processes is primarily technological progress. Supporters see globalisation as the inevitable consequence of modern technological developments in transportation and communication. Sceptics argue that an explanation based upon technological determinism is too limited. Technologies undoubtedly play an enabling role but the crucial variables are decisions made by public and private institutions.

Related to this is also a serious disagreement about the significance of the national state. Supporters suggest that the national state has lost its sovereign powers. Economic processes propelled by transborder financial flows, offshore electronic markets and worldwide marketing of cultural products affect the decision-making powers of individual states.

Sceptics say this is true only in a limited way. The financial capacities and political power of major transnational corporations have certainly increased. Some of these corporations have revenues that exceed the gross domestic product of important industrial nations. However, sceptics find the claim that governments have become impotent greatly exaggerated. Many powerful companies could not survive without state subsidies (e.g., Renault and McDonnell Douglas) or without state purchases of defence products (e.g., General Electric, Boeing, IBM) or of non-defence products (e.g., Siemens and Alcatel).

Moreover, the role of law enforcement institutions is crucial for the efficient performance of large companies. National sovereignty helps transnational corporations to avoid the creation of genuine supranational regulatory institutions that might control their restrictive business practices. Transnational corporations need national governments to guarantee safe investment environments, to create market opportunities through foreign aid or to promote the trade of their "national" companies through their diplomatic missions. They may also benefit from supportive national regulations on technical standards, patent and trademark protection, or acquisitions and mergers.

In the analysis of the sceptics, powerful governments have voluntarily delegated primacy to the marketplace. The state is still decisive in determining the quality of health care, social services and education. The retreat of the state tends to be partial and from selected social domains such as social services, and not from intervention on behalf of the holders of intellectual property rights, for example.

Sceptics may not deny that states today play a lesser role, but they argue that this is not an inevitable process. National states have for a variety of political and economic reasons assisted in their own demise.

Globalisation: The Political Agenda

As a political programme, too, globalisation represents an agenda that has both its advocates and critics.

The advocates claim that globalisation creates worldwide open and competitive markets which promote global prosperity. The key justification of their political programme is that a global free market leads to greater employment, better quality of goods and services and lower consumer prices.

For critics, the globalisation agenda is a neoliberal political programme that primarily promotes the interests of the world's most powerful players:

Globalisation has meant different things, at different levels, for different categories of people. Millions of farmers, immigrants, poorly qualified urban workers, youth and women suffer globalisation's negative consequences; they are marginalised and excluded from the new world economy.

Against Leon Brittan, the former EU Commissioner for external trade, who believes that "globalisation is good for the planet", the critics argue that the globalisation programme has disastrous consequences for sustainable development since it promotes the unhindered growth of consumer expenditure.

Globalisation advocates see the process as unstoppable and as ultimately beneficial. It will make all the world's people more prosperous.

The critics disagree and say that if there is any globalisation at all, it is the "globalisation of poverty". Among the empirical figures they cite for their argument is the sevenfold rise of poverty in eastern Europe since 1989. They also point to the fact that the ratio of the richest 20 per cent of people in the world to the poorest 20 per cent rose from 1:30 in 1960 to 1:80 in 1995. They further note that in the United States 1 per cent of the population owns 50 per cent of the wealth, whereas 60 per cent owns nothing.

Advocates and critics also disagree about the cultural dimensions of the globalisation programme. Advocates say globalisation promotes cultural differentiation while critics claim globalisation is merely a new guise for old-fashioned cultural imperialism.

Both advocates and critics may have a point here as the global landscape is made up of homogenising global tendencies, heterogenising local developments and hybrid forms that are sometimes referred to as "glocalisation". The worldwide proliferation of standardised food, clothing, music and TV shows, and the spread of Anglo-Saxon business style and linguistic conventions, create the impression of an unprecedented cultural homogenisation. Yet, despite the McDonaldisation of the world, there remain forcefully distinct cultural entities, to which the manifold inter-ethnic conflicts that beset the globe are dramatic testimony. There has certainly been an increase in cultural contacts and of cultural movements that go beyond national boundaries, but this has not yet brought about a global culture. Parallel with the homogenisation of consumer lifestyles there is also local cultural differentiation.

Whereas advocates see a positive link between globalisation and employment, critics argue that employment conditions worldwide are rapidly worsening. The demand for labour diminishes and the supply increases. Neoliberal capitalism can make do with a very limited labour force. Economic growth does not lead to more but rather to less employment ("jobless growth"). Characteristic of the capitalist economic system, particularly since the Industrial Revolution, is that more economic productivity is achieved with less input of labour. There is no empirical indication that the new so-called service economies provide higher-skilled jobs for more people. What they do is create large numbers of data processors in poor countries at minimal wages.

It is precisely in such new service industries as telecommunications that increasing numbers of people are being laid off. It has been suggested that in some countries (e.g., the United States) employment figures have risen, but this refers mainly to part-time, flexible and temporary jobs that are usually low paid and have limited social security.

The critics thus conclude that in the end the globalisation programme is a propagandistic ploy to mask the politico-economic objectives of neoliberal capitalism. It diverts public attention from the fact that this agenda creates new monopolists and oligopolists rather than free competitive markets, and that it increases unemployment worldwide as privatised enterprises – no longer controlled by employment policy objectives – tend to lay off large numbers of people because they find it possible to operate with a smaller labour force and hence reduce costs.

Globalisation as Humanitarian Concern

Positions on the use of the globalisation concept as an analytical tool and/or as the central plank of a political agenda are thus strongly divided. Even so, it would seem worthwhile to explore briefly whether the concept could derive meaning as a guide to the kind of world we want to live in and in which we want to see our children grow up.

The concept "globalisation" could be used to represent the aspiration of a world community that respects universal standards of fundamental human rights and is characterised by a sensitivity to the need for global solidarity and a recognition and acceptance of sociocultural differences.

This aspiration requires the worldwide development of a human rights culture. This is a tall order. We have to learn to become global citizens. People around the world need to learn the sensitivity for living in a multicultural arena. Global citizenship does not come with our genetic structure but is acquired only through extensive training.

Global citizenship implies knowledge about the world that is different from what today's mass media and educational systems offer. Our educational systems pose formidable obstacles to the goal of global citizenship because of their highly specialised, fragmented, piecemeal approaches to knowledge. Our current university systems do much to discourage any unconventional, multidisciplinary exploration.

Multidisciplinarity, which would be a prerequisite of any attempt at global understanding and knowledge, remains a solemn recommendation in numerous academic memorandums. In reality, most universities do not train students to speak the language of sciences other than those they study.

The mass media are equally ill equipped to enhance global consciousness. They commonly stress the priority of the local over the global, deal with problems as isolated incidents, leave large parts of the globe outside their audience's reach and report in superficial, often biased if not racist ways, about foreign peoples and cultures.

If we aspire to "global citizenship" and want to educate ourselves to implement it, it is essential to overcome a complex moral challenge.

The Moral Challenge

The philosopher Richard Rorty argues that in today's international reality,

> no foreseeable applications of technology could make every family rich enough to give their children anything like the chances that are taken for granted in the lucky parts of the world. Nor can we expect that the people in the industrialised democracies will redistribute their wealth in creating bright prospects for children of the underdeveloped countries in such a way as to threaten the prospects of their own children…The only way the rich can think of themselves as part of the same moral community with the poor is through some scenario which gives hope to the children of the poor without threatening that of their own children.

In other words: the rich are only willing to act in accordance with such moral principles as human solidarity provided their own interests are not threatened. If the prospects of their own children are at stake the choice will be against the moral principles.

The challenge here is that the aspiration of a globalisation for the poor cannot be realised without seriously limiting the prospects of the rich. This represents a classical case of a hard moral choice since, given the ecological constraints of our globe, the prospects of the poor can only improve at the expense of those of the rich. It is impossible to raise the living standards of the majority of "unlucky people" in the world to those of the privileged minorities without creating an unprecedented ecological disaster! The plight of the poor cannot be changed without reducing the privileges of the rich. If the poor and rich continue to live in different moral universes, education to produce global citizens is doomed to fail.

[…]

4

Jihad vs. McWorld

Benjamin R. Barber

Just beyond the horizon of current events lie two possible political futures – both bleak, neither democratic. The first is a retribalization of large swaths of humankind by war and bloodshed: a threatened Lebanonization of national states in which culture is pitted against culture, people against people, tribe against tribe – a Jihad in the name of a hundred narrowly conceived faiths against every kind of interdependence, every kind of artificial social cooperation and civic mutuality. The second is being borne in on us by the onrush of economic and ecological forces that demand integration and uniformity and that mesmerize the world with fast music, fast computers, and fast food – with MTV, Macintosh, and McDonald's, pressing nations into one commercially homogenous global network: one McWorld tied together by technology, ecology, communications, and commerce. The planet is falling precipitantly apart *AND* coming reluctantly together at the very same moment.

These two tendencies are sometimes visible in the same countries at the same instant: thus Yugoslavia, clamoring just recently to join the New Europe, is exploding into fragments; India is trying to live up to its reputation as the world's largest integral democracy while powerful new fundamentalist parties like the Hindu nationalist Bharatiya Janata Party, along with nationalist assassins, are imperiling its hard-won unity. States are breaking up or joining up: the Soviet Union has disappeared almost overnight, its parts forming new unions with one another or with like-minded nationalities in neighboring states. The old interwar national state based on territory and political sovereignty looks to be a mere transitional development.

Original publication details: Benjamin R. Barber, "Jihad vs. McWorld," in *The Atlantic*, 269, 3, March 1992, pp. 53–65. Reproduced with permission from B. R. Barber.

The Globalization Reader, Fifth Edition. Edited by Frank J. Lechner and John Boli.
Editorial material and organization © 2015 John Wiley & Sons, Ltd.
Published 2015 by John Wiley & Sons, Ltd.

The tendencies of what I am here calling the forces of Jihad and the forces of McWorld operate with equal strength in opposite directions, the one driven by parochial hatreds, the other by universalizing markets, the one re-creating ancient subnational and ethnic borders from within, the other making national borders porous from without. They have one thing in common: neither offers much hope to citizens looking for practical ways to govern themselves democratically. If the global future is to pit Jihad's centrifugal whirlwind against McWorld's centripetal black hole, the outcome is unlikely to be democratic – or so I will argue.

McWorld, or the Globalization of Politics

Four imperatives make up the dynamic of McWorld: a market imperative, a resource imperative, an information-technology imperative, and an ecological imperative. By shrinking the world and diminishing the salience of national borders, these imperatives have in combination achieved a considerable victory over factiousness and particularism, and not least of all over their most virulent traditional form – nationalism. It is the realists who are now Europeans, the utopians who dream nostalgically of a resurgent England or Germany, perhaps even a resurgent Wales or Saxony. Yesterday's wishful cry for one world has yielded to the reality of McWorld.

THE MARKET IMPERATIVE. Marxist and Leninist theories of imperialism assumed that the quest for ever-expanding markets would in time compel nation-based capitalist economies to push against national boundaries in search of an international economic imperium. Whatever else has happened to the scientist predictions of Marxism, in this domain they have proved farsighted. All national economies are now vulnerable to the inroads of larger, transnational markets within which trade is free, currencies are convertible, access to banking is open, and contracts are enforceable under law. In Europe, Asia, Africa, the South Pacific, and the Americas such markets are eroding national sovereignty and giving rise to entities – international banks, trade associations, transnational lobbies like OPEC and Greenpeace, world news services like CNN and the BBC, and multinational corporations that increasingly lack a meaningful national identity – that neither reflect nor respect nationhood as an organizing or regulative principle.

The market imperative has also reinforced the quest for international peace and stability, requisites of an efficient international economy. Markets are enemies of parochialism, isolation, fractiousness, war. Market psychology attenuates the psychology of ideological and religious cleavages and assumes a concord among producers and consumers – categories that ill fit narrowly conceived national or religious cultures. Shopping has little tolerance for blue laws, whether dictated by pub-closing British paternalism, Sabbath-observing Jewish Orthodox fundamentalism, or no-Sunday-liquor-sales Massachusetts puritanism. In the context of common markets, international law ceases to be a vision of justice and becomes a workaday framework for getting things done – enforcing contracts, ensuring that governments abide by deals, regulating trade and currency relations, and so forth.

Common markets demand a common language, as well as a common currency, and they produce common behaviors of the kind bred by cosmopolitan city life everywhere. Commercial pilots, computer programmers, international bankers, media specialists, oil riggers, entertainment celebrities, ecology experts, demographers, accountants, professors, athletes – these compose a new breed of men and women for whom religion, culture, and nationality can seem only marginal elements in a working identity. Although sociologists of everyday life will no doubt continue to distinguish a Japanese from an American mode, shopping has a common signature throughout the world. Cynics might even say that some of the recent revolutions in Eastern Europe have had as their true goal not liberty and the right to vote but well-paying jobs and the right to shop (although the vote is proving easier to acquire than consumer goods). The market imperative is, then, plenty powerful; but, notwithstanding some of the claims made for "democratic capitalism," it is not identical with the democratic imperative.

THE RESOURCE IMPERATIVE. Democrats once dreamed of societies whose political autonomy rested firmly on economic independence. The Athenians idealized what they called autarky, and tried for a while to create a way of life simple and austere enough to make the polis genuinely self-sufficient. To be free meant to be independent of any other community or polis. Not even the Athenians were able to achieve autarky, however: human nature, it turns out, is dependency. By the time of Pericles, Athenian politics was inextricably bound up with a flowering empire held together by naval power and commerce – an empire that, even as it appeared to enhance Athenian might, ate away at Athenian independence and autarky. Master and slave, it turned out, were bound together by mutual insufficiency.

The dream of autarky briefly engrossed nineteenth-century America as well, for the underpopulated, endlessly bountiful land, the cornucopia of natural resources, and the natural barriers of a continent walled in by two great seas led many to believe that America could be a world unto itself. Given this past, it has been harder for Americans than for most to accept the inevitability of interdependence. But the rapid depletion of resources even in a country like ours, where they once seemed inexhaustible, and the maldistribution of arable soil and mineral resources on the planet, leave even the wealthiest societies ever more resource-dependent and many other nations in permanently desperate straits.

Every nation, it turns out, needs something another nation has; some nations have almost nothing they need.

THE INFORMATION-TECHNOLOGY IMPERATIVE. Enlightenment science and the technologies derived from it are inherently universalizing. They entail a quest for descriptive principles of general application, a search for universal solutions to particular problems, and an unswerving embrace of objectivity and impartiality.

Scientific progress embodies and depends on open communication, a common discourse rooted in rationality, collaboration, and an easy and regular flow and exchange of information. Such ideals can be hypocritical covers for power-mongering by elites, and they may be shown to be wanting in many other ways, but they are entailed by the very idea of science and they make science and globalization practical allies.

Business, banking, and commerce all depend on information flow and are facilitated by new communication technologies. The hardware of these technologies tends to be systemic and integrated – computer, television, cable, satellite, laser, fiber-optic, and microchip technologies combining to create a vast interactive communications and information network that can potentially give every person on earth access to every other person, and make every datum, every byte, available to every set of eyes. If the automobile was, as George Ball once said (when he gave his blessing to a Fiat factory in the Soviet Union during the Cold War), "an ideology on four wheels," then electronic telecommunication and information systems are an ideology at 186,000 miles per second – which makes for a very small planet in a very big hurry. Individual cultures speak particular languages; commerce and science increasingly speak English; the whole world speaks logarithms and binary mathematics.

Moreover, the pursuit of science and technology asks for, even compels, open societies. Satellite footprints do not respect national borders; telephone wires penetrate the most closed societies. With photocopying and then fax machines having infiltrated Soviet universities and *samizdat* literary circles in the eighties, and computer modems having multiplied like rabbits in communism's bureaucratic warrens thereafter, *glasnost* could not be far behind. In their social requisites, secrecy and science are enemies. [...]

Yet in all this high-tech commercial world there is nothing that looks particularly democratic. It lends itself to surveillance as well as liberty, to new forms of manipulation and covert control as well as new kinds of participation, to skewed, unjust market outcomes as well as greater productivity. The consumer society and the open society are not quite synonymous. Capitalism and democracy have a relationship, but it is something less than a marriage. An efficient free market after all requires that consumers be free to vote their dollars on competing goods, not that citizens be free to vote their values and beliefs on competing political candidates and programs. The free market flourished in junta-run Chile, in military-governed Taiwan and Korea, and, earlier, in a variety of autocratic European empires as well as their colonial possessions.

THE ECOLOGICAL IMPERATIVE. The impact of globalization on ecology is a cliche even to world leaders who ignore it. We know well enough that the German forests can be destroyed by Swiss and Italians driving gas-guzzlers fueled by leaded gas. We also know that the planet can be asphyxiated by greenhouse gases because Brazilian farmers want to be part of the twentieth century and are burning down tropical rain forests to clear a little land to plough, and because Indonesians make a living out of converting their lush jungle into toothpicks for fastidious Japanese diners, upsetting the delicate oxygen balance and in effect puncturing our global lungs. Yet this ecological consciousness has meant not only greater awareness but also greater inequality, as modernized nations try to slam the door behind them, saying to developing nations, "The world cannot afford your modernization; ours has wrung it dry!"

Each of the four imperatives just cited is transnational, transideological, and transcultural. Each applies impartially to Catholics, Jews, Muslims, Hindus, and Buddhists; to democrats and totalitarians; to capitalists and socialists. The Enlightenment dream of a universal rational society has to a remarkable degree been realized – but in a form that is commercialized, homogenized, depoliticized, bureaucratized, and, of course, radically incomplete, for the movement toward McWorld is in competition with forces of global breakdown, national dissolution, and centrifugal corruption. These forces, working in the opposite direction, are the essence of what I call Jihad.

Jihad, or the Lebanonization of the World

OPEC, the World Bank, the United Nations, the International Red Cross, the multinational corporation ... there are scores of institutions that reflect globalization. But they often appear as ineffective reactors to the world's real actors: national states and, to an ever greater degree, subnational factions in permanent rebellion against uniformity and integration – even the kind represented by universal law and justice. The headlines feature these players regularly: they are cultures, not countries; parts, not wholes; sects, not religions; rebellious factions and dissenting minorities at war not just with globalism but with the traditional nation-state. Kurds, Basques, Puerto Ricans, Ossetians, East Timoreans, Quebecois, the Catholics of Northern Ireland, Abkhasians, Kurile Islander Japanese, the Zulus of Inkatha, Catalonians, Tamils, and, of course, Palestinians – people without countries, inhabiting nations not their own, seeking smaller worlds within borders that will seal them off from modernity.

A powerful irony is at work here. Nationalism was once a force of integration and unification, a movement aimed at bringing together disparate clans, tribes, and cultural fragments under new, assimilationist flags. But as Ortega y Gasset noted more than sixty years ago, having won its victories, nationalism changed its strategy. In the 1920s, and again today, it is more often a reactionary and divisive force, pulverizing the very nations it once helped cement together. The force that creates nations is "inclusive," Ortega wrote in *The Revolt of the Masses*. "In periods of consolidation, nationalism has a positive value, and is a lofty standard. But in Europe everything is more than consolidated, and nationalism is nothing but a mania ..."

This mania has left the post-Cold War world smoldering with hot wars; the international scene is little more unified than it was at the end of the Great War, in Ortega's own time. There were more than thirty wars in progress last year, most of them ethnic, racial, tribal, or religious in character, and the list of unsafe regions doesn't seem to be getting any shorter. Some new world order!

The aim of many of these small-scale wars is to redraw boundaries, to implode states and resecure parochial identities: to escape McWorld's dully insistent imperatives. The mood is that of Jihad: war not as an instrument of policy but as an emblem of identity, an expression of community, an end in itself. Even where there is no shooting war, there is fractiousness, secession, and the quest for ever smaller communities. Add to the list of dangerous countries those at risk: In Switzerland and Spain, Jurassian and Basque separatists still argue the virtues of ancient identities, sometimes in the language of bombs. Hyperdisintegration in the former Soviet Union may well continue unabated – not just a Ukraine independent from the Soviet Union but a Bessarabian Ukraine independent from the Ukrainian republic; not just Russia severed from the defunct union but Tatarstan severed from Russia. Yugoslavia makes even the disunited, ex-Soviet, nonsocialist republics that were once the Soviet Union look integrated, its sectarian fatherlands springing up within factional motherlands like weeds within weeds within weeds. Kurdish independence would threaten the territorial integrity of four Middle Eastern nations. Well before the current cataclysm Soviet Georgia made a claim for autonomy from the Soviet Union, only to be faced with its Ossetians (164,000 in a republic of 5.5 million) demanding their own self-determination within Georgia. The Abkhasian minority in Georgia has followed suit. [...]

The passing of communism has torn away the thin veneer of internationalism (workers of the world unite!) to reveal ethnic prejudices that are not only ugly and deep-seated but increasingly murderous. Europe's old scourge, anti-Semitism, is back with a vengeance, but it is only one of many antagonisms. It appears all too easy to throw the historical gears into reverse and pass from a Communist dictatorship back into a tribal state.

Among the tribes, religion is also a battlefield. ("Jihad" is a rich word whose generic meaning is "struggle" – usually the struggle of the soul to avert evil. Strictly applied to religious war, it is used only in reference to battles where the faith is under assault, or battles against a government that denies the practice of Islam. My use here is rhetorical, but does follow both journalistic practice and history.) Remember the Thirty Years War? Whatever forms of Enlightenment universalism might once have come to grace such historically related forms of monotheism as Judaism, Christianity, and Islam, in many of their modern incarnations they are parochial rather than cosmopolitan, angry rather than loving, proselytizing rather than ecumenical, zealous rather than rationalist, sectarian rather than deistic, ethnocentric rather than universalizing. As a result, like the new forms of hypernationalism, the new expressions of religious fundamentalism are fractious and pulverizing, never integrating. This is religion as the Crusaders knew it: a battle to the death for souls that if not saved will be forever lost.

The atmospherics of Jihad have resulted in a breakdown of civility in the name of identity, of comity in the name of community. International relations have sometimes taken on the aspect of gang war – cultural turf battles featuring tribal factions that were supposed to be sublimated as integral parts of large national, economic, postcolonial, and constitutional entities.

The Darkening Future of Democracy

These rather melodramatic tableaux vivants do not tell the whole story, however. For all their defects, Jihad and McWorld have their attractions. Yet, to repeat and insist, the attractions are unrelated to democracy. Neither McWorld nor Jihad is remotely democratic in impulse. Neither needs democracy; neither promotes democracy.

McWorld does manage to look pretty seductive in a world obsessed with Jihad. It delivers peace, prosperity, and relative unity – if at the cost of independence, community, and identity (which is generally based on difference). The primary political values required by the global market are order and tranquillity, and freedom – as in the phrases "free trade," "free press," and "free love." Human rights are needed to a degree, but not citizenship or participation – and no more social justice and equality than are necessary to promote efficient economic production and consumption. Multinational corporations sometimes seem to prefer doing business with local oligarchs, inasmuch as they can take confidence from dealing with the boss on all crucial matters. Despots who slaughter their own populations are no problem, so long as they leave markets in place and refrain from making war on their neighbors (Saddam Hussein's fatal mistake). In trading partners, predictability is of more value than justice.

The Eastern European revolutions that seemed to arise out of concern for global democratic values quickly deteriorated into a stampede in the general direction of free markets and their ubiquitous, television-promoted shopping malls. East Germany's Neues Forum, that courageous gathering of intellectuals, students, and workers which overturned the Stalinist regime in Berlin in 1989, lasted only six months in Germany's mini-version of McWorld. Then it gave way to money and markets and monopolies from the West. By the time of the first all-German elections, it could scarcely manage to secure three percent of the vote. Elsewhere there is growing evidence that glasnost will go and perestroika – defined as privatization and an opening of markets to Western bidders – will stay. So understandably anxious are the new rulers of Eastern Europe and whatever entities are forged from the residues of the Soviet Union to gain access to credit and markets and technology – McWorld's flourishing new currencies – that they have shown themselves willing to trade away democratic prospects in pursuit of them: not just old totalitarian ideologies and command-economy production models but some possible indigenous experiments with a third way between capitalism and socialism, such as economic cooperatives and employee stock-ownership plans, both of which have their ardent supporters in the East.

Jihad delivers a different set of virtues: a vibrant local identity, a sense of community, solidarity among kinsmen, neighbors, and countrymen, narrowly conceived. But it also guarantees parochialism and is grounded in exclusion. Solidarity is secured through war against outsiders. And solidarity often means obedience to a hierarchy in governance, fanaticism in beliefs, and the obliteration of individual selves in the name of the group. Deference to leaders and intolerance toward outsiders (and toward "enemies within") are hallmarks of tribalism – hardly the attitudes required for the cultivation of new democratic women and men capable of governing themselves. Where new democratic experiments have been conducted in retribalizing societies, in both Europe and the Third World, the result has often been anarchy, repression, persecution, and the coming of new, noncommunist forms of very old kinds of despotism. During the past year, Havel's velvet revolution in Czechoslovakia was imperiled by partisans of "Czechland" and of Slovakia as independent entities. India seemed little less rent by Sikh, Hindu, Muslim, and Tamil infighting than it was immediately after the British pulled out, more than forty years ago.

To the extent that either McWorld or Jihad has a NATURAL politics, it has turned out to be more of an antipolitics. For McWorld, it is the antipolitics of globalism: bureaucratic, technocratic, and meritocratic, focused (as Marx predicted it would be) on the administration of things – with people, however, among the chief things to be administered. In its politico-economic imperatives McWorld has been guided by laissez-faire market principles that privilege efficiency, productivity, and beneficence at the expense of civic liberty and self-government.

For Jihad, the antipolitics of tribalization has been explicitly antidemocratic: one-party dictatorship, government by military junta, theocratic fundamentalism – often associated with a version of the *Führerprinzip* that empowers an individual to rule on behalf of a people. Even the government of India, struggling for decades to model democracy for a people who will soon number a billion, longs for great leaders; and for every Mahatma Gandhi, Indira Gandhi, or Rajiv Gandhi taken from them by zealous assassins, the Indians appear to seek a replacement who will deliver them from the lengthy travail of their freedom.

The Confederal Option

How can democracy be secured and spread in a world whose primary tendencies are at best indifferent to it (McWorld) and at worst deeply antithetical to it (Jihad)? My guess is that globalization will eventually vanquish retribalization. The ethos of material "civilization" has not yet encountered an obstacle it has been unable to thrust aside. [...]

Jihad may be a last deep sigh before the eternal yawn of McWorld. [...] if retribalization is inhospitable to democracy, there is nonetheless a form of democratic government that can accommodate parochialism and communitarianism, one that can even save them from their defects and make them more tolerant and participatory: decentralized participatory democracy. And if McWorld is indifferent to democracy, there is nonetheless a form of democratic government that suits global markets passably well – representative government in its federal or, better still, confederal variation.

With its concern for accountability, the protection of minorities, and the universal rule of law, a confederalized representative system would serve the political needs of McWorld as well as oligarchic bureaucratism or meritocratic elitism is currently doing. As we are already beginning to see, many nations may survive in the long term only as confederations that afford local regions smaller than "nations" extensive jurisdiction. Recommended reading for democrats of the twenty-first century is not the US Constitution or the French Declaration of Rights of Man and Citizen but the Articles of Confederation, that suddenly pertinent document that stitched together the thirteen American colonies into what then seemed a too loose confederation of independent states but now appears a new form of political realism, as veterans of Yeltsin's new Russia and the new Europe created at Maastricht will attest.

By the same token, the participatory and direct form of democracy that engages citizens in civic activity and civic judgment and goes well beyond just voting and accountability – the system I have called "strong democracy" – suits the political needs of decentralized communities as well as theocratic and nationalist party dictatorships have done. Local neighborhoods need not be democratic, but they can be. Real democracy has flourished in diminutive settings: the spirit of liberty, Tocqueville said, is local. Participatory democracy, if not naturally apposite to tribalism, has an undeniable attractiveness under conditions of parochialism.

Democracy in any of these variations will, however, continue to be obstructed by the undemocratic and antidemocratic trends toward uniformitarian globalism and intolerant retribalization which I have portrayed here. For democracy to persist in our brave new McWorld, we will have to commit acts of conscious political will – a possibility, but hardly a probability, under these conditions. Political will requires much more than the quick fix of the transfer of institutions. Like technology transfer, institution transfer rests on foolish assumptions about a uniform world of the kind that once fired the imagination of colonial administrators. Spread English justice to the colonies by exporting wigs. Let an East Indian trading company act as the vanguard to Britain's free parliamentary institutions. Today's well-intentioned quick-fixers in the National Endowment for Democracy and the Kennedy School of Government, in the unions and foundations and universities zealously nurturing contacts in Eastern Europe and the Third World, are hoping to democratize by long distance. Post Bulgaria a parliament by first-class mail. Fed Ex the Bill of Rights to Sri Lanka. Cable Cambodia some common law. [...]

Democrats need to seek out indigenous democratic impulses. There is always a desire for self-government, always some expression of participation, accountability, consent, and representation, even in traditional hierarchical societies. These need to be identified, tapped, modified, and incorporated into new democratic practices with an indigenous flavor. The tortoises among the democratizers may ultimately outlive or outpace the hares, for they will have the time and patience to explore conditions along the way, and to adapt their gait to changing circumstances. Tragically, democracy in a hurry often looks something like France in 1794 or China in 1989.

It certainly seems possible that the most attractive democratic ideal in the face of the brutal realities of Jihad and the dull realities of McWorld will be a confederal union of semi-autonomous communities smaller than nation-states, tied together into regional economic associations and markets larger than nation-states – participatory and self-determining in local matters at the bottom, representative and accountable at the top. The nation-state would play a diminished role, and sovereignty would lose some of its political potency. The Green movement adage "Think globally, act locally" would actually come to describe the conduct of politics.

This vision reflects only an ideal, however – one that is not terribly likely to be realized. Freedom, Jean-Jacques Rousseau once wrote, is a food easy to eat but hard to digest. Still, democracy has always played itself out against the odds. And democracy remains both a form of coherence as binding as McWorld and a secular faith potentially as inspiriting as Jihad.

5

The Clash of Civilizations?

Samuel P. Huntington

The Next Pattern of Conflict

World politics is entering a new phase, and intellectuals have not hesitated to prolif-erate visions of what it will be – the end of history, the return of traditional rivalries between nation states, and the decline of the nation state from the conflicting pulls of tribalism and globalism, among others. Each of these visions catches aspects of the emerging reality. Yet they all miss a crucial, indeed a central, aspect of what global politics is likely to be in the coming years.

It is my hypothesis that the fundamental source of conflict in this new world will not be primarily ideological or primarily economic. The great divisions among humankind and the dominating source of conflict will be cultural. Nation states will remain the most powerful actors in world affairs, but the principal conflicts of global politics will occur between nations and groups of different civilizations. The clash of civilizations will dominate global politics. The fault lines between civilizations will be the battle lines of the future.

Conflict between civilizations will be the latest phase in the evolution of conflict in the modern world. For a century and a half after the emergence of the modern inter-national system with the Peace of Westphalia, the conflicts of the Western world were largely among princes – emperors, absolute monarchs and constitutional mon-archs attempting to expand their bureaucracies, their armies, their mercantilist economic strength and, most important, the territory they ruled. In the process they

Original publication details: Samuel P. Huntington, "The Clash of Civilizations?" in *Foreign Affairs*, 72, 3, Summer 1993. pp. 22–3, 25–32, 39–41, 49. Reproduced with permission from Foreign Affairs.

The Globalization Reader, Fifth Edition. Edited by Frank J. Lechner and John Boli.
Editorial material and organization © 2015 John Wiley & Sons, Ltd.
Published 2015 by John Wiley & Sons, Ltd.

created nation states, and beginning with the French Revolution the principal lines of conflict were between nations rather than princes. In 1793, as R. R. Palmer put it, "The wars of kings were over; the wars of peoples had begun." This nineteenth-century pattern lasted until the end of World War I. Then, as a result of the Russian Revolution and the reaction against it, the conflict of nations yielded to the conflict of ideologies, first among communism, fascism-Nazism and liberal democracy, and then between communism and liberal democracy. During the Cold War, this latter conflict became embodied in the struggle between the two superpowers, neither of which was a nation state in the classical European sense and each of which defined its identity in terms of its ideology.

These conflicts between princes, nation states and ideologies were primarily conflicts within Western civilization, "Western civil wars," as William Lind has labeled them. This was as true of the Cold War as it was of the world wars and the earlier wars of the seventeenth, eighteenth and nineteenth centuries. With the end of the Cold War, international politics moves out of its Western phase, and its centerpiece becomes the interaction between the West and non-Western civilizations and among non-Western civilizations. In the politics of civilizations, the peoples and governments of non-Western civilizations no longer remain the objects of history as targets of Western colonialism but join the West as movers and shapers of history. [...]

Why Civilizations Will Clash

Civilization identity will be increasingly important in the future, and the world will be shaped in large measure by the interactions among seven or eight major civilizations. These include Western, Confucian, Japanese, Islamic, Hindu, Slavic-Orthodox, Latin American and possibly African civilizations. The most important conflicts of the future will occur along the cultural fault lines separating these civilizations from one another.

Why will this be the case?

First, differences among civilizations are not only real; they are basic. Civilizations are differentiated from each other by history, language, culture, tradition and, most important, religion. The people of different civilizations have different views on the relations between God and man, the individual and the group, the citizen and the state, parents and children, husband and wife, as well as differing views of the relative importance of rights and responsibilities, liberty and authority, equality and hierarchy. These differences are the product of centuries. They will not soon disappear. They are far more fundamental than differences among political ideologies and political regimes. Differences do not necessarily mean conflict, and conflict does not necessarily mean violence. Over the centuries, however, differences among civilizations have generated the most prolonged and the most violent conflicts.

Second, the world is becoming a smaller place. The interactions between peoples of different civilizations are increasing; these increasing interactions intensify civilization consciousness and awareness of differences between civilizations and commonalities within civilizations. North African immigration to France generates hostility among Frenchmen and at the same time increased receptivity to immigration by "good" European Catholic Poles. Americans react far more negatively to Japanese investment than to larger investments from Canada and European countries. Similarly, as Donald Horowitz has pointed out, "An Ibo may be ... an Owerri Ibo or an Onitsha Ibo in what was the Eastern region of Nigeria. In Lagos, he is simply an Ibo. In London, he is a Nigerian. In New York, he is an African." The interactions among peoples of different civilizations enhance the civilization-consciousness of people that, in turn, invigorates differences and animosities stretching or thought to stretch back deep into history.

Third, the processes of economic modernization and social change throughout the world are separating people from longstanding local identities. They also weaken the nation state as a source of identity. In much of the world religion has moved in to fill this gap, often in the form of movements that are labeled "fundamentalist." Such movements are found in Western Christianity, Judaism, Buddhism and Hinduism, as well as in Islam. In most countries and most religions the people active in fundamentalist movements are young, college-educated, middle-class technicians, professionals and business persons. The "unsecularization of the world," George Weigel has remarked, "is one of the dominant social facts of life in the late twentieth century." The revival of religion, "la revanche de Dieu," as Gilles Kepel labeled it, provides a basis for identity and commitment that transcends national boundaries and unites civilizations.

Fourth, the growth of civilization-consciousness is enhanced by the dual role of the West. On the one hand, the West is at a peak of power. At the same time, however, and perhaps as a result, a return to the roots phenomenon is occurring among non-Western civilizations. Increasingly one hears references to trends toward a turning inward and "Asianization" in Japan, the end of the Nehru legacy and the "Hinduization" of India, the failure of Western ideas of socialism and nationalism and hence "re-Islamization" of the Middle East, and now a debate over Westernization versus Russianization in Boris Yeltsin's country. A West at the peak of its power confronts non-Wests that increasingly have the desire, the will and the resources to shape the world in non-Western ways.

In the past, the elites of non-Western societies were usually the people who were most involved with the West, had been educated at Oxford, the Sorbonne or Sandhurst, and had absorbed Western attitudes and values. At the same time, the populace in non-Western countries often remained deeply imbued with the indigenous culture. Now, however, these relationships are being reversed. A de-Westernization and indigenization of elites is occurring in many non-Western countries at the same time that Western, usually American, cultures, styles and habits become more popular among the mass of the people.

Fifth, cultural characteristics and differences are less mutable and hence less easily compromised and resolved than political and economic ones. In the former Soviet Union, communists can become democrats, the rich can become poor and the poor rich, but Russians cannot become Estonians and Azeris cannot become Armenians. In class and ideological conflicts, the key question was "Which side are you on?" and people could and did choose sides and change sides. In conflicts between civilizations, the question is "What are you?" That is a given that cannot be changed. And as we know, from Bosnia to the Caucasus to the Sudan, the wrong answer to that question can mean a bullet in the head. Even more than ethnicity, religion discriminates sharply and exclusively among people. A person can be half-French and half-Arab and simultaneously even a citizen of two countries. It is more difficult to be half-Catholic and half-Muslim.

Finally, economic regionalism is increasing. The proportions of total trade that were intraregional rose between 1980 and 1989 from 51 percent to 59 percent in Europe, 33 percent to 37 percent in East Asia, and 32 percent to 36 percent in North America. The importance of regional economic blocs is likely to continue to increase in the future. On the one hand, successful economic regionalism will reinforce civilization-consciousness. On the other hand, economic regionalism may succeed only when it is rooted in a common civilization. The European Community rests on the shared foundation of European culture and Western Christianity. The success of the North American Free Trade Area depends on the convergence now underway of Mexican, Canadian and American cultures. Japan, in contrast, faces difficulties in creating a comparable economic entity in East Asia because Japan is a society and civilization unique to itself. However strong the trade and investment links Japan may develop with other East Asian countries, its cultural differences with those countries inhibit and perhaps preclude its promoting regional economic integration like that in Europe and North America.

Common culture, in contrast, is clearly facilitating the rapid expansion of the economic relations between the People's Republic of China and Hong Kong, Taiwan, Singapore and the overseas Chinese communities in other Asian countries. With the Cold War over, cultural commonalities increasingly overcome ideological differences, and mainland China and Taiwan move closer together. If cultural commonality is a prerequisite for economic integration, the principal East Asian economic bloc of the future is likely to be centered on China. This bloc is, in fact, already coming into existence. As Murray Weidenbaum has observed,

> Despite the current Japanese dominance of the region, the Chinese-based economy of Asia is rapidly emerging as a new epicenter for industry, commerce and finance. This strategic area contains substantial amounts of technology and manufacturing capability (Taiwan), outstanding entrepreneurial, marketing and services acumen (Hong Kong), a fine communications network (Singapore), a tremendous pool of financial capital (all three), and very large endowments of land, resources and labor (mainland China) … From Guangzhou to Singapore, from Kuala Lumpur to Manila, this influential network – often based on extensions of the traditional clans – has been described as the backbone of the East Asian economy.

Culture and religion also form the basis of the Economic Cooperation Organization, which brings together ten non-Arab Muslim countries: Iran, Pakistan, Turkey, Azerbaijan, Kazakhstan, Kyrgyzstan, Turkmenistan, Tadjikistan, Uzbekistan and Afghanistan. One impetus to the revival and expansion of this organization, founded originally in the 1960s by Turkey, Pakistan and Iran, is the realization by the leaders of several of these countries that they had no chance of admission to the European Community. Similarly, Caricom, the Central American Common Market and Mercosur rest on common cultural foundations. Efforts to build a broader Caribbean-Central American economic entity bridging the Anglo-Latin divide, however, have to date failed.

As people define their identity in ethnic and religious terms, they are likely to see an "us" versus "them" relation existing between themselves and people of different ethnicity or religion. The end of ideologically defined states in Eastern Europe and the former Soviet Union permits traditional ethnic identities and animosities to come to the fore. Differences in culture and religion create differences over policy issues, ranging from human rights to immigration to trade and commerce to the environment. Geographical propinquity gives rise to conflicting territorial claims from Bosnia to Mindanao. Most important, the efforts of the West to promote its values of democracy and liberalism as universal values, to maintain its military predominance and to advance its economic interests engender countering responses from other civilizations. Decreasingly able to mobilize support and form coalitions on the basis of ideology, governments and groups will increasingly attempt to mobilize support by appealing to common religion and civilization identity.

The clash of civilizations thus occurs at two levels. At the micro-level, adjacent groups along the fault lines between civilizations struggle, often violently, over the control of territory and each other. At the macro-level, states from different civilizations compete for relative military and economic power, struggle over the control of international institutions and third parties, and competitively promote their particular political and religious values.

The Fault Lines between Civilizations

The fault lines between civilizations are replacing the political and ideological boundaries of the Cold War as the flash points for crisis and bloodshed. The Cold War began when the Iron Curtain divided Europe politically and ideologically. The Cold War ended with the end of the Iron Curtain. As the ideological division of Europe has disappeared, the cultural division of Europe between Western Christianity, on the one hand, and Orthodox Christianity and Islam, on the other, has reemerged. The most significant dividing line in Europe, as William Wallace has suggested, may well be the eastern boundary of Western Christianity in the year 1500. This line runs along what are now the boundaries between Finland and Russia and between the Baltic states and Russia, cuts through Belarus and Ukraine separating the more Catholic western Ukraine from Orthodox eastern Ukraine, swings westward separating Transylvania from the rest of Romania, and then goes through Yugoslavia almost exactly along the line now separating Croatia and Slovenia from the rest of Yugoslavia. In the Balkans this line, of course, coincides with the historic boundary between the Hapsburg and Ottoman empires. The peoples to the north and west of this line are Protestant or Catholic; they shared the common experiences of European history – feudalism, the Renaissance, the Reformation, the Enlightenment, the French Revolution, the Industrial Revolution; they are generally economically better off than the peoples to the east; and they may now look forward to increasing involvement in a common European economy and to the consolidation of democratic political systems. The peoples to the east and south of this line are Orthodox or Muslim; they historically belonged to the Ottoman or Tsarist empires and were only lightly touched by the shaping events in the rest of Europe; they are generally less advanced economically; they seem much less likely to develop stable democratic political systems. The Velvet Curtain of culture has replaced the Iron Curtain of ideology as the most significant dividing line in Europe. As the events in Yugoslavia show, it is not only a line of difference; it is also at times a line of bloody conflict.

Conflict along the fault line between Western and Islamic civilizations has been going on for 1,300 years. After the founding of Islam, the Arab and Moorish surge west and north only ended at Tours in 732. From the eleventh to the thirteenth century the Crusaders attempted with temporary success to bring Christianity and Christian rule to the Holy Land. From the fourteenth to the seventeenth century, the Ottoman Turks reversed the balance, extended their sway over the Middle East and the Balkans, captured Constantinople, and twice laid siege to Vienna. In the nineteenth and early twentieth centuries as Ottoman power declined Britain, France, and Italy established Western control over most of North Africa and the Middle East.

After World War II, the West, in turn, began to retreat; the colonial empires disappeared; first Arab nationalism and then Islamic fundamentalism manifested themselves; the West became heavily dependent on the Persian Gulf countries for its energy; the oil-rich Muslim countries became money-rich and, when they wished to, weapons-rich. Several wars occurred between Arabs and Israel (created by the West). France fought a bloody and ruthless war in Algeria for most of the 1950s; British and French forces invaded Egypt in 1956; American forces went into Lebanon in 1958; subsequently American forces returned to Lebanon, attacked Libya, and engaged in various military encounters with Iran; Arab and Islamic terrorists, supported by at least three Middle Eastern governments, employed the weapon of the weak and bombed Western planes and installations and seized Western hostages. This warfare between Arabs and the West culminated in 1990, when the United States sent a massive army to the Persian Gulf to defend some Arab countries against aggression by another. In its aftermath NATO planning is increasingly directed to potential threats and instability along its "southern tier."

This centuries-old military interaction between the West and Islam is unlikely to decline. It could become more virulent. The Gulf War left some Arabs feeling proud that Saddam Hussein had attacked Israel and stood up to the West. It also left many feeling humiliated and resentful of the West's military presence in the Persian Gulf, the West's overwhelming military dominance, and their own apparent inability to shape their destiny. Many Arab countries, in addition to the oil exporters, are reaching levels of economic and social development where autocratic forms of government become inappropriate and efforts to introduce democracy become stronger. Some openings in Arab political systems have already occurred. The principal beneficiaries of these openings have been Islamist movements. In the Arab world, in short, Western democracy strengthens anti-Western political forces. This may be a passing phenomenon, but it surely complicates relations between Islamic countries and the West. […]

The West versus the Rest

The west is now at an extraordinary peak of power in relation to other civilizations. Its superpower opponent has disappeared from the map. Military conflict among Western states is unthinkable, and Western military power is unrivaled. Apart from Japan, the West faces no economic challenge. It dominates international political and security institutions and with Japan international economic institutions. Global political and security issues are effectively settled by a directorate of the United States, Britain and France, world economic issues by a directorate of the United States, Germany and Japan, all of which maintain extraordinarily close relations with each other to the exclusion of lesser and largely non-Western countries. Decisions made at the UN Security Council or in the International Monetary Fund that reflect the interests of the West are presented to the world as reflecting the desires of the world community. The very phrase "the world community" has become the euphemistic collective noun (replacing "the Free World") to give global legitimacy to actions reflecting the interests of the United States and other Western powers. Through the IMF and other international economic institutions, the West promotes its economic interests and imposes on other nations the economic policies it thinks appropriate. In any poll of non-Western peoples, the IMF undoubtedly would win the support of finance ministers and a few others, but get an overwhelmingly unfavorable rating from just about everyone else, who would agree with Georgy Arbatov's characterization of IMF officials as "neo-Bolsheviks who love expropriating other people's money, imposing undemocratic and alien rules of economic and political conduct and stifling economic freedom."

Western domination of the UN Security Council and its decisions, tempered only by occasional abstention by China, produced UN legitimation of the West's use of force to drive Iraq out of Kuwait and its elimination of Iraq's sophisticated weapons and capacity to produce such weapons. It also produced the quite unprecedented action by the United States, Britain and France in getting the Security Council to demand that Libya hand over the Pan Am 103 bombing suspects and then to impose sanctions when Libya refused. After defeating the largest Arab army, the West did not hesitate to throw its weight around in the Arab world. The West in effect is using international institutions, military power and economic resources to run the world in ways that will maintain Western predominance, protect Western interests and promote Western political and economic values.

That at least is the way in which non-Westerners see the new world, and there is a significant element of truth in their view. Differences in power and struggles for military, economic and institutional power are thus one source of conflict between the West and other civilizations. Differences in culture, that is basic values and beliefs, are a second source of conflict. V. S. Naipaul has argued that Western civilization is the "universal civilization" that "fits all men." At a superficial level much of Western culture has indeed permeated the rest of the world. At a more basic level, however, Western concepts differ fundamentally from those prevalent in other civilizations. Western ideas of individualism, liberalism, constitutionalism, human rights, equality, liberty, the rule of law, democracy, free markets, the separation of church and state, often have little resonance in Islamic, Confucian, Japanese, Hindu, Buddhist or Orthodox cultures. Western efforts to propagate such ideas produce instead a reaction against "human rights imperialism" and a reaffirmation of indigenous values, as can be seen in the support for religious fundamentalism by the younger generation in non-Western cultures. The very notion that there could be a "universal civilization" is a Western idea, directly at odds with the particularism of most Asian societies and their emphasis on what distinguishes one people from another. Indeed, the author of a review of 100 comparative studies of values in different societies concluded that "the values that are most important in the West are least important worldwide." In the political realm, of course, these differences are most manifest in the efforts of the United States and other Western powers to induce other peoples to adopt Western ideas concerning democracy and human rights. Modern democratic government originated in the West. When it has developed in non-Western societies it has usually been the product of Western colonialism or imposition.

The central axis of world politics in the future is likely to be, in Kishore Mahbubani's phrase, the conflict between "the West and the Rest" and the responses of non-Western civilizations to Western power and values. Those responses generally take one or a combination of three forms. At one extreme, non-Western states can, like Burma and North Korea, attempt to pursue a course of isolation, to insulate their societies from penetration or "corruption" by the West, and, in effect, to opt out of participation in the Western-dominated global community. The costs of this course, however, are high, and few states have pursued it exclusively. A second alternative, the equivalent of "band-wagoning" in international relations theory, is to attempt to join the West and accept its values and institutions. The third alternative is to attempt to "balance" the West by developing economic and military power and cooperating with other non-Western societies against the West, while preserving indigenous values and institutions; in short, to modernize but not to Westernize. […]

Western civilization is both Western and modern. Non-Western civilizations have attempted to become modern without becoming Western. To date only Japan has fully succeeded in this quest. Non-Western civilizations will continue to attempt to acquire the wealth, technology, skills, machines and weapons that are part of being modern. They will also attempt to reconcile this modernity with their traditional culture and values. Their economic and military strength relative to the West will increase. Hence the West will increasingly have to accommodate these non-Western modern civilizations whose power approaches that of the West but whose values and interests differ significantly from those of the West. This will require the West to maintain the economic and military power necessary to protect its interests in relation to these civilizations. It will also, however, require the West to develop a more profound understanding of the basic religious and philosophical assumptions underlying other civilizations and the ways in which people in those civilizations see their interests. It will require an effort to identify elements of commonality between Western and other civilizations. For the relevant future, there will be no universal civilization, but instead a world of different civilizations, each of which will have to learn to coexist with the others.

Part I Questions

1. What is the "hidden promise" of globalization, according to Micklethwait and Wooldridge? How do they counter the "vengeful howls" against globalization? What kinds of globalization gains, in addition to the ones they mention, could you cite in support of their position?
2. How does Sen show that globalization is not a western "curse"? By what criteria should "globalism" be judged? What is the "central issue of contention" in the debate about globalization?
3. Hamelink presents the views of skeptics of globalization, who question its newness and significance. What arguments do the skeptics present? Are their arguments more convincing about some aspects of globalization rather than others?
4. What are the key features of "McWorld" and "Jihad"? How does McWorld provoke and support Jihad? What does Barber find most threatening about globalization?
5. What is new about world politics today, according to Huntington? Does this image of a world embroiled in clashes of civilizations contradict the conventional view that globalization is a process that creates new bonds across cultural boundaries? Does he demonstrate that civilizations are now the primary forms of identity and organization in world society?

Part II

Explaining Globalization

Introduction

How can we best explain globalization? This question has no easy answer because, as we suggested in our introduction, globalization has many layers and dimensions. A good explanation must come to grips with this complexity. In addition, the world society that is still under formation presents a moving target, so any theory must be adaptable in dealing with new dimensions and characteristics of globalization. Explanation is all the more difficult because, as globalization refashions the world, theoretical tools once used to make sense of earlier historical periods may no longer be adequate. The "global age," Martin Albrow argued in his book by that title, calls for new theory, new thinking, and new departures in social science, especially if the discontinuity between old and new is as profound as many observers claim. In this part, we illustrate the new forms of theorizing that have emerged in recent decades by presenting selections from four major perspectives on globalization.

These perspectives propose quite varied accounts of globalization. We can illustrate the differences between them by comparing their answers to a hypothetical question (taken from the excerpt by John W. Meyer et al.): how would a newly discovered island society be incorporated into world society? One perspective's proponents would reply that transnational corporations would stake a claim to the island's natural resources, send engineers to create infrastructure, and build plants to take advantage of cheap labor. Another perspective's proponents would argue that agents of powerful countries would assist the society in building a functioning but limited state and tempt it to form alliances with them; international organizations would provide support and advice so that the society could become a stable

The Globalization Reader, Fifth Edition. Edited by Frank J. Lechner and John Boli.
Editorial material and organization © 2015 John Wiley & Sons, Ltd.
Published 2015 by John Wiley & Sons, Ltd.

participant in global politics. From a third perspective, the answer would involve the wholesale refashioning of the island society – it would be invaded by experts of many sorts who would help build not only a state but also the full range of modern institutions that any proper country is expected to develop. A final group would focus on the way the society would balance its own heritage against the intrusions of world culture, aided by outside organizations concerned about preserving its unique culture. Incorporation into world society can thus take the form of economic exploitation, state building and alliances, broad institutional restructuring according to global models, or self-reflexive cultural identification. The selections show that such answers derive from different views of the motive forces and characteristic features of globalization.

World-System Theory and Related Perspectives

To scholars inspired by Marx, globalization is essentially the expansion of the capitalist system around the globe. At the time Marx was writing in the mid-nineteenth century, the world was becoming unified via thickening networks of communication and economic exchange. A world economy, guided by liberal philosophy with global aspirations, provided the framework for a single world that since has grown more integrated and standardized. Sociologist Immanuel Wallerstein, author of the multivolume landmark study *The Modern World-System*, puts this historical claim in context. What happened in the mid-nineteenth century, he suggests, was a phase in a centuries-old process. The capitalist world-system originated in the sixteenth century, when European traders established enduring connections with Asia, Africa, and the Americas. From the outset, this system consisted of a single economy – a market and a regional division of labor – but many states, and no one power was strong enough to gain control and stifle dynamic competition. In the "core" of the system, the dominant classes were supported by strong states as they exploited labor, resources, and trade opportunities, most notably in "peripheral" areas. Buffer countries in the "semiperiphery" helped mitigate tensions between core and periphery, and a set of political and economic norms that favored core countries helped to keep the system remarkably stable. The central purpose of the world-system is capital accumulation by competing firms, which go through cycles of growth and decline.

Leslie Sklair, a British sociologist, complements this long-term perspective by stressing the role of transnational corporations and classes as the prime movers in the contemporary global system. He argues that a global consumerist ideology supports the exploitative structure commanded by transnational corporations and helps the dominant transnational class get ever stronger. This class-based view is reinforced by British-American geographer David Harvey in his discussion of neoliberalism, which he characterizes as an economic ideology devoted above all to property rights, free trade, and free markets. This prominent ideology, Harvey insists, is primarily a means for upper classes around the world to increase their economic supremacy at the expense of the middle and lower classes.

World Polity Theory

In this third theoretical perspective, states remain an important component of world society, but primary attention goes to the global cultural and organizational environment in which states are embedded. What is new in world society, from this perspective, is the all-encompassing "world polity" and its associated world culture, which supplies a set of cultural rules or scripts that specify how institutions around the world should deal with common problems. Globalization is the formation and enactment of this world polity and culture. One of the world polity's key elements, as American sociologist John W. Meyer and colleagues explain, is a general, globally legitimated model of how to form a state. Guided by this model, particular states in widely varying circumstances organize their affairs in surprisingly similar fashion. Because world society is structured as a polity with an intensifying global culture, new organizations – business enterprises, educational institutions, social movements, leisure and hobby groups, and so on – spring up in all sorts of countries to enact its precepts. As carriers of global principles, these organizations then help to build and elaborate world culture and world society further.

World Culture Theory

This perspective agrees that world culture is indeed new and important, but it is less homogeneous than world-polity scholars imply. Globalization is a process of relativization, as Roland Robertson puts it. Societies must make sense of themselves in relation to a larger system of societies, while individuals make sense of themselves in relation to a sense of humanity as a larger whole. World society thus consists of a complex set of relationships among multiple units in the "global field." In this model, world society is governed not by a particular set of values but by the confrontation of different ways of organizing these relationships. Globalization compresses the world into a single entity, and people necessarily become more and more aware of their relationship to this global presence. Of central importance to this process is the problem of "globality": how to make living together in one global system meaningful or even possible. Not surprisingly, religious traditions take on new significance insofar as they address the new global predicament that compels societies and individuals to "identify" themselves in new ways. Robertson concludes that a "search for fundamentals" is inherent in globalization.

Arjun Appadurai, an American anthropologist of Indian origin, analyzes the cultural compression of the globe by showing how ideas, money, and people flow through disjoint "scapes." These flows intersect in different ways in particular societies, where identity construction becomes a matter of making local sense of their collisions. While the flows homogenize the world to some extent, the disjunctures in globalization also produce heterogeneity. Sameness and difference "cannibalize" each other.

As even this brief sketch makes clear, scholars offer varied understandings of the key dimensions, sources, and consequences of globalization. These theories have made substantial advances in accounting for transformations of the world. They all express a distinctly global point of view, even though they also still rely on ideas familiar from earlier social theory. As orienting perspectives, they guide much current research. But explaining globalization is necessarily work in progress, a collective effort to clarify the problems posed by the rise of a new world society as much as an attempt to produce satisfying accounts of how the world has become a global whole.

6

The Modern World-System as a Capitalist World-Economy

Immanuel Wallerstein

The world in which we are now living, the modern world-system, had its origins in the sixteenth century. This world-system was then located in only a part of the globe, primarily in parts of Europe and the Americas. It expanded over time to cover the whole globe. It is and has always been a *world-economy*. It is and has always been a *capitalist* world-economy. We should begin by explaining what these two terms, world-economy and capitalism, denote. It will then be easier to appreciate the historical contours of the modern world-system – its origins, its geography, its temporal development, and its contemporary structural crisis.

What we mean by a world-economy (Braudel's *économie-monde*) is a large geographic zone within which there is a division of labor and hence significant internal exchange of basic or essential goods as well as flows of capital and labor. A defining feature of a world-economy is that it is *not* bounded by a unitary political structure. Rather, there are many political units inside the world-economy, loosely tied together in our modern world-system in an interstate system. And a world-economy contains many cultures and groups – practicing many religions, speaking many languages, differing in their everyday patterns. This does not mean that they do not evolve some common cultural patterns, what we shall be calling a geoculture. It does mean that neither political nor cultural homogeneity is to be expected or found in a world-economy. What unifies the structure most is the division of labor which is constituted within it.

Capitalism is not the mere existence of persons or firms producing for sale on the market with the intention of obtaining a profit. Such persons or firms have existed for

Original publication details: Immanuel Wallerstein, "The Modern World-Systems as a Capitalist World-Economy," in *World-Systems Analysis: An Introduction*. Durham, NC: Duke University Press, 2004. pp. 23–30. Reproduced with permission from Duke University Press.

The Globalization Reader, Fifth Edition. Edited by Frank J. Lechner and John Boli.
Editorial material and organization © 2015 John Wiley & Sons, Ltd.
Published 2015 by John Wiley & Sons, Ltd.

thousands of years all across the world. Nor is the existence of persons working for wages sufficient as a definition. Wage-labor has also been known for thousands of years. We are in a capitalist system only when the system gives priority to the *endless* accumulation of capital. Using such a definition, only the modern world-system has been a capitalist system. Endless accumulation is a quite simple concept: it means that people and firms are accumulating capital in order to accumulate still more capital, a process that is continual and endless. If we say that a system "gives priority" to such endless accumulation, it means that there exist structural mechanisms by which those who act with other motivations are penalized in some way, and are eventually eliminated from the social scene, whereas those who act with the appropriate motivations are rewarded and, if successful, enriched.

A world-economy and a capitalist system go together. Since world-economies lack the unifying cement of an overall political structure or a homogeneous culture, what holds them together is the efficacy of the division of labor. And this efficacy is a function of the constantly expanding wealth that a capitalist system provides. Until modern times, the world-economies that had been constructed either fell apart or were transformed *manu militari* into world-empires. Historically, the only world-economy to have survived for a long time has been the modern world-system, and that is because the capitalist system took root and became consolidated as its defining feature.

Conversely, a capitalist system cannot exist within any framework except that of a world-economy. We shall see that a capitalist system requires a very special relationship between economic producers and the holders of political power. If the latter are too strong, as in a world-empire, their interests will override those of the economic producers, and the endless accumulation of capital will cease to be a priority. Capitalists need a large market (hence minisystems are too narrow for them) but they also need a multiplicity of states, so that they can gain the advantages of working with states but also can circumvent states hostile to their interests in favor of states friendly to their interests. Only the existence of a multiplicity of states within the overall division of labor assures this possibility.

A capitalist world-economy is a collection of many institutions, the combination of which accounts for its processes, and all of which are intertwined with each other. The basic institutions are the market, or rather the markets; the firms that compete in the markets; the multiple states, within an interstate system; the households; the classes; and the status-groups (to use Weber's term, which some people in recent years have renamed the "identities"). They are all institutions that have been created within the framework of the capitalist world-economy. Of course, such institutions have some similarities to institutions that existed in prior historical systems to which we have given the same or similar names. But using the same name to describe institutions located in different historical systems quite often confuses rather than clarifies analysis. It is better to think of the set of institutions of the modern world-system as contextually specific to it.

Let us start with markets, since these are normally considered the essential feature of a capitalist system. A market is both a concrete local structure in which individuals or firms sell and buy goods, and a virtual institution across space where the same kind of exchange occurs. How large and widespread any virtual market is depends on the realistic alternatives that sellers and buyers have at a given time. In principle, in a capitalist world-economy the virtual market exists in the world-economy as a whole. But as we shall see, there are often interferences with these boundaries, creating narrower and more "protected" markets. There are of course separate virtual markets for all commodities as well as for capital and different kinds of labor. But over time, there can also be said to exist a single virtual world market for all the factors of production combined, despite all the barriers that exist to its free functioning. One can think of this complete virtual market as a magnet for all producers and buyers, whose pull is a constant political factor in the decision-making of everyone – the states, the firms, the households, the classes, and the status-groups (or identities). This complete virtual world market is a reality in that it influences all decision making, but it never functions fully and freely (that is, without interference). The totally free market functions as an ideology, a myth, and a constraining influence, but never as a day-to-day reality.

One of the reasons it is not a day-to-day reality is that a totally free market, were it ever to exist, would make impossible the endless accumulation of capital. This may seem a paradox because it is surely true that capitalism cannot function without markets, and it is also true that capitalists regularly say that they favor free markets. But capitalists in fact need not totally free markets but rather markets that are only partially free. The reason is clear. Suppose there really existed a world market in which all the factors of production were totally free, as our textbooks in economics usually define this – that is, one in which the factors flowed without restriction, in which there were a very large number of buyers and a very large number of sellers, and in which there was perfect information (meaning that all sellers and all buyers knew the exact state of all costs of production). In such a perfect market, it would always be possible for the buyers to bargain down the sellers to an absolutely minuscule level of profit (let us think of it as a penny), and this low level of profit would make the capitalist game entirely uninteresting to producers, removing the basic social underpinnings of such a system.

What sellers always prefer is a monopoly, for then they can create a relatively wide margin between the costs of production and the sales price, and thus realize high rates of profit. Of course, perfect monopolies are extremely difficult to create, and rare, but quasi-monopolies are not. What one needs most of all is the support of the machinery of a relatively strong state, one which can enforce a quasi-monopoly. There are many ways of doing this. One of the most fundamental is the system of patents which reserves rights in an "invention" for a specified number of years. This is what basically makes "new" products the most expensive for consumers and the most profitable for their producers. Of course, patents are often violated and in any case they eventually expire, but by and large they protect a quasi-monopoly for a time. Even so, production protected by patents usually remains only a quasi-monopoly, since there may be other similar products on the market that are not covered by the patent. This is why the normal situation for so-called leading products (that is, products that are both new and have an important share of the overall world market for commodities) is an oligopoly rather than an absolute monopoly. Oligopolies are however good enough to realize the desired high rate of profits, especially since the various firms often collude to minimize price competition.

Patents are not the only way in which states can create quasi-monopolies. State restrictions on imports and exports (so-called protectionist measures) are another. State subsidies and tax benefits are a third. The ability of strong states to use their muscle to prevent weaker states from creating counter-protectionist measures is still another. The role of the states as large-scale buyers of certain products willing to pay excessive prices is still another. Finally, regulations which impose a burden on producers may be relatively easy to absorb by large producers but crippling to smaller producers, an asymmetry which results in the elimination of the smaller producers from the market and thus increases the degree of oligopoly. The modalities by which states interfere with the virtual market are so extensive that they constitute a fundamental factor in determining prices and profits. Without such interferences, the capitalist system could not thrive and therefore could not survive.

Nonetheless, there are two inbuilt anti-monopolistic features in a capitalist world-economy. First of all, one producer's monopolistic advantage is another producer's loss. The losers will of course struggle politically to remove the advantages of the winners. They can do this by political struggle within the states where the monopolistic producers are located, appealing to doctrines of a free market and offering support to political leaders inclined to end a particular monopolistic advantage. Or they do this by persuading other states to defy the world market monopoly by using their state power to sustain competitive producers. Both methods are used. Therefore, over time, every quasi-monopoly is undone by the entry of further producers into the market.

Quasi-monopolies are thus self-liquidating. But they last long enough (say thirty years) to ensure considerable accumulation of capital by those who control the quasi-monopolies. When a quasi-monopoly does cease to exist, the large accumulators of capital simply move their capital to new leading products or whole new leading industries. The result is a cycle of leading products. Leading products have moderately short lives, but they are constantly succeeded by other leading industries. Thus the game continues. As for the once-leading industries past their prime, they become more and more "competitive," that is, less and less profitable. We see this pattern in action all the time.

Firms are the main actors in the market. Firms are normally the competitors of other firms operating in the same virtual market. They are also in conflict with those firms from whom they purchase inputs and those firms to which they sell their products. Fierce intercapitalist rivalry is the name of the game. And only the strongest and the most agile survive. One must remember that bankruptcy, or absorption by a more powerful firm, is the daily bread of capitalist enterprises. Not all capitalist entrepreneurs succeed in accumulating capital. Far from it. If they all succeeded, each would be likely to obtain very little capital. So, the repeated "failures" of firms not only weed out the weak competitors but are a condition sine qua non of the endless accumulation of capital. That is what explains the constant process of the concentration of capital.

To be sure, there is a downside to the growth of firms, either horizontally (in the same product), vertically (in the different steps in the chain of production), or what might be thought of as orthogonally (into other products not closely related). Size brings down costs through so-called economies of scale. But size adds costs of administration and coordination, and multiplies the risks of managerial inefficiencies. As a result of this contradiction, there has been a repeated zigzag process of firms getting larger and then getting smaller. But it has not at all been a simple up-and-down cycle. Rather, worldwide there has been a secular increase in the size of firms, the whole historical process taking the form of a ratchet, two steps up then one step back, continuously. The size of firms also has direct political implications. Large size gives firms more political clout but also makes them more vulnerable to political assault – by their competitors, their employees, and their consumers. But here too the bottom line is an upward ratchet, toward more political influence over time.

The axial division of labor of a capitalist world-economy divides production into core-like products and peripheral products. Core-periphery is a relational concept. What we mean by core-periphery is the degree of profitability of the production processes. Since profitability is directly related to the degree of monopolization, what we essentially mean by core-like production processes is those that are controlled by quasi-monopolies. Peripheral processes are then those that are truly competitive. When exchange occurs, competitive products are in a weak position and quasi-monopolized products are in a strong position. As a result, there is a constant flow of surplus-value from the producers of peripheral products to the producers of core-like products. This has been called unequal exchange.

To be sure, unequal exchange is not the only way of moving accumulated capital from politically weak regions to politically strong regions. There is also plunder, often used extensively during the early days of incorporating new regions into the world-economy (consider, for example, the conquistadores and gold in the Americas). But plunder is self-liquidating. It is a case of killing the goose that lays the golden eggs. Still, since the consequences are middle-term and the advantages short-term, there still exists much plunder in the modern world-system, although we are often "scandalized" when we learn of it. When Enron goes bankrupt, after procedures that have moved enormous sums into the hands of a few managers, that is in fact plunder. When "privatizations" of erstwhile state property lead to its being garnered by mafia-like businessmen who quickly leave the country with destroyed enterprises in their wake, that is plunder. Self-liquidating, yes, but only after much damage has been done to the world's productive system, and indeed to the health of the capitalist world-economy.

Since quasi-monopolies depend on the patronage of strong states, they are largely located – juridically, physically, and in terms of ownership – within such states. There is therefore a geographical consequence of the core-peripheral relationship. Core-like processes tend to group themselves in a few states and to constitute the bulk of the production activity in such states. Peripheral processes tend to be scattered among a large number of states and to constitute the bulk of the production activity in these states. Thus, for shorthand purposes we can talk of core states and peripheral states, so long as we remember that we are really talking of a relationship between production processes. Some states have a near even mix of core-like and peripheral products. We may call them semiperipheral states. They have, as we shall see, special political properties. It is however not meaningful to speak of semiperipheral production processes.

Since, as we have seen, quasi-monopolies exhaust themselves, what is a core-like process today will become a peripheral process tomorrow. The economic history of the modern world-system is replete with the shift, or downgrading, of products, first to semiperipheral countries, and then to peripheral ones. If circa 1800 the production of textiles was possibly the preeminent core-like production process, by 2000 it was manifestly one of the least profitable peripheral production processes. In 1800 these textiles were produced primarily in a very few countries (notably England and some other countries of northwestern Europe); in 2000 textiles were produced in virtually every part of the world-system, especially cheap textiles. The process has been repeated with many other products. Think of steel, of automobiles, or even computers. This kind of shift has no effect on the structure of the system itself. In 2000 there were other core-like processes (e.g., aircraft production or genetic engineering) which were concentrated in a few countries. There have always been new core-like processes to replace those which become more competitive and then move out of the states in which they were originally located.

The role of each state is very different vis-à-vis productive processes depending on the mix of core–peripheral processes within it. The strong states, which contain a disproportionate share of core-like processes, tend to emphasize their role of protecting the quasi-monopolies of the core-like processes. The very weak states, which contain a disproportionate share of peripheral production processes, are usually unable to do very much to affect the axial division of labor, and in effect are largely forced to accept the lot that has been given them.

The semiperipheral states which have a relatively even mix of production processes find themselves in the most difficult situation. Under pressure from core states and putting pressure on peripheral states, their major concern is to keep themselves from slipping into the periphery and to do what they can to advance themselves toward the core. Neither is easy, and both require considerable state interference with the world market. These semiperipheral states are the ones that put forward most aggressively and most publicly so-called protectionist policies. They hope thereby to "protect" their production processes from the competition of stronger firms outside, while trying to improve the efficiency of the firms inside so as to compete better in the world market. They are eager recipients of the relocation of erstwhile leading products, which they define these days as achieving "economic development." In this effort, their competition comes not from the core states but from other semiperipheral states, equally eager to be the recipients of relocation which cannot go to all the eager aspirants simultaneously and to the same degree. In the beginning of the twenty-first century, some obvious countries to be labeled semiperipheral are South Korea, Brazil, and India – countries with strong enterprises that export products (for example steel, automobiles, pharmaceuticals) to peripheral zones, but that also regularly relate to core zones as importers of more "advanced" products.

The normal evolution of the leading industries – the slow dissolution of the quasi-monopolies – is what accounts for the cyclical rhythms of the world-economy. A major leading industry will be a major stimulus to the expansion of the world-economy and will result in considerable accumulation of capital. But it also normally leads to more extensive employment in the world-economy, higher wage-levels, and a general sense of relative prosperity. As more and more firms enter the market of the erstwhile quasi-monopoly, there will be "overproduction" (that is, too much production for the real effective demand at a given time) and consequently increased price competition (because of the demand squeeze), thus lowering the rates of profit. At some point, a buildup of unsold products results, and consequently a slowdown in further production.

When this happens, we tend to see a reversal of the cyclical curve of the world-economy. We talk of stagnation or recession in the world-economy. Rates of unemployment rise worldwide. Producers seek to reduce costs in order to maintain their share of the world market. One of the mechanisms is relocation of the production processes to zones that have historically lower wages, that is, to semiperipheral countries. This shift puts pressure on the wage levels in the processes still remaining in core zones, and wages there tend to become lower as well. Effective demand which was at first lacking because of overproduction now becomes lacking because of a reduction in earnings of the consumers. In such a situation, not all producers necessarily lose out. There is obviously acutely increased competition among the diluted oligopoly that is now engaged in these production processes. They fight each other furiously, usually with the aid of their state machineries. Some states and some producers succeed in "exporting unemployment" from one core state to the others. Systemically, there is contraction, but certain core states and especially certain semiperipheral states may seem to be doing quite well. [...]

7

Sociology of the Global System

Leslie Sklair

The Conceptual Space for Transnational Practices (TNP)

The concept of transnational practices refers to the effects of what people do when they are acting within specific institutional contexts that cross state borders. Transnational practices create globalizing processes. TNPs focus attention on observable phenomena, some of which are measurable, instead of highly abstract and often very vague relations between conceptual entities. [...]

The global system is most fruitfully conceptualized as a system that operates at three levels, and knowledge about which can be organized in three spheres, namely the economic, the political, and the culture-ideology. Each sphere is typically characterized by a representative institution, cohesive structures of practices, organized and patterned, which can only be properly understood in terms of their transnational effects. The dominant form of globalization in the present era is undoubtedly capitalist globalization. This being the case, the primary agents and institutional focus of economic transnational practices are the transnational corporations.

However, there are others. The World Bank, the IMF, WTO, commodity exchanges, the G7 (political leaders of the seven most important economies), the US Treasury and so on are mostly controlled by those who share the interests of the major TNCs and the major TNCs share their interests. In a revealing report on 'IMF: Efforts to Advance US Policies at the Fund' by the US General Accounting Office (GAO-01-214, January 23, 2001) we discover that the US Treasury and the Executive Director actively

Original publication details: Leslie Sklair, *Globalization: Capitalism and Its Alternatives*, 3rd edn. Oxford: Oxford University Press, 2002. Chapter 5. Reproduced with permission from Oxford University Press.

The Globalization Reader, Fifth Edition. Edited by Frank J. Lechner and John Boli.
Editorial material and organization © 2015 John Wiley & Sons, Ltd.
Published 2015 by John Wiley & Sons, Ltd.

promoted US policies on sound banking, labour issues, and audits of military expenditures. The report concluded that it was difficult to determine the precise significance of US influence, because other countries generally support the same policies. This phenomenon is widely known as the Washington Consensus, a term coined by John Williamson of the Institute for International Economics.

> By 'Washington' Williamson meant not only the US government, but all those institutions and networks of opinion leaders centered in the world's de facto capital – the IMF, World Bank, think-tanks, politically sophisticated investment bankers, and worldly finance ministers, all those who meet each other in Washington and collectively define the conventional wisdom of the moment ... [One may roughly] summarize this consensus as ... the belief that Victorian virtue and economic policy – free markets and sound money – is the key to economic development.

This is the transnational capitalist class at work. The underlying goal of keeping global capitalism on course is in constant tension with the selfish and destabilizing actions of those who cannot resist system-threatening opportunities to get rich quick or to cut their losses. It is, however, the direct producers, not the transnational capitalist class who usually suffer most when this occurs as, for example, the tin miners of Bolivia and the rest of the world found out when the London Metal Exchange terminated its tin contract in 1985 and when the Association of Coffee Producing Countries collapsed late in 2001. [...]

It may be helpful to spell out who determine priorities for economic, political and culture-ideology transnational practices, and what they actually do. Those who own and control the TNCs organize the production of commodities and the services necessary to manufacture and sell them. The state fraction of the transnational capitalist class produces the political environment within which the products and services can be successfully marketed all over the world irrespective of their origins and qualities. Those responsible for the dissemination of the culture-ideology of consumerism produce the values and attitudes that create and sustain the need for the products. These are analytical rather than empirical distinctions. In the real world they are inextricably mixed. TNCs get involved in host country politics, and the culture-ideology of consumerism is largely promulgated through the transnational corporations involved in mass media and advertising. Members of the transnational capitalist class often work directly for TNCs, and their life styles are exemplary for the spread of consumerism. Nevertheless, it is useful to make these analytical distinctions, particularly where the apparent and real empirical contradictions are difficult to disentangle.

The thesis on which this conceptual apparatus rests and on which any viable theory of the current dominant global system depends is that capitalism is changing qualitatively from an international to a globalizing system. This is the subject of a heated debate in academic, political and cultural circles. The idea that capitalism has entered a new global phase (whether it be organized or disorganized) clearly commands a good deal of support though, unsurprisingly, there are considerable differences on the details. The conception of capitalism of Ross and Trachte convincingly locates the emergence of global capitalism in a series of technological revolutions (primarily in transportation, communications, electronics, biotechnology), and this provides a key support to the global system theory being elaborated here. My focus on transnational corporations draws on a large and rich literature on the global corporation, again full of internal disputes, but based on the premise, well expressed by Howells and Wood that 'the production processes within large firms are being decoupled from specific territories and being formed into new global systems'. [...]

Economic Transnational Practices

Economic transnational practices are economic practices that transcend state boundaries. These may seem to be entirely contained within the borders of a single country even though their effects are transnational. For example, within one country there are consumer demands for products that are unavailable, in general or during particular seasons, from domestic sources. Retailers place orders with suppliers who fill the orders from foreign sources. Neither the retailer nor the consumer needs to know or care where the product comes from, though some countries now have country of origin rules making mandatory the display of this information. Many campaigning groups make sure that customers know, for example, that some products come from sweatshops in Asia or the USA. There may be a parallel situation in the supplier country. Local producers may simply sell their products to a domestic marketing board or wholesaler and neither know nor care who the final consumer is. Transnational corporations, big or small, enter the scene when sellers, intermediaries, and buyers are parts of the same transnational network.

Hundreds of thousands of companies based all over the world export goods and services. In the US alone in the late 1990s there were more than 200,000 exporting companies according to the website of the US Department of Commerce. Of this large number of exporters only about 15 percent operated from multiple locations, but these accounted for about 80 percent of exports from the US and almost half of manufacturing exports were from the top 50 firms. They, of course, are the major TNCs, comprising the less than one percent of US manufacturers that export to 50 or more countries. Over half of all US export value derives from their transnational economic practices and, significantly, much of their business is comprised of intra-firm transactions. The picture is similar in many other countries with firms that export manufactured goods. The global economy is dominated by a few gigantic transnational corporations marketing their products, many of them global brands, all over the world, some medium-sized companies producing in a few locations and selling in multiple markets, while many many more small firms sell from one location to one or a few other locations.

One important consequence of the expansion of the capitalist world economy has been that individual economic actors (like workers and entrepreneurs) and collective economic actors (like trade unions and TNCs) have become much more conscious of the transnationality of their practices and have striven to extend their global influence. As capitalist globalization spread, anti-globalization researchers and activists focused on imports and exports, and vested some products with great political and culture-ideology significance. Increasing numbers of consumers now register where what they are buying comes from, and producers now register where what they are producing will go to, and this knowledge may affect their actions. An important example of this process is the rapid growth of ethical and organic marketing between Third World producers and First World consumers. These transnational practices must be seen within the context of an unprecedented increase in the volume of economic transnational practices since the 1950s, as evidenced by the tremendous growth of cross-border trade. According to the World Bank, global exports rose from US\$94 billion in 1965, to \$1,365 billion in 1986, \$3,500 billion in 1993 and over \$5,400 billion in 1999. Foreign investment and other types of capital flows have increased even more rapidly. This means that even some quite poor people in some poor countries now have access to many non-local consumer goods, and through their use of the mass media are becoming more aware of the status-conferring advantages that global branded goods and services have over others. [...]

The Transnational Capitalist Class

The transnational capitalist class is not made up of capitalists in the traditional Marxist sense. Direct ownership or control of the means of production is no longer the exclusive criterion for serving the interests of capital, particularly not the global interests of capital.

The transnational capitalist class (TCC) is transnational in at least five senses. Its members tend to share global as well as local economic interests; they seek to exert economic control in the workplace, political control in domestic and international politics, and culture-ideology control in everyday life; they tend to have global rather than local perspectives on a variety of issues; they tend to be people from many countries, more and more of whom begin to consider themselves citizens of the world as well as of their places of birth; and they tend to share similar lifestyles, particularly patterns of luxury consumption of goods and services. In my formulation, the transnational capitalist class includes the following four fractions:

- TNC executives and their local affiliates (corporate fraction);
- globalizing state and inter-state bureaucrats and politicians (state fraction);
- globalizing professionals (technical fraction); and
- merchants and media (consumerist fraction).

This class sees its mission as organizing the conditions under which its interests and the interests of the global system (which usually but do not always coincide) can be furthered within the transnational, inter-state, national and local contexts. The concept of the transnational capitalist class implies that there is one central transnational capitalist class that makes system-wide decisions, and that it connects with the TCC in each community, region and country.

Political transnational practices are not primarily conducted within conventional political organizations. Neither the transnational capitalist class nor any other class operates primarily through transnational political parties. However, loose transnational political groupings do exist and they do have some effects on, and are affected by, the political practices of the TCC in most countries. There are no genuine transnational political parties, though there appears to be a growing interest in international associations of parties, which are sometimes mistaken for transnational parties. [...]

There are, however, various transnational political organizations through which fractions of the TCC operate locally, for example, the Rotary Club and its offshoots and the network of American, European and Japan-related Chambers of Commerce that straddles the globe. As Errington and Gewertz show in their study of a Rotary Club in Melanesia as well as my own research on AmCham in Mexico, these organizations work as crucial transmission belts and lines of communication between global capitalism and local business. [...]

At a more elevated level are the Trilateral Commission of the great and good from the United States, Europe and Japan whose business is 'Elite Planning for World Management'; the World Economic Forum which meets at Davos in Switzerland and the annual global conferences organized by *Fortune* magazine that bring together the corporate and the state fractions of the TCC. Many other similar but less well-known networks for capitalist globalization exist, for example the Bilderberg Group and Caux Round Table of senior business leaders. There are few major cities in any First or Third World (and now New Second World) country that do not have members of or connections with one or more of these organizations. They vary in strength from the major First World political and business capitals, through important Third World cities like Cairo, Singapore and Mexico City, to nominal presences in some of the poorer countries in Africa, Asia and Latin America. They are backed up by many powerful official bodies, such as foreign trade and economics departments of the major states. Specialized agencies of the World Bank and the IMF, WTO, US Agency for International Development (USAID), development banks, and the UN work with TNCs, local businesses, and NGOs (willing and not so willing) in projects that promote the agenda of capitalist globalization. [...]

Labour and the Transnational Capitalist Class

The relative strength of the transnational capitalist class can be understood in terms of the relative weakness of transnational labour. Labour is represented by some genuinely transnational trade unions.... In addition, there are some industrially based transnational union organizations, for example the International Metalworkers Federation, and the International Union of Food and Allied Workers' Associations. These have been involved in genuine transnational labour struggles, and have gained some short-term victories. However, they face substantial difficulties in their struggles against organized capital, locally and transnationally, and they have little influence. [...]

While most TNCs in most countries will follow the local rules regarding the unions, host governments, particularly those promoting export processing industries (not always under pressure from foreign investors), have often suspended national labour legislation in order to attract TNCs and/or to keep production going and foreign currency rolling in. With very few exceptions, most globalizing bureaucrats and politicians wanting to take advantage of the fruits of capitalist globalization will be unhelpful towards labour unions, if not downright hostile to them when they dare to challenge the transnational capitalist class. [...]

Culture-Ideology Transnational Practices

[...] Bagdikian characterized those who control this system [world media] as the lords of the global village. They purvey their product (a relatively undifferentiated mass of news, information, ideas, entertainment and popular culture) to a rapidly expanding public, eventually the whole world. He argued that national boundaries are growing increasingly meaningless as the main actors (five groups at the time he was writing) strive for total control in the production, delivery, and marketing of what we can call the culture-ideology goods of the capitalist global system. Their goal is to create a buying mood for the benefit of the global troika of media, advertising and consumer goods manufacturers. 'Nothing in human experience has prepared men, women, and children for the modern television techniques of fixing human attention and creating the uncritical mood required to sell goods, many of which are marginal at best to human needs'. Two symbolic facts: by the age of 16, the average North American youth has been exposed to more than 300,000 television commercials; and the former Soviet Union sold advertising slots on cosmonaut suits and space ships! In order to connect and explain these facts, we need to generate a new framework, namely the culture-ideology of consumerism.

The Culture-Ideology of Consumerism

The transformation of the culture-ideology of consumerism from a sectional preference of the rich to a globalizing phenomenon can be explained in terms of two central factors, factors that are historically unprecedented. First, capitalism entered a qualitatively new globalizing phase in the 1960s.... [I]n the second half of the twentieth century, for the first time in human history, the dominant economic system, capitalism, was sufficiently productive to provide a basic package of material possessions and services to almost everyone in the First World and to privileged groups elsewhere.... A rapidly globalizing system of mass media was also geared up to tell everyone what was available and, crucially, to persuade people that this culture-ideology of consumerism was what a happy and satisfying life was all about....

Mass media perform many functions for global capitalism. They speed up the circulation of material goods through advertising, which reduces the time between production and consumption. They begin to inculcate the dominant ideology into the minds of viewers, listeners and readers from an early age, in the words of Esteinou Madrid, 'creating the political/cultural demand for the survival of capitalism'. The systematic blurring of the lines between information, entertainment, and promotion of products lies at the heart of this practice. This has not in itself created consumerism, for consumer cultures have been in place for centuries. What it has created is a reformulation of consumerism that transforms all the mass media and their contents into opportunities to sell ideas, values, products, in short, a consumerist worldview. [...]

Contemporary consumer culture would not be possible without the shopping mall, both symbolically and substantively. As Crawford argued, the merging of the architecture of the mall with the culture of the theme park has become the key symbol and the key spatial reference point for consumer capitalism, not only in North America but increasingly all over the world. What Goss terms the magic of the mall has to be understood on several levels, how the consuming environment is carefully designed and controlled, the seductive nature of the consuming experience, the transformation of nominal public space into actual private terrain. Although there are certainly anomalies of decaying city districts interspersed with gleaming malls bursting with consumer goods in the First World, it is in the poorer parts of the Third World that these anomalies are at their most stark. Third World malls until quite recently catered mainly to the needs and wants of expatriate TNC executives and officials, and local members of the transnational capitalist class. The success of the culture-ideology of consumerism can be observed all over the world in these malls, where now large numbers of workers and their families flock to buy, usually with credit cards, thus locking themselves into the financial system of capitalist globalization. [...]

The Theory of the Global System: A Summary

The theory of the global system can be summarized, graphically, as follows. All global systems rest on economic transnational practices and at the highest level of abstraction these are the building blocks of the system. Concretely, in the capitalist global system they are mainly located in the major transnational corporations. Transnational political practices are the principles of organization of the system. Members of the transnational capitalist class drive the system, and by manipulating the design of the system they can build variations into it. Transnational culture-ideology practices are the nuts and bolts and the glue that hold the system together. Without them, parts of the system would drift off into space. This is accomplished through the culture-ideology of consumerism. [...]

In order to work properly the dominant institutions in each of the three spheres have to take control of key resources. Under the conditions of capitalist globalization, the transnational corporations strive to control global capital and material resources, the transnational capitalist class strives to control global power, and the transnational agents and institutions of the culture-ideology of consumerism strive to control the realm of ideas. Effective corporate control of global capital and resources is almost complete. There are few important natural resources that are entirely exempt from the formal or effective control of the TNCs or official agencies with whom they have strategic alliances. The transnational capitalist class and its local affiliates exert their rule through its connections with globalizing bureaucrats and politicians in pro-capitalist political parties or social democratic parties that choose not to fundamentally challenge the global capitalist project. The local affiliates of the TCC exert authority in non-capitalist states indirectly to a greater or lesser extent. This is the price levied as a sort of entrance fee into the capitalist global system. In the last resort, it is the corporate control of capital and labour that is the decisive factor for those who do not wish to be excluded from the system.

The struggle for control of ideas in the interests of capitalist consumerism is fierce, the goal is to create the one-dimensional man within the apparently limitless vistas of consumerism that Marcuse prophesied. Ideas that are antagonistic to the global capitalist project can be reduced to one central counter-hegemonic idea, the rejection of the culture-ideology of consumerism itself, and they get little exposure in the mass media, as opposed to alternative media where they are at the core of an exciting cultural diversity for minority groups all over the world. Without consumerism, the rationale for continuous capitalist accumulation dissolves. It is the capacity to commercialize and commodify all ideas and the products in which they adhere, television programmes, advertisements, newsprint, books, tapes, CDs, videos, films, the Internet and so on, that global capitalism strives to appropriate. [...]

8

A Brief History of Neoliberalism

David Harvey

Introduction

[...]

Neoliberalism is in the first instance a theory of political economic practices that proposes that human well-being can best be advanced by liberating individual entrepreneurial freedoms and skills within an institutional framework characterized by strong private property rights, free markets, and free trade. The role of the state is to create and preserve an institutional framework appropriate to such practices. The state has to guarantee, for example, the quality and integrity of money. It must also set up those military, defence, police, and legal structures and functions required to secure private property rights and to guarantee, by force if need be, the proper functioning of markets. Furthermore, if markets do not exist (in areas such as land, water, education, health care, social security, or environmental pollution) then they must be created, by state action if necessary. But beyond these tasks the state should not venture. State interventions in markets (once created) must be kept to a bare minimum because, according to the theory, the state cannot possibly possess enough information to second-guess market signals (prices) and because powerful interest groups will inevitably distort and bias state interventions (particularly in democracies) for their own benefit.

There has everywhere been an emphatic turn towards neoliberalism in political-economic practices and thinking since the 1970s. Deregulation, privatization, and withdrawal of the state from many areas of social provision have been all too common. Almost all states, from those newly minted after the collapse of the Soviet

Original publication details: David Harvey, *A Brief History of Neoliberalism*. Oxford: Oxford University Press, 2005. pp. 2–3, 87–90, 91–3. Reproduced with permission from Oxford University Press.

The Globalization Reader, Fifth Edition. Edited by Frank J. Lechner and John Boli.
Editorial material and organization © 2015 John Wiley & Sons, Ltd.
Published 2015 by John Wiley & Sons, Ltd.

Union to old-style social democracies and welfare states such as New Zealand and Sweden, have embraced, sometimes voluntarily and in other instances in response to coercive pressures, some version of neoliberal theory and adjusted at least some policies and practices accordingly. Post-apartheid South Africa quickly embraced neoliberalism, and even contemporary China, as we shall see, appears to be headed in this direction. Furthermore, the advocates of the neoliberal way now occupy positions of considerable influence in education (the universities and many 'think tanks'), in the media, in corporate boardrooms and financial institutions, in key state institutions (treasury departments, the central banks), and also in those international institutions such as the International Monetary Fund (IMF), the World Bank, and the World Trade Organization (WTO) that regulate global finance and trade. Neoliberalism has, in short, become hegemonic as a mode of discourse. It has pervasive effects on ways of thought to the point where it has become incorporated into the common-sense way many of us interpret, live in, and understand the world.

The process of neoliberalization has, however, entailed much 'creative destruction', not only of prior institutional frameworks and powers (even challenging traditional forms of state sovereignty) but also of divisions of labour, social relations, welfare provisions, technological mixes, ways of life and thought, reproductive activities, attachments to the land and habits of the heart. In so far as neoliberalism values market exchange as 'an ethic in itself, capable of acting as a guide to all human action, and substituting for all previously held ethical beliefs', it emphasizes the significance of contractual relations in the marketplace. It holds that the social good will be maximized by maximizing the reach and frequency of market transactions, and it seeks to bring all human action into the domain of the market.

[…]

The Moving Map of Neoliberalization

A moving map of the progress of neoliberalization on the world stage since 1970 would be hard to construct. To begin with, most states that have taken the neoliberal turn have done so only partially – the introduction of greater flexibility into labour markets here, a deregulation of financial operations and embrace of monetarism there, a move towards privatization of state-owned sectors somewhere else. Wholesale changes in the wake of crises (such as the collapse of the Soviet Union) can be followed by slow reversals as the unpalatable aspects of neoliberalism become more evident. And in the struggle to restore or establish a distinctive upper-class power all manner of twists and turns occur as political powers change hands and as the instruments of influence are weakened here or strengthened there. Any moving map would therefore feature turbulent currents of uneven geographical development that need to be tracked in order to understand how local transformations relate to broader trends.

Competition between territories (states, regions, or cities) as to who had the best model for economic development or the best business climate was relatively insignificant in the 1950s and 1960s. Competition of this sort heightened in the more fluid and open systems of trading relations established after 1970. The general progress of neoliberalization has therefore been increasingly impelled *through* mechanisms of uneven geographical developments. Successful states or regions put pressure on everyone else to follow their lead. Leapfrogging innovations put this or that state (Japan, Germany, Taiwan, the US, or China), region (Silicon Valley, Bavaria, Third Italy, Bangalore, the Pearl River delta, or Botswana), or even city (Boston, San Francisco, Shanghai, or Munich) in the vanguard of capital accumulation. But the competitive advantages all too often prove ephemeral, introducing an extraordinary volatility into global capitalism. Yet it is also true that powerful impulses of neoliberalization have emanated, and even been orchestrated, from a few major epicentres.

Clearly, the UK and the US led the way. But in neither country was the turn unproblematic. While Thatcher could successfully privatize social housing and the public utilities, core public services such as the national health-care system and public education remained largely immune. In the US, the 'Keynesian compromise' of the 1960s had never got close to the achievements of social democratic states in Europe. The opposition to Reagan was therefore less combative. Reagan was, in any case, heavily preoccupied with the Cold War. He launched a deficit-funded arms race ('military Keynesianism') of specific benefit to his electoral majority in the US south and west. While this certainly did not accord with neoliberal theory, the rising Federal deficits did provide a convenient excuse to gut social programmes (a neoliberal objective).

In spite of all the rhetoric about curing sick economies, neither Britain nor the US achieved high levels of economic performance in the 1980s, suggesting that neoliberalism was not the answer to the capitalists' prayers. To be sure, inflation was brought down and interest rates fell, but this was all purchased at the expense of high rates of unemployment (averaging 7.5 per cent in the US during the Reagan years and more than 10 per cent in Thatcher's Britain). Cutbacks in state welfare and infrastructural expenditures diminished the quality of life for many. The overall result was an awkward mix of low growth and increasing income inequality. And in Latin America, where the first wave of forced neoliberalization struck in the early 1980s, the result was for the most part a whole 'lost decade' of economic stagnation and political turmoil.

The 1980s in fact belonged to Japan, the East Asian 'tiger' economies, and West Germany as competitive powerhouses of the global economy. Their success in the absence of any wholesale neoliberal reforms makes it difficult to argue that neoliberalization progressed on the world stage as a proven palliative of economic stagnation. To be sure, the central banks in these countries generally followed a monetarist line (the West German Bundesbank was particularly assiduous in combating inflation). And gradual reductions in trade barriers created competitive pressures that resulted in a subtle process of what might be called 'creeping neoliberalization' even in countries generally resistant to it. The Maastricht agreement of 1991, for example, which set a broadly neoliberal framework for the internal organization of the European Union, would not have been possible had there not been pressure from those states, such as Britain, that had committed themselves to neoliberal reforms. But in West Germany the trade unions remained strong, social protections were kept in place, and wage levels continued to be relatively high. This stimulated the technological innovation that kept West Germany well ahead of the field in international competition in the 1980s (though it also produced technologically induced unemployment).

Export-led growth powered the country forward as a global leader. In Japan, independent unions were weak or non-existent and rates of labour exploitation were high, but state investment in technological change and the tight relationship between corporations and banks (an arrangement that also proved felicitous in West Germany) generated an astonishing export-led growth performance in the 1980s, very much at the expense of the UK and the US. Such growth as there was in the 1980s did not depend, therefore, on neoliberalization except in the shallow sense that greater openness in global trade and markets provided the context in which the export-led success stories of Japan, West Germany, and the Asian 'tigers' could more easily unfold in the midst of intensifying international competition. By the end of the 1980s those countries that had taken the stronger neoliberal path still seemed to be in economic difficulty. It was hard not to conclude that the West German and Asian 'regimes' of accumulation were deserving of emulation. Many European states therefore resisted neoliberal reforms and embraced the West German model. In Asia, the Japanese model was broadly emulated first by the 'Gang of Four' (South Korea, Taiwan, Hong Kong, and Singapore) and then by Thailand, Malaysia, Indonesia, and the Philippines.

The West German and the Japanese models did not, however, facilitate the restoration of class power. The increases in social inequality to be found in the UK and particularly in the US during the 1980s were held in check. While rates of growth were low in the US and the UK, the standard of living of labour was declining significantly and the upper classes were beginning to do well. The rates of remuneration of US CEOs, for example, were becoming the envy of Europeans in comparable positions. In Britain, a new wave of entrepreneurial financiers began to consolidate large fortunes. If the project was to restore class power to the top elites, then neoliberalism was clearly the answer. Whether or not a country could be pushed towards neoliberalization then depended upon the balance of class forces (powerful union organization in West Germany and Sweden held neoliberalization in check) as well as upon the degree of dependency of the capitalist class on the state (very strong in Taiwan and South Korea).

The means whereby class power could be transformed and restored were gradually but unevenly put into place during the 1980s and consolidated in the 1990s. Four components were critical in this. First, the turn to more open financialization that began in the 1970s accelerated during the 1990s. Foreign direct investment and portfolio investment rose rapidly throughout the capitalist world. But it was spread unevenly, often depending on how good the business climate was here as opposed to there. Financial markets experienced a powerful wave of innovation and deregulation internationally. Not only did they become far more important instruments of coordination, but they also provided the means to procure and concentrate wealth. They became the privileged means for the restoration of class power. The close tie between corporations and the banks that had served the West Germans and the Japanese so well during the 1980s was undermined and replaced by an increasing connectivity between corporations and financial markets (the stock exchanges). Here Britain and the US had the advantage. In the 1990s, the Japanese economy went into a tailspin (led by a collapse in speculative land and property markets), and the banking sector was found to be in a parlous state. The hasty reunification of Germany created stresses, and the technological advantage that the Germans had earlier commanded dissipated, making it necessary to challenge more deeply its social democratic tradition in order to survive.

Secondly, there was the increasing geographical mobility of capital. This was in part facilitated by the mundane but critical fact of rapidly diminishing transport and communications costs. The gradual reduction in artificial barriers to movement of capital and of commodities, such as tariffs, exchange controls, or, even more simply, waiting times at borders (the abolition of which in Europe had dramatic effects) also played an important role. While there was considerable unevenness (Japan's markets remained highly protected, for example), the general thrust was towards standardization of trade arrangements through international agreements that culminated in the World Trade Organization agreements that took effect in 1995 (more than a hundred countries had signed on within the year). This greater openness to capital flow (primarily US, European, and Japanese) put pressures on all states to look to the quality of their business climate as a crucial condition for their competitive success. Since a degree of neoliberalization was increasingly taken by the IMF and the World Bank as a measure of a good business climate, the pressure on all states to adopt neoliberal reforms ratcheted upwards.

Thirdly, the Wall Street–IMF–Treasury complex that came to dominate economic policy in the Clinton years was able to persuade, cajole, and (thanks to structural adjustment programmes administered by the IMF) coerce many developing countries to take the neoliberal road. The US also used the carrot of preferential access to its huge consumer market to persuade many countries to reform their economies along neoliberal lines (in some instances through bilateral trade agreements). These policies helped produce a boom in the US in the 1990s. The US, riding a wave of technological innovation that underpinned the rise of a so-called 'new economy', looked as if it had the answer and that its policies were worthy of emulation, even though the relatively full employment achieved was at low rates of pay under conditions of diminishing social protections (the number of people without health insurance grew). Flexibility in labour markets and reductions in welfare provision (Clinton's draconian overhaul of 'the welfare system as we know it') began to pay off for the US and put competitive pressures on the more rigid labour markets that prevailed in most of Europe (with the exception of Britain) and Japan. The real secret of US success, however, was that it was now able to pump high rates of return into the country from its financial and corporate operations (both direct and portfolio investments) in the rest of the world. It was this flow of tribute from the rest of the world that founded much of the affluence achieved in the US in the 1990s.

Lastly, the global diffusion of the new monetarist and neoliberal economic orthodoxy exerted an ever more powerful ideological influence. As early as 1982, Keynesian economics had been purged from the corridors of the IMF and the World Bank. By the end of the decade most economics departments in the US research universities – and these helped train most of the world's economists – had fallen into line by broadly cleaving to the neoliberal agenda that emphasized the control of inflation and sound public finance (rather than full employment and social protections) as primary goals of economic policy.

All of these strands came together in the so-called 'Washington Consensus' of the mid-1990s. The US and UK models of neoliberalism were there defined as the answer to global problems. Considerable pressure was put even on Japan and Europe (to say nothing of the rest of the world) to take the neoliberal road. It was, therefore, Clinton and then Blair who, from the centre-left, did the most to consolidate the role of neo-liberalism both at home and internationally. The formation of the World Trade Organization was the high point of this institutional thrust (though the creation of NAFTA and the earlier signing of the Maastricht accords in Europe were also significant regional institutional adjustments). Programmatically, the WTO set neo-liberal standards and rules for interaction in the global economy. Its primary objective, however, was to open up as much of the world as possible to unhindered capital flow (though always with the caveat clause of the protection of key 'national interests'), for this was the foundation of the capacity of the US financial power as well as that of Europe and Japan, to exact tribute from the rest of the world.

[...]

9

World Society and the Nation-State

John W. Meyer, John Boli, George M. Thomas, and Francisco O. Ramirez

This essay reviews arguments and evidence concerning the following proposition: *Many features of the contemporary nation-state derive from worldwide models constructed and propagated through global cultural and associational processes.* These models and the purposes they reflect (e.g., equality, socioeconomic progress, human development) are highly rationalized, articulated, and often surprisingly consensual. Worldwide models define and legitimate agendas for local action, shaping the structures and policies of nation-states and other national and local actors in virtually all of the domains of rationalized social life – business, politics, education, medicine, science, even the family and religion. The institutionalization of world models helps explain many puzzling features of contemporary national societies, such as structural iso-morphism in the face of enormous differences in resources and traditions, ritualized and rather loosely coupled organizational efforts, and elaborate structuration to serve purposes that are largely of exogenous origins. World models have long been in oper-ation as shapers of states and societies, but they have become especially important in the postwar era as the cultural and organizational development of world society has intensified at an unprecedented rate.

The operation of world society through peculiarly cultural and associational processes depends heavily on its statelessness. The almost feudal character of parcel-ized legal-rational sovereignty in the world has the seemingly paradoxical result of diminishing the causal importance of the organized hierarchies of power and inter-ests celebrated in most "realist" social scientific theories. The statelessness of world

Original publication details: John W. Meyer, John Boli, George M. Thomas, and Francisco O. Ramirez, "World Society and the Nation-State," *in American Journal of Sociology*, 1997. pp. 144–6, 150–1, 152–3, 157–61, 173–5. Reproduced with permission from the author and University of Chicago Press.

society also explains, in good measure, the lack of attention of the social sciences to the coherence and impact of world society's cultural and associational properties. Despite Tocqueville's well-known analysis of the importance of cultural and associational life in the nearly stateless American society of the 1830s, the social sciences are more than a little reluctant to acknowledge patterns of influence and conformity that cannot be explained solely as matters of power relations or functional rationality. This reluctance is most acute with respect to global development. Our effort here represents, we hope, a partial corrective for it.

We are trying to account for a world whose societies, organized as nation-states, are structurally similar in many unexpected dimensions and change in unexpectedly similar ways. A hypothetical example may be useful to illustrate our arguments, and we shall carry the example throughout the essay. If an unknown society were "discovered" on a previously unknown island, it is clear that many changes would occur. A government would soon form, looking something like a modern state with many of the usual ministries and agencies. Official recognition by other states and admission to the United Nations would ensue. The society would be analyzed as an economy, with standard types of data, organizations, and policies for domestic and international transactions. Its people would be formally reorganized as citizens with many familiar rights, while certain categories of citizens – children, the elderly, the poor – would be granted special protection. Standard forms of discrimination, especially ethnic and gender based, would be discovered and decried. The population would be counted and classified in ways specified by world census models. Modern educational, medical, scientific, and family law institutions would be developed. All this would happen more rapidly, and with greater penetration to the level of daily life, in the present day than at any earlier time because world models applicable to the island society are more highly codified and publicized than ever before. Moreover, world-society organizations devoted to educating and advising the islanders about the models' importance and utility are more numerous and active than ever.

What would be unlikely to happen is also clear. Theological disputes about whether the newly discovered *Indios* had souls or were part of the general human moral order would be rare. There would be little by way of an imperial rush to colonize the island. Few would argue that the natives needed only modest citizenship or human rights or that they would best be educated by but a few years of vocational training.

Thus, without knowing anything about the history, culture, practices, or traditions that obtained in this previously unknown society, we could forecast many changes that, upon "discovery," would descend on the island under the general rubric of "development." Our forecast would be imprecise because of the complexity of the interplay among various world models and local traditions, but the likely range of outcomes would be quite limited. We can identify the range of possibilities by using the institutionalist theoretical perspective underlying the analysis in this essay to interpret what has already happened to practically all of the societies of the world after their discovery and incorporation into world society. [...]

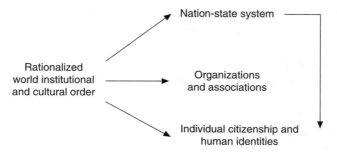

Figure 9.1 The world as enactment of culture.

Explanatory Models

Most analyses see nation-states as collective actors – as products of their own histories and internal forces. We emphasize instead models of the sort depicted in figure 9.1.

Figure 9.1 presents the view that nation-states are more or less exogenously constructed entities – the many individuals both inside and outside the state who engage in state formation and policy formulation are enactors of scripts rather more than they are self-directed actors. The social psychology at work here is that of Goffman or Snow, emphasizing dramaturgical and symbolic processes in place of the hard-boiled calculation of interests assumed by rationalistic actor-centric approaches.

We have deliberately oversimplified figure 9.1 because the proposition we are examining focuses on the enactment dimension of world-societal development. Of course, states, organizations, and individuals also contribute to the content and structure of world culture, and much world-cultural change and elaboration occur within transnational organizations and associations independent of lower-level units. A more complete figure would depict recursive processes among the constituent parts of world society, but here we concentrate on enactment processes.

The exogenous cultural construction of the nation-state model makes it easy and "natural" for standard sociopolitical forms to arise in our island society. Models and measures of such national goals as economic progress and social justice are readily available and morally compelling. Also available are model social problems, defined as the failure to realize these goals, that make it easy to identify and decry such failures as inefficient production methods or violations of rights. Alongside these are prescriptions about standardized social actors and policies that are to be engaged in the effort to resolve these newly recognized problems. All this is widely known and ready for implementation. [...]

Isomorphism and Isomorphic Change

Given other perspectives' emphases on the heterogeneity of economic and political resources (realist theories) or on local cultural origins (microphenomenological theories), most lines of thought anticipate striking diversity in political units around the world and in these units' trajectories of change. Our argument accounts for the similarities researchers often are surprised to find. It explains why our island society, despite all the possible configurations of local economic forces, power relationships, and forms of traditional culture it might contain, would promptly take on standard-ized forms and soon appear to be similar to a hundred other nation-states around the world.

Take the example of women in higher education. Microrealist or functional actor-centric models suggest that female enrollments in universities would increase in developed economies much more than elsewhere. Macrorealist arguments imply that female enrollments would expand in the core much more than the periphery, while micro-phenomenological arguments point to rising female enrollments in Western but not Islamic countries. However, female enrollments have expanded rapidly every-where, and in about the same time period – a period in which world societal discourse has emphasized female equality. This finding makes sense only if common world forces are at work.

Isomorphic developments leading to the same conclusion are reported in studies of many other nation-state features: constitutional forms emphasizing both state power and individual rights, mass schooling systems organized around a fairly standard curriculum, rationalized economic and demographic record keeping and data systems, antinatalist population control policies intended to enhance national development, formally equalized female status and rights, expanded human rights in general, expansive environmental policies, develop-ment-oriented economic policy, universalistic welfare systems, standard defini-tions of disease and health care, and even some basic demographic variables. Theories reasoning from the obviously large differences among national econ-omies and cultural traditions have great difficulty accounting for these observed isomorphisms, but they are sensible outcomes if nation-states are enactments of the world cultural order. [...]

Processes of World Society's Impact on Nation-States

So far we have argued that the observable isomorphism among nation-states supports our proposition that these entities derive from models embedded in an overarching world culture. What processes in world society construct and shape these "actors" to produce such isomorphism? The usual approach to answering this question would seek to identify mechanisms whereby actors rationally pursuing their interests make similar choices and decisions. This approach implicitly assumes that actor definitions and interests are largely fixed and independent of culture. We find it more useful and revealing to focus on processes that produce or reconstruct the actors themselves. We identify three processes by which world-societal elements authorize and fashion national states: the construction of identity and purpose, systemic maintenance of actor identity, and legitimation of the actorhood of such subnational units as individ-uals and organized interests.

Construction of nation-state identity and purpose

World society contains much cultural material authoritatively defining the nation-state as the preferred form of sovereign, responsible actor. The external recognition and construction of sovereign statehood has been a crucial dimension of the Western system for centuries, with new claimants especially dependent on obtaining formal recognition from dominant powers. With the anticolonial and self-determination movements of the twentieth century, all sorts of collectivities have learned to organize their claims around a nation-state identity, and the consolidation of the United Nations system has provided a central forum for identity recognition that diminishes the importance of major states. Entry into the system occurs, essentially, via application forms (to the United Nations and other world bodies) on which the applicant must demonstrate appropriately formulated assertions about sovereignty and control over population and territory, along with appropriate aims and purposes.

More than 130 new nation-state entities have formed since 1945. They consistently proclaim, both internally and externally, their conformity to worldwide models of national identity and state structure. So, too, would our island society. But older states, too, have learned to adapt to changes in these models. Thus, through both selection and adaptation, the system has expanded to something close to universality of the nation-state form. Realist theories, grounding their analyses in each country's particular resources and history, would predict a much wider variety of forms, including the retention of older statuses such as formal dependency or indirect incorporation of small or weak entities.

World-cultural models of sovereign identity take concrete form in particular state structures, programs, and policies. As described above, worldwide models of the rationalized nation-state actor define appropriate constitutions, goals, data systems, organization charts, ministry structures, and policies. Models also specify standard forms for the cultural depiction of national identity. Methods of constructing national culture through traditions, museums, tourism, and national intellectual culture are highly stylized. Nation-states are theorized or imagined communities drawing on models that are lodged at the world level.

Often, copying world models or conventions amounts to simple mimesis that has more to do with knowing how to fill in forms than with managing substantive problems. For instance, to compile comparable educational enrollment data in the 1950s, UNESCO statisticians chose to report enrollments for a six-year primary level and three-year junior and senior secondary levels. In ensuing decades, many countries structured their mass schooling systems around this six-year/three-year/three-year model, generally without investigating whether it would best meet any of the presumed purposes of schooling.

Strang shows the extraordinary impact of the legitimized identity system on the survival and stability of states. Throughout modern history, dependent territories have moved to sovereign statehood at a steadily increasing rate that accelerated rapidly in the postwar period. Once sovereign, countries almost never revert to dependence. Even the breakup of the Soviet Union produced not dependent territories but formally sovereign nation-states, unprepared as some of the former republics were for this status. Thus, it is highly unlikely that our island society would be incorporated as a dependent territory of an extant nation-state; this would be too great a violation of the legitimized right to self-determination. Moreover, establishing the island society's sovereign status in the international system would stabilize its new state, though it would not preclude, and might even increase, instability in the state's government.

Orientation to the identity and purposes of the nation-state model increases the rate at which countries adopt other prescribed institutions of modernity. Having committed themselves to the identity of the rationalizing state, appropriate policies follow – policies for national development, individual citizenship and rights, environmental management, foreign relations. These policies are depicted as if they were autonomous decisions because nation-states are defined as sovereign, responsible, and essentially autonomous actors. Taking into account the larger culture in which states are embedded, however, the policies look more like enactments of conventionalized scripts. Even if a state proclaims its opposition to the dominant world identity models, it will nevertheless pursue many purposes within this model. It will develop bureaucratic authority and attempt to build many modern institutions, ranging from a central bank to an educational system. It will thereby find itself modifying its traditions in the direction of world-cultural forms.

Systemic maintenance of nation-state actor identity

If a specific nation-state is unable to put proper policies in place (because of costs, incompetence, or resistance), world-society structures will provide help. This process operates more through authoritative external support for the legitimate purposes of states than through authoritarian imposition by dominant powers or interests. For example, world organizations and professionalized ideologies actively encourage countries to adopt population control policies that are justified not as good for the world as a whole but as necessary for national development. National science policies are also promulgated as crucial to national development; before this link was theorized, UNESCO efforts to encourage countries to promote science failed to diffuse. As this example illustrates, international organizations often posture as objective disinterested others who help nation-states pursue their exogenously derived goals.

Resistance to world models is difficult because nation-states are formally committed, as a matter of identity, to such self-evident goals as socioeconomic development, citizen rights, individual self-development, and civil international relations. If a particular regime rhetorically resists world models, local actors can rely on legitimacy myths (democracy, freedom, equality) and the ready support of activist external groups to oppose the regime. Nation-state "choices" are thus less likely to conflict with world-cultural prescriptions than realist or microphenomenological theories anticipate because both nation-state choices and world pressures derive from the same overarching institutions.

Legitimation of subnational actors and practices

World-cultural principles license the nation-state not only as a managing central authority but also as an identity-supplying nation. Individual citizenship and the sovereignty of the people are basic tenets of nationhood. So too are the legitimacy and presumed functional necessity of much domestic organizational structure, ranging from financial market structures to organizations promoting individual and collective rights (of labor, ethnic groups, women, and so on). World-society ideology thus directly licenses a variety of organized interests and functions. Moreover, in pursuing their externally legitimated identities and purposes by creating agencies and programs, nation-states also promote the domestic actors involved. Programs and their associated accounting systems increase the number and density of types of actors, as groups come forward to claim newly reified identities and the resources allocated to them.

A good example is the rise of world discourse legitimating the human rights of gays and lesbians, which has produced both national policy changes and the mobilization of actors claiming these rights. As nation-states adopt policies embodying the appropriate principles, they institutionalize the identity and political presence of these groups. Of course, all these "internally" generated changes are infused with world-cultural conceptions of the properly behaving nation-state.

Hence, if a nation-state neglects to adopt world-approved policies, domestic elements will try to carry out or enforce conformity. General world pressures favoring environmentalism, for example, have led many states to establish environmental protection agencies, which foster the growth of environmental engineering firms, activist groups, and planning agencies. Where the state has not adopted the appropriate policies, such local units and actors as cities, schools, scout troops, and religious groups are likely to practice environmentalism and call for national action. Thus, world culture influences nation-states not only at their centers, or only in symbolic ways, but also through direct connections between local actors and world culture. Such connections produce many axes of mobilization for the implementation of world-cultural principles and help account for similarities in mobilization agendas and strategies in highly disparate countries.

Explicit rejection of world-cultural principles sometimes occurs, particularly by nationalist or religious movements whose purported opposition to modernity is seen as a threat to geopolitical stability. While the threat is real enough, the analysis is mistaken because it greatly underestimates the extent to which such movements conform to rationalized models of societal order and purpose. These movements mobilize around principles inscribed in world-cultural scripts, derive their organizing capacity from the legitimacy of these scripts, and edit their supposedly primordial claims to maximize this legitimacy. By and large, they seek an idealized modern community undergoing broad-based social development where citizens (of the right sort) can fully exercise their abstract rights. While they violate some central elements of world-cultural ideology, they nonetheless rely heavily on other elements. For example, religious "fundamentalists" may reject the extreme naturalism of modernity by making individuals accountable to an unchallengeable god, but they nevertheless exhort their people to embrace such key world-cultural elements as nation building, mass schooling, rationalized health care, and professionalization. They also are apt to reformulate their religious doctrine in accordance with typical modern conceptions of rational-moral discipline. In general, nationalist and religious movements intensify isomorphism more than they resist it. [...]

Conclusion

A considerable body of evidence supports our proposition that world-society models shape nation-state identities, structures, and behavior via worldwide cultural and associational processes. Carried by rationalized others whose scientific and professional authority often exceeds their power and resources, world culture celebrates, expands, and standardizes strong but culturally somewhat tamed national actors. The result is nation-states that are more isomorphic than most theories would predict and change more uniformly than is commonly recognized. As creatures of exogenous world culture, states are ritualized actors marked by extensive internal decoupling and a good deal more structuration than would occur if they were responsive only to local cultural, functional, or power processes.

As the Western world expanded in earlier centuries to dominate and incorporate societies in the larger world, the penetration of a universalized culture proceeded hesitantly. Westerners could imagine that the locals did not have souls, were members of a different species, and could reasonably be enslaved or exploited. Inhabiting a different moral and natural universe, non-Western societies were occasionally celebrated for their noble savagery but more often cast as inferior groups unsuited for true civilization. Westerners promoted religious conversion by somewhat parochial and inconsistent means, but broader incorporation was ruled out on all sorts of grounds. Education and literacy were sometimes prohibited, rarely encouraged, and never generally provided, for the natives were ineducable or prone to rebellion. Rationalized social, political, and economic development (e.g., the state, democracy, urban factory production, modern family law) was inappropriate, even unthinkable. Furthermore, the locals often strongly resisted incorporation by the West. Even Japan maintained strong boundaries against many aspects of modernity until the end of World War II, and Chinese policy continues a long pattern of resistance to external "aid."

The world, however, is greatly changed. Our island society would obviously become a candidate for full membership in the world community of nations and individuals. Human rights, state-protected citizen rights, and democratic forms would become natural entitlements. An economy would emerge, defined and measured in rationalized terms and oriented to growth under state regulation. A formal national polity would be essential, including a constitution, citizenship laws, educational structures, and open forms of participation and communication. The whole apparatus of rationalized modernity would be mobilized as necessary and applicable; internal and external resistance would be stigmatized as reactionary unless it was couched in universalistic terms. Allowing the islanders to remain imprisoned in their society, under the authority of their old gods and chiefs and entrapped in primitive economic technologies, would be unfair and discriminatory, even though the passing of their traditional society would also occasion nostalgia and regret.

Prevailing social theories account poorly for these changes. Given a dynamic socio-cultural system, realist models can account for a world of economic and political absorption, inequality, and domination. They do not well explain a world of formally equal, autonomous, and expansive nation-state actors. Microcultural or phenomenological lines of argument can account for diversity and resistance to homogenization, not a world in which national states, subject to only modest coercion or control, adopt standard identities and structural forms.

We argue for the utility of recognizing that rationalized modernity is a universalistic and inordinately successful form of the earlier Western religious and post-religious system. As a number of commentators have noted, in our time the religious elites of Western Christendom have given up on the belief that there is no salvation outside the church. That postulate has been replaced by the belief among almost all elites that salvation lies in rationalized structures grounded in scientific and technical knowledge – states, schools, firms, voluntary associations, and the like. The new religious elites are the professionals, researchers, scientists, and intellectuals who write secularized and unconditionally universalistic versions of the salvation story, along with the managers, legislators, and policymakers who believe the story fervently and pursue it relentlessly. This belief is worldwide and structures the organization of social life almost everywhere.

The colossal disaster of World War II may have been a key factor in the rise of global models of nationally organized progress and justice, and the Cold War may well have intensified the forces pushing human development to the global level. If the present configuration of lowered systemic (if not local) tensions persists, perhaps both the consensuality of the models and their impact on nation-states will decline. On the other hand, the models' rationalized definitions of progress and justice (across an ever broadening front) are rooted in universalistic scientific and professional definitions that have reached a level of deep global institutionalization. These definitions produce a great deal of conflict with regard to their content and application, but their authority is likely to prove quite durable.

Many observers anticipate a variety of failures of world society, citing instances of gross violations of world-cultural principles (e.g., in Bosnia), stagnant development (e.g., in Africa), and evasion of proper responsibility (in many places). In our view, the growing list of perceived "social problems" in the world indicates not the weakness of world-cultural institutions but their strength. Events like political torture, waste dumping, or corruption, which not so long ago were either overlooked entirely or considered routine, local, specific aberrations or tragedies, are now of world-societal significance. They violate strong expectations regarding global integration and propriety and can easily evoke world-societal reactions seeking to put things right. A world with so many widely discussed social problems is a world of Durkheimian and Simmelian integration, however much it may also seem driven by disintegrative tendencies.

10

Globalization as a Problem

Roland Robertson

The Crystallization of a Concept and a Problem

Globalization as a concept refers both to the compression of the world and the intensification of consciousness of the world as a whole. The processes and actions to
which the concept of globalization now refers have been proceeding, with some
interruptions, for many centuries, but the main focus of the discussion of globalization is on relatively recent times. In so far as that discussion is closely linked to the
contours and nature of modernity, globalization refers quite clearly to recent developments. In the present book globalization is conceived in much broader terms than
that, but its main empirical focus is in line with the increasing acceleration in both
concrete global interdependence and consciousness of the global whole in the twentieth century. But it is necessary to emphasize that globalization is not equated with
or seen as a direct consequence of an amorphously conceived modernity.

Use of the noun 'globalization' has developed quite recently. Certainly in academic
circles it was not recognized as a significant concept, in spite of diffuse and intermit-
tent usage prior to that, until the early, or even middle, 1980s. During the second half
of the 1980s its use increased enormously, so much so that it is virtually impossible to
trace the patterns of its contemporary diffusion across a large number of areas of
contemporary life in different parts of the world. By now, even though the term is
often used very loosely and, indeed, in contradictory ways, it has *itself* become part
of 'global consciousness,' an aspect of the remarkable proliferation of terms centred

Original publication details: Roland Robertson, *Globalization: Social Theory and Global Culture*. London:
Sage, 1992. pp. 8–9, 25–9, 174–80.

upon 'global.' Although the latter adjective has been in use for a long time (meaning, strongly, worldwide; or, more loosely, 'the whole'), it is indicative of our contemporary concern with globalization that the *Oxford Dictionary of New Words* (1991) actually includes 'global' as a *new* word, focusing specifically, but misleadingly, on its use in 'environmental jargon.' That same *Dictionary* also defines 'global consciousness' as 'receptiveness to (and understanding) of cultures other than one's own, often as part of an appreciation of world socio-economic and ecological issues.' It maintains that such a use has been much influenced by Marshall McLuhan's idea of 'the global village,' introduced in his book *Explorations in Communication* (1960). The notion of compression, or 'shrinking,' is indeed present in that influential book about the shared simultaneity of media, particularly televisual, experience in our time. There can be little doubt that McLuhan both reflected and shaped media trends, so much so that in time we have come to witness (self-serving) media attempts to consolidate the idea of the global *community*. On the other hand the media fully acknowledge the 'nationality' of particular media systems, and report at length on the tough realities of international relations, wars and so on. Such realities are far from the communal connotations which some have read into McLuhan's imagery. In the same period when McLuhan's notion of the global village was becoming influential there occurred the 'expressive revolution' of the 1960s. That was, to put it very simply, a 'revolution' in consciousness among the young in numerous parts of the world, centred upon such themes as liberation and love, in both individual and collective terms. In fact the *Oxford Dictionary of New Words* maintains that the current term 'global consciousness … draws on the fashion for *consciousness-raising* in the sixties' (1991).

Undoubtedly the 1960s 'revolution' in consciousness had an important effect in many parts of the world, in its sharpening of the sense of what was supposedly common to all in an increasingly tight-knit world. Yet, as we will see more fully, this sense of global interdependence has rapidly become recognized in numerous other, relatively independent, domains and fora. World wars, particularly World War II with its 'humanity-shaking' events and its aftermath, the rise of what became known as the Third World, the proliferation of international, transnational and supranational institutions and the attempts to coordinate what has become known as the global economy have played crucial parts in the twofold process of 'objective' and 'subjective' 'globalization.' And surely McLuhan's own Catholic-tinged observations concerning the media-centred 'global village' were partly shaped by such developments. [...]

Coming to Terms with the World as a Whole

[...] My model of what, in the most flexible terms, may be called the global field is centred on the way(s) in which we think about globality in relation to the basic makeup of that field. My formulation is more multifaceted than that of Dumont, in that I think in terms of four major aspects, or reference points, rather than two. These are *national societies*; *individuals*, or more basically, *selves*; *relationships between national societies*, or *the world system of societies*; and, in the generic sense, *mankind*, which, to avoid misunderstanding, I frequently call *humankind*. [...]

In the broadest sense I am concerned with the way(s) in which the world is ordered. Whereas I am setting out this model of order in what may appear to be formal terms, the intent which actually guides it is to inject *flexibility* into our considerations of 'totality.' In so far as we think about the world as a whole, we are inevitably involved in a certain kind of what is sometimes pejoratively called totalistic analysis. But even though my scheme does involve a 'totalizing' tendency, it does so partly in order to comprehend *different* kinds of orientation to the global circumstance. It will be seen that movements, individuals and other actors perceive and construct the order (or disorder) of the world in a number of different ways. In *that* sense what my model does is to facilitate interpretation and analysis of such variation. So there is a crucial difference between imposing a model of the global field on all the present and potential actors in that field and setting out a model which facilitates comprehension of variation in that field. The latter is an important consideration. My interest is in how order is, so to speak, *done*; including order that is 'done' by those seeking explicitly to establish legal principles for the ordering of the world. To put it yet another way, my model is conceived as an attempt to make analytical and interpretive sense of how quotidian actors, collective or individual, go about the business of conceiving of the world, including attempts to *deny* that the world is one.

Nevertheless, in spite of my acknowledgment of certain denials of global wholeness, I maintain that the trends towards the unicity of the world are, when all is said and done, inexorable. […]

Globalization refers in this particular sense to the coming into, often problematic, conjunction of different forms of life. This cannot be accurately captured in the simple proposition that globalization is 'a consequence of modernity,' which I consider specifically towards the end of this volume. Present concern with globality and globalization cannot be comprehensively considered simply as an aspect or outcome of the Western 'project' of modernity or, except in very broad terms, enlightenment. In an increasingly globalized world there is a heightening of civilizational, societal, ethnic, regional and, indeed individual, self-consciousness. There are constraints on social entities to locate themselves within world history and the global future. Yet globalization in and of itself also involves the diffusion of the *expectation* of such identity declarations.

This model, which is presented diagrammatically in Figure 10.1, gives the basic outline of what I here call the global field but which for other purposes I call the global-human condition. The figure indicates the four major components, or reference points, of the conception of globality, the basic way in which we are able as empirically informed analysts to 'make sense' of globality, as well as the form in terms of which globalization has in the last few centuries actually proceeded. Discussion of different, or alternative, forms in terms of which globalization *might* have occurred or, indeed, did partially occur are discussed in later chapters. To provide an example at this stage, it is clear that Islam historically has had a general 'globalizing' thrust; but had that potential form of globalization succeeded we would now almost certainly comprehend contemporary 'globality' differently. There would be a need for a different kind of model.

The model is presented in primary reference to twentieth-century developments. In that it partly summarizes such developments it draws attention to increasing,

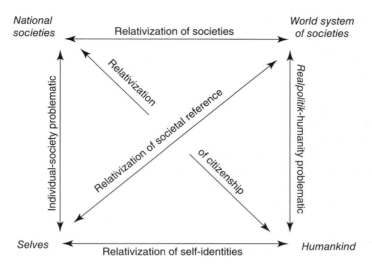

Figure 10.1 The global field.

interrelated thematizations of societies, individual selves, international relations and humankind. At the same time, it opens the way to the discussion and study of the ways in which the general pattern came historically to prevail. It also allows for different, indeed conflicting, empirical emphases within 'the field' [...]

First, while I have emphasized that my perspective allows for empirical variation with respect to what later I call images of world order and that my primary task in analyzing globalization is to lay bare and open up relatively neglected aspects of that theme, there are clearly moral and critical dimensions of my approach to globalization. I will only mention the most general here. There is certainly a sense in which I am trying to tackle directly the problem of *global complexity*, a point which will become even clearer when I address the question of the shifting contents of the four major components of my model. It will, I hope, also become clear that I am arguing for the moral acceptance of that complexity. In other words, complexity becomes something like a moral issue in its own right. Specifically, the way in which I tackle the issues of globality and globalization suggests that in order for one to have a 'realistic' view of the world as a whole one must, at least in the contemporary circumstance, accept in principle the relative autonomy of each of the four main components and that, by the same token, one should acknowledge that each of the four is in one way or another constrained by the other three. In one sense, then, overemphasis on one to the expense of attention to the other three constitutes a form of 'fundamentalism.' Simply put, one cannot and should not wish away the reality of one or more aspects of the terms in which globalization has been proceeding. This certainly does not exhaust the issue of the extent to which my approach to globalization is moral and critical. But it must suffice for the moment.

Second, there is the issue of the processes which bring about globalization – the 'causal mechanisms' or the 'driving forces.' What happens here to arguments about the dynamics of capitalism and the forces of imperialism which have undoubtedly played a large part in bringing the world into an increasingly compressed condition?

In arguing that mine is a cultural perspective on globalization I do not wish to convey the idea that I consider the matter of 'the forces' or 'the mechanisms' of globalization unimportant. However, I am well aware that that is well-trodden ground. The spread of Western capitalism and the part played by imperialism have been addressed at great length, as has the increasingly complex crystallization of the contemporary global economy. In contrast, the discussion of the disputed terms in which globalization has occurred and is occurring has been greatly neglected. It is that and directly related issues which form the main concern ..., and it is hoped that such a cultural focus will place work in the more traditional vein in a new light. While the use of the term 'culture' here is certainly not as broad and all-embracing as is to be found in some tendencies within the relatively new field of cultural studies, it is employed much more fluidly and adventurously than in conventional sociological work. In particular, my approach is used to demonstrate discontinuities and differences, rather than the traditional sociological view of culture as integrating. It is also meant to indicate a particular way of doing sociology, rather than a sociology that concentrates on culture as such.

Third, in my representation of the global field I have emphasized a number of processes of *relativization*. That term is meant to indicate the ways in which, as globalization proceeds, challenges are increasingly presented to the stability of particular perspectives on, and collective and individual participation in, the overall globalization process. As I have said, this picture of the global field has been produced in primary reference to contemporary globality and globalization. It is an ideal-typical representation of what is meant here by global complexity. In one important respect it indicates overall processes of differentiation in so far as global complexity is concerned. Broadly speaking, application of the model involves the view that processes of differentiation of the main spheres of globality increase over time. Thus differentiation between the spheres was much lower in earlier phases of globalization; while the effects of such differentiation have been encountered unevenly and with different responses in different parts of the world. [...]

Globalization and the Search for Fundamentals

The approach to globalization which I have been advocating takes its departure from empirical generalizations concerning the rapidly increasing compression of the entire world into a single, global field and conceptual ideas about the ways in which the world as a whole should be 'mapped' in broadly sociological terms. The two strands of elaboration are, of course, closely linked. In the relatively early stage of my attempts to theorize the topic of globalization the issue of 'fundamentalism' was conspicuous. Indeed it was partly in order to account for the resurgence of religious fundamentalism in the late 1970s and early 1980s that I revitalized my longstanding interest in 'international' phenomena. Coming to terms with fundamentalism and related issues has been a prominent aspect of my work on globalization, even though over the last ten years or so I have revised my thinking about the relationship between globalization and fundamentalism (more generally 'the search for fundamentals').

Whereas my first formulations tended to see politicoreligious fundamentalism as resulting largely from compression of the *inter-societal system* (fundamentalism as an attempt to express society identity), my more recent attempts to grasp analytically the more general problem of the assertion of 'deep particularity' on the global scene have centred upon the global construction and dissemination of ideas concerning the value of particularism. The first perspective involves an emphasis on space-time compression leading to the felt necessity for societies (and regions and civilizations, as well as 'subnational' entities) to declare their identities for both internal and external purposes. It tends to involve a focus on fundamentalism as a *reaction* to, rather than as an aspect – or, indeed, a creation – of, globalization; although that was not the exclusive focus of my earlier perspective. The second approach involves a more definite stress on the idea that the expectation of identity declaration is built into the general process of globalization. This does not mean that the notion of fundamentalism as reaction or resistance is thereby relinquished, but that that possibility is now viewed in a more general frame.

There have been four major focal points of the dominant globalization process since the sixteenth century: *nationally constituted societies*; *the international system of societies*; *individuals*; and *humankind*. At the risk of repetition, my argument in this respect can be restated. It is largely in terms of the enhancement of each of these reference points, in the sense of their being tangibly crystallized, and the raising of problems about the relationships between them that the globalization process has proceeded in recent centuries. At the same time there have been changes in the ways in which each of these major components of the overall global circumstance has been operatively constructed. All of this means that we have to conceive of the concept of globalization as having primarily to do with *the form* in terms of which the world has moved towards unicity. So when we speak of globalization we must realize that we are referring above all to a relatively specific path that the world has taken in the direction of it becoming singular. The world could in theory, as I have argued, have become a single entity along different trajectories – without, for example, involving the salience of the national society which has *actually* been a vital ingredient of the overall globalization process. [...]

Universalism and Particularism Globalized

In my perspective globalization in what I call its primary sense is a relatively autonomous process. Its central *dynamic* involves the twofold process of the particularization of the universal and the universalization of the particular. The particularization of the universal, defined as the global concretization of the problem of universality, has become the occasion for the search for *global* fundamentals. In other words, the current phase of very rapid globalization facilitates the rise of movements concerned with the 'real meaning' of the world, movements (and individuals) searching for the meaning of the world as a whole. The universalization of the particular refers to the global universality of the search for the particular, for increasingly fine-grained modes of identity presentation. To put it as sharply as possible, I propose that 'fundamentalism' is a mode of thought and practice which has become almost globally institutionalized, in large part, as far as the twentieth century is concerned, in terms of the norm of national self-determination, announced after World War I by Woodrow Wilson, given new life after World War II with respect to what became known as the Third World, and then expanded on a global scale to all manner of 'entities' from the 1960s onwards. In so far as analysts see 'the search' entirely in terms of an atavistic response to globalization they are failing to deal with the participatory aspect of globalization. This does not mean that there are no atavistic, isolationist or anti-global responses to globalization. But we have to be very careful in delineating these. They are by no means self-evident. [...]

In addressing globalization I have paid particular attention to what I have called the take-off period of modern globalization, lasting from about 1870 through to the mid-1920s; and I have been struck by the extent to which in that period the general issue of the coordination of the particular and the universal received widespread practical and political attention. This was a time when there was great emphasis on the need to invent tradition and national identity within the context of an increasingly compressed, globalized world. Indeed much of the desire to invent tradition and identity derived from the contingencies of global compression and the concomitant spread of expectations concerning these. During the period lasting from about 1870 to 1925 basic geohuman contingencies were formally worked out in such terms as the time-zoning of the world and the establishment of the international dateline; the near-global adoption of the Gregorian calendar and the adjustable seven-day week; and the establishment of international telegraphic and signaling codes. At the same time, there arose movements which were specifically concerned with the relationship between the local and the panlocal, one of the most notable being the ecumenical movement which sought to bring the major 'world' religious traditions into a coordinated, concultural discourse. On the secular front, the international socialist movement had parallel aims, but it was even more ambitious in that it sought to overcome *strong* particularism in the name of internationalism. A more specific case is provided by the rise at the end of the nineteenth century of the International Youth Hostel movement, which attempted an international coordination of particularistic, 'back to nature' ventures. Other particular–universal developments of the time include the modern Olympic Games and Nobel prizes. The contemporary use of such terms as 'fundamentals' and 'fundamentalism' was also established, mainly in the USA, in the same period.

What is particularly significant about this period is that the material circumstance of the world (as a heliocentric globe) was, as it were, dealt with in relationship to the rapidly spreading consciousness of the global world as such, greatly facilitated by recently developed rapid means of travel and communication, such as the airplane and the wireless. One crucial aspect of these trends was that events and circumstances previously segregated in space and time increasingly came to be considered as simultaneous in terms of categories which were universalistically particular and particularistically universal. Spatial and temporal categories and measures were globally institutionalized so as to both accentuate consciousness of difference and to universalize difference.

Needless to say, such developments did not emerge *de novo* during the period in question. The steady growth in map-making and its globalization, the interpenetration of modes of 'travelers' tales,' the growth of postal services, the increase in the spread of travel, the early rise of tourism – all these, and still other, developments lay in the background to the rapid trends of the crucial take-off period of modern globalization. One particularly important development of a somewhat different kind concerned what has been called the politicization of archeology in the mid-nineteenth century. As we have seen, in that earlier period the monuments of classical and biblical civilization in Egypt, Mesopotamia, Greece and other areas of the Near and Middle East became national quests, within the context of increasingly international and industrialized society. In turn these monuments have become the bases of the official national symbols of the peoples of the Middle East and the eastern Mediterranean. Now in those areas both local and non-local archeologists are shaping 'a new past for the peoples of that region.' All of this began, it should be remembered, in a period of great (often imperial) concern with the unification of humankind.

In sum I argue that the search for fundamentals – in so far as it exists on any significant scale – is to a considerable degree both a contingent feature of globalization and an aspect of global culture. In a sense 'fundamentalism within limits' makes globalization work. [...]

11

Disjuncture and Difference in the Global Cultural Economy

Arjun Appadurai

It takes only the merest acquaintance with the facts of the modern world to note that it is now an interactive system in a sense that is strikingly new. Historians and sociologists, especially those concerned with translocal processes and the world systems associated with capitalism, have long been aware that the world has been a congeries of large-scale interactions for many centuries. Yet today's world involves interactions of a new order and intensity. Cultural transactions between social groups in the past have generally been restricted, sometimes by the facts of geography and ecology, and at other times by active resistance to interactions with the Other (as in China for much of its history and in Japan before the Meiji Restoration). Where there have been sustained cultural transactions across large parts of the globe, they have usually involved the long-distance journey of commodities (and of the merchants most concerned with them) and of travelers and explorers of every type. The two main forces for sustained cultural interaction before this century have been warfare (and the large-scale political systems sometimes generated by it) and religions of conversion, which have sometimes, as in the case of Islam, taken warfare as one of the legitimate instruments of their expansion. Thus, between travelers and merchants, pilgrims and conquerors, the world has seen much long-distance (and long-term) cultural traffic. This much seems self-evident.

But few will deny that given the problems of time, distance, and limited technologies for the command of resources across vast spaces, cultural dealings between socially and spatially separated groups have, until the past few centuries, been bridged

Original publication details: Arjun Appadurai, "Disjuncture and Difference in the Global Cultural Economy," in *Public Culture*, 2, 2, 1990. pp. 1–24. Reproduced with permission from Duke University Press.

at great cost and sustained over time only with great effort. The forces of cultural gravity seemed always to pull away from the formation of large-scale ecumenes, whether religious, commercial, or political, toward smaller-scale accretions of intimacy and interest.

Sometime in the past few centuries, the nature of this gravitational field seems to have changed. Partly because of the spirit of the expansion of Western maritime interests after 1500, and partly because of the relatively autonomous developments of large and aggressive social formations in the Americas (such as the Aztecs and the Incas), in Eurasia (such as the Mongols and their descendants, the Mughals and Ottomans), in island Southeast Asia (such as the Buginese), and in the kingdoms of precolonial Africa (such as Dahomey), an overlapping set of ecumenes began to emerge, in which congeries of money, commerce, conquest, and migration began to create durable cross-societal bonds. This process was accelerated by the technology transfers and innovations of the late eighteenth and nineteenth centuries, which created complex colonial orders centered on European capitals and spread throughout the non-European world. This intricate and overlapping set of Eurocolonial worlds (first Spanish and Portuguese, later principally English, French, and Dutch) set the basis for a permanent traffic in ideas of peoplehood and selfhood, which created the imagined communities of recent nationalisms throughout the world.

With what Benedict Anderson has called "print capitalism," a new power was unleashed in the world, the power of mass literacy and its attendant large-scale production of projects of ethnic affinity that were remarkably free of the need for face-to-face communication or even of indirect communication between persons and groups. The act of reading things together set the stage for movements based on a paradox – the paradox of constructed primordialism. There is, of course, a great deal else that is involved in the story of colonialism and its dialectically generated nationalisms, but the issue of constructed ethnicities is surely a crucial strand in this tale.

But the revolution of print capitalism and the cultural affinities and dialogues unleashed by it were only modest precursors to the world we live in now. For in the past century, there has been a technological explosion, largely in the domain of transportation and information, that makes the interactions of a print-dominated world seem as hard-won and as easily erased as the print revolution made earlier forms of cultural traffic appear. For with the advent of the steamship, the automobile, the airplane, the camera, the computer, and the telephone, we have entered into an altogether new condition of neighborliness, even with those most distant from ourselves. Marshall McLuhan, among others, sought to theorize about this world as a "global village," but theories such as McLuhan's appear to have overestimated the communitarian implications of the new media order. We are now aware that with media, each time we are tempted to speak of the global village, we must be reminded that media create communities with "no sense of place." The world we live in now seems rhizomic, even schizophrenic, calling for theories of rootlessness, alienation, and psychological distance between individuals and groups on the one hand, and fantasies (or nightmares) of electronic propinquity on the other. Here, we are close to the central problematic of cultural processes in today's world.

Thus, the curiosity that drove Pico Iyer to Asia (in 1988) is in some ways the product of a confusion between some ineffable McDonaldization of the world and the much subtler play of indigenous trajectories of desire and fear with global flows of people and things. Indeed, Iyer's own impressions are testimony to the fact that, if *a* global cultural system is emerging, it is filled with ironies and resistances, sometimes camouflaged as passivity and a bottomless appetite in the Asian world for things Western.

Iyer's own account of the uncanny Philippine affinity for American popular music is rich testimony to the global culture of the hyperreal, for somehow Philippine renditions of American popular songs are both more widespread in the Philippines, and more disturbingly faithful to their originals, than they are in the United States today. An entire nation seems to have learned to mimic Kenny Rogers and the Lennon sisters, like a vast Asian Motown chorus. But *Americanization* is certainly a pallid term to apply to such a situation, for not only are there more Filipinos singing perfect renditions of some American songs (often from the American past) than there are Americans doing so, there is also, of course, the fact that the rest of their lives is not in complete synchrony with the referential world that first gave birth to these songs.

In a further globalizing twist on what Fredric Jameson has called "nostalgia for the present," these Filipinos look back to a world they have never lost. This is one of the central ironies of the politics of global cultural flows, especially in the arena of entertainment and leisure. [...]

The central problem of today's global interactions is the tension between cultural homogenization and cultural heterogenization. A vast array of empirical facts could be brought to bear on the side of the homogenization argument, and much of it has come from the left end of the spectrum of media studies, and some from other perspectives. Most often, the homogenization argument subspeciates into either an argument about Americanization or an argument about commoditization, and very often the two arguments are closely linked. What these arguments fail to consider is that at least as rapidly as forces from various metropolises are brought into new societies they tend to become indigenized in one or another way: this is true of music and housing styles as much as it is true of science and terrorism, spectacles and constitutions. The dynamics of such indigenization have just begun to be explored systemically, and much more needs to be done. But it is worth noticing that for the people of Irian Jaya, Indonesianization may be more worrisome than Americanization, as Japanization may be for Koreans, Indianization for Sri Lankans, Vietnamization for the Cambodians, and Russianization for the people of Soviet Armenia and the Baltic republics. Such a list of alternative fears to Americanization could be greatly expanded, but it is not a shapeless inventory: for polities of smaller scale, there is always a fear of cultural absorption by polities of larger scale, especially those that are nearby. One man's imagined community is another man's political prison.

This scalar dynamic, which has widespread global manifestations, is also tied to the relationship between nations and states. For the moment let us note that the simplification of these many forces (and fears) of homogenization can also be exploited by nation-states in relation to their own minorities, by posing global commoditization (or capitalism, or some other such external enemy) as more real than the threat of its own hegemonic strategies.

The new global cultural economy has to be seen as a complex, overlapping, disjunctive order that cannot any longer be understood in terms of existing center – periphery models (even those that might account for multiple centers and peripheries). Nor is it susceptible to simple models of push and pull (in terms of migration theory), or of surpluses and deficits (as in traditional models of balance of trade), or of consumers and producers (as in most neo-Marxist theories of development). Even the most complex and flexible theories of global development that have come out of the Marxist tradition are inadequately quirky and have failed to come to terms with what Scott Lash and John Urry have called disorganized capitalism. The complexity of the current global economy has to do with certain fundamental disjunctures between economy, culture, and politics that we have only begun to theorize.

I propose that an elementary framework for exploring such disjunctures is to look at the relationship among five dimensions of global cultural flows that can be termed (a) *ethnoscapes*, (b) *mediascapes*, (c) *technoscapes*, (d) *financescapes*, and (e) *ideoscapes*. The suffix *-scape* allows us to point to the fluid, irregular shapes of these landscapes, shapes that characterize international capital as deeply as they do international clothing styles. These terms with the common suffix *-scape* also indicate that these are not objectively given relations that look the same from every angle of vision but, rather, that they are deeply perspectival constructs, inflected by the historical, linguistic, and political situatedness of different sorts of actors: nation-states, multinationals, diasporic communities, as well as subnational groupings and movements (whether religious, political, or economic), and even intimate face-to-face groups, such as villages, neighborhoods, and families. Indeed, the individual actor is the last locus of this perspectival set of landscapes, for these landscapes are eventually navigated by agents who both experience and constitute larger formations, in part from their own sense of what these landscapes offer.

These landscapes thus are the building blocks of what (extending Benedict Anderson) I would like to call *imagined worlds*, that is, the multiple worlds that are constituted by the historically situated imaginations of persons and groups spread around the globe. An important fact of the world we live in today is that many persons on the globe live in such imagined worlds (and not just in imagined communities) and thus are able to contest and sometimes even subvert the imagined worlds of the official mind and of the entrepreneurial mentality that surround them.

By *ethnoscape*, I mean the landscape of persons who constitute the shifting world in which we live: tourists, immigrants, refugees, exiles, guest workers, and other moving groups and individuals constitute an essential feature of the world and appear to affect the politics of (and between) nations to a hitherto unprecedented degree. This is not to say that there are no relatively stable communities and networks of kinship, friendship, work, and leisure, as well as of birth, residence, and other filial forms. But it is to say that the warp of these stabilities is everywhere shot through with the woof of human motion, as more persons and groups deal with the realities of having to move or the fantasies of wanting to move. What is more, both these realities and fantasies now function on larger scales, as men and women from villages in India think not just of moving to Poona or Madras but of moving to Dubai and Houston, and refugees from Sri Lanka find themselves in South India as well as in Switzerland, just as the Hmong are driven to London as well as to Philadelphia. And as international capital shifts its needs, as production and technology generate different needs, as nation-states shift their policies on refugee populations, these moving groups can never afford to let their imaginations rest too long, even if they wish to.

By *technoscape*, I mean the global configuration, also ever fluid, of technology and the fact that technology, both high and low, both mechanical and informational, now moves at high speeds across various kinds of previously impervious boundaries. Many countries now are the roots of multinational enterprise: a huge steel complex in Libya may involve interests from India, China, Russia, and Japan, providing different components of new technological configurations. The odd distribution of technologies, and thus the peculiarities of these technoscapes, are increasingly driven not by any obvious economies of scale, of political control, or of market rationality but by increasingly complex relationships among money flows, political possibilities, and the availability of both un- and highly-skilled labor. So, while India exports waiters and chauffeurs to Dubai and Sharjah, it also exports software engineers to the United States – indentured briefly to Tata-Burroughs or the World Bank, then laundered through the State Department to become wealthy resident aliens, who are in turn objects of seductive messages to invest their money and know-how in federal and state projects in India. [...]

It is useful to speak as well of *financescapes*, as the disposition of global capital is now a more mysterious, rapid, and difficult landscape to follow than ever before, as currency markets, national stock exchanges, and commodity speculations move mega-monies through national turnstiles at blinding speed, with vast, absolute implications for small differences in percentage points and time units. But the critical point is that the global relationship among ethnoscapes, technoscapes, and financescapes is deeply disjunctive and profoundly unpredictable because each of these landscapes is subject to its own constraints and incentives (some political, some informational, and some technoenvironmental), at the same time as each acts as a constraint and a parameter for movements in the others. Thus, even an elementary model of global political economy must take into account the deeply disjunctive relationships among human movement, technological flow, and financial transfers.

Further refracting these disjunctures (which hardly form a simple, mechanical global infrastructure in any case) are what I call *mediascapes* and *ideoscapes*, which are closely related landscapes of images. *Mediascapes* refer both to the distribution of the electronic capabilities to produce and disseminate information (newspapers, magazines, television stations, and film-production studios), which are now available to a growing number of private and public interests throughout the world, and to the images of the world created by these media. These images involve many complicated inflections, depending on their mode (documentary or entertainment), their hardware (electronic or preelectronic), their audiences (local, national, or transnational), and the interests of those who own and control them. What is most important about these mediascapes is that they provide (especially in their television, film, and cassette forms) large and complex repertoires of images, narratives, and ethnoscapes to viewers throughout the world, in which the world of commodities and the world of news and politics are profoundly mixed. What this means is that many audiences around the world experience the media themselves as a complicated and interconnected repertoire of print, celluloid, electronic screens, and billboards. The lines between the realistic and the fictional landscapes they see are blurred, so that the farther away these audiences are from the direct experiences of metropolitan life, the more likely they are to construct imagined worlds that are chimerical, aesthetic, even fantastic objects, particularly if assessed by the criteria of some other perspective, some other imagined world. [...]

Ideoscapes are also concatenations of images, but they are often directly political and frequently have to do with the ideologies of states and the counterideologies of movements explicitly oriented to capturing state power or a piece of it. These ideoscapes are composed of elements of the Enlightenment worldview, which consists of a chain of ideas, terms, and images, including *freedom, welfare, rights, sovereignty, representation,* and the master term *democracy*. The master narrative of the Enlightenment (and its many variants in Britain, France, and the United States) was constructed with a certain internal logic and presupposed a certain relationship between reading, representation, and the public sphere. But the diaspora of these terms and images across the world, especially since the nineteenth century, has loosened the internal coherence that held them together in a Euro-American master narrative and provided instead a loosely structured synopticon of politics, in which different nation-states, as part of their evolution, have organized their political cultures around different keywords. [...]

This globally variable synaesthesia has hardly even been noted, but it demands urgent analysis. Thus *democracy* has clearly become a master term, with powerful echoes from Haiti and Poland to the former Soviet Union and China, but it sits at the center of a variety of ideoscapes, composed of distinctive pragmatic configurations of rough translations of other central terms from the vocabulary of the Enlightenment. This creates ever new terminological kaleidoscopes, as states (and the groups that seek to capture them) seek to pacify populations whose own ethnoscapes are in motion and whose mediascapes may create severe problems for the ideoscapes with which they are presented. The fluidity of ideoscapes is complicated in particular by the growing diasporas (both voluntary and involuntary) of intellectuals who continuously inject new meaning-streams into the discourse of democracy in different parts of the world.

This extended terminological discussion of the five terms I have coined sets the basis for a tentative formulation about the conditions under which current global flows occur: they occur in and through the growing disjunctures among ethnoscapes, technoscapes, financescapes, mediascapes, and ideoscapes. This formulation, the core of my model of global cultural flow, needs some explanation. First, people, machinery, money, images, and ideas now follow increasingly nonisomorphic paths; of course, at all periods in human history there have been some disjunctures in the flows of these things, but the sheer speed, scale, and volume of each of these flows are now so great that the disjunctures have become central to the politics of global culture. The Japanese are notoriously hospitable to ideas and are stereotyped as inclined to export (all) and import (some) goods, but they are also notoriously closed to immigration, like the Swiss, the Swedes, and the Saudis. Yet the Swiss and the Saudis accept populations of guest workers, thus creating labor diasporas of Turks, Italians, and other circum-Mediterranean groups. Some such guest-worker groups maintain continuous contact with their home nations, like the Turks, but others, like

Explaining Globalization

high-level South Asian migrants, tend to desire lives in their new homes, raising anew the problem of reproduction in a deterritorialized context.

Deterritorialization, in general, is one of the central forces of the modern world because it brings laboring populations into the lower-class sectors and spaces of relatively wealthy societies, while sometimes creating exaggerated and intensified senses of criticism or attachment to politics in the home state. Deterritorialization, whether of Hindus, Sikhs, Palestinians, or Ukrainians, is now at the core of a variety of global fundamentalisms, including Islamic and Hindu fundamentalism. In the Hindu case, for example, it is clear that the overseas movement of Indians has been exploited by a variety of interests both within and outside India to create a complicated network of finances and religious identifications, by which the problem of cultural reproduction for Hindus abroad has become tied to the politics of Hindu fundamentalism at home.

At the same time, deterritorialization creates new markets for film companies, art impresarios, and travel agencies, which thrive on the need of the deterritorialized population for contact with its homeland. Naturally, these invented homelands, which constitute the mediascapes of deterritorialized groups, can often become sufficiently fantastic and one-sided that they provide the material for new ideoscapes in which ethnic conflicts can begin to erupt. The creation of Khalistan, an invented homeland of the deterritorialized Sikh population of England, Canada, and the United States, is one example of the bloody potential in such mediascapes as they interact with the internal colonialisms of the nation-state. The West Bank, Namibia, and Eritrea are other theaters for the enactment of the bloody negotiation between existing nation-states and various deterritorialized groupings.

It is in the fertile ground of deterritorialization, in which money, commodities, and persons are involved in ceaselessly chasing each other around the world, that the mediascapes and ideoscapes of the modern world find their fractured and fragmented counterpart. For the ideas and images produced by mass media often are only partial guides to the goods and experiences that deterritorialized populations transfer to one another. In Mira Nair's brilliant film *India Cabaret,* we see the multiple loops of this fractured deterritorialization as young women, barely competent in Bombay's metropolitan glitz, come to seek their fortunes as cabaret dancers and prostitutes in Bombay, entertaining men in clubs with dance formats derived wholly from the prurient dance sequences of Hindi films. These scenes in turn cater to ideas about Western and foreign women and their looseness, while they provide tawdry career alibis for these women. Some of these women come from Kerala, where cabaret clubs and the pornographic film industry have blossomed, partly in response to the purses and tastes of Keralites returned from the Middle East, where their diasporic lives away from women distort their very sense of what the relations between men and women might be. These tragedies of displacement could certainly be replayed in a more detailed analysis of the relations between the Japanese and German sex tours to Thailand and the tragedies of the sex trade in Bangkok, and in other similar loops that tie together fantasies about the Other, the conveniences and seductions of travel, the economics of global trade, and the brutal mobility fantasies that dominate gender politics in many parts of Asia and the world at large. [...]

One important new feature of global cultural politics, tied to the disjunctive relationships among the various landscapes discussed earlier, is that state and nation are at each other's throats, and the hyphen that links them is now less an icon of conjuncture than an index of disjuncture. This disjunctive relationship between nation and state has two levels: at the level of any given nation-state, it means that there is a battle of the imagination, with state and nation seeking to cannibalize one another. Here is the seedbed of brutal separatisms – majoritarianisms that seem to have appeared from nowhere and microidentities that have become political projects within the nation-state. At another level, this disjunctive relationship is deeply entangled with various global disjunctures: ideas of nationhood appear to be steadily increasing in scale and regularly crossing existing state boundaries, sometimes, as with the Kurds, because previous identities stretched across vast national spaces or, as with the Tamils in Sri Lanka, the dormant threads of a transnational diaspora have been activated to ignite the micropolitics of a nation-state. [...]

States find themselves pressed to stay open by the forces of media, technology, and travel that have fueled consumerism throughout the world and have increased the craving, even in the non-Western world, for new commodities and spectacles. On the other hand, these very cravings can become caught up in new ethnoscapes, mediascapes, and, eventually, ideoscapes, such as democracy in China, that the state cannot tolerate as threats to its own control over ideas of nationhood and peoplehood. States throughout the world are under siege, especially where contests over the ideoscapes of democracy are fierce and fundamental, and where there are radical disjunctures between ideoscapes and technoscapes (as in the case of very small countries that lack contemporary technologies of production and information); or between ideoscapes and financescapes (as in countries such as Mexico or Brazil, where international lending influences national politics to a very large degree); or between ideoscapes and ethnoscapes (as in Beirut, where diasporic, local, and translocal filiations are suicidally at battle); or between ideoscapes and mediascapes (as in many countries in the Middle East and Asia) where the lifestyles represented on both national and international TV and cinema completely overwhelm and undermine the rhetoric of national politics. In the Indian case, the myth of the law-breaking hero has emerged to mediate this naked struggle between the pieties and realities of Indian politics, which has grown increasingly brutalized and corrupt.

The transnational movement of the martial arts, particularly through Asia, as mediated by the Hollywood and Hong Kong film industries is a rich illustration of the ways in which long-standing martial arts traditions, reformulated to meet the fantasies of contemporary (sometimes lumpen) youth populations, create new cultures of masculinity and violence, which are in turn the fuel for increased violence in national and international politics. Such violence is in turn the spur to an increasingly rapid and amoral arms trade that penetrates the entire world. The worldwide spread of the AK-47 and the Uzi, in films, in corporate and state security, in terror, and in police and military activity, is a reminder that apparently simple technical uniformities often conceal an increasingly complex set of loops, linking images of violence to aspirations for community in some imagined world.

Returning then to the ethnoscapes with which I began, the central paradox of ethnic politics in today's world is that primordia (whether of language or skin color or neighborhood or kinship) have become globalized. That is, sentiments, whose greatest force is in their ability to ignite intimacy into a political state and turn locality into a staging ground for identity, have become spread over vast and irregular spaces as groups move yet stay linked to one another through sophisticated media capabilities. This is not to deny that such primordia are often the product of invented traditions or retrospective affiliations, but to emphasize that because of the disjunctive and unstable interplay of commerce, media, national policies, and consumer fantasies, ethnicity, once a genie contained in the bottle of some sort of locality (however large), has now become a global force, forever slipping in and through the cracks between states and borders.

But the relationship between the cultural and economic levels of this new set of global disjunctures is not a simple one-way street in which the terms of global cultural politics are set wholly by, or confined wholly within, the vicissitudes of international flows of technology, labor, and finance, demanding only a modest modification of existing neo-Marxist models of uneven development and state formation. There is a deeper change, itself driven by the disjunctures among all the landscapes I have discussed and constituted by their continuously fluid and uncertain interplay, that concerns the relationship between production and consumption in today's global economy. Here, I begin with Marx's famous (and often mined) view of the fetishism of the commodity and suggest that this fetishism has been replaced in the world at large (now seeing the world as one large, interactive system, composed of many complex subsystems) by two mutually supportive descendants, the first of which I call *production fetishism* and the second, the *fetishism of the consumer*.

By *production fetishism* I mean an illusion created by contemporary transnational production loci that masks translocal capital, transnational earning flows, global management, and often faraway workers (engaged in various kinds of high-tech putting-out operations) in the idiom and spectacle of local (sometimes even worker) control, national productivity, and territorial sovereignty. To the extent that various kinds of free-trade zones have become the models for production at large, especially of hightech commodities, production has itself become a fetish, obscuring not social relations as such but the relations of production, which are increasingly transnational. The locality (both in the sense of the local factory or site of production and in the extended sense of the nation-state) becomes a fetish that disguises the globally dispersed forces that actually drive the production process. This generates alienation (in Marx's sense) twice intensified, for its social sense is now compounded by a complicated spatial dynamic that is increasingly global.

As for the *fetishism of the consumer*, I mean to indicate here that the consumer has been transformed through commodity flows (and the mediascapes, especially of advertising, that accompany them) into a sign, both in Baudrillard's sense of a simulacrum that only asymptotically approaches the form of a real social agent, and in the sense of a mask for the real seat of agency, which is not the consumer but the producer and the many forces that constitute production. Global advertising is the key technology for the worldwide dissemination of a plethora of creative and culturally well-chosen ideas of consumer agency. These images of agency are increasingly distortions of a world of merchandising so subtle that the consumer is consistently helped to believe that he or she is an actor, where in fact he or she is at best a chooser.

The globalization of culture is not the same as its homogenization, but globalization involves the use of a variety of instruments of homogenization (armaments, advertising techniques, language hegemonies, and clothing styles) that are absorbed into local political and cultural economies, only to be repatriated as heterogeneous dialogues of national sovereignty, free enterprise, and fundamentalism in which the state plays an increasingly delicate role: too much openness to global flows, and the nation-state is threatened by revolt, as in the China syndrome; too little, and the state exits the international stage, as Burma, Albania, and North Korea in various ways have done. In general, the state has become the arbitrageur of this *repatriation of difference* (in the form of goods, signs, slogans, and styles). But this repatriation or export of the designs and commodities of difference continuously exacerbates the internal politics of majoritarianism and homogenization, which is most frequently played out in debates over heritage.

Thus the central feature of global culture today is the politics of the mutual effort of sameness and difference to cannibalize one another and thereby proclaim their successful hijacking of the twin Enlightenment ideas of the triumphantly universal and the resiliently particular. This mutual cannibalization shows its ugly face in riots, refugee flows, state-sponsored torture, and ethnocide (with or without state support). Its brighter side is in the expansion of many individual horizons of hope and fantasy, in the global spread of oral rehydration therapy and other low-tech instruments of well-being, in the susceptibility even of South Africa to the force of global opinion, in the inability of the Polish state to repress its own working classes, and in the growth of a wide range of progressive, transnational alliances. Examples of both sorts could be multiplied. The critical point is that both sides of the coin of global cultural process today are products of the infinitely varied mutual contest of sameness and difference on a stage characterized by radical disjunctures between different sorts of global flows and the uncertain landscapes created in and through these disjunctures. […]

Part II Questions

1. Why can capitalism exist only in a world-economy, according to Wallerstein? What role do strong states play in the world-system? Why does the modern world-system propagate universalist and anti-universalist principles? Does Wallerstein think the world-system of today still resembles that of the sixteenth century?

2. Although Sklair notes that the current global system is "not synonymous with the global capitalist system," he regards specific features of world capitalism as driving forces of globalization. What are these features, and what do they add to Wallerstein's analysis of world capitalism?

3. What are the principal features of neoliberalism, according to Harvey? What negative consequences of neoliberalism does he identify? How does his analysis complement the views of Wallerstein and Sklair? Is it in conflict with their views in any way?

4. What do Meyer and his colleagues mean when they say that nation-states are not "collective actors"? What surprising similarities among nation-states do they note, and how do they account for them? With their view of culture as the driving force in globalization, how does their approach differ from that of world-system theory?

5. How does Robertson define globalization, and how does his "model of order" capture its key features? What is the "take-off period of modern globalization"? How does globalization trigger debate about world order and a "search for fundamentals"?

6. What views of cultural globalization does Appadurai challenge when he describes the process as an "infinitely varied contest of sameness and difference" in a complex "disjunctive order"? How can (or must) any group draw on the flows in different "scapes" to construct its identity?

Part III

Experiencing Globalization

Introduction

In *Golden Arches East*, James L. Watson reports that, as older residents of Hong Kong revel in the quality of Cantonese cuisine, their offspring avidly consume Big Macs, pizza, and Coca-Cola. Not long ago, travelers on British Rail's first-class Pullman service could enjoy dishes from India, the Middle East, China, Greece, and so on, as Allison James reports in a volume on *Cross-Cultural Consumption*. From personal experience, we can attest that, in urban areas of the American South, Thai cuisine successfully competes with traditional fare and supermarkets abound with produce from most continents. To be sure, these examples refer to privileged areas of the world. They are not unprecedented, as the earlier European adoption of New World potatoes and sugar demonstrates. Yet they illustrate one way in which globalization affects people concretely, namely, through changes in diet and taste. Such changes express new linkages, new transnational structures, and a new global culture. More and more people can literally get a taste of what it means to be part of world society.

No one experiences globalization in all its complexity, but globalization is significant insofar as it reshapes the daily lives of billions of people. Increasingly, the larger world is present locally. This obviously applies to a Ban Ki-moon (the UN secretary-general) or a Bill Gates (founding chairman of Microsoft), conscious contributors to globalization, but it is also true for the Thai prostitutes, minions in a global industry, who are now suffering from AIDS. American textile workers sense the global in the local through the impact of intense foreign competition and outsourcing to overseas companies. Soccer fans regard as routine the fact that a large portion of the world's population directs its attention to the World Cup every four years. Business people traveling internationally witness globalization daily in the media offerings in their hotel rooms. Migrants who call home, send money back, or make return visits bring a bit of that wider world to the villages they left.

The Globalization Reader, Fifth Edition. Edited by Frank J. Lechner and John Boli.
Editorial material and organization © 2015 John Wiley & Sons, Ltd.
Published 2015 by John Wiley & Sons, Ltd.

Introduction

107

These people, and many more, experience globalization. Experiencing globalization, as the examples indicate, does not mean that some abstract, impersonal force overwhelms individuals. People participate and respond in different ways. They can shape, resist, absorb, or try to avoid globalization. They can seek opportunity in it, feel the harm of it, or lament the power of it. For some, globalization is a central reality; for others, it is still on the margins of their lives. In short, there is no one experience of globalization. That, in itself, is an important aspect of the process. The formation of a new world society does not involve all people in the same way, and it does not create the same texture in everyone's everyday life. But there are some commonalities in the global experience of globalization. To one degree or another, globalization is real to almost everyone. It transforms the prevailing sense of time and space, now globally standardized. It envelops everyone in new institutions. It poses a challenge, in the sense that even marginally affected groups must take a stance toward the world. Globalization raises identity problems for societies and individuals alike.

The selections in this part illuminate the experience of globalization from different vantage points. We begin with a historical perspective in Dutch-American sociologist Frank J. Lechner's discussion of early and later "waves of globalization." Tracing the development of the colonial sugar industry in Jamaica beginning in the 1670s, on the one hand, and the development of capital-intensive agriculture in North Dakota in the 1870s, on the other, Lechner shows how the early phase brought far-flung regions of the world into the European economy while the later phase entailed deeper penetration of globalizing forces that both expanded national markets and integrated local farmers into the world economy.

The contemporary experience of globalization involves creative adaptation to global processes, new mixtures of cultural frameworks, and the growth of a variable global consciousness. Theodore C. Bestor, an American anthropologist, describes the intricate links among many players in the global production of sushi, as fishers in New England supply freshly caught tuna to Japanese buyers, who ship it to a Japanese market from which it is distributed further to chefs around the world. Consumers develop a shared taste for raw fish prepared a certain way, tuna farming becomes a globally organized business, and everyone involved is aware of taking part in a globalized version of a slice of Japanese culture. Focusing on a different kind of global food, James L. Watson, another American anthropologist, describes McDonald's customers in Hong Kong, including children, as critical consumers to whose expectations about food and service the multinational corporation must adapt. Far from imposing a new dietary standard, McDonald's blended into an already heterogeneous urban landscape. Watson concludes that in places like Hong Kong, the transnational is the local.

Even more "transnational" is the experience of immigrants like the Dominicans studied closely by Peggy Levitt, an American sociologist. Moving from the town of Miraflores in the Dominican Republic to cities like Boston, they keep close ties with their community of origin. While growing new roots, they also do much to improve life in Miraflores, for example through a development committee that sponsors civic projects. By virtue of their many ties across the sea, places like Miraflores are not what they used to be either: Levitt calls them "transnational villages."

One almost ubiquitous pastime in these transnational villages is soccer (football), the most globalized game of all and a prominent way in which billions feel themselves connected to the wider world. As British journalist David Goldblatt recounts, soccer had the benefit of an imperial boost at a time when "the British were everywhere." But as the game was taken up first by elites, then by other groups in many different places, it also was decentered: Britain lost its place as the center of the soccer universe. That is precisely why soccer, more than anything else in world culture, provides opportunities for what Goldblatt calls the "collective dramatization of identities and social relationships."

Our next two selections present glimpses of the extremes of wealth and poverty characterizing world society. American journalist and essayist Mike Davis takes us on a tour of Dubai, the largest city in the oil-rich United Arab Emirates. Dubai has become a global business and shopping mecca packed with spectacular high-rise buildings and ultra-luxurious hotels and resorts. However, the lavish lifestyle it encourages is well out of the reach of the host of migrant workers from Asia whose labor is essential to Dubai's futuristic development. Even in a small city-state like Dubai, globalization is experienced in very different ways by residents at different ends of the social scale.

In sharp contrast to Dubai, Haiti is a locus of grinding poverty and illness, an enduring "skein of tragedies," as Paul Farmer, an American anthropologist and physician, puts it. Farmer's focus is the high prevalence of AIDS and tuberculosis in a country with woefully inadequate health care. He argues that AIDS came to Haiti mainly as a result of American sex tourists visiting the island, and he characterizes the Haitian situation as an instance of "structural violence." This term is used to capture the death, illness, and stigmatization that result from structural inequalities and marginalizing ideologies that subjugated peoples face in their everyday lives.

In the last selection, American journalist Ethan Watters explores the spread of Western (largely American) conceptions of mental health and illness to a society with a quite different understanding of the human psyche. Before the 1990s, the category of "depression" had no place in Japanese culture. But, as Watters sketches in intriguing detail, vigorous and imaginative "mega-marketing" methods by global pharmaceutical countries achieved remarkable success in redefining common Japanese states of mind as depression – and in inducing a sizeable proportion of the population to turn to Zoloft, Prozac, and Proxil for help with their newly redefined woes.

12

Waves in the History of Globalization

Frank J. Lechner

The First Wave of Globalization: Jamaica

In 1670, one Francis Price, a former British officer, filed a patent on a piece of land in central Jamaica he named Worthy Park, which was to become a large sugar plantation that survived into the twentieth century. Fifteen years before, British troops had expelled the Spanish from the island; with the government's encouragement, would-be planters like Price now moved into the countryside to make the victory pay off. That proved difficult. As in other parts of the New World, the island's native inhabitants had been decimated by European germs, leaving no indigenous labor force. In spite of modest Spanish efforts to grow sugar in the West Indies, Jamaica had no viable economy, which meant that the British had to start nearly from scratch. The island lacked the infrastructure that would make plantations immediately profitable. To purchase land, prepare it for production, and buy provisions, entrepreneurs needed capital, which they had to borrow on stiff terms from financiers back home. From the outset, they were in debt to bankers and merchants, for whom risky loans at high interest were good business. While the home country provided capital, it offered few willing or even indentured workers. Soon after, slaves solved the labor shortage: in 1670 Jamaica already had nearly 8,000 out of a total population of about 13,700, within half a century they would outnumber whites ten to one. In the 1700s some 600,000 entered Jamaica altogether, with several hundred laboring at Worthy Park itself in any one year. As sugar production there shifted into high gear after 1700, under the direction of Francis Price's son Charles, Worthy Park became a major node in a transatlantic network.

Original publication details: Frank J. Lechner, *Globalization: The Making of World Society*. Oxford: Wiley-Blackwell, 2009. pp. 18–26. Reproduced with permission from John Wiley & Sons. Note: This text has been edited and all notes and references to third party sources removed. Please refer to the original source text for clarification on what has been omitted.

Worthy Park kept some cattle for fertilizer, had some small vegetable plots, and set aside land for a house, offices, and slave quarters, but most of it was devoted to one thing only: growing sugar cane. In an annual cycle, slaves supervised by an overseer would tend to the fields and cut the cane, to be processed in the on-site factory run by more skilled slaves who squeezed the juice from the cane and then boiled it to crystallize the sugar, using the by-product for rum. All metal equipment came from Britain. Because Worthy Park did not grow its own food, that had to be imported as well: some supplies came from the American mainland colonies, salted herring for the slaves from the Dutch. Since few slave infants survived to working age, planters like the Prices constantly had to buy new arrivals from Africa. They rarely had ready cash to pay for all this and borrowed money instead, pledging part of their land or crops as collateral. Capital flowed through their hands to food suppliers and slave traders and African slave sellers – and often right back to other home-country financiers. Sugar made the network work: as the British public developed its sweet tooth, sugar imports exceeded all other colonial crops in volume and value, reaching 100,000 "hogsheads" by 1730, most of which the British consumed themselves. Worthy Park produced several hundred of these hogsheads, earning up to about £10,000 a year.

Many parties, on all sides of the Atlantic, had a piece of the sugar action. They were actors in a globalizing market, at the crest of the first wave of globalization. In this wave, a taste for sweetened food spread in Europe, which consumed more than 240,000 tons a year by 1800. In England alone, consumption increased by more than 400 percent, from four to eighteen pounds per person, in the eighteenth century. Everyone involved in the Britain–Africa–New World triangle depended on the others, seeking riches through commerce, producing commodities for distant markets, and financially tied to a few sources of capital. Rules of production and finance were gradually worked out, turning the slave-sugar trade into a new economic system. At the heart of it all, the sugar plantation was a "pioneer institution of capitalist development". While the Atlantic triangle was not strictly global, many participants expanded their horizons, literally and figuratively. Jamaica itself was in a sense a product of this early globalization, a "sugar island" in the "West Indies," defined by Europeans in terms of its function for the emerging system but also a "creole" community resulting from cultural exchange in which slaves had an important role.

The wave had started not with a desire for sugar but with a search for spices (though sugar itself was long considered a "spice"). Seeking access to the Asian spice trade by sailing west to evade Mongol blockage, circumvent Islamic lands, and outrace the Portuguese, Christopher Columbus had landed on a nearby island, thinking he had reached India. Others followed, lured not by spices but by the prospect of finding silver and gold. Besides precious metals they brought new foods home: potatoes and tomatoes entered the European diet. In the early part of the wave, far-flung regions for the first time exchanged foods globally. When the Portuguese reached China, for example, they introduced maize, sweet potatoes, and peanuts, crops that later would help to sustain China's population boom. They brought back sugar cane from Asia for planting on São Tomé and other islands. On his second voyage, Columbus himself took sugar cane from the Canary Islands to the New World, where in the 1500s it proved a suitable crop first on Santo Domingo, then in Brazil. From modest beginnings, it grew into a major crop. On the other side of the globe, meanwhile, Europeans gained a foothold in Asia, using their superior power to enforce positive terms of trade in spices, tea, and other goods. The fruits of global ventures in both hemispheres mixed in British cups in the form of sweetened tea, its combination of exotic ingredients eventually defined as typically British. European trade thus linked the hemispheres in an entirely new way. Aware of the connections, at least the elite began to see the world whole, a global consciousness evident in geographical treatises and in maps and globes made for European seafarers and power brokers that for the first time included most regions of the world.

Some Patterns in the First Wave

Commerce and Christian fervor, the lust for money and the urge to save souls, channeled the first wave. But states were deeply involved from the beginning, starting with Iberian monarchs Ferdinand and Isabella sponsoring Columbus's journey. Sugar, too, reflected state power. After all, British force claimed Caribbean islands for British planters. Sugar production there resulted from a power struggle with Spain. Having seized control of Jamaica, the British government stimulated sugar production via land grants. It controlled the trade by requiring planters to sell in the home market while at the same time protecting them against foreign competition – a hallmark of the "mercantile" system. As an interest group, the plantocracy gained influence in Parliament, which passed favorable laws. In Jamaica itself, they dominated the Assembly, using public power to serve their interests. British naval forces patrolled shipping lanes and British power long backed the slave trade as well. By charging duties, the Crown more than made up for its expenses. If the colonial trade worked to the disadvantage of the British public, since freer trade might have lowered prices and stimulated innovation, both special interest groups and the government itself profited handsomely. In part due to sugar's appeal, the Caribbean became one focus in the struggle for global dominance between Britain and France. Immediately after Britain prevailed in 1763, depressing French production, Jamaican sugar experienced its golden age. Throughout the first wave, the process of making and selling sugar thus unfolded "under the wing of the state". Not just the sugar trade flourished. With "the full weight of the state behind them," English traders did well in many parts of the world, as Britain turned from plain old conquest to building a commercial empire.

In the first wave of globalization, more people became more globally connected in more ways than ever before. They could taste the links in the tea drunk in Britain, the tobacco smoked in France, the peanuts in Chinese dishes, or the herring given to Jamaican slaves. Global connections thus changed the daily lives of millions. The links grew along with new crops in new places – potatoes in the Netherlands, maize in China, sugar in the Caribbean. Globalization thus also changed the world in a very physical sense, especially through New World crops in China and India. The new links benefited some and harmed many others. British planters and traders were among the winners, Native Americans and African slaves among the losers. Early globalization thus began to create a global hierarchy. The links were mostly the work of Europeans, with Britain gaining a leading role. British power served as a driving force in and was much enhanced by globalization. Though there were still few "international rules of engagement", Britain began to make some. The case of Jamaica illustrates the legacy of the first wave, when in more parts of the globe economic activity focused on producing commodities for the world market, whites came to view themselves as superior to other races, and English began to serve as the lingua franca.

Caught up in several long-distance flows of people, money, and goods, Worthy Park was part and parcel of this globalization. But we cannot make too much of the example. Though over time more Europeans used more sugar, it remained a luxury product through the 1600s and even by 1800 was still a small part of their overall diet. Most people got most of their food from places nearby, and foreign trade overall comprised only a few percent of the British economy. For all the brutal drama of the slave trade, only a small minority of Africans moved across the ocean; relatively few white Europeans made similar treks as migrants or sailors. Information and goods moved slowly – it took a Jamaican shipment of sugar several weeks to reach London, and by modern standards the speed did not increase greatly for centuries – effectively separating regions and societies in spite of the growing links. Britain came to dominate the "Euro-American world system" that included Jamaica but in the 1700s it had yet to make its mark on the very different "China-centered East Asian world system".

The continents were connected, to be sure, partly because Europeans used New World resources to gain advantage in Asia, which has tempted some to argue that the start of direct shipments of silver from South America to the Philippines makes 1571 the year globalization was "born". But the link was still fairly loose, and since European powers had further carved up the world into imperial zones, the world market was weakly integrated at best. So was world culture: "Western" religion and practices took hold in the New World, but the encounters of civilizations in Asia left regional cultures there mostly intact. Westerners learned much about others but many others did not reciprocate this interest: "[o]utside Europe, interest in foreign lands remained relatively small". In spite of the new maps and globes available to a Western reading public, this was still "a world that did not understand itself" – the maps and globes themselves contained many blank spots. Its web of connection was still small, thin, and fragile.

None of this detracts from the significance of the first wave. Its legacy set the stage for the next one, in which industrializing Western countries dramatically diverged from others. Early globalization concentrated greater power and resources in the hands of Europeans, helping to create the conditions for further advances. "[T]he remarkable innovations of the Industrial Revolution would not have had the deep and sustained consequences that they did if British industry had not operated within the [previously developed] global framework of sources of raw materials and markets for finished products". To embellish the point slightly, "[g]lobalization made the Industrial Revolution," not least by giving British textile makers a powerful incentive to compete with more efficient Indian exporters. The prime, though unintended, British creation of the first wave, the newly independent United States, would also come to play a global role.

The Second Wave of Globalization: North Dakota

In 1875, the Amenia and Sharon Land Company, a group of American investors, bought 28,000 acres from the Northern Pacific Railroad in Cass County, North Dakota. In return for the right to sell large tracts along new lines – 25,600 acres for each mile of railroad – the company had built track from Minnesota into the Dakota Territory in the early 1870s, crossing the Red River of the North in 1872 and reaching Bismarck by June 1873. Where the railroad went, settlers quickly followed: in 1870, the Dakota side of the river valley counted only 2,405 residents, by 1890 the population of the new state of North Dakota had grown to over 190,000. They came not only from more crowded states to the east but also from Britain, Germany, and Scandinavia, where the railroad company advertised its good land. As an agent for the railroad company put it, the settlers "rapidly converted the raw prairie into a great field of waving grain". Wheat proved a hardy and bountiful crop in the relatively arid and flat North Central region. By the end of the century, the area produced over 440 million bushels or about two-thirds of America's wheat crop. In North Dakota alone, over 4 million acres were devoted to wheat, increasing to over 8 million by 1910. When the railroad company ran into financial difficulty, investors like those who made up the Amenia and Sharon exchanged their bonds for portions of its land grants, joining the Great Dakota Boom and eventually accumulating some 58,000 acres. The boom was really a global one, just one instance of how new means of transportation and communication helped new people settle distant places in ways that would link them far more tightly to the world at large.

Rather than divide its holdings into traditional family farms – a tenant system did develop in the 1890s – the Amenia and Sharon created a new kind of business, the large-scale, professionally managed, for-profit "bonanza" farm. Most of the absentee owners in Connecticut knew and cared little about farming but one of the company directors, E. W. Chaffee, went west to make a go of farming the land it had acquired. Though instructed simply to prepare the property for profitable sale, Chaffee was seized by a vision of the land's potential. He hired a professional sod buster to get started. He built lodging for the workers he hired as needed, season by season. To make optimal use of the workers and increase the return on capital, he bought new machinery – ploughs, binders, and threshers, some steam-powered. Given the scale of the operation, with dozens of horses and more than a hundred men in the fields during busy periods, he had to institute clear procedures. Strict accounting by a full-time bookkeeper was essential to keep track of costs and revenues; any activity that was not profitable would have to be changed. Chaffee branched out into elevators, creating an agricultural company that encompassed many phases of food production. In the 1890s, his son added an experimental plot designed to test new varieties of grain to be supplied to tenants. In everything they did, the Chaffees aimed for optimal efficiency, applying the latest techniques. They thus built one of the first "factory farms", demonstrating the benefits of agriculture run as a rational business.

The bonanza farms did not last in their original form, partly due to their sheer scale, but they show how the second wave of globalization rolled across the American prairies in the late nineteenth century. Even before the arrival of railroads, still hampered by distance, American farmers had already ventured into the "Great West," but trains that "broke much more radically with geography" helped them conquer that huge space. They could bring their produce to market more cheaply, save time by avoiding muddy roads, and obtain supplies more reliably. Going from New York City to the Fargo area might have taken about three weeks as late as 1857, two decades later it would take less than a week. Information also moved more quickly: telegraph and later telephone lines were built along with the railroad tracks, enabling people like the Chaffees to communicate across their far-flung holdings, keep in touch with company directors, and stay abreast of wheat prices. News from New York, or from London or Argentina for that matter, could reach Fargo in mere minutes.

The Amenia and Sharon operation was unusually large, but even smaller ones required much capital. Individual settlers from Europe might have enough to start on their own but, like their predecessors in Jamaica, many needed credit. Laying track cost even more, requiring huge infusions of capital from domestic and foreign lenders. The Dakota Boom was also a Capitalist Boom, connecting lenders, companies, farmers, and all sorts of middlemen across America and across the Atlantic. Most Dakota grain went to Chicago, the key node in the network where from the 1850s onward revolutionary new ways to store, move, and sell grain were invented. Though family-run farms by no means disappeared, the Amenia and Sharon pointed to a new form of enterprise, relying on wage labor rather than household or slave labor. On an even larger scale than the bonanza farms, the railroads ran their business in a new way, using very precise accounting to set rates and manage costs, if only to hold bankruptcy at bay. This wave of globalization involved millions of people moving millions of miles. Many were native-born, but in America immigrants helped to settle the prairies, build the railroads, and enlarge the cities. They followed the tracks of trains and capital.

Just as Jamaica was shaped by its special role in the first wave of globalization, the Dakotas, and the whole North-Central US, developed thanks to their role in the second wave. Domestic investors, settlers, and consumers provided the key impetus, to be sure, but foreign money, immigrants, and markets pushed the second wave as well. North Dakota became bread basket to the world. Still on the very periphery of world affairs in 1850, it was fully involved by 1900. The same goes for large swaths of Canada, Argentina, and Australia: places linked by new technology, occupied by people from afar, and brought into cultivation to become a source of food and profit; by 1913 they produced more wheat than all of Europe and held more people than all of France. In a truly global market, each country could specialize. In fact, they had to specialize: whatever the exact form of their operations, farms turned into businesses competing in the global market. By practicing monoculture, as on the Dakota farms, they also altered the land. The waving grain that marked this wave of globalization physically changed the world.

Some Patterns in the Second Wave

The story of America's western expansion involves more than hardy pioneers, greedy speculators, and innovative businessmen, all looking for the main chance in a growing market opened up by new technology. As British power did in Jamaica, the American state played a key role behind the scenes, at times much more overtly. By granting land to railroads and selling public land cheaply to settlers, most notably with the Homestead Act of 1862, the federal government encouraged the expansion. In various ways, the state used its military power of persuasion to clear lands that were inconveniently occupied by Native Americans, losers in this round of globalizing ventures as slaves had been previously. Property rights guaranteed by the state, enforceable in court, provided the incentive for development, whether by farmers or railroads. Expansion happened in part because Congress wanted it to happen. Conquering people, space, and nature itself was a matter of deliberate effort. Bringing new people, new practices, and new principles, backed by new power, to new lands created an empire of sorts. Though not exactly comparable, this had much in common with the scramble for empire by the European powers in Africa and Asia. The "developmental states" of this phase of globalization, America included, were committed both to industrialization and to territorial control in a global quest for wealth and power. At a critical time in globalization, when new kinds of connections quickly sprouted, America had advantages of scale and structure that helped it sow the seeds of future dominance.

The entry of the Amenia and Sharon Company into Dakota Territory in 1875 was but one small step in the very large process of unifying the world that had already unfolded by that time, the "drawing together of all parts of the globe into a single world". In the preceding 35 years, British trade with the other continents had increased sixfold, and in the 1870s the leading nations annually exchanged some 88 million tons of seaborne goods, by comparison with 20 million in 1840. Thanks to the work of explorers, most blank spots on the maps of 1848 had been filled in, so that in 1875 educated people knew their world much better. In 1848 a journey around the world would have taken 11 months – the American prairies were one obstacle – but by 1872, with the benefit of steamships and railroads nearly everywhere, Jules Verne's Phileas Fogg might indeed have done it in 80 days.

The very food people ate, perhaps the most tangible object of diffusion, illustrates most plainly the drawing together. At least in the industrializing countries, globalization meant more food for more people and, in spite of tariffs, at lower prices. A global food system emerged, tying all participants into a network of interdependence. Specialized farms and regions, using the latest machines and fertilizers, fed their products into an elaborate system for processing and distribution, creating a "social division of labor [that] has taken on a truly global dimension". Its new "market geography" depended less on local soils and climate, more on "prices and information flows of the economy as a whole". Global economic integration "reinforced itself" – as more countries developed more ties, more wanted to join in more ways. Judged by the convergence of prices for global staples such as wheat, this integration or "big bang" of globalization had unfolded only since the 1820s. The network operated according to some common rules, or at least Britain tried to impose some, with support from others – for example, that trade ought to be free and currencies backed by gold. Its infrastructure, too, needed common rules, developed by organizations like the International Telegraph Union (1865). To coordinate their services, railroads in the US (1883) and elsewhere set their clocks to the same time in the same zones, standards that would soon be extended to the world as a whole. By the late nineteenth century, then, the web of connectivity had become stronger, wider, and more intricate. Exposed to news from abroad, aware of those who left for distant parts, enjoying new foods from new places, more people knew they were connected in a single global space where the rhythm of daily life depended on globally set times.

[...]

13

How Sushi Went Global

Theodore C. Bestor

A 40-minute drive from Bath, Maine, down a winding two-lane highway, the last mile
on a dirt road, a ramshackle wooden fish pier stands beside an empty parking lot. At
6:00 p.m. nothing much is happening. Three bluefin tuna sit in a huge tub of ice on
the loading dock.

Between 6:45 and 7:00, the parking lot fills up with cars and trucks with license
plates from New Jersey, New York, Massachusetts, New Hampshire, and Maine.
Twenty tuna buyers clamber out, half of them Japanese. The three bluefin, ranging
from 270 to 610 pounds, are winched out of the tub, and buyers crowd around them,
extracting tiny core samples to examine their color, fingering the flesh to assess the fat
content, sizing up the curve of the body.

After about 20 minutes of eyeing the goods, many of the buyers return to their
trucks to call Japan by cellphone and get the morning prices from Tokyo's Tsukiji
market – the fishing industry's answer to Wall Street – where the daily tuna auctions
have just concluded. The buyers look over the tuna one last time and give written bids
to the dock manager, who passes the top bid for each fish to the crew that landed it.

The auction bids are secret. Each bid is examined anxiously by a cluster of young
men, some with a father or uncle looking on to give advice, others with a young
woman and a couple of toddlers trying to see Daddy's fish. Fragments of concerned
conversation float above the parking lot: "That's all?" "Couldn't we do better if we
shipped it ourselves?" "Yeah, but my pickup needs a new transmission now!" After a
few minutes, deals are closed and the fish are quickly loaded onto the backs of trucks
in crates of crushed ice, known in the trade as "tuna coffins." As rapidly as they

Original publication details: Theodore C. Bestor, "How Sushi Went Global," in *Foreign Policy*,
November–December, 2000. pp. 54–5, 56–8, 59, 60, 61–2, 63. Reproduced with permission from
Foreign Policy.

arrived, the flotilla of buyers sails out of the parking lot – three bound for New York's John F. Kennedy Airport, where their tuna will be airfreighted to Tokyo for sale the day after next.

Bluefin tuna may seem at first an unlikely case study in globalization. But as the world rearranges itself – around silicon chips, Starbucks coffee, or sashimi-grade tuna – new channels for global flows of capital and commodities link far-flung individuals and communities in unexpected new relationships. The tuna trade is a prime example of the globalization of a regional industry, with intense international competition and thorny environmental regulations, centuries-old practices combined with high technology; realignments of labor and capital in response to international regulation; shifting markets; and the diffusion of culinary culture as tastes for sushi, and bluefin tuna, spread worldwide. [...]

Japan's emergence on the global economic scene in the 1970s as the business destination du jour, coupled with a rejection of hearty, redmeat American fare in favor of healthy cuisine like rice, fish, and vegetables, and the appeal of the high-concept aesthetics of Japanese design all prepared the world for a sushi fad. And so, from an exotic, almost unpalatable ethnic specialty, then to haute cuisine of the most rarefied sort, sushi has become not just cool, but popular. The painted window of a Cambridge, Massachusetts, coffee shop advertises "espresso, cappuccino, carrot juice, lasagna, and sushi." Mashed potatoes with wasabi (horseradish), sushi-ginger relish, and seared sashimi-grade tuna steaks show Japan's growing cultural influence on upscale nouvelle cuisine throughout North America, Europe, and Latin America. Sushi has even become the stuff of fashion, from "sushi" lip gloss, colored the deep red of raw tuna, to "wasabi" nail polish, a soft avocado green. [...]

Japan remains the world's primary market for fresh tuna for sushi and sashimi; demand in other countries is a product of Japanese influence and the creation of new markets by domestic producers looking to expand their reach. Perhaps not surprisingly, sushi's global popularity as an emblem of a sophisticated, cosmopolitan consumer class more or less coincided with a profound transformation in the international role of the Japanese fishing industry. From the 1970s onward, the expansion of 200-mile fishing limits around the world excluded foreign fleets from the prime fishing grounds of many coastal nations. And international environmental campaigns forced many countries, Japan among them, to scale back their distant water fleets. With their fishing operations curtailed and their yen for sushi still growing, Japanese had to turn to foreign suppliers.

Jumbo jets brought New England's bluefin tuna into easy reach of Tokyo, just as Japan's consumer economy – a byproduct of the now disparaged "bubble" years – went into hyperdrive. The sushi business boomed. During the 1980s, total Japanese imports of fresh bluefin tuna worldwide increased from 957 metric tons (531 from the United States) in 1984 to 5,235 metric tons (857 from the United States) in 1993. The average wholesale price peaked in 1990 at 4,900 yen (US$34) per kilogram, bones and all, which trimmed out to approximately US$33 wholesale per edible pound.

Not surprisingly, Japanese demand for prime bluefin tuna – which yields a firm red meat, lightly marbled with veins of fat, highly prized (and priced) in Japanese cuisine – created a gold-rush mentality on fishing grounds across the globe wherever bluefin tuna could be found. But in the early 1990s, as the US bluefin industry was taking off, the Japanese economy went into a stall, then a slump, then a dive. US producers suffered as their high-end export market collapsed. Fortunately for them, the North American sushi craze took up the slack. US businesses may have written off Japan, but Americans' taste for sushi stuck. An industry founded exclusively on Japanese demand survived because of Americans' newly trained palates and a booming US economy. [...]

In New England waters, most bluefin are taken one fish at a time, by rod and reel, by hand line, or by harpoon – techniques of a small-scale fisher, not of a factory fleet. On the European side of the Atlantic, the industry operates under entirely different conditions. Rather than rod and reel or harpooning, the typical gear is industrial – the purse seiner (a fishing vessel closing a large net around a school of fish) or the long line (which catches fish on baited hooks strung along lines played out for many miles behind a swift vessel). The techniques may differ from boat to boat and from country to country, but these fishers are all angling for a share of the same Tsukiji yen – and in many cases, some biologists argue, a share of the same tuna stock. Fishing communities often think of themselves as close-knit and proudly parochial; but the sudden globalization of this industry has brought fishers into contact – and often into conflict – with customers, governments, regulators, and environmentalists around the world.

Two miles off the beach in Barbate, Spain, a huge maze of nets snakes several miles out into Spanish waters near the Strait of Gibraltar. A high-speed, Japanese-made workboat heads out to the nets. On board are five Spanish hands, a Japanese supervisor, 2,500 kilograms of frozen herring and mackerel imported from Norway and Holland, and two American researchers. The boat is making one of its twice-daily trips to Spanish nets, which contain captured Mediterranean tuna being raised under Japanese supervision for harvest and export to Tsukiji.

Behind the guard boats that stand watch over the nets 24 hours a day, the headlands of Morocco are a hazy purple in the distance. Just off Barbate's white cliffs to the northwest, the light at the Cape of Trafalgar blinks on and off. For 20 minutes, the men toss herring and mackerel over the gunwales of the workboat while tuna the size (and speed) of Harley-Davidsons dash under the boat, barely visible until, with a flash of silver and blue, they wheel around to snatch a drifting morsel.

The nets, lines, and buoys are part of an *almadraba*, a huge fish trap used in Spain as well as Sicily, Tunisia, and Morocco. The *almadraba* consists of miles of nets anchored to the channel floor suspended from thousands of buoys, all laid out to cut across the migration routes of bluefin tuna leaving the strait. This *almadraba* remains in place for about six weeks in June and July to intercept tuna leaving the Mediterranean after their spawning season is over. Those tuna that lose themselves in the maze end up in a huge pen, roughly the size of a football field. By the end of the tuna run through the strait, about 200 bluefin are in the pen.

Two hundred fish may not sound like a lot, but if the fish survive the next six months, if the fish hit their target weights, if the fish hit the market at the target price, these 200 bluefin may be worth $1.6 million dollars. In November and December, after the bluefin season in New England and Canada is well over, the tuna are harvested and shipped by air to Tokyo in time for the end-of-the-year holiday spike in seafood consumption. [...]

Inside the Strait of Gibraltar, off the coast of Cartagena, another series of tuna farms operates under entirely different auspices, utilizing neither local skills nor traditional technology. The Cartagena farms rely on French purse seiners to tow captured tuna to their pens, where joint ventures between Japanese trading firms and large-scale Spanish fishing companies have set up farms using the latest in Japanese fishing technology. The waters and the workers are Spanish, but almost everything else is part of a global flow of techniques and capital: financing from major Japanese trading companies; Japanese vessels to tend the nets; aquacultural techniques developed in Australia; vitamin supplements from European pharmaceutical giants packed into frozen herring from Holland to be heaved over the gunwales for the tuna; plus computer models of feeding schedules, weight gains, and target market prices developed by Japanese technicians and fishery scientists.

These "Spanish" farms compete with operations throughout the Mediterranean that rely on similar high-tech, high-capital approaches to the fish business. In the Adriatic Sea, for example, Croatia is emerging as a formidable tuna producer. In Croatia's case, the technology and the capital were transplanted by émigré Croatians who returned to the country from Australia after Croatia achieved independence from Yugoslavia in 1991. Australia, for its part, has developed a major aquacultural industry for southern bluefin tuna, a species closely related to the Atlantic bluefin of the North Atlantic and Mediterranean and almost equally desired in Japanese markets. [...]

Globalization doesn't necessarily homogenize cultural differences nor erase the salience of cultural labels. Quite the contrary, it grows the franchise. In the global economy of consumption, the brand equity of sushi as Japanese cultural property adds to the cachet of both the country and the cuisine. A Texan Chinese-American restaurateur told me, for example, that he had converted his chain of restaurants from Chinese to Japanese cuisine because the prestige factor of the latter meant he could charge a premium; his clients couldn't distinguish between Chinese and Japanese employees (and often failed to notice that some of the chefs behind his sushi bars were Latinos).

The brand equity is sustained by complicated flows of labor and ethnic biases. Outside of Japan, having Japanese hands (or a reasonable facsimile) is sufficient warrant for sushi competence. Guidebooks for the current generation of Japanese global *wandervogel* sometimes advise young Japanese looking for a job in a distant city to work as a sushi chef; US consular offices in Japan grant more than 1,000 visas a year to sushi chefs, tuna buyers, and other workers in the global sushi business. A trade school in Tokyo, operating under the name Sushi Daigaku (Sushi University), offers short courses in sushi preparation so "students" can impress prospective employers with an imposing certificate. Even without papers, however, sushi remains firmly linked in the minds of Japanese and foreigners alike with Japanese cultural identity. Throughout the world, sushi restaurants operated by Koreans, Chinese, or Vietnamese maintain Japanese identities. In sushi bars from Boston to Valencia, a customer's simple greeting in Japanese can throw chefs into a panic (or drive them to the far end of the counter).

On the docks, too, Japanese cultural control of sushi remains unquestioned. Japanese buyers and "tuna techs" sent from Tsukiji to work seasonally on the docks of New England laboriously instruct foreign fishers on the proper techniques for catching, handling, and packing tuna for export. A bluefin tuna must approximate the appropriate *kata*, or "ideal form," of color, texture, fat content, body shape, and so forth, all prescribed by Japanese specifications. Processing requires proper attention as well. Special paper is sent from Japan for wrapping the fish before burying them in crushed ice. Despite high shipping costs and the fact that 50 percent of the gross weight of a tuna is unusable, tuna is sent to Japan whole, not sliced into salable portions. Spoilage is one reason for this, but form is another. Everyone in the trade agrees that Japanese workers are much more skilled in cutting and trimming tuna than Americans, and no one would want to risk sending botched cuts to Japan.

Not to impugn the quality of the fish sold in the United States, but on the New England docks, the first determination of tuna buyers is whether they are looking at a "domestic" fish or an "export" fish. On that judgment hangs several dollars a pound for the fisher, and the supply of sashimi-grade tuna for fishmongers, sushi bars, and seafood restaurants up and down the Eastern seaboard. Some of the best tuna from New England may make it to New York or Los Angeles, but by way of Tokyo – validated as top quality (and top price) by the decision to ship it to Japan by air for sale at Tsukiji, where it may be purchased by one of the handful of Tsukiji sushi exporters who supply premier expatriate sushi chefs in the world's leading cities. [...]

Such mystification of a distant market's motivations for desiring a local commodity is not unique. For decades, anthropologists have written of "cargo cults" and "commodity fetishism" from New Guinea to Bolivia. But the ability of fishers today to visualize Japanese culture and the place of tuna within its demanding culinary tradition is constantly shaped and reshaped by the flow of cultural images that now travel around the globe in all directions simultaneously, bumping into each other in airports, fishing ports, bistros, bodegas, and markets everywhere. In the newly rewired circuitry of global cultural and economic affairs, Japan is the core, and the Atlantic seaboard, the Adriatic, and the Australian coast are all distant peripheries. Topsy-turvy as Gilbert and Sullivan never imagined it.

Japan is plugged into the popular North American imagination as the sometimes inscrutable superpower, precise and delicate in its culinary tastes, feudal in its cultural symbolism, and insatiable in its appetites. Were Japan not a prominent player in so much of the daily life of North Americans, the fishers outside of Bath or in Seabrook would have less to think about in constructing their Japan. As it is, they struggle with unfamiliar exchange rates for cultural capital that compounds in a foreign currency.

14

McDonald's in Hong Kong

James L. Watson

[…] How does one explain the phenomenal success of American-style fast food in Hong Kong and, increasingly, in Guangzhou – the two epicenters of Cantonese culture and cuisine? Seven of the world's ten busiest McDonald's restaurants are located in Hong Kong. When McDonald's first opened in 1975, few thought it would survive more than a few months. By January 1, 1997, Hong Kong had 125 outlets, which means that there was one McDonald's for every 51,200 residents, compared to one for every 30,000 people in the United States. Walking into these restaurants and looking at the layout, one could well be in Cleveland or Boston. The only obvious differences are the clientele, the majority of whom are Cantonese-speakers, and the menu, which is in Chinese as well as English.

Transnationalism and the Fast Food Industry

Does the roaring success of McDonald's and its rivals in the fast food industry mean that Hong Kong's local culture is under siege? Are food chains helping to create a homogeneous, "global" culture better suited to the demands of a capitalist world order? Hong Kong would seem to be an excellent place to test the globalization hypothesis, given the central role that cuisine plays in the production and maintenance of a distinctive local identity. Man Tso-chuen's great-grandchildren are today avid

Original publication details: James L. Watson, "McDonald's in Hong Kong: Consumerism, Dietary Change, and the Rise of a Children's Culture," in *Golden Arches East: McDonald's in East Asia,* ed. James L. Watson. Redwood City: Stanford University Press, 1997. pp. 79–80, 84–7, 89–95, 100–4, 107–8. Reproduced with permission from Stanford University Press.

consumers of Big Macs, pizza, and Coca-Cola; does this somehow make them less "Chinese" than their grandfather?

It is my contention that the cultural arena in places like Hong Kong is changing with such breathtaking speed that the fundamental assumptions underlining such questions are themselves questionable. Economic and social realities make it necessary to construct an entirely new approach to global issues, one that takes the consumers' own views into account. Analyses based on neomarxian and dependency (center/periphery) models that were popular in the 1960s and 1970s do not begin to capture the complexity of emerging transnational systems.

This chapter represents a conscious attempt to bring the discussion of globalism down to earth, focusing on one local culture. The people of Hong Kong have embraced American-style fast foods, and by so doing they might appear to be in the vanguard of a worldwide culinary revolution. But they have not been stripped of their cultural traditions, nor have they become "Americanized" in any but the most superficial of ways. Hong Kong in the late 1990s constitutes one of the world's most heterogeneous cultural environments. Younger people, in particular, are fully conversant in transnational idioms, which include language, music, sports, clothing, satellite television, cybercommunications, global travel, and – of course – cuisine. It is no longer possible to distinguish what is local and what is not. In Hong Kong, as I hope to show in this chapter, the transnational *is* the local. [...]

Mental Categories: Snack versus Meal

As in other parts of East Asia, McDonald's faced a serious problem when it began operation in Hong Kong: Hamburgers, fries, and sandwiches were perceived as snacks (Cantonese *siu sihk*, literally "small eats"); in the local view these items did not constitute the elements of a proper meal. This perception is still prevalent among older, more conservative consumers who believe that hamburgers, hot dogs, and pizza can never be "filling." Many students stop at fast food outlets on their way home from school; they may share hamburgers and fries with their classmates and then eat a full meal with their families at home. This is not considered a problem by parents, who themselves are likely to have stopped for tea and snacks after work. Snacking with friends and colleagues provides a major opportunity for socializing (and transacting business) among southern Chinese. Teahouses, coffee shops, bakeries, and ice cream parlors are popular precisely because they provide a structured yet informal setting for social encounters. Furthermore, unlike Chinese restaurants and banquet halls, snack centers do not command a great deal of time or money from customers.

Contrary to corporate goals, therefore, McDonald's entered the Hong Kong market as a purveyor of snacks. Only since the late 1980s has its fare been treated as the foundation of "meals" by a generation of younger consumers who regularly eat non-Chinese food. Thanks largely to McDonald's, hamburgers and fries are now a recognized feature of Hong Kong's lunch scene. The evening hours remain, however, the weak link in McDonald's marketing plan; the real surprise was breakfast, which became a peak traffic period (more on this below).

The mental universe of Hong Kong consumers is partially revealed in the everyday use of language. Hamburgers are referred to, in colloquial Cantonese, as *han bou bao* – *han* being a homophone for "ham" and *bao* the common term for stuffed buns or bread rolls. *Bao* are quintessential snacks, and however excellent or nutritious they might be, they do not constitute the basis of a satisfying (i.e., filling) meal. In South China that honor is reserved for culinary arrangements that rest, literally, on a bed of rice (*fan*). Foods that accompany rice are referred to as *sung*, probably best translated as "toppings" (including meat, fish, and vegetables). It is significant that hamburgers are rarely categorized as meat (*yuk*); Hong Kong consumers tend to perceive anything that is served between slices of bread (Big Macs, fish sandwiches, hot dogs) as *bao*. In American culture the hamburger is categorized first and foremost as a meat item (with all the attendant worries about fat and cholesterol content), whereas in Hong Kong the same item is thought of primarily as bread.

From Exotic to Ordinary: McDonald's Becomes Local

Following precedents in other international markets, the Hong Kong franchise promoted McDonald's basic menu and did not introduce items that would be more recognizable to Chinese consumers (such as rice dishes, tropical fruit, soup noodles). Until recently the food has been indistinguishable from that served in Mobile, Alabama, or Moline, Illinois. There are, however, local preferences: the best-selling items in many outlets are fish sandwiches and plain hamburgers; Big Macs tend to be the favorites of children and teenagers. Hot tea and hot chocolate outsell coffee, but Coca-Cola remains the most popular drink.

McDonald's conservative approach also applied to the breakfast menu. When morning service was introduced in the 1980s, American-style items such as eggs, muffins, pancakes, and hash brown potatoes were not featured. Instead, the local outlets served the standard fare of hamburgers and fries for breakfast. McDonald's initial venture into the early morning food market was so successful that Mr. Ng hesitated to introduce American-style breakfast items, fearing that an abrupt shift in menu might alienate consumers who were beginning to accept hamburgers and fries as a regular feature of their diet. The transition to eggs, muffins, and hash browns was a gradual one, and today most Hong Kong customers order breakfasts that are similar to those offered in American outlets. But once established, dietary preferences change slowly: McDonald's continues to feature plain hamburgers (but not the Big Mac) on its breakfast menu in most Hong Kong outlets.

Management decisions of the type outlined above helped establish McDonald's as an icon of popular culture in Hong Kong. From 1975 to approximately 1985, McDonald's became the "in" place for young people wishing to associate themselves with the laid-back, nonhierarchical dynamism they perceived American society to embody. The first generation of consumers patronized McDonald's precisely because it was *not* Chinese and was *not* associated with Hong Kong's past as a backward-looking colonial outpost where (in their view) nothing of consequence ever happened. Hong Kong was changing and, as noted earlier, a new consumer culture was beginning to take shape. McDonald's caught the wave of this cultural movement and has been riding it ever since.

Anthropological conventions and methodologies do not allow one to deal very well with factors such as entrepreneurial flair or managerial creativity. Ethnographers are used to thinking in terms of group behavior, emphasizing coalitions and communities rather than personalities. In studies of corporate culture, however, the decisive role of management – or, more precisely, individual managers – must be dealt with in a direct way. This takes us into the realm of charisma, leadership, and personality.

Thanks largely to unrelenting efforts by Mr. Ng and his staff, McDonald's made the transition from an exotic, trendy establishment patronized by self-conscious status seekers to a competitively priced chain offering "value meals" to busy, preoccupied consumers. Today, McDonald's restaurants in Hong Kong are packed – wall-to-wall – with people of all ages, few of whom are seeking an American cultural experience. Twenty years after Mr. Ng opened his first restaurant, eating at McDonald's has become an ordinary, everyday experience for hundreds of thousands of Hong Kong residents. The chain has become a local institution in the sense that it has blended into the urban landscape; McDonald's outlets now serve as rendezvous points for young and old alike. [...]

Sanitation and the Invention of Cleanliness

Besides offering value for money, another key to McDonald's success was the provision of extra services, hitherto unavailable to Hong Kong consumers. Until the mid-1980s, a visit to any Hong Kong restaurant's toilet (save for those in fancy hotels) could best be described as an adventure. Today, restaurant toilets all over the territory are in good working order and, much to the surprise of visitors who remember the past, they are (relatively) clean. Based on conversations with people representing the full range of social strata in Hong Kong, McDonald's is widely perceived as the catalyst of this dramatic change. The corporation maintained clean facilities and did not waver as new outlets opened in neighborhoods where public sanitation had never been a high priority. Daniel Ng recalled how, during the early years of his business, he had to re-educate employees before they could even begin to comprehend what corporate standards of cleanliness entailed. Many workers, when asked to scrub out a toilet, would protest that it was already cleaner than the one in their own home, only to be told that it was not clean enough. McDonald's set what was perceived at the time to be an impossible standard and, in the process, raised consumers' expectations. Rivals had to meet these standards in order to compete. Hong Kong consumers began to draw a mental equation between the state of a restaurant's toilets and its kitchen. In pre-1980s public eateries (and in many private homes), the toilet was located inside the kitchen. One was not expected to see any contradiction in this arrangement; the operative factor was that both facilities had to be near the water supply. Younger people, in particular, have begun to grow wary of these arrangements and are refusing to eat at places they perceive to be "dirty."

Without exception my informants cited the availability of clean and accessible toilets as an important reason for patronizing McDonald's. Women, in particular, appreciated this service; they noted that, without McDonald's, it would be difficult to find public facilities when they are away from home or office. A survey of one Hong Kong outlet in June 1994 revealed that 58 percent of the consumers present were women. For many Hong Kong residents, therefore, McDonald's is more than just a restaurant; it is an oasis, a familiar rest station, in what is perceived to be an inhospitable urban environment.

What's in a Smile? Friendliness and Public Service

American consumers expect to be served "with a smile" when they order fast food, but … this is not true in all societies. In Hong Kong people are suspicious of anyone who displays what is perceived to be an excess of congeniality, solicitude, or familiarity. The human smile is not, therefore, a universal symbol of openness and honesty. "If you buy an apple from a hawker and he smiles at you," my Cantonese tutor once told me, "you know you're being cheated."

Given these cultural expectations, it was difficult for Hong Kong management to import a key element of the McDonald's formula – service with a smile – and make it work. Crew members were trained to treat customers in a manner that approximates the American notion of "friendliness." Prior to the 1970s, there was not even an indigenous Cantonese term to describe this form of behavior. The traditional notion of friendship is based on loyalty to close associates, which by definition cannot be extended to strangers. Today the concept of *public* friendliness is recognized – and verbalized – by younger people in Hong Kong, but the term many of them use to express this quality is "friendly," borrowed directly from English. McDonald's, through its television advertising, may be partly responsible for this innovation, but to date it has had little effect on workers in the catering industry.

During my interviews it became clear that the majority of Hong Kong consumers were uninterested in public displays of congeniality from service personnel. When shopping for fast food most people cited convenience, cleanliness, and table space as primary considerations; few even mentioned service except to note that the food should be delivered promptly. Counter staff in Hong Kong's fast food outlets (including McDonald's) rarely make great efforts to smile or to behave in a manner Americans would interpret as friendly. Instead, they project qualities that are admired in the local culture: competence, directness, and unflappability. In a North American setting the facial expression that Hong Kong employees use to convey these qualities would likely be interpreted as a deliberate attempt to be rude or indifferent. Workers who smile on the job are assumed to be enjoying themselves at the consumer's (and management's) expense: In the words of one diner I overheard while standing in a queue, "They must be playing around back there. What are they laughing about?"

Consumer Discipline?

[A] hallmark of the American fast food business is the displacement of labor costs from the corporation to the consumers. For the system to work, consumers must be educated – or "disciplined" – so that they voluntarily fulfill their side of an implicit bargain: We (the corporation) will provide cheap, fast service, if you (the customer) carry your own tray, seat yourself, and help clean up afterward. Time and space are also critical factors in the equation: Fast service is offered in exchange for speedy consumption and a prompt departure, thereby making room for others. This system has revolutionized the American food industry and has helped to shape consumer expectations in other sectors of the economy. How has it fared in Hong Kong? Are Chinese customers conforming to disciplinary models devised in Oak Brook, Illinois?

The answer is both yes and no. In general Hong Kong consumers have accepted the basic elements of the fast food formula, but with "localizing" adaptations. For instance, customers generally do not bus their own trays, nor do they depart immediately upon finishing. Clearing one's own table has never been an accepted part of local culinary culture, owing in part to the low esteem attaching to this type of labor. […]

Perhaps the most striking feature of the American-inspired model of consumer discipline is the queue. Researchers in many parts of the world have reported that customers refuse, despite "education" campaigns by the chains involved, to form neat lines in front of cashiers. Instead, customers pack themselves into disorderly scrums and jostle for a chance to place their orders. Scrums of this nature were common in Hong Kong when McDonald's opened in 1975. Local managers discouraged this practice by stationing queue monitors near the registers during busy hours and, by the 1980s, orderly lines were the norm at McDonald's. The disappearance of the scrum corresponds to a general change in Hong Kong's public culture as a new generation of residents, the children of refugees, began to treat the territory as their home. Courtesy toward strangers was largely unknown in the 1960s: Boarding a bus during rush hour could be a nightmare and transacting business at a bank teller's window required brute strength. Many people credit McDonald's with being the first public institution in Hong Kong to enforce queuing, and thereby helping to create a more "civilized" social order. McDonald's did not, in fact, introduce the queue to Hong Kong, but this belief is firmly lodged in the public imagination.

Hovering and the Napkin Wars

Purchasing one's food is no longer a physical challenge in Hong Kong's McDonald's but finding a place to sit is quite another matter. The traditional practice of "hovering" is one solution: Choose a group of diners who appear to be on the verge of leaving and stake a claim to their table by hovering nearby, sometimes only inches away. Seated customers routinely ignore the intrusion; it would, in fact, entail a loss of face to notice. Hovering was the norm in Hong Kong's lower- to middle-range restaurants during the 1960s and 1970s, but the practice has disappeared in recent years. Restaurants now take names or hand out tickets at the entrance; warning signs, in Chinese and English, are posted: "Please wait to be seated." Customers are no longer allowed into the dining area until a table is ready.

Fast food outlets are the only dining establishments in Hong Kong where hovering is still tolerated, largely because it would be nearly impossible to regulate. Customer traffic in McDonald's is so heavy that the standard restaurant design has failed to reproduce American-style dining routines: Rather than ordering first and finding a place to sit afterward, Hong Kong consumers usually arrive in groups and delegate one or two people to claim a table while someone else joins the counter queues. Children make ideal hoverers and learn to scoot through packed restaurants, zeroing in on diners who are about to finish. It is one of the wonders of comparative ethnography to witness the speed with which Hong Kong children perform this reconnaissance duty. Foreign visitors are sometimes unnerved by hovering, but residents accept it as part of everyday life in one of the world's most densely populated cities. It is not surprising, therefore, that Hong Kong's fast food chains have made few efforts to curtail the practice.

Management is less tolerant of behavior that affects profit margins. In the United States fast food companies save money by allowing (or requiring) customers to collect their own napkins, straws, plastic flatware, and condiments. Self-provisioning is an essential feature of consumer discipline, but it only works if the system is not abused. In Hong Kong napkins are dispensed, one at a time, by McDonald's crew members who work behind the counter; customers who do not ask for napkins do not receive any. This is a deviation from the corporation's standard operating procedure and adds a few seconds to each transaction, which in turn slows down the queues. Why alter a well-tested routine? The reason is simple: napkins placed in public dispensers disappear faster than they can be replaced. [...]

Children as Consumers

[...] McDonald's has become so popular in Hong Kong that parents often use visits to their neighborhood outlet as a reward for good behavior or academic achievement. Conversely, children who misbehave might lose their after-school snacking privileges or be left at home while their siblings are taken out for a McDonald's brunch on Sunday. During interviews parents reported that sanctions of this type worked better than anything they could think of to straighten out a wayward child: "It is my nuclear deterrent," one father told me, in English.

Many Hong Kong children of my acquaintance are so fond of McDonald's that they refuse to eat with their parents or grandparents in Chinese-style restaurants or *dim sam* teahouses. This has caused intergenerational distress in some of Hong Kong's more conservative communities. In 1994, a nine-year-old boy, the descendant of illustrious ancestors who settled in the New Territories eight centuries ago, talked about his concerns as we consumed Big Macs, fries, and shakes at McDonald's: "A-bak [uncle], I like it here better than any place in the world. I want to come here every day." His father takes him to McDonald's at least twice a week, but his grandfather, who accompanied them a few times in the late 1980s, will no longer do so. "I prefer to eat *dim sam*," the older man told me later. "That place [McDonald's] is for kids." Many grandparents have resigned themselves to the new consumer trends and take their preschool grandchildren to McDonald's for midmorning snacks – precisely the time of day that local teahouses were once packed with retired people. Cantonese grandparents have always played a prominent role in child minding, but until recently the children had to accommodate to the proclivities of their elders. By the 1990s grandchildren were more assertive and the midmorning *dim sam* snack was giving way to hamburgers and Cokes.

The emergence of children as full-scale consumers has had other consequences for the balance of domestic power in Hong Kong homes. Grade school children often possess detailed knowledge of fast foods and foreign (non-Chinese) cuisines. Unlike members of the older generation, children know what, and how, to eat in a wide variety of restaurants. Specialized information is shared with classmates: Which chain has the best pizza? What is ravioli? How do you eat a croissant? Food, especially fast food, is one of the leading topics of conversation among Hong Kong school children. Grandchildren frequently assume the role of tutors, showing their elders the proper way to eat fast food. Without guidance, older people are likely to disassemble the Big Mac, layer by layer, and eat only those parts that appeal to them. Hong Kong adults also find it uncomfortable to eat with their hands and devise makeshift finger guards with wrappers. Children, by contrast, are usually expert in the finer points of fast food etiquette and pay close attention to television ads that feature young people eating a variety of foods. It is embarrassing, I was told by an 11-year-old acquaintance, to be seen at McDonald's with a grandfather who does not know how to eat "properly."

Many Hong Kong kindergartens and primary schools teach culinary skills, utilizing the lunch period for lessons in flatware etiquette, menu reading, and food awareness (taste-testing various cuisines, including Thai, European, and Indian). Partly as a consequence, Hong Kong's youth are among the world's most knowledgeable and adventurous eaters. One can find a wide range of cuisines in today's Hong Kong, rivaling New York City for variety. South Asian, Mexican, and Spanish restaurants are crowded with groups of young people, ages 16 to 25, sharing dishes as they graze their way through the menu. Culinary adventures of this nature are avoided by older residents (people over 50), who, in general, have a more restricted range of food tolerance.

Ronald McDonald and the Invention of Birthday Parties

Until recently most people in Hong Kong did not even know, let alone celebrate, their birthdates in the Western calendrical sense; dates of birth according to the lunar calendar were recorded for divinatory purposes but were not noted in annual rites. By the late 1980s, however, birthday parties, complete with cakes and candles, were the rage in Hong Kong. Any child who was anyone had to have a party, and the most popular venue was a fast food restaurant, with McDonald's ranked above all competitors. The majority of Hong Kong people live in overcrowded flats, which means that parties are rarely held in private homes.

Except for the outlets in central business districts, McDonald's restaurants are packed every Saturday and Sunday with birthday parties, cycled through at the rate of one every hour. A party hostess, provided by the restaurant, leads the children in games while the parents sit on the sidelines, talking quietly among themselves. For a small fee celebrants receive printed invitation cards, photographs, a gift box containing toys and a discount coupon for future trips to McDonald's. Parties are held in a special enclosure, called the Ronald Room, which is equipped with low tables and tiny stools – suitable only for children. Television commercials portray Ronald McDonald leading birthday celebrants on exciting safaris and expeditions. The clown's Cantonese name, Mak Dong Lou Suk-Suk ("Uncle McDonald"), plays on the intimacy of kinship and has helped transform him into one of Hong Kong's most familiar cartoon figures. [...]

Conclusions: Whose Culture Is It?

[...] Having watched the processes of culture change unfold for nearly thirty years, it is apparent to me that the ordinary people of Hong Kong have most assuredly *not* been stripped of their cultural heritage, nor have they become the uncomprehending dupes of transnational corporations. Younger people – including many of the grandchildren of my former neighbors in the New Territories – are avid consumers of transnational culture in all of its most obvious manifestations: music, fashion, television, and cuisine. At the same time, however, Hong Kong has itself become a major center for the *production* of transnational culture, not just a sinkhole for its *consumption*. Witness, for example, the expansion of Hong Kong popular culture into China, Southeast Asia, and beyond: "Cantopop" music is heard on radio stations in North China, Vietnam, and Japan; the Hong Kong fashion industry influences clothing styles in Los Angeles, Bangkok, and Kuala Lumpur; and, perhaps most significant of all, Hong Kong is emerging as a center for the production and dissemination of satellite television programs throughout East, Southeast, and South Asia.

A lifestyle is emerging in Hong Kong that can best be described as postmodern, postnationalist, and flamboyantly transnational. The wholesale acceptance and appropriation of Big Macs, Ronald McDonald, and birthday parties are small, but significant aspects of this redefinition of Chinese cultural identity. In closing, therefore, it seems appropriate to pose an entirely new set of questions: Where does the transnational end and the local begin? Whose culture is it, anyway? In places like Hong Kong the postcolonial periphery is fast becoming the metropolitan center, where local people are consuming and simultaneously producing new cultural systems. [...]

15

The Transnational Villagers

Peggy Levitt

The top part of the avenue leading from the Dominican city of Baní to the village of Miraflores is bordered by thick, leafy mimosa trees. Throughout the year, they are covered by orange blossoms and blanket the street with a delicious shade. On the way out of town, the sidewalks are busy with women shopping and children returning home from school. The streets grow quiet as the beauty parlors, small grocery stores (*colmados*), and lawyers' offices closest to the town square gradually give way to residential neighborhoods. On one corner is Mayor Carlos Peña's feed store, where he and his coworkers from the Partido Revolucionario Dominicano (PRD) meet to talk about politics every late afternoon. Farther down the street, members of the Partido Reformista Social Cristiano (PRSC) also sit in front of their party's headquarters, drinking sweet cups of coffee and discussing the current election campaign. At the edge of town, the buildings end abruptly in overgrown fields. The avenue goes silent except for a lone motorcycle driver. The countryside is overwhelmingly beautiful.

A few hundred yards ahead, two sights unexpectedly interrupt this peaceful landscape. On the right side of the road, four partially complete mansions stand behind large iron gates. Their crumbling marble pillars and large cracked windows, so out of character with the rest of the scene, mock onlookers from the street. A little farther down the avenue, at the edge of a large, uncultivated field, a billboard proclaims, "Viaje a Boston con Sierra Travel" – Travel to Boston with Sierra Travel. Telephone numbers in Boston and Baní, coincidentally beginning with the same exchange, are hidden by grasses so tall they almost cover the sign completely.

Original publication details: Peggy Levitt, *The Transnational Villagers*. Oakland: University of California Press, 2001. pp. 1–3, 11–12, 184–91.

The Globalization Reader, Fifth Edition. Edited by Frank J. Lechner and John Boli.

A small restaurant, its rusting metal chairs and tables glinting brightly in the sun, announces the entrance to Miraflores. Turning off the road into this village of close to four thousand residents reveals further discontinuities. While some of the homes resemble miniature, finished versions of the empty mansions along the avenue, one out of five families still lives in a small, two-room wooden house. Four in ten use outdoor privies. Though the electricity goes off nightly for weeks at a stretch, nearly every household has a television, VCR, or compact-disc player. And although it takes months to get a phone installed in Santo Domingo, the Dominican capital, Mirafloreños can get phone service in their homes almost immediately after they request it.

What explains these sharp contrasts? Who is responsible for these half-finished homes that differ so completely in style and scale from the other houses in the area? Who is the audience for the billboards in the middle of fields that advertise international plane flights? How is it that people who must collect rainwater in barrels so they can wash when the water supply goes off are watching the latest videos in the comfort of their living rooms?

Transnational migration is at the root of these contradictions. The billboard speaks to the nearly two-thirds of Mirafloreño families who have relatives in the greater Boston metropolitan area. These migrants pay for the home improvements and buy the appliances. They create such a lucrative market for long-distance phone service that CODETEL (the Dominican phone company) installs phone lines in Miraflores almost immediately after they are requested. And some built the dream palaces on the avenue, which they completed only halfway before their money dried up.

Mirafloreños began migrating to Boston, Massachusetts, in the late 1960s. Most settled in and around Jamaica Plain, traditionally a white-ethnic neighborhood until Latinos and young white professionals replaced those who began leaving the city in the 1960s. Over the years, migrants from the Dominican Republic and the friends and family they left behind have sustained such strong, frequent contacts with one another it is as if village life takes place in two settings. Fashion, food, and forms of speech, as well as appliances and home decorating styles, attest to these strong connections. In Miraflores, villagers often dress in T-shirts emblazoned with the names of businesses in Massachusetts, although they do not know what these words or logos mean. They proudly serve their visitors coffee with Cremora and juice made from Tang. The local *colmados* stock SpaghettiOs and Frosted Flakes. Many of the benches in the Miraflores park are inscribed with the names of villagers who moved to Boston years ago. And almost everyone, including older community members who can count on their fingers how many times they have visited Santo Domingo, can talk about "La Mozart" or "La Centre" – Mozart Street Park and Centre Street, two focal points of the Dominican community in Jamaica Plain.

In Boston, Mirafloreños have re-created their premigration lives to the extent that their new physical and cultural environment allows. Particularly during the early years of settlement, but even today, a large number of migrants lived within the same twenty-block radius. There are several streets where people from Miraflores live in almost every triple-decker house. Community members leave their apartment doors open so that the flow between households is as easy and uninhibited as it is in Miraflores. They decorate their refrigerators with the same plastic fruit magnets they used in Miraflores, and they put the same sets of ceramic animal families on the shelves of their living rooms. Women continue to hang curtains around the door frames; these provide privacy without keeping in the heat in the Dominican Republic but are merely decorative in Boston. Because someone is always traveling between Boston and the island, there is a continuous, circular flow of goods, news, and information. As a result, when someone is ill, cheating on his or her spouse, or finally granted a visa, the news spreads as quickly in Jamaica Plain as it does on the streets of Miraflores.

Many Americans expect migrants like Mirafloreños to sever their ties to their homeland as they become assimilated into the United States. They assume that migrants will eventually transfer their loyalty and community membership from the countries they leave behind to the ones that receive them. But increasing numbers of migrants continue to participate in the political and economic lives of their homelands, even as they are incorporated into their host societies. Instead of loosening their connections and trading one membership for another, some individuals are keeping their feet in both worlds. They use political, religious, and civic arenas to forge social relations, earn their livelihoods, and exercise their rights across borders. [...]

Miraflores is just one type of transnational community, which I call a transnational village. Transnational villages have several unique characteristics. First, actual migration is not required to be a member. Migrants' continued participation in their home communities transforms the sending-community context to such an extent that nonmigrants also adapt many of the values and practices of their migrant counterparts, engage in social relationships that span two settings, and participate in organizations that act across borders. This is not to say that those who migrate and those who remain behind live in an imagined, third, transnational space. Instead, they are all firmly rooted in a particular place and time, though their daily lives often depend upon people, money, ideas, and resources located in another setting.

A second characteristic of transnational villages is that they emerge and endure partially because of social remittances. Social remittances are the ideas, behaviors, and social capital that flow from receiving to sending communities. They are the tools with which ordinary individuals create global culture at the local level. They help individuals embedded in a particular context and accustomed to a particular set of identities and practices to imagine a new cartography, encouraging them to try on new gender roles, experiment with new ideas about politics, and adopt new organizing strategies. Once this process has begun, daily life in the village is changed to such an extent, and migrants and nonmigrants often become so dependent on one another, that transnational villages are likely to endure.

A third feature distinguishing transnational villages is that they create and are created by organizations that themselves come to act across borders. These political, religious, and civic organizations arise or are reorganized to meet the needs of their newly transnational members, enabling migrants to continue to participate in both settings and encouraging community perpetuation. This also means that migrants have multiple channels through which to pursue transnational belonging. Dual citizenship is just one way to be a transnational actor. Religious, civic, and political groups allow migrants to express and act upon dual allegiances.

Migrants organize groups across borders in several ways. They may establish hometown associations, like the Miraflores Development Committee, with chapters in the sending community and in the areas where migrant residents cluster. They may form receiving-country divisions of national political parties. Or, as in the case of the Catholic Church, they may extend an already established international institution to incorporate new connections resulting from relations between migrants and nonmigrants. [...]

Mirafloreños living in Boston ... began getting together informally during the mid-1970s. At first these gatherings were primarily social events until someone suggested that the group organize activities to better the community.

> Our meetings were a place we could feel at home because at work and on the street we were still having a hard time getting adjusted. Then Pepe had the idea to try to do something for Miraflores. We had a big meeting on Mozart Street, where he was living. One of the people wrote a letter back saying we wanted to work with the Movimiento and help them. The idea to build the park originated in Boston. And after that we were always doing something. We would finish a project and the group would stop meeting. But then someone would come up with a different idea and we would get going once again. (Carlos, 42, return migrant, Miraflores)

All Mirafloreños are automatically members of the MDC, regardless of their place of residence. Each chapter has its own leadership and organizational structure. In 1994 seven *directores* (leaders) in Miraflores and eight leaders in Boston ran the organization. In addition to their weekly meetings, the group periodically organized larger meetings when a new project was starting or when committee members felt they needed additional help. The MDC in Miraflores organized community-wide *asambleas* (assemblies) about once a year to elect new leadership. Community-wide meetings also took place when a particularly difficult problem arose or a decision had to be made requiring a broader consensus. Members in Boston communicated their views by phone before these events, though they did not actually vote. Migrants chose their leaders separately, by informal agreement. When members of either chapter visited Boston or Miraflores, they were expected to attend the meetings held during their visits. As Rosita, a thirty-two-year-old nonmigrant, described it:

> Last summer, I went to visit my sister in Boston for two months. While I was there, I used to go to the *comité* meetings every Sunday night. People expected me to do this. And it helped. I could tell the people in Boston what was going on in Miraflores, and when I got home I was able to give the other members of the committee a better idea about what was going on.

When migrant leaders returned to the village to live, the community expected them to assume a leadership role in the MDC. "We are just waiting for Marcial to get settled," said Alfredo about a new returnee. "He's been back only five months, but when he's ready, we are counting on him to be very active with us."

The MDC does not receive technical assistance or financial support regularly from the Dominican government. It does not belong to a national or international nongovernmental organization (NGO) network. Independence has its advantages and disadvantages. Clearly these kinds of relationships can produce needed resources and enhance migrants' influence. In the Mexican case, however, while the government's Program for Mexican Communities Abroad extended resources and invited greater participation among immigrants, it also formalized and standardized many of these activities under the direction of the Mexican government. Some argue that these transnational activities reproduce long-standing inequities because those already in power and an emerging migrant elite monopolize their benefits. Though migrant leaders' increased social status and economic weight earns them substantive citizenship rights they did not enjoy as residents of Mexico, it is at nonmigrants' expense.

The MDC is, however, operating in an environment that is favorable to NGOs. In the past two decades, international development agendas have devoted significant resources toward strengthening civil society and building institutions. The United States Agency for International Development supported such programs in the Dominican Republic as a way to circumvent government corruption and encourage the growth of alternative political forums. Organizations have also been created that directly address migrants' concerns. The Fundación para la Defensa de Dominicanos Residentes en el Exterior (Foundation for the Defense of Dominicans Living Abroad), a group formed primarily by return migrants, works to improve the image of Dominicanos Ausentes because they are so often associated with the drug trade and prostitution.

The MDC's Accomplishments

For twenty-five years various incarnations of the MDC have strategized, raised funds, and implemented projects across borders. These activities produced significant improvements in village life. Monies raised by the MDC purchased more than 80 percent of the land that the communal facilities were built on. The MDC also constructed the community center, health clinic, park, cemetery, and bridges over the irrigation canals that traverse Miraflores. In 1993, in addition to renovating the school and health clinic, the MDC also funded physicians' salaries and medical supplies.

Some combination of community and state resources generally supports these projects. The MDC funds at least some portion of all its projects, by either paying for the entire project or leveraging monies it raises to secure matching funds from the government. Fund-raising generally took two forms. The groups in Boston and on the island organized large fund-raising events, such as dances and fairs, which often took place simultaneously. The radio telethon in Boston, for example, during which Mirafloreños called in to pledge donations to the MDC, was broadcast at the same time in Miraflores. The Boston group held its big dinner dance during the village's *fiestas patronales* (patron saint celebration), which was also the most important fund-raising time for the MDC on the island. In Boston committee members also recruited villagers to contribute a $10 *cuota*, or donation, to the MDC each week. They visited their contributors every weekend to collect money, exchange news, and offer updates on the committee's progress. During this study, anywhere from 40 to 150 community members contributed money on a regular basis.

The MDC's contributions to community development in Miraflores, however, go far beyond physical improvements and fund-raising. The committee fosters positive change in the community in several other ways. First, the MDC solidified and expanded upon the informal solidarity that was such an integral part of Mirafloreño community life. Despite their regular exchanges of labor, food, child care, and clothing, attempts to formalize this social capital and use it systematically had generally failed. In addition to the previously mentioned co-op story, respondents recalled a number of other incidents in which they felt they had been taken advantage of. It was simply a fact of life, many said, that when funds are raised, someone pockets something for themselves.

> I remember I was living in Boston and they came around asking for donations. They wanted to build a sewing workshop where they could teach women in the village how to sew and they could earn some extra income. I said I would donate the machines but not money. I was not going to give money and have it stolen another time. I never heard back from them. And now, look around you, do you see anyone making dresses anywhere? (Rolando, 46, return migrant, Miraflores)

As a result, the community was very suspicious of its leadership and had difficulty working together as a formal group. There were few community members considered honest enough to be leaders. After all, in a world where everyone must struggle to make ends meet, why wouldn't someone take advantage of an opportunity that presented itself? Don Miguel went so far as to say, "If you don't want to be called a thief, then you shouldn't belong to any organization." Added Juline, a sixty-seven-year-old nonmigrant:

> It is very curious because we are a very generous people. We give to each other all the time. But any time someone tries to get us to work together as a group on some joint project, we all get suspicious of one another. We accuse each other of cheating and stealing or of trying to get something for ourselves. The people are right in this. There are too many instances where people cheated their fellow community members. That makes it very hard to trust someone who is not part of your family.

In the MDC's case, however, both the social remittances migrants introduced and the clear rewards resulting from the MDC's efforts helped convince a critical mass of Mirafloreños that community organization could work. In the same way that migrants encouraged calls for a different kind of politics, they also contributed to demands for an MDC that was more accountable to its members. Some of the management and administrative techniques they introduced made this possible. Furthermore, increasing numbers became convinced once the MDC established a successful track record of completing projects that clearly made a difference in the community. The committee's activities stood in sharp contrast to the corruption and inefficiencies pervading Dominican life. While these examples could not counteract years of disillusionment with the state, they did provide models of success that could be emulated.

We still do not trust one another. And every time we start a new project, you know by the end that someone will be the bad guy. But we also have seen that if we work together, we can succeed. People see that we are finishing the funeral home. We're finishing the baseball stadium. These are clear examples that people see and say to themselves, we can do this. We can make things better around here without someone profiting for themselves. (Laura, 58, nonmigrant, Miraflores)

A second way that the MDC promoted community development was by fostering organizational growth. The community took on more projects, addressing a wider variety of concerns, because of the large sums migrants raised in Boston. As a result, greater numbers of migrants and nonmigrants participated in a more diverse set of activities, which in turn required a wide variety of skills.

In 1993, for example, committee leaders restructured the MDC in Miraflores to be able to manage its activities more effectively. They created health, education, and sports subcommittees supervised by an overarching coordinating committee. Someone uninterested in sports could work on health. A person worried about schools could go to the education subcommittee's meetings without having to sit through the entire meeting of the MDC. This made it easier and more attractive for Mirafloreños to focus their time and energies. Leaders estimated that participation in some kind of group rose from about 10 to 20 percent of all community members. More people also participated in Boston. Though the Boston chapter continued to meet as a whole, rather than dividing around specific activities, leaders felt that more migrants either attended meetings or kept informed about the group's activities because the MDC addressed a wider set of concerns.

Participation taught some respondents a new set of skills. Maribel, a twenty-six-year-old nonmigrant, said she learned some basic accounting and that this helped her manage her finances better at home. Mayra, a thirty-four-year-old nonmigrant, improved her social skills:

I gained a lot more confidence about speaking in front of a group. It used to be that I hardly ever went out, let alone got up in front of people and said what I had to say. But little by little, after going to meetings, I started feeling more comfortable. We were working together and it began to feel like a team. And one day, I finally raised my hand and said something. After that, they couldn't keep me quiet.

The creation of subcommittees particularly encouraged women to participate. As the MDC became more prominent and respected for its accomplishments, community members became more open to the idea that *mujeres serias* could be active in its work. Decentralizing the organization created "windows of opportunity" where women could assume more responsibility and have more say. Though in general men continued to dominate the organization and women took on traditionally female roles, their participation increased.

Women have always participated in the church. It is considered okay for even a woman who is married to go to mass and to attend meetings of the parish council. But very few women were active in the MDC. It wasn't considered proper. Now, though, that they have the health committee and the education committee – these are things that people feel it is okay for women to be involved in. They will not accuse a woman of going to a meeting to flirt with men. They will say she is there because she cares about her children. (Pedro, 58, return migrant, Miraflores) [...]

Finally, the efforts of MDC members in Boston and Miraflores enhanced villagers' ability to make demands of the Dominican state. In some areas, such as health care, the community was able to provide for itself what the government did not provide for them. Before the PRD government (1978–86) built rural health clinics throughout the country, it was the MDC that financed health care provision in Miraflores. In other cases, the community leveraged the monies it raised to secure additional funds. Leaders convinced municipal authorities in Baní, for example, to match the $10,000 they collected to build the community's park.

Migrant support also ultimately enabled the MDC to pressure the government to provide for them. The committee raised approximately $50,000 to construct its aqueduct. Members planned to finance and implement the entire project on their own because they were tired of waiting for the government to do it for them. After the MDC raised enough money to begin work, committee members visited provincial water supply authorities to get the permits they needed. When months passed and no permits arrived, they began making weekly trips to Santo Domingo to complain at the National Palace. Though each time officials assured them that the permits were on their way, they never materialized. Finally, after several months, the MDC learned that President Balaguer was coming to Baní to inaugurate another public-works project and they arranged to meet with him.

We found out that Balaguer would be coming to Baní, so we asked the Reformistas in town to arrange a meeting for us. As the MDC president, I went as the representative of the entire group. I said, Dr. Balaguer, our village goes without water for days at a time. We want to build an aqueduct, and with the help of those who are living in Boston we have raised the money to do so. We have been asking the provincial water authorities for months to give us the permits we need, but there is always some excuse. We would like you to help us. And the old man looked at me and he said, "You can tell your community members to keep their money. I will build your aqueduct." (Ramón, 48, nonmigrant, Miraflores) [...]

16

The Great Game and the Informal Empire

David Goldblatt

[…] Before the First World War, football spread as the game of the *fin-de-siècle* urban elites of Europe and Latin America. The game also made its first tentative appearance in those parts of Africa and Asia most closely linked to Europe; the first indigenous football clubs had been formed in elite circles in Egypt, Algeria, South Africa and the Ghanaian Cape Coast before 1914. Working-class players never stayed long enough in any of these places to give the locals more than a glimpse of their unusual ball game. More importantly this kind of company lent no social cachet to football; quite the opposite. That required the participation of the eclectic elites and technicians of Britain's informal empire.

In the half century before the cataclysm of the First World War the British were everywhere. Obviously enough Britons staffed the military and bureaucratic machines of the empire, but the pink that coloured over one-quarter of the earth's surface on the conventional maps of the day had been quietly seeping out into almost every region of the world. British merchant seamen criss-crossed every ocean and in every port that they stopped in a British community of merchants, entrepreneurs, middlemen and speculators was gathered. These circuits of trade created a de facto British economic empire that reached to China, South America, Mexico and right the way across Europe, from Lisbon to Moscow, from Oslo to Constantinople. More than just trade, the British exported capital to these unofficial economic outposts, establishing banks, investing in railways, infrastructure and factories. Where local skills and technologies were

Original publication details: David Goldblatt, *The Ball Is Round: A Global History of Soccer.* London: Penguin, 2006. pp. 114–19, 901–3. Reproduced with permission from Riverhead Books, an imprint of Penguin Group (USA) LLC and Penguin Books Ltd.

The Globalization Reader, Fifth Edition. Edited by Frank J. Lechner and John Boli.
Editorial material and organization © 2015 John Wiley & Sons, Ltd.
Published 2015 by John Wiley & Sons, Ltd.

insufficient, Britain exported technicians, techniques and machines too, most notably for the funding and constructing of Latin America's entire railway network.

While economic relationships were at the core of British influence, the informal empire was always more than just pounds, shillings and pence. British teachers, schools and educational philosophies were in vogue and in demand among many of the elites of Europe and the Rio de la Plata, for Britain was not just the most powerful player in world affairs, it was the most modern. While for much of the twentieth century Britain saw itself as imperturbably tranquil and able successfully to preserve the archaic and traditional, that is not how it looked to others in the late nineteenth century. On the contrary, the whirlwind of its industrial revolution, the modernist might of its iron-hulled navy, its development of new technologies of communication like the telegraph, suggested a society in a process of tumultuous change, riding the very edge of a revolutionary wave of social and economic transformation. Britain meant wealth, power and modernity and who did not wish to be rich, powerful and modern?

In the realms of politics, high culture and football, the terms British and English became synonymous. Despite the obvious contribution of Scotland to the creation of both empire and football, and the existence of separate Home Countries football associations, the nuances were too complex and of little interest to most of Continental Europe. British, English, it made no difference; either way the island empire's place in the great power politics of the era evoked reactions. On the one hand it created significant and powerful pockets of jealousy, suspicion and Anglophobia among the most nationalist political forces in Europe, the Far East and Latin America. An Italian gymnastics magazine of 1906 could write: 'they dress, eat, drink and abuse in English … people only play football to look like an Englishman and to be able to use an exotic vocabulary. For some time this was considered fashionable and a sign of good taste. Fortunately, everyone recognizes now the grotesqueness of this attitude.' Perhaps not everyone, for almost everywhere these voices were drowned out by a great wave of Anglophilia; and to embrace England and Englishness was to embrace sport.

The key agents of this sporting diaspora were the peculiar expatriate elites that staffed the economic and educational outposts of the informal empire, or mingled as travellers, gadflies and adventurers in its ambience. Long-standing British colonies in São Paulo, Rio, Lima, Buenos Aires, Oporto and Lisbon sent their sons to be educated at home where they acquired a taste for games that was sufficiently unquenchable that they set up sports clubs on their return. They were joined in the later part of the century by fresh waves of migrant Britons engaged in trade, business and banking in Scandinavia, Italy, Switzerland, France, Russia and the cities of the Austro-Hungarian Empire. The social mix included the sons of both aristocratic and bourgeois families but was heavily weighted towards public-school old boys and in its upper echelons Oxbridge graduates. Alongside them a new class of highly educated technical specialists, particularly engineers, factory managers, railway technicians and teachers were recruited to Belgium, Russia, Spain, Germany and Mexico. All took the fashion and the passion for sport with them.

Consequently, from the 1860s to the 1880s football was just one of a whole panoply of English sports that were played and watched for the first time across the informal empire. While cricket won the affections of some local elites, most notably in the

Netherlands, and rugby was immensely successful in south-west France, it was football that seemed most to engage the imagination.

But whose imagination? Who were the first generation of pioneering football players? They were almost exclusively male; there is scant recorded evidence of women's football in England, France, the Netherlands, Russia and Sweden, describing isolated and sporadic events. Above all they were urban, sometimes titled, always moneyed and usually highly educated. [...]

Football also attracted many of the more intellectually inclined, and university students were at the core of the new football clubs in Rio, Copenhagen and Prague. Dr James Spensley, the leading force and player at Genoa Cricket, was the kind of multi-talented, cosmopolitan Englishman who inspired these scholar-players. Spensley was described in his obituary as having 'widespread interest[s] in philosophical studies, Greek language, Egyptian Papyrus, football, boxing and popular university. He even initiated an evening school in Genoa.' Reflecting on the dense network of formal and informal connections among this emergent transnational class the Frenchman Paul Adam wrote in his 1907 book *La morale des sports*:

> Over the last fifty years, a general type of elite has emerged. They share a number of common ideas about philosophy, science, arts and morality. They reign and prosper in spa towns, winter resorts and where international conferences take place. This elite is composed of doctors, bankers, professors, rentiers, authors, diplomats, dandies, artists, princes and dilettantes of various kinds ... they consider themselves brothers of the same intellectual family and have faith in universality and rationalism ... through sport they may unite and soon dominate the world.

But football was not the only game competing for the attention of this transnational class. Cricket, rugby, tennis, hockey, athletics and gymnastics were all in circulation at the same time. Cricket, rugby and hockey were certainly English enough in their origins and social trappings to serve many of the cultural and status functions that the uptake of football satisfied. What was it about football, above all about playing football, that captured the imaginations of so many youthful European and Latino elites? On the one hand, the game was successful in this milieu for the same reasons that the British working classes took to the game with such speed and enthusiasm: the simplicity of its rules and scoring system; its flexibility in terms of numbers that can play, how long they can play for and the space required to play in; its lack of equipment; and the lower likelihood of serious injury, compared to rugby especially. But these are the traditional explanations for football's success among the world's urban poor. The *fin-de-siècle* gentleman player could have played whatever he wanted – football was not the only option left after financial and social costs had been discounted. People played because they just loved to play. Once seen, the prospect of trying it out for yourself was irresistible. [...]

Once the game had been established as an amateur pastime of the young and rich in the informal empire, a second wave of Britons helped shape its growth. In the two decades before the First World War, both professional and amateur British teams toured extensively in Europe and Latin America, providing inspiration, reflection and paying crowds wherever they went. A handful of more adventurous figures from within the otherwise rather conservative world of British professional football took the plunge and stayed overseas. Jimmy Hogan, an itinerant Lancastrian professional, had played for Rochdale, Burnley, Fulham, Swindon Town and Bolton Wanderers before moving to Holland and Vienna to coach before the war. The Glaswegian John Madden ran Slavia Prague for over thirty years starting in 1905.

The Great Game was coming to a close. Kipling, no friend or lover of team sports, recognized that for much of his generation that world of imperial rivalry and great power politics was cast in the frame of sport. As tensions rose in the last years of peace, there was, even among the Anglophile footballers, resentment over the exclusivity and haughty air of superiority of expatriate British clubs which saw the formation of breakaway and alternative sporting organizations to challenge their hegemony. Nacional in Montevideo, Stade Français in Paris, and Independiente in Buenos Aires were all created in opposition to English-dominated clubs in their cities and inevitably came to carry a nationalist flag onto the pitch. Simultaneously in Central Europe, Latin America and Sweden the game was spreading beyond the circle of the privileged and on to the toes and heels of the urban working class – who knew nothing of England and cared even less for its modernity or sophistication. But for them to take possession of football, as their English and Scottish equivalents had done thirty years before, the old order would have to be broken, the great game would have to stop, and if not everyone, then around 10 million young men would have to die first. [...]

Football's status as the most popular global sport was not inevitable. It is a consequence of both historical forces beyond the game, and the intrinsic qualities of its own structure, rhythms and appearance. Football emerged and spread in an era when many other sports were also being codified: rugby, hockey, tennis and golf in Britain; baseball, American football and basketball in the United States; martial arts in Japan, and gymnastics in Germany. The political and military fate of these great powers determined much of the initial distribution of sports. Baseball was established as the leading sport where the USA was an occupying or intervening military power – Cuba, Venezuela, the Philippines, Guatemala, post-war Japan and South Korea. The spread and status of Japanese martial arts and German *Turnen* were terminated by their ultimate military defeats and subsequent loss of empire. British sports, by contrast, spread through both the formal empire and the immense informal empire of Britain's global economic and cultural connections.

However, the geographical reach and cultural cachet of Britain and British sports did not guarantee their adoption in general, let alone that it would be football that would catch on. In an age of explosive industrialization, the mass societies of the nineteenth and twentieth centuries were unlikely to embrace individual sports – not only did they betoken a world quite separate from the majority of those publics, but the spaces that they are played in do not offer the possibility of a truly huge spectacle. Tennis and other racquet sports can only physically accommodate a limited number of spectators around their courts. Basketball suffers from the same problem. You just cannot build a stadium of 100,000 around a basketball court. Golf necessarily separates both spectators and players.

The appeal of football among team sports as a game to play, watch and follow is well rehearsed: it is simple, cheap and flexible in terms of numbers and playing spaces;

it is easy to learn, accommodating of a great diversity of physiques, and favours no single set of skills, attributes or virtues but requires a command of many. Its insistence on the use of feet and head over hands has proved an infectious and enticing prospect. As a spectacle it offers space for inspired individuals and dogged collectives, creates instantaneously comprehensible narratives, operates in a perpetually changing three-dimensional space and balances the exhilaration of flow with the orgasmic punctuation of the goal.

These lines of reasoning help us explain the scale of football's reach and its victory in the competitive struggle among modern sports for hegemony. What it does not explain is why having taken hold it should exert such an extraordinary level of social fervour. Few have been bold enough to venture such a general theory; to wonder what it is that sustains and animates the spectacular at the heart of modern life. Some have cast football as the circus, a theatre of distraction, an elite conspiracy devoted to the manufacture of consent and the marginalization of dissent. Some see football as the universal religion for an age of disenchantment. Others see its elevation as the triumph of the empty pleasure, the conversion of the ephemeral to the status of the transcendent where, in the ultimate joke at the end of history, ideology is replaced by vacuity.

The notion of football as the bread and circuses of the industrial city is not entirely fanciful. The records of European fascism and communism, Latin American populists and military oligarchies and authoritarian ultra-nationalists all over the developing world, demonstrate the degree to which political power has sought directly to control football and use it as an instrument of legitimacy, distraction or glorification. However, all of these political forms are in decline, if not extinct. They have been replaced by variants, more or less savoury, of representative liberal democracy and bureaucratic authoritarianism that are the dominant polities of the twenty-first century. Everywhere, beyond the tiniest enclaves of actually disintegrating socialism, variants of capitalism and the market constitute the economic order. For the most part, neither liberal democracy nor advanced capitalism requires the degree of active allegiance and collective acclaim that authoritarian and penurious regimes demand of their subjects. They have no need for conscript armies, militias or incendiary mobs. They can sustain their legitimacy without epics and supermen. And if citizens choose not to participate and consumers continue to passively consume, that is enough. Consent is sustained on the Valium of affluence. Only Silvio Berlusconi's experiment in televisual authoritarian demagogy with its umbilical connection to Italian football approximates to the old model. Elsewhere, at worst, modern commercial football could be seen as the mall rather than the circus; insidiously bland, decaffeinated and pre-packed, its relentless formulaic repetition an instrument for disabling consciousness rather than manipulating it.

If the conditions under which football could be used as a form of crude populist propaganda are past, the image of the circus still points us to the intensely dramatic quality of the football spectacle. The theatre has certainly been offered as an alternative model and football could credibly be seen as a parallel but infinitely more popular art form, offering live and improvised performance, narrative twist, character and plot. Yet this captures only a fraction of the practices and pleasures of football cultures, minimizing the non-narrative qualities of a game whose shapes and choreographies are closer to dance than drama. Despite the best attempts of experimental theatre companies, actors and audiences remain rigidly separated in the stage's division of labour. In football the crowd is unquestionably the chorus, not only supplying ambience, commentary and income, but actively shaping the tone and the course of the game. When in full carnival mode, the crowd can even move from out of the wings and take a place on stage. The opportunity that this provides for the collective dramatization of identities and social relationships, both spontaneous and organized, is without parallel in the field of global popular culture. [...]

17

Fear and Money in Dubai

Mike Davis

'As your jet starts its descent, you are glued to your window. The scene below is aston-ishing: a 24-square-mile archipelago of coral-coloured islands in the shape of an almost-finished puzzle of the world. In the shallow green waters between continents, the sunken shapes of the Pyramids of Giza and the Roman Colosseum are clearly visible. In the distance, three other large island groups are configured as palms within crescents and planted with high-rise resorts, amusement parks and a thousand mansions built on stilts over the water. The 'Palms' are connected by causeways to a Miami-like beachfront crammed with mega-hotels, apartment skyscrapers and yachting marinas.

'As the plane slowly banks toward the desert mainland, you gasp at the even more improbable vision ahead. Out of a chrome forest of skyscrapers soars a new Tower of Babel. It is an impossible half-mile high: taller than the Empire State Building stacked on top of itself. You are still rubbing your eyes with wonderment as the plane lands and you are welcomed into an airport shopping emporium where seductive goods entice: Gucci bags, Cartier watches and one-kilogram bars of solid gold. The hotel driver is waiting for you in a Rolls Royce Silver Seraph. Friends had recommended the Armani Inn in the 170-storey tower, or the 7-star hotel with an atrium so huge that the Statue of Liberty would fit inside it, and service so exclusive that the rooms come with personal butlers; but instead you have opted to fulfill a childhood fantasy. You always have wanted to play Captain Nemo in *Twenty Thousand Leagues Under the Sea*.

'Your jellyfish-shaped hotel, the Hydropolis, is, in fact, exactly 66 feet below the surface of the sea. Each of its 220 luxury suites has clear plexiglass walls that provide spectacular views of passing mermaids and of the famed 'underwater fireworks': a hallucinatory exhibition of 'water bubbles, swirled sand and carefully deployed

Original publication details: Mike Davis, "Fear and Money in Dubai," in *New Left Review* 41, September/October, 2006. pp. 47–51, 53, 58–60. Reproduced with permission from New Left Review.

lighting'. Any initial anxiety about the safety of your sea-bottom resort is dispelled by the smiling concierge. The structure has a multi-level fail-safe security system which includes protection against terrorist submarines as well as missiles and aircraft.

'Although you have an important business meeting at Internet City with clients from Hyderabad and Taipei, you have arrived a day early to treat yourself to one of the famed adventures at the 'Restless Planet' themepark. After a soothing night's sleep under the sea, you board a monorail for this Jurassic jungle. Your first encounter is with some peacefully grazing brontosaurs. Next you are attacked by a flock of velociraptors, the animatronic beasts – designed by experts from the British Natural History Museum – so flawlessly lifelike that you shriek in fear and delight. With your adrenaline pumped up by this close call, you round off the afternoon with some snowboarding on the local indoor snow mountain (outdoors, the temperature is 105°). Nearby is the world's largest mall – the altar of the city's famed Shopping Festival, which attracts millions of frenetic consumers each January – but you postpone the temptation. Instead, you indulge in some expensive Thai fusion cuisine. The gorgeous Russian blonde at the restaurant bar stares at you with vampirish hunger, and you wonder whether the local sin is as extravagant as the shopping ...'

Fantasy Levitated

Welcome to a strange paradise. But where are you? Is this a new Margaret Atwood novel, Philip K. Dick's unpublished sequel to *Blade Runner* or Donald Trump on acid? No. It is the Persian Gulf city-state of Dubai in 2010. After Shanghai (current population 15 million), Dubai (current population 1.5 million) is the planet's biggest building site: an emerging dreamworld of conspicuous consumption and what the locals boast as 'supreme lifestyles'. Despite its blast-furnace climate (on typical 120° summer days, the swankier hotels refrigerate their swimming pools) and edge-of-the-war-zone location, Dubai confidently predicts that its enchanted forest of 600 skyscrapers and malls will attract 15 million overseas visitors a year by 2010, three times as many as New York City. Emirates Airlines has placed a staggering $37 billion order for new Boeings and Airbuses to fly these tourists in and out of Dubai's new global air hub, the vast Jebel Ali airport. Indeed, thanks to a dying planet's terminal addiction to Arabian oil, this former fishing village and smugglers' cove proposes to become one of the world capitals of the 21st century. Favouring diamonds over rhinestones, Dubai has already surpassed that other desert arcade of capitalist desire, Las Vegas, both in sheer scale of spectacle and the profligate consumption of water and power.

Dozens of outlandish mega-projects – including the artificial 'island world' (where Rod Stewart has reportedly spent $33 million to buy 'Britain'), the earth's tallest building (Burj Dubai, designed by Skidmore, Owings & Merrill), the underwater luxury hotel, the carnivorous dinosaurs, the domed ski resort and the hyper-mall – are already under construction or about to leave the drawing board. The 7-star hotel, the spinnaker-shaped Burj Al-Arab – looking much like the set of a James Bond film – is already world-famous for its $5,000 per-night rooms with 100-mile views and an exclusive clientele of Arab royalty, English rock stars and Russian billionaires. And the dinosaurs, according to the finance director of the Natural History Museum, 'will have the full stamp of authority of the Museum in London, and will demonstrate that education and science can be fun'; and profitable, since the 'only way into the dinosaur park will be through the shopping mall'.

The biggest project, Dubailand, represents a vertiginous new stage in fantasy environments. Literally a 'themepark of themeparks', it will be more than twice the size of Disney World and employ 300,000 workers who, in turn, will entertain 15 million visitors per year (each spending a minimum of $100 per day, not including accommodation). Like a surrealist encyclopaedia, its 45 major 'world class' projects include replicas of the Hanging Gardens of Babylon, the Taj Mahal and the Pyramids, as well as a snow mountain with ski lifts and polar bears, a centre for 'extreme sports', a Nubian village, 'Eco-Tourism World', a vast Andalusian spa and wellness complex, golf courses, autodromes, race tracks, 'Giants' World', 'Fantasia', the largest zoo in the Middle East, several new 5-star hotels, a modern art gallery and the Mall of Arabia.

Gigantism

Under the enlightened despotism of its Emir and CEO, 58-year-old Sheikh Mohammed al-Maktoum, Dubai has become the new global icon of imagineered urbanism. Multi-billionaire Sheikh Mo – as he is known to Dubai's expats – has a straightforward if immodest goal: 'I want to be Number One in the world'. Although he is an ardent collector of thoroughbreds (the world's largest stable) and super-yachts (the 525-foot-long 'Project Platinum', which has its own submarine and flight deck), his consuming passion is over-the-top, monumental architecture. Indeed, he seems to have imprinted Scott and Venturi's bible of hyper-reality, *Learning From Las Vegas*, in the same way that pious Muslims memorize the *Qur'an*. One of his proudest achievements, he often tells visitors, is to have introduced gated communities to Arabia, the land of nomads and tents.

Thanks to his boundless enthusiasm for concrete and steel, the coastal desert has become a huge circuit board upon which the elite of transnational engineering firms and retail developers are invited to plug in high-tech clusters, entertainment zones, artificial islands, glass-domed 'snow mountains', *Truman Show* suburbs, cities within cities – whatever is big enough to be seen from space and bursting with architectural steroids. The result is not a hybrid but an eerie chimera: a promiscuous coupling of all the cyclopean fantasies of Barnum, Eiffel, Disney, Spielberg, Jon Jerde, Steve Wynn and Skidmore, Owings & Merrill. Although compared variously to Las Vegas, Manhattan, Orlando, Monaco and Singapore, the sheikhdom is more like their collective summation and mythologization: a hallucinatory pastiche of the big, the bad and the ugly.

The same phantasmagoric but generic Lego blocks, of course, can be found in dozens of aspiring cities these days (including Dubai's envious neighbours, the wealthy oil oases of Doha and Bahrain), but al-Maktoum has a distinctive and invio-lable criterion: everything must be 'world class', by which he means Number One in the Guinness Book of Records. Thus Dubai is building the world's largest theme park, the biggest mall (and within it, the largest aquarium), the tallest building, the largest international airport, the biggest artificial island, the first sunken hotel and so on. Although such architectural megalomania is eerily reminiscent of Albert Speer and his patron's vision of imperial Berlin, it is not irrational. Having 'learned from Las Vegas', al-Maktoum understands that if Dubai wants to become the luxury-consumer paradise of the Middle East and South Asia (its officially defined 'home market' of 1.6 billion), it must ceaselessly strive for visual and environmental excess. If, as Rowan Moore has suggested, immense, psychotic assemblages of fantasy kitsch inspire vertigo, then al-Maktoum wants us to swoon.

From a booster's viewpoint, the city's monstrous caricature of futurism is simply shrewd branding for the world market. As one developer told the *Financial Times*, 'If there was no Burj Dubai, no Palm, no World, would anyone be speaking of Dubai today? You shouldn't look at projects as crazy stand-alones. It's part of building the brand'. And its owners love it when architects and urbanists, like George Katodrytis, anoint it as the cutting edge:

> Dubai is a prototype of the new post-global city, which creates appetites rather than solves problems ... If Rome was the 'Eternal City' and New York's Manhattan the apotheosis of twentieth-century congested urbanism, then Dubai may be considered the emerging prototype for the 21st century: prosthetic and nomadic oases presented as isolated cities that extend out over the land and sea.

In its exponential quest to conquer the architectural record-books, moreover, Dubai has only one real rival: China – a country that now has 300,000 millionaires and is predicted to become the world's largest market for luxury goods (from Gucci to Mercedes) in a few years. [...]

War Zone

[...]

In many complex and surprising ways, Dubai actually earns its living from fear. Its huge port complex at Jebel Ali, for example, has profited immeasurably from the trade generated by the US invasion of Iraq, while Terminal Two at the Dubai airport, always crowded with Halliburton employees, private mercenaries and American soldiers en route to Baghdad or Kabul, has been described as 'the busiest commercial terminal in the world' for America's Middle East wars. Post-9/11 developments have also shifted global investment patterns to Dubai's benefit. Thus after al-Qaeda's attacks on America, the Muslim oil states, traumatized by the angry Christians in Washington and lawsuits by WTC survivors, no longer considered the United States the safest harbour for their petrodollars. Panicky Saudis alone are estimated to have repatriated at least one-third of their trillion-dollar overseas portfolio. Although nerves are now calmer, Dubai has benefited enormously from the continuing inclination of the oil sheikhs to invest within, rather than outside, the region. As Edward Chancellor has emphasized, 'unlike the last oil boom of the late 1970s, relatively little of the current Arab oil surplus has been directly invested in US assets or even deposited in the international banking system. This time much of the oil money has remained at home where a classic speculative mania is now being played out.'

[…]

Much of this money, of course, dances to an old tune. 'A majority of new Dubai properties', explains *Business Week*, 'are being acquired for speculative purposes, with only small deposits put down. They are being flipped in the contemporary Miami manner.' But what is too often 'flipped', some economists predict, may ultimately flop. Will Dubai someday fall from the sky when this real-estate balloon bursts, or will peak oil keep this desert Laputa floating above the contradictions of the world economy? Al-Maktoum remains a mountain of self-confidence: 'I would like to tell capitalists that Dubai does not need investors; investors need Dubai. And I tell you that the risk lies not in using your money, but in letting it pile up.'

Dubai's philosopher-king (one of the huge offshore island projects will actually spell out an epigram of his in Arabic script) is well aware that fear is also the most dynamic component of the oil revenues that turn his sand dunes into malls and sky-scrapers. Every time insurgents blow up a pipeline in the Niger Delta, a martyr drives his truck bomb into a Riyadh housing complex, or Washington and Tel Aviv rattle their sabres at Tehran, the price of oil (and thus Dubai's ultimate income) increases by some increment of anxiety in the all-important futures market. The Gulf economies, in other words, are now capitalized not just on oil production, but also on the fear of its disruption. According to a recent survey of experts by *Business Week*, 'the world paid the Persian Gulf oil states an extra $120 billion or so last year because of the premium in prices due to fear of unexpected supply disruptions. Some cynics argue that oil producers welcome the fear of disruption because it boosts their revenues'. 'Fear', according to one of the senior energy analysts that the magazine consulted, 'is a gift to oil producers'.

But it is a gift that the oil rich would rather spend in a tranquil oasis surrounded by very high walls. With its sovereignty ultimately guaranteed by the American nuclear super-carriers usually berthed at Jebel Ali, as well as by whatever secret protocols (negotiated during falcon hunting trips in Afghanistan?) govern the Emiratis' relation-ship to Islamic terrorism, Dubai is a paradise of personal security, from the Swiss-style laws governing financial secrecy to the armies of concierges, watchmen and bodyguards who protect its sanctums of luxury. Tourists are customarily ordered away by the security guards if they attempt to sneak a peek at Burj Al-Arab on its private island. Hotel guests, of course, arrive in Rolls Royces.

[…]

18

An Anthropology of Structural Violence

Paul Farmer

The ethnographically visible, central Haiti, September 2000: Most hospitals in the region are empty. This is not because of a local lack of treatable pathology; rather, patients have no money to pay for such care. One hospital – situated in a squatter settlement just 8 kilometers from a hydroelectric dam that decades ago flooded a fertile valley – is crowded. Medicines and laboratory studies are free. Every bed is filled, and the courtyard in front of the clinic is mobbed with patients waiting to be seen. Over a hundred have slept on the grounds the night before and are struggling to smooth out wrinkles in hand-me-down dresses or pants or shirts; hats are being adjusted, and some are massaging painful cricks in the neck. The queue of those waiting to have a new medical record created is long, snaking toward the infectious-disease clinic I am hoping to reach. First, however, it is better to scan the crowd for those who should be seen immediately.

Less ethnographically visible is the fact that Haiti is under democratic rule. For the first time in almost two centuries, democratic elections are planned and could result in a historic precedent: President René Préval, elected some years earlier, could actually survive his presidency to transfer power to another democratically elected president. If Préval succeeds, he will be the first president in Haitian history ever to serve out his mandate, not a day more, not a day less.

To local eyes, the prospect of this victory (which later did indeed come to pass) is overwhelmed by the vivid poverty seeping into the very seams of Haitian society. For the rural poor, most of them peasants, this means erosion and lower crop yields; it means hunger and sickness. And every morning the crowd in front of the clinic seems to grow.

To foreign eyes, the Haitian story has become a confused skein of tragedies, most of them seen as local. Poverty, crime, accidents, disease, death – and more often than

Original publication details: Paul Farmer, "An Anthropology of Structural Violence," in *Current Anthropology*, 45, 3, June 2004. pp. 305–7, 316–17.

not their causes – are also seen as problems locally derived. The transnational tale of slavery and debt and turmoil is lost in the vivid poverty, the understanding of which seems to defeat the analyses of journalists and even many anthropologists, focused as we are on the ethnographically visible – what is there in front of us.

Making my way through this crowd has become a daily chore and triage – seeking out the sickest – a ritual in the years since I became medical director of the clinic. Now the morning sun angles into the courtyard, but the patients are shaded by tall ficus trees, planted there years before. The clinic and hospital were built into the hillside over the previous 15 years, but the dense foliage gives the impression that the buildings have been there for decades.

I see two patients on makeshift stretchers; both are being examined by auxiliary nurses armed with stethoscopes and blood-pressure cuffs. Perhaps this morning it will take less than an hour to cross the 600 or so yards that separate me from another crowd of patients already diagnosed with tuberculosis or AIDS. These are the patients I am hoping to see, but it is also my duty to see to the larger crowd, which promises, on this warm Wednesday morning, to overwhelm the small Haitian medical staff.

A young woman takes my arm in a common enough gesture in rural Haiti. "Look at this, doctor." She lifts a left breast mass. The tumor is not at all like the ones I was taught to search for during my medical training in Boston. This lesion started as an occult lump, perhaps, but by this September day has almost completely replaced the normal breast. It is a "fungating mass," in medical jargon, and clear yellow fluid weeps down the front of a light-blue dress. Flies are drawn to the diseased tissue, and the woman waves them away mechanically. On either side of her, a man and a woman help her with this task, but they are not kin, simply other patients waiting in the line.

"Good morning," I say, although I know that she is expecting me to say next to nothing and wants to be the speaker. She lifts the tumor toward me and begins speaking rapidly.

"It's hard and painful," she says. "Touch it and see how hard it is." Instead, I lift my hand to her axilla and find large, hard lymph nodes there – likely advanced and metastatic cancer – and I interrupt her as politely as I can. If only this were a neglected infection, I think. Not impossible, only very unlikely. I need to know how long this woman has been ill.

But the woman, whose name is Anite, will have none of it. She is going to tell the story properly, and I will have to listen. We are surrounded by hundreds, and at least 40 can hear every word of the exchange. I think to pull her from the line, but she wants to talk in front of her fellow sufferers. For years I have studied and written about these peculiarly Haitian modes of declaiming about one's travails, learning how such jeremiads are crafted for a host of situations and audiences. There is so much to complain about. Now I have time only to see patients as a physician and precious little time for interviewing them. I miss this part of my work, but although I want to hear Anite's story, I want even more to attend to her illness. And to do that properly will require a surgeon, unless she has come with a diagnosis made elsewhere. I look away from the tumor. She carries, in addition to a hat and a small bundle of oddments, a white vinyl purse. Please, I think, let there be useful information in there. Surely she has seen other doctors for a disease process that is, at a minimum, months along?

I interrupt again to ask her where she has come from and if she has sought care elsewhere. We do not have a surgeon on staff just now. We have been promised, a weary functionary at the Ministry of Health has told me, that the Cuban government will soon be sending us a surgeon and a pediatrician. But for this woman, Anite, time has run out.

"I was about to tell you that, doctor." She has let go of my arm to lift the mass, but now she grips it again. "I am from near Jérémie," she says, referring to a small city on the tip of Haiti's southern peninsula – about as far from our clinic as one could be and still be in Haiti. To reach us, Anite must have passed through Port-au-Prince, with its private clinics, surgeons, and oncologists.

"I first noticed a lump in my breast after falling down. I was carrying a basket of millet on my head. It was not heavy, but it was large, and I had packed it poorly, perhaps. The path was steep, but it had not rained on that day, so I don't know why I fell. It makes you wonder, though." At least a dozen heads in line nod in assent, and some of Anite's fellow patients make noises encouraging her to continue.

"How long ago was that?" I ask again.

"I went to many clinics," she says in front of dozens of people she has met only that morning or perhaps the night before. "I went to 14 clinics." Again, many nod assent. The woman to her left says "Adjè!" meaning something along the lines of "You poor thing!" and lifts a finger to her cheek. This crowd response seems to please Anite, who continues her narrative with gathering tempo. She still has not let me know how long she has been ill.

"Fourteen clinics," I respond. "What did they say was wrong with you? Did you have an operation or a biopsy?" The mass is now large and has completely destroyed the normal architecture of her breast; it is impossible to tell if she has had a procedure, as there is no skin left to scar.

"No," replies Anite. "Many told me I needed an operation, but the specialist who could do this was in the city, and it costs $700 to see him. In any case, I had learned in a dream that it was not necessary to go to the city." ("The city" means Port-au-Prince, Haiti's capital.)

More of the crowd turns to listen; the shape of the line changes subtly, beginning to resemble more of a circle. I think uncomfortably of the privacy of a US examination room and of the fact that I have never seen there a breast mass consume so much flesh without ever having been biopsied. But I have seen many in Haiti, and almost all have proven malignant.

Anite continues her narrative. She repeats that on the day of the fall, she discovered the mass. It was "small and hard," she says. "An abscess, I thought, for I was breast-feeding and had an infection while breastfeeding once before." This is about as clinical as the story is to get, for Anite returns to the real tale. She hurt her back in the fall. How was she to care for her children and for her mother, who was sick and lived with her? "They all depend on me. There was no time."

And so the mass grew slowly "and worked its way under my arm." I give up trying to establish chronology. I know it had to be months or even years ago that she first discovered this "small" mass. She had gone to clinic after clinic, she says, "spending our very last little money. No one told me what I had. I took many pills."

"What kind of pills?" I ask.

Anite continues. "Pills. I don't know what kind." She had given biomedicine its proper shot, she seems to say, but it had failed her. Perhaps her illness had more mysterious origins? "Maybe someone sent this my way," she says. "But I'm a poor woman – why would someone wish me ill?"

"Unlikely," says an older man in line. "It's God's sickness." Anite had assumed as much – "God's sickness" being shorthand for natural illness rather than illness associated with sorcery – but had gone to a local temple, a *houmfor*, to make sure. "The reason I went was because I'd had a dream. The mass was growing, and there were three other small masses growing under my arm. I had a dream in which a voice told me to stop taking medicines and to travel far away for treatment of this illness."

She had gone to a voodoo priest for help in interpreting this dream. Each of the lumps had significance, said the priest. They represented "the three mysteries," and to be cured she would have to travel to a clinic where doctors "worked with both hands" (this term suggesting that they would have to understand both natural and supernatural illness).

The story would have been absurd if it were not so painful. I know, and once knew more, about some of the cultural referents; I am familiar with the style of illness narrative dictating some of the contours of her story and the responses of those in line. But Anite has, I am almost sure, metastatic breast cancer. What she needs is surgery and chemotherapy if she is lucky (to my knowledge, there is no radiation therapy in Haiti at this time). She does not need, I think, to tell her story publicly for at least the fifteenth time.

Anite seems to gather strength from the now-rapt crowd, all with their own stories to tell the harried doctors and nurses once they get into the clinic. The semi-circle continues to grow. Some of the patients are straining, I can tell, for a chance to tell their own stories, but no one interrupts Anite. "In order to cure this illness, he told me, I would have to travel far north and east."

It has taken Anite over a week to reach our clinic. A diagnosis of metastatic breast cancer is later confirmed.

[…]

[…] Since the syndrome was first described, AIDS has also been termed a "social disease" and has been studied by social scientists, including anthropologists. Theses and books have been written. One scholar wrote, early on, of an "epidemic of signification". When AIDS was first recognized, in the early eighties, it was soon apparent that it was an infectious disease, even though other, more exotic interpretations abounded at the time. Well before Luc Montagner discovered HIV, many believed that the etiologic agent was a never-before described virus, and people wanted to know, as they so often do, where this new sickness came from. During the eighties the hypotheses circulating in the United States suggested that HIV came to the United States from Haiti. Newspaper articles, television reports, and even scholarly publications confidently posited a scenario in which Haitian professionals who had fled the Duvalier regime ended up in western Africa and later brought the new virus back to Haiti, which introduced it to the Americas. AIDS was said to proliferate in Haiti because of strange practices involving voodoo blood rituals and animal sacrifice.

These theories are ethnographically absurd, but they are wrong in other ways, too. First, they happened to be incorrect epidemiologically. AIDS in Haiti had nothing to do with voodoo or Africa. Second, they had an adverse effect on Haiti – the tourism industry collapse in the mid-eighties was due in large part to rumors about HIV – and on Haitians living in North America and Europe. The perception that "Haitian" was almost synonymous with "HIV-infected" in the minds of many US citizens, has been well documented.

How, then, was HIV introduced to the island nation of Haiti? An intracellular organism must necessarily cross water in a human host. It was clear from the outset that HIV did not come to Haiti from Africa. None of the first Haitians diagnosed with the new syndrome had ever been to Africa; most had never met an African. But many did have histories of sexual contact with North Americans. In a 1984 paper published in a scholarly journal, the Haitian physician Jean Guérin and colleagues revealed that 17% of their patients reported a history of sexual contact with tourists from North America. These exchanges involved the exchange of money, too, and so "sexual tourism" – which inevitably takes place across steep grades of economic inequality – was a critical first step in the introduction of HIV to Haiti. In fact, the viral subtype ("clade") seen in Haiti is a reflection of the fact that the Haitian AIDS epidemic is a subepidemic of the one already existing in the United States (see Farmer 1992, 1999).

There is more, of course, to the "hidden history" of AIDS in Haiti. By the time HIV was circulating in the Americas, Haiti was economically dependent not on France, as in previous centuries, but on the United States. From the time of the US military occupation through the Duvalier dictatorships (1957–86), the United States had come to occupy the role of chief arbiter of Haitian affairs. After the withdrawal of troops in 1934, US influence in Haiti grew rather than waned. US-Haitian agribusiness projects may have failed, deepening social inequalities throughout Haiti as the rural peasantry became poorer, but US-Haitian ties did not. Haiti became a leading recipient of US "aid," and the United States and the "international financial institutions" were the Duvalier family's most reliable source of foreign currency. Haiti became, in turn, the ninth-largest assembler of US goods in the world and bought almost all of its imports from the United States. Tourism and *sous-traitance* (offshore assembly) replaced coffee and other agricultural products as the chief sources of foreign revenue in Haiti.

Haiti is the extreme example of a general pattern. If one uses trade data to assess the degree of Caribbean-basin countries' dependency on the United States at the time HIV appeared in the region, one sees that the five countries with the tightest ties to the United States were the five countries with the highest HIV prevalence. Cuba is the only country in the region not linked closely to the United States. Not coincidentally, Cuba was and remains the country with the lowest prevalence of HIV in the Americas. It was possible to conclude an earlier book on the subject by asserting that "AIDS in Haiti is about proximity rather than distance. AIDS in Haiti is a tale of ties to the United States, rather than to Africa; it is a story of unemployment rates greater than 70 percent. AIDS in Haiti has far more to do with the pursuit of trade and tourism in a dirt-poor country than with, to cite Alfred Métraux again, "dark saturnalia celebrated by 'blood-maddened, sex-maddened, god-maddened' negroes."

But this was merely the beginning of a biosocial story of the virus. The Haitian men who had been the partners of North Americans were by and large poor men; they were trading sex for money. The Haitians in turn transmitted HIV to their wives and girlfriends. Through affective and economic connections, HIV rapidly became entrenched in Haiti's urban slums and then spread to smaller cities, towns, and, finally, villages like the one in which I work. Haiti is now the most HIV-affected country in the Americas, but the introduction and spread of the new virus has a history – a bio-social history that some would like to hide away.

Like many anthropologists, I was not always careful to avoid stripping away the social from the material. But HIV, though hastened forward by many social forces, is as material as any other microbe. Once in the body, its impact is profound both biologically and socially. As cell-mediated immunity is destroyed, poor people living with HIV are felled more often than not by tuberculosis. Last year, HIV was said to surpass tuberculosis as the leading infectious cause of adult death, but in truth these two epidemics are tightly linked. Further, merely looking at the impact of HIV on life expectancy in certain sub-Saharan African nations lets us know that this virus has had, in the span of a single generation, a profound effect on kinship structure.

All this is both interesting and horrible. What might have been done to avert the deaths caused by these two pathogens? What might be done right now? One would think that the tuberculosis question, at least, could be solved. Because there is no non-human host, simply detecting and treating promptly all active cases would eventually result in an end to deaths from this disease. Money and political will are what is missing – which brings us back to structural violence and its supporting hegemonies: the materiality of the social.

AIDS, one could argue, is thornier. There is no cure, but current therapies have had a profound impact on mortality among favored populations in the United States and Europe. The trick is to get therapy to those who need it most. Although this will require significant resources, the projected cost over the next few years is less than the monies allocated in a single day for rescuing the US airlines industry. But the supporting hegemonies have already decreed AIDS an unmanageable problem. The justifications are often byzantine. For example, a high-ranking official within the US Department of the Treasury (who wisely declined to be named) has argued that Africans have "a different concept of time" and would therefore be unable to take their medications on schedule; hence, no investment in AIDS therapy for Africa. The head of the US Agency for International Development later identified a lack of wristwatches as the primary stumbling block. Cheap wristwatches are not unheard of, but, as I have said, the primary problem is a matter of political will. Others have underlined, more honestly, the high costs of medications or the lack of health-care infrastructure in the countries hit hardest by HIV. Still others point to fear of acquisition of resistance to antiretroviral medications. The list is familiar to those interested in tuberculosis and other treatable, chronic diseases that disproportionately strike the poor.

The distribution of AIDS and tuberculosis – like that of slavery in earlier times – is historically given and economically driven. What common features underpin the afflictions of past and present centuries? Social inequalities are at the heart of structural violence. Racism of one form or another, gender inequality, and above all brute poverty in the face of affluence are linked to social plans and programs ranging from slavery to the current quest for unbridled growth. These conditions are the cause and result of displacements, wars both declared and undeclared, and the seething, submerged hatreds that make the irruption of *Schadenfreude* a shock to those who can afford to ignore, for the most part, the historical underpinnings of today's conflicts. Racism and related sentiments – disregard, even hatred, for the poor – underlie the current lack of resolve to address these and other problems squarely. It is not sufficient to change attitudes, but attitudes do make other things happen.

Structural violence is the natural expression of a political and economic order that seems as old as slavery. This social web of exploitation, in its many differing historical forms, has long been global, or almost so, in its reach. [...]

19

Crazy Like Us

The Globalization of the American Psyche

Ethan Watters

[...]

The Japanese public's impression that the country was behind the times in addressing mental health got a boost after the devastating earthquake in the city of Kobe in January 1995. The government response to the disaster was criticized by Western mental health experts for being lackluster on many fronts. Researchers from the United States were soon on the scene and garnered much press attention by suggesting that the population needed not just food and shelter but more attention paid to their emotional and mental health.

Several prominent Japanese psychiatrists and mental health advocates used the authority of the visiting mental health experts to make a broad argument that Japanese culture discouraged talking about emotionally loaded issues. "The comparison, quite unfavorable to Japan, was often made to the United States, where the emphasis on psychological issues is generally believed to be culturally strong and given proper priority," the anthropologist Joshua Breslau reported. "One well-known newspaper critic noted that his friend told him how nearly everyone in US cities has a psychological counselor."

A critical turning point came just three months after the Kobe quake. A TV producer named Kenichiro Takiguchi was browsing through the English-language section of a Tokyo bookstore and started to flip through a paperback copy of Peter Kramer's American best seller *Listening to Prozac*. Always on the lookout for good ideas for programs, he took the book to his bosses at Japan's largest television network and persuaded them to let him produce a fifty-minute special. The message of the special was similar to the beliefs made popular after the Kobe earthquake, namely, that Americans were far advanced in their recognition and treatment of emotional disorders such as depression and anxiety. The show hit a nerve. Millions

Original publication details: Ethan Watters, *Crazy Like Us: The Globalization of the American Psyche*. New York: Free Press, 2010. pp. 220–8, 245–6. Reproduced with permission from SLL/Sterling Lord Literistic. Copyright Ethan Watters.

The Globalization Reader, Fifth Edition. Edited by Frank J. Lechner and John Boli.
Editorial material and organization © 2015 John Wiley & Sons, Ltd.
Published 2015 by John Wiley & Sons, Ltd.

watched and more than two thousand viewers called in afterward to praise the net-work for running the program.

Japanese psychiatrists were largely taken by surprise at this turn in public interest. Up to that point the public had eschewed the intrusion of psychiatry into daily life. As the small population of psychiatrists had mostly limited their practice to the severely mentally ill, the call to address common unhappiness and anxiety that came with bad economic times caught them off-guard. Like many people in the country up to that point, they had not considered unhappiness (or divorce or suicide) a mental health issue. They were in need of a new and compelling explanation for what was going on. Fortunately for them, GlaxoSmithKline and several other major psychopharmaceuti-cal companies were just then preparing to throw them a lifeline.

Junk Science and First World Medicine

Kalman Applbaum, a professor at the University of Wisconsin in Milwaukee, is an anthropologist, but he doesn't study little-known tribes in far-off lands. His interest is closer at hand: the rituals and practices of international corporations. His specialty, the anthropology of the boardroom, has led to teaching posts both in anthropology departments and at business schools, including Harvard and Kellogg. He is also fluent in Japanese and often consults with companies interested in the Asian markets. When he heard in the late 1990s that major players in the pharmaceutical industry were attempting to introduce SSRIs to Japan, he knew he had the topic for his next set of research papers.

At the beginning of the new millennium, Applbaum went out of his way to visit the headquarters of GlaxoSmithKline, Lilly, and Pfizer, the major international players who were at various stages of trying to get their drugs into Japan. At the time both Pfizer and Lilly were playing catch-up to GlaxoSmithKline, which was just then launching Paxil in the country. Although he had to sign non-disclosure agreements promising that he wouldn't identify the executives by name or company affiliation, Applbaum managed to get remarkable access to the inner workings of these com-panies. Several of his former MBA students who were then working in these firms helped make key introductions, but in the end these executives proved more than willing to talk. When I asked Applbaum why they were so forthcoming, he told me it was simple: because of his business school credentials and his extensive experience in the Japanese market, they thought he might be able to give them some free advice.

Applbaum discovered that the companies intent on entering the SSRI market in Japan were not battling each other like Coke and Pepsi for market share – or at least not at the beginning. Instead he found wide acknowledgment within the ranks of drug company executives that the best way for companies to create a market was for competing companies to join forces.

A critical player in this joint effort was the trade organization Pharmaceutical Manufacturers of America, or PhRMA, which functions as the national and interna-tional lobby and public relations organization for a coalition of major drug com-panies. In the late 1990s Applbaum found PhRMA working on a number of levels in

Japan to influence what they considered to be a backward and bureaucratic drug approval process. As one PhRMA executive based in Chiyoda-Ku, Tokyo, told Applbaum, their job was to create "a market based upon competitive, customer choice and a transparent pricing structure that supports innovation." The lobby wanted drugs such as Paxil to be able to enter new markets based on "global, objective, scientific standards."

The more Applbaum talked to drug company insiders, the more righteous frustration he found. When he visited the offices of a leading SSRI manufacturer in November 2001, he discovered a wellspring of anger directed at what they perceived as Japanese resistance to pharmaceutical progress. These executives criticized scientific standards for clinical testing in Japan as "quite poor" and asserted that there was no "good clinical practice" in the country. Why, they asked Applbaum rhetorically, should their company be forced to retest these drugs in exclusively Japanese populations? The assumption was that the science behind the American human trials was unassailable – certainly better than anything the Japanese would attempt.

No doubt that annoyance at having to retest drugs was so intense because a couple of recent large-scale human trials of SSRIs in Japan had *failed* to show any positive effects. Drugs such as Pfizer's Zoloft, which were widely prescribed in the United States, had at least one large-scale human trial failure in Japan in the 1990s. Instead of considering the meaning of such results, the drug company executives railed at Japanese testing practices, calling them second rate. "There is no sense of urgency about patient need in Japan," one executive complained to Applbaum.

The Mega-Marketing of Depression

Although drug company executives clearly would have preferred to avoid the expensive and time-consuming process of retesting their SSRIs in Japan, they ultimately found a way to put those trials to good use as the first step in their marketing campaign. The drug makers often bought full-page ads in newspapers in the guise of recruiting test subjects. Applbaum believes that this was one of several savvy methods the drug companies employed to sidestep the prohibitions in Japan on marketing prescription drugs directly to the consumer. These advertisements, supposedly designed only to recruit people for the trials, were well worth the cost, as they both featured the brand name of the drug and promoted the idea of depression as a common ailment. One company scored even more public attention when it recruited a well-known actress to take part in the trials.

But getting the drug approved for market was only the first step. Talking with these executives, it became clear to Applbaum that they were intent on implementing a complex and multifaceted plan to, as he put it, "alter the total environment in which these drugs are or may be used." Applbaum took to calling this a "mega-marketing" campaign – an effort to shape the very consciousness of the Japanese consumer.

The major problem GlaxoSmithKline faced was that Japanese psychiatrists and mental health professionals still translated the diagnosis of "depression" as *utsubyô*, and in the mind of many Japanese that word retained its association with an incurable and inborn depression of psychotic proportions. In hopes of softening the connotations of the word, the marketers hit upon a metaphor that proved remarkably effective. Depression, they repeated in advertising and promotional material, was *kokoro no kaze*, like "a cold of the soul." It is not clear who first came up with the phrase. It is possible that it originated from Kenichiro Takiguchi's prime-time special on depression. In that show, it was said that Americans took anti-depressants the way other cultures took cold medicine.

Whatever its origin, the line *kokoro no kaze* appealed to the drug marketers, as it effectively shouldered three messages at the same time. First, it implied that *utsubyô* was not the severe condition it was once thought to be and therefore should carry no social stigma. Who would think less of someone for having a cold? Second, it suggested that the choice of taking a medication for depression should be as simple and worry-free as buying a cough syrup or an antihistamine. Third, the phrase communicated that, like common colds, depression was ubiquitous. Everyone, after all, from time to time suffers from a cold.

Although advertising couldn't mention particular drugs, companies could run spots in the guise of public service announcements encouraging people to seek professional help for depression. In these ads SSRI makers attempted to distance depression further from the endogenous depression as it was understood by Japanese psychiatrists for most of the century. One GlaxoSmithKline television advertisement showed an attractive young woman standing in a green field, asking, "How long has it been? How long has it been since you began to worry that it might be depression?" The scene then shows a woman on an escalator and then a middle-aged office worker staring out a bus window. The voiceover then recommends that if you've been feeling down for a month, "do not endure it. Go see a doctor."

[…]

Depression was so broadly defined by the marketers that it clearly encompassed classic emotions and behaviors formerly attributed to the melancholic personality type. The label of depression then took on some laudable characteristics, such as being highly sensitive to the welfare of others and to discord within the family or group. Being depressed in this way became a testament to one's deeply empathic nature.

To get these messages out to the Japanese public, the SSRI makers employed a variety of techniques and avenues. Company marketers quickly reproduced and widely disseminated articles in newspapers and magazines mentioning the rise of depression, particularly if those pieces touted the benefits of SSRIs. The companies also sponsored the translation of several best-selling books first published in the United States on depression and the use of antidepressants.

Given all the ways that GlaxoSmithKline and the other SSRI makers managed to make the average Japanese aware of their drugs, the official ban on direct-to-consumer marketing became almost meaningless. If there was any doubt about this, one only had to look at how these companies used the Internet. "The best way to reach patients today is not via advertising but the Web," one Tokyo-based marketing manager told Applbaum. "The Web basically circumvents [direct-to-consumer advertising] rules, so there is no need to be concerned over these. People go to the company website and take a quiz to see whether they might have depression. If yes, then they go to the doctor and ask for medication."

The mega-marketing campaign often came in disguised forms, such as patient advocacy groups that were actually created by the drug companies themselves. The website utu-net.com, which appeared to be a coalition of depressed patients and their advocates, was funded by GlaxoSmithKline, although visitors to the site would have had no clue of the connection. What they would have found was a series of articles on depression driving home the key points of the campaign, including the idea that it was a common illness and that antidepressants bring the brain's natural chemistry back into balance.

The public interest in the new diagnosis brought a remarkable amount of media attention. Often in back-to-back months, the major magazines *Toyo Keizai* and *DaCapo* ran pieces on depression and the new drugs. In 2002 a leading Japanese business magazine ran a twenty-six-page cover story encouraging businesspeople to seek professional help for depression. The article rather perfectly mirrored the key points of the SSRI makers' mega-marketing campaign and in many ways reflected the early conceptions of neurasthenia a century before. The article suggested that it was the more talented and hard-charging workers who were the most susceptible to depression. Estimates of how many Japanese secretly suffered from depression, which ranged from 3 to 17 percent of the population, seemed to increase every month.

[…]

The SSRI makers made much of one public relations windfall in particular. It was rumored for years (and finally confirmed by the Imperial Household Agency) that Crown Princess Masako suffered from depression. Soon it was revealed that she was taking antidepressants as part of her treatment. This was a huge boost for the profile of depression and SSRIs in the country. Princess Masako's personal psychiatrist was none other than Yutaka Ono, one of the field's leaders that GlaxoSmithKline had feted at the Kyoto conference in 2001.

[…]

Early Adopters Have Second Thoughts

There is no doubt that the efforts of GlaxoSmithKline in Japan proved profitable. In just the first year on the market Paxil sales brought in over 100 million dollars. At the end of 2002 the company reported, "Sales of Seroxat/Paxil, GSK's leading product for depression and anxiety disorders, was the driver of growth in the CNS (Central Nervous System) therapy area, with sales of 3.1 billion, up 15% globally and 18% in the USA. International Sales of Paxil Grew 27% to $401 million led by continued strong growth in Japan, where the product was launched only two years ago." By 2008 sales of Paxil were over one billion dollars per year in Japan.

Kitanaka has been stunned to see how fast things have changed in Japan since SSRIs were introduced. "The whole culture surrounding psychiatry has changed drastically," she told me. "From a stigmatizing notion that no one talked about, depression has become one of the top concerns of people. It has become a legitimate disease at so many different levels and at the same time these changes have transformed the nature of depression as an experience itself."

Some Japanese psychiatrists, even Ono and Tajima, whom the company feted in 2000, felt they were not leading this new trend but reacting to it. Ono reports that starting in 2001 he suddenly had a rush of patients showing up at his office with either a magazine article or an advertisement in hand and wanting to talk about their depression. It was clear to him that the mild symptoms these patients described would not previously have been considered an illness. As more and more Japanese began to identify themselves as depressed and as the risks of SSRIs came to his attention, he has wondered if there were ways to reverse the trend.

"The marketing campaign has been in many ways too successful. The slogan, depression is like a 'cold of the soul,' has convinced far too many people to seek medical treatment for something that is often not an illness," Ono told me. "Perhaps we could start saying that depression is like a 'cancer of the soul.' That would be more accurate and perhaps not so many people would be willing to adopt that belief."

[…]

Part III Questions

1. What are the two "waves of globalization," in Lechner's analysis? How was the expansion of the world economy in the first wave different from that of the second wave? In what ways did the second wave result in connectivity that was "stronger, wider, and more intricate"?
2. How does the tuna trade exemplify key features of contemporary globalization, according to Bestor? Why are tuna farms a kind of global enterprise? Does the globalization of sushi show that cultural differences are disappearing?
3. How does the experience of McDonald's customers in Hong Kong resemble and differ from that of their counterparts in the West? How does Watson use his case study to argue that "the transnational is the local"? What assumptions about cultural globalization does he challenge?
4. How do migrants like the ones described by Levitt lead "bifocal" lives, attached to two places at once? Concretely, how do Dominican migrants in the United States affect life "back home"? What makes their villages of origin "transnational"?
5. How did soccer spread as part of Britain's former "informal empire," according to Goldblatt? Who exactly were its chief promoters? Did soccer's success also show signs of imperial weakness? Do you agree with the reasons that Goldblatt gives for soccer's "victory in the competitive struggle of modern sports for hegemony"? What examples might illustrate his point about the game's role in the "collective dramatization of identities"?
6. Sheikh Mohammed al-Maktoum of Dubai insists that everything in his futuristic city-state be "world class." What does this term mean? How does it reflect globalization? How has fear helped create the "strange paradise" that has made this desert city a major business center and tourist destination?

7. What does Farmer mean by saying that Haiti has been subject to "structural violence?" What role does sex tourism play in the plight of Haiti's people? What factors account for the extreme poverty of Haiti, in contrast with the extreme affluence of Dubai?
8. How does Watters explain the process by which the concept of depression gained a foothold in Japan? Is this "globalization of the American psyche" destructive of other cultures? Why would American concepts of mental illness and treatment be especially likely to spread to other countries?

Part IV

Globalization and the World Economy

Introduction

Since World War II, economic globalization has been far-reaching and intensive. The value of world trade has increased more than a thousand-fold, growing considerably faster than the overall economy. Foreign investment has soared far beyond earlier levels, as companies have established plants in other countries and investors have added foreign stocks to their portfolios. Corporations with global reach have become dominant in many economic sectors, from oil to computers, from automobiles to retail. The financial world has also grown smaller, as new technologies have enabled traders to track information globally and to shift assets instantaneously. While cross-border transactions are by no means friction-free, barriers of all sorts, especially tariffs on goods and services, have come down. In contrast with the initial decades after World War II, when many countries still pursued inwardly oriented growth strategies, almost all parts of the world are highly integrated into a single world economy in which several "developing" countries, notably the "BRIC" group of Brazil, Russia, India, and China, now play a much more significant role.

In this more integrated system, events in one place can quickly ripple through the rest of the world, as was dramatically demonstrated in the global economic crisis that hammered the world economy starting in 2007. The initial blow was the bursting of the unsustainable price bubble in the US housing market, which had ballooned during years of low interest rates, careless lending by banks and other financial institutions, and carefree borrowing by consumers who blithely assumed that housing prices would rise forever. The bursting of the bubble sent shock waves through the world economy as financial institutions suddenly found themselves facing a severe liquidity crunch. What made the shock waves all the more damaging was the fact that housing prices had also ballooned in many other countries, rendering their financial systems highly vulnerable to a credit squeeze.

The Globalization Reader, Fifth Edition. Edited by Frank J. Lechner and John Boli.
Editorial material and organization © 2015 John Wiley & Sons, Ltd.
Published 2015 by John Wiley & Sons, Ltd.

During 2008, the crisis became a calamity. Banks began to fail, lending was sparse, and markets for many sorts of exotic financial instruments – collateralized debt obligations, credit-default swaps, and other privately traded derivatives often created to avoid the scrutiny of regulators – became so constricted that valuations could not be determined for tens of trillions of US dollars' worth of investment vehicles. The viability of even the oldest and most respected financial institutions became suspect. As losses mounted and capital markets stalled, US Treasury and banking officials brokered the sale at deeply discounted prices of several high-profile companies, among them the largest US mortgage lender, Countrywide Financial (in January, to Bank of America), and the prominent investment bank Bear Stearns (in March, to JP Morgan). But when officials refused to rescue another prominent investment bank, Lehman Brothers, in September 2008, the entire global financial system suffered a major seizure. Global credit markets virtually froze as the trust that is essential to the financial system evaporated almost overnight. The damage was worldwide and severe; hardest hit were small countries with heavily leveraged banks, such as Ireland and, particularly, Iceland, all of whose banks went under. Iceland's financial collapse led to the first International Monetary Fund bail-out of a developed country's economy since a loan package to Britain in 1976.

The crisis provoked a rapid response of unprecedented proportions by governments, which stepped in with stupendous amounts of capital, credit, and credit guarantees for the ailing financial institutions, in some cases taking direct ownership of them. In Britain, China, France, Germany, India, Japan, Sweden, Switzerland, Taiwan, and many other countries, governments cut interest rates, bailed out banks, flooded capital markets with low-interest loans, launched enormous economic stimulus packages, and expanded compensation to deal with rapidly rising unemployment. The lessons of the worst previous global economic crisis, the Great Depression of the 1930s, clearly had not been lost on public officials: When credit markets dry up and panic hits the stock markets (most of the world's stock markets fell by more than half during the crisis), only states have the resources, authority, and credibility to take effective action that can restore investor, employer, and consumer confidence. Yet state support is not magical; it could not prevent steep declines in global capital investment, trade, and overall economic output that, as of early 2014, still have yet to recover fully in many places. Such support also came at a price. Many governments that incurred large debts found their access to credit restricted, triggering further crisis intervention, especially in Europe, and a negative reaction in global markets – yet further confirmation of global economic integration.

The Great Recession hit only seven years after another spectacular boom-and-bust, the "dot.com" mania (investment in internet companies) that imploded in March 2000. That bust came on the heels of yet another implosion, the 1997 crisis that plunged many Asian countries (especially Thailand, Malaysia, the Philippines, Indonesia, Taiwan, South Korea, and Singapore) into recession and eventually hurt economies as far away as Brazil and Russia. All of these economic downturns demonstrate the highly interdependent nature of the world economy: flows of raw materials, finished goods, services, and capital itself are now organized in global markets that are integrated far more tightly than ever before, and the volumes of these flows are many orders of magnitude greater than they were in the "take-off" period of globalization in the second half of the nineteenth century.

These upheavals in the world economy reveal the reality and the danger of globalization. They also obscure the fact that, in the decades prior to the Asian crisis, economic globalization had been generally welcomed. Business leaders, economists, and politicians cheered as world trade grew faster than world GDP, foreign direct investment grew faster than domestic investment, and the volume of international currency transactions increased exponentially. Many formerly marginal "Third World" countries became growing, exporting tigers, particularly in Asia. The production of goods once monopolized by the industrialized West spread across the globe, linking companies, workers, and whole countries in transnational "commodity chains." Not only did economic exchange intensify, but also it was increasingly managed by international organizations, such as the GATT and its successor, the World Trade Organization, that promulgated global rules, and the IMF, which sought to maintain stability in the global financial system. Economic integration had become a hallmark of globalization, deliberately promoted by governments, corporations, and international organizations alike.

At the same time, skeptical voices began to challenge the prevailing view of globalization's beneficial effects. Like Immanuel Wallerstein in Part II, scholars question the uniqueness of the late twentieth century. The sixteenth and the nineteenth centuries, they argue, already witnessed dramatic integration that set the stage for all subsequent developments. Financial markets may operate differently due to new computer technology, and the geopolitical context may be different due to the demise of the Soviet Union, but these are not qualitative changes. Other skeptics, by contrast, argue not that capitalism has always been global but that it is not yet fully globalized. For example, they suggest that the real roots of economic crises, such as the recent Great Recession and the Asian "contagion" of the 1990s, lay in bad domestic policies. International markets can exploit and aggravate poor policies and practices, but they are not the primary cause of a contagious crisis. The involvement of countries in the world economy varies greatly in any case. While some small economies, such as the Netherlands, are highly dependent on exports, for large countries, especially the United States, imports and exports still represent only a relatively small portion of total GDP. For these skeptics, the whole notion of integration is misleading, since the core of the world economy is only perhaps 30 of the world's 200 countries – Western Europe and North America, and a few countries of Pacific Asia, which account for the vast bulk of world capital and nearly all of the largest multinational corporations. Globalization, from this perspective, amounts to only modestly more intense ties among countries, corporations, and consumers in the industrialized democracies.

We think the skeptics make some good empirical points but underestimate the significance of recent qualitative changes. Our purpose, however, is not to settle these debates. Instead, we present illustrations of integration, an analysis of different measures of global inequality, and a trenchant look at the poorest segment of the world's population. These are followed by two largely complementary analyses of the causes of the Great Recession. This part concludes with a provocative assessment of economic globalization by an influential economist.

The first selection by American journalist James Fallows highlights the most striking change in the world economy of the past three decades – the extraordinarily rapid expansion of China's economy, which has grown about 10 percent a year during that period. Fallows takes us inside the factories and corporate offices of the area of Shenzen, north of Hong Kong, one of the vital centers of the new China that has emerged. He recounts the great progress China has made in lifting many of its people out of poverty while noting that this upward swing has entailed arduous working conditions and heavy worker subordination in many sectors of the economy. He also finds reason to believe that, so far, China's rise has been largely beneficial for Western countries, though continued Chinese expansion could eventually pose a serious challenge to the West.

Next, Miguel Korzeniewicz, an American sociologist, demonstrates how global production actually works in one highly visible sector. The Nike corporation relied on Asian production and American marketing from the outset, but production in Asia diversified as Korean producers began to manage sites in Vietnam and Indonesia. The Nike commodity chain thus pulled in cheaper workers in new countries while most profits still flowed to corporate owners in the West. Since the 1990s, this disparity has motivated various groups to protest the treatment of Asian workers producing Nike shoes. Gary Gereffi, also an American sociologist, provides a more general assessment of global production networks (value and commodity chains), illustrated by case studies of industrial upgrading in three economic sectors – apparel, electronics, and fresh vegetables. The apparel and electronics cases concentrate on East Asia, with Nike as an important player in the former, while the brief discussion of fresh vegetables covers one of the few sectors in which African countries are prominent in global production networks.

That more people and organizations are becoming better connected through buying similar products, engaging in trade, or following common economic rules is not in doubt. There is less agreement on the consequences of economic globalization. Does it lessen poverty? Could it aggravate inequality? These are the questions that Branko Milanovic, a World Bank economist, addresses in the next selection. Milanovic shows that different concepts of inequality – as an average across countries, as a country average weighted by population, and as a measure of inequality across individuals – yield different answers to these questions. Averaged across countries, inequality has declined dramatically since 1950. But weighted by population, inequality across countries rose just as dramatically at the same time, though it has declined modestly since 2000. When inequality among all the world's individuals is considered, the situation is bleakest: this measure indicates greater inequality than either of the country-based concepts and it has changed little since 1990. The richest 8 percent of the world's people garner 50 percent of the world's income, a higher proportion than for any individual country in the world.

A central concern of global development aid organizations since the 1990s is the poorest of the world's poor, the "Bottom Billion." Paul Collier, a British economist and former World Bank official, explores four "traps" that make it extremely difficult for the poorest countries to climb out of poverty: the conflict trap, the natural resources trap, the dual trap of being landlocked and having bad neighbors, and the trap of bad governance. Some of the poorest countries are trapped in two or more ways, with the result that they are poorer now than they were in 1970. Collier points out that some countries have managed to escape the traps, and huge numbers of people have escaped poverty in China and India, but even a recent upsurge in economic growth in some of these countries has not improved the prospects of the bottom billion to any significant degree.

The next two selections, by Australian economist Malcolm Edey and Indian-American economist Ashok Bardhan, analyze the genesis of the Great Recession that began in 2007. Edey offers a brief chronology of the events in 2007 and 2008 before discussing the complex set of circumstances that led to the crisis, which was sparked by the collapsing US housing market. Writing in April 2009, just after world stock markets reached their lowest point, Edey documents the severity of the ensuing economic contraction. Presciently, he predicts a gradual recovery, thanks in large part to the extraordinary actions by governments to flood the world economy with money and undertake massive deficit spending programs that averted a repeat of the Great Depression of the 1930s. This analysis is complemented by Bardhan's more explicitly global perspective, in which "over-financialization" and "over-globalization" were the culprits. The former refers to the disproportionate growth of the global financial sector in recent decades and that sector's increasing reliance on complex and poorly understood financial instruments. The latter entails too-rapid foreign investment, export growth, and outsourcing in emerging market economies, especially China, which led to severe global imbalances in trade and consumption patterns. Bardhan observes that these problems have been reduced by the global crisis but suggests that inherent tensions in world society are making a permanently stable world economy unlikely.

Joseph E. Stiglitz, formerly chief economist at the World Bank, concludes this part with his argument that thus far economic globalization has been unjust, undemocratic, and disadvantageous to developing nations. Capital liberalization has created undue volatility, and trade liberalization has put large groups of workers at risk. He attributes the downside of globalization especially to the policies of international financial institutions, which he accuses of advocating "market fundamentalism," that is, the neoliberalism decried by David Harvey in Part II. Stiglitz calls for a new global economic agenda and a new form of global governance.

20

China Makes, the World Takes

James Fallows

[…] The factories where more than 100 million Chinese men and women toil, and from which cameras, clothes, and every other sort of ware flow out to the world, are to me the most startling and intense aspect of today's China. For now, they are also the most important. They are startling above all in their scale. I was prepared for the skyline of Shanghai and its 240-mph Maglev train to the airport, and for the nonstop construction, dust, and bustle of Beijing. Every account of modern China mentions them. But I had no concept of the sweep of what has become the world's manufacturing center: the Pearl River Delta of Guangdong province (the old Canton region), just north of Hong Kong. That one province might have a manufacturing workforce larger than America's. Statistics from China are largely guesses, but Guangdong's population is around 90 million. If even one-fifth of its people hold manufacturing jobs, as seems likely in big cities, that would be 18 million – versus 14 million in the entire United States.

One facility in Guangdong province, the famous Foxconn works, sits in the middle of a conurbation just outside Shenzhen, where it occupies roughly as much space as a major airport. Some 240,000 people (the number I heard most often; estimates range between 200,000 and 300,000) work on its assembly lines, sleep in its dormitories, and eat in its company cafeterias. I was told that Foxconn's caterers kill 3,000 pigs each day to feed its employees. The number would make sense – it's one pig per 80 people, in a country where pigs are relatively small and pork is a staple meat (I heard no estimate for chickens). From the major ports serving the area, Hong Kong and Shenzhen harbors, cargo ships left last year carrying the equivalent of more than

Original publication details: James Fallows, "China Makes, the World Takes," in *The Atlantic*, July–August 2007. pp. 49–50, 52, 57–60, 62. © The Atlantic Media Co as first published in The Atlantic Magazine. Reproduced with permission from Tribune Content Agency.

The Globalization Reader, Fifth Edition. Edited by Frank J. Lechner and John Boli.
Editorial material and organization © 2015 John Wiley & Sons, Ltd.
Published 2015 by John Wiley & Sons, Ltd.

40 million of the standard 20-foot-long metal containers that end up on trucks or railroad cars. That's one per second, round the clock and year-round – and it's less than half of China's export total. What's in the containers that come back from America? My guess was, "dollars"; in fact, the two leading ship-borne exports from the United States to China, by volume, are scrap paper and scrap metal, for recycling.

And the factories are important, for China and everyone else. Someday China may matter internationally mainly for the nature of its political system or for its strategic ambitions. Those are significant even now, of course, but China's success in manufacturing is what has determined its place in the world. Most of what has been good about China over the past generation has come directly or indirectly from its factories. The country has public money with which to build roads, houses, and schools – especially roads. The vast population in the countryside has what their forebears acutely lacked, and peasants elsewhere today still do: a chance at paying jobs, which means a chance to escape rural poverty. Americans complain about cheap junk pouring out of Chinese mills, but they rely on China for a lot that is not junk, and whose cheap price is important to American industrial and domestic life. Modern consumer culture rests on the assumption that the nicest, most advanced goods – computers, audio systems, wall-sized TVs – will get cheaper year by year. Moore's Law, which in one version says that the price of computing power will be cut in half every 18 months or so, is part of the reason, but China's factories are a big part too. [...]

Shenzhen, which is the part of China immediately north of Hong Kong and its "New Territories," did not exist as a city as recently as Ronald Reagan's time in the White House. It was a fishing town of 70,000 to 80,000 people, practically unnoticeable by Chinese standards. Today's other big coastal manufacturing centers, such as Xiamen, Guangzhou, Hangzhou, and Shanghai, were for centuries consequential Chinese cities. Not Shenzhen. Its population has grown at least a hundredfold in the past 25 years – rather than merely tripled or quadrupled, as in other cities. It is roughly as populous as New York, like many Chinese cities I keep coming across. Shenzhen has scores of skyscrapers and many, many hundreds of factories.

The story of Shenzhen's boom is in a sense the first chapter in modern China's industrialization. "During the founding period, Shenzhen people were bold and resolute in smashing the trammels of the old ideas," says the English version of the city's history, as recounted in Shenzhen's municipal museum in an odd, modern-Chinese combination of Maoist bombast and supercapitalist perspective. "With the market-oriented reforms as the breakthrough point, they shook off the yoke of the planned economy, and gradually built up new management systems."

What all this refers to is the establishment, in the late summer of 1980, of Shenzhen as a "special economic zone," where few limits or controls would apply and businesses from around the world would be invited to set up shop. Shenzhen was attractive as an experimental locale, not just because it was so close to Hong Kong, with its efficient harbor and airport, but also because it was so far from Beijing. If the experiment went wrong, the consequences could be more easily contained in this southern extremity of the country. Nearly every rule that might restrict business development was changed or removed in Shenzhen. Several free-trade processing zones were established, where materials and machinery coming in and exports going out would be exempt from the usual duties or taxes.

Modern Shenzhen has traits that Americans would associate with a booming Sun Belt city – transient, rough, unmannered, full of opportunity – and that characterized Manchester, Detroit, Chicago, Los Angeles at their times of fastest growth. […]

In 1996, just after he turned 30, Liam Casey went to Taipei for an electronics trade show. It was his first trip to Asia, and, he says, "I could see this is where the opportunity was." Within a year, he had set up operations in the Shenzhen area and started the company now known as PCH China Solutions. The initials stand for Pacific Coast Highway, in honor of his happy Southern California days.

What does this company do? The short answer is outsourcing, which in effect means matching foreign companies that want to sell products with Chinese suppliers who can make those products for them. Casey describes his mission as "helping innovators leverage the manufacturing supply chain here in China." To see how this works, consider the great human flows that now converge in southern China, which companies like Casey's help mediate.

One is the enormous flow of people, mainly young and unschooled, from China's farms and villages to Shenzhen and similar cities. Some arrive with a factory job already arranged by relatives or fixers; some come to the cities and then look for work. In the movie version of *Balzac and the Little Chinese Seamstress*, two teenaged men from the city befriend a young woman in the mountain village where they have been sent for rustication during the Cultural Revolution. One day the young woman unexpectedly leaves. She has gone to "try her luck in a big city," her grandfather tells them. "She said she wanted a new life." The new life is in Shenzhen.

Multiplied millions of times, and perhaps lacking the specific drama of the *Balzac* tale, this is the story of the factory towns. As in the novel, many of the migrants are young women. In the light-manufacturing operations I have seen in the Pearl River Delta and around Shanghai, the workforce is predominantly female. Signing on with a factory essentially means making your job your life. Workers who come to the big coastal factory centers either arrive, like the little seamstress, before they have a spouse or children, or leave their dependents at home with grandparents, aunts, or uncles. At the electronics and household-goods factories, including many I've seen, the pay is between 900 and 1,200 RMB per month, or about $115 to $155. In the villages the workers left, a farm family's cash earnings might be a few thousand RMB per year. Pay is generally lowest, and discipline toughest, at factories owned and managed by Taiwanese or mainland Chinese companies. The gigantic Foxconn (run by its founder, Terry Guo of Taiwan) is known for a militaristic organization and approach. Jobs with Western firms are the cushiest but are also rare, since the big European and American companies buy mainly from local subcontractors. Casey says that monthly pay in some factories he owns is several hundred RMB more than the local average. His goal is to retain workers for longer than the standard few-year stint, allowing them to develop greater skills and a sense of company spirit.

A factory work shift is typically 12 hours, usually with two breaks for meals (subsidized or free), six or seven days per week. Whenever the action lets up – if the assembly line is down for some reason, if a worker has spare time at a meal break – many people place their heads down on the table in front of them and appear to fall asleep instantly. Chinese law says that the standard workweek is 40 hours, so this means a lot of overtime, which is included in the pay rates above. Since their home village may be several days' travel by train and bus, workers from the hinterland usually go back only once a year. They all go at the same time – during the "Spring Festival," or Chinese New Year, when ports and factories effectively close for a week or so and the nation's transport system is choked. "The people here work hard," an American manager in a US-owned plant told me. "They're young. They're quick. There's none of this 'I have to go pick up the kids' nonsense you get in the States."

At every electronics factory I've seen, each person on an assembly line has a bunch of documents posted by her workstation: her photo, name, and employee number, often the instructions she is to follow in both English and Chinese. Often too there's a visible sign of how well she's doing. For the production line as a whole there are hourly totals of target and actual production, plus allowable and actual defect levels. At several Taiwanese-owned factories I've seen, the indicator of individual performance is a childish outline drawing of a tree with leaves. After each day's shift one of the tree's leaves is filled in with a colored marker, either red or green. If the leaf is green, the worker has met her quota and caused no problems. If it's red, a defect has been traced back to her workstation. One red leaf per month is within tolerance; two is a problem.

As in all previous great waves of industrialization, many people end up staying in town; that's why Shenzhen has grown so large. But more than was the case during America's or England's booms in factory work, many rural people, especially the young women, work for two or three years and then go back to the country with their savings. In their village they open a shop, marry a local man and start a family, buy land, or use their earnings to help the relatives still at home.

Life in the factories is obviously hard, and in the heavy-industry works it is very dangerous. In the same week that 32 people were murdered at Virginia Tech, 32 Chinese workers at a steel plant in the north were scalded to death when a ladleful of molten steel was accidentally dumped on them. Even in Chinese papers, that story got less play than the US shooting – and fatal coal-mine disasters are so common that they are reported as if they were traffic deaths. By comparison, the light industries that typify southern China are tedious but less overtly hazardous. As the foreman of a Taiwanese electronics factory put it to me when I asked him about rough working conditions, "Have you ever seen a Chinese farm?" [...]

In decades of reporting on military matters, I have rarely encountered people as concerned about keeping secrets as the buyers and suppliers who meet in Shenzhen and similar cities. What information are they committed to protect? Names, places, and product numbers that would reveal which Western companies obtain which exact products from which Chinese suppliers. There are high-and low-road reasons for their concern.

The low-road reason is the "Nike problem." This is the buyers' wish to minimize their brands' association with outsourcing in general and Asian sweatshops in particular, named for Nike's PR problems because of its factories in Indonesia. By Chinese standards, the most successful exporting factories are tough rather than abusive, but those are not the standards Western customers might apply.

The high-road reason involves the crucial operational importance of the "supply chain." It is not easy to find the right factory, work out the right manufacturing system, ensure the right supply of parts and raw material, impose the right quality standards, and develop the right relationship of trust and reliability. Companies that have solved these problems don't want to tell their competitors how they did so. "Supply chain *is* intellectual property," is the way Liam Casey put it. Asking a Western company to specify its Chinese suppliers is like asking a reporter to hand over a list of his best sources.

Because keeping the supply chain confidential is so important to buyers, they try to impose confidentiality on their suppliers. When an outside company's reputation for design and quality is strong – Sony, Braun, Apple – many Chinese contractors like to drop hints that they are part of its supply chain. But the ones who really are part of it must be more discreet if they want to retain the buying company's trust (and business).

So I will withhold details, but ask you to take this leap: If you think of major US or European brand names in the following businesses, odds are their products come from factories like those I'm about to describe. The businesses are: computers, including desktops, laptops, and servers; telecom equipment, from routers to mobile phones; audio equipment, including anything MP3-related, home stereo systems, most portable devices, and headsets; video equipment of all sorts, from cameras and camcorders to replay devices; personal-care items and high-end specialty-catalog goods; medical devices; sporting goods and exercise equipment; any kind of electronic goods or accessories; and, for that matter, just about anything else you can think of. Some of the examples I'll give come from sites in Shenzhen, but others are from facilities near Shanghai, Hangzhou, Guangzhou, Xiamen, and elsewhere.

Why does a foreign company come to our Mr. China? I asked Casey what he would tell me if I were in, say, some branch of the steel industry in Pittsburgh and was looking to cut costs. "Not interested," he said. "The product's too heavy, and you've probably already automated the process, so one person is pushing a button. It would cost you almost as much to have someone push the button in China."

But what is of intense interest to him, he said, is a company that has built up a brand name and relationships with retailers, and knows what it wants to promote and sell next – and needs to save time and money in manufacturing a product that requires a fair amount of assembly. "That is where we can help, because you will come here and see factories that are better than the ones you've been working with in America or Germany."

Here are a few examples, all based on real-world cases: You have announced a major new product, which has gotten great buzz in the press. But close to release time, you discover a design problem that must be fixed – and no US factory can adjust its production process in time.

The Chinese factories can respond more quickly, and not simply because of 12-hour workdays. "Anyplace else, you'd have to import different raw materials and components," Casey told me. "Here, you've got nine different suppliers within a mile, and they can bring a sample over that afternoon. People think China is cheap, but really, it's *fast*." Moreover, the Chinese factories use more human labor, and fewer expensive robots or assembly machines, than their counterparts in rich countries. "People are the most adaptable machines," an American industrial designer who works in China told me. "Machines need to be reprogrammed. You can have people doing something entirely different next week."

Or: You are an American inventor with a product you think has "green" potential for household energy savings. But you need to get it to market fast, because you think big companies may be trying the same thing, and you need to meet a target retail price of $100. "No place but China to do this," Mr. China said, as he showed me the finished product.

Or: You are a very famous American company, and you worry that you've tied up too much capital keeping inventory for retail stores at several supply depots in America. With Mr. China's help, you start emphasizing direct retail sales on your Web site – and do all the shipping and fulfillment from one supply depot, run by young Chinese women in Shenzhen, who can ship directly to specific retail stores. [...]

21

Commodity Chains
and Marketing Strategies
Nike and the Global Athletic Footwear Industry

Miguel Korzeniewicz

The world-economic trends and cycles of the past two decades have made it increasingly apparent that the production and distribution of goods take place in complex global networks that tie together groups, organizations, and regions. The concept of commodity chains is helpful in mapping these emerging forms of capitalist organization. Most often, analysts depict global commodity chains (GCCs) by focusing primarily on production processes and their immediate backward and forward linkages. Less attention has been paid to the crucial role played by the design, distribution, and marketing nodes within a GCC. These nodes are important because they often constitute the epicenter of innovative strategies that allow enterprises to capture greater shares of wealth within a chain. Furthermore, a GCC perspective helps us understand how marketing and consumption patterns in core areas of the world shape production patterns in peripheral and semiperipheral countries. Thus an analysis of the design, distribution, and marketing segments within a commodity chain can provide unique insights into the processes through which core-like activities are created, and competitive pressures are transferred elsewhere in the world-economy.

To provide such an analysis, this chapter focuses on the distribution segment of a particular commodity chain: athletic footwear. In particular, this chapter examines the marketing strategy of one corporation within the global athletic shoe industry (Nike) to refine our understanding of the dynamic nature of global commodity

Original publication details: Miguel Korzeniewicz, "Commodity Chains and Marketing Strategies: Nike and the Global Athletic Footwear Industry," in *Commodity Chains and Global Capitalism,* ed. Gary Gereffi and Miguel Korzeniewicz. Westport, CT: Greenwood Press, 1994. pp. 247–61.

chains. The example of athletic footwear is useful in exploring how commodity chains are embedded in cultural trends. The social organization of advertising, fashion, and consumption shapes the networks and nodes of global commodity chains. The athletic footwear case shows that the organization of culture itself is an innovative process that unevenly shapes patterns of production and consumption in core, semiperipheral, and peripheral areas of the world-economy. [...]

Trends in the US Athletic Shoe Market

The athletic footwear market in the United States has been characterized over the past two decades by phenomenal rates of growth. As indicated by Figure 21.1, wholesale revenues of athletic shoes in the United States tripled between 1980 and 1990. In the past six years, consumers in the United States more than doubled their expenditures on athletic shoes: In 1985 they spent $5 billion and bought 250 million pairs of shoes, whereas by the end of 1991 retail sales totaled $12 billion for nearly 400 million pairs of shoes. Three-fourths of all Americans bought athletic shoes in 1991, compared with two-thirds in 1988. In 1990, athletic shoes accounted for about a third of all shoes sold. The athletic footwear industry today generates $12 billion in retail sales, with at least twenty-five companies earning $20 million or more in annual sales. From the point of view of Schumpeterian innovations, the trajectory of the athletic footwear commodity chain over recent times provides valuable insights into the creation of a modern consumer market.

Retail markets for athletic shoes are highly segmented according to consumer age groups. Teenagers are the most important consumers of athletic shoes. A study sponsored by the Athletic Footwear Association found that the average American over twelve years of age owns at least two pairs of athletic shoes, worn for both athletic and casual purposes. As experienced by many parents and youngsters during the

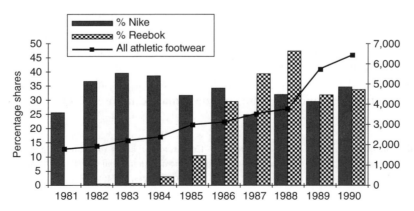

Figure 21.1 Total wholesale revenues of athletic footwear and Nike's and Reebok's shares, 1981–90.
Source: National Sporting Goods Association.

1980s and 1990s, athletic shoes have been constructed and often promoted among teenagers as an important and visible symbol of social status and identity.

The products in this commodity chain also are highly differentiated according to models and the particular sport for which they are purportedly designed. By 1989, Nike was producing shoes in 24 footwear categories, encompassing 300 models and 900 styles. Reebok sold 175 models of shoes in 450 colors, and planned to add 250 new designs. Adidas and LA Gear sell 500 different styles each. The two fastest-growing segments of athletic shoes in the late 1980s were basketball shoes and walking shoes, while the volume of sales for tennis and running shoes declined. In 1991, basketball shoes accounted for 22 percent of sales, and cross trainers for 14 percent of sales. Product differentiation provides an important vehicle both for competition among enterprises and price stratification.

Finally, the sports footwear market is highly segmented according to price. Indicative of this segmentation, the price distribution of athletic shoes has a very wide range. In 1989 the average cost of basketball, walking, and running shoes was between $40 and $47, while top-of-the-line shoes cost about $175. The bulk of production is oriented toward sales of the lower-priced shoes, while the market for the higher-priced commodities is substantially smaller. In 1990, more than 80 percent of athletic shoe purchases were priced under $35, with only 1.4 percent of shoes bought costing more than $65. Price rather than appearance or functionality often constitutes the primary matrix differentiating athletic shoes as status symbols.

Since displacing Adidas in the early 1980s, and after falling behind Reebok in the mid-1980s, Nike Corporation has become the largest and most important athletic shoe company in the United States. Nike's sales have grown from $2 million in 1972 to $270 million in 1980, and to over $3 billion in 1991. Reebok, the number two brand in the United States today, experienced similar rates of growth – in fact, Reebok has been the fastest-growing company in the history of American business. Between 1981 and 1987, Reebok's sales grew from $1.5 million to $1.4 billion, experiencing an average annual growth rate of 155 percent. Similarly, LA Gear grew at a dazzling rate, from $11 million in 1985 to $535 million in 1989. Between 1985 and 1990, Nike's share of the athletic footwear market in the United States declined from 30 to 25 percent, Reebok's rose from 14 to 24 percent; LA Gear's increased from a minimal share to 11 percent, and Converse's share declined from 9 to 5 percent. These data suggest that a limited number of large firms compete within the athletic footwear market in the United States, but also that the organization of the market provides considerable permeability for successful entry and competition by new enterprises.

What are the factors that explain the enormous growth of the athletic shoe industry? The evidence suggests, in part, that the most important enterprises within this commodity chain have grown by increasing their control over the nodes involved in the material production of athletic shoes. The most fundamental innovation of these enterprises, however, has been the *creation* of a market, and this has entailed the construction of a convincing world of symbols, ideas, and values harnessing the desires of individuals to the consumption of athletic shoes. By focusing on the marketing and circulation nodes of a commodity chain, greater analytical precision can be gained in identifying the crucial features of these innovations.

Rather than analyzing the athletic footwear chain as a whole, the next section focuses on a single enterprise, Nike Corporation. Although a comparative analysis of other enterprises would yield greater insights into possible differences in organizational trajectories, the focus on a single firm allows a more detailed exploration of the innovative strategies that have characterized the athletic footwear commodity chain. This approach also highlights the relevance of world-systems theory, and the concept of commodity chains, to the study of economic and social processes at a microlevel of observation. Nike's rise to prominence has been based on its ability to capture a succession of nodes along the commodity chain, increasing its expertise and control over the critical areas of design, distribution, marketing, and advertising. This strategy also involved a fundamental reshaping of production and consumption, hence contributing to the recent transformation of the athletic footwear commodity chain.

Nike Corporation: Competition, Upgrading, and Innovation in a Commodity Chain

The activities of Nike Corporation created a quintessential American product that has captured a large share of the giant US athletic footwear market. Nike Corporation increased its revenues tenfold in the past ten years, from $270 million in 1980 to an estimated $3 billion in 1991. Nike sells tens of millions of athletic shoes in the United States every year, yet all of the firm's manufacturing operations are conducted overseas, making the company an archetype of a global sourcing strategy. Nike Corporation never relocated domestic production abroad, as many American companies have done, because the firm actually originated by importing shoes from Japan. It has subcontracted nearly all of its production overseas ever since: currently, "all but 1 percent of the millions of shoes Nike makes each year are manufactured in Asia." In the United States, Nike has developed essentially as a design, distribution, and marketing enterprise.

Nike's successful implementation of its overseas sourcing strategy can best be understood as part of the firm's effort to retain control over highly profitable nodes in the athletic footwear commodity chain, while avoiding the rigidity and pressures that characterize the more competitive nodes of the chain. "We don't know the first thing about manufacturing," says Neal Lauridsen, Nike's vice-president for Asia-Pacific. "We are marketers and designers." Nike's practice of overseas sourcing provides strategic and geographical mobility to the firm by developing a complex division of labor among the components of a global subcontracting network. The way these characteristics are linked to consumer demand and marketing strategies helps explain the tremendous growth and success of Nike. [...]

Marketing as an upgrading strategy (1976–84)

During this second period, Nike Corporation introduced major innovations in marketing, distribution, and subcontracting for the production of athletic footwear. First, between 1976 and 1984, Nike was shaped by (and helped to shape) the "fitness boom" – the phenomenal growth of jogging, running, and exercise as a common activity by millions of Americans. Nike was part of this phenomenon by implementing a marketing strategy that involved the development of a vast and visible network of endorsement contracts with basketball, baseball, and football players and coaches. Second, Nike's distribution network was enhanced by the establishment of a strategic alliance with Foot Locker, a rapidly growing chain of retail stores marketing athletic products. Finally, Nike Corporation sought to further enhance its control over subcontractors and lower production costs by shifting most manufacturing activities from Japan to South Korea and (to a lesser extent) Taiwan. Combined, these innovations provided a significant competitive edge to Nike Corporation.

Beginning in the mid-1970s, running, jogging, and exercise in general became part of mainstream American culture. Nike Corporation was in the right place at the right time to capitalize on this phenomenon by outperforming competing brands and becoming the most important athletic shoe company in the United States. But the ability to gain from this phenomenon required a major reorientation in the marketing of the company's products: Nike Corporation's main customer base had to shift, as one observer puts it, from "running geeks to yuppies." To achieve this shift, Nike's promotional efforts in the 1970s moved slowly but consistently away from amateur sports to professional sports, and from lesser-known track and field runners to highly visible sports figures. In 1977 and 1978 Nike developed a strategy to sign visible college basketball coaches; by 1979 it had signed over fifty college coaches. One measure of Nike's promotional success was the cover of *Sports Illustrated* of March 26, 1979, which showed Larry Bird (at the time a player in the NCAA tournament) wearing Nike shoes. In the late 1970s, Nike also began to promote heavily in baseball, and by 1980 a Nike representative had signed over fifty players in different baseball teams – as well as eight players in the Tampa Bay team that made it to the 1980 Super Bowl. This new marketing strategy enhanced Nike's image in its new market niche.

Nike's rise as the largest athletic shoe company in the United States also involved creating a more effective distribution network. Foot Locker, an emerging chain of sport equipment retailers, became the most important distributor of Nike shoes. As a way to solve inventory and financial bottlenecks, Nike people devised an advance-order purchase system they called "futures." The system required major distributors to commit themselves to large orders six months in advance, in return for a 5–7 percent discount and a guaranteed delivery schedule. Foot Locker was one of the first dealers to try the futures contracts, and to benefit from them, eventually becoming Nike's most important retailer. Another reason for Foot Locker's close relationship with Nike was the latter's flexibility, and its willingness to change design specifications on request from dealers. This responsiveness of Nike contrasted with Adidas' generally inflexible approach to their supply of shoes, and further extended the company's competitive edge.

Finally, the phenomenal growth in the demand for athletic shoes changed Nike's subcontracting patterns. Nike now needed larger outputs, lower labor prices, and more control over the manufacturing process. In 1974 the great bulk of BRS's [Blue Ribbon Sports'] $4.8 million in sales was still coming from Japan. Phil Knight, aware of rising labor costs in Japan, began to look for sourcing alternatives. One of these alternatives was the United States. In early 1974, BRS rented space in an empty old factory in Exeter, New Hampshire, and later opened a second factory in Saco, New Hampshire. Domestic facilities also fulfilled a critical R&D function that Nike would later use to gain greater control over production processes abroad. However, by 1984 imported shoes (mostly from Korea and Taiwan) rose to 72 percent of the US shoe market, and US-based factories were forced to close. The collapse of the US production base was due primarily to its limited manufacturing capacity and its economic implausibility. Product timelines lagged and American-based manufacturing found itself unable to compete with lower Asian labor costs.

While Nippon Rubber (Nike's Japanese supplier) reportedly made the decision to relocate part of its production to South Korea and Taiwan, Nike also began to look for new sources of its own. In October 1975, Phil Knight flew to Asia to search for alternative supply sources to lessen his dependency on both Nissho Iwai and Nippon Rubber without losing either company. In Japan, Knight met a Chinese trader who agreed to set up a Nike-controlled corporation called Athena Corporation that established production facilities in Taiwan. In South Korea the Sam Hwa factory of Pusan became the main partner, which began 1977 making 10,000 pairs of Nike shoes a month, and ending the year by making about 100,000 pairs a month. By 1980, nearly 90 percent of Nike's shoe production was located in Korea and Taiwan.

The consolidation of South Korea and Taiwan as the main geographical centers of manufacturing also involved the emergence of a complex system of stratification among Nike's suppliers. Donaghu and Barff identify three main classes of factories supplying Nike: developed partners, volume producers, and developing sources. "Developed partners" are the upper tier of Nike suppliers, responsible for the most innovative and sophisticated shoes. "Volume producers" are those that manufacture a specific type of product in large quantities. These factories are typically less flexible than developed partners in their manufacturing organization. Finally, "developing sources" are the newer factories that attracted Nike because of their low labor costs, entering into a series of tutelary arrangements both with Nike and the more experienced Nike suppliers.

The geographical dynamism of Nike's shifts in subcontracting arrangements interacted with this complex stratification system in interesting ways. As labor costs in Japan rose in the 1970s, Nike Corporation shifted production to emerging semiperipheral countries such as South Korea and Taiwan. As labor costs in the established semiperipheral supply locations began to rise in the 1980s, Nike tried to shift some of the labor-intensive, technologically less advanced segments of its production to new locations in peripheral areas (such as China). It is interesting to note, however, that linkages with developed partners remained critical for two reasons. First, several of Nike's more sophisticated models required the expertise and flexibility of older, more reliable partners. Second, the technological expertise and capital of the older partners was often necessary to bring newer production facilities up to Nike standards, leading to joint ventures between the older, more established sources and the newer ones. From this point of view, centralization and decentralization of subcontracting arrangements were constrained by marketing requirements.

Design, advertising, and the return to the semiperiphery (post-1985)

After 1985, Nike entered into another period of high growth, based on innovations in product design (the creation of the "Air Nike" models, which quickly became immensely popular) and advertising strategies (signing its most popular endorser, Michael Jordan). Also, Nike Corporation continued to target new market niches, entering the aerobics segment of the market, where Reebok had become increasingly dominant, and the growing and profitable athletic apparel markets. Finally, Nike Corporation altered its subcontracting arrangements, shifting important segments in the manufacture of Nike's athletic shoes to the People's Republic of China, Thailand, and Indonesia. However, the need for specialized and sophisticated production runs once again forced Nike to return to more experienced manufacturers in South Korea and Taiwan.

The ability to produce high-performance, sophisticated footwear models became critical to Nike because the company was able to pull out of its early 1980s stagnation through its "Nike Air" technological innovation. By 1984 the phenomenal growth of a mass market for jogging shoes began to stabilize, particularly in the men's segment of the market. Other companies, like Reebok and LA Gear, were becoming more effective in selling to the female and aerobics segments of the market. Nike Corporation, accustomed to years of high growth, was in crisis. Many endorsement contracts were canceled, the Athletics West program cut down its sponsored athletes from 88 to 50, and by the end of 1984, Nike had laid off 10 percent of its 4,000-person work force. Another indication of Nike's bad fortunes was its declining influence among sports coaches and agents. To reverse this decline, Nike Corporation once again turned toward introducing a drastic product innovation.

Nike's declining fortunes in the mid-1980s were reversed by the introduction of Air Nike (a new technology that allowed a type of gas to be compressed and stored within the sole) and by the phenomenal success of its "Air Jordan" line of basketball shoes, as well as the success of the endorser they were named after, Michael Jordan. In Nike's Los Angeles store, the first two shipments of Air Jordans sold out in three days. By 1985 it was clear that Air Jordan shoes were a huge success. Nike sold in three months what had been projected for the entire year. The first contract between Nike Corporation and Michael Jordan was worth $2.5 million over five years, and it included (among other things) a royalty to the athlete on all Air Jordan models sold by the company.

The several advertising campaigns featuring Michael Jordan highlight Nike's capacity to influence market demand for its shoes. Nike's video and print advertisements have been among the most innovative and controversial in recent years, adding to Nike's visibility and undoubtedly contributing to its phenomenal growth. Part of the appeal of Nike advertising is its success in tapping and communicating a consistent set of values that many people in the 1970s and 1980s identified with: hipness, irreverence, individualism, narcissism, self-improvement, gender equality, racial equality, competitiveness, and health.

But there also have been several allegations made that by targeting inner-city youths in its advertising and marketing campaigns, Nike has profited substantially from sales directly related to drug and gang money, showing little concern for the social and financial stability of the predominantly black, poor communities, where sales account for 20 percent of the total athletic footwear market. The relationship between the athletic footwear industry and drug money has become increasingly evident by the alarming rate of robberies and killings over expensive sports shoes. Some store owners claim that Nike is not only aware that drug money contributes heavily to its sales, but that Nike representatives adamantly encourage distributors in the inner cities to specifically target and cater to this market.

Nike commercials tend to be subtle. The trademark "swoosh" logo is often far more prominent than dialogue or a straightforward pitch. They are also controversial. Nike's use of the Beatles' song "Revolution" to advertise its new "Nike Air" was startling, and so has been its recent use of John Lennon's song "Instant Karma." Some of the most distinctive Nike advertisements contain themes that can best be described as postmodern: the rapid succession of images, image self-consciousness, and "ads-within-ads" themes. The "Heritage" Nike commercial, showing a white adult runner training in an urban downtown area while images of sports heroes are projected on the sides of buildings, is particularly striking because it seeks to identify the viewer with an idealized figure (the runner) who is in turn identifying with idealized figures (the sports heroes). This ninety-second advertisement cost over $800,000 to run once in its entirety during the 1991 Superbowl. Though there is no dialogue, the product is identifiable (it is seen almost subliminally several times), and the message of the commercial is clear. Postmodern theory, given its sensitivity to new cultural phenomena, can be helpful in understanding advertising as a crucial element in the athletic footwear global commodity chain. An understanding of consumption must be based on commodity aesthetics because consumption is increasingly the consumption of signs. Similarly, Featherstone has noted the increasing importance of the production of symbolic goods and images. In a sense, Nike represents an archetype of a firm selling to emerging postmodern consumer markets that rest on segmented, specialized, and dynamic features.

As in the previous periods, these drastic changes in marketing and distribution strategies were accompanied by shifts in the firm's subcontracting strategy. In 1980 Nike began a process of relocation to the periphery (particularly China, Indonesia, and Thailand) that most other companies would gradually follow in the course of the decade. This relocation was driven by cost advantages: "a mid-priced shoe made in South Korea which costs Nike US $20 when it leaves the docks of Pusan will only cost about US $15 to make in Indonesia or China." Nike Corporation was one of the very first companies to enter the People's Republic of China. In 1980, Phil Knight began to set up a manufacturing base in China. Soon an agreement between Nike Corporation and the Chinese government was finalized, and shoes began to be produced in the PRC. This rapid success can be explained by the fact that Nike used a Chinese-born representative (David Chang) who was thoroughly familiar with the local environment, which meant that proposals were quickly translated into Chinese and attuned to the negotiating style and objectives of the Chinese government. Also, Nike's objectives were long-term and the volumes of production being negotiated were significant, which coincided with the development priorities of the Chinese government at the time.

Just as Nike led the trend of entry into China, later in the mid-1980s it led a reevaluation of the benefits and disadvantages of associating directly with developing partners. By late 1984, production in Chinese factories totaled 150,000 pairs a month, one-seventh of the originally projected 1 million pairs a month. The early 1980s also signaled a slowdown in the rapid growth of conventional athletic footwear markets at a time when competition from other athletic footwear firms (LA Gear, Reebok) was increasing. By 1983 Nike terminated its subcontracting arrangement with the Shanghai factory, and in 1984 negotiated an early termination of its contract with the Tianjin factory.

In the mid-1980s Nike briefly considered shifting production back to established manufacturing sources in South Korea and Taiwan. The advantages of lower labor costs in the developing manufacturing areas had to be weighed against disadvantages in production flexibility, quality, raw material sourcing, and transportation. The development of a new shoe model from technical specifications to shoe production was four months in South Korea, compared to eight months in China. The ratio of perfect-quality (A-grade) shoes to aesthetically flawed, but structurally sound (B-grade) shoes was 99 : 1 in Korea, 98 : 2 in Taiwan, and 80 : 20 in China. While Taiwan and South Korea sourced 100 percent of the raw materials needed for production, China was only able to source 30 percent. Finally, shipping from Taiwan and South Korea was 20–25 days; from Shanghai it was 35–40 days.

The mid-1980s also marked the introduction of the "Nike Air" technology and especially the "Air Jordan" model. Being more sophisticated, secretive, and expensive, this model required more experienced and trustworthy suppliers of the "developed partners" type that had been developed in South Korea over the years. One Reebok executive argued that "as the complexity of our product increases, it continues to go to [South Korea]. The primary reason is that product development out of Korean factories is quick and accurate for athletic footwear, better than any place in the world." An observer concluded in the mid-1980s that after the trend of relocation to low-wage locations like Thailand, Indonesia, and China, "buyers are starting to return [to Pusan] after finding that the extra cost of doing business in South Korea is offset by reliability and the large capacity of its factories." This need for more established suppliers coincided with the adjustments that the Korean shoe producers themselves made in an effort to adapt to rising labor costs and the migration of many firms to other countries. Many Pusan firms shrunk in size but also increased the unit value of their production.

However, the relative importance of South Korean firms has continued to decline. Thus, "at least one-third of the lines in Pusan have shut down in the past three years. Only a handful of South Korean companies are expected to remain significant shoe exporters in a couple of years." Similar changes have affected shoe-producing firms in Taiwan, where "since 1988, the number of footwear companies has fallen from 1,245 to 745. Athletic shoe exports slipped from US $1.5 billion in 1988 to US $1 billion (in 1991)." Taiwanese and South Korean-based firms, on the other hand, are used for managing and mediating the relocation of production facilities to the periphery.

The shift of Nike's production to the periphery has become significant. "In the fiscal year to 31 May 1988, Nike bought 68 percent of its shoes from South Korea but only 42 percent in 1991–92. China, Indonesia and Thailand produced 44 percent of Nike's shoes last fiscal year; against less than 10 percent in 1987–88." This same trend is expected to continue in the future: "now, Vietnam looks like the next country on the list. Two major Taiwanese suppliers, Feng Tay and Adi Corporation, are interested in starting production in Vietnam if and when the U.S. trade embargo of its old adversary is lifted."

The advantages of Nike Corporation that have enabled it to become a powerful and profitable link in the athletic footwear commodity chain are the expertise of its designers in finding technological advances in shoe comfort and performance, the distribution networks built over the past twenty-five years, and the effectiveness of its marketing, promotion and advertising campaigns.

Overall assessment

To summarize the arguments made in this section, Nike's development of its twin strategies of overseas subcontracting and domestic marketing can best be understood as involving three distinct periods, each corresponding to different patterns of market demand, geographical locus of production, and marketing strategies. In the first period, between 1962 and 1975, Nike Corporation emphasized control over the import and distribution nodes of its commodity chain. Between 1976 and 1984, Nike Corporation enhanced its relative competitive position by extending control to marketing, and by redesigning its subcontracting strategy to take advantage of new opportunities in Southeast Asia (in South Korea and Taiwan initially, later in China, Thailand, and Indonesia). Finally, beginning in the mid-1980s, Nike Corporation successfully extended control to product design and advertising, further upgrading the firm's organizational structure. As a whole, these three periods suggest that Nike Corporation has sustained and enhanced its competitive edge through the implementation of frequent innovations in the nodes and networks of its commodity chain.

Conclusions

This chapter has examined the organizational strategies of Nike Corporation within the global athletic shoe industry. Nike's uncommon success and growth is due in part to social and cultural trends that have made leisure and fitness more important in our contemporary society. It is also the outcome of Nike's strategy of responding to these trends by accumulating expertise and control over the increasingly important service nodes of the athletic footwear commodity chain: import, distribution, marketing, and advertising.

Nike Corporation (and the athletic footwear industry in general) are excellent case studies of how goods emerge from complex, transnational linkages at different stages of production and distribution. Nike Corporation was born a globalized company. The study confirms a division of labor between core or postindustrial societies (that will presumably specialize in services over time) and noncore societies at different levels of industrialization (that will increasingly specialize in manufacturing). While Korean and Chinese firms are producing the actual shoe, US-based Nike promotes the symbolic nature of the shoe and appropriates the greater share of the value result-ing from its sales.

Nike and the athletic shoe industry show that there are emerging patterns of con-sumption that have enormous consequences for social and economic organization. Linkages between consumption and production must be explored in greater detail. While a consensus has been building for some time that there are new patterns in the organization of production (alternatively called flexible specialization, flexible production, or post-Fordist production), we also need a better understanding of what may be called "post-Fordist consumption" – that is, the emerging patterns of consumption and distribution that are the counterpart to transformations in the realm of production.

22

The Global Economy
Organization, Governance, and Development

Gary Gereffi

The Emergence of International Trade
and Production Networks

The growth of world trade has probably received the most attention in the global-ization literature because of its direct relevance to employment, wages, and the rising number of free trade agreements around the world. The most common causes usually given to explain expanding world trade are technological (improvements in transportation and communication technologies) and political (e.g., the removal of protectionist barriers, such as tariffs, import quotas, and exchange controls, which had restricted world markets from 1913 until the end of the Second World War). It is also important to acknowledge that the volume of international trade depends to a considerable degree on how boundaries are drawn, both for different geographies of production and according to whether trade covers final products only or whether it also includes intermediate inputs. However, even though the share of trade in world output surpassed its 1913 peak in the 1980s and 1990s, the sheer volume of trade is probably not sufficient to argue for a qualitative break with the past.

Of far greater significance are several novel features in the *nature* of international trade that do not have counterparts in previous eras. These suggest the need for a new framework to understand both patterns of competition among international firms and the development prospects of countries that are trying to upgrade their

Original publication details: Gary Gereffi, "The Global Economy: Organization, Governance, and Development," in *The Handbook of Economic Sociology*, ed. Neil J. Smelser and Richard Swedberg. Russell Sage Foundation, published by Princeton University Press, 2005. pp. 166–8, 171–5. Reproduced with permission from Princeton University Press.

position in diverse global industries. The three new aspects of modern world trade relevant here are (1) the rise of intraindustry and intraproduct trade in intermediate inputs; (2) the ability of producers to "slice up the value chain," in Krugman's phrase, by breaking a production process into many geographically separated steps; and (3) the emergence of a global production networks framework that highlights how these shifts have altered governance structures and the distribution of gains in the global economy.

Intraindustry trade in parts and components

Arndt and Kierzkowski use the term *fragmentation* to describe the international division of labor that allows producers located in different countries and often with different ownership structures to form cross-border production networks for parts and components. Specialized "production blocks" are coordinated through service links, which include activities such as transportation, insurance, telecommunications, quality control, and management specifications. Yeats, analyzing detailed trade data for the machinery and transport equipment group (SITC 7), finds that trade in components made up 30 percent of total OECD exports in SITC 7 in 1995, and that trade in these goods was growing at a faster pace than the overall SITC 7 total. Similarly, Hummels, Rapaport, and Yi argue that the "vertical specialization" of global trade, which occurs when a country uses imported intermediate parts to produce goods it later exports, accounted for about 14.5 percent of all trade among OECD countries in the early 1990s. Vertical specialization captures the idea that countries link sequentially in production networks to produce a final good, although vertical trade itself does not require the vertical integration of firms.

Feenstra takes this idea one step further, and explicitly connects the "integration of trade" with the "disintegration of production" in the global economy. The rising integration of world markets through trade has brought with it a disintegration of the production process of multinational firms, since companies are finding it profitable to outsource (domestically or abroad) an increasing share of their noncore manufacturing and service activities. This represents a breakdown of the vertically integrated mode of production – the so-called Fordist model, originally exemplified by the automobile industry – on which US industrial prowess had been built for much of the twentieth century. The success of the Japanese model of "lean production" in the global economy since the 1980s, pioneered by Toyota in automobiles, reinforces the central importance of coordinating exceptionally complex interfirm trading networks of parts and components as a new source of competitive advantage in the global economy.

Slicing up the value chain

The notion of a value-added chain has been a useful tool for international business scholars who have focused on the strategies of both firms and countries in the global economy. Bruce Kogut, a professor at the Wharton School of Business, University of

Pennsylvania, was one of the first to argue that value chains are a key element in the new framework of competitive analysis that is needed because of the globalization of world markets: "The formulation of strategy can be fruitfully viewed as placing bets on certain markets and on certain links of the value-added chain. ... The challenge of global strategy formulation is to differentiate between the various kinds of economies, to specify which link and which factor captures the firm's advantage, and to determine where the value-added chain would be broken across borders." In a subsequent paper, Kogut elaborates the central role of the value-added chain in the design of international business strategies, which are based upon the interplay between the comparative advantage of countries and the competitive advantage of firms. While the logic of comparative advantage helps to determine *where* the value-added chain should be broken across national borders, competitive (or firm-specific) advantage influences the decision on *what* activities and technologies along the value-added chain a firm should concentrate its resources in.

Michael Porter of Harvard Business School also developed a value-chain framework that he applied both at the level of individual firms and as one of the bases for determining the competitive advantage of nations. At the firm level, a value chain refers to a collection of discrete activities performed to do business, such as the physical creation of a product or service, its delivery and marketing to the buyer, and its support after sale. On the basis of these discrete activities, firms can establish two main types of competitive advantage: low relative cost (a firm's ability to carry out the activities in its value chain at lower cost than its competitors); or differentiation (performing in a unique way relative to competitors). While competitive advantage is determined at the level of a firm's value chain, Porter argues, "The appropriate unit of analysis in setting international strategy is the industry because the industry is the arena in which competitive advantage is won or lost."

The pattern of competition differs markedly across industries: at one extreme are "multidomestic" industries, in which competition in each country is basically independent of competition in other countries; and at the other end of the spectrum are "global industries," in which a firm's competitive position in one country is significantly impacted by its position in other countries. Since international competition is becoming the norm, Porter believes that firms must adopt "global strategies" in order to decide how to spread the activities in the value chain among countries. A very different set of scholars, studying the political economy of advanced industrial societies, highlighted the transformation from "organized capitalism" to "disorganized" or "competitive" capitalism. This approach is based on dramatic shifts in the strategic and institutional contexts of the global economy in the 1980s toward deregulated national markets and unhampered international exchanges. According to Schmitter, sectors or industries are the key unit for comparative analysis in this setting because they represent a meso level where a number of changes in technology, market structure, and public policy converge.

Our review of the contemporary global economy thus far has highlighted two distinctive shifts: the unparalleled fragmentation and reintegration of global production and trade patterns since the 1970s; and the recognition by Kogut and Porter, among others, of the power of value-chain or industry analysis as a basis for formulating global strategies that can integrate comparative (location-specific) advantage and competitive (firm-specific) advantage. However, the third transformation in the global economy that needs to be addressed as a precursor to the global value chain perspective is the remarkable growth of manufactured exports from low-wage to high-wage nations in the past several decades. This phenomenon has produced a range of reactions – from anxiety by producers in developed countries who believe they cannot compete with the flood of low-cost imports, to hope among economies in the South that they can catch up with their neighbors in the North by moving up the ladder of skill-intensive activities, to despair that global inequality and absolute levels of poverty have remained resistant to change despite the rapid progress of a relative handful of developing nations.

Production networks in the global economy

In the 1990s, a new framework, called global commodity chains (GCC), tied the concept of the value-added chain directly to the global organization of industries. This work was based on an insight into the growing importance of global buyers (mainly retailers and brand companies, or "manufacturers without factories") as key drivers in the formation of globally dispersed production and distribution networks. Gereffi contrasted these buyer-driven chains to what he termed producer-driven chains. The latter are the production systems created by vertically integrated transnational manufacturers, while the former term recognizes the role of global buyers, highlighting the significance of design and marketing in initiating the activities of global production systems. The GCC approach drew attention to the variety of actors that could exercise power within global production and distribution systems. It was the field-based methodology of GCC research, in particular, that provided new insights into the statistics showing an increase in trade involving components and other intermediate inputs. The trade data alone mask important organizational shifts because they differentiate neither between intrafirm and interfirm trade nor between the various ways in which global outsourcing relationships were being constructed.

A variety of overlapping terms has been used to describe the complex network relationships that make up the global economy. Each of the contending concepts, however, has particular emphases that are important to recognize for a chain analysis of the global economy:

Supply chains. A generic label for an input–output structure of value-adding activities, beginning with raw materials and ending with a finished product

International production networks. A focus on the international production networks in which TNCs act as "global network flagships"

Global commodity chains. An emphasis on the internal governance structure of supply chains (especially the producer-driven vs. buyer-driven distinction) and on the role of diverse lead firms in setting up global production and sourcing networks

French "filière" approach. A loosely knit set of studies that used the *filière* (i.e., channel or network) of activities as a method to study primarily agricultural export commodities such as rubber, cotton, coffee, and cocoa

Global value chains. Emphasis on the relative value of those economic activities that are required to bring a good or service from conception, through the different phases of production (involving a combination of physical transformation and the input of various producer services), delivery to final consumers, and final disposal after use.

The "value chain" concept has recently gained popularity as an overarching label for this body of research because it focuses on value creation and value capture across the full range of possible chain activities and end products (goods and services), and because it avoids the limiting connotations of the word *commodity,* which to some implies the production of undifferentiated goods with low barriers to entry. Like the GCC framework, global value chain (GVC) analysis accepts many of the observations made previously on geographical fragmentation, and it focuses primarily on the issues of industry (re)organization, coordination, governance, and power in the chain. Its concern is to understand the nature and consequences of organizational fragmentation in global industries. The GVC approach offers the possibility of understanding how firms are linked in the global economy, but also acknowledges the broader institutional context of these linkages, including trade policy, regulation, and standards. More generally, the global production networks paradigm has been used to join scholarly research on globalization with the concerns of both policymakers and social activists, who are trying to harness the potential gains of globalization to the pragmatic concerns of specific countries and social constituencies that feel increasingly marginalized in the international economic arena.

The next section of this chapter looks at different perspectives on governance at the meso level of the global economy, and it will be followed by a discussion of industrial upgrading, which analyzes the trajectories by which countries seek to upgrade their positions in the global economy. [...]

Industrial Upgrading and Global Production Networks

Major changes in global business organization during the last several decades of the twentieth century have had a significant impact on the upgrading possibilities of developing countries. This section will illustrate how the reorganization of international trade and production networks affects the capability of developing countries in different regions of the world to improve their positions in the value chains of diverse industries.

Industrial upgrading refers to the process by which economic actors – nations, firms, and workers – move from low-value to relatively high-value activities in global production networks. Different mixes of government policies, institutions, corporate strategies, technologies, and worker skills are associated with upgrading success. However, we can think about upgrading in a concrete way as linked to a series of economic roles associated with production and export activities, such as assembly, original equipment manufacturing (OEM), original brand name manufacturing (OBM), and original design manufacturing (ODM). This sequence of economic roles involves an expanding set of capabilities that developing countries must attain in pursuing an upgrading trajectory in diverse industries. In the remainder of this section, we will look at evidence from several sectors to see how global production networks have facilitated or constrained upgrading in developing nations.

Apparel

The global apparel industry contains many examples of industrial upgrading by developing countries. The lead firms in this buyer-driven chain are retailers (giant discount stores like Walmart and Target, department stores like J.C. Penney and Marks & Spencer, specialty retailers like The Limited and Gap), marketers (who control major apparel brands, such as Liz Claiborne, Tommy Hilfiger, Polo/Ralph Lauren, Nike), and brand name manufacturers (e.g., Wrangler, Phillips – van Heusen). These lead firms all have extensive global sourcing networks, which typically encompass 300 to 500 factories in various regions of the world. Because apparel production is quite labor intensive, manufacturing is typically carried out in countries with very low labor costs.

The main stages for firms in developing countries are first, to be included as a supplier (i.e., exporter) in the global apparel value chain; and then to upgrade from assembly to OEM and OBM export roles within the chain. Because of the Multi-Fiber Arrangement (MFA) associated with the GATT, which used quotas to regulate import shares for the United States, Canada, and much of Europe, at least 50 to 60 different developing countries have been significant apparel exporters since the 1970s, many just assembling apparel from imported inputs using low-wage labor in local export-processing zones.

The shift from assembly to the OEM export role has been the main upgrading challenge in the apparel value chain. It requires the ability to fill orders from global buyers, which includes making samples, procuring or manufacturing the needed inputs for the garment, meeting international standards in terms of price, quality, and delivery, and assuming responsibility for packing and shipping the finished item. Since fabric supply is the most important input in the apparel chain, virtually all countries that want to develop OEM capabilities need to develop a strong textile industry. The OBM export role is a more advanced stage because it involves assuming the design and marketing responsibilities associated with developing a company's own brands.

East Asian newly industrializing economies (NIEs) of Hong Kong, Taiwan, South Korea, and Singapore, which are generally taken as the archetype for industrial upgrading among developing countries, made a rapid transition from assembly to OEM production in the 1970s. Hong Kong clothing companies were the most successful in making the shift from OEM to OBM production in apparel, and Korean and Taiwanese firms pursued OBM in other consumer goods industries like appliances, sporting goods, and electronics. After mastering the OEM role, leading apparel export firms in Hong Kong, Taiwan, and South Korea began to set up their own international production networks in the 1980s, using the mechanism of "triangle manufacturing" whereby orders were received in the East Asian NIEs, apparel production was carried out in lower-wage countries in Asia and elsewhere (using textiles from the

NIEs), and the finished product was shipped to the United States or other overseas buyers using the quotas assigned to the exporting nation.

Thus, international production networks facilitated the upgrading of East Asian apparel firms in two ways: first, they were the main source of learning from US and European buyers about how to make the transition from assembly to OEM and OBM; and second, the East Asian NIEs established their own international production networks when faced with rising production costs and quota restrictions at home, and in order to take advantage of lower labor costs and a growing supply base in their region. Asian apparel manufacturers thus made the coordination of the apparel supply chain into one of their own core competences for export success.

Figure 22.1 presents a stylized model of industrial upgrading in the Asian apparel value chain. The main segments of the apparel chain – garments, textiles, fibers, and machinery – are arranged along the horizontal axis from low to high levels of relative value added in the production process. Countries are grouped on the vertical axis by their relative level of development, with Japan at the top and the least-developed exporters like Bangladesh, Sri Lanka, and Vietnam at the bottom.

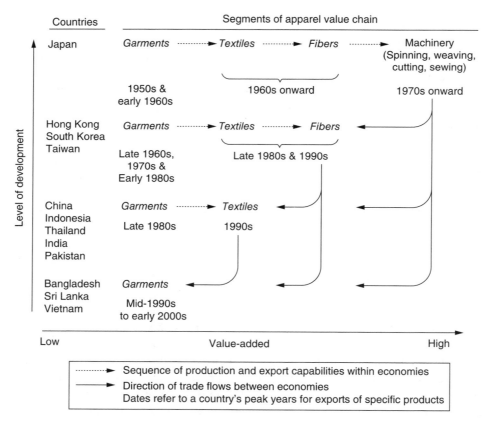

Figure 22.1　Industrial upgrading in the Asian apparel value chain. Dotted arrows refer to the sequence of production and export capabilities within economies. Solid arrows refer to the direction of trade flows between economies. Dates refer to a country's peak years for exports of specific products.

Figure 22.1 reveals several important dynamics about the apparel value chain in Asia, and the GVC approach more generally. First, individual countries progress from low- to high-value-added segments of the chain in a sequential fashion over time. This reinforces the importance in GVC research of looking at the entire constellation of value-added steps in the supply chain (raw materials, components, finished goods, related services, and machinery), rather than just the end product, as traditional industry studies are wont to do. Second, there is a regional division of labor in the apparel value chain, whereby countries at very different levels of development form a multitiered production hierarchy with a variety of export roles (e.g., the United States generates the designs and large orders, Japan provides the sewing machines, the East Asian NIEs supply fabric, and low-wage Asian economies like China, Indonesia, or Vietnam sew the apparel). Industrial upgrading occurs when countries change their roles in these export hierarchies. Finally, advanced economies like Japan and the East Asian NIEs do not exit the industry when the finished products in the chain become mature, as the "product cycle" model implies, but rather they capitalize on their knowledge of production and distribution networks in the industry and thus move to higher-value-added stages in the apparel chain. This strategic approach to upgrading requires that close attention be paid to competition within and between firms occupying all segments of global value chains.

It is important to note, in closing this section, the key role played by international regulation in the organization of the apparel value chain. The MFA and its apparel quotas will be eliminated in 2005 as a result of the Agreement on Textiles and Clothing in the WTO, and many of the smaller apparel exporters that only do assembly will probably be forced out of the world export market. This should greatly increase export concentration in the global apparel industry, with China likely to be the major winner, along with other large countries such as Mexico, India, Turkey, Romania, and Vietnam that have developed considerable expertise in OEM production. Mexico's rapid move in the 1990s to the top of list as the leading apparel exporter to the United States owes a great deal to the passage of NAFTA in 1994, which allowed the creation of textile production and other backward linkages in Mexico, and thereby facilitated the entry of the US retailers and apparel marketers that previously shunned Mexico in order to import apparel from Asia. In addition, employment in the apparel export industry increased in Mexico from 73,000 in 1994 to nearly 300,000 in 2000, mainly because Mexico coupled its relatively low wage rates with its recently acquired ability to carry out "full-package" (or OEM) production. However, China regained the lead from Mexico in 2001 and 2002, as Mexico has been unable to match the volume and low price of Chinese apparel exports, and because of the intense competition from new suppliers that continue to enter the US market.

Electronics

Global production networks have been a central feature in the development and upgrading of Asia's large, dynamic electronics sector. In the case of electronics, there have been competing cross-border production networks set up by US, Japanese, and European firms, led by TNCs that span the entire value chain in various industries.

For high-tech industries like electronics, these producer-driven chains must combine cost competitiveness with product differentiation and speed to market. Cross-border networks not only allow firms to combine these very different market demands effectively, but they also permit the integration of Asia's four distinct development tiers: Japan occupies the first tier; the East Asian NIEs are in the second tier; the major Southeast Asian countries of Malaysia, Thailand, the Philippines, and Indonesia are in the third tier; and the fourth tier contains China and late-developers such as Vietnam. While the economic crisis of 1997 called East Asia's economic miracle into question, it appears that the structural changes associated with recovery from the crisis will reinforce and increase the opportunities for networked production, as the process of corporate restructuring leads firms to focus on core activities and supplement these with the increasingly specialized technology, skills, and know-how that are located in different parts of Asia.

The diverse upgrading dynamics in Asian electronics can best be seen by contrasting the US and Japanese production networks. In the mid-1990s, US networks were considered to be relatively open and conducive to local development in host countries, while Japanese networks were perceived as closed and hierarchical with activities confined within affiliates that were tightly controlled by the parent company. US electronics multinationals typically set up Asian networks based on a complementary division of labor: US firms specialized in "soft" competencies (the definition of standards, designs, and product architecture), and the Taiwanese, Korean, and Singaporean firms specialized in "hard" competencies (the provision of components and basic manufacturing stages). The Asian affiliates of US firms in turn developed extensive subcontracting relationships with local manufacturers, who became increasingly skilled suppliers of components, subassemblies, and even entire electronics systems. Japanese networks, by contrast, were characterized by market segmentation: electronics firms in Japan made high-value, high-end products, while their offshore subsidiaries in Asia continued to make low-value, low-end products. In terms of Asian upgrading, the US production networks were definitely superior: US networks maximized the contributions from their Asian affiliates, and Japanese networks minimized the value added by their regional suppliers. Although there is some evidence that Japanese firms tried to open up their production networks in the late 1990s, at best there has been partial convergence, with persistent diversity.

Taiwan's achievements in electronics are especially notable for several reasons. During the 1990s, Taiwan established itself as the world's largest supplier of computer monitors, main boards, mouse devices, keyboards, scanners, and notebook personal computers (PCs), among other items. About 70 percent of the notebook PCs sold under OEM arrangements to American and Japanese computer companies, which resell them under their own logos, have been designed by Taiwanese firms. Acer, Taiwan's leading computer maker, is successful at both OEM and OBM production. Progress has been equally remarkable in the field of electronic components, and Taiwan also boasts one of the world's leading silicon foundry companies, the Taiwan Semiconductor Manufacturing Corporation. What is especially impressive about these accomplishments is that small and medium enterprises have played a central role as a source of flexibility in Taiwan's production networks. The role of small and medium enterprises as engines of growth and industrial transformation sets Taiwan apart from South Korea, which has relied extensively on huge, diversified conglomerates (*chaebol*) as the cornerstone of its electronics sector. The Taiwanese model in the computer industry draws on a combination of several factors: government policies that facilitated market entry and upgrading; strong linkages with large Taiwanese firms and business groups; and organizational innovations, such as the shift from relatively simple, production-based OEM to more complex "turn-key production" arrangements that encompass a wide variety of high-end support services, including design and global supply chain management.

One of the most striking features of the electronics industry in recent years has been the rise of global contract manufacturers. A significant share of the world's electronics manufacturing capacity is now contained in a handful of huge contractors, such as Solectron, Flextronics, and Celestica. These firms are pure manufacturers. They sell no products under their own brand names and instead focus on providing global manufacturing services to a diverse set of lead firms, such as Hewlett Packard, Nortel, and Ericsson. All have operations that are truly global in scope, and all have grown dramatically since the early 1990s. Solectron, the largest contractor, expanded from a single Silicon Valley location with 3,500 employees and $256 million in revenues in 1988 to a global powerhouse with more than 80,000 employees in 50 locations and nearly $20 billion in revenues in 2000. Although they have global reach, all of the largest contract manufacturers are based in North America. Except for the personal computer industry, Asian and European contract manufacturers have not developed, and the few that did were acquired by North American contractors during their buying spree fueled by the inflated stock prices of the 1990s. Global contract manufacturers introduce a high degree of modularity into value chain governance because the large scale and scope of their operations create comprehensive bundles of standardized value chain activities that can be accessed by a variety of lead firms through modular networks.

Fresh vegetables

A final example of the role of global production networks in promoting industrial upgrading involves the production of fresh vegetables in Kenya and Zimbabwe for export to UK supermarkets. Africa has very few success stories in the realm of export-oriented development, but some countries of sub-Saharan Africa seem to have found a niche in the fresh vegetables market. Several factors tie this case to our previous examples. First, fresh vegetables are a buyer-driven value chain, albeit in the agricultural sector. As with apparel, there is a high level of concentration at the retail end of the chain. The largest UK supermarkets and other food retailers control 70 to 90 percent of fresh produce imports from Africa. These retailers have avoided direct involvement in production; they just specialize in marketing and in the coordination of their supply chains.

Second, a major stimulus for local upgrading in Africa comes from UK retailers ratcheting up the standards that exporters must meet. UK supermarkets have moved beyond compliance with product quality and legislative (or due diligence) requirements for how produce is grown, processed, and transported. They now are focusing on broader standards that exporters must meet, such as integrated crop management, environmental protection, and human rights. In addition, retailers are beginning to use third-party auditors paid for by producers to ensure compliance with these standards.

Third, more stringent UK requirements have led to a decline in the market share of smallholder production and small export firms, which have been excluded from the supermarket supply chain. The horticulture industry in sub-Saharan Africa is dominated by a few large exporters that source predominantly from large-scale production units. In both Kenya and Zimbabwe, the top five exporters controlled over three-quarters of all fresh vegetable exports in the late 1990s.

Fourth, as in apparel and electronics, market power in the horticultural chain has shifted from those activities that lower production costs to those that add value in the chain. In fresh vegetables, the latter include investing in postharvest facilities, such as cold storage; barcoding products packed in trays to differentiate varieties, countries, and suppliers; moving into high-value-added items such as ready-prepared vegetables and salads; and treating logistics as a core competence in the chain in order to reduce the time between harvesting, packing, and delivery. Pushing back these functions into Africa can reduce the cost for UK supermarkets because adding value to vegetables is labor-intensive and African labor is relatively cheap, but taken together these high-end services can become a new source of competitiveness and an opportunity to add value in Africa.

23

Global Income Inequality by the Numbers: In History and Now

An Overview

Branko Milanovic

[...]

As the world becomes more integrated the global dimension of inequality is likely to become increasingly relevant. This is for at least two reasons: because of much greater movement of factors of production across borders, and because of greater influence of other people's (foreigners') standard of living and way of life on one's perceived income position and aspirations. Greater movement of capital, goods, technology and ideas from one end of the globe to another implies greater connectivity with people who are not one's compatriots, and greater dependence on other nations for generation of one's income. Movements of labor which illustrate this interdependence in a most obvious fashion are still less important than movements of capital, but they are increasing. The knowledge of how other people live and how much money they make influences strongly our perception of our own income and position in the income pyramid. An imaginary community of world citizens is thus gradually built. And once this is done, comparisons of actual incomes and welfare between different members of that imaginary community acquire importance. This is why global inequality, even if not as relevant and important for an average individual as inequality within her political community (nation state) will gain in importance. Once we compare ourselves with people from other parts of the world, we are indeed interested in global income distribution. Global inequality begins to matter.

When we talk about inequality that transcends national borders, we really often have in mind not one but three different concepts – even when we are not fully aware of it. I am going to articulate these three concepts.

Original publication details: Branko Milanovic, "Global Income Inequality by the Numbers: In History and Now." Washington, DC: The World Bank Development Research Group, Poverty and Inequality Team, November 2012. pp. 2–9. Licensed under the Creative Commons Attribution 3.0 Generic license.

The first concept of inequality (let's call it *Inequality 1*) is focused on inequality between nations of the world. It is an inequality statistic calculated across GDPs or mean incomes obtained from household surveys of all countries in the world, without population-weighting.

To show how this is done, consider the three individuals in the top row of Figure 23.1: the height of each person represents the GDP or mean income of his or her country. Somebody from a poor country would be represented as a short person, somebody from a middle-income country as a person of medium height, and somebody from a rich country as a very tall person. When we calculate this concept of inequality, we take all countries with their mean incomes – we have some 150 countries in the world with such data – and calculate the Gini coefficient. China and Luxembourg have the same importance, because we do not take population sizes into account. Every country counts the same, somewhat like in the UN General Assembly.

Consider now the second row of the figure which would help us define Concept 2 inequality or *Inequality 2*. There, individuals from poor countries are all equally short as before and those from rich countries all equally tall, but the difference lies in the fact that countries' population sizes are now taken into account. We do exactly the same as we did in Inequality 1, but now China and Luxemburg (or any other country) enter the calculation with their populations. In Figure 23.1, the poor country is the most populous (5 individuals out of total of 10 displayed there), and the middle-income country, the least populous (2 individuals). Introducing population is very important. As we shall

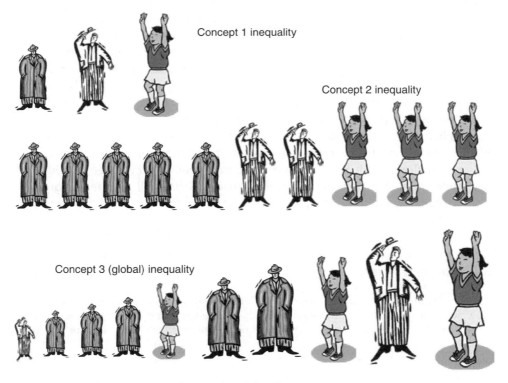

Figure 23.1   Three concepts of inequality defined.

see in the next section, during the past 25 years, the movements in Concept 1 and Concept 2 inequalities were very different. Recall, however, that in both cases the calculation takes into account not actual incomes of individuals, but country averages.

Inequality 3 is the global inequality, which is the most important concept for those interested in the world as composed of individuals, not nations. Unlike the first two concepts, this one is individual-based: each person, regardless of her country, enters in the calculation with her actual income. In Figure 23.1, this is represented by the different heights of individuals who belong to the same country. Not all Americans have the average income of the United States, nor do all Chinese have the average income of China. And indeed in Figure 23.1, the poorest person is from the middle-income country, while her compatriot is the second richest (the second tallest) in our group of ten individuals.

[…]

Figure 23.2 displays the movements of the three types of inequalities after the Second World War. The Gini coefficient is on the vertical axis. Inequality 1 was stable from 1960 to 1980. This means that there was no systematically faster or slower growth of poor or rich countries. Neither were poor catching on with the rich, nor were the two groups growing further apart. Divergence started only at the beginning of globalization, around 1980, and went on until the turn of the century. These two decades were very bad as far as convergence, or catching up by poor countries, is concerned: rich countries grew, on average, faster than poor countries. However China and India, which are the huge success cases of that period and the two most populous countries in the world, do not enter into calculation of Inequality 1 with greater weights than any other country.

Let us now consider further Figure 23.2. Why is it called "the mother of all inequality disputes"? To see what the dispute is about, consider the difference in the

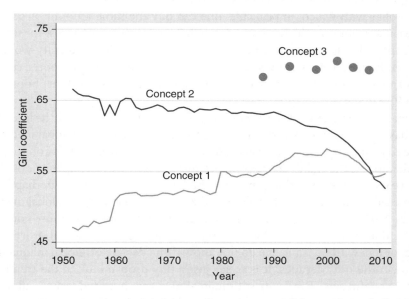

Figure 23.2 International and global inequality, 1952–2011: "The mother of all inequality disputes".

movements of Inequality 1 and Inequality 2. While the first, as we just saw, rose during the globalization era, the second declined, at times even dramatically. Measured by Inequality 2, the world has certainly become a much better ("more convergent" or more equal) place precisely during the same period. Thus, those who desire to emphasize the unevenness of globalization tend to focus on growing inter-country gaps, not taking into account sizes of population, and prefer Inequality 1. Those who, on the contrary, wish to focus on positive aspects of globalization tend to favor Concept 2, and to point to the indubitable successes of China and India. In effect, to grasp intuitively why and how Concept 2 inequality declined, we need just to recall that in these calculations, China counts a lot because of its large population size. And China, starting in the 1980s from an extremely low level of income, has during the past three decades grown very fast, converging on the rich world. Until recently, it was China alone that had been preventing a rise in global inequality as measured by Concept 2. But now it has "support" from India which is also registering high rates of growth, and is also starting from a very low baseline. High rates of growth of these two countries are thus the major factor underlying the downward trend of Inequality 2.

Inequality 3 can be calculated only from the mid-1980s because we do not have household surveys going further back in time. Figure 23.2 shows that Inequality 3 is higher than Inequality 2. This is true by definition because in Inequality 3 people enter the calculations with their actual incomes, not with country averages. A quick glance at Figure 23.1 shows that the variability of heights is greater in the third row than in the second. Averaging-out reduces measured inequality.

To calculate "true" global inequality or Concept 3 inequality, we have to adjust people's incomes with the price levels they face and which, of course, differ between countries. We are interested in real welfare of people and those living in "cheaper" countries will get a boost in their incomes compared to what they make in nominal dollar terms. The currency we use is international (or "PPP" for purchasing power parity) dollar with which, in principle, one can buy the same amount of goods and services in any country of the world. Indeed, if we were not to adjust for the differences in price levels, and were to use nominal dollars, global inequality would have been even higher. This is because price levels tend to be lower in poorer countries, and income of people living in poorer countries thus gets a significant "boost" when we use PPP dollars.

Often, a key issue of concern regarding global inequality is not only its level, but its trend: has it been going up or down during the globalization era? Global inequality is calculated at approximately five-year intervals, from 1988 (the first dot on the left) to 2008 (the dot on the right). If we compare this last dot with a couple of dots for the earlier years, we see something that may be historically important: perhaps for the first time since the Industrial Revolution, there may be a decline in global inequality. Between 2002 and 2008, global Gini decreased by 1.4 points. We must not rush to conclude that what we see in the most recent years represents a real or irreversible decline, or a new trend, since we do not know if the decline of global inequality will continue in the next decades. It is so far just a tiny drop, a kink in the trend, but is indeed a hopeful sign. For the first time in almost two hundred years – after a long period during which global inequality rose and then reached a very high plateau – it may be setting onto a downward path.

The main reason for this break in the previous trend is what also underlies the decrease in Concept 2 inequality: fast growth of relatively poor and very populous countries, most notably China and India. Their growth, reflected in the rising real incomes of their populations, has not only curbed the rise in global inequality, but pushed it slightly down. China's and India's roles stand in marked contrast to the two other factors that influence global inequality and which have both been clearly pro-inequality. The first is the divergence of countries' mean incomes which lasted from around 1980 to 2000; the second were rising within-national inequalities in many countries. The catching-up of poor and large countries has been the sole factor offsetting these upward pressures. But it has been such a strong factor that it has either kept global inequality from rising or, more recently with the acceleration of Indian growth, reduced it.

What can we say about the level of global inequality? What does the Gini of about 70, which is the value of global inequality (see Figure 23.2), mean? One way to look at it is to take the whole income of the world and divide it into two halves: the richest 8% will take one-half and the other 92% of the population will take another half. So, it is a 92-8 world. Applying the same type of division to the US income, the numbers are 78 and 22. Or using Germany, the numbers are 71 and 29. Another way to look at it is to compare what percentage of world population, ranked from the poorest to the richest, is needed to get to the cumulative one-fifths of global income. Three-quarters of (the poorer) world population are needed to get to the first one-fifth of total income, but only 1.7% of those at the top suffice to get to the last one-fifth.

Global inequality is much greater than inequality within any individual country. [...]

24

The Bottom Billion

Why the Poorest Countries Are Failing and What Can Be Done About It

Paul Collier

The third world has shrunk. For forty years the development challenge has been a rich world of one billion people facing a poor world of five billion people. The Millennium Development Goals established by the United Nations, which are designed to track development progress through 2015, encapsulate this thinking. By 2015, however, it will be apparent that this way of conceptualizing development has become outdated. Most of the five billion, about 80 percent, live in countries that are indeed developing, often at amazing speed. The real challenge of development is that there is a group of countries at the bottom that are falling behind, and often falling apart.

The countries at the bottom coexist with the twenty-first century, but their reality is the fourteenth century: civil war, plague, ignorance. They are concentrated in Africa and Central Asia, with a scattering elsewhere. Even during the 1990s, in retrospect the golden decade between the end of the Cold War and 9/11, incomes in this group declined by 5 percent. We must learn to turn the familiar numbers upside down: a total of five billion people who are already prosperous, or at least are on track to be so, and one billion who are stuck at the bottom.

This problem matters, and not just to the billion people who are living and dying in fourteenth-century conditions. It matters to us. The twenty-first-century world of material comfort, global travel, and economic interdependence will become increasingly vulnerable to these large islands of chaos. And it matters now. As the bottom billion diverges from an increasingly sophisticated world economy, integration will become harder, not easier.

[...]

Original publication details: Paul Collier, *The Bottom Billion*. New York: Oxford University Press, 2007. pp. 3–10, 79–80, 95–6. Reproduced with permission from Oxford University Press.

All societies used to be poor. Most are now lifting out of it; why are others stuck? The answer is traps. Poverty is not intrinsically a trap, otherwise we would all still be poor. Think, for a moment, of development as chutes and ladders. In the modern world of globalization there are some fabulous ladders; most societies are using them. But there are also some chutes, and some societies have hit them. The countries at the bottom are an unlucky minority, but they are stuck.

Traps, and the Countries Caught in Them

Suppose your country is dirt poor, almost stagnant economically, and that few people are educated. You don't have to try that hard to imagine this condition – our ancestors lived this way. With hard work, thrift, and intelligence, a society can gradually climb out of poverty, unless it gets trapped. Development traps have become a fashionable area of academic dispute, with a fairly predictable right-left divide. The right tends to deny the existence of development traps, asserting that any country adopting good policies will escape poverty. The left tends to see global capitalism as inherently generating a poverty trap.

The concept of a development trap has been around for a long time and is most recently associated with the work of the economist Jeffrey Sachs, who has focused on the consequences of malaria and other health problems. Malaria keeps countries poor, and because they are poor the potential market for a vaccine is not sufficiently valuable to warrant drug companies making the huge investment in research that is necessary. This book is about four traps that have received less attention: the conflict trap, the natural resources trap, the trap of being landlocked with bad neighbors, and the trap of bad governance in a small country. Like many developing countries that are now succeeding, all the countries that are the focus of this book are poor. Their distinctive feature is that they got caught in one or another of the traps. These traps are not inescapable, however, and over the years some countries have broken free of them and then started to catch up. Unfortunately, that process of catching up has itself recently stalled. Those countries that have only broken clear of the traps during the last decade have faced a new problem: the global market is now far more hostile to new entrants than it was in the 1980s. The countries newly escaped from the traps may have missed the boat, finding themselves in a limbo-like world in which growth is constrained by external factors; this will be the theme in my discussion of globalization. When Mauritius escaped the traps in the 1980s it rocketed to middle-income levels; when neighboring Madagascar finally escaped the traps two decades later, there was no rocket.

Most countries have stayed clear of any of the traps that are the subject of this book. But countries with a combined population of around one billion people have got caught in them. Underlying that statement are some definitions. For example, one of the traps involves being landlocked – although being landlocked is not sufficient to constitute the trap. But when is a country landlocked? You might think that such a matter is clear enough from an atlas. But what about Zaire, which after the ruinous reign of President Mobutu understandably rebranded itself as the

Democratic Republic of the Congo? It is *virtually* landlocked but has a tiny sliver of coast. And Sudan has some coast, but most of its people live far away from it.

[...]

As of 2006 there are around 980 million people living in these trapped countries. Since their populations are growing, by the time you read this the figure will be hovering around the one billion mark. Seventy percent of these people are in Africa, and most Africans are living in countries that have been in one or another of the traps. Africa is therefore the core of the problem.

[...]

But the countries of the bottom billion do not form a group with a convenient geographic label. When I want to use a geographic label for them I describe them as "Africa +," with the + being places such as Haiti, Bolivia, the Central Asian countries, Laos, Cambodia, Yemen, Burma, and North Korea. They all either are still in one of the traps or escaped too late.

[...]

So, how have the countries of the bottom billion been doing? First, consider how people live, or rather die. In the bottom billion average life expectancy is fifty years, whereas in the other developing countries it is sixty-seven years. Infant mortality – the proportion of children who die before their first birthday – is 14 percent in the bottom billion, whereas in the other developing countries it is 4 percent. The proportion of children with symptoms of long-term malnutrition is 36 percent in the bottom billion as against 20 percent for the other developing countries.

The Role of Growth in Development

Has this gap between the bottom billion and the rest of the developing world always been there, or has it come about because the bottom billion have been trapped? To find out, we have to disaggregate the statistics that have been used in the past to describe all the countries that we label as "developing." Here's a hypothetical example. Prosperia has a big economy that is growing at 10 percent, but the country has only a small population. Catastrophia is a small economy declining at 10 percent, but it has a large population. The usual approach – employed, for example, by the International Monetary Fund (IMF) in its flagship publication *World Economic Outlook* – is to average figures that relate to the size of a country's economy. On this approach, Prosperia's large, growing economy skews the average upward, and so in aggregate the two countries are described as growing. The problem is that this describes what is going on from the perspective of the typical unit of income, not from the perspective of the typical person. Most units of income are in Prosperia, but most people are in Catastrophia. If we want to describe what the typical person experiences in the countries of the bottom billion, we need to work with figures based not on a country's income but on its population. Does it matter? Well, it does if the poorest countries are diverging from the rest, which is the thesis of this book, because averaging by income dismisses the poorest countries as unimportant. The experience of their people does not count for much precisely because they are poor – their income is negligible.

When we get the data appropriately averaged, what do we find? Those developing countries that are not part of the bottom billion – the middle four billion – have experienced rapid and accelerating growth in per capita income. Let's take it decade by decade. During the 1970s they grew at 2.5 percent a year, hopeful but not remarkable. During the 1980s and 1990s their growth rate accelerated to 4 percent a year. During the first few years of the twenty-first century it accelerated again to over 4.5 percent. These growth rates may not sound sensational, but they are without precedent in history. They imply that children in these countries will grow up to have lives dramatically different from those of their parents. Even where people are still poor, these societies can be suffused with hope: time is on their side.

But how about the bottom billion? Let's again take it decade by decade. During the 1970s their per capita income rose at 0.5 percent a year, so they were becoming slightly better off in absolute terms but at a rate that was likely to be barely perceptible. Given the high degree of volatility of individual incomes in these societies, the slight overall tendency to improvement is likely to have been drowned by these individual risks. The overall tenor of the society will have been dominated by individual fears of falling rather than hope coming from society-wide progress. But in the 1980s the performance of the bottom billion got much worse, *declining* at 0.4 percent a year. In absolute terms, by the end of the 1980s they were back to where they had been in 1970. If you had been living in these societies over that full sweep of twenty years, the only economic experience was of individual volatility: some people went up and some went down. There was no society-wide reason for hope. And then came the 1990s. This is now seen as the golden decade, between the end of the Cold War and 9/11 – the decade of the cloudless sky and booming markets. It wasn't so golden for the bottom billion: their rate of absolute decline accelerated to 0.5 percent a year. By the turn of the millennium they were therefore poorer than they had been in 1970.

[...]

Think about what these two sets of growth rates imply. During the 1970s the bottom billion diverged in growth from the rest of the developing world by 2 percent a year. So even then the main feature of the societies in the bottom billion was divergence, not development. But the situation soon became alarmingly worse. During the 1980s the divergence accelerated to 4.4 percent a year, and during the 1990s it accelerated further to an astonishing 5 percent a year. Taking the three decades as a whole, the experience of the societies in the bottom billion was thus one of massive and accelerating divergence. Given the power of compound growth rates, these differences between the bottom billion and the rest of the developing world will rapidly cumulate into two different worlds. Indeed, the divergence has indeed already pushed most of the countries of the bottom billion to the lowest spot in the global pile.

It was not always that way. Before globalization gave huge opportunities to China and India, they were poorer than many of the countries that have been caught in the traps. But China and India broke free in time to penetrate global markets, whereas other countries that were initially less poor didn't. For the last two decades this has produced a growth pattern that appears confusing. Some initially poor countries are growing very well, and so it can easily look as if there is not really a problem: the bottom appears to be growing as fast as the rest. Over the next two decades the true nature of the problem is going to become apparent, however, because the countries that are trapped in stagnation or decline are now pretty well the poorest. The average person in the societies of the bottom billion now has an income only around one-fifth that of the typical person in the other developing countries, and the gap will just get worse with time. Picture this as a billion people stuck in a train that is slowly rolling backward downhill. By 2050 the development gulf will no longer be between a rich billion in the most developed countries and five billion in the developing countries; rather, it will be between the trapped billion and the rest of humankind.

[…]

All the people living in the countries of the bottom billion have been in one or another of the traps that I have described […]. Seventy-three percent of them have been through civil war, 29 percent of them are in countries dominated by the politics of natural resource revenues, 30 percent are landlocked, resource-scarce, and in a bad neighborhood, and 76 percent have been through a prolonged period of bad governance and poor economic policies. Adding up these percentages, you will realize that some countries have been in more than one trap, either simultaneously or sequentially.

But when I speak of traps, I am speaking figuratively. These traps are probabilistic; unlike black holes, it is not impossible to escape from them, just difficult. Take as an example the trap of bad governance and poor policies, and remember that the mathematical expectation of being stuck with bad policies is nearly sixty years. That expectation is built up from the very small chance, less than 2 percent, of escaping from the trap in any single year. But of course that small change implies that periodically countries do escape. This is true of all the traps: a peace holds (as is currently the case in Angola), natural resources get depleted (as is looming in Cameroon, which has nearly exhausted its oil reserves), reformers succeed in transforming governance and policies (as is now under way in Nigeria). And such transformations have implications for the landlocked: as Nigeria turns itself around, Niger, though still landlocked, is now in a better neighborhood. The focus of this chapter is to ask what happens next.

You might think that if a country escapes from a trap, it can then start to catch up – it will begin to grow, and grow pretty fast. The professional term for catch-up is "convergence." The best-studied example of convergence is the European Union. The countries that were initially the poorest members, such as Portugal, Ireland, and Spain, have grown the fastest, whereas the country that was initially richest, Germany, has grown slowly, and so the states that make up the European Union have converged. That is partly why relatively poor countries such as Poland and the other countries of Eastern Europe have been keen to join, whereas the countries that are richer than the European Union, Norway and Switzerland, have decided not to do so. Convergence is also working on a global scale: the lower-income countries are, on the whole, growing faster than the developed countries. People in the developed world are starting to get worried that China is converging on us so fast. The fact that the countries of the bottom billion have bucked this trend to convergence is the puzzle with which I started. And so far my explanation has been that they have been stuck in one or another of the four traps.

[…]

To get a chance to play in the global economy, you need to break free of the traps, and that is not easy. Remember, in order to turn a country around it helps to have a pool of educated people, but the global labor market is draining the bottom billion of their limited pool of such people. Even once they reform, many of these economies find it difficult to attract private investment inflows, and may continue to hemorrhage their own modest private wealth. And they face a high hurdle in trying to break into diversified markets for exports because China, India, and the other successful developing countries have already done so. Even once free of the traps, countries are liable to be stuck in a kind of limbo – no longer falling apart, but not able to replicate the rapid growth of Asia, and so failing to converge.

This indeed seems to describe a lot of bottom-billion countries that have recently come out of the traps. Remember that in the past four years the average country of the bottom billion has at last started to grow. I have interpreted that as a temporary phenomenon linked to the global boom in commodities. But suppose you were to put the most favorable gloss on it – that they have broken free of the traps. Well, although they are growing, it is at a very sedate pace – much more slowly than the other developing countries even during the slow decade of the 1970s. Even if their present growth rate is sustained, they will continue to diverge rapidly. It will take them many decades to reach what we now consider to be the threshold of middle income, and by that time the rest of the world will have moved on.

There is also a yet more depressing variant of the future for these limbo countries: the traps still await them. As long as they have low incomes and slow growth they continue to play Russian roulette. Côte d'Ivoire survived low income and slow growth for a couple of decades but then fell into conflict as the result of a coup. Zimbabwe survived the same and then fell into bad governance. Tanzania, currently among the most hopeful low-income countries, is about to become resource-rich due to new discoveries of gas and gold. Malawi grew remarkably well for the first decade of its independence, considering that is landlocked and resource-scarce, but then its neighbors fell into the conflict trap and, being dependent upon them, it too began to decline. And so a miserable but possible scenario is that countries in the bottom billion oscillate between the traps and limbo, perhaps switching in the process from one trap to another.

25

The Global Financial Crisis and Its Effects

Malcolm Edey

A Brief Chronology

As is now well known, the immediate background to the crisis was the emergence of problems in the US market for sub-prime housing loans in the first half of 2007. Sub-prime loans, in US terminology, are loans that do not meet standard criteria for good credit quality, such as a sound credit history on the part of the borrower, good income documentation and/or a conservative loan-to-valuation ratio. Sub-prime lending became very significant in the United States from around the middle part of this decade; by 2006, these loans were around one-fifth of new housing lending and an estimated 15 per cent of the stock of housing loans outstanding in the United States.

An important feature of this period was the securitization of sub-prime and other loans by their original lenders and their subsequent sale to other investors. This occurred partly through conventional mortgage-backed securities but also, increasingly, through more complex products such as collateralised debt obligations (or CDOs), which came to play an important part in the spreading of the crisis. CDOs work by layering the claims in a pool of mortgages into tranches, with the most senior tranches provided the most protection against potential losses. That structure enabled some of these securities to gain high credit ratings even when the average quality of the underlying loans was poor. In combination with their relatively high yields, these features made them attractive to investors. What was not

Original publication details: Malcolm Edey, "The Global Financial Crisis and Its Effects," in *Economic Papers*, 28, 3, September 2009. pp. 186–9, 191, 193–5. Reproduced with permission from John Wiley & Sons. Note: This text has been edited and all notes and references to third party sources removed. Please refer to the original source text for clarification on what has been omitted.

well-understood, however, was that the layering structure could result in substantial losses, even to the senior tranches, in the event of a generalised downturn in the US housing market, which is what subsequently occurred.

When these problems first became apparent, in the first half of 2007, the effects seemed to be confined largely to the US financial sector. The first significant impacts on global markets began in August 2007. It was at that time that the major French bank BNP-Paribas announced the suspension of three of its funds that were investing in US mortgage securities. That announcement drew attention to the fact that a number of European banks, or off-balance-sheet vehicles associated with them, had invested heavily in these securities and could therefore be exposed to significant losses. Further, uncertainty about the size and location of these exposures, along with the general opaqueness of many of these securities, meant that financial institutions in general suffered a serious loss of investor confidence. The result was that risk spreads in global credit markets widened markedly, and banks found it more difficult, and more expensive, to obtain funding through financial markets. These developments placed already strained institutions under further pressure.

In the months that followed, the crisis widened as more information about the scale of losses was revealed. Some of the more significant developments were the run on the British bank Northern Rock in September 2007, which led to its nationalisation; a string of large-scale losses announced by major banks and investment banks in the United States and Europe shortly thereafter; and the rescue of Bear Stearns in March 2008. The latter appeared for a while to mark a turning point, and for a few months market conditions began to settle down and credit spreads to narrow, although they remained well above their pre-crisis levels.

However, the crisis intensified sharply in September 2008, particularly following the failure of the US investment bank Lehman Brothers, which was the first time in the crisis that losses were incurred by creditors of a major financial institution. The Lehman collapse followed the effective nationalisation of the two US federal mortgage agencies Fannie Mae and Freddie Mac – that together had more than $5 trillion in mortgages under management or guarantee – a week earlier. These events were followed in quick succession by the nationalisation of the world's largest insurance company American International Group (AIG) along with a string of other announcements of the failure or near-failure of financial institutions in the United States and Europe. Uncertainty about the nature, scope and passage of the various proposed rescue packages through this period added to the general turmoil.

These events sparked a severe loss of confidence, not just in the financial sector, but also across households and businesses. In the weeks that followed the Lehman Brothers' collapse, world equity markets experienced extreme volatility, with prices falling in net terms to eventually reach levels around 50 per cent below their earlier peaks. It was also during this period that governments around the world moved to guarantee deposits and in some cases wholesale borrowing by their banks, in conjunction with a series of other measures designed to support their financial systems. The crisis also spread quickly to other vulnerable countries; towards the end of 2008, the International Monetary Fund (IMF) announced stabilisation packages for Iceland, Pakistan and several Eastern European countries.

Underlying Causes

This brief chronology gives an idea of how the crisis happened in a mechanical sense, but does not address the deeper question of its underlying causes. This issue has been extensively debated over the past year – and no doubt will continue to be so for many years ahead – and hence our understanding of the roles and importance of each of the various factors is still developing. Nonetheless, at this stage the explanations have centred around three broad sets of factors, and it is probably fair to say that each played a significant role.

The first set of factors stresses aspects that have in fact been common to past financial bubbles, in particular the combination of cheap credit that increased demand for debt along with a general increase in the appetite for risk by potential lenders. Central to this line of explanation is the low interest rate structure that prevailed in the major economies for much of the early part of this decade. The United States, the euro area and Japan all ran unusually low interest rates during the period. While the specific reasons for doing so vary amongst this group, and are still subject to considerable debate, they were partly related to cyclical economic conditions in those economies and, at a deeper level, to the large global savings imbalances that emerged around the turn of this decade. However, whatever the ultimate driving factor behind the low interest rates of that period, the low cost of funds contributed to an increasing demand for debt, especially by households.

This environment was also one in which perceptions of risk were declining, in part for sound reasons associated with strong economic growth, falling unemployment and rising house prices. More generally, the low interest environment encouraged a 'search for yield' in financial markets, in which investors sought to increase returns by taking on more risk. This led to a significant compression of risk spreads across a range of credit markets around the world. While a financial crisis was not inevitable in these circumstances, history suggests that this situation was conducive to a kind of financial cycle that can quickly get out of hand.

The second set of explanations focuses on features of the financial system that encouraged the particular types of risk-taking that were prevalent on this occasion, and which made this financial cycle different from earlier crises. Included in this confluence of events were the growth of the originate-and-distribute model in mortgage lending, the increasing use of structured securities such as CDOs, weaknesses in risk controls on those activities, and the unhelpful role played by credit-rating agencies in ensuring these products were marketable. Over time, conflicts of interest by loan generators and rating agencies became more prominent in a climate that was characterised by high optimism and rising leverage. The wide-spread sale of these products, both in the United States and abroad, set up the conditions for international transmission of the crisis once their values started to decline. This in turn led to a major reappraisal of attitudes to risk and willingness to lend. These effects were exacerbated by the efforts of financial firms to quickly reduce the level of their leverage and exposures to risk, which contributed to an evaporation of liquidity in many markets.

The third (and related) factor concerns the ineffectiveness of regulatory regimes in containing the growth of financial risk-taking in the major countries. To give one example, the growth of the originate-and-distribute model can be seen in part as a response to capital adequacy regulations that gave banks an incentive to economise on capital by shifting their activities into off-balance-sheet vehicles. In this way, a set of regulations intended to contain a certain type of risk actually had the effect of shifting risk into unregulated vehicles, where it was not well controlled. While there is still much to consider in this area, it is apparent in retrospect that regulatory gaps had opened up in a number of areas as monitoring lagged the pace and complexity of financial innovation. This failure may have been exacerbated by the climate at the time, which was generally to encourage home-ownership rates and reduce regulation.

The Initial Economic Impact

The pace of global activity had already been softening before the most intense phase of the financial crisis began in September 2008. The large run up in home construction and dwelling prices in the United States had started to turn by mid-2006 – partly in response to rising policy rates – and this was dampening the overall growth of the US economy. The pace of activity had also started to soften for much the same reason in the United Kingdom. However, other parts of the world continued to look resilient through the first half of 2008. China and the other emerging economies in Asia and elsewhere mostly kept growing at a firm pace during that period, and world commodity prices were still close to their peaks.

However, with the deterioration in financial conditions following the Lehman Brothers' collapse in September, the level of activity in the major economies took a sharp turn for the worse. In the climate of extreme uncertainty, business and consumer confidence collapsed. Households responded by cutting discretionary spending, especially demand for manufactured goods. The result was an exceptionally sharp fall in global industrial production towards the end of 2008, and significant contractions in GDP in most of the major economies. The downturn in the G7 economies intensified during the December quarter – especially in Japan – and spread to other parts of the world, including Asia, Latin America and eastern Europe. Some countries in east Asia saw GDP declines of more than 5 per cent in the December quarter. While the Chinese and Indian economies continued to expand through this period, their rates of growth were significantly reduced.

[…]

Several reasons have been proposed to explain this sudden and synchronised deterioration in global macroeconomic conditions. The first, which was already touched on above, was the wide-spread loss of confidence in the wake of the collapse of Lehman Brothers and the associated period of exceptional turmoil in global financial markets. This deterioration was clearly seen in survey-based measures of business and consumer confidence in the major economies. It is plausible that improvements in communication and the more rapid transmission of economic news contributed to making this swing in confidence more highly synchronised than in earlier major cycles. As a consequence of the deterioration in confidence, along with the decline in housing and equity wealth and rising unemployment, households around the world made a rapid re-evaluation of their spending plans, cutting back in particular on discretionary spending. Private consumption fell sharply in the industrialised and emerging market economies in late 2008. One very clear example was a sharp drop in the demand for cars, with sales in the major economies falling from their early 2008 levels by around 25 per cent. Similarly, business investment contracted in a number of countries in late 2008/early 2009.

A second factor, also related to the Lehman Brothers' collapse, was the further tightening of credit standards by lenders in the major economies and a marked additional increase in the price of risk. This manifested itself, amongst other things, in disruptions to trade credit and insurance, and in a tightening of lending for consumer and business spending. Reflecting these developments, the pace of credit growth fell sharply in a range of countries in late 2008 or early 2009, although part of this is likely to have reflected a pull back in demand for credit. Adverse feedback loops appeared to be operating during this period as a weakening economy undermined asset prices, which further diminished confidence and the capacity of banks to lend.

Third, these effects seem to have been transmitted quickly around the world – especially to Asia – through the trade channel as businesses cut back on production in response to reduced orders. Falls in exports and production were particularly pronounced for certain manufactured goods such as cars, steel and electronics, and industrial production declined by exceptionally large magnitudes in countries where these types of goods are a large share in total production. More generally, firms around the world sought to economise on inventories in response to weaker expected demand and reduced availability of working capital. This effect appears to have been amplified by internal cyclical dynamics in some countries. In China, for example, the economy had for some time been growing at a faster-than-trend pace, and the authorities had already taken steps to rein in growth during 2007 and the first half of 2008, long before China's economy was affected by the decline in global trade as the rest of the world slowed.

Finally, part of the slowdown in the pace of global activity reflected the inevitable pullback in some sectors that had become overextended. The most obvious of these were the housing and financial sectors in the major countries, although the point could also be extended to the high levels of household debt in many countries in advance of the crisis. Inevitably, the reallocation of resources within the economy following such adjustments has taken some time to run its course.

Policy responses

While the financial crisis had a significant negative effect on the level of global activity, a number of forces have been working in the opposite direction and can be expected to support recovery over time. The most important have been the wide ranging set of monetary, fiscal and other policy measures. These can be considered under two broad headings: those directed at the immediate issues of repairing damaged credit markets and restoring growth in demand and activity; and those directed at the medium-term agenda of reducing the risk of similar crises in the future.

In regard to the immediate issues, authorities in all the major economies took a range of steps to provide direct assistance to their financial sectors to offset the effective tightening of financial conditions faced by the private sector. These measures took several forms including central bank facilities to improve access to liquidity, targeted facilities to unclog credit in particular financial markets, direct injections of capital into financial institutions and the provision of various forms of government guarantees. In the United States there were significant measures to remove bad assets from the balance sheets of affected financial institutions and to purchase longer dated securities in order to support mortgage and private credit markets. Significant steps have also been taken internationally to provide official funds to emerging and developing countries in the period ahead, notably through initiatives of multilateral organisations such as the IMF.

Early signs were that these steps were contributing to an improvement in the functioning of financial markets. The extreme volatility that followed the Lehman Brothers' collapse began to ease in early 2009, and the availability of government guarantees enabled a recovery in bond issuance by banks around the world. This helped to put banks in a position where they could be more confident of their long-term funding. Nonetheless, these efforts are likely to take some time to be fully effective. In the interim, credit spreads have remained high and lending to date has still been hampered by the cumulative erosion of asset prices and its accompanying pressure on balance sheets.

In addition, interest rates in major and emerging-market countries were cut sharply as the crisis unfolded. In some major countries, policy rates were reduced to close to zero and central banks moved to quantitative easing approaches to provide additional stimulus to particular markets and to the economy more generally. [...]

Fiscal policy has also provided a substantial stimulus. Many countries, including all the large countries such as the United States, United Kingdom, Germany and China, announced major packages to support demand in 2009 and 2010. In total, discretionary fiscal measures announced since late 2008 provided for a stimulus of up to 2 per cent of world GDP in 2009, as governments have stepped in to fill part of the contraction in private spending. This support has taken the form of direct financial assistance to households, tax reductions for businesses and direct spending by governments, such as for infrastructure projects. This is in addition to the effects of the automatic fiscal stabilisers – such as the typical reduction in the level of taxes paid by the private sector during downturns and the increase in unemployment benefit spending – which in some countries have also been very substantial.

In regard to the medium-term agenda, considerable work has been underway on reforming financial regulatory policies. At a broad level, this work addresses an old issue: where (and how) to strike the balance between adequate government regulation that protects the economic system and allowing market innovation, in this case with respect to the financial sector. The overarching issue is the need to better contain financial risk taking, and to do so in a way that remains effective as the financial system evolves. Experience from the present crisis suggests that regulations aimed at containing risk-taking can result in risk being pushed out to the unregulated part of the system. It is also in the nature of markets that they will tend to innovate around regulations, and the nature of risk-taking will inevitably keep changing as financial systems get more sophisticated. This highlights the need for regulatory frameworks to be adaptable to changing circumstances. While there is still much to be considered in this area, better risk management techniques could include aspects such as requiring banks to hold more liquidity and capital and to adjust capital requirements over the course of the cycle, along with enhanced stress-testing models, greater transparency of financial products and ensuring appropriate incentives for rating agencies. Because of the interdependency among financial systems, it makes sense for these issues to be tackled cooperatively at a global level.

26

The Twin Excesses – Financialization and Globalization – Caused the Crash

Ashok Bardhan

In their effort to explain the global crisis analysts have identified lax regulation and other attributes of the financial system as the principal culprits. To grasp fully the reason it also needs to be recognized that this is the first crisis of the modern era of globalization. If the proximate cause is the "laissez faire" to "laissez financer" progression in free-market idolatry, leading to bubbles in asset prices and the subsequent crash, then the facilitating condition was yet another quasi-bubble – a bubble in globalization. It may be easier to appreciate the virulence and speed with which the crisis has spread if we recognize that in addition to over-financialization domestically, there was perhaps over-globalization internationally.

While over-globalization was evident in ever-faster trade and capital flows and increasing off-shoring of production, over-financialization could be seen in the rise in the size of financial assets relative to the real economy as indicated by gross domestic product. Globally, the holdings of financial assets, comprising equities, government and private bonds and bank deposits, ballooned way out of proportion to global GDP, the primary underlying measure of real economic activity (see Figure 26.1). Similarly, the gross market value of outstanding derivative contracts more than doubled between mid-2006 and mid-2008. The share of financial services in GDP has increased dramatically in the US and UK in recent years; in the latter it has doubled in the last decade alone. In many countries, the financial sector grew to a size disproportionate to its primary raison d'être – to efficiently bring savers and borrowers together,

Original publication details: Ashok Bardhan, "Two Views on the Cause of the Global Crisis: Part 2: The Twin Excesses – Financialization and Globalization – Caused the Crash," YaleGlobal, 2009. http://yaleglobal.yale.edu/content/two-views-global-crisis-2, accessed July 21, 2014.

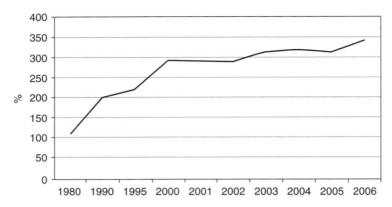

Figure 26.1   Global Financial Assets to Global GDP Ratio.
Source: McKinsey Global Institute.

allocate savings to viable investments, and manage diversification of risk. Liquid and deep financial markets are necessary; indeed, they are the lifeblood of economic activity, but to extend the analogy, not if they cause high blood pressure to the economy!

Globalization too has played its role. A large part of the new trade volumes generated were a result of diversion from potential consumption by domestic consumers to consumption by consumers half-way across the world. There is an ongoing debate in China, for example, whether the economic wisdom of having nearly a 40 percent share of exports in GDP has served the developmental goals of the country well. At least some of the blame for income inequality, lopsided development and consumption stagnation in the country can be laid at the feet of the overgrown external sector.

Global imbalances, on which reams have been written, provided the financing for the insatiable appetite of US and other consumers, met by the unbounded capacity of China's manufacturing machine. Footloose capital ran hither and thither for better returns and ended up in high-risk investments. The US–China globalization axis may have been critical but by no means was it the only game in town. Reckless lending by western banks to East European clients drove much of the importing frenzy in those countries. It was finance that drove and propelled international trade, in addition to that generated by underlying patterns of global specialization and competitiveness.

Together with the financial sector, globalization, as we know it – global trade in goods and services, capital flows and off-shoring of production – seems destined to decline in the short term. The total market value of financial assets held worldwide has declined by about a third, or more than $50 trillion, in 2008 according to a report by the Asian Development Bank. Container traffic in the world's busiest ports is down by more than 20 percent. While trade volumes show greater volatility than GDP, the figures for the former show a near precipitous decline relative to the former. The IMF expects global GDP to decrease by 1.3 percent in 2009, while economists from the World Trade Organization forecast a 9 percent decline for global trade in the same year, both the largest drops on record since World War II. Export volumes are expected to decrease in every major region of the world. Indeed, double-digit declines in real national variables are so rare that declines in export volumes of over 30 percent, such as in the case of Japan, make one wonder about the "bubble-like" nature of the underlying demand. On the other hand, while Euro area GDP and US GDP are both expected to contract in 2009, emerging economies are the one bright spot with a GDP growth forecast of 1.6 percent.

In addition to trade, global financial flows and cross-border investments are also expected to be adversely affected. The most dynamic economic region of the world, Emerging Asia, is expected to attract 40 percent less net private capital flows (which include portfolio and direct investments) in 2009. It is as if both ships and funds in search of a safe harbor are docked at home ports.

The prospect of offshoring, that recent offspring of globalization, presents a mixed picture. While any downturn can only serve to further intensify the ever-present cost-cutting impulse on the part of management, the fundamental nature of downsizing and restructuring underway in the US in key sectors, and the sharp cutbacks in many parent operations in the financial services sector, suggest that even the seemingly unstoppable phenomenon of offshoring may slow down. Already, there have been some cutbacks in the number of employees of offshore call centers.

Increasing interventions by national governments in the economic management of individual nation-states also tend to slow down the globalization process. National stimulus packages have a domestic stance and are inward-oriented, regardless of whether there is an explicit "buy domestic" provision, since greater reliance on government spending inevitably leads to less "leakage" internationally. The mounting job losses, complexity of the financial crisis, increasing range of conflicting interests, issues of inequality and fairness, and, last but not least, compulsions of electoral politics in an increasingly democratic world will all lead to greater state intervention, curbing the power of the market.

Far too rapid and distorted growth in global economic linkages and the financial services sector, as well as their mutual feeding off each other, have brought into sharper focus contradictions facing the future evolution of the global economy, the resolution of which is bound to affect globalization. While the future shape of regulatory reform is being vigorously debated, it is not clear how continued global-ization will be affected in the medium term by the crisis.

All of this leads us to the following question: can we eat our cake, have it too, and trade it in on the global markets? Dani Rodrik has long pointed out the "inescapable trilemma of the world economy," that "democracy, national sovereignty and global economic integration are mutually incompatible." The present crisis shows that it is actually a quadrilemma. The international policy establishment must manage and reconcile simultaneously conflicting pulls and pushes. To begin with there are the universal free-market guiding principles. These operate in individual nation-states, which are the primary arena of economic policy. Economic policies, in turn, are largely shaped by a democratic polity that is apprehensive and insecure about increasing free trade and international economic integration. It is difficult to see how the tenuous co-habitation of these four – globalization, free-market principles, democracy, and national policy independence – can survive in the present circum-stances. Something may have to give way, if just a little…

27

Globalism's Discontents

Joseph E. Stiglitz

Few subjects have polarized people throughout the world as much as globalization. Some see it as the way of the future, bringing unprecedented prosperity to everyone, everywhere. Others, symbolized by the Seattle protestors of December 1999, fault globalization as the source of untold problems, from the destruction of native cultures to increasing poverty and immiseration. In this article, I want to sort out the different meanings of globalization. In many countries, globalization has brought huge benefits to a few with few benefits to the many. But in the case of a few countries, it has brought enormous benefit to the many. Why have there been these huge differences in experiences? The answer is that globalization has meant different things in different places.

The countries that have managed globalization on their own, such as those in East Asia, have, by and large, ensured that they reaped huge benefits and that those benefits were equitably shared; they were able substantially to control the terms on which they engaged with the global economy. By contrast, the countries that have, by and large, had globalization managed for them by the International Monetary Fund and other international economic institutions have not done so well. The problem is thus not with globalization but with how it has been managed.

The international financial institutions have pushed a particular ideology – market fundamentalism – that is both bad economics and bad politics; it is based on premises concerning how markets work that do not hold even for developed countries, much less for developing countries. The IMF has pushed these economics policies without a broader vision of society or the role of economics within society. And it has pushed these policies in ways that have undermined emerging democracies.

Original publication details: Joseph E. Stiglitz, from "Globalism's Discontents," in *The American Prospect*, 13, 1, January 2002. pp. 1–14. Reproduced with permission from J. E. Stiglitz.

More generally, globalization itself has been governed in ways that are undemocratic and have been disadvantageous to developing countries, especially the poor within those countries. The Seattle protestors pointed to the absence of democracy and of transparency, the governance of the international economic institutions by and for special corporate and financial interests, and the absence of countervailing democratic checks to ensure that these informal and *public* institutions serve a general interest. In these complaints, there is more than a grain of truth.

Beneficial Globalization

Of the countries of the world, those in East Asia have grown the fastest and done most to reduce poverty. And they have done so, emphatically, via "globalization." Their growth has been based on exports – by taking advantage of the global market for exports and by closing the technology gap. It was not just gaps in capital and other resources that separated the developed from the less-developed countries, but differences in knowledge. East Asian countries took advantage of the "globalization of knowledge" to reduce these disparities. But while some of the countries in the region grew by opening themselves up to multinational companies, others, such as Korea and Taiwan, grew by creating their own enterprises. Here is the key distinction: Each of the most successful globalizing countries determined its own pace of change; each made sure as it grew that the benefits were shared equitably; each rejected the basic tenets of the "Washington Consensus," which argued for a minimalist role for government and rapid privatization and liberalization.

In East Asia, government took an active role in managing the economy. The steel industry that the Korean government created was among the most efficient in the world – performing far better than its private-sector rivals in the United States (which, though private, are constantly turning to the government for protection and for subsidies). Financial markets were highly regulated. My research shows that those regulations promoted growth. It was only when these countries stripped away the regulations, under pressure from the US Treasury and the IMF, that they encountered problems.

During the 1960s, 1970s, and 1980s, the East Asian economies not only grew rapidly but were remarkably stable. Two of the countries most touched by the 1997–1998 economic crisis had had in the preceding three decades not a single year of negative growth; two had only one year – a better performance than the United States or the other wealthy nations that make up the Organization for Economic Cooperation and Development (OECD). The single most important factor leading to the troubles that several of the East Asian countries encountered in the late 1990s – the East Asia crisis – was the rapid liberalization of financial and capital markets. In short, the countries of East Asia benefited from globalization because they made globalization work for them; it was when they succumbed to the pressures from the outside that they ran into problems that were beyond their own capacity to manage well.

Globalization can yield immense benefits. Elsewhere in the developing world, globalization of knowledge has brought improved health, with life spans increasing at a rapid pace. How can one put a price on these benefits of globalization? Globalization has brought still other benefits: Today there is the beginning of a globalized civil society that has begun to succeed with such reforms as the Mine Ban Treaty and debt forgiveness for the poorest highly indebted countries (the Jubilee movement). The globalization protest movement itself would not have been possible without globalization.

The Darker Side of Globalization

How then could a trend with the power to have so many benefits have produced such opposition? Simply because it has not only failed to live up to its potential but frequently has had very adverse effects. But this forces us to ask, why has it had such adverse effects? The answer can be seen by looking at each of the economic elements of globalization as pursued by the international financial institutions and especially by the IMF.

The most adverse effects have arisen from the liberalization of financial and capital markets – which has posed risks to developing countries without commensurate rewards. The liberalization has left them prey to hot money pouring into the country, an influx that has fueled speculative real-estate booms; just as suddenly, as investor sentiment changes, the money is pulled out, leaving in its wake economic devastation. Early on, the IMF said that these countries were being rightly punished for pursuing bad economic policies. But as the crisis spread from country to country, even those that the IMF had given high marks found themselves ravaged.

The IMF often speaks about the importance of the discipline provided by capital markets. In doing so, it exhibits a certain paternalism, a new form of the old colonial mentality: "We in the establishment, we in the North who run our capital markets, know best. Do what we tell you to do, and you will prosper." The arrogance is offensive, but the objection is more than just to style. The position is highly undemocratic: There is an implied assumption that democracy by itself does not provide sufficient discipline. But if one is to have an external disciplinarian, one should choose a good disciplinarian who knows what is good for growth, who shares one's values. One doesn't want an arbitrary and capricious taskmaster who one moment praises you for your virtues and the next screams at you for being rotten to the core. But capital markets are just such a fickle taskmaster; even ardent advocates talk about their bouts of irrational exuberance followed by equally irrational pessimism.

Lessons of Crisis

Nowhere was the fickleness more evident than in the last global financial crisis. Historically, most of the disturbances in capital flows into and out of a country are not the result of factors inside the country. Major disturbances arise, rather, from influences outside the country. When Argentina suddenly faced high interest rates in

1998, it wasn't because of what Argentina did but because of what happened in Russia. Argentina cannot be blamed for Russia's crisis.

Small developing countries find it virtually impossible to withstand this volatility. I have described capital-market liberalization with a simple metaphor: Small countries are like small boats. Liberalizing capital markets is like setting them loose on a rough sea. Even if the boats are well captained, even if the boats are sound, they are likely to be hit broadside by a big wave and capsize. But the IMF pushed for the boats to set forth into the roughest parts of the sea before they were seaworthy, with untrained captains and crews, and without life vests. No wonder matters turned out so badly!

To see why it is important to choose a disciplinarian who shares one's values, consider a world in which there were free mobility of skilled labor. Skilled labor would then provide discipline. Today, a country that does not treat capital well will find capital quickly withdrawing; in a world of free labor mobility, if a country did not treat skilled labor well, it too would withdraw. Workers would worry about the quality of their children's education and their family's health care, the quality of their environment and of their own wages and working conditions. They would say to the government: If you fail to provide these essentials, we will move elsewhere. That is a far cry from the kind of discipline that free-flowing capital provides.

The liberalization of capital markets has not brought growth: How can one build factories or create jobs with money that can come in and out of a country overnight? And it gets worse: Prudential behavior requires countries to set aside reserves equal to the amount of short-term lending; so if a firm in a poor country borrows $100 million at, say, 20 percent interest rates short-term from a bank in the United States, the government must set aside a corresponding amount. The reserves are typically held in US Treasury bills – a safe, liquid asset. In effect, the country is borrowing $100 million from the United States and lending $100 million to the United States. But when it borrows, it pays a high interest rate, 20 percent; when it lends, it receives a low interest rate, around 4 percent. This may be great for the United States, but it can hardly help the growth of the poor country. There is also a high *opportunity* cost of the reserves; the money could have been much better spent on building rural roads or constructing schools or health clinics. But instead, the country is, in effect, forced to lend money to the United States. [...]

The Costs of Volatility

Capital-market liberalization is inevitably accompanied by huge volatility, and this volatility impedes growth and increases poverty. It increases the risks of investing in the country, and thus investors demand a risk premium in the form of higher-than-normal profits. Not only is growth not enhanced but poverty is increased through several channels. The high volatility increases the likelihood of recessions – and the poor always bear the brunt of such downturns. Even in developed countries, safety nets are weak or nonexistent among the self-employed and in the rural sector. But these are the dominant sectors in developing countries. Without adequate safety nets, the recessions that follow from capital-market liberalization lead to impoverishment.

In the name of imposing budget discipline and reassuring investors, the IMF invariably demands expenditure reductions, which almost inevitably result in cuts in outlays for safety nets that are already threadbare.

But matters are even worse – for under the doctrines of the "discipline of the capital markets," if countries try to tax capital, capital flees. Thus, the IMF doctrines inevitably lead to an increase in tax burdens on the poor and the middle classes. Thus, while IMF bailouts enable the rich to take their money out of the country at more favorable terms (at the overvalued exchange rates), the burden of repaying the loans lies with the workers who remain behind.

The reason that I emphasize capital-market liberalization is that the case against it – and against the IMF's stance in pushing it – is so compelling. It illustrates what can go wrong with globalization. Even economists like Jagdish Bhagwati, strong advocates of free trade, see the folly in liberalizing capital markets. Belatedly, so too has the IMF – at least in its official rhetoric, though less so in its policy stances – but too late for all those countries that have suffered so much from following the IMF's prescriptions.

But while the case for trade liberalization – when properly done – is quite compelling, the way it has been pushed by the IMF has been far more problematic. The basic logic is simple: Trade liberalization is supposed to result in resources moving from inefficient protected sectors to more efficient export sectors. The problem is not only that job destruction comes before the job creation – so that unemployment and poverty result – but that the IMF's "structural adjustment programs" (designed in ways that allegedly would reassure global investors) make job creation almost impossible. For these programs are often accompanied by high interest rates that are often justified by a single-minded focus on inflation. Sometimes that concern is deserved; often, though, it is carried to an extreme. In the United States, we worry that small increases in the interest rate will discourage investment. The IMF has pushed for far higher interest rates in countries with a far less hospitable investment environment. The high interest rates mean that new jobs and enterprises are not created. What happens is that trade liberalization, rather than moving workers from low-productivity jobs to high-productivity ones, moves them from low-productivity jobs to unemployment. Rather than enhanced growth, the effect is increased poverty. To make matters even worse, the unfair trade-liberalization agenda forces poor countries to compete with highly subsidized American and European agriculture.

The Governance of Globalization

By contrast, […] in the current process of globalization we have a system of what I call global governance without global government. International institutions like the World Trade Organization, the IMF, the World Bank, and others provide an ad hoc system of global governance, but it is a far cry from global government and lacks democratic accountability. Although it is perhaps better than not having any system of global governance, the system is structured not to serve general interests or assure equitable results. This not only raises issues of whether broader values are given short shrift; it does not even promote growth as much as an alternative might.

Governance through Ideology

Consider the contrast between how economic decisions are made inside the United States and how they are made in the international economic institutions. In this country, economic decisions within the administration are undertaken largely by the National Economic Council, which includes the secretary of labor, the secretary of commerce, the chairman of the Council of Economic Advisers, the treasury secretary, the assistant attorney general for antitrust, and the US trade representative. The Treasury is only one vote and often gets voted down. All of these officials, of course, are part of an administration that must face Congress and the democratic electorate. But in the international arena, only the voices of the financial community are heard. The IMF reports to the ministers of finance and the governors of the central banks, and one of the important items on its agenda is to make these central banks more independent – and less democratically accountable. It might make little difference if the IMF dealt only with matters of concern to the financial community, such as the clearance of checks; but in fact, its policies affect every aspect of life. It forces countries to have tight monetary and fiscal policies: It evaluates the trade-off between inflation and unemployment, and in that trade-off it always puts far more weight on inflation than on jobs.

The problem with having the rules of the game dictated by the IMF – and thus by the financial community – is not just a question of values (though that is important) but also a question of ideology. The financial community's view of the world predominates – even when there is little evidence in its support. Indeed, beliefs on key issues are held so strongly that theoretical and empirical support of the positions is viewed as hardly necessary.

Recall again the IMF's position on liberalizing capital markets. As noted, the IMF pushed a set of policies that exposed countries to serious risk. One might have thought, given the evidence of the costs, that the IMF could offer plenty of evidence that the policies also did some good. In fact, there was no such evidence; the evidence that was available suggested that there was little if any positive effect on growth. Ideology enabled IMF officials not only to ignore the absence of benefits but also to overlook the evidence of the huge costs imposed on countries.

An Unfair Trade Agenda

The trade-liberalization agenda has been set by the North, or more accurately, by special interests in the North. Consequently, a disproportionate part of the gains has accrued to the advanced industrial countries, and in some cases the less-developed countries have actually been worse off. After the last round of trade negotiations, the Uruguay Round that ended in 1994, the World Bank calculated the gains and losses to each of the regions of the world. The United States and Europe gained enormously. But sub-Saharan Africa, the poorest region of the world, lost by about 2 percent because of terms-of-trade effects: The trade negotiations opened their markets to manufactured goods produced by the industrialized countries but did not open up the markets of Europe and the United States to the agricultural goods in which poor countries often have a comparative advantage. Nor did the trade agreements eliminate the subsidies to agriculture that make it so hard for the developing countries to compete.

The US negotiations with China over its membership in the WTO displayed a double standard bordering on the surreal. The US trade representative, the chief negotiator for the United States, began by insisting that China was a developed country. Under WTO rules, developing countries are allowed longer transition periods in which state subsidies and other departures from the WTO strictures are permitted. China certainly wishes it were a developed country, with Western-style per capita incomes. And since China has a lot of "capitas," it's possible to multiply a huge number of people by very small average incomes and conclude that the People's Republic is a big economy. But China is not only a developing economy; it is a low-income developing country. Yet the United States insisted that China be treated like a developed country! China went along with the fiction; the negotiations dragged on so long that China got some extra time to adjust. But the true hypocrisy was shown when US negotiators asked, in effect, for developing-country status for the United States to get extra time to shelter the American textile industry.

Trade negotiations in the service industries also illustrate the unlevel nature of the playing field. Which service industries did the United States say were *very* important? Financial services – industries in which Wall Street has a comparative advantage. Construction industries and maritime services were not on the agenda, because the developing countries would have a comparative advantage in these sectors.

Consider also intellectual-property rights, which are important if innovators are to have incentives to innovate (though many of the corporate advocates of intellectual property exaggerate its importance and fail to note that much of the most important research, as in basic science and mathematics, is not patentable). Intellectual-property rights, such as patents and trademarks, need to balance the interests of producers with those of users – not only users in developing countries, but researchers in developed countries. If we underprice the profitability of innovation to the inventor, we deter invention. If we overprice its cost to the research community and the end user, we retard its diffusion and beneficial effects on living standards.

In the final stages of the Uruguay negotiations, both the White House Office of Science and Technology Policy and the Council of Economic Advisers worried that we had not got the balance right – that the agreement put producers' interests over users'. We worried that, with this imbalance, the rate of progress and innovation might actually be impeded. After all, knowledge is the most important input into research, and overly strong intellectual-property rights can, in effect, increase the price of this input. We were also concerned about the consequences of denying life-saving medicines to the poor. This issue subsequently gained international attention in the context of the provision of AIDS medicines in South Africa. The international outrage forced the drug companies to back down – and it appears that, going forward, the most adverse consequences will be circumscribed. But it is worth noting that initially, even the Democratic US administration supported the pharmaceutical companies.

What we were not fully aware of was another danger – what has come to be called "biopiracy," which involves international drug companies patenting traditional medicines. Not only do they seek to make money from "resources" and knowledge that rightfully belong to the developing countries, but in doing so they squelch domestic firms who long provided these traditional medicines. While it is not clear whether these patents would hold up in court if they were effectively challenged, it is clear that the less-developed countries may not have the legal and financial resources required to mount such a challenge. The issue has become the source of enormous emotional, and potentially economic, concern throughout the developing world. This fall, while I was in Ecuador visiting a village in the high Andes, the Indian mayor railed against how globalization had led to biopiracy. [...]

Global Social Justice

Today, in much of the developing world, globalization is being questioned. For instance, in Latin America, after a short burst of growth in the early 1990s, stagnation and recession have set in. The growth was not sustained – some might say, was not sustainable. Indeed, at this juncture, the growth record of the so-called post-reform era looks no better, and in some countries much worse, than in the widely criticized import-substitution period of the 1950s and 1960s when Latin countries tried to industrialize by discouraging imports. Indeed, reform critics point out that the burst of growth in the early 1990s was little more than a "catch-up" that did not even make up for the lost decade of the 1980s.

Throughout the region, people are asking: "Has reform failed or has globalization failed?" The distinction is perhaps artificial, for globalization was at the center of the reforms. Even in those countries that have managed to grow, such as Mexico, the benefits have accrued largely to the upper 30 percent and have been even more concentrated in the top 10 percent. Those at the bottom have gained little; many are even worse off. The reforms have exposed countries to greater risk, and the risks have been borne disproportionately by those least able to cope with them. Just as in many countries where the pacing and sequencing of reforms has resulted in job destruction outmatching job creation, so too has the exposure to risk out-matched the ability to create institutions for coping with risk, including effective safety nets.

In this bleak landscape, there are some positive signs. Those in the North have become more aware of the inequities of the global economic architecture. The agreement at Doha to hold a new round of trade negotiations – the "Development Round" – promises to rectify some of the imbalances of the past. There has been a marked change in the rhetoric of the international economic institutions – at least they talk about poverty. At the World Bank, there have been some real reforms; there has been some progress in translating the rhetoric into reality – in ensuring that the voices of the poor are heard and the concerns of the developing countries are listened to. But elsewhere, there is often a gap between the rhetoric and the reality. Serious reforms in governance, in who makes decisions and how they are made, are not on the table. If one of the problems at the IMF has been that ideology, interests, and perspectives of the financial community in the advanced industrialized countries have been given disproportionate weight (in matters whose effects go well beyond finance), then the prospects for success in the current discussions of reform, in which the same parties continue to predominate, are bleak. They are more likely to result in slight changes in the shape of the table, not changes in who is *at* the table or what is on the agenda.

September 11 has resulted in a global alliance against terrorism. What we now need is not just an alliance *against* evil, but an alliance *for* something positive – a global alliance for reducing poverty and for creating a better environment, an alliance for creating a global society with more social justice.

Part IV Questions

1. How has China's rapid economic expansion in recent decades been beneficial to both China and the United States, according to Fallows? What negative aspects of this expansion does he mention? What "perils" for the United States does he foresee in the long run, if China's economy continues to expand as it has?

2. What is a global "commodity chain"? What does the rise of such chains in many sectors reveal about the division of labor around the globe? Who benefits most from the work done in such chains? What general lessons can you draw from Korzeniewicz's case study of the Nike Corporation?

3. What is new about contemporary world trade, according to Gereffi? How are developing countries involved in the three production networks he discusses? How do trends in the apparel and electronics industry demonstrate that the integration of the global economy entails a more geographically fragmented division of labor in these ever-expanding global production networks and commodity chains?

4. What are the three concepts of global inequality that Milanovic analyzes? What trends does he find? Which concept best captures the amount of inequality in the world? Is it reasonable to expect that inequality will decline in coming decades?

5. The "bottom billion" live in countries that are caught in one or more "development traps," according to Collier. What are the four traps? How much economic growth have countries caught in development traps experienced in recent decades? What do these traps imply for their prospects of development in the future?

6. How does Edey explain the global economic crisis that began in 2007? How did governments respond to the crisis? What does Bardhan add to Edey's explanation in his analysis? What might be done in terms of national and global regulation to help prevent such crises in the future? Can regulatory changes ensure that another crisis will not erupt?

7. What are the "discontents" and the "darker side" of globalization, according to Stiglitz? How does he assess the consequences of market liberalization? What does he mean by "governance through ideology," and what should replace it?

Part V

Globalization and the Nation-State

Introduction

The topic of this part is political globalization, in particular the implications of globalization for the nation-state. In a world made up of powerful and highly stable nation-states, political globalization might seem like a contradiction in terms. A state (more commonly called "government" in the United States) is the sovereign authority in a specified territory, with the right to use force both to maintain internal order and to defend its territory against aggression. Sovereignty, in turn, implies that the state is the ultimate authority in its territory, exercising legal jurisdiction over its citizens and the groups and organizations they form in the conduct of daily life. The sovereign state is not subject to any higher authority; no state has the right to expect compliance from any other state, and no all-encompassing world state has emerged with authority over all national states. Sometimes the United Nations is described as the potential nucleus of a world state, but it has no compelling authority over its member states and it relies entirely on the action of its members to enforce compliance with its resolutions and the sanctions it imposes on misbehaving states.

In times past, world maps contained many different kinds of political unit, from small dukedoms and principalities to large empires ruled by powerful states. Nearly all of the small units have been absorbed in larger nation-states, and all but a few of the colonies held by former imperial powers like Britain and France have become independent sovereign states. With the dissolution of the last great empire, the Soviet Union, in the 1990s, the world is now composed almost entirely of sovereign nation-states.

What sense does it make, then, to speak of political globalization? First, the very fact that the entire world, with the exception of the arctic areas and a few small colonies and dependencies, is organized by a single type of political unit, the nation-state, is a sign of globalization. Never before has the world been composed of only one type

The Globalization Reader, Fifth Edition. Edited by Frank J. Lechner and John Boli.
Editorial material and organization © 2015 John Wiley & Sons, Ltd.
Published 2015 by John Wiley & Sons, Ltd.

of political unit. The rapid decolonization of the twentieth century, when more than 130 colonies or dependencies became independent states, was a great political surprise, since most of these new states are too small and weak to defend themselves effectively from more powerful states. This indicates that the principle of state sovereignty itself has become a central feature of global society, and that a particular model of political organization, the sovereign state, has achieved global status as the most desirable, viable, and legitimate way of structuring political life.

Second, political globalization is indicated by the considerable uniformity exhibited by sovereign states in terms of their goals, structures, programs, and internal operations. Almost all states assume responsibility for a wide range of activities, including education, health care, management of the economy and finance, retirement pensions, environmental protection, and poverty alleviation, alongside the classic core concerns of states, foreign policy and military defense. Almost all states have elaborate bureaucratic structures to administer the many programs they operate to meet their responsibilities. And almost all states are formally structured (in their constitutions and legislation) as democracies in which all citizens have an equal right to vote in elections that determine the holders of executive and legislative positions. Thus, a common basic model of the state is in place everywhere in the world, though states vary considerably in how they implement the model.

A third dimension of political globalization is the emergence in the past hundred years of intergovernmental organizations (IGOs). IGOs are associations of states created to deal with problems and manage issues that affect many countries at once or involve high levels of interdependence among countries. Of the approximately 300 global IGOs and more than a thousand regional or subregional IGOs, most are concerned with economic, technical, or political matters. Most prominent are the United Nations and its associated agencies (UNESCO, the World Health Organization, the International Labour Organization, the Food and Agriculture Organization, and so on), which constitute a central world political forum within which states conduct their international relations. Other prominent bodies include the World Trade Organization (WTO) and International Monetary Fund (IMF), which help manage the world economy; the International Telecommunication Union and INTELSAT, which supervise global telecommunications and satellite systems; the International Civil Aviation Organization, which oversees commercial air transportation; and the Universal Postal Union, which coordinates international postal services.

As economic globalization has increased, as technology and technical systems have become more encompassing and complex, as problems like pollution and narcotics trafficking and terrorism have also become global, the adequacy of states to cope with the rapidly integrating world has increasingly been called into question. Many transnational corporations (TNCs) have larger sales revenues than the entire economies of most countries, and global financial transactions amount to trillions of dollars per day – so the world economy is beyond the control of states. Global warming and environmental degradation are inevitable byproducts of economic development, and states are too much concerned with their own development to take serious action about such problems. Religious and ethnic groups within countries are increasingly militant and well armed, threatening the viability of the states they oppose. These and numerous other factors have led many observers to speak of repeated "crises" of the state and to predict the breakdown or irrelevance of states.

Other observers caution that the death of the state has been announced prematurely. Problems may be increasingly global in scale, but states are also larger and more capable than ever before. Their tax revenues constitute a larger share of gross national product than ever before; they have larger and better trained bureaucracies than ever; and they are remarkably effective in operating national health care systems, pension plans, postal services, road and air transportation systems, and many other programs, at least in the more developed countries. The demands on states are certainly growing, perhaps even faster than states can keep up with them, but it is by no means certain that states are as incapable of dealing with their responsibilities as many critics claim. Only in smaller and poorer countries do we find clearly weak states that fall far short of global expectations for their performance.

Our selections in this part begin with the view that the nation-state is incapacitated by globalization. Susan Strange, a British international relations scholar, argues that the power and authority of the state are declining due to technological change and the rapid escalation of capital costs for successful innovation. These factors force states to do the bidding of transnational corporations, whose massive resources are seen as necessary to maintain national competitiveness in the global economy. Strange notes the paradox that declining state effectiveness has been accompanied by growing state intervention into people's daily lives, but such intervention has less to do with fundamental responsibilities and increasingly focuses on marginal issues.

Strange's analysis is complemented by American international relations professor James H. Mittelman's work on global organized crime. Mittelman describes transnational criminal organizations as operating both above and below the state, in the first instance as transnational corporations taking full advantage of globalized technologies that put them beyond the reach of states, in the second instance as a means by which poor and marginalized groups try to cope with globalization's dislocations. Concentrated in global cities, organized crime destabilizes the global economy and makes the task of governance ever more problematic for states.

Dani Rodrik, an American economist, provides evidence that economic globalization may indeed have undermined the capacity of states to give adequate support to citizens. The problem, Rodrik says, is that companies in the developed countries can move their operations to places where labor costs are lower and unions are weak. This practice lowers wages, diminishes labor's bargaining power, and lowers government revenues so that welfare and social security programs become more difficult to support. The developed countries' economies are also undercut by the low-cost imports available to consumers, which further intensifies this downward spiral. Rodrik argues that states should respond by being more skeptical of free trade and capital flows, so a balance can be struck between openness and social responsibility.

A contrary view emerges in the selection by British political scientist John Glenn on state "social spending" (for education, pensions, health care, income support, and the like) in recent decades. Glenn finds little evidence of retrenchment by the state in the developed countries (the "global North"): in the 1990s, when scholars were proclaiming the death or irrelevancy of the state, both overall state spending and social spending were higher than ever (though they declined slightly in the latter part of the decade). The same generally holds for less developed countries in the "global South," but an important "North–South divide" prevails: states in the South, particularly poorer and more peripheral states, engage in much more restricted social spending. Glenn explores features of the world economy that help explain why this is so.

In the last selection in this part, American sociologists David P. Baker and Gerald K. LeTendre add another corrective to claims about the purported decline of the state. They point out that mass schooling has expanded dramatically almost everywhere in the world, as a global process that engages all states and results in remarkably similar educational systems in most places. States pursue education to make their citizens literate and economically productive, loyal to the nation, and capable of managing their own lives, and they do so despite often severe resource limitations. Poorer and weaker countries may have inadequate school systems, but they are fully committed to improving them to the extent that they can.

28

The Declining Authority of States

Susan Strange

Today it seems that the heads of governments may be the last to recognise that they and their ministers have lost the authority over national societies and economies that they used to have. Their command over outcomes is not what it used to be. Politicians everywhere talk as though they have the answers to economic and social problems, as if they really are in charge of their country's destiny. People no longer believe them. Disillusion with national leaders brought down the leaders of the Soviet Union and the states of central Europe. But the disillusion is by no means confined to socialist systems. Popular contempt for ministers and for the head of state has grown in most of the capitalist countries – Italy, Britain, France and the United States are leading examples. Nor is the lack of confidence confined to those in office; opposition parties and their leaders are often no better thought of than those they wish to replace. In the last few years, the cartoonists and the tabloid press have been more bitter, less restrained critics of those in authority in government than at any other time this century. Although there are exceptions – mostly small countries – this seems to be a worldwide phenomenon of the closing years of the twentieth century, more evident in some places than others, but palpable enough to suggest that some common causes lie behind it.

[I write] in the firm belief that the perceptions of ordinary citizens are more to be trusted than the pretensions of national leaders and of the bureaucracies who serve them; that the commonsense of common people is a better guide to understanding than most of the academic theories being taught in universities. The social scientists,

Original publication details: Susan Strange, *The Retreat of the State*. Cambridge: Cambridge University Press, 1996. pp. 3–8, 9–10, 12–14.

in politics and economics especially, cling to obsolete concepts and inappropriate theories. These theories belong to a more stable and orderly world than the one we live in. It was one in which the territorial borders of states really meant something. But it has been swept away by a pace of change more rapid than human society had ever before experienced.

For this reason I believe the time has come to reconsider a few of the entrenched ideas of some academic colleagues in economics, politics, sociology and international relations. The study of international political economy has convinced me that we have to rethink some of the assumptions of conventional social science, and especially of the study of international relations. These concern: firstly, the limits of politics as a social activity; secondly, the nature and sources of power in society; thirdly, the necessity and also the indivisibility of authority in a market economy; and fourthly, the anarchic nature of international society and the rational conduct of states as the unitary actors within that society. The first and second are assumptions commonly taken for granted in political science. The third is an assumption of much liberal, or neo-classical economic science. And the last is an assumption of much so-called realist or neo-realist thinking in international relations. Each of these assumptions will be examined more closely later.

But first it may help to outline briefly the argument of the book as a whole. That will show the context in which these more fundamental questions about politics and power arise and have to be reconsidered. The argument put forward is that the impersonal forces of world markets, integrated over the postwar period more by private enterprise in finance, industry and trade than by the cooperative decisions of governments, are now more powerful than the states to whom ultimate political authority over society and economy is supposed to belong.

Where states were once the masters of markets, now it is the markets which, on many crucial issues, are the masters over the governments of states. And the declining authority of states is reflected in a growing diffusion of authority to other institutions and associations, and to local and regional bodies, and in a growing asymmetry between the larger states with structural power and weaker ones without it.

There are, to be sure, some striking paradoxes about this reversal of the state–market balance of power. One, which disguises from many people the overall decline of state power, is that the *intervention* of state authority and of the agencies of the state in the daily lives of the citizen appears to be growing. Where once it was left to the individual to look for work, to buy goods or services with caution in case they were unsafe or not what they seemed to be, to build or to pull down houses, to manage family relationships and so on, now governments pass laws, set up inspectorates and planning authorities, provide employment services, enforce customer protection against unclean water, unsafe food, faulty buildings or transport systems. The impression is conveyed that less and less of daily life is immune from the activities and decisions of government bureaucracies.

That is not necessarily inconsistent with my contention that state *power* is declining. It is less effective on those basic matters that the market, left to itself, has never been able to provide – security against violence, stable money for trade and investment, a clear system of law and the means to enforce it, and a sufficiency of public goods like drains, water supplies, infrastructures for transport and communications. Little wonder that it is less respected and lacks its erstwhile legitimacy. The need for a political authority of some kind, legitimated either by coercive force or by popular consent, or more often by a combination of the two, is the fundamental reason for the state's existence. But many states are coming to be deficient in these fundamentals. Their deficiency is not made good by greater activity in marginal matters, matters that are optional for society, and which are not absolutely necessary for the functioning of the market and the maintenance of social order. Trivialising government does not make its authority more respected; often, the contrary is true.

The second paradox is that while the governments of established states, most notably in North America and western Europe, are suffering this progressive loss of real authority, the queue of societies that want to have their own state is lengthening. This is true not only of ethnic groups that were forcibly suppressed by the single-party government of the former Soviet Union. It is true of literally hundreds of minorities and aboriginal peoples in every part of the world – in Canada and Australia, in India and Africa, even in the old so-called nation-states of Europe. Many – perhaps the majority – are suppressed by force, like the Kurds or the Basques. Others – like the Scots or the Corsicans – are just not strong enough or angry enough to offer a serious challenge to the existing state. Still others such as the native Americans, the Aboriginals, the Samis or the Flemish are pacified by resource transfers or by half-measures that go some way to meet their perceived need for an independent identity. Only a few, such as the Greenlanders, the Slovaks or Slovenes or the unwanted, unviable Pacific island-states, have succeeded in getting what they wanted – statehood. But once achieved, it does not seem to give them any real control over the kind of society or the nature of their economy that they might have preferred. In short, the desire for ethnic or cultural autonomy is universal; the political means to satisfy that desire within an integrated world market economy is not. Many, perhaps most, societies have to be content with the mere appearance of autonomy, with a facade of statehood. The struggle for independence has often proved a pyrrhic victory.

The final paradox which can be brought as evidence against my basic contention about the hollowness of state authority at the end of this century is that this is a western, or even an Anglo-Saxon phenomenon, and is refuted by the Asian experience of the state. The Asian state, it is argued, has in fact been the means to achieve economic growth, industrialisation, a modernised infrastructure and rising living standards for the people. Singapore might be the prime example of a strong state achieving economic success. But Japan, Korea and Taiwan are all states which have had strong governments, governments which have successfully used the means to restrict and control foreign trade and foreign investment, and to allocate credit and to guide corporate development in the private sector. Is it not premature – just another instance of Eurocentrism therefore – to assume the declining authority of the state?

There are two answers to this third paradox. One is that all these Asian states were exceptionally fortunate. They profited in three ways from their geographical position on the western frontier of the United States during the Cold War. Their strategic importance in the 1950s and after was such that they could count on generous military and economic aid from the Americans, aid which was combined with their exceptionally high domestic savings and low patterns of consumption. The combination gave a head start to rapid economic development. Secondly, and also for strategic reasons, they could be – almost had to be – exempted from the pressure to conform to the norms of the open liberal economy. They were allowed, first formally and then informally, to limit foreign imports and also to restrict the entry of the foreign firms that might have proved too strong competitors for their local enterprises. At the same time, they were given relatively open access first to the large, rich US market for manufactures, and later, under some protest, to the European one. And thirdly, the technology necessary to their industrialisation was available to be bought on the market, either in the form of patents, or in the person of technical advisors from Europe and America or through corporate alliances which brought them the technology without the loss of managerial control.

Now, I would argue, these special dispensations are on the way out, and not only because the Cold War is over. The Asian governments will be under increasing pressure from Washington to adopt more liberal non-discriminatory policies on trade and investment. And they will also be under pressure from within to liberalise and to allow more competition, including foreign competition, for the benefit of consumers and of other producers. In short, the exceptionalism of the Asian state during the Cold War has already been substantially eroded, and will continue to be so. As it has been at other times, and in other places, there will be contests for control over the institutions and agencies of government in most of the Asian countries. There will be contests between factions of political parties, between vested interests both in the private sectors and in the public sector. There will be power struggles between branches of the state bureaucracy. Both the unity and the authority of government is bound to suffer.

The Neglected Factor – Technology

The argument depends a good deal on the accelerating pace of technological change as a prime cause of the shift in the state–market balance of power. Since social scientists are, not, by definition, natural scientists, they have a strong tendency to overlook the importance of technology which rests, ultimately, on advances in physics, in chemistry and related sciences like nuclear physics or industrial chemistry. In the last 100 years, there has been more rapid technological change than ever before in human history. On this the scientists themselves are generally agreed. It took hundreds – in some places, thousands – of years to domesticate animals so that horses could be used for transport and oxen (later heavy horses) could be used to replace manpower to plough and sow ground for the production of crops in agriculture. It has taken less than 100 years for the car and truck to replace the horse and for aircraft to partly take over from road and rail transport. The electric telegraph as a means of communication was invented in the 1840s and remained the dominant system in Europe until the 1920s. But in the next eighty years, the telegraph gave way to the telephone, the telephone gave way to radio, radio to television and cables to satellites and optic fibres linking computers to other computers. No one under the age of thirty or thirty-five today needs convincing that, just in their own lifetime, the pace of technological change has been getting faster and faster. The technically unsophisticated worlds of business, government and education of even the 1960s would be unrecognisable to them. No fax, no personal computers, no accessible copiers, no mobile phones, no video shops, no DNA tests, no cable TV, no satellite networks connecting distant markets, twenty-four hours a day. The world in which their grandparents grew up in the 1930s or 1940s is as alien to them as that of the Middle Ages. There is no reason to suppose that technological change in products and processes, driven by profit, will not continue to accelerate in future.

This simple, everyday, commonsense fact of modern life is important because it goes a long way to explaining both political and economic change. It illuminates the changes both in the power of states and in the power of markets. Its dynamism, in fact, is basic to my argument, because it is a continuing factor, not a once-for-all change.

For the sake of clarity, consider first the military aspects of technical change, and then the civilian aspects – although in reality each spills over into the other. In what are known as strategic studies circles, no one doubts that the development of the atom bomb in the middle of the twentieth century, and later of nuclear weapons carried by intercontinental missiles, has brought about a major change in the nature of warfare between states. Mutual assured destruction was a powerful reason for having nuclear weapons – but equally it was a good reason for not using them. After the paradoxical long peace of the Cold War, two things began to change. The expectation that, sooner or later, nuclear war would destroy life on the planet began to moderate. And confidence began to wane that the state could, by a defensive strategy, prevent this happening. Either it would or it wouldn't, and governments could do little to alter the probabilities. Thus, technology had undermined one of the primary reasons for the existence of the state – its capacity to repel attack by others, its responsibility for what Adam Smith called 'the defence of the realm'. [...]

The Second Neglect – Finance

Not the least of the TNC's attractions to host states is its ability to raise finance both for the investment itself and – even more important – for the development of new technology. Another key part of [my] argument is that, besides the accelerating pace of technological change, there has been an escalation in the capital cost of most technological innovations – in agriculture, in manufacturing and the provision of services, and in new products and in new processes. In all of these, the input of capital has risen while the relative input of labour has fallen. It is this increased cost which has raised the stakes, as it were, in the game of staying up with the competition. This is so whether we look at competition from other firms who are also striving for larger market shares, or whether we look at governments trying to make sure that the economies for whose performance they are held responsible stay up with the competition in wealth-creation coming from other economies. Thus, to the extent that a government can benefit from a TNC's past and future investments without itself bearing the main cost of it, there are strong reasons for forging such alliances.

But the escalating costs of technological change are also important for a more fundamental reason, and not just because it explains the changing policies of host states to TNCs. It has to do with change in the world system. The cost of new technology in the production structure has added to the salience of money in the international political economy. It is no exaggeration to say that, with a few notable exceptions, scholars in international relations for the past half-century have grossly neglected the political aspects of credit-creation, and of changes in the global financial structure. In much theorising about international relations or even international political economy there is no mention at all of the financial structure (as distinct from the international monetary order governing the exchange relations of national currencies.) Briefly, the escalating capital costs of new technologies could not have been covered at all without, firstly, some very fundamental changes in the volume and nature of credit created by the capitalist market economy; and secondly, without the added mobility that in recent years has characterised that created credit. The *supply* of capital to finance technological innovation (and for other purposes) has been as important in the international political economy as the *demand* from the innovators for more money to produce ever more sophisticated products by ever more capital-intensive processes of production.

These supply and demand changes take place, and take effect, in the market. And it is markets, rather than state–state relations that many leading texts in international political economy tend to overlook. Much more emphasis is put on international monetary relations between governments and their national currencies. To the extent that attention is paid at all to the institutions creating and marketing credit in the world economy, they are held to be important chiefly for the increased volatility they may cause to exchange rates, or to the impact they may have on the ability of governments to borrow abroad to finance development or the shortfall between revenue and spending, or between export earnings and import bills. [...]

Politics, Power and Legitimacy

There are three premises underlying [my] argument. Each relates directly to – indeed, challenges – some of the conventional assumptions of economics, social and political science and international relations. The first premise is that politics is a common activity; it is not confined to politicians and their officials. The second is that power over outcomes is exercised impersonally by markets and often unintentionally by those who buy and sell and deal in markets. The third is that authority in society and over economic transactions is legitimately exercised by agents other than states, and has come to be freely acknowledged by those who are subject to it.

[...] dealing with recent changes in international political economy, readers will encounter three general propositions about the patterns of legitimate authority now developing in the international political economy towards the end of the twentieth century. One is that there is growing asymmetry among allegedly sovereign states in the authority they exercise in society and economy. In international relations, back to Thucydides, there has always been some recognition of a difference between small states and great powers, in the way each behaves to others and in the options available to them in their relations with other states. But there has been a tendency all along to assume a certain uniformity in the nature and effectiveness of the control which each state has over social and economic relations within their respective territorial boundaries. The attributes of domestic sovereignty, in other words, were assumed automatically to go with the regulation accorded each state by its peers. Now, I shall argue, that assumption can no longer be sustained. What was regarded as an exceptional anomaly when in 1945 the United States conceded two extra votes in the UN General Assembly for the Soviet Union – one for the 'sovereign' republic of the Ukraine and one for Byelorussia – now hardly attracts comment. The micro-states of Vanuatu and the Republic of San Marino are admitted to the select circle of member-states of the United Nations. But no one really believes that recognition of their 'sovereignty' is more than a courteous pretence. It is understood that there is only a difference of degree between these and many of the smaller and poorer members of the international society of states who are established occupants of seats in the UN.

The second proposition is that the authority of the governments of all states, large and small, strong and weak, has been weakened as a result of technological and financial change and of the accelerated integration of national economies into one single global market economy. Their failure to manage the national economy, to maintain employment and sustain economic growth, to avoid imbalances of payments with other states, to control the rate of interest and the exchange rate is not a matter of technical incompetence, nor moral turpitude nor political maladroitness. It is neither in any direct sense their fault, nor the fault of others. None of these failures can be blamed on other countries or on other governments. They are, simply, the victims of the market economy.

The third proposition complements the second. It is that some of the fundamental responsibilities of the state in a market economy – responsibilities first recognised, described and discussed at considerable length by Adam Smith over 200 years ago – are not now being adequately discharged by anyone. At the heart of the international political economy, there is a vacuum, a vacuum not adequately filled by intergovernmental institutions or by a hegemonic power exercising leadership in the common interest. The polarisation of states between those who retain some control over their destinies and those who are effectively incapable of exercising any such control does not add up to a zero-sum game. What some have lost, others have not gained. The diffusion of authority away from national governments has left a yawning hole of non-authority, ungovernance it might be called. [...]

29

Global Organized Crime

James H. Mittelman

The New Criminality

Clearly, there is a long history of organized crime transcending national borders; however, traditional patterns explain only part of the surge of illegal activities today. Globalizing tendencies emerging since the 1970s are transforming organized crime. There are newly prominent forms of illegality, such as computer crimes, money laundering, stealing nuclear materials mainly from the former Soviet Union, and "sophisticated fraud" (technological complexity among several parties using counterfeit bank instruments, credit cards, letters of credit, computer intrusion, and ingenuity of design – such as stock market "pump and dump" scams and pyramid schemes) that crop up between the established codes of international law, challenge existing norms, infiltrate licit businesses, and extend into international finance. Although some types of crime remain localized, what drives organized crime groups increasingly are efforts to exploit the growth mechanisms of globalization.

To take a single example of these dynamics at work, consider Chinese emigration to the United States. Triads (Chinese criminal networks) have smuggled people to America since the California gold rush in the 1840s. Moreover, there is a tradition of Chinese from the coastal province of Fujian, across from Taiwan, to draw on their extended families in California and other states and to move to America. As many as 90 percent of Chinese boat people originate in Fujian and in Guangdong province immediately to the south, where the major smuggling groups are concentrated.

Original publication details: James H. Mittelman, *The Globalization Syndrome: Transformation and Resistance*. Princeton: Princeton University Press, 2000. pp. 208–12, 214–15. Reproduced with permission from Princeton University Press.

The problem of the boat people – which captured public attention in 1993 when would-be Chinese immigrants died aboard the Panamanian vessel *Golden Venture*, a rusty old freighter that ran aground on a sandbar in sight of New York City – is largely rooted in China's explosive economic growth in recent years. The transition to a market economy, which in China has been likened to a runaway train, has sparked uneven gains and losses in income, with the rural areas, especially those in the interior, lagging far behind the urban centers and coastal regions. In the first phase of a classic Polanyian double movement, millions of low-income farm workers, have been pushed off the land to make way for large-scale industrial and commercial projects, triggering massive internal migration that coastal municipalities, now surrounded by burgeoning shantytowns, cannot absorb. China's labor supply is of enormous proportions – 452 million "surplus" workers, according to the Chinese Ministry of Labor. This crisis has fueled rural resentment and peasant uprisings in some parts of China, perhaps constituting an early stage of a Polanyian backlash.

A response to the poverty trap of the relative decline of incomes in the countryside and limited opportunities for finding legal employment in the cities is to break the cycle by seeking emigration "services" that meet the demand from a desperate and impoverished sector of the economy. Where poverty is severe, criminal gangs flourish. In China today, smuggling groups feed on a marginalized layer of people, substrata subject to an overheated market economy, and are globalizing their spatial domain.

The smuggling operations would not be possible, however, without the involvement of powerful and wealthy criminals, who have the resources to corrupt state officials. The corruption of political authorities is the crucible in which customs officers, police, and tax inspectors assist in criminal operations or merely look the other way. This is true of not only alien smuggling, but also drug smuggling, intellectual property counterfeiting, illegal currency transactions, and other black- and gray-market activities. In this web of criminals, the rich, and politicians, the holders of public office provide "legal" protection for their partners, as with the Golden Triangle – at the intersection of the borders of Laos, Thailand, and Myanmar – during the Cold War (an example of what Cox calls the machinations of the "covert world"). The high risk and high demand involved in these operations offer potentially large profits, creating incentives for the shrewdest and most ruthless criminal organizations to "supply" their services.

These trends are explicable in terms of the nexus of organized crime and globalization. The rise of transnational organized crime groups is spurred by technological innovations, especially advances in commercial airline travel, telecommunications, and the use of computers in business, allowing for increased mobility of people – some of them carriers of contraband – and the flow of illicit goods. Central to this process are innovations in satellite technology, fiber-optic cable, and the miniaturization of computers, all of which facilitate operations across frontiers. Hypercompetition is accelerating these cross-border flows. Deregulation, in turn, furthers this tendency, because it lowers state barriers to free flows of capital, goods, services, and labor.

Like global firms, transnational organized crime groups operate both above and below the state. Above the state, they capitalize on the globalizing tendencies of permeable borders and deregulation. Embracing the processes of globalization, these groups create demand for their services. They become actors in their own right in the

GDLP, organized along zonal or regional and subregional lines, such as in the Golden Triangle, a major production and distribution site for morphine and heroin.

At the same time, transnational organized crime groups operate below as well as beside the state by offering incentives to the marginalized segments of the population trying to cope with the adjustment costs of globalization. These groups reach down and out to the lower rungs of social structures – the impoverished – a substratum that does not lend itself to the easy strategies prescribed by the state and interstate institutions. These strategies are often cloaked as part of the national development project, but today are overtaken by the globalization process. The marginalized represent labor supply in the form of social forces participating in the parallel economy of organized (and unorganized) crime and *impairing the licit channels of neoliberalism*. The supply side, then, may be regarded as a *disguised form of resistance* to the dominant mode of globalization. Triads, a phenomenon noted earlier, bring this dynamic into stark relief. They originated as resistance movements battling to overthrow alien invaders who dominated the Manchu Qing Dynasty during the seventeenth century. At the end of Qing rule in 1911, these groups did not dissolve, but instead evolved into criminal societies, with some of the newest and most potent ones responding to the recurrent lack of order and social disruptions in China. Nowadays, from their main base in Hong Kong, the triads engage several "ethnic Chinese" and Thai groups linked to opium producers in Myanmar, and also deal with their affiliated gangs in cities in the United States, Western Europe, and across the Pacific Rim.

Insofar as the purpose of organized crime is to make money, these groups are typically regarded as predominantly economic actors. Their profit comes not merely from theft, but also today from emulating market mechanisms – forming strategic alliances, investing (and laundering) their capital, plowing it into new growth areas (e.g., dumping toxic wastes that abuse the environment in developing countries and then negotiating lucrative contracts for the cleanup industry), directing a share of their returns into R&D, adopting modern accounting systems, using global information networks that have no frontiers, and insuring (protecting) themselves against risks or threats to their organizations. Whereas these groups may have ostensibly economic objectives, to the extent that they undermine the main actors in the globalization process – transborder firms and dominant states that acquiesce to it – then transnational organized crime groups are both a political component of, and a response to, globalization.

Crime groups are similar to legitimate businesses in that they embrace the logic of the market, show great flexibility in initiative, and are also hierarchically structured. For example, the Hong Kong triads provide leadership, while the commercial *tongs* (merchants' guilds), many of them based in Chinatowns, act as local subsidiaries. Enhanced by *guanxi* (connections) in Eastern Asia, which has its counterpart in other cultures, this fluidity suggests that organized crime can also be disorganized.

Although some crime groups, such as the Cali cartels in Colombia, are highly centralized, they typically draw on loose networks of familial and ethnic relations. These networks reduce the transaction costs of acquiring information about illegal activities and provide a framework of trust. Hence, operating where there are neither clear rules nor laws, new entrants such as Nigerian organizations, which first joined the ranks of major transnational crime groups in the 1980s, arise. They have relied on family and ethnic ties in the diaspora, developing links between domestic bases and compatriots abroad. The 1980s drop in oil prices and cuts in government spending precipitated a crime wave in Nigeria and left numerous Nigerian students stranded overseas when their funding was terminated, turning many of them to fraudulent activities.

So, too, transnational organized crime groups heighten uncertainty, contributing to a larger trend of what James Rosenau conceptualizes as turbulence in the global political economy. New hubs of global organized crime – with Johannesburg and Cape Town linked to the Nigerian chain and rapidly emerging as regional centers – are key nodes in these networks. In fact, Nigerians – no longer parvenus in their profession – have penetrated the entire subregion of Southern Africa, and are involved in heroin and cocaine trafficking, various types of fraud, car theft, alien smuggling (aided by illegals who work as couriers), and gang activities, prompting US officials to refuse to train Nigerian police and central bankers because antifraud instruction is deemed only to increase the sophistication of Nigerian criminals. Now, the Nigerian trafficking groups fan out beyond Africa and have become major actors in drug smuggling in Southeast and Southwest Asia, with increasing involvement in Latin America as well.

Global cities, more than states, are the main loci of transnational criminal organizations. Some cities – such as Hong Kong and Istanbul – have formed a second tier and serve as transshipment points. However, it is global cities – especially New York, London, and Tokyo – that offer agglomerations of financial services (which provide vast opportunities for disguising the use and flow of money), sources of technological innovation, and advanced communications and transportation systems. In these locales and elsewhere, a new breed of cybercriminals can exploit inherent vulnerabilities in the electronic infrastructure of global finance through computer intrusions for the purposes of theft, blackmail, and extortion. Given the vast scope of the Internet, cybergangs can assault a global city from virtually anywhere and remain anonymous, thus crippling the capacity of the state to apprehend and prosecute perpetrators. Yet these cities are epicenters of globalization.

Home to large, diverse populations, global cities allow criminals, and even entire criminal organizations, to blend into legitimate institutions in ethnic neighborhoods. These shelters pose a problem for the police insofar as they do not know the many languages and diasporic cultures harboring criminals or are not trusted by segments of society outside the mainstream. Nigerian criminal gangs in London and Asian criminal gangs in New York are among those able to exploit these advantages, which is testimony to the embeddedness of transnational organized crime in neoliberal economic globalization.

Criminalization and the Rise of the State as a Courtesan

The state is most often understood in the Weberian sense of exercising a monopoly over the legitimate use of force. Building on this foundation, pluralists have regarded the state as an arbiter, a neutral referee, among different interests in society. In this tradition, pluralists hark back to *The Federalist Papers,* whose authors – John Jay, Alexander Hamilton, and James Madison – developed the idea that the role of the state is to balance and restrain the passions of its citizens. More recently, political scientists from David Easton to present-day writers have built a concept of the state based on the notion that its major function is the authoritative allocation of values. The role of the public sphere as an allocator of material values is a theme pursued by both conventionally and critically minded social scientists.

Although the foregoing notation about a complex literature is but a conceptual benchmark, one need not explore the subtleties of theories of the state more fully to demonstrate that the globalization of organized crime weakens the very basis of government and constrains its capacity. On the one hand, criminal elements do not seek to take over the state; they are obviously not revolutionary movements seeking to seize its apparatuses. On the other hand, transnational and subnational criminal groups contest the rationale of the state, especially in terms of its legitimate control over violence and the maintenance of justice. These groups are central to the recurrent problem in what Joel Migdal terms maintaining "state social control": "the successful subordination of people's own inclinations of social behavior or behavior sought by other social organizations in favor of the behavior prescribed by state rules." To be sure, criminal groups are alternative social organizations that, in some respects, challenge the power and authority of the state to impose its standards, codified as law. These groups constitute an alternative system by offering commerce and banking in black and gray markets that operate outside the regulatory framework of the state; buying, selling, and distributing controlled or prohibited commodities, such as narcotics; providing swift and usually discreet dispute resolution and debt collection without resorting to the courts; creating and maintaining cartels when state laws proscribe them; and arranging security for the so-called protection of businesses, as well as sheltering them from competitors, the state, and rival criminals.

Adding to the concentration of unaccountable power amassing with economic globalization, organized crime groups are tapping into a global system of arms trade, as well as raising and channeling immense amounts of money for this purpose. Insurgents in different regions rely increasingly on organized crime groups, and their armed forces are now intermingled with Serbs, Croats, and other soldiers of fortune, demobilized at home and seeking new employment opportunities. In a twist, parasitic states such as Mobutu's Zaire (today, Kabila's Democratic Republic of Congo, challenged at home by rebel forces), like their opponents, have drawn on former police officers and a flourishing business of mercenaries with their own corporate organizations, recruiting networks, and journals. (Among the companies selling arms and other forms of military assistance are Sandline International in the United Kingdom; Military Professional Resources Inc. of Alexandria, Virginia; and Executive Outcomes of South Africa, which had two thousand contract soldiers on call and its own fleet of aircraft until the post-apartheid government passed antimercenary laws in 1998). By hiring these people for protection, some states are privatizing portions of enforcement and defense. Although ex-police officers and mercenaries themselves may not be criminals, their involvement in regional conflicts accentuates the tendency whereby growing connections between the state and organized crime give rise to more state-sanctioned violence.

Many instances of war and conflict mask transnational organized crime. While the media have, by and large, one-sidedly portrayed Somalia's conflict as warfare among clans causing the collapse of the state, surely cross-border drug trafficking in khat (leaves from a shrub, used as a narcotic when chewed) is a major element in that poverty-stricken country's deadly competition over resources. Similarly, in Lebanon, Sri Lanka, Pakistan, and other locales, much of the fighting ostensibly over religious differences and ethnic loyalties is also about drug trafficking, a source of enormous revenues. Put differently, the violence and urban anarchy in these countries typically melds unlawful, organized arms and drug trafficking, and religious and ethnic cleavages.

Heavily laden with the trappings of force, circumscribed but not disempowered, the state is less autonomous, with diminished ability to control borders. Not only is the state porous in terms of flows of knowledge and information, but also, increasingly, transnational criminal elements are entrants. In the face of such cross-border flows, the traditional notion of jurisdiction based on territoriality is progressively brought into question. New forms of criminality infringe on the principle of sovereignty, the centerpiece of the Westphalian interstate system. [...]

30

Has Globalization Gone Too Far?

Dani Rodrik

The process that has come to be called "globalization" is exposing a deep fault line between groups who have the skills and mobility to flourish in global markets and those who either don't have these advantages or perceive the expansion of unregulated markets as inimical to social stability and deeply held norms. The result is severe tension between the market and social groups such as workers, pensioners, and environmentalists, with governments stuck in the middle. [...]

While I share the idea that much of the opposition to trade is based on faulty premises, I also believe that economists have tended to take an excessively narrow view of the issues. To understand the impact of globalization on domestic social arrangements, we have to go beyond the question of what trade does to the skill premium. And even if we focus more narrowly on labor-market outcomes, there are additional channels, which have not yet come under close empirical scrutiny, through which increased economic integration works to the disadvantage of labor, and particularly of unskilled labor. This book attempts to offer such a broadened perspective. As we shall see, this perspective leads to a less benign outlook than the one economists commonly adopt. One side benefit, therefore, is that it serves to reduce the yawning gap that separates the views of most economists from the gut instincts of many laypeople.

Original publication details: Dani Rodrik, from "Has Globalization Gone Too Far?" in *Has Globalization Gone Too Far?* Institute for International Economics, March 1997. pp. 2, 4–7, 77–81. Reproduced with permission from D. Rodrik.

Sources of Tension

I focus on three sources of tension between the global market and social stability and offer a brief overview of them here.

First, reduced barriers to trade and investment accentuate the asymmetry between groups that can cross international borders (either directly or indirectly, say through outsourcing) and those that cannot. In the first category are owners of capital, highly skilled workers, and many professionals, who are free to take their resources where they are most in demand. Unskilled and semiskilled workers and most middle managers belong in the second category. Putting the same point in more technical terms, globalization makes the demand for the services of individuals in the second category *more elastic* – that is, the services of large segments of the working population can be more easily substituted by the services of other people across national boundaries. Globalization therefore fundamentally transforms the employment relationship.

The fact that "workers" can be more easily substituted for each other across national boundaries undermines what many conceive to be a postwar social bargain between workers and employers, under which the former would receive a steady increase in wages and benefits in return for labor peace. This is because increased substitutability results in the following concrete consequences:

- Workers now have to pay a larger share of the cost of improvements in work conditions and benefits (that is, they bear a greater incidence of nonwage costs).
- They have to incur greater instability in earnings and hours worked in response to shocks to labor demand or labor productivity (that is, volatility and insecurity increase).
- Their bargaining power erodes, so they receive lower wages and benefits whenever bargaining is an element in setting the terms of employment.

These considerations have received insufficient attention in the recent academic literature on trade and wages, which has focused on the downward shift in demand for unskilled workers rather than the increase in the elasticity of that demand.

Second, globalization engenders conflicts within and between nations over domestic norms and the social institutions that embody them. As the technology for manufactured goods becomes standardized and diffused internationally, nations with very different sets of values, norms, institutions, and collective preferences begin to compete head on in markets for similar goods. And the spread of globalization creates opportunities for trade between countries at very different levels of development.

This is of no consequence under traditional multilateral trade policy of the WTO and the General Agreement on Tariffs and Trade (GATT): the "process" or "technology" through which goods are produced is immaterial, and so are the social institutions of the trading partners. Differences in national practices are treated just like differences in factor endowments or any other determinant of comparative advantage. However, introspection and empirical evidence both reveal that most people attach values to processes as well as outcomes. This is reflected in the norms that shape and constrain the domestic environment in which goods and services are produced – for example, workplace practices, legal rules, and social safety nets.

Trade becomes contentious when it unleashes forces that undermine the norms implicit in domestic practices. Many residents of advanced industrial countries are uncomfortable with the weakening of domestic institutions through the forces of trade, as when, for example, child labor in Honduras displaces workers in South Carolina or when pension benefits are cut in Europe in response to the requirements of the Maastricht treaty. This sense of unease is one way of interpreting the demands for "fair trade." Much of the discussion surrounding the "new" issues in trade policy – that is, labor standards, environment, competition policy, corruption – can be cast in this light of procedural fairness.

We cannot understand what is happening in these new areas until we take individual preferences for processes and the social arrangements that embody them seriously. In particular, by doing so we can start to make sense of people's uneasiness about the consequences of international economic integration and avoid the trap of automatically branding all concerned groups as self-interested protectionists. Indeed, since trade policy almost always has redistributive consequences (among sectors, income groups, and individuals), one cannot produce a principled defense of free trade without confronting the question of the fairness and legitimacy of the practices that generate these consequences. By the same token, one should not expect broad popular support for trade when trade involves exchanges that clash with (and erode) prevailing domestic social arrangements.

Third, globalization has made it exceedingly difficult for governments to provide social insurance – one of their central functions and one that has helped maintain social cohesion and domestic political support for ongoing liberalization throughout the postwar period. In essence, governments have used their fiscal powers to insulate domestic groups from excessive market risks, particularly those having an external origin. In fact, there is a striking correlation between an economy's exposure to foreign trade and the size of its welfare state. It is in the most open countries, such as Sweden, Denmark, and the Netherlands, that spending on income transfers has expanded the most. This is not to say that the government is the sole, or the best, provider of social insurance. The extended family, religious groups, and local communities often play similar roles. My point is that it is a hallmark of the postwar period that governments in the advanced countries have been expected to provide such insurance.

At the present, however, international economic integration is taking place against the background of receding governments and diminished social obligations. The welfare state has been under attack for two decades. Moreover, the increasing mobility of capital has rendered an important segment of the tax base footloose, leaving governments with the unappetizing option of increasing tax rates disproportionately on labor income. Yet the need for social insurance for the vast majority of the population that remains internationally immobile has not diminished. If anything, this need has become greater as a consequence of increased integration. The question therefore is how the tension between globalization and the pressures for socialization of risk can be eased. If the tension is not managed intelligently and creatively, the danger is that the domestic consensus in favor of open markets will ultimately erode to the point where a generalized resurgence of protectionism becomes a serious possibility.

Each of these arguments points to an important weakness in the manner in which advanced societies are handling – or are equipped to handle – the consequences of globalization. Collectively, they point to what is perhaps the greatest risk of all, namely that the cumulative consequence of the tensions mentioned above will be the solidifying of a new set of class divisions – between those who prosper in the globalized economy and those who do not, between those who share its values and those who would rather not, and between those who can diversify away its risks and those who cannot. This is not a pleasing prospect, even for individuals on the winning side of the divide who have little empathy for the other side. Social disintegration is not a spectator sport – those on the sidelines also get splashed with mud from the field. Ultimately, the deepening of social fissures can harm all. [...]

The Role of National Governments

Policymakers have to steer a difficult middle course between responding to the concerns discussed here and sheltering groups from foreign competition through protectionism. I can offer no hard-and-fast rules here, only some guiding principles.

Strike a balance between openness and domestic needs

There is often a trade-off between maintaining open borders to trade and maintaining social cohesion. When the conflict arises – when new liberalization initiatives are under discussion, for example – it makes little sense to sacrifice social concerns completely for the sake of liberalization. Put differently, as policymakers sort out economic and social objectives, free trade policies are not automatically entitled to first priority.

Thanks to many rounds of multilateral trade liberalization, tariff and nontariff restrictions on goods and many services are now at extremely low levels in the industrial countries. Most major developing countries have also slashed their trade barriers, often unilaterally and in conformity with their own domestic reforms. Most economists would agree that the efficiency benefits of further reductions in these existing barriers are unlikely to be large. Indeed, the dirty little secret of international economics is that a tiny bit of protection reduces efficiency only a tiny bit. A logical implication is that the case for further liberalization in the traditional area of manufactured goods is rather weak.

Moreover, there is a case for taking greater advantage of the World Trade Organization's existing escape clause, which allows countries to institute otherwise-illegal trade restrictions under specified conditions, as well as for broadening the scope of these multilateral safeguard actions. In recent years, trade policy in the United States and the European Union has gone in a rather different direction, with increased use of antidumping measures and limited recourse to escape clause actions. This is likely because WTO rules and domestic legislation make the petitioning industry's job much easier in antidumping cases: there are lower evidentiary hurdles than in escape clause actions, no determinate time limit, and no requirement for compensation for affected trade partners, as the escape clause provides. Also, escape clause actions, unlike antidumping duties, require presidential approval in the United States. This is an undesirable situation because antidumping rules are, on the whole, consistent neither with economics principles nor, as discussed below, with fairness. Tightening the rules on antidumping in conjunction with a reconsideration and reinvigoration of the escape clause mechanism would make a lot of sense.

Do not neglect social insurance

Policymakers have to bear in mind the important role that the provision of social insurance, through social programs, has played historically in enabling multilateral liberalization and an explosion of world trade. As the welfare state is being pruned, there is a real danger that this contribution will be forgotten.

This does not mean that fiscal policy has to be profligate and budget deficits large. Nor does it mean a bigger government role. Enhanced levels of social insurance, for better labor-market outcomes, can be provided in most countries within existing levels of spending. This can be done, for example, by shifting the composition of income transfers from old-age insurance (i.e., social security) to labor-market insurance (i.e., unemployment compensation, trade adjustment assistance, training programs). Because pensions typically constitute the largest item of social spending in the advanced industrial countries, better targeting of this sort is highly compatible with responsible fiscal policies. Gearing social insurance more directly toward labor markets, without increasing the overall tax burden, would be one key step toward alleviating the insecurities associated with globalization.

There is a widespread feeling in many countries that, in the words of Tanzi and Schuknecht, "[s]ocial safety nets have ... been transformed into universal benefits with widespread free-riding behavior, and social insurance has frequently become an income support system with special interests making any effective reform very difficult." Further, "various government performance indicators suggest that the growth in spending after 1960 may not have brought about significantly improved economic performance or greater social progress." However, social spending has had the important function of buying social peace. Without disagreeing about the need to eliminate waste and reform in the welfare state more broadly, I would argue that the need for social insurance does not decline but rather increases as global integration increases. So the message to reformers of the social welfare system is, don't throw the baby out with the bath water.

Do not use "competitiveness" as an excuse for domestic reform

One of the reasons globalization gets a bad rap is that policymakers often fall into the trap of using "competitiveness" as an excuse for needed domestic reforms. Large fiscal deficits or lagging domestic productivity are problems that drag living standards down in many industrial countries and would do so even in closed economies. Indeed, the term "competitiveness" itself is largely meaningless when applied to whole economies, unless it is used to refer to things that already have a proper name – such as productivity, investment, and economic growth. Too often, however, the need to resolve fiscal or productivity problems is presented to the electorate as the consequence of global competitive pressures. This not only makes the required policies a harder sell – why should we adjust just for the sake of becoming better competitors against the Koreans or the Mexicans? – it also erodes the domestic support for international trade – if we have to do all these painful things because of trade, maybe trade isn't such a wonderful thing anyhow!

The French strikes of 1995 are a good case in point. What made the opposition to the proposed fiscal and pension reforms particularly salient was the perception that fundamental changes in the French way of life were being imposed for the sake of international economic integration. The French government presented the reforms as required by the Maastricht criteria, which they were. But presumably, the Maastricht criteria themselves reflected the policymakers' belief that a smaller welfare state would serve their economies better in the longer run. By and large, the French government did not make the case for reform on its own strengths. By using the Maastricht card, it turned the discussion into a debate on European economic integration. Hence the widespread public reaction, which extended beyond just those workers whose fates would be immediately affected.

The lesson for policymakers is, do not sell reforms that are good for the economy and the citizenry as reforms that are dictated by international economic integration.

Do not abuse "fairness" claims in trade

The notion of fairness in trade is not as vacuous as many economists think. Consequently, nations have the right – and should be allowed – to restrict trade when it conflicts with *widely held* norms at home or undermines domestic social arrangements that enjoy *broad* support.

But there is much that is done in the name of "fair trade" that falls far short of this criterion. There are two sets of practices in particular that should be immediately suspect. One concerns complaints made against other nations when very similar practices abound at home. Antidumping proceedings are a clear example: standard business practices, such as pricing over the life of a product or pricing over the business cycle, can result in duties being imposed on an exporting firm. There is nothing "unfair" about these business practices, as is made abundantly clear by the fact that domestic firms engage in them as well.

The second category concerns cases in which other nations are unilaterally asked to change *their* domestic practices so as to equalize competitive conditions. Japan is frequently at the receiving end of such demands from the United States and the European Union. A more recent example concerns the declaration by the US Trade Representative that corruption in foreign countries will henceforth be considered as unfair trade. While considerations of fairness and legitimacy will guide a country's own social arrangements, even by restricting imports if need be, such considerations should not allow one country to impose its own institutions on others. Proponents of fair trade must bear this key distinction in mind. Thus, it is perfectly legitimate for the United States to make it illegal for domestic firms to engage in corrupt practices abroad (as was done with the Foreign Corrupt Practices Act of 1977). It is also legitimate to negotiate a multilateral set of principles with other countries in the Organization for Economic Cooperation and Development (OECD) with broadly similar norms. It may also be legitimate to restrict imports from a country whose labor practices broad segments of the domestic population deem offensive. But it is not acceptable to unilaterally threaten retaliation against other countries because their business practices do not comply with domestic standards at home *in order to force these countries to alter their own standards*. Using claims of fairness to advance competitive aims is coercive and inherently contradictory. Trying to "export" norms by asking other countries to alter their social arrangements to match domestic ones is inappropriate for the same reason. [...]

31

Welfare Spending in an Era of Globalization
The North–South Divide

John Glenn

This paper examines the contention that economic globalization has led to the decline of welfare spending in recent decades. In so doing, it is argued that the experience of the industrialized and less industrialized states has been radically different. The OECD countries have experienced little, if any, downturn in either levels of state expenditure in general or in levels of welfare spending in particular. In contradistinction, many of the developing states have experienced significant declines in welfare spending, particularly during the period of structural adjustment implementation. In order to explain these two divergent outcomes, the paper examines the way in which the behaviour of international investors, multinational companies and the international financial institutions differs in relation to these two sets of countries.

It is argued that the current period of economic globalization, i.e., the intensification of economic relations between states, was actually initiated by the highly industrialized countries themselves following the economic stagnation of the 1970s. During this period, many OECD countries moved towards full liberalization of their capital accounts. Many have also encouraged the expansion of their domestic companies' overseas operations in order to take advantage of lower production costs and to lower their own trade imbalances. In addition to capital account liberalization, these countries have also promoted trade liberalization since 1947 through a raft of agreements under the auspices of GATT and the WTO. At the same time, the debt crisis afflicting the less industrialized countries in the 1980s provided political leverage for the United States and other G7 countries to foist neo-liberal economic policies on

Original publication details: John Glenn, "Welfare Spending in an Era of Globalization: The North–South Divide," in *International Relations*, 23, 1, 2009. pp. 27–8, 30–1, 36–9, 45–6. Reprinted by permission of SAGE.

countries in the South using the IMF and World Bank to do so. As a result, these countries have also become more integrated into the international financial and trade system.

The highly industrialized countries have therefore been important agents of change where economic globalization is concerned. However, this is not to say that they are immune to the pressures of globalization that they themselves initiated. Now that the genie is out of the bottle, multinational companies and international financial investors are able to move their investments from country to country with relative ease. This freedom has meant that these actors have also become important agents in their own right and now exert pressures on states using their economic wherewithal. Their ability to 'vote with their feet' by moving their capital to those states with the most favourable economic environments furnishes them with the potential to exert influence on the policies of states. However, it is argued that their influence is far greater on the less industrialized states of the South than on the states that promoted the globalized world that we now live in.

The paper examines two hypotheses. The first hypothesis argues that states are actively re-configuring themselves in order to produce environments conducive to business. The competition state hypothesis claims that economic globalization exerts certain pressures upon states so as to induce ever greater efficiency in core areas of competence. An alternative hypothesis argues that states compensate those worst affected by greater economic openness, and as a result a decline in social spending will not occur. In fact, there are overlaps between the two. Both models emphasize the importance of state investment in human capital in order to compete in the more open world that we now find ourselves in. The following argues that highly industrialized states exhibit characteristics of both the competition and the compensation model. Aggregate social expenditure shows little sign of decreasing and the welfare state continues to be alive and well. But large-scale privatization has occurred in many countries – with regard to both previously nationalized industries and social service provision. In addition, much stricter qualifying conditions have been introduced for those wishing to avail themselves of these social services/benefits. Yet, the highly industrialized countries continue to invest heavily in human capital, thereby maintaining their competitive edge vis-à-vis other countries. In the South welfare spending is generally low in comparison to the North. Moreover, the rapid expansion of welfare programmes that occurred in the North after the Second World War has not been repeated in several developing regions. It is argued that this stagnation in social spending may be at least partially explained by the more globalized environment that these states now find themselves in. [...] [T]here has been little change in the welfare expenditure of the key industrialized states in the last two decades.

Table 31.1 corroborates such a conclusion: Sweden has experienced the most dramatic decline in state expenditure since 1995 (from 67.1 per cent of GDP to 56.7 per cent in 2006). This is closely followed by Norway (from 51.5 per cent of GDP in 1995 to 41.8 per cent), another relatively high spending state that has traditionally followed the 'Scandinavian welfare model'. But overall, there has been very little change in patterns of state expenditure. For the OECD countries in general, since 1995 there has been a slight decline from 42.1 per cent of GDP to 40.6 per cent in 2006. Levels of government expenditure, therefore, may well have fallen slightly

Table 31.1 The growth of government expenditure (as a percentage of GDP).

	1961	1965	1970	1975	1980	1985	1990	1995	2000	2006
Austria	32.3	37.9	39.2	46.1	48.7	51.1	51.5	56.0	51.4	48.6
Belgium	29.8	32.3	36.5	44.5	51.6	61.9	52.2	51.9	49.1	50.1
Canada	30.0	29.1	35.7	40.8	40.8	47.1	48.8	48.5	41.1	38.9
France	35.7	38.4	38.9	43.5	46.4	52.2	49.3	54.4	51.6	54.5
Germany	33.8	36.7	38.7	49.0	48.3	47.6	44.5	48.3	45.1	46.1
Italy	29.4	34.3	34.2	43.2	46.0	51.6	53.5	52.5	46.1	47.8
Japan	17.4	20.0	19.4	27.2	33.1	32.3	31.8	36.5	39.2	36.7
Netherlands	35.4	38.7	46.0	56.6	59.7	60.7	53.1	49.7	43.7	46.5
Norway	29.7	34.2	41.0	46.6	49.1	42.9	54.0	51.5	42.7	41.8
Spain	13.0	19.6	22.2	24.7	32.6	42.2	42.6	44.2	39.0	38.2
Sweden	31.0	36.1	43.7	49.0	62.0	64.9	61.3	67.1	56.8	56.7
Switzerland	18.0	19.7	21.3	28.7	29.3	31.0	30.0	34.5	33.9	36.1
United Kingdom	33.4	36.4	39.3	46.9	45.6	46.0	42.2	45.0	37.5	45.6
United States	29.0	27.9	32.3	35.5	34.9	36.0	37.1	37.0	34.2	36.6
Average	28.4	31.5	34.9	41.6	44.9	47.7	46.6	48.4	43.7	44.6

Source: OECD Economic Outlook, 2006, 1983.

Refer to *OECD Economic Outlook*, vol. 79, June 2006, Table 25, p. 189 and *OECD Economic Outlook*, vol. 33, July 1983, Table R8, p. 165.

since their peaks in the early to mid 1990s, but the data does not support the belief that we are witnessing a dramatic decline of state intervention. Moreover, the figures are taken from a period of relatively high spending – over the *longue durée* the pattern has been one of increasing levels of spending. Indeed, the current period may be most accurately seen as a minor correction after unprecedented levels of spending, after all 'the much-vaunted era of globalization has witnessed the development of the largest states the world has ever seen and there is little evidence of this trend being reversed'. However, there are two points worth noting. It could be that the overall expenditure of these states has remained relatively constant, but that less of the budget has been allocated to welfare issues. Table 31.2 therefore confirms the earlier finding, indicating that the actual social spending for these states has remained surprisingly stable in the last two decades and indeed the average has increased slightly. [...]

Are similar patterns exhibited in the case of the developing states? Historically, levels of state spending, and in particular levels of welfare spending, have been much lower in these countries. Even in Latin America, where social spending has been historically high, the average for the region was still 15.1 per cent of GDP in 2005 compared to the norm for the OECD of over 20 per cent. Moreover, for many states the level of welfare spending actually declined from the mid 1970s to the mid 1990s. Nita Rudra, for example, examines the spending patterns of 53 developing countries over the last quarter of a century, and concludes that, compared to the industrialized countries, spending levels 'began much lower and fell lower still'. This is despite the fact that sub-Saharan Africa and Asia are the most affected by the

Table 31.2   Social spending as a percentage of GNP for seventeen industrialized countries.

	1960	1980	1990	1995	2001
Austria	15.9	23.8	24.1	26.6	26.0
Germany	18.1	20.3	22.8	27.5	27.4
Belgium	13.8	24.2	25.4	25.8	24.7
France	13.4	22.7	26.6	29.2	28.5
Netherlands	11.7	27.3	27.7	25.6	21.8
Italy	13.1	18.4	23.3	23.0	24.5
Sweden	10.8	29.0	30.8	33.2	29.8
Denmark	10.6	29.1	29.3	32.4	29.2
United Kingdom	10.2	18.2	19.6	23.0	21.8
Finland	8.8	18.5	24.8	31.1	24.8
Norway	7.8	18.6	24.7	26.0	23.9
New Zealand	10.4	19.2	21.9	18.9	18.5
Switzerland	4.9	15.2	17.9	23.9	25.4
Canada	9.1	13.3	16.6	19.6	17.3
Australia	7.4	11.3	14.2	17.8	15.7
United States	7.3	13.1	13.4	15.4	14.7
Japan	4.1	10.1	11.2	13.5	16.9
Average	10.4	19.5	22.0	24.3	22.7

Source: F. Castles, *The Future of the Welfare State*, 2004, Table 2.1 and *OECD Factbook*, 2006

HIV/AIDS epidemic. For sub-Saharan Africa, the figures are staggering with '60 per cent of all people living with HIV – 25.8 million' residing within the region.

Table 31.3 indicates that the level of social security spending within the South varies considerably and the pattern largely depends on the region under consideration. The southern states of Latin America tend to have the highest levels of social spending, reflecting both their history of populism, with its emphasis on redistribution, and possibly their economic wherewithal, allowing them to withstand some of the worst excesses of structural adjustment. The core East Asian states also exhibit relatively high social spending (around 9 per cent GDP) reflecting their adoption of the export-orientated developmental state model that produced high growth levels and relatively low debt burdens. However, many states of Central America, South Asia and sub-Saharan Africa have historically exhibited very low levels of social spending, at times constituting just a few per cent of GDP.

The actual pattern of spending also varies from region to region. East Asian states place greatest emphasis on education (over half of social spending) and the family unit is given far more responsibility for social support in economic downturns. But,

Table 31.3 Central government social spending as a percentage of GDP for selected less industrialized countries.

	1985	1990	1995	2000
Botswana	12.8[a]	10.2	12.7	
Egypt	8.8[d]	8.3	10.0	6.4
Ghana	3.3[e]	5.4	3.8	
Kenya	7.6[a]	7.0	6.8[g]	7.7
Zambia	5.1[a]	4.4	6.8	7.2[c]
Colombia	6.8	4.5	5.5	6.8
Guatemala	3.5[b]	2.3[f]	2.6[h]	3.1
Belize	6.9[b]	7.1	9.3	8.6[c]
Chile	12.6[b]	11.7	11.0	20.8
Argentina	9.6[a]	10.0[f]	14.9	15.6
Dominican Republic	3.5[a]	3.3	3.3[g]	3.8
Panama	14.0[a]	13.0	14.3	13.2
Uruguay	15.2[b]	14.5	21.0	23.2
Costa Rica[a]	13.9[a]	15.1	12.9	
Hong Kong*	8.9	8.7	9.5	13.1
Taiwan*	2.5	3.0	5.3	8.7
Singapore*	9.2	7.0	6.4	8.3[j]
South Korea*	5.1	7.0	6.7	8.4
Philippines	2.6	4.1	4.0	4.7
Indonesia	1.9	1.3	1.3	1.2
Nepal	3.1	3.8	3.8	4.5
Bangladesh	1.7	2.1	3.4	3.3

Source: IMF International Financial Statistics online; *Government Financial Statistics Yearbook*, Washington D.C.: IMF, various years; *Key Indicators of Developing Asian and Pacific Countries*, Oxford: OUP, various years. [a]1987, [b]1988, [c]1999, [d]1986, [e]1984, [f]1991, [g]1994, [h]1994, [i]1997, [j]2002. * Includes social housing. Social spending here is the amount spent on health, education and social security.

in addition, most of the East Asian states have relatively young populations and have therefore not had to allocate great sums to pensions. The developmental model's emphasis on attracting capital by investing in infrastructure and human capital has resulted in a relatively high proportion of spending dedicated to education. In addition, a high level of social housing provision has provided a competitive edge by containing wage inflation. Intra-regional differences are clearly apparent. For example, the fact that Taiwan had to dedicate 40 per cent of its budget to national defence in the 1950s/1960s meant that welfare programmes, such as comprehensive health coverage, were slow to be introduced (1995). On the other hand, in many Latin American countries social security constitutes almost half of total social expenditure. Much of this is dedicated to pension payments, despite the fact that these countries also have a relatively young population compared to the OECD countries and unemployment is generally high. This can be explained by the fact that many Latin American countries have 'extremely early retirement ages for selected public sector occupations' [...]

However, if East Asia and southern Latin America are taken out of the equation, the differences in government spending between the industrialized and developing states are striking, with the latter registering extremely low levels of spending. Taking the extreme poles, social expenditure as a proportion of GDP for Indonesia or the Dominican Republic registers around the 2–3 per cent mark, compared to Sweden or France which at the moment hover just under the 30 per cent mark. It is also noteworthy that, in contrast to the industrialized states, from 1980 to 1990 many southern states experienced a decline in social spending as a percentage of overall government spending (Table 31.4). However, this decline seems to have abated and many developing states are now endeavouring to increase the amount they spend on the general welfare of their populations. [...] [T]his most likely reflects the fact that during this period these countries were burdened with very high levels of debt and most of these countries had therefore implemented, or had begun implementing, a series of structural adjustment policies in order to receive loans from the IMF. [...]

In contrast to the North, the developing states are therefore far more vulnerable to the pressures arising from economic globalization. Overall, social spending is far lower in the South, with some regions registering just a few per cent of GDP. Despite this, many of these states experienced further reductions in their spending, particularly in the 1980s, thus mirroring Cerny's description of the decline of the welfare state and its paring back of welfare provision (its re-distributive function). The reason for this divergent outcome is that these two sets of countries confront rather different external economic environments. Multinational companies and financial investors employ a different set of criteria depending on a state's position within the world system, but the international financial institutions and their structural adjustment policies have also had a significant impact on levels of welfare expenditure in the developing states. [...]

A more accurate depiction is of globalization (whether it be economic liberalization or structural adjustment) having a differential impact across the industrializing world. Trade and capital account liberalization will affect countries very differently depending on a host of factors: levels of debt; economic ranking; political institutions; historical legacies, etc. Those countries offering stability, high-quality infrastructure and healthy, well-educated populations will clearly be seen as better investment opportunities. In

Globalization and the Nation-State

Table 31.4   Central government expenditure 1980–98.

	Social service expenditure (as percentage of overall expenditure)		
	1980	*1990*	*1998*
Kenya	36.0	28.5	29.6
Lesotho	31.4	34.3	35.7
Botswana	41.5	33.9	42.7
Turkey	33.0	26.3	25.7
Tunisia	53.7	36.9	46.6
Jordan	38.5	36.6	44.6
Egypt	32.1	32.1	23.6
Sri Lanka	40.5	27.5	30.0
India	8.8	19.2	20.1
Indonesia	23.7	13.2	26.2
Philippines	25.4	22.5	26.5
Malaysia	31.0	35.6	42.5
Thailand	37.8	32.2	38.3
Mexico	57.6	30.6	48.1
Panama	48.5	66.7	65.2
Chile	65.3	63.9	71.3
Dominican Republic	53.0	44.0	44.2
Uruguay	67.6	61.6	75.8
Brazil	43.5	33.0	34.5
Costa Rica	73.9	58.7	59.6
Colombia	58.5	32.1	45.2

Source: World Development Reports 1997 & 2000/2001. Table 14.

addition, those countries with relatively low levels of debt will not be burdened by punitive repayments, structural adjustment programmes and relatively high interest rates. For the most vulnerable countries, the competition state, rather than the compensatory state, best describes their situation, with the pressures of globalization acting to stop or even roll back social spending. […]

32

World Culture and the Future of Schooling

David P. Baker and Gerald K. LeTendre

[...]

By and large, most people most of the time think about education as solely a national undertaking. The trends we examine here, however, lead to quite a different vision, one where there is a considerable global process at work. To make sense of this contrasting globalized world of education, it is helpful first to describe the common image of schooling as a national enterprise. It is a vision with several components.

The everyday vision of schooling as a national enterprise sees it as chiefly a unique product of a nation's culture and governmental effort to foster prosperity for its citizens. This is thought to be true regardless of the particular level of governance of schools within the nation. It is common, then, to refer to French, Chilean, Japanese, American, and South African (or any nation's) schools as separate national entities. After all, what could be more deeply embedded in a nation's society than its schools preparing children for future adult lives in that country? The reigning image of education today is that schools are designed and managed within a national context for the specific needs and goals of a particular nation.

This vision also assumes that schooling is organized to educate and socialize children in a specific way that is directly linked to the future welfare of a particular nation. For example, German schools are thought to produce German adults with the technical skills, linguistic capabilities, and cultural awareness necessary to carry forth the entity of Germany into the future. A national product of educated citizens issuing forth from the school system is the main image of what schooling does in every

Original publication details: David P. Baker and Gerald K. LeTendre, *National Differences, Global Similarities: World Culture and the Future of Schooling*. Redwood City: Stanford University Press, 2005. pp. 1–4, 6–10, 12. Reproduced with permission from Stanford University Press.

nation. Educators may be aware of the larger global world, but their predominant image of a nation's schools is as a means to pass on a sense of national uniqueness and heritage, as well as meet the technical needs of its particular labor market. This image implies that schooling is limited to the specific needs of a nation, therefore schooling would not expand except as is needed for national reasons. Nor would schools engage in education that is separable from traditional values of the nation. Additionally, this image of schooling holds that because labor markets are hierarchical, so should schooling be hierarchical. For efficiency, the argument continues, the best and the brightest of a nation deserve the best educational opportunities for the best national outcomes, and those with lesser endowments should receive less. All of this is wrapped up in the picture of a national system of education operating uniquely to produce efficiently adults with the kind of skill necessary for a range of tasks in the labor market and adult life within a national context. [...]

This image of national schooling is how many think the educational world works, but ultimately it is mostly inaccurate, and becoming more so every moment. In spite of the fact that nations (and their subunits, provinces, and states) have immediate political and fiduciary control over schooling, education as an institution has become a global enterprise. We show here that there are all kinds of trends suggesting that ideas and demands and expectations for what school can, and should, do for a society have developed well beyond any particular national context. The same global ideas, demands, and expectations filter into nations, greatly shaping their schools in union with school all over the world. Over the last century, there have been both steady expansion of schooling into our daily lives and deepening of education's meaning for things people hold dear. The current situation in schooling across nations is wholly unpredictable from the image of unique national models of schooling.

All the while that schooling has been considered a national technical project, from nation to nation considerable global forces are at work shaping and changing schooling in fundamental ways that many people are unaware of as they view education mostly from a national perspective. But just like the shrinking of the world's marketplace, media, and politics, education too is undergoing intensive globalization. Whether you find them in Mexico City, a small town in Pennsylvania, or in rural Kenya, schools all over the world appear to run in much the same way everywhere. Whether we were educated in a public school in New York City or a Catholic school in Tokyo, we experienced the same basic patterns of education. Today we can walk into almost any public school around the world and be able to understand what is going on, even though the specifics of the lesson might be totally incomprehensible. Even if we do not know the language, social mores, or dominant religious dogma of a country, we can still identify central features and make sense of the general patterns when we step into a school there. We all recognize schooling just about everywhere because it entails a similar set of ideas about education held consistently throughout the world. This commonality – and the amazing story of what produces it – often goes unobserved, and its substantial consequences on the everyday world of students, parents, teachers, and administrators remain mostly unappreciated. [...]

Subplot One: The Worldwide Success of Mass Schooling

[...] [W]e are struck by how successful schooling is in the world. But we don't mean just any kind of schooling; rather, we refer to a particularly successful type of schooling that has spread around the world and has become the *singular model* of educating children, regardless of a nation's political regime, level of economic wealth, cultural heritage, and social problems. This is often referred to as *state-sponsored mass schooling,* or "mass schooling" for short. It is mostly public schooling for large masses of children, hence the name.

The history of the spread of public mass schooling and its accompanying mass enrollments around the world is the biggest success story ever known about the implementation of education. Funding for schooling now rivals military and other social welfare expenditures in most national budgets, and educational spending continues to grow worldwide.

Comparing mass schooling with that of the education in premodern societies that has gone on throughout most of the history of human civilization shows how revolutionary an idea mass schooling really is. For most of recorded history, education was practical, situational, and highly limited – as with an apprenticeship to gain a set of skills – and it often did not require literacy. Most of the time, children learned all they needed to know within their family, clan, or tribe. Much of the content of premodern formal schooling was "religious" in nature: learning the legends, beliefs, and sacred traditions of a people or culture, and some limited literacy for reading religious texts. It was in this situation that premodern schooling became most elaborated; a small, elite group of students were taught how to read, write, and memorize the texts important to that culture. Practical apprenticeships were education for some nonelites, but this was not available for all and was aimed at a specific craft.

This all started to change some 150 to 200 years ago with the rise of mass schooling in many Western nations. There were still elite forms of education, but over time schooling was developed in principle for all children to learn academic skills through a more or less common curricula. Since then mass schooling has become one of the most impressive cases of successful transmission of a cultural model in the history of human society, developing and spreading in a relatively short time without limitations. Using mass schooling, most nations have achieved mass literacy within just the last hundred years, and currently there are no real alternatives to mass schooling anywhere. Full enrollment in elementary education was achieved before the middle of the twentieth century in wealthier nations and over the next forty years in poorer nations. Mass secondary education expanded to the same full enrollment a decade or two after elementary reached full enrollment, and the growth of higher education continues unabated in many nations today. Mass schooling has developed and intensified over time as an institution, deepening its meaning for everyday life. A big part of our story is what effects this resilient institution has on students, families, teachers, and school administrators.

Subplot Two: Schooling Is an Institution

At the core of the spread of mass schooling is a set of fundamental ideas that were unique just a short time ago but now have become widely accepted and even cherished. For instance, the ideas that all children should be educated; that the nation has an interest in this and should furnish funds; that education is for the collective good; that children should start early and receive continuous instruction for a relatively large number of years; that tradition of statuses such as race, gender, religion, or language should not be barriers to mass schooling; and that academic cognitive skills are useful to all children are institutional foundations that underpin and give modern schooling widespread meaning in society. Adding to these powerful ideas is the rise of the exclusive currency of the educational credential, required to hold almost any position in labor markets all over the world. Now in human society, formal schooling has an unprecedented monopoly on the issuing and control of these credentials that lead to so many aspects of adult life.

Our stories lead us to appreciate how these ideas about mass schooling have formed a broad globalizing process making schooling a pervasive and powerful institution. As we have just described, the schooling-as-a-national-enterprise perspective tends not to appreciate the complex institutional nature of education, or its ability to reach across national borders as easily as the ideas behind modern capitalism and democratic government have spread worldwide. A big part of this underlying subplot is what is happening to the institution of mass education, more than what is happening educationally in any one nation, or even type of nation.

Education is an institution, like modern health care or the family, that may take on differing forms from nation to nation and even from region to region within a nation, but that at a deeper level is strongly affixed to global norms and rules about what education is and how schools should operate. If one turns a blind eye toward the image of schooling as a world institution, one is easily led astray in interpreting trends in schools, particularly cross-national trends that appear to differ so much from our individual experience (chiefly with a particular nation's schooling). [...]

Our point here is that to a large extent the grammar of schooling is global. This means that much of the grammar of schools and the ideas behind it are reproduced and reinforced at a global level. Every individual school is still influenced by local, regional, and national factors, but the basic image of a school – what it is and what it should do – is commonly defined in the same way globally. Consequently, the organization of national school systems (French, German, American, and so on) is now influenced by transnational forces that are beyond the control of national policy makers, politicians, and educators themselves yet appear to be part of their everyday world. We do not mean to say that the United Nations or other powerful multinational agencies overtly force nations to do and think in the same way about schooling. Rather, widespread understanding repeatedly communicated across nations, resulting in common acceptance of ideas, leads to standardization and similar meanings, all happening in a soft, almost imperceptible, taken-for-granted way.

As a global institution, schooling has developed powerful world values and beliefs about children, learning, teaching, and the administration of schools. Over a thirty-year research program with colleagues, institutional theorist and comparative sociologist John Meyer has convincingly established a strong case for thinking about schooling as a product of a world culture that renders education as a resilient and powerful institution in modern society. They have shown that mass schooling takes similar forms throughout the world, and that there are common beliefs in what schooling can and should do for society. This process, they argue, has to a large degree been driven by a dynamic world culture.

By *world culture*, we do not mean a culture that is void, ersatz, or not historical. Institutionalists see a dynamic world culture that (for better or worse) evolved out of Western ideals of rationality and purposeful action. Rationality as a pervasive cultural product (some would say even a hegemonic product) of the historical rise of the West serves to bureaucratize, marketize, individuate, and homogenize the institutions of the world. Homogenization produces consistent norms of behavior across a set of modern institutions, thus tying institutions such as the modern nation state and formal education together in a tight political sphere. Rationality, along with its off-shoots of marketization, individualization, bureaucratization, and homogenization, plays the tune that all modern global institutions march to, but it is itself a cultural product and acts as such throughout the social system. [...]

Mass schooling is the predominant model of education in the world today. It pervades every part of people's lives in modern society and creates a cultural of education unparalleled in human existence. Although nations have made, and will continue to make, their own modifications to the model, mass education chiefly develops as a world institution. But it is far from static or monolithic; global forces dynamically interact with national ones and schooling often changes unpredictably. [...]

Part V Questions

1. Identify and explain several aspects of globalization that make it more difficult for states to manage their societies. Then explain how some aspects of globalization can improve states' capacity to manage their societies.

2. Strange argues that rapid technological change and the extensive resources required for technological innovation force states to do the bidding of transnational corporations. Explain this argument, while also showing how technological change can also work to the benefit of states.

3. What happens to the territory of an empire when it collapses? Think about the case of the Soviet Union after 1989, when many new states appeared. Did any former Soviet republics choose not to become independent states? Can you explain why?

4. How can intergovernmental organizations (IGOs) help solve the problems that states face in dealing with globalization? Are IGO policies likely to benefit all states equally? Explain.

5. In what ways does global organized crime diminish the capacity of states to manage their affairs, in Mittelman's analysis? How do states respond to the challenge posed by global criminal organizations?

6. Rodrik suggests that globalization may have gone too far. In your opinion, should business and markets be totally free of government regulation and oversight? How large a role should government play in managing the economy and seeking solutions to social problems?

7. Explain Glenn's argument that the decline of the state has been exaggerated with regard to both total state spending and social (welfare) spending. How does the "North–South divide" affect state spending? Among less developed countries, why is social spending greater in Latin American and East Asian countries than in South Asian, Central American, and sub-Saharan African countries?

8. Mass schooling is highly expanded in most countries of the world, according to Baker and LeTendre. What does this tell us about the purported decline of the state in an era of globalization? How do Baker and LeTendre make the case that mass schooling has become a global institution? What features of globalization help to promote this institution?

Part VI

Global Governance

Introduction

No world government runs world society; no world president or prime minister can issue binding decisions. Much as the UN General Assembly might like to take on this role, no legislature makes global policy. Some international courts impose sanctions for some violations of international norms, but their authority hardly matches that of domestic judicial systems. Yet the world faces many problems that no single government can tackle by itself. Some problems spill across borders, as in the case of national financial troubles that endanger global markets. Others have to do with easing exchanges between countries, such as the case of devising common shipping methods to facilitate trade. Still other problems are really of planetary scope, most clearly in the case of environmental issues such as ozone depletion or global warming. If anything, globalization has helped to increase the number of such problems. The tighter web of global connections entails new risks as well as opportunities. But old political forms are poorly tailored to cope with several twenty-first-century problems. What is to be done about the mismatch? "Global governance" is the term used to describe the various efforts to find effective solutions for common problems, in the form of new norms, agreements, and institutions, all in the absence of an authoritative center or policy-making body.

As commonly used, the term suffers from fuzziness. Introducing a volume on *Globalization and Governance* (1999), Aseem Prakash and Jeffrey A. Hart define governance as "organizing collective action," which in turn "entails the establishing of institutions" made up of "rules of the game that permit, prescribe, or prohibit certain actions." In their introduction to a similar book on *Governance in a Globalizing World* (2000), Robert O. Keohane and Joseph S. Nye define governance as "the processes and institutions, both formal and informal, that guide and restrain the collective activities of a group." Global governance then minimally refers to organizing the collective

The Globalization Reader, Fifth Edition. Edited by Frank J. Lechner and John Boli.
Editorial material and organization © 2015 John Wiley & Sons, Ltd.
Published 2015 by John Wiley & Sons, Ltd.

action of many countries or guiding the collective activities of people from many places. To some extent, the fuzziness of the term is deliberate. Strictly speaking, governance includes government, but the point of invoking global "governance" is to highlight ways of doing things, of carrying out joint decisions affecting many people or places, without relying on conventional government as such and without claiming the mantle of a single global authority. In other words, the term is used broadly to encompass many border-crossing or space-spanning collective activities in the sphere between what states used to claim as their prerogatives and what a full-fledged world government might claim as its proper domain. That sphere is large and growing – the key point that students of global governance try to convey. A somewhat fuzzy designation has the benefit of being inclusive.

Institutions of global governance come in many shapes and sizes. One is illustrated in the global environmentalism section (Part XI), namely, the regime intended to reduce the use of chemicals that harm the ozone layer in the atmosphere, arrived at through negotiations among states, strong backing by scientific experts, and pressure from NGO activists. It is just one of many such environmental "regimes," that is, sets of norms and procedures addressing specific issues and typically implemented by designated organizations or officials. In our book *World Culture* (2005), we describe another governance institution, the International Criminal Court (ICC), established by a treaty among state members, backed by legal experts and supportive NGOs, and now in business in The Hague as the first global institution empowered to hold state officials individually responsible for war crimes or crimes against humanity. Though not a formal part of the UN system, it reflects the growth of law and law-making in many bodies related to the United Nations, most notably the propagation of the human rights "regime" in the last several decades. A third example relates to the world economy. The Bank for International Settlements (BIS), founded before World War II, has evolved as the prime agency through which many central banks cooperate to assure global financial stability. Its Basel Committee on Banking Supervision has become perhaps the most important institution setting guidelines for banking operations. In response to the credit crisis and bank losses of the late 2000s, for example, it proposed stricter capital and liquidity requirements to prevent banks from overextending themselves, giving them a stronger cushion in case of new setbacks.

When it comes to protecting the environment, ensuring basic rights, or bolstering economic confidence, to mention only some prominent instances, "the world" has taken action through new institutions carrying out new responsibilities with new resources and authority. Precisely how well they do this is a matter of debate. Environmental regimes vary in effectiveness; the ICC has yet to demonstrate its clout; for all its influence, the BIS could not stem major bank losses. The factors that foster or hinder success within and across such arenas remain poorly understood. The autonomy of these global governance bodies, which purportedly are not beholden to traditional state interests, is also in question. This issue still afflicts the United Nations, for example, because it often does the bidding of powerful members rather than promote common interests. Directly or indirectly, many institutions of global governance are still accountable to specific governments. At the same time, it is fair to say that such governments often lose some of their hold over institutions in the long run. The UN is again a case in point, as its activities have greatly expanded beyond those contemplated in its Charter and the key founding member, the United States, often finds itself at odds with UN policies. How much autonomy global governance institutions actually achieve is a current topic for study.

Finally, while scholars are learning much more about individual institutions – many of which are intergovernmental organizations, or IGOs – the overall shape of global governance is far from settled. In some ways, the United Nations remains at the core of the emerging system, but governance institutions have proliferated across many fields in many directions. For lack of a common direction, some analysts, like Anne-Marie Slaughter, view global governance as fragmented or disaggregated – an uncoordinated mishmash. Others view this state of affairs as simply inevitable bumps on the long road to a more full-fledged world government. Sorting out the forces that ultimately determine the overall shape of global governance is another key item on the scholarly agenda.

The first selection in this section covers one of the most important governance institutions, the International Monetary Fund. Reviewing data from studies of the IMF's programs, American political scientist James Vreeland describes how an institution originally intended to bolster financial stability by assisting countries with balance-of-payments problems – an area where it has had some success – has taken on a broader role to promote economic development, an area where its effects appear weak and have come at the cost of greater inequality. Its conditional lending is controversial, in part because it infringes on state sovereignty, but Vreeland finds that IMF involvement in state finances need not lead to drastic cuts in social spending. Another key economic governance institution is the World Trade Organization, founded in 1995 with the primary goals of promoting free trade and settling trade disputes peacefully. Ann Capling, a Canadian-Australian political scientist, and Richard Higgott, a British-Australian political scientist, show that the WTO faces numerous challenges – for example, how to avoid protectionist reactions to economic downturns in rich countries, how to give a stronger voice to emerging economies, and how to balance demands for further liberalization with fairness to workers.

Anne-Marie Slaughter, an American international relations scholar, presents a broader picture of global governance, showing how networks of government officials such as regulators, judges, and central bankers have crystallized to address common problems, acquiring at least some of the authority to "perform many of the functions of a world government . . . without the form." This institutional bridge-building, she argues, is gradually shaping a new world order in which states remain key players but become embedded in a wider set of relationships. An example of such embedding is the work of the International Organization for Standardization (ISO), described by Americans Craig N. Murphy, an international political economy scholar, and JoAnne Yates, a management and communications professor. ISO is a nongovernmental organization that brings government experts together with industry representatives in standard-setting bodies that, through voluntary consensus building, decide on guidelines for a wide range of activities, from manufacturing processes to specifications for screw threads to quality control. A striking example of its impact, recounted here, is the standardization it achieved years ago for the dimensions of freight containers, which greatly stimulated the expansion of cross-ocean trade.

Our final two selections address new developments in the governance of global health. Three British health researchers, Richard Dodgson, Kelley Lee, and Nick Drager, suggest that globalization makes it more difficult for governments to take care of their citizens' health; "transborder health risks," such as new epidemics, are a case in point. Instead of relying on intergovernmental cooperation, they advocate a more ambitious governance system in which states cooperate with nonstate actors, for example through public–private partnerships, to address a wider range of issues. This approach is exemplified by global campaigns against the marketing of breast milk substitutes and against tobacco use. One increasingly important "nonstate actor" is the Gates Foundation, the largest private philanthropic organization in the world. British physician David McCoy and his colleagues show that, by virtue of its considerable assets, the foundation helps to set priorities in global health governance, for example by emphasizing issues like HIV/AIDS and malaria rather than other health problems. Its policy leverage shapes global public health efforts and more broadly illustrates a new trend in global governance.

33

The International Monetary Fund

James Vreeland

At the writing of this book, 49 developing countries around the world – whose popu-lations account for more than one billion people – are participating in economic programs supported by the International Monetary Fund (IMF or Fund). These "IMF programs" grant the governments of these countries access to IMF loans, but access to the loans can be cut off if the governments fail to comply with specific policy con-ditions. IMF policy conditions impact the lives of individuals living in these countries in intimate ways: the policy conditions address government expenditures, so IMF programs help determine whether roads, schools, or debt repayment take priority. The policy conditions also address interest rates, so they may affect one's ability to borrow to purchase a home or invest in a business. IMF policy conditions often address the value of the national currency, so IMF programs may impact the very purchasing power of the money in people's pockets.

Not surprisingly, the IMF is well known throughout the developing world – to the elites and the masses alike. The organization often appears to exercise as much or even more authority than their own governments. Yet, the IMF is less familiar to average citizens in the developed world. And, to many throughout the world, the actual functioning of the organization is unknown or misunderstood. Unfounded opinion about the IMF abounds among people who often lump it together with other international institutions like the World Bank and the World Trade Organization, even though the administration and purposes of the IMF are quite distinct from these other international institutions.

Original publication details: James Raymond Vreeland, *The International Monetary Fund: Politics of Conditional Lending*. Abingdon: Routledge, 2007. pp. 1–3, 84–5, 87–92, 94. Reproduced with permission from Taylor & Francis.

Founded in the wake of the Great Depression, the IMF can be thought of as an international credit union with access to a pool of resources provided by the subscriptions of its members, which include nearly every country in the world. The size of a country's contribution depends on the country's economic dominance, hence, the bulk of the resources of the IMF come from the developed world. The Fund can lend from this pool of resources to countries facing economic problems. These days, the only countries that borrow from the IMF come from the developing world.

IMF loans can be thought of as a form of insurance for governments against the possibility of an economic crisis. Such insurance, however, introduces something economists call "moral hazard": the prospect of receiving assistance in the face of an economic crisis in the form of an IMF loan may itself lower a government's incentive to avoid the bad economic policies that cause economic crises in the first place.

To counter moral hazard, the IMF imposes *conditionality*: governments are required to follow what the IMF deems as "good" policies in return for the continued disbursements of the IMF loan. Thus, one can think of an IMF program as having two components: the *loan* and the *conditions* attached to the loan. The goal of this arrangement is to first stabilize a country facing a balance of payments crisis and then to promote growth and the reduction of poverty.

Yet, conditionality is controversial. If the policies imposed by the IMF are so good for countries, why must governments be enticed through conditional lending? At the heart of this question is national sovereignty, and beyond purely economic guidelines, the imposition of IMF programs is heavily influenced by international and domestic politics.

International politics play a role because powerful members sometimes use their influence at the IMF to pursue political goals. Votes at the IMF, like contributions, are pegged to a country's economic size, so economically powerful countries have more say at the IMF than other countries, and can pressure the Fund to do their bidding. Governments who are considered important allies of the IMF's most influential members – like the United States – sometimes receive preferential treatment from the IMF. The IMF may bail them out of economic crises with large loans even if they fail to comply with IMF conditions of changing economic policy.

Yet, at the domestic level of politics in developing countries, there are other cases where governments actually want IMF conditions to be imposed. These governments seek the assistance of the international institution to get around domestic political constraints and force changes in economic policy. Governments can use IMF conditionality to gain leverage over domestic opposition to policy change. Sometimes, such policy changes result in superior outcomes for society, but often IMF leverage is used to protect elites and make others bear the cost of an economic crisis.

Unfortunately, there is scant evidence of the success of IMF conditionality. Studies have even found that IMF programs hurt economic growth. A further effect of IMF programs is the increase of income inequality. This is not just because the IMF is involved with countries that already have economic problems – even accounting for this fact, these disappointing results hold.

There is little consensus over why IMF programs have the perverse effects that they do. Some argue that the influence of international political pressures has led to low levels of compliance with IMF conditionality. As a result, IMF lending simply subsidizes the continuation of bad economic policies. Others argue that the economic policies imposed by the IMF are the wrong ones. Instead of imposing austerity, the IMF should promote economic stimulus packages so that developing countries can grow their way out of economic problems. Still others argue that failure is due to domestic politics. Policy may change under IMF programs, but governments implement only selected reforms or impose partial reform with the goal of insulating domestic political elites and placing the burden of the economic crisis on labor and the poor. Strangely, with all of these various points of view, there is a broad based consensus that the IMF should scale back its operations. Many feel that the IMF should get out of the development business.

Recently, however, the IMF has made a bold new commitment to promote economic development through continued conditional lending. Thus, IMF programs remain a presence throughout most of the developing world. In some countries, participation in IMF programs is business as usual, a routine way of life. [...]

The Effects of IMF Programs on the Balance of Payments

If IMF programs have any effect, it should be on the balance of payments (BOP). First and foremost, the Articles of Agreement mandate the IMF to address problems in this area. What is the balance of payments? The IMF defines a country's overall balance of payments as the sum of the "current account," the "capital account," and the "financial account" plus "net errors and omissions." The *current account* of the balance of payments is the credits minus the debits of goods, services, income, and current transfers. The *capital account* refers mainly to transfers of fixed assets and nonproduced, nonfinancial assets. The *financial account* is the net sum of the balance of direct investment, portfolio investment and other investment transactions. *Net errors and omissions* reflect statistical inconsistencies in the recording of entries and are included so that all debit and credit entries in the balance of payments statement sum to zero. By construction (of net errors and omissions), the overall balance of payments is equal to net changes in "reserves and related items," the sum of transactions in reserve assets, exceptional financing, and use of Fund credit and loans.

Many studies have looked at the effect of IMF programs on both the overall BOP and the current account component of the BOP. The IMF mandate to address BOP problems has been clear throughout its history. The Articles of Agreement are explicit that IMF lending should go to countries experiencing BOP problems. The deficit country is taking in more imports or fixed assets or finance than it is generating through exports – the immediate purpose of an IMF arrangement is to provide a loan so that foreign debts can continue to be serviced and necessary imports can be purchased. The loan is intended to soften the blow as adjustments are made as the demand for imports and foreign financing is cut. Demand can be addressed in many ways: devaluation, where the demand for imports is cut by effectively raising their domestic price; the reduction of money supply by raising interest rates or limiting credit creation; and fiscal austerity, where governments reduce consumption both by raising taxes and by spending less. Yet it is not obvious that the IMF program will help. If governments fail to comply with IMF policy conditions, or if the IMF policies are not sufficient, BOP problems can persist. Indeed, if the IMF program causes a drastic contraction of the economy, it is possible for the BOP situation to worsen.

What have studies found? The broad consensus is that the IMF has had success in addressing balance of payments problems. For example, in an early study conducted by economist and professor of Latino Studies at the University of California, Santa Cruz, Manuel Pastor, IMF programs were found to have a positive, statistically significant effect on the BOP, using a before–after methodology analyzing Latin American countries during 1965–81. Another early study using a before–after approach to study Latin America, by Tony Killick, along with colleagues Moazzam Malik and Marcus Manuel, also found a statistically significant positive effect of IMF programs on the BOP. [...]

Economic Growth

What is the effect of IMF programs on economic development? For some, this is the most important question. Sustainable economic development and prosperity address many of the other economic problems discussed above. An economy that is growing can avoid or afford to sustain BOP and fiscal deficits, and can afford to maintain some degree of inflation. Economic development is also associated with numerous important indicators of quality of life for people. Some argue, however, that economic growth is not and should not be a goal of the IMF. They point out that the original purpose of the IMF was to address balance of payments problems and that the focus on economic growth is something that developed over time. The claim is that the IMF was never intended to promote economic growth.

Yet, this is not completely true. The Articles of Agreement call upon the IMF to provide members "with opportunity to correct maladjustments in their balance of payments *without resorting to measures destructive of national or international prosperity*" [emphasis added]. This certainly indicates that the IMF should at least not hurt prospects for economic growth.

The Report of the Executive Directors for the First Annual Meeting of the Board of Governors in 1946 was even more explicit:

> The function of the Fund is to aid members in maintaining arrangements that promote the balanced expansion of international trade and investment and in this way *contribute to the maintenance of high levels of employment and real income*.

Right from the first meeting of the governing body of the IMF, high levels of employment and income were central.

Even though the IMF shifted its focus from the industrialized world to the developing world, the importance of promoting national prosperity remained. In fact, the IMF has become increasingly concerned with promoting growth and addressing poverty over time. As Michel Camdessus, the IMF Managing Director from 1987 to 2000, described,

> Our primary objective is growth … It is toward growth that our programs and their conditionality are aimed. It is with a view toward growth that we carry out our special responsibility of helping to correct balance of payments disequilibria and, more generally, to eliminate obstructive macroeconomic imbalances. When I refer to growth, I mean high-quality growth, not … growth for the privileged few, leaving the poor with nothing but empty promises.

Managing Director Horst Köhler, who took the helm at the IMF after Camdessus, emphasized the importance of promoting world financial stability, but he also echoed the views of his predecessor, contending that "the IMF should strive to promote non-inflationary economic growth that benefits all people of the world."

How effective has the IMF been at promoting economic growth? Not very. Not only is evidence of growth promotion weak, recent studies even show that IMF programs have a significant *negative* effect on economic growth. Early studies consistently showed no statistically significant effect. Out of nine before–after studies from 1978 to 1995, covering different countries, regions, and time spans, only one reported a significant positive effect. Four of the others reported no effect; two reported a statistically insignificant negative effect; and one reported an insignificant positive effect. Using with–without comparisons, results were similar – some show insignificant positive effects, others insignificant negative effects, still others show no effect at all, but none of them show a statistically significant effect.

With more sophisticated methodology, new results emerged. Khan's 1990 study, which addressed nonrandom selection, showed a significant negative effect on growth in the short run, with the adverse effects on growth diminishing thereafter. In his study published in 1994, Conway built upon this result using an advanced technique to control for nonrandom selection on observed variables. He showed that IMF programs have an initial significant negative effect on growth, but a significant *positive* effect within three years. The take-away point of Conway's study is that IMF programs start out badly but end well.

The Conway study had a profound impact. The result made a lot of sense. As IMF economists Nadeem Ul Haque and Mohsin Khan reported in 1998: "In the case of growth, the consensus seems to be that output will be depressed in the short run as the demand-reducing elements of the policy package dominate. Over time the structural reform elements of the program start to take effect and growth begins to rise." A subsequent study by IMF economists Louis Dicks-Mireaux, Mauro Mecagni, and Susan Schadler provided further evidence, showing that ESAF programs from the 1986–91 period appeared to have a statistically significant positive effect on output growth. This study used an advanced methodology to deal with the selection problem. It then went further, however, by testing some of the statistical assumptions underlying the model. They found that many of the assumptions were dubious, and this caused them to raise doubts about the reliability of the statistical findings.

Then a series of studies found a statistically significant negative effect on growth, using similarly advanced statistical techniques. The 2000 study by political scientist Adam Przeworski and me controlled for nonrandom selection on unobserved variables like "political will" and "trust." The analysis on 79 countries from 1971 to 1990 showed a statistically significant negative effect on annual output growth of about 1.5

percent. Similar results were obtained on a larger sample including 135 countries from 1951 to 1990. No evidence of a long run positive effect was found.

In their 2003 study of Latin America, economists Michael Hutchison of University of California, Santa Cruz, and Ilan Noy of University of Hawaii show that IMF programs have a negative effect on economic growth. In fact, they show that the effect is worse for countries that "successfully" complete programs. This raises an important point that is addressed in the next chapter on compliance: even – indeed, *especially* – countries that complete IMF programs experience lower growth.

In their study, published in 2005, economists Robert Barro and Jong-Wha Lee also found disappointing results. Using an instrumental variable approach to address the selection problem, they found that IMF programs have a negative effect in the short run that is not statistically significant, and a strong statistically significant *negative* effect on economic growth in the long run. This result runs directly counter to the consensus described by Haque and Khan in 1998. Finally, in a study published in 2006 that also uses an instrumental variables approach to the selection problem, economist Axel Dreher further confirms that IMF programs lower growth – his results also deal with compliance and are discussed in the next chapter. Dreher finds that compliance somewhat mitigates this effect, but even for countries that comply the effect is negative.

So, the newly emerging consensus is that IMF programs hurt economic growth. The initial contractionary effect of IMF programs is really not surprising. Some economists at the IMF have been quite forthright about why. IMF economist Vito Tanzi, for example, has argued that IMF programs induce governments to save on public investment, with nefarious consequences for growth. IMF economists Mario Blejer and Adrienne Cheasty point out that the high real interest rates induce good firms to shut down along with bad ones, which can also hurt growth. Plus, there is the straightforward effect of IMF austerity cutting demand, which drives down economic growth. [...]

Income Distribution and Social Spending

It is notable that studies of the effect of IMF programs on BOP, budget deficits, inflation, and growth reach different conclusions, depending on the methodology and data employed. This is not so with respect to income distribution. There have been three studies using three different methodologies and three different data sets. All come to the same conclusion: typically, IMF programs exacerbate income inequality.

Pastor conducted the first study in 1987, using the before–after approach to analyze labor's share of income in Latin America during 1965–81. His conclusion was strong: "The single most consistent effect the IMF seems to have is the redistribution of income away from workers." Pastor's study was path breaking, but the early study was limited by the methodology, which did not account for nonrandom selection, and because it looked only at Latin America. These limitations were addressed by a young scholar at Harvard University, Gopal Garuda, who published in 2000 his study of the effect of IMF programs on overall income distribution. Garuda looked at a standard index of overall income inequality called the "Gini coefficient." He addressed the selection problem by estimating the propensity of countries to participate in IMF programs, using a statistical model similar to the one presented in Chapter 3. Then he compared countries with and without IMF programs that had similar circumstances or "propensities" to participate in IMF programs. One interesting new finding Garuda discovered is that when countries unlikely to participate in IMF programs do participate, income inequality does not increase. However, for countries that are likely to participate, IMF programs exacerbate income inequality. The Garuda study was limited by the small amount of data on Gini coefficients that are available – this is why he incorporated a selection model within a with–without framework. He did not have enough data to employ a standard selection model.

In a study I published in 2002, the limited data problem was resolved by just looking at the manufacturing sector of the economy. The data on labor's share of earnings from manufacturing are available for 2,095 observations of 110 countries from 1961 to 1993. With these data, a fully parameterized selection model is possible. The result of the study confirmed the two it built upon: IMF programs increase income inequality. [...]

Conclusion

Evaluating the effects of IMF programs is analogous to evaluating the effects of medical treatments. If one were to compare the health of people undergoing medical treatment to people not, one might come to the quick conclusion that medical treatments hurt patients, because they are much less healthy than the rest of the population. This is obviously because people only go to the doctor when they are sick. Yet, some medical treatments have been found to be helpful, while others are benign or even malignant. Before coming to such conclusions, one must address the selection problem – under what circumstances is treatment applied?

Researchers have addressed the selection problem when analyzing the effects of IMF programs in various ways with increasing degrees of sophistication. Nevertheless, the conclusions in the literature are tentative. With each generation of studies come new and often contradictory findings.

According to the most recent studies and reviews, the IMF seems to be most effective in addressing balance of payments problems. It is less effective in addressing inflation. And recent studies show pernicious effects on economic growth. IMF programs exacerbate income inequality according to all studies that look directly at this question. In the area of social spending, the most recent study shows that spending on health and education may increase in dictatorships, where little is spent to begin with, but IMF programs make democracies that participate in IMF programs look more like dictatorships when it comes to spending on the poor.

34

The Future of the Multilateral Trade System – What Role for the World Trade Organization?

Ann Capling and Richard Higgott

[…] As we come to the end of the first decade of the twenty-first century, we live in a period of acute economic crisis – by common agreement, the worst since the Great Depression of the 1930s. The attention of global leaders is focused on providing the necessary fiscal stimuli to reboot the world's major economies and securing the necessary level of global institutional reform to both underwrite and regulate the global banking system. But the WTO is under duress. Its problems were identifiable prior to the eruption of the financial crisis, but they have been exacerbated by the current crisis as much as they are part of the current crisis – notwithstanding that, for once, no one thinks that trade is a contributory factor.

The dramatic problems in the financial sector are accompanied by a dramatic decline in cross-border trade; indeed, the first such decline since 1982. This has affected all of the world's major economic powers including the wealthy countries of the Organisation for Economic Co-operation and Development (OECD) and the emerging economies, including Brazil, Russia, India, and China (BRIC). In 2008, global trade grew by 2 percent in volume, but the WTO expects it to fall by 9 percent in 2009 – the biggest contraction in trade since World War II. Whereas most members of the WTO appear to have kept the worst domestic protectionist pressures under control, there is growing evidence of countries adopting, or threatening to adopt, trade-restricting or trade-distorting measures to protect key national businesses and jobs. Since the beginning of the financial crisis, governments have enacted scores of trade-restricting measures, including tariff increases, new import licensing

Original publication details: Ann Capling and Richard Higgott, "The Future of the Multilateral Trade System – What Role for the World Trade Organization?" in *Global Governance*, 15, 2009. pp. 313–19, 323. Reproduced with permission from Lynne Rienner Publishers.

requirements, and new agricultural export subsidies. Antidumping cases are also on the increase and bailouts to car and automotive component manufacturers in many countries can also have a trade-distorting effect. These activities have taken place across a range of countries including the United States, the members of the European Union (EU), China, Russia, India, Indonesia, and Argentina. The financial crisis also inhibits trade expansion through the negative effects of reduced liquidity on access to and sharp increases in the cost of trade credit for exporters. This problem is particularly acute for developing country exporters. The cost of trade credit has tripled in the six months between the November 2008 and April 2009 G-20 summits.

For some scholars and practitioners, the current financial crisis questions the utility of the WTO in addressing its elements. While recognizing the primacy of the financial crisis, the articles in this special issue resist the assertion of irrelevance. Rather, we would suggest that the financial crisis throws into sharp relief some of the issues that the WTO needs to address if it is to remain relevant in the twenty-first century. Specifically, are WTO rules sufficient to withstand the pressures for retaliation that will ensue if domestic protectionist policies are enacted? This is particularly important given the increasingly hidden or murky nature of much contemporary protectionism. [...]

In its initial guise as the General Agreement on Tariffs and Trade (GATT), the multilateral trade system had the dual aims of preventing a retreat to the discriminatory economic blocs that fragmented the world in the 1930s and of promoting economic recovery and growth through the promotion of international trade. The challenge for the architects of the trade system was to establish rules that enabled a compromise between the quest for open and nondiscriminatory markets and the domestic welfare and development objectives of states. This compromise, which navigated a middle ground between domestic interventionism and unfettered economic liberalism, was famously described by John Ruggie as "embedded liberalism." The new rules were embodied in the charter for the International Trade Organization (ITO), which was to be the third pillar of the Bretton Woods system alongside the IMF and the World Bank. But opposition from the US Senate meant that ITO did not come into being and, instead, the rules for commercial policy were extracted from the charter and incorporated into GATT.

With no formal organizational status, no administrative capacity to deal with problems between meetings of the contracting parties, and only a tiny secretariat, GATT nonetheless proved to be a robust and adaptable institution. From its original twenty-three contracting parties in 1947, its membership expanded steadily, ongoing liberalization of trade in manufactured goods was achieved through multiple rounds of trade negotiations, and new trade rules were established in response to continuing transformations in the international political economy. At the high-water mark of GATT, the Uruguay Round negotiations (1986–94) produced new agreements in areas such as trade in services, intellectual property, investment, and agriculture, which represented the development and extension of global trade rules on an unprecedented scale. At the same time, the process for resolving trade disputes between nations was reformed to make it more predictable and effective, and to give it real teeth. These agreements and the new dispute settlement mechanism were brought together into a new World Trade Organization, which at long last put the multilateral trade system on an equal footing with the other Bretton Woods institutions, the IMF and the World Bank.

The WTO Today

At the time of its birth in 1995, there were great expectations for the future of the WTO and its role in the governance of the global economy. For the first time ever, the global trade regime now had a firm legal foundation, a strong organizational basis, and an effective dispute settlement mechanism to ensure the enforcement of multilateral trade rules and disciplines. But this optimism has proved to be misplaced and the multilateral trade regime has been subjected to immense pressures and strains since the late 1990s. This has been especially evident in the current Doha Development Round of negotiations, which was launched in the shadow of the September 11, 2001, terrorist attacks. Since its inception, the Doha Round has lurched from crisis to crisis, with the major players (the United States, the EU, Brazil, India, and China) deadlocked over the perennial issue of agricultural subsidies and protection.

The pervasive sense of crisis in the Doha Round culminated in the breakdown of the marathon mini-ministerial meeting in Geneva in July 2008, which had come agonizingly close to reaching a significant breakthrough agreement. These developments, on top of the ongoing pressures and strains within the WTO, have led many to question the future relevance of the WTO. Some argue that other forces in the global economy are now more important than multilateral trade negotiations in maintaining an open, liberal trade system, thus obviating the need for the WTO. Others argue that the proliferation of regional trade agreements and bilateral investment treaties undermine the WTO's role in rule making and dispute settlement.

In the wake of the failure at Geneva in July 2008, there was no shortage of explanations for what ailed the WTO in the op-ed pages and the blogosphere alike: lack of leadership by the major economic powers; the clash of interests and values that comes from having a more diverse membership; the increasing propensity for governments to liberalize unilaterally or bilaterally; the growing backlash against liberalization that is evident in some Western countries; the contested nature of the WTO's mandate; the WTO's cumbersome approach to decision making; and, more generally, the climate of mistrust that is said to exist within the WTO. The problem with such diagnoses is that they are rarely accompanied with forward-looking proposals for addressing these problems.

There are exceptions, of course, and among the recent and comprehensive inquiries into the challenges confronting the multilateral trade system are the Report of the Consultative Board (the Sutherland report) of 2004, commissioned by then WTO director-general Supachai Panitchpakdi, and the Warwick Commission report of 2007, an independent inquiry chaired by former Canadian trade minister Pierre Pettigrew. [...]

[T]he Warwick Commission report identified five central challenges facing the world trading system and the dilemmas they pose for policymakers. Identified before the outbreak of the financial crisis, all challenges are central to the present global economic woes. First, the commission noted a paradox between the continued liberalization and internationalization of the economies of the major OECD countries on the one hand and an attendant marked reduction in popular support for open markets in significant sections of the populations of these countries on the other. Concern about stagnant wages, job losses, growing income inequality, and environmental degradation are now central to the political debate in most rich countries, and some sections of the community see trade as part of the problem rather than part of the solution – a situation exacerbated in the frenzied climate of 2009. Ironically, this development was contrasted in the report with the growing support occurring at the same time for economic liberalization in many of the larger and faster-growing developing countries.

The second challenge identified by the report is the increasingly multipolar nature of the global trade system. In the past, the GATT system was very much a rich man's club, with dealmaking dominated by the Quad – the United States, the EU, Japan, and Canada. The transformation of the old Quad into the new G4 (the United States, the EU, India, and Brazil) demonstrates the ongoing adaptability of the WTO, especially compared to the other Bretton Woods institutions. But unlike the old Quad, the G4 is not a club of like-minded countries, and together with China which joined the WTO in 2001, the role of India and Brazil in the WTO reflects a significant readjustment of power relations in the global economy. Moreover, WTO members have shown a marked propensity to engage in coalitional activity for the purpose of asserting their commercial objectives, thus adding greater complexity to both agenda formation and negotiation. In this context, policymakers need to think about how to ensure the sustained participation of all major groups of WTO members in its activities. With these realities in mind, the report identified the need to ensure that the fast-growing, large emerging markets take up leadership roles in the global trading system while, at the same time, ensuring that the originally dominant economic actors, the United States and the EU, do not disengage. Importantly, it is also crucial to ensure that the smallest and poorest WTO members continue to retain a valued stake in the system. The report concluded that tackling these potentially competing imperatives will require a new modus operandi across the spectrum of negotiations, content, and form of WTO agreements. These same priorities have emerged in the context of the financial crisis as the constitution of the appropriate group (G8, G-20, G-22, G-24) to address the problems again occupies central stage in the global conversation in 2009.

The third distinct challenge facing policymakers is the need to reconcile the sometimes competing objectives of the WTO. Accompanying their growing weight in the WTO, developing countries have rightly demanded that certain matters of particular importance to them be addressed. At the same time, many WTO members want multilateral trade rules to continue to evolve, in order to keep up with fast-moving commercial developments in the world economy. Moreover, there are calls by some for the WTO's agenda to be expanded to include issues such as the environment and human rights. This tension between unfinished business and new agendas has often led to conflict within the WTO; indeed, the boundaries of the WTO agenda are contested, as was evident in the bitter debate over the so-called Singapore issues. This raises important questions about the remit of the WTO, about how decisions should be made about its boundaries, and about its future role in economic regulation in an increasingly integrated global economy.

A fourth challenge concerns issues of justice and fairness. Criticisms of decision-making processes in the WTO by nongovernmental organizations (NGOs) and many developing country governments came to a head at the Seattle ministerial meeting in 1999. Since then, the WTO has instituted several substantial reforms, especially in relation to improving internal transparency, thus putting the WTO well ahead of many other international organizations in this regard. Nevertheless, problems persist. The Warwick Commission identified the need for the WTO to continue its efforts to build a more just multilateral trade system. In particular, WTO members need to balance the potentially competing demands of efficiency, fairness, and legitimacy within the system in such a way as to keep the diverse membership of the WTO engaged. Moreover, the WTO faces a significant challenge in establishing a balance of rights and obligations among its members that will be perceived as legitimate, sufficiently flexible, and also capable of addressing the trade-related development needs and priorities of individual members.

The fifth and final challenge identified in the report relates to the challenge posed by preferential trade agreements, which are inherently discriminatory and thus at odds with the WTO's fundamental norms of nondiscrimination. Governments around the world are turning to other vehicles for trade reform – notably bilateral and regional trade agreements that establish preferential trade relationships among their signatories. To be sure, frustration with the slow pace of multilateral trade negotiations and the WTO's cumbersome approach to decisionmaking is not the only spur toward preferential trade agreements, but research shows that these alternative vehicles for reciprocal trade liberalization have important consequences for the multilateral trading system. Reconciling these approaches to trade reform is, and will continue to be, a significant challenge for the WTO and its membership. [...]

Conclusion

[We] argue for the central and ongoing importance of the WTO as an institution for global governance. For the most part, we have not sought to emphasize either the juridical or trade liberalization functions of the WTO; indeed, to focus narrowly on the WTO as a vehicle for free trade – as its most ardent critics and supporters alike are wont to do – is to neglect the central role of the WTO in providing other global public goods through collective action problem solving. To be sure, many of the public goods provided by the WTO are those that are valued primarily for their contribution to economic efficiency; these include the reduction of transaction costs, the enhancement of policy transparency, confidence-building measures, and information collection and dissemination. But there are other public good dimensions of the WTO that relate to normative concerns such as fairness, including the universality of rules to protect the weak and rules about nondiscrimination. Moreover, from a more sociological perspective, the WTO can be seen to provide a forum for the expression of fundamental differences in national cultures, values, and economic systems; for deliberation and learning; and for the generation of common norms and values. These are among the benefits that collective action through the WTO uniquely provides: there is no other institution or trade agreement that provides these goods on an almost universal basis. Indeed, if the WTO did not exist, the challenges of managing globalization, in these times of acute economic crisis, would demand that it be reinvented.

35

A New World Order

Anne-Marie Slaughter

What is possible is not independent of what we believe to be possible. The possibility of such developments in the practical world depends upon their being grasped imaginatively by the people who make the practical world work.

– Neil MacCormick

Terrorists, arms dealers, money launderers, drug dealers, traffickers in women and children, and the modern pirates of intellectual property all operate through global networks. So, increasingly, do governments. Networks of government officials – police investigators, financial regulators, even judges and legislators – increasingly exchange information and coordinate activity to combat global crime and address common problems on a global scale. These government networks are a key feature of world order in the twenty-first century, but they are underappreciated, undersupported, and underused to address the central problems of global governance.

Consider the examples just in the wake of September 11. The Bush administration immediately set about assembling an ad hoc coalition of states to aid in the war on terrorism. Public attention focused on military cooperation, but the networks of financial regulators working to identify and freeze terrorist assets, of law enforcement officials sharing vital information on terrorist suspects, and of intelligence operatives working to preempt the next attack have been equally important. Indeed, the leading expert in the "new security" of borders and container bombs insists that the domestic agencies responsible for customs, food safety, and regulation of all kinds

Original publication details: Anne-Marie Slaughter, *A New World Order*. Princeton: Princeton University Press, 2004. pp. 1–4, 8–9, 13–18. Reproduced with permission from Princeton University Press.

must extend their reach abroad, through reorganization and much closer cooperation with their foreign counterparts. And after the United States concluded that it did not have authority under international law to interdict a shipment of missiles from North Korea to Yemen, it turned to national law enforcement authorities to coordinate the extraterritorial enforcement of their national criminal laws. Networked threats require a networked response.

Turning to the global economy, networks of finance ministers and central bankers have been critical players in responding to national and regional financial crises. The G-8 is as much a network of finance ministers as of heads of state; it is the finance ministers who make key decisions on how to respond to calls for debt relief for the most highly indebted countries. The finance ministers and central bankers hold separate news conferences to announce policy responses to crises such as the East Asian financial crisis in 1997 and the Russian crisis in 1998. The G-20, a network specifically created to help prevent future crises, is led by the Indian finance minister and is composed of the finance ministers of twenty developed and developing countries. More broadly, the International Organization of Securities Commissioners (IOSCO) emerged in 1984. It was followed in the 1990s by the creation of the International Association of Insurance Supervisors and a network of all three of these organizations and other national and international officials responsible for financial stability around the world called the Financial Stability Forum.

Beyond national security and the global economy, networks of national officials are working to improve environmental policy across borders. Within the North American Free Trade Agreement (NAFTA), US, Mexican, and Canadian environmental agencies have created an environmental enforcement network, which has enhanced the effectiveness of environmental regulation in all three states, particularly in Mexico. Globally, the Environmental Protection Agency (EPA) and its Dutch equivalent have founded the International Network for Environmental Compliance and Enforcement (INECE), which offers technical assistance to environmental agencies around the world, holds global conferences at which environmental regulators learn and exchange information, and sponsors a website with training videos and other information.

Nor are regulators the only ones networking. National judges are exchanging decisions with one another through conferences, judicial organizations, and the Internet. Constitutional judges increasingly cite one another's decisions on issues from free speech to privacy rights. Indeed, Justice Anthony Kennedy of the US Supreme Court cited a decision by the European Court of Justice (ECJ) in an important 2003 opinion overturning a Texas antisodomy law. Bankruptcy judges in different countries negotiate minitreaties to resolve complicated international cases; judges in transnational commercial disputes have begun to see themselves as part of a global judicial system. National judges are also interacting directly with their supranational counterparts on trade and human rights issues.

Finally, even legislators, the most naturally parochial government officials due to their direct ties to territorially rooted constituents, are reaching across borders. International parliamentary organizations have been traditionally well meaning though ineffective, but today national parliamentarians are meeting to adopt and publicize common positions on the death penalty, human rights, and environmental issues. They support one another in legislative initiatives and offer training programs and technical assistance.

Each of these networks has specific aims and activities, depending on its subject area, membership, and history, but taken together, they also perform certain common functions. They expand regulatory reach, allowing national government officials to keep up with corporations, civic organizations, and criminals. They build trust and establish relationships among their participants that then create incentives to establish a good reputation and avoid a bad one. These are the conditions essential for long-term cooperation. They exchange regular information about their own activities and develop databases of best practices, or, in the judicial case, different approaches to common legal issues. They offer technical assistance and professional socialization to members from less developed nations, whether regulators, judges, or legislators.

In a world of global markets, global travel, and global information networks, of weapons of mass destruction and looming environmental disasters of global magnitude, governments must have global reach. In a world in which their ability to use their hard power is often limited, governments must be able to exploit the uses of soft power: the power of persuasion and information. Similarly, in a world in which a major set of obstacles to effective global regulation is a simple inability on the part of many developing countries to translate paper rules into changes in actual behavior, governments must be able not only to negotiate treaties but also to create the capacity to comply with them.

Understood as a form of global governance, government networks meet these needs. As commercial and civic organizations have already discovered, their networked form is ideal for providing the speed and flexibility necessary to function effectively in an information age. But unlike amorphous "global policy networks" championed by UN Secretary General Kofi Annan, in which it is never clear who is exercising power on behalf of whom, these are networks composed of national government officials, either appointed by elected officials or directly elected themselves. Best of all, they can perform many of the functions of a world government – legislation, administration, and adjudication – without the form. [...]

The Globalization Paradox: Needing More Government and Fearing It

Peoples and their governments around the world need global institutions to solve collective problems that can only be addressed on a global scale. They must be able to make and enforce global rules on a variety of subjects and through a variety of means. Further, it has become commonplace to claim that the international institutions created in the late 1940s, after a very different war and facing a host of different threats from those we face today, are outdated and inadequate to meet contemporary challenges. They must be reformed or even reinvented; new ones must be created.

Yet world government is both infeasible and undesirable. The size and scope of such a government presents an unavoidable and dangerous threat to individual liberty.

Further, the diversity of the peoples to be governed makes it almost impossible to conceive of a global demos. No form of democracy within the current global repertoire seems capable of overcoming these obstacles.

This is the globalization paradox. We need more government on a global and a regional scale, but we don't want the centralization of decision-making power and coercive authority so far from the people actually to be governed. It is the paradox identified in the European Union by Renaud Dehousse and by Robert Keohane in his millennial presidential address to the American Political Science Association. The European Union has pioneered "regulation by networks," which Dehousse describes as the response to a basic dilemma in EU governance: "On the one hand, increased uniformity is certainly needed; on the other hand, greater centralization is politically inconceivable, and probably undesirable." The EU alternative is the "transnational option" – the use of an organized network of national officials to ensure "that the actors in charge of the implementation of Community policies behave in a similar manner."

Worldwide, Keohane argues that globalization "creates potential gains from cooperation" if institutions can be created to harness those gains; however, institutions themselves are potentially oppressive. The result is "the Governance Dilemma: although institutions are essential for human life, they are also dangerous." The challenge facing political scientists and policymakers at the dawn of the twenty-first century is discovering how well-structured institutions could enable the world to have "a rebirth of freedom."

Addressing the paradox at the global level is further complicated by the additional concern of accountability. In the 1990s the conventional reaction to the problem of "world government" was instead to champion "global governance," a much looser and less threatening concept of collective organization and regulation without coercion. A major element of global governance, in turn, has been the rise of global policy networks, celebrated for their ability to bring together all public and private actors on issues critical to the global public interest.

Global policy networks, in turn, grow out of various "reinventing government" projects, both academic and practical. These projects focus on the many ways in which private actors now can and do perform government functions, from providing expertise to monitoring compliance with regulations to negotiating the substance of those regulations, both domestically and internationally. The problem, however, is ensuring that these private actors uphold the public trust. […]

Looking at the international system through the lens of unitary states leads us to focus on traditional international organizations and institutions created by and composed of formal state delegations. Conversely, however, thinking about states the way we think about domestic governments – as aggregations of distinct institutions with separate roles and capacities – provides a lens that allows us to see a new international landscape. Government networks pop up everywhere.

Horizontal government networks – links between counterpart national officials across borders – are easiest to spot. Far less frequent, but potentially very important, are vertical government networks, those between national government officials and their supranational counterparts. The prerequisite for a vertical government network is the relatively rare decision by states to delegate their sovereignty to an institution above them with real power – a court or a regulatory commission. That institution can then be the genuine counterpart existence of a national government institution. Where these vertical networks exist, as in the relations between national courts and the ECJ in the European Union, they enable the supranational institution to be maximally effective. [...]

A New World Order

Appreciating the extent and nature of existing government networks, both horizontal and vertical, makes it possible to envision a genuinely new world order. "World order," for these purposes, describes a system of global governance that institutionalizes cooperation and sufficiently contains conflict such that all nations and their peoples may achieve greater peace and prosperity, improve their stewardship of the earth, and reach minimum standards of human dignity. The concept of a "new world order" has been used and overused to refer to everything from George H. W. Bush's vision of a post-Cold War world to the post-9/11 geopolitical landscape. Nevertheless, I use it to describe a different conceptual framework for the actual infrastructure of world order – an order based on an intricate three-dimensional web of links between disaggregated state institutions.

Recall Atlas and his globe at Rockefeller Center. A disaggregated world order would be a world latticed by countless government networks. These would include horizontal networks and vertical networks; networks for collecting and sharing information of all kinds, for policy coordination, for enforcement cooperation, for technical assistance and training, perhaps ultimately for rule making. They would be bilateral, plurilateral, regional, or global. Taken together, they would provide the skeleton or infrastructure for global governance.

To appreciate the full implications of this vision, consider again our implicit mental maps of "the international system" or even "world order." It's a flat map, pre-Columbian, with states at the level of the land and the international system floating above them somewhere. International organizations also inhabit this floating realm – they are apart from and somehow above the states that are their members. To the extent that they are actually seen as governing the international system or establishing global order, they must constitute an international bureaucracy equivalent in form and function to the multiple domestic bureaucracies of the states "underneath" them.

In a world of government networks, by contrast, the same officials who are judging, regulating, and legislating domestically are also reaching out to their foreign counterparts to help address the governance problems that arise when national actors and issues spill beyond their borders. Global governance, from this perspective, is not a matter of regulating states the way states regulate their citizens, but rather of addressing the issues and resolving the problems that result from citizens going global – from crime to commerce to civic engagement. Even where genuinely supranational officials participate in vertical government networks – meaning judges or regulators who exercise actual sovereign authority delegated to them by a group of states – they must work very closely with their national counterparts and must harness national coercive power to be effective.

Scholars and commentators in different issue areas have begun to identify various pieces of this infrastructure. Financial regulators, for instance, are becoming accustomed to describing the new international financial architecture as a combination of networks – G-7, G-8, and G-20, the Basel Committee, and IOSCO among them – with traditional international institutions, such as the International Monetary Fund (IMF) and the World Bank. Scholars of the European Union, as noted above, are increasingly familiar with the concept of "regulation by network." Environmental activists would readily recognize some of the institutions associated with the North American Free Trade Agreement (NAFTA) as "environmental enforcement networks" composed of the environmental protection agencies of the United States, Canada, and Mexico. And constitutional law scholars, human rights activists, and transnational litigators would not balk at the idea of transnational judicial networks to describe the various ways in which courts around the world are increasingly interacting with one another. [...]

Premises

There can, of course, be no one blueprint for world order. The proposal advanced here is part of an active and ongoing debate. In the spirit of such debate, it is important to acknowledge that the model of world order I put forward rests on a combination of descriptive and predictive empirical claims, which can be summarized in basic terms:

- The state is not the only actor in the international system, but it is still the most important actor.
- The state is not disappearing, but it is disaggregating into its component institutions, which are increasingly interacting principally with their foreign counterparts across borders.
- These institutions still represent distinct national or state interests, even as they also recognize common professional identities and substantive experience as judges, regulators, ministers, and legislators.
- Different states have evolved and will continue to evolve mechanisms for reaggregating the interests of their distinct institutions when necessary. In many circumstances, therefore, states will still interact with one another as unitary actors in more traditional ways.
- Government networks exist alongside and sometimes within more traditional international organizations. [...]

36

ISO and the Infrastructure
for a Global Market

Craig N. Murphy and JoAnne Yates

ISO's leaders have, at times, spoken about the organization as if it were almost part of the United Nations (UN) family, but current practice is to call it "a non-governmental organization [NGO] that *forms a bridge between the public and private sectors* ... [M]any of its member[s] ... are part of the governmental structure of their countries ... [O]ther members have their roots uniquely in the private sector, having been set up by national partnerships of industry associations." About two-thirds of ISO's 158 member organizations are part of their country's central government; the rest are NGOs.

ISO conducts almost all of its work through technical committees that focus on specific topics. Each of its about 230 committees and 500 subcommittees has a rotating secretariat provided by one of the ISO member bodies. The committees conduct much of their discussion electronically and when they meet face-to-face, they usually do so only for a day or two at a time. In 2008, about one-third of ISO's technical committees and subcommittees met in more than 90 cities spread across 34 countries and six continents.

On top of the large committee structure rests a 150-person secretariat in Geneva, one much smaller than those of most of the UN Specialized Agencies based in the same city. Nonetheless, the vastness and complexity of ISO's decentralized structure means that the number of people actively working on establishing new international agreements throughout the ISO network is probably larger than the staff of the entire UN system.

Original publication details: Craig N. Murphy and JoAnne Yates, *The International Organization for Standardization: Global Governance through Voluntary Consensus*. Abingdon: Routledge, 2009. pp. 25–6, 46–7, 50–8. Reproduced with permission from Taylor & Francis.

The organization's highly decentralized structure somewhat obscures the relatively complex way in which the work of voluntary standard setting is funded. Ultimately, much of the funding comes from the major consumers of standards, the firms and other organizations that adopt them.

Similarly, ISO's insistence on the *voluntary* nature of its standards – for example, the ISO web site states that *"ISO itself does not regulate or legislate"* – somewhat obscures a more complex reality. Most ISO standards become obligatory for at least some organizations because the standards are cited in national legislation and international conventions. [...]

The ISO Network and Its Voluntary Consensus Process: The Actors and Why They Are Involved

ISO has 158 national standard setting bodies, spread across the world, as members. Of these, about 35 unusually active members, which may be designated major member bodies, each take part in hundreds of different technical committees and their subcommittees. Together, this group provides almost all the secretariats. About twice as many member bodies, around 70 of the remaining 123, are more selectively active; they each take part in the limited number of technical committees that affect the economic sectors in which their country is the most involved. For example, the Ghana Standards Board represents a country whose major exports include cocoa and other products of the tropical rainforest. The board takes part in only 12 committees and subcommittees overall, and is especially active in the committees concerned with food products (TC-34), timber (TC-218), and environmental management (TC-207).

In addition to these 105 regular members, ISO has 42 "correspondent members" from countries that are just developing independent national standards activities. These members rarely take an active part in technical committees and are usually involved in only a few. Correspondent members do not have a right to take part in developing ISO's overall policies, but they are kept informed about all of the work that is of interest to them. Members in this group include countries that are not sovereign, but that have well established communities of engineers (e.g., Hong Kong and Palestine); some former Soviet republics with significant numbers of engineers but whose independent standards' bodies are relatively new; and many developing countries with almost no industrial base. [...]

On 25 April 2006, BBC (British Broadcasting Corporation) business correspondent Toby Poston launched into a surprisingly long feature with this apology:

> There is perhaps no obvious reason to get excited about the fiftieth anniversary of a large metal box. Such containers are now an everyday sight, hauled by trucks, trains, and ships all over the world. But without them, it is very unlikely that we would all be buying Japanese TVs, Costa Rican bananas, Chinese underwear, or New Zealand lamb. In fact, globalization would probably not exist and the World Trade Organization [WTO] would have a lot less to talk about.

And, of course, without ISO, there wouldn't be all those standard boxes.

When people in the standards movement enumerate the ISO's accomplishments, often the first thing they mention is the shipping container – and the resulting transformation of the physical infrastructure of international trade that enabled the integration and massive growth of the global economy over the last 30 years. ISO's role was not just that of securing agreement on standard sizes for those boxes; ISO was also involved in setting standards for the ships and trains that carried the containers, the docks where they were loaded and unloaded, the cranes that lifted them, the training of the women and men who operated those cranes – the list of *physical* infrastructure goes on and on.

ISO also provided – and continues to provide – the standards needed to complete other aspects of the *technical* infrastructure of this new, global economy: standard documents for the transit of goods, standard bar-codes that could summarize and allow a quick electronic perusal of all that was in those documents, and even the standardized bank cards whose secure codes are the catalyst that starts the journey of so many of those boxes. [...]

A Standard and Its Consequences

In 1956 when the first container ship – a converted World War II oil tanker – left the dock in Newark, New Jersey, the world had neither the physical nor the technical infrastructure for a global consumer economy. Shipping costs were just too high.

It was not that the cost of moving a bunch of heavy objects across the oceans was, itself, prohibitive. Far from it: nature provided a normally smooth highway for free. The excessive costs had to do with packing and unpacking and loading and unloading any commodities that could not be shipped in bulk, the way oil or grains could be. In the 1950s, any manufactured product – in fact, anything other than some basic raw materials – was sent in a "break-bulk" ship that typically would be packed with 200,000 separate items: say, 70,000 cartons of mixed goods, 24,000 bags of papers and mail, 3,000 drums of different chemicals, 900 barrels of dishes, etc. Each of the 200,000 items would have to be separately lifted into and out of the ship by crews of longshoremen. In the 1950s, port costs – the costs of all that movement in and out of the ship – made up over half the cost of sending cloth and clothes and most "Second Industrial Revolution" goods from an inland manufacturer on one continent to consumers on another. Such goods included medicines and other chemical products, electrical goods, and branded consumer products, which – together with the manufactured cloth and clothes of the original Industrial Revolution, make all the sorts of things one might find today in a US Walmart or a French Carrefour.

Before the container revolution, the cost of loading cargo into an average ship was US$5.86 per ton. Today, that cost is 16 cents.

The proximate cause of this 93 percent reduction in cost was the publication, in 1965, of the ISO draft standards that define the most important parts of the containers that we see today – a metal box, eight feet wide and about eight feet high, usually 20 or 40 feet long, with doors at one end and reinforced corners that allow it to be clamped to other containers and to be stacked. Between 1956 and 1965, a tiny group of companies converted a few small ships to proprietary containers, but in the years immediately after the publication of the standard, the building of ever-larger ships for the sole purpose of carrying ISO standard containers took off (Figure 36.1).

Both the growing number of ships and their increasing capacity are equally important. The combined capacity of the approximately 600 containerships that were built in the first decade of the boom (by the mid-1970s) is the about the same as the combined capacity of three "super containerships" launched in 2007 and 2008, each of which can hold 11,000 to 12,000 of the standard containers.

One historian of this change, Hugo van Driel, calls it, quite aptly, a "transportation revolution." Yet, when containerization began, the revolutionary implications of shipping in standard boxes were far from fully recognized. In 1967, proponents estimated that perhaps, one day, 75 percent of the general cargo shipped across the North Atlantic could be transported in containers, and, by 1995, the growing containerized proportion of the tonnage of general goods handled by Europe's largest port (Rotterdam) reached that level. The proportion has continued to grow. What is more important is that the cost savings from containerization have allowed the total tonnage of general goods through Rotterdam to increase tenfold in just 40 years. Globally, container traffic continues to grow 10–15 percent each year, outstripping the growth rates of even the fastest growing economies, such as China. Of course, the 13 percent average annual growth in container shipping over the last two decades was one of the key factors that allowed China's 9 percent average annual growth rate over the same period. John Fossey, a shipping industry observer, says that the container revolution explains, "[W]hy a person in Northern Europe who wants to eat strawberries on Christmas day can find them in their supermarket"; more generally, the revolution has been "a key enabler of the rapid industrialization and globalization we are seeing in the world today." […]

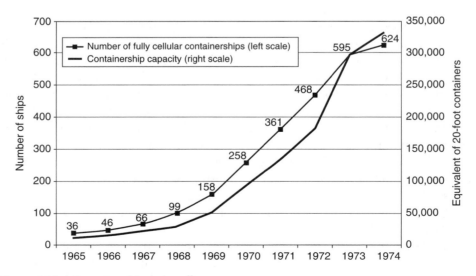

Figure 36.1   Containerships take off.
Source: UNCTAD, *Review of Maritime Transport*, 1973–4, 146.

Setting the Standard

Yet, even the briefest glance back at the history of containerized shipping reveals that the massive reductions in transportation costs were far from inevitable. Recall the argument of the contemporary French standard setter, Jean-Daniel Merlet, that there is a "triangular" relationship among standardization, regulation, and innovation, in which the regulatory environment often shapes efforts at standardization, which, in turn, can enable or constrain different forms of innovation.

Tineke Egyedi, who has looked at the history of container standards in great depth, points out that standardization can play a particularly transformative role (for good or for ill) when it, "facilitate[s] change in large technical systems. More specific[ally], the flexibility, which is required for system innovation, lies in the standardization of *gateway technologies*, [technologies that effectuate] whatever technical connections between distinct production sub-systems are required in order for them to be utilized in conjunction, within a larger integrated production system." The standardized container, Egyedi argues, is a quintessential gateway technology. It is "a gateway between different subsystems of transportation" that enhances the "efficiency of the system as a whole."

This "gateway" had been envisioned for decades before the work of an ISO technical committee, TC-104, finally made it possible. [...]

The container story is a major leitmotiv in the personal stories of many leaders in the standards movement after the Second World War. For example, Olle Sturén, the long-serving ISO secretary general, led the Swedish delegation to the first ISO meeting on container standards in 1959 – one of his first forays into global standard setting – and the Swedish records of those meetings are one of the few sets of technical committee documents maintained from the beginning with their historical significance in mind. Similarly, the American standard setter, Vince Grey, who eventually played a major role in ISO's early work on information technology, was regularly called upon by the organization to explain how he, and ISO, moved from focusing on ships and marine technology to playing a role in every aspect of the global economy of the last decade.

Grey was a US Merchant Marine engineering officer who entered graduate school in 1952 and at the same time took a job with the American Standards Association (ASA, as today's ANSI, the American National Standards Institute, was then known) where he got a taste of ISO standard setting as a US representative on ISO technical committees. After a short stint in the Navy, Grey arrived back at ASA in 1956, at just about the same moment that the first container ship left Newark harbor.

Within a few months, two US companies, Matson and Sea-Land, had become the major competitors in the new trans-oceanic container shipping business, but their containers were incompatible and neither company envisioned a competitive, integrated intermodal system that could transfer boxes among the trucks, the railroad cars, the barges, and the ships owned by any company. However, businesses in many fields did envision such a system so, by the end of 1957, ASA had put together a huge (75-member) technical committee and was urging ISO to do the same.

Initially, ASA was not the only American standard setter. The US government agencies that regulated ocean shipping and subsidized the building of US ships also wanted a standard. Ironically, because neither Sea-Land nor Matson were seeking subsidies, the US regulators did not consult them. The ocean shippers were part of the ASA process, but that process was dominated by container manufacturers, truckers, and railroads, who wanted to reach an agreement as rapidly as possible.

Most accounts of the process agree that the chair of the ASA process, a retired Aluminum Company of America engineer, Herbert Hall, played the decisive role in getting agreement on the sizes of containers, including the most contentious issue of length. Hall was fascinated by what he called "preferred numbers," arguing for 10-, 20-, and 40-foot standard lengths. A shipper could use the appropriate size for a particular customer, but, because two of the small containers would fit in the space of the next larger container, the problem of packing them on ships would be minimized. By late 1959, ASA had a proposed US standard that it sent forward to ISO's TC-104 as a working document.

Hall's 1959 standard meant that latecomers to containerization would be favored. Matson and Sea-Land, on the other hand, would have to write off tens of millions of dollars of recent investment. Yet, it was clear that if they did not accept the standard, they would lose US government contracts and would never be able to apply for subsidies, a point that was made clear immediately when the American Hawaiian Steamship Company was turned down for US federal mortgage insurance on a planned ship that would not accommodate the new standard containers.

Not surprisingly, Matson and Sea-Land tried to change the ASA standard, but Hall, who continued to chair the committee for many years, persisted in his ruling that only the multiples of 10 feet had received sufficient support, including that of the US government agencies represented on the committee. The companies then turned to Congress, which acquiesced to them in 1965 by amending the Merchant Marine Act so that no preference was given to firms following the ASA standard.

However, by that point it was too late. The ISO process had greatly strengthened the ASA standard. Unlike ASA, ISO concentrated on "performance standards," on what containers should do rather than on how they should be constructed. That meant ISO could avoid long debates about the different benefits of aluminum (the favorite material in the US) versus steel (more popular in the rest of the world). It also meant that ISO had to face, head-on, one of the problems that still plagued the US standard, that of corner fittings and corner locks, the bits that "provide the place where the container is lifted and where it is secured during transport."

A major breakthrough on this subject had been made in 1963, when Sea-Land, despite its anger over ASA's decision on standard sizes, released its patent rights to the corner fittings that were working successfully on the world's largest fleet of carriers. This example of the collective spirit that sometimes animates voluntary consensus standard setting proved decisive, but it was by no means unique. A sequence of events played into Sea-Land's decision. Two years earlier, the designer of the Sea-Land fitting had offered royalty-free use of a more recent fitting he had designed for one of Sea-Land's competitors, Fruehauf, for whom he was now chief engineer. Although, the Fruehauf design had not been proven in use, Fruehauf's example – and the desire for a common technology that would stimulate the growth of the industry – convinced Sea-Land to give up its own intellectual property.

Nevertheless, even though the Sea-Land corners had proved adequate in many months of trans-oceanic shipping, they had not been tested under all of the conditions that would exist in a global intermodal transportation system. Part of ISO's job was to set up tests that simulate conditions in every part of the world, on railways bouncing down Swiss mountains or trucks in India's weaving stop-and-go traffic. Vince Grey writes about a key 1965 ISO meeting in The Hague that agreed upon the test criteria and then waited as the American standard fittings were tested by a lab in Detroit, "How did the container do? Did it survive?" Unfortunately, no. The American standard was not adequate to take the loads that a container would experience in a world-wide intermodal system. The Sea-Land corner would have to be further redesigned. "So," Grey recounts,

> we spun off a committee. We created an ad hoc committee to design a corner fitting with greater strength in whatever areas were needed so that it would pass the test. It was probably one of the most expensive sets of drawings that have ever been prepared in ISO. In that ad hoc committee, there were the Executive Vice-Presidents of these major companies, and they sat at a drafting board and drew these drawings. The ad hoc committee came back with its work and it was adopted … for the next year containers were ordered and the purchase specification said "the corner fitting shall be the ad hoc committee corner fitting."

It was after this Hague meeting that the container revolution took off. Yet, Grey adds, it took another two years, after a meeting in London, before, "someone could really go out in the manufacturing field and say, 'I want an ISO container.' We had a set of different documents which, when assembled, defined what is today 95% of the population of containers – a standard box, you know, with doors at one end and a closed roof."

The final step before the ISO standard involved another set of emergency tests of the 1965 corner fitting, which had sometimes failed under heavy loads. Another ad hoc committee set up new tests and a British and a US engineer were sent off to a London "hotel room with their slide rules and told to redesign the fitting." Over the "bitter" objections of the many shipping companies that had had no problems with the 1965 standard, ISO approved the strengthened standard in a second 1967 meeting (this one in Moscow), even though the amendment required container owners to spend millions of dollars welding new fittings on the thousands of boxes that were only a few months old. […]

37

Global Health Governance
A Conceptual Review

Richard Dodgson, Kelley Lee, and Nick Drager

[...]

Introduction

In today's world of changing health risks and opportunities, the capacity to influence health determinants, status and outcomes cannot be assured through national actions alone because of the intensification of crossborder and transborder flows of people, goods and services, and ideas. The need for more effective collective action by governments, business and civil society to better manage these risks and opportunities is leading us to reassess the rules and institutions that govern health policy and practice at the subnational, national, regional and global levels. This is particularly so as a range of health determinants are increasingly affected by factors outside of the health sector – trade and investment flows, collective violence and conflict, illicit and criminal activity, environmental change and communication technologies. There is an acute need to broaden the public health agenda to take account of these globalizing forces, and to ensure that the protection and promotion of human health is placed higher on other policy agendas. There is a widespread belief that the current system of international health governance (IHG) does not sufficiently meet these needs and, indeed, has a number of limitations and gaps. In light of these perceived shortcomings, the

Original publication details: Richard Dodgson, Kelley Lee, and Nick Drager, "Global Health Governance: A Conceptual Review," in Discussion Paper No. 1, Department of Health & Development, World Health Organization, February 2002. pp. 5, 7–8, 17–20. Reproduced with permission from WHO and London School of Hygiene & Tropical Medicine.

The Globalization Reader, Fifth Edition. Edited by Frank J. Lechner and John Boli.

Published 2015 by John Wiley & Sons, Ltd.

concept of global health governance (GHG) has become a subject of interest and debate in the field of international health. [...]

Many argue that globalization is reducing the capacity of states to provide for the health of their domestic populations and, by extension, intergovernmental health cooperation is also limited. The impact of globalization upon the capacity of states and other actors to co-operate internationally to protect human health is fourfold. First, globalization has introduced or intensified **transborder health risks** defined as risks to human health that transcend national borders in their origin or impact. Such risks may include emerging and reemerging infectious diseases, various noncommunicable diseases (e.g. lung cancer, obesity, hypertension) and environmental degradation (e.g. global climate change). The growth in the geographical scope and speed in which transborder health risks present themselves directly challenge the existing system of IHG that is defined by national borders. The mechanisms of IHG, in other words, may be constrained by its statecentric nature to tackle global health effectively.

Second, as described above, globalization is characterised by a growth in the number, and degree of influence, of nonstate actors in health governance. Many argue that the relative authority and capacity of national governments to protect and promote the health of domestic populations has declined in the face of globalizing forces beyond national borders that affect the basic determinants of health as well as erode national resources for addressing their consequences. Nonstate actors, including civil society groups, global social movements, private companies, consultancy firms, think tanks, religious movements and organized crime, in turn, have gained relatively greater power and influence both formally and informally. The emerging picture is becoming more complex, with the distinct roles of state and nonstate actors in governance activities such as agenda setting, resource mobilisation and allocation, and dispute settlement becoming less clear. New combinations of both state and nonstate actors are rapidly forming, in a myriad of forms such as partnerships, alliances, coalitions, networks and joint ventures. This apparent "hybridisation" of governance mechanisms around certain health issues is a reflection of the search for more effective ways of cooperation to promote health in the face of new institutions. At the same time, however, it throws up new challenges for creating appropriate and recognised institutional mechanisms for, *inter alia,* ensuring appropriate representation, participation, accountability and transparency.

Third, current forms of globalization appear to be problematic for sustaining, and even worsening existing socioeconomic, political and environmental problems. UNDP, for example, reports that neoliberal forms of globalization have been accompanied by widening inequalities between rich and poor within and across countries. In a special issue of *Development,* authors cite experiences of worsening poverty, marginalisation and health inequity as a consequence of globalization. In some respects, these problems can be seen as "externalities" or "global public bads" that are arising as a result of globalizing processes that are insufficiently managed by effective health governance. As Fidler writes, these deeply rooted problems "feed off" the negative consequences of the globalization of health, creating a reciprocal relationship between health and the determinants of health. Although many of these problems are most acute in the developing world, they are of concern to all countries given their transborder nature (i.e. unconfined to national borders).

Fourth, globalization has contributed to a decline in both the political and practical capacity of the national governments, acting alone or in cooperation with other states, to deal with global health challenges. While globalization is a set of changes occurring gradually over several centuries, its acceleration and intensification from the late twentieth century has brought attention to the fact that states alone cannot address many of the health challenges arising. Infectious diseases are perhaps the most prominent example of this diminishing capacity, but equally significant are the impacts on noncommunicable diseases (e.g. tobacco-related cancers), food and nutrition, lifestyles and environmental conditions. This decapitating of the state has been reinforced by initiatives to further liberalise the global trade of goods and services. The possible health consequences of more open global markets have only begun to be discussed within trade negotiations and remain unaddressed by proposed governance mechanisms for the emerging global economy.

The fourth of the above points is perhaps the most significant because it raises the possibility of the need for a change in the fundamental nature of health governance. As mentioned above, IHG is structured on the belief that governments have primary responsibility for the health of its people and able, in co-operation with other states, to protect its population from health risks. Globalization, however, means that the state may be increasingly undermined in its capacity to fulfil this role alone, that IHG is necessary but insufficient, and that additional or new forms of health governance may be needed. Some scholars and practitioners believe that this new system of health governance needs to be global in scope, so that it can deal effectively with problems caused by the globalization of health. [...]

[W]e can identify some essential elements of GHG and the challenges for achieving them. The first is the "deterritorialisation" of how we think about and promote health, and thus *the need to address factors which cross, and even ignore, the geographical boundaries of the state*. The formation of the international system of states in the sixteenth century, the birth of public health during the nineteenth century, and the creation of national health systems in the twentieth century have contributed to a system of governance that is premised on protecting the integrity of the state. IHG has been historically focused on those health issues that cross national borders, with the aim of protecting domestic populations within certain defined geographical boundaries through such practices as quarantine, cordon sanitaire, and internationally agreed standards governing the reporting of infectious disease, trade and population mobility. All of these efforts have been focused on the point of contact, the national border of states.

However, forces of global change, in various forms, have intensified crossborder activity to such an extent as to undermine the capacity of states to control them. The increased levels of international trade and movement of people are examples. Moreover, a wide range of other forces render national borders irrelevant. The worldwide flows of information and communication across the Internet; the ecological impacts of global environmental change; the frenzied exchange of capital and finance via electronic media; the illicit trade in drugs, food products and even people; and the global mobility of other life forms (e.g. microbes) through natural (e.g. bird migration) and manmade (e.g. bulk shipping) means render border controls irrelevant. Many of these global changes impact on health and requires forms of cooperation that go beyond IHG.

A second essential element of GHG is *the need to define and address the determinants of health from a multi-sectoral perspective.* Biomedical approaches to health have dominated historically in the form of disease-focused research and policy, the skills mix of international health experts and officials, and the primacy given to working through ministries of health and health professionals. A global system of health governance begins with the recognition that a broad range of determinants impact on population health including social and natural environments. In recent decades, this has been recognised to some extent through the increased involvement of other forms of expertise in health policy making (e.g. economics, anthropology) and links with other social sectors (e.g. education, labour). More recently, ministries of health and international health organizations have sought to engage more directly with sectors traditionally seen as relatively separate from health (e.g. trade, environment, agriculture) in recognition of "cross sectoral" policy issues at play. Informal consultations between WHO and WTO, for example, have been prompted by the importance of multilateral trade agreements to health.

The main challenge to achieving greater cross sectoral collaboration lies in the danger of casting the health "net" so widely that everything becomes subsumed within the global health umbrella. Opening up GHG too indiscriminately can dilute policy focus and impact, and raise questions about feasibility. The linking of traditional health and non-health issues also demands a clear degree of understanding and empirical evidence about cause and effect. Defining the scope of GHG, therefore, remains a balance between recognising the interconnectedness of health with a varied range of globalizing forces, and the need to define clear boundaries of knowledge and action.

The third essential element of GHG is *the need to involve, both formally and informally, a broader range of actors and interests.* As described above, while nonstate actors have long been an important part of the scene, IHG has been firmly state-defined. Health-related regional organizations (e.g. PAHO, European Union), along with major international health organizations such as WHO and the World Bank are formally governed by member states. Their mandates, in turn, are defined by their role in supporting the national health systems of those member states. The universality of their activities is measured by the number of member states participating in them. Defining criteria and measures of progress to address the burden of disease, health determinants and health status are focused on the state or groups of states.

GHG, however, is distinguished by the starting point that globalization is creating health needs and interests that increasingly cut across and, in some cases, are oblivious to state boundaries. To effectively address these global health challenges, there is a need to strengthen, supplement and even replace existing forms of IHG. Importantly, this does not mean that the role of the state or IHG will disappear or become redundant, but that they will rather need to become part of a wider system of GHG. Many existing institutions will be expected to play a significant role in GHG, and states will continue to be key actors. However, states and state-defined governance alone is not enough. Forms of governance that bring together more concertedly state and non-state actors will be central in a global era. As described by the Commission on Global Governance, "[global governance] must ... be understood as also involving NGOs, citizen's movements, multinational corporations, and the global capital market," as well as a "global mass media of dramatically enlarged influence."

As described above, state and nonstate actors have long interacted on health governance. The difference for GHG will lie in their degree of involvement and nature of their respective roles, varying with the health issue concerned. Three brief examples illustrate this. First, relations among the diverse NGO community are constantly changing depending on the issue. On certain issues, they may be willing to form strategic networks or alliances with other NGOs, thus representing an important governance mechanism within GHG. Such a mechanism was formed around the global campaign against the marketing of breastmilk substitutes that led to the formation of the International Baby Food Action Network. Cooperation among the International Baby Food Action Network, UNICEF, WHO and selected governments led to the International Code of Marketing on Breast-Milk Substitutes in 1981. Like-minded NGOs also came together to form more permanent, but still highly fluid, global social movements around the environment and women's health. These movements opposed each other at the UN Conference on the Environment and Development, yet worked together to propose an alternative view of development at the World Summit for Social Development in 1995. Close relations among the women's health movement, national governments and UNFPA was also a defining feature of the International Conference on Population and Development. Relations between the women's health movement and some states, in particular the US, were so close that members of the women's health movement served on some of the official government delegations. Parties involved in the conference believed that such close relations played a key role in shaping the resultant commitment to reproductive health.

A second example is the closer relations among state and nonstate actors characterising the emerging global strategy on tobacco control. Under the auspices of WHO, negotiations for a Framework Convention on Tobacco Control (FCTC) have been attended by officially recognised NGOs, along with state delegations. [...] WHO maintains that NGO participation is central to the overall success of the FCTC, and has supported the creation of a global NGO network to support the FCTC (i.e. Framework Convention Alliance). Links were also formed with representatives of the women's movement to ensure that tobacco and women's health was discussed during the Beijing Plus 5 process. At the same time, TFI has developed links with the business community, in particular, the pharmaceutical industry, to explore how nicotine replacement treatments can be made more widely available. Other coordination efforts have been focused on bringing together different UN organizations through the formation of a UN Ad Hoc Inter-Agency Task Force on tobacco control, and the holding of public hearings to encourage the submission of a wide range of evidence from different interest groups.

These efforts to build formal links with such a diverse range of stakeholders to support global tobacco control policy is unprecedented for WHO, and a good example of emerging forms of GHG. It represents an important challenge to traditional ways of working for WHO in its efforts to tackle health issues with global dimensions. Ensuring state and nonstate actors work collectively on different levels of governance (i.e. global, regional, national and subnational), the FCTC is an example of how "behind-the-border" convergence could be promoted in the future. The goal of adopting a legally binding treaty and associated protocols is also a new development in institutionalising global governance in the health sector. The FCTC is based on international regimes that have emerged to promote collective action on global environmental problems. These international regimes can be defined as "sets of implicit or explicit principles, norms, rules and decision-making procedures around which actors expectations converge in a given area of international relations." In addition to the FCTC, other examples of international regimes in the field of health are the International Health Regulations, the International Code for the Marketing of Breast Milk Substitutes and the Codex Alimentarius. These examples of international health regimes demonstrate that they have played a significant role in IHG. The remit and organizational structure of the FCTC and its implementation suggest that such regimes will be a core feature of GHG in future.

A third example of state–nonstate governance is so-called global public–private partnerships (GPPPs) defined as "a collaborative relationship which transcends national boundaries and brings together at least three parties, among them a corporation (and/or industry association) and inter-governmental organizations, so as to achieve a shared health creating goal on the basis of a mutually agreed division of labour." Among the most prominent GPPPs are the Albendazole Donation Programme, Medicines for Malaria Venture and International AIDS Vaccine Initiative. The idea of building partnerships with business is at the centre of UN-wide views on the governance of globalization (Global Compact). For this reason, and the fact that GPPPs bring much needed resources to major health issues, the number of GPPPs is likely to grow in future. [...]

38

The Bill & Melinda Gates Foundation's Grant-Making Programme for Global Health

David McCoy, Gayatri Kembhavi, Jinesh Patel, and Akish Luintel

Introduction

The Bill & Melinda Gates Foundation (henceforth referred to as the Gates Foundation) is the largest private grant-making foundation in the world. It has three main programmes: a US programme that focuses on secondary and post-secondary education; a global development programme that focuses on hunger and poverty (with an emphasis on small farmers and financial services for the poor); and a global health programme. The total amount paid out by the foundation for all grants in 2007 was US$2.01 billion, of which $1.22 billion (61%) was for global health.

Although there is a long history of private philanthropic funding in global health – notably by the Rockefeller Foundation and the Ford Foundation – the influence of the Gates Foundation is of a different order. In 2007, the amount spent by the Gates Foundation on global health was almost as much as WHO's annual budget (approximately $1.65 billion), and was substantially more than the total grant spending of the Rockefeller Foundation across all programmatic areas in the same year ($0.17 billion). The Gates Foundation's effect on global health is evident in malaria research. In the late 1990s, only $84 million was spent on malaria research yearly; since 2000, the Gates Foundation has helped to roughly treble this amount. However, there have been concerns about the role, effect, and lack of accountability of the Gates Foundation (and of private foundations in general). So far, the foundation's global health programme has not been properly assessed. In this report, therefore, we

Original publication details: David McCoy, Gayatri Kembhavi, Jinesh Patel, and Akish Luintel, "The Bill & Melinda Gates Foundation's Grant-Making Programme for Global Health," in *The Lancet*, 373, May 9, 2009. pp. 1645, 1647, 1651–2. Reproduced from The Lancet with permission from Elsevier.

describe and discuss the foundation's grant-making programme for global health. Although we do not assess the impact or cost-effectiveness of the programme, this analysis provides a useful starting point. [...]

The Gates Foundation's Grant-Making Programme

Between January, 1998, and December, 2007, 1,094 grants were awarded for global health by the Gates Foundation; the total value of these grants was $8.95 billion. Table 38.1 shows the number and total value of new global health grants awarded every year, and the actual expenditure on grants per year. The amount of funding committed to new global health grants fell from 1999 to 2002, before rising until 2006 and then falling again in 2007. Although the number and value of new grants awarded in 2007 was lower than in 2005 and 2006, actual expenditure grew.

The size of individual grants varied substantially. The smallest grant was for $3,500, whereas the largest was for $750 million. The length of grants varied from less than 1 year to more than 5 years, but most (777 [71%]) were awarded for periods of between 2 years and 5 years. [...]

65% ($5.82 billion) of all Gates Foundation global health funding was shared by 20 organisations, including five global health partnerships – such as the Global Fund to Fight AIDS, Tuberculosis and Malaria and GAVI Alliance, which together received a quarter of all funding through ten grants. Global health partnerships were the second largest category of recipient. Other global health partnerships that received funding between 1998 and 2007 were the Global Alliance for Improved Nutrition (which directly received about $58 million but also benefited from a grant of $50 million that was channelled through the World Bank), the International Partnership for Microbicides (about $60 million), the International Trachoma Initiative (about $31 million), and the Global Alliance to Eliminate Lymphatic Filariasis (about $20 million, but channelled through the World Bank).

Table 38.1 Number and total value of new global health grants between 1998 and 2007 (and total disbursements per year) made by the Bill & Melinda Gates Foundation.

	1998	1999	2000	2001	2003	2004	2005	2006	2007	Total
Number of new grants	34	68	81	68	108	137	200	197	129	1094
Total value of grants awarded (US$, millions)	151	1132	632	388	477	780	1981	1991	1079	8949
Amount disbursed (US$, millions)*	–	686	554	856	577	442	844	916	1220	6602

Data for annual disbursements were obtained from annual reports or financial statements on the Gates Foundation website. The Gates Foundation's operational and administrative costs are excluded.
*The amount disbursed in 1998 was unavailable on the Gates Foundation website

The category of organisation that received the largest proportion of funding was non-governmental or non-profit organisations. Between 1998 and 2007, the Gates Foundation awarded grants worth $3.30 billion to a wide range of over 100 such organisations, including those that are mainly research-based, those that are mainly involved in health-care delivery, and those with a focus on public awareness or advocacy. The non-governmental or non-profit organisation that received the most amount of funding was the Program for Appropriate Technology in Health (PATH; Seattle, WA, USA), which was awarded 47 grants worth a total of $949 million, mostly for medical research and development. The Gates Foundation has helped to increase PATH's annual expenditure from less than $20 million to over $150 million during the past decade. The next three largest recipients in this category were the Institute for OneWorld Health (a non-profit pharmaceutical company set up in San Francisco, CA, USA, to discover and develop new drugs for neglected diseases), the Save the Children Federation, and the Aeras Global TB Vaccine Foundation (a non-profit product development partnership focused on tuberculosis). Other non-governmental organisations that received large amounts of funding were Family Health International, Care International, and World Vision, which received grants worth $56 million, $41 million, and $8 million, respectively.

Public awareness and advocacy organisations were also major recipients. The US-based ONE Campaign, which focuses on poverty and preventable global disease, received a grant worth $22 million in 2007; and DATA, an advocacy organisation for Africa, received two grants (in 2003 and 2006) worth a total of $26 million. In 2008, the ONE Campaign and DATA merged to become a single organisation known as ONE, which is now led by a former executive of the Gates Foundation. The International HIV/AIDS Alliance, which supports community action within developing countries as well as international research, policy analysis, and advocacy, received grants worth about $42 million. ActionAid International received a grant of just under $11 million to develop a network of non-governmental organisations to monitor and lobby European governments and the European Commission to support the right to health. [...]

Recent changes to collaboration in global health have been characterised by the emergence of loose horizontal networks, where it is unclear who is making decisions and who is accountable to whom. Indeed, the Gates Foundation has helped to promote the emergence of these networks. One investigation that would bring greater clarity to the structure of global health governance is the critical examination of the nature and effects of the relationship between the Gates Foundation and the World Bank, WHO, and key global health partnerships.

A notable finding was that 42% of all funding was spent on either health-care delivery (including humanitarian relief) or increasing access to drugs, vaccines, and other medical commodities. However, the foundation's reputation for focusing on biotechnological developments was also confirmed. More than a third (37%) of funding was for research and development, or basic sciences research. Furthermore, the size of grants for research and development seems to have increased in recent years compared with those for health-care delivery. Similar findings were reported in a previous analysis of the foundation's support for child health research, which concluded that funding was disproportionately allocated to the development of new technologies rather than towards overcoming the barriers to the use of existing technologies. This technological bias reflects the priorities of Bill Gates himself. In his recent annual letter, he stated that "optimism about technology is a fundamental part of the foundation's approach" and he described the key approach to eliminating the main causes of early childhood mortality as "the invention of a handful of new vaccines and getting them into widespread usage". Although we did not calculate a composite figure for all vaccine-related funding (i.e., for research and development, basic science research, health-care delivery, purchase and supply, advocacy or policy development), we estimate that at least half of all funding was linked to vaccination.

The allocation of funding by disease or health issue reflects the explicit strategy of the Gates Foundation to focus on several priority diseases – namely, diarrhoeal disease, pneumonia, malaria, HIV/AIDS, and tuberculosis, as well as vaccine-preventable diseases in general. A key question that emerges from these data is whether the foundation allocates its funding according to need, both in selection of diseases and health issues, and in the focus on vaccines and technology.

A cursory look at the data suggests a prioritisation of HIV/AIDS and malaria over maternal health or mental illness, even though these conditions together make up five of the ten leading causes of disease burden in women aged 15–44 years in low-income and middle-income countries, whereas prematurity, low birthweight, birth trauma, and birth asphyxia together contribute 8% of the total burden of disease in low-income countries. However, the issue of priority setting cannot be answered by looking at the Gates Foundation in isolation. The foundation might after all be choosing to fill a gap that has been neglected by the market or other funders. Additionally, the foundation's allocation of funding for research and development will be determined by factors other than measures of the burden of disease, such as the state and cost of science and the type of research and development needed. Nevertheless, other analyses of global health funding suggest a need to examine the priorities of the Gates Foundation. One study that assessed spending on global health by the World Bank, the Gates Foundation, the US Government, and the Global Fund in 2005 found that funding per death varied substantially across types of disease – for example, $1,029.10 for HIV/AIDS compared with $3.21 for non-communicable diseases. Another study that analysed global spending on neglected diseases (including private sector investment) found that only three diseases (HIV/AIDS, malaria, and tuberculosis) accounted for 80% of the total expenditure. The investigators also found that much more was spent on drugs and vaccines than on diagnostics and calculated that the Gates Foundation contributed about a fifth of all funding for research and development for neglected diseases. They concluded that factors beyond science, technology, and opportunity were clearly playing a part in decisions about funding.

One argument used to make the case that the Gates Foundation over-emphasises technology and new vaccine development is that many existing cost-effective technologies do not reach the people who need them because of poverty or health system failings. Additionally, most of the high child mortality in poor countries results from an underlying lack of access to basic needs such as food, housing, water, and safe employment. Thus, rather than viewing the hundreds of thousands of child deaths from rotavirus infection as a clinical problem that needs a vaccine solution, a better approach might be to view it as a public health problem that needs a social, economic, or political intervention to ensure universal access to clean water and sanitation. However, these concerns about the foundation's technology-based approach need to be considered alongside three counter-arguments. First, as previously mentioned, a substantial amount of funding is spent on service delivery (albeit largely through vertical programmes) or increasing access to existing technologies. Second, the responsibility for funding and developing delivery systems belongs to governments and other types of donors. Third, the Gates Foundation has a separate programme of funding aimed at addressing malnutrition and chronic hunger through various agricultural interventions. Nonetheless, there should be more data-driven discussion about the overall effect of the Gates Foundation's approach to global health improvement. In view of its receipt of public subsidies in the form of tax exemptions, there should also be an expectation that the foundation is subject to some public scrutiny.

The Gates Foundation is a major contributor to global health with enormous financial power and policy leverage. Its decisions can have a substantial influence on other organisations. The foundation's emphasis on technology, however, can detract attention from the social determinants of health while promoting an approach to health improvement that is heavily dependent on clinical technologies. The support of vertical, disease-based programmes can undermine coherent and long-term development of health systems, and its sponsorship of global health policy networks and think tanks can diminish the capabilities of Ministries of Health in low-income and middle-income countries. Additionally, the foundation's generous funding of organisations in the UK and USA accentuates existing disparities between developed and developing countries while neglecting support for the civic and public institutional capacities of low-income and middle-income countries. Although Bill Gates' annual letter indicates a genuine desire of the foundation to help the poor and to do good, further independent research and assessment are needed to ensure that this desire is translated into the right and most cost-effective set of approaches, strategies, and investments for improving the health of the poor.

Part VI Questions

1. What are "IMF programs," what is their intended purpose, and how does Vreeland show that they often have "perverse effects"? How might IMF critics or supporters use the information he provides?
2. Why is the WTO "under duress"? How might economic recessions aggravate that duress? Do Capling and Higgott convince you that the WTO or its members are willing and able to meet the challenges they outline? What other information could you find, for example with regard to the so-called Doha round, that might shed light on this issue?
3. How do governments use networks to extend their "global reach," according to Slaughter? Why does she say that these networks perform "functions of a world government … without the form"? Could globalization lay the groundwork for the real thing (i.e., an actual "world government")? If so, would you consider that desirable?

4.   As Murphy and Yates point out, ISO claims that it "does not regulate or legis-
     late." What does ISO do and how does it do it? What features of its procedures
     account for its relative success, in Murphy and Yates's description? What does the
     container story tell us about the distinct role of ISO in governance of the world
     economy?

5.   Why do Dodgson et al. make a plea for stronger global health governance? What
     specific problems might motivate their case? What do they consider "essential
     elements" of global health governance? Apart from the examples they mention,
     can you think of a campaign, policy, or initiative that illustrates the promise of
     the system they have in mind?

6.   Considering the role of the Gates Foundation in global health, would it be fair to
     say that "money talks"? How do McCoy et al. assess the pros and cons of the
     foundation's role in health promotion, and how would you assess it yourself? Is
     the role of private organizations in governance inherently problematic?

7.   Reflect on the items in this section. Taken together, what do they tell you about
     issues in global governance – for example, about the role of states, the collective
     capacity to address cross-border problems, and possible steps toward "world
     government"?

Part VII

Globalization, INGOs, and Civil Society

Introduction

In conflict zones where governments fear to tread, volunteers working with Doctors Without Borders rush to the rescue of people in need. Environmental activists have long banded together in organizations like Greenpeace and Friends of the Earth to try to protect whales and tropical rain forests. Since the 1960s, people imprisoned by oppressive regimes have looked to Amnesty International to take up their cause. Sports aficionados take for granted that the International Olympic Committee sets the rules for the Olympic Games. Professionals in many fields join their peers in organizations like the International Sociological Association. As these examples show, international nongovernmental organizations (INGOs) have become actively involved in a wide range of global issues. While many INGOs focus on matters that do not draw much public attention, others help identify and publicize new issues and exert pressure on states and other organizations to deal with them.

INGOs are voluntary associations of individuals, groups, or corporations who band together to pursue specific goals and activities on a worldwide or regional basis. As a complement to Part VI, the selections in this part focus in particular on the role of INGOs, and the global social movements and international conferences with which they are often associated, in world politics and global governance. While most analysts of world politics see states as the primary actors, stressing their jockeying for power as the driving force behind world development (or, as we saw in Part V, raising doubts about the capacity of states to meet the challenges posed by globalization), in these selections states are not so much "in the driver's seat" regarding world affairs. Instead, states are only one among many types of global actor, and they often are influenced substantially by other actors in ways they may hardly recognize.

Many INGOs act as self-authorized global governance bodies, in such arenas as science, engineering, knowledge management, sports, hobbies, management

The Globalization Reader, Fifth Edition. Edited by Frank J. Lechner and John Boli.
Editorial material and organization © 2015 John Wiley & Sons, Ltd.
Published 2015 by John Wiley & Sons, Ltd.

techniques, medical specialties, and much more. Global authority is exercised, for example, for the game of chess by the World Chess Federation; for volleyball, by the Fédération Internationale de Volleyball; for physics, by the International Union of Pure and Applied Physics and its member national associations; and for psychiatrists, by the World Psychiatric Association. Most INGOs of this sort receive little public attention and are familiar only to their members, but they have important governance functions. They make global rules, disseminate knowledge throughout the world, establish codes of ethics, propagate technical and environmental standards, organize world championships, and so on. In their respective sectors, they are the peak global organizations.

INGOs and the movements they represent are core elements of what is often referred to as global civil society. Analogous to national civil societies, global civil society is the vast network of voluntary organizations, formal and informal, that "world citizens" fashion to pursue common interests, share knowledge, promote professions, address social problems, and so on. Civil society organizations are non-profit associations, largely or wholly independent of the state, governed by democratic structures and committed to encouraging widespread and active participation by their members. Local and national organizations – what are often called domestic nongovernmental organizations, or NGOs – concentrate on local and national issues, but increasingly they are linked to INGOs and thereby to their counterparts in other countries. They thus form complex networks of ties, sharing information about their respective areas of concern and coordinating their programs in line with global organizations, policies, and standards. Of particular interest are INGOs engaged in global social activism and mobilization. INGOs are the key players in most global social movements, and larger movements can involve coalitions of hundreds of INGOs; for example, the International Campaign to Ban Landmines was supported by more than 1,200 organizations.

The best-known social movement INGOs are human rights organizations like Amnesty International and Human Rights Watch, environmental bodies like the World Wildlife Fund and Greenpeace, and business-reforming INGOs like the International Forum on Globalization and the Clean Clothes Campaign. These groups work to improve conditions in countries all around the world and draw on members from all parts of the world. Many other global movements are also driven by INGOs, almost always in conjunction with domestic NGOs – movements for women's rights, for democracy and free elections, for the rights of indigenous peoples, for improved labor practices by global corporations like Nike or The Gap, for fair trade principles in agricultural production, and so on.

Social movement INGOs stand out because they engage extensively with and often challenge states, trying to change state policies or prompt state action on specific problems. They usually have little choice but to work through states because their own resources are meager and states are the only actors capable of – and responsible for – solving broad social problems. They also, and increasingly, become involved with intergovernmental organizations (IGOs), which were introduced in Part VI. Of special importance are the United Nations and its agencies, which formally incorporate INGOs in their work through what is known as "consultative status." Thousands of INGOs have consultative status with UN bodies, and they are key participants in many UN programs. The UNAIDS Programme even seats an INGO representative on its governing board.

The most important IGO, the United Nations, was formed after World War II as the successor to the League of Nations. Unlike the league, which the United States never joined, the UN mandate from the beginning was much broader than the issues of security and peace. Very quickly the UN became the focal point for global governance in many domains, and by the 1960s it had assumed a major role in promoting decolonization, the formation of new states in the former colonies, and the development of education, health care, and other modern systems in the less developed world. One of the UN's more striking activities has been its sponsorship of major world conferences on emerging issues, such as the conferences on women's issues during the UN Decade for Women (1975–85) and the later Beijing conference in 1995, as well as global conferences on the environment, including the highly publicized "Earth Summit" in Rio de Janeiro in 1992 and the UN Climate Change Conference in Copenhagen in 2009. In every instance, the official UN conferences, attended by delegates from states, have vied for attention with the parallel and much larger INGO/NGO conferences that speak not for governments but, in the broadest sense, for humanity as a whole.

To amplify a point we made in the previous section, we therefore find a complex and highly decentralized global governance structure that involves much cooperation among civil-society INGOs, IGOs (led by the UN), and states – but also much divisiveness, disagreement, and controversy about specific policies, programs, and lines of development in many domains. Global consensus is often hard to reach, but the globalization of issues – the degree to which issues and policies are debated and settled at the global level – is continually on the rise.

In the first selection, Israeli sociologist Nitza Berkovitch discusses the global women's movement, which originated in the late nineteenth century and became an increasingly coherent and effective social movement after World War I as it concentrated its efforts on the International Labour Organization, a new IGO set up to promote and standardize labor law and policy. Berkovitch analyzes the rise of new sets of global rules and expectations pertaining to women, crystallizing after World War II in a powerful ideology calling for women's full equality with men. Sparked by the UN Decade for Women, women's INGOs have proliferated rapidly, making the movement both more global and more divided as the voices of Third World women have become increasingly prominent.

Elizabeth Heger Boyle, an American sociologist, shows how the concern regarding female genital cutting (FGC) first arose among Western activists as a feminist issue but was later redefined as a medical problem, in large part because of resistance to the feminist stance by women in places where FGC is practiced. This recasting of the issue brought FGC onto the official agenda of major intergovernmental organizations, particularly the World Health Organization, but the growing importance of the idea that "women's rights are human rights" led to a further recasting of FGC as a human rights issue. This framework remains dominant to the present day.

The human rights framework is a key element in the selection by Rebecca L. Barlow, an Australian international relations scholar, on the women's movement in Iran. Barlow challenges the oft-repeated claim that the international human rights regime was a Western creation, pointing out that the original proposals for a UN Charter barely mentioned human rights and both the United States and Britain resisted the establishment of a human rights regime. Many non-Western countries pushed successfully for an explicit rights declaration, and non-Western countries were a majority of the members of the first Human Rights Commission. Barlow then recounts the origins and development of the One Million Signatures Campaign in Iran, a massive effort by women's groups – both secular and religious – pushing for gender equality in Iran. Despite the patriarchal theocratic regime, the women's movement is posing a greater challenge to the subordinate position of women than most outside observers recognize.

In the next selection, American sociologists John Boli and George M. Thomas present a high-level overview of the entire population of international nongovernmental organizations since 1875. After charting the enormous increase in INGO formation and its ups and downs with the two world wars, they set INGOs in a world cultural context by showing how they foster and enact increasingly widespread global principles. Their article finds considerable evidence that INGOs can and do influence IGOs and states, though the extent of such influence varies greatly from issue to issue.

Peter Eigen, a German lawyer and former official at the World Bank, builds the case for global action to eliminate government corruption, including the bribing of public officials by companies seeking contracts or investment opportunities. As chairman of Transparency International (TI), the INGO he founded to identify and challenge corruption, he reviews the problems caused by corruption and the measures that TI believes can reduce its prevalence if a strong partnership among INGOs, states, and such IGOs as the OECD can be mobilized effectively.

A different kind of partnership – among NGOs, states, and corporations – takes center stage in the study by Swiss sociologist Franziska Bieri and John Boli of the global campaign to end the trade in conflict (blood) diamonds. They show how two small INGOs were key participants in the origins and development of the Kimberley Process, which produced a certification scheme to keep conflict diamonds off the world market. At issue here is the expanding ideology of corporate social responsibility (CSR), which imposes moral obligations on companies to consider not just profits but the "triple bottom line." CSR thinking proved to be a strong lever by which to induce the industry to embrace the certification scheme. While far from perfect, the scheme has been remarkably successful, greatly reducing the global market share of conflict diamonds.

Finally, we return to the issue of the "bottom billion" discussed in Part IV. In the 1990s, microfinance emerged as an exciting new approach to lifting people out of poverty, thanks largely to the efforts of Muhammud Yunus and his Grameen Bank in Bangladesh. But, as Indian-American urban studies scholar Ananya Roy shows, the microfinance industry has come under strident attack for charging high interest rates, benefitting investors more than the poor, and doing little to reduce long-term poverty. Roy presents a rather different view of microfinance. While it may not have achieved much in terms of spurring development, she argues, it has been quite effective as a form of social protection, helping the poor through hard times and reducing their vulnerability to the ups and downs of world prices for life's necessities, especially food.

39

The Emergence and Transformation of the International Women's Movement

Nitza Berkovitch

The Interwar Period: Lobbying for Expansion of the World Agenda

The world polity after World War I differed markedly from that of the previous period. Earlier dreams of establishing permanent international cooperative bodies were realized with the creation of the League of Nations and the International Labour Organization (ILO), which ushered in a new phase of world-polity construction. The League and the ILO, both created at the Paris Peace Conference of 1919, constituted the first stable organizational basis for inter-state cooperation. They opened a new arena for women's mobilization by offering a central world focal point that theretofore had been lacking. In so doing, they changed the context in which women's organizations operated, consequently provoking changes in their modes of operation as well. Their main effort now targeted the newly created international bodies.

By turning their attention to the new world bodies, women's organizations conferred legitimacy on them and thus helped institutionalize their centrality. At the same time, the degree of organization and cooperation among women's groups increased. Many women's organizations moved their headquarters to Geneva to facilitate contacts with the various bodies of the League, while others established specialized bureaus expressly to deal with the League. In addition, a new type of organization

Original publication details: Nitza Berkovitch, "The Emergence and Transformation of the International Women's Movement," in *Constructing World Culture: International Nongovernmental Organizations since 1875*, ed. John Boli and George M. Thomas. Redwood City: Stanford University Press, 1999. pp. 109–10, 119–21, 124–6. Reproduced with permission from Stanford University Press.

emerged, the multi- or supra-international organization consisting of representatives of a number of international organizations. For example, in 1925 the Joint Committee of Representative Organizations was founded, and in 1931 ten of the largest women's groups formed the Liaison Committee of Women's International Organizations. Members of the Committee established close contacts with high officials in the League Secretariat, cooperating with the League on various welfare-related and other activities.

The increased global mobilization of women within the formally organized global arena sharpened tensions within the international women's movement. Bitter conflict emerged between those who supported action on behalf of women's equality and those who favored laws that gave women special protection, especially in the area of work. Both camps focused their efforts on getting the League and ILO to take action on women's issues, but with quite different emphases.

The League's limited mandate did not allow women's issues to be considered in full; regulation of the relationships between states and their respective citizens was not included in its jurisdiction. Instead, the League concentrated on regulating relations among states. Individual "rights," a construct that had mobilized social movements for more than a century, were not considered an international concern that could be regulated by international standards. It was only through a sustained effort lasting almost two decades that women's international organizations were able to place the heart of their social concerns, the legal status of women, on the League's agenda.

The exclusion of the issue of women's rights from the League's jurisdiction was explicitly stipulated by officials during the Paris Peace Conference. Facing continuous pressure from women's organizations, however, and after much hesitation and deliberation on the part of the politicians, Conference officials agreed that "women's organizations could be heard," but only "by commissions occupying themselves especially with questions touching on women's interests." The women's delegation to the Conference presented seven resolutions covering moral, political, and educational issues. For the most part, they were ignored. [...]

Development Ideology

During the 1970s, the discourse of women's rights encountered that of development. This encounter was the result of the most significant event in global organizing on women's issues: the United Nation's Decade for Women (1976–1985). The Women's Decade coincided with the Second United Nations Development Decade, during which development started to dominate global discourse and activity. The two events melded into each other in the sense that a core dimension for grappling with women's issues became the concern for "incorporating women into development"; women's issues came to the fore in many development documents and projects. Framing women's issues in the context of development brought about qualitative and quantitative changes on both national and international fronts. It led to an intensification of world activity on women's issues that in turn had an enormous impact on nation-states, while it stimulated the establishment of women's movements in many countries and led most governments in the world to create an official state agency for the promotion of women's issues. Women's issues became a state concern.

Before discussing these interrelated developments, I should note that the catalyst for the Decade for Women is believed to have been a women's organization, not any of the UN bodies. Hilkka Pietila, who was herself involved in some of the activities she documents, refers to "an oral tradition in the UN family" that identifies the Women's International Democratic Federation (WIDF) as the source of the proposal for an International Women's Year. As observers on the UN Commission on the Status of Women, the WIDF's president and a number of other WINGO leaders drafted a proposal that the Commission recommended to the General Assembly. Despite initial resistance, the Assembly eventually endorsed the idea in 1972, proclaiming 1975 as International Women's Year (IWY) with the themes of equality, development, and peace.

In 1975 the World Conference of the International Women's Year was held in Mexico City. One hundred and thirty-three states participated, endorsing two major documents: the "Declaration of Mexico on the Equality of Women and Their Contribution to Development and Peace" and the "World Plan of Action for the Implementation of the Objectives of IWY." The conference designated the 1976–1985 period as the UN Decade for Women. Representatives from 145 countries attended the 1980 Mid-Decade Conference in Copenhagen, convened as a "mid-point review of progress and obstacles in achieving the goals of the Decade," and adopted a Programme of Action. The end of the Decade was marked by the 1985 World Conference to Review and Appraise the Achievements of the UN Decade for Women, held in Nairobi. Drawing representatives from 157 countries, the conference adopted a document titled "The Nairobi Forward-Looking Strategies for the Advancement of Women."

It was during the Women's Decade that the status of women was linked to the development of their countries. As a result, both the form and content of global organizing has changed. Official bodies and the international women's movement shifted their focus from legal standards and international law to concrete projects, further organizational expansion, greater research efforts, and network enhancement to coordinate these numerous endeavors.

Within the new framework, elevating women's status and achieving equality between the sexes were conceptualized as necessary conditions for full national – economic and social – development. Women were now considered important human resources essential to comprehensive rationalization. Eradicating discrimination was an integral part of the global plan to improve the well-being of national societies and of the world as a whole. "Human rights" as a leading concept lost its prominence, though it did not disappear. Thus, for example, the sweepingly broad Convention for the Elimination of All Forms of Discrimination Against Women (adopted by the General Assembly in 1979) incorporates, side by side, the principles of abstract social justice and a more "instrumental" principle of development. In 1982, a commission under the same name was established to monitor the Convention's implementation. By 1990, this convention had been ratified by 101 countries, one of the highest rates of ratification of any UN convention. [...]

Summary

The story of "united womanhood" must be understood within the larger framework of the changing world polity. The existence of the international women's movement as such, its huge conferences, its plethora of documents and resolutions, and its ubiquitous lobbying visibly enact the concept of transnationalism and thus boost our tendency to see the world as a single global social system. As Roland Robertson notes: "Indeed this is one among many movements and organizations which have helped to compress the world as a whole." Thus, the international women's movement did not only reflect world culture but also helped shape its content and structure.

What started in earlier periods as moral crusades led by women's groups eventually culminated in highly legitimized and rationalized actions enacted by official world bodies on behalf of women. Around the turn of the century, the women's movement, being part of the transnational reform movement, reflected and reinforced the emphasis on moral reform and universalism. However, these early groups also promoted elements of equality, rights, and suffrage. One way of resolving the tension between the notions of individual rights and moral regeneration was subsuming the former in the latter. The international women's movement promoted women's rights as a necessary condition for enacting and bringing about desired changes in society. However, in the early period there were no world bodies to act on behalf of women.

With the establishment of the ILO as a global organization with the mandate to set international standards, the women's movement found a central target for its advocacy of the principle of equality alongside the principle of "protection," with growing tension between the two principles. The League of Nations also helped shape the mode of action and agenda of the women's groups when it became the focus for their lobbying efforts for and against an international equal rights treaty. However, it was only after World War II, when world-level organizing intensified and a more authoritative world center was established, that the principle of equality began to guide world activities regarding women. The changing agenda of the ILO regarding women's employment is striking. The sole focus on protective legislation was widened to include binding standards on equality in employment. Nation-states joined the campaign, and the majority of them revised their national labor codes to be consistent with the new spirit of women's rights.

In the 1970s another layer was added: an instrumental discourse of development that brought with it further rationalizing and organizing of world activities on women's issues. The encounter between the two discourses shaped much of the activity and spirit of the UN Decade for Women (1976–1985). The international women's movement began to operate in a much more complicated environment, with more options but also more constraints. Thanks to the initiatives of women's organizations, regular world women's conferences were held both during the Decade and after, the latest in Beijing in 1995.

The three UN conferences indicate a great deal about the worldwide construction of women's issues. First, official world organizing and activities regarding women's issues have expanded tremendously in comparison with previous periods. Second, the effects are not limited to the international level. Nation-states put "women" on their agenda, altering existing laws and establishing official bureaus and departments to deal with women's issues. Third, world-cultural ideas about women have penetrated developing countries as well, leading to the emergence of women's movements in almost every country in the world.

All the while, the international women's movement has expanded in size and transformed in content and composition. It became truly global as it grew to incorporate women from the Third World, with their specific concerns and perspectives. This process, however, was not unproblematic. Rather, it was accompanied by rising tension between women from the South and women from the North. This shows that, in contrast to conventionally held wisdom, transnational movements in general and the women's movement in particular cannot be reduced to the interests of one hegemonic region. National and regional factors can affect international organizing agenda, but the wider context affects, to a large degree, the legitimacy and effectiveness of international organizing. Once international organizing emerges and gains a degree of legitimacy and operational capacity, however, new organizational dynamics are set in motion that reshape the wider context itself.

Women everywhere have been integrated into the ongoing global campaign. The international women's movement has emerged as a visible and viable global force. The overarching result is, indeed, a reconceptualization of feminism as

> a movement of people working for change across and despite national boundaries, not of representatives of nation states or national governments … we must be global, recognising that the oppression of women in one part of the world is often affected by what happens in another, and that no woman is free until the conditions of oppression of women are eliminated everywhere.

40

The Evolution of Debates over Female Genital Cutting

Elizabeth Heger Boyle

In 1958, the Economic and Social Council of the United Nations formally requested that the World Health Organization (WHO) study FGC [female genital cutting]. WHO refused, claiming the practice was outside the organization's competence because it was of a "social and cultural rather than medical nature." Three years later, African women attending a UN seminar in Addis Ababa reiterated the request to study FGC, but WHO's response was the same. The organization had a policy of not intervening in domestic politics without an explicit invitation from a state, and invitations were not forthcoming.

By the mid-1990s, the situation had changed completely. The international community was centrally involved in eradicating FGC. Amnesty International included private abuses in its annual country reports for the first time, specifically referring to the practice. The International Monetary Fund and the World Bank (with impetus from the United States) linked aid to reform efforts. Four other prominent international governmental organizations (IGOs, including WHO) issued a joint statement condemning the practice as a violation of women's rights. In a short span of decades, the ancient practice of FGC had become the target of unified international action. How did this change come about? [...]

Original publication details: Elizabeth Heger Boyle, *Female Genital Cutting: Cultural Conflict in the Global Community*. Baltimore: Johns Hopkins University Press, 2002. pp. 41, 45–6, 47–9, 49–52, 53–5. Reproduced with permission from Johns Hopkins University Press.

The Health Compromise

In the early years of the UN system, international intervention into local politics was highly circumscribed. The cherished right of each nation to govern its own people was heralded as nation after new nation threw off the bonds of colonialism and claimed independence. In this context, the international community defined the domestic jurisdictions of nation-states broadly. In addition, international organizations did not define FGC as a health risk at this time, perhaps because the practice was passed on "voluntarily" from generation to generation. Furthermore, the negative consequences of early attempts to eradicate the practice in Kenya and Sudan might have made members of the international community reluctant to take up the issue. These factors combined to keep the international community out of the FGC controversy in the decades following World War II.

Western feminists, including Fran Hosken, Mary Daly, and Gloria Steinem, and women's international organizations were critically important in raising international interest in the practice. (African opponents to the practice had been present for some time but had been unsuccessful at getting IGOs such as WHO involved in eradication efforts.) Initially, Western women and groups were vocal and confrontational. Advocates of sovereign autonomy continually raised the question of whether the West and international organizations should be involved in the eradication of FGC. Feminists responded by arguing that FGC was a serious problem requiring immediate international attention. Feminist mobilization in the 1970s spurred the international system to take a new look at FGC.

Early second-wave feminists argued that FGC was a tool of patriarchy and a symbol of women's subordination. These feminists argued that FGC was sadistic and part of a global patriarchal conspiracy. Seeing sadism in FGC actually predates feminist mobilization. For example, in one early account, Worsley claimed that the women who performed FGC "always" did so with a "sadistic smile of delight." In adopting this explanation for FGC, Western women were implicitly assuming that no one would voluntarily choose to undergo the practice. African women were portrayed as victims who made "incorrect" choices because they were burdened by patriarchy. [...]

Many African women found the discourse offensive. For example, at the international women's conference in Copenhagen in 1980, African women boycotted the session featuring Fran Hosken, calling her perspective ethnocentric and insensitive to African women. Often, individuals in cultures where FGC is practiced were offended by their characterization in anti-FGC discourse. Seble Dawit and Salem Mekuria criticized Alice Walker for failing to treat African women as efficacious and self-aware individuals: she "portrays an African village, where women and children are without personality, dancing and gazing blankly through some stranger's script of their lives." Occasionally these individuals claimed that anti-FGC rhetoric was exaggerated, but more typically they argued that African women were not assigned the attributes of modern individuals. In other words, they were not assumed to be self-directed, autonomous, and efficacious.

Feminist arguments were also criticized for being ineffective at the local level. Melissa Parker, who lived with a tribe in Sudan while conducting medical research, argued that this type of discourse was doomed to fail locally:

> Of course women do not circumcise their daughters to create problems for them later on. They do so to protect them. An uncircumcised girl is unmarriageable and would bring undying shame to her and her family. People would call her *kaaba* (bad), *waskhan* (dirty) and *nigsa* (unclean). Her life would be intolerable, as she would be taunted by friends and relatives wherever she went. In brief, the practice of circumcision is bound up with beliefs of honour, shame, purity and cleanliness. It is these beliefs which need to be examined and interrogated if any headway is to be made in bringing an end to such a custom. It seems almost comical that Western and Sudanese feminists have spent so much time tackling it simply at the level of female oppression when it is rooted in so much else as far as those women who experience it are concerned.

Parker's perspective was essentially acknowledging that FGC was institutionalized in some areas. In these areas, history could not be ignored and "interests" had to be understood as including not only those defined by "universal" standards but also those important to the local context.

Despite the criticism, the feminist rhetoric captured the attention of the global community. By 1979, UN subcommittees had begun to study and provide outlets for national governments to discuss FGC. This occurred despite explicit opposition from some women in practicing cultures. Nevertheless, perhaps because the feminist rhetoric was so controversial, when IGOs finally decided to intervene to stop FGC around this time, they did not explicitly rely on the feminists' arguments.

Instead, IGOs relied on scientific arguments about women's health to justify their initial intervention to eradicate FGC. WHO and nongovernmental organizations were already intervening in national arenas to assist in birth control programs. Programs to eliminate FGC fit well within this mobilization. For example, international actors placed FGC in a category termed Traditional Practices Affecting the Health of Women and Children. This was also the title given to a 1979 WHO seminar held in Khartoum and the term used to describe FGC in the UN annual reports. African nation-states also tended to root their eradication policies in a scientific health discourse. The major joint effort of nations was named the Inter-African Committee on Traditional Practices Affecting the Health of Women and Children. Health problems were a universal concern, affecting every nation. By placing FGC within this framework, international actors did not appear to be singling out African nations for reform. Health rhetoric permitted a compromise between rights and sovereignty.

Thus, FGC became a health issue despite WHO's early assessment that it was not. This reframing of the practice may reflect the increasing importance assigned to medicine (and science in general) in the international system. Because health issues were universally applicable to all nation-states and yet narrowly tailored to easily identifiable "problems," they were viewed as apolitical. Intervening for medical reasons did not threaten sovereignty because medicine was seen as neutral and existing apart from politics. Further, medicine was intimately linked with modernization and progress. It would be irrational and hence inconceivable for a culture to reject modern medicine. [...]

Initially, feminists were willing to reframe their arguments in the terms adopted by IGOs. Themes of human rights and medicine began to appear in the feminist literature. For example, in her 1981 report, Hosken reframed her arguments justifying Western involvement, locating them in notions of human rights and health. She cited a letter she had sent to the secretary-general of the United Nations, Kurt Waldheim, which had been signed by "many thousands of concerned women and men from all over the world": "The mutilation of genital organs of the female body for any reason whatsoever is a fundamental offense against the human rights of all women in general, and specifically against the female children and women who are mutilated. The RIGHT TO HEALTH is a basic human right that cannot be abridged." (Ironically, even the "neutral" medical discourse became the basis for distinguishing a hierarchy of values. For example, Hosken asserted in the same report that although Africans continued to call the practice "female circumcision," the "medically correct" term was "genital mutilation.") In the 1980s, feminists and other international actors reached consensus through an implicit agreement to focus on the medical consequences of FGC. FGC was a violation of the right to health, and therefore it was appropriate for the international community to intervene in local politics to reduce the occurrence of the practice.

In sum, radical feminists prompted the international community to take action against FGC. Realizing that they must act but unwilling to embrace the caustic feminist discourse, community leaders had difficulty developing their own justification for intervention. Science, in the form of medicine, became a seemingly neutral basis for invoking the human rights frame and intervening in national politics. In fact, however, the worldwide adoption of this perspective without debate was a monumental step toward global homogeneity. Individualism carried through medical science was acceptable to international actors; individualism in the form of assertive arguments about gender relationships smacked of bias and was initially too provocative for these same actors.

Women's Rights as Human Rights

Once adopted, medical arguments were the sole basis for international intervention against FGC until 1990 (WHO, UNICEF, UN Family Planning Association (UNFPA), and UN Development Program (UNDP) 1995; UN Population Fund 1996). A number of medical organizations were at the forefront of mobilization, including WHO, the Sudanese Obstetrical and Gynecological Society, International Planned Parenthood Federation, the International Organization of Gynecologists, and Doctors without Borders. Thus, from the late 1960s until 1990, the primary goal of international organizations was to reduce the negative health consequences of the practice.

A review of the literature suggests that the medical discourse was somewhat effective in making individuals aware of health problems associated with FGC. For example, Demographic and Health Survey data show that in Kenya only 31 percent of circumcised women aged forty-five to forty-nine were circumcised by trained medical personnel, but 57 percent of circumcised women aged twenty to twenty-nine were. Likewise, only 9 percent of Egyptian women aged forty-five to forty-nine were circumcised by trained medical personal, but 50 percent of those women had their daughters circumcised by trained medical personnel. This trend is not universal, however. In some countries, such as Mali and Tanzania, medicalization has been, and continues to be, minimal. Ethnographies suggest more subtle forms of medicalization as well – changes that might not be picked up in official statistics. For example, over time, ethnographies increasingly refer to the use of antiseptics to clean the wound after FGC. Regardless of whether the medical discourse actually reduced the incidence of FGC, in many areas it had the overall favorable effect of making the procedure medically safer.

Given the success of the medical mobilization against FGC, it is easy to imagine mobilization around the practice diminishing. This did not happen. Instead, mobilization increased in the 1990s – but under a rights model rather than a medical model.

Although the international community in the postwar era had been hesitant to address gender issues, a relationship between gender equality and human rights had been developing; gender equality was becoming an appropriate basis for international action. In the 1950s, 1960s, and 1970s, the United Nations and its various subunits proposed many conventions and declarations relating to gender and human rights. (Conventions are binding for the states that have ratified them; declarations are non-binding statements of aspirations.) During this time, women came to be defined less in terms of their familial role as mothers and more in terms of their rights as individuals. Most countries in the modern world have signaled their receptivity to these various conventions and declarations. The conventions and declarations provide a backdrop for understanding the policy development related specifically to FGC.

Thus, the increased attention to FGC coincided with greater attention to women's issues in general. The international system had begun to create formal mechanisms for dealing with gender inequality around this time. The Convention for the Elimination of All Forms of Discrimination against Women (CEDAW) is a case in point. The history of CEDAW goes back to 1963, when twenty-two countries introduced a resolution at the eighteenth UN General Assembly calling for international cooperation to eliminate discrimination against women. The resolution noted that discrimination against women still existed "in fact if not in law" despite the equality provision of the UN Charter and the UDHR. On December 18, 1979, the CEDAW Convention was adopted by the General Assembly, and it came into force on September 3, 1981, when twenty countries had ratified it. As of June 2002, 170 countries had ratified the convention. Within the international treaty system, CEDAW stands distinctly as the symbol that women's rights are human rights.

The preamble to CEDAW reaffirms faith in fundamental human rights and respect for human dignity. Article 1 defines discrimination against women broadly to include both intentional and de facto discrimination in human rights and fundamental freedoms. Article 2 mandates that states parties pursue, "by all appropriate means and without delay," a policy of eliminating discrimination against women. Articles 2 through 5 set out the kind of measures to be taken by the state – legislative, judicial, administrative, and other measures, including affirmative action and modification of social and cultural patterns of conduct. Articles 6 through 16 address specific issues as they relate to women: sexual slavery, political and public life, nationality, education, employment, health care, economic and social life, rural life, equality in terms of civil law, and marriage and family relations. [...]

By the mid-1990s, feminist arguments concerning women's rights as human rights and violence against women became the dominant basis for action by IGOs. A critical component of the feminist argument was to expand the idea of human rights to incorporate a positive requirement on states to protect individuals against harmful actions that occur in the "private" realm. MacKinnon argued that the privacy doctrine undermined gender equality generally: "The very place (home, body), relations (sexual), activities (intercourse and reproduction), and feelings (intimacy, selfhood) that feminism finds central to women's subjection form the core of the privacy doctrine. But when women are segregated in private, one at a time, a law of privacy will tend to protect the right of men 'to be let alone,' to oppress us one at a time." This laid the groundwork for later arguments that the idea of human rights should be expanded to encompass private abuses.

Once "privacy" became contested terrain, human rights activists were able to transcend cultural boundaries by grouping a number of private actions and practices under the broad title "violence against women." At the international level, activists who promoted this idea were successful in increasing attention to issues such as FGC, wife beating, marital rape, child abuse, and sexual harassment. [...]

FGC was featured prominently among these "new" human rights abuses, and feminists also began to pressure states directly about the practice. Dorothy Stetson suggested that governments in countries where FGC occurred represented only male interests. Priscilla Warren stated the case even more strongly: "Often the victim's own government cannot or will not control the perpetrator; the state then also becomes a perpetrator." Ultimately, national governments succumbed to the pressure. This is evident, for example, in the Egyptian state's abrupt turnaround on the practice. In its 1996 report to the CEDAW Committee, the Egyptian state implicitly acknowledged its responsibility in the fight against FGC.

By the mid-1990s, the transition from a medical model to a human rights model was complete. The FGC issue skipped from committee to committee in the organization, assigned first to a committee dealing with slavery, then moving on to a committee dealing with discrimination. Ultimately, the issue settled within the jurisdiction of the committee responsible for protecting human rights. By the time the issue reached the committee on human rights, the framing was complete: the international community had to eradicate FGC because the practice violated fundamental human rights. FGC offended the institutionalized construction of individuals as efficacious promoters of their own self-interest.

In even more dramatic terms, the joint statement of WHO, UNICEF, UNFPA, and UNDP in 1995 labeled the medical basis for anti-FGC policies a "mistake." The reasoning of the joint statement suggested that much of the medical discourse – at least as it was applied locally – was exaggerated and consequently counterproductive. The second problem with the medical reasoning was more surprising. Essentially, medicalization had been *too* effective. By making FGC safer, the international community had undermined the urgency that originally motivated the eradication of the practice. The organizations attempted to recapture some of that urgency in their repackaged message: FGC had negative health consequences, but – more importantly – it was a violation of women's rights.

Thus, in the mid-1990s, responsibility for eradicating FGC was once again reassessed. At that time, the right to health took a backseat to the human right to be free from abuse – including abuse from intimates.

41

Women's Human Rights and the Muslim Question

Iran's One Million Signatures Campaign

Rebecca L. Barlow

At the root of many investigations into Islam's relationship with modernity is a commonly held view that human rights are the legacy of Western culture. This logic is often stretched to suggest that whereas Western societies embody a cultural predisposition towards the international human rights framework, it is considered foreign, unfamiliar, and extraneous in other cultural settings. For relativists, human rights represent a culturally constrained project: a product of enlightenment theory and European individualism with little applicability in non-Western contexts. In a world that took a paradigmatic turn on 11 September 2001, the non-Western 'other' in this political master narrative has increasingly come to imply 'Muslim'. Now we are faced with a philosophical, and sometimes theological, debate surrounding the universality of human rights norms on the one hand, and Islam as a 'complete way of life' on the other.

Nowhere is this debate more entrenched than in terms of gender relations and women's status. According to the modern principle of gender equality, any distinction made on the basis of sex that has the intention or outcome of according women unequal rights to men is ipso facto discriminatory and unjust. But from the relativist viewpoint, gender equality is considered context dependent, or worse, a lofty ideal of women who are white, Western, and privileged. It is often presumed peripheral to Muslim societies organised around 'traditional' family relations, and, further, undesirable to Muslim women whose identities hinge on religious tradition within the family structure. These presumptions emerge at least in part from images of the 'Muslim woman' as a dutiful, and often submissive, wife, daughter, or mother. Such notions are not solely the result of the Western imagination, since there is a strong insistence from within some Muslim countries that women's human rights are inauthentic to Muslim societies, and by

Original publication details: Rebecca L. Barlow, *Women's Human Rights and the Muslim Question: Iran's One Million Signatures Campaign*. Carlton, Victoria: Melbourne University Press, 2012. pp. 1–3, 21–6, 124–30, 132.

definition 'un-Islamic'. The problem lies with the acceptance of such claims as the 'Muslim view' on human rights – as if there is a homogenous and uncontested position that has somehow made its way into every Muslim society and community around the globe. Subsequently, restrictions on women's freedom in Muslim societies come to be externally viewed as reflecting a community belief in Islamic principles – instead of the result of patriarchal political calculations by those in power. It is adherence to Islam, according to the relativist position, that precludes the resonance of universal human right norms with those following a Muslim way of life.

[. . .]

Popular assumption holds that as the victors of World War II, it was the Great Powers who championed the idea of human rights as a central axis for the post-conflict structure of international governance. The master narrative reads as follows: Western countries, represented by the emerging American superpower, led the world in the development of the human rights regime. Those same powers ensured that the emerging framework would have a Western bias, and provide a tool for the spread of Western interests and values. On close inspection, however, this narrative sits uneasily with the historical events and circumstances of the time. It is true that 'freedom' became the rallying call for Americans and the Allied powers under the leadership of President Franklin D Roosevelt. However, by many accounts, in the immediate months following the end of World War II, Roosevelt's 'four freedoms' speech was relegated to the status of wartime rhetoric. Some have argued that at the end of World War II the Great Powers sought to arrest the rising interest in the development of human rights norms, or to restrict it at the very least.

[. . .]

Early resistance to the international codification of human rights by the world's leading powers demonstrates a crucial point: there is nothing inherent in human rights as a concept, nor the human rights system, that provides a tool for Western cultural hegemony. In fact, one could argue that the case is quite the opposite. In the mid-twentieth century, the Great Powers knew the formalisation of specific requirements on all states to observe individual human rights would require significant abrogation of authority. For Britain and the Soviet Union, a doctrine of human rights would pose a fundamental challenge to essential political orientations: colonialism in one instance, and Stalinism in the other. For the United States, formal recognition of human rights would bring the discriminatory domestic policies towards African-Americans and the indigenous population to international scrutiny.

[. . .]

State delegates to the first meeting of the United Nations found themselves under intense public pressure to include a precise mandate for human rights in the organisation's charter. The United States took steps to indicate some recognition of public sentiment. Under-Secretary of State Sumner Welles made a public statement guaranteeing that nothing would be finalised in the United Nations Charter until all countries absent from the Dumbarton Oaks discussions were given opportunity to express their views. Thus, in subsequent symposia held in San Francisco, smaller and less powerful countries capitalised on the opportunity to contribute. The governments of Cuba, Egypt, France, Guatemala, India, Lebanon, Mexico, New Zealand, Norway, Paraguay, and South Africa submitted amendments to the Dumbarton proposals that called for the explicit recognition of human rights as the motivating and organising principle of the United Nations. After two months of deliberation, the Great Powers decided they could not ignore the extraordinary amount of public pressure to reformulate the Charter proposal. By the time the Charter of the United Nations was signed on 26 June 1945, the language of human rights had been mainstreamed throughout the document. This occurred not under the leadership or insistence of the powerful, but through the strong sentiment and persistence of small and less powerful states.

Article 68 of the Charter charged the Economic and Social Council (ECOSOC) with the task of establishing the Human Rights Commission (HRC). Soon after, ECOSOC developed the terms of reference that would guide the work of the Council, mandating it to submit proposals, recommendations, and reports regarding the establishment of an 'international bill of rights'. But when the HRC met for the first time in January 1947, diverging interpretations came to light regarding ECOSOC's proposal. The United States and the Soviet Union insisted that the terminology 'international bill of rights' required the Human Rights Commission to develop a declaration of human rights principles. Other delegates – according to Morsink, a majority of states – were sure that ECOSOC's recommendations meant nothing less than a legal covenant, with implementation machinery attached.

The imperative of dealing with intense political and social problems of the time led delegates from smaller and less powerful states to insist on a declaration with authoritative character. Indian delegate Hansa Metha expressed distaste at the prospects of 'a vague resolution including mystic and psychological principles'. She argued that the United Nations Charter and pursuant ECOSOC resolutions called for a human rights declaration with 'imperative character' that should be 'binding on all Member States'. Fernand Dehousse of Belgium argued that an 'academic vote' for an inspirational statement 'might even endanger the Commission's existence and would cause immense disappointment to a world that was awaiting positive solutions capable of influencing human destiny'.

As elected Chair of the Human Rights Commission, Eleanor Roosevelt had the final word, instructing members that any written formulation of rights 'should not be drawn up in such as way as to give the impression that Governments would have a contractual obligation to guarantee human rights'. This unequivocal position was something of an enigma from the woman who had developed a reputation as the 'first lady' of the world for her arrant dedication to the human rights cause following the end of World War II. Her ruling provides an insight into the realpolitik of late 1940s America. According to Waltz, Roosevelt did not enjoy great popularity in the decision-making circles of her own country, where right-wing opponents to the idea of human rights held significant political sway. Known as the 'Old Guard', these men expressed concern that a human rights doctrine would disturb the balance of power between state and federal government in the United States, and impede the president's capacity to make international agreements. At root, this anxiety may have more accurately reflected an implicit recognition that a robust and binding human rights system would fundamentally alter the United States' racial hierarchy. Despite strong personal identification with the human rights cause, Roosevelt's public position on the Human Rights Commission was thus constrained by the US State Department. The final document adopted by the United Nations General Assembly in 1948 was a non-binding declaration of principles. This reflected the intents of the

US and Soviet governments, and occurred in spite of the demands of many smaller and less powerful states for de jure human rights requirements.

Importantly, however, despite a lack of legal clout, the Universal Declaration has taken on great political weight as the apex of rights-based standards required for meaningful participation in global civil society. It is not outside the boundaries of logic to argue that, in some ways, the non-prescriptive nature of the UDHR has worked in favour of the human rights cause. As a proclamation of internationally agreed-upon standards, the Universal Declaration is available for re-appropriation in diverse cultures and societies all around the world. While human rights are formalised at the international level, they are protected first and foremost at the local level. The implementation of human rights at the local level can take various forms according to different priorities of reality – so long as the normative function of the right is maintained. Furthermore, the non-legal nature of the Universal Declaration has served as a safeguard against dogmatic reification. As such, human rights are widely understood to be constantly evolving, with the dynamic to respond to new rights-based problems and challenges as they emerge within the variables of time and place. The Universal Declaration has been the catalyst for many finely nuanced treaties, protocols, and conventions, which together form a sophisticated comprehensive framework on international human rights. This reflects the declaration's normative function and content, which has allowed it to stand alone in international relations as an independent statement of ethics.

The temporal history of the human rights project defies its subjection as a Western imposition. In dealing with the emerging international framework in the mid-twentieth century, the Great Powers sought to ensure the outcome was as non-impacting as possible. The protection of individual human rights that transcended race, ethnicity, religion (and later, gender), implied an abrogation of state and colonialist authority; this was a point on which the Great Powers were unwilling to negotiate. What this suggests is that it is a weak human rights system that fosters Western cultural hegemony – rather than a robust system of legally sanctified rights. And indeed, in 1953, only four years after the Universal Declaration of Human Rights was adopted by the General Assembly, the United States announced its formal intention to retreat from participating in the further development of the international human rights system. The US superpower was completely removed from the development of the International Covenant on Civil and Political Rights (ICCPR), and took nearly thirty years to ratify the document after its adoption in the General Assembly in 1966. The historical master narrative of universal human rights thus obscures a crucial detail: the most forthright proponents of a robust human rights system following World War II were not the Great Powers, but rather small states and representatives of non-Western countries.

Human Rights Discourse in Practice: The One Million Signatures Campaign

The One Million Signatures Campaign was launched in August 2006, presenting one of the clearest expressions of human rights activism in the history of the Iranian women's movement. The method and aim of the campaign are clear: after the collection of one million local Iranian signatures in protest of all discriminatory laws on women, the petition will be presented to parliament, along with a draft bill to bring all local laws into line with international standards on women's rights and gender equality. The state has predictably responded to the Campaign with claims that it is both 'un-Islamic' and 'un-Iranian'. Many of the women involved have been accused of 'endangering national security' and spreading 'propaganda against the state'. Underlying this reaction is the charge that expressions of solidarity with international norms could not possibly represent a truly home-grown initiative.

[. . .]

Despite the regime's insistence to the contrary, the One Million Signatures Campaign comprises a diverse cross-section of Iranian women. Feminists of both secular and religious orientations back the campaign in principle and action. The campaign may not represent the dissolution of differences between secular feminists and Islamic feminists, but it does indicate the will of both groups to move away from ideological idealism in favour of a common strategic umbrella with clearly defined goals. The human rights discourse expressed through the One Million Signatures Campaign represents a practical move beyond the boundaries of the Islamic/secular feminist debate towards a common call for universal standards on gender equality.

Campaign beginnings

The birth of the One Million Signatures Campaign can be traced to the 22nd Khordad event in 2006. Following the state's crackdown on the International Women's Day celebration in March, some members of the women's movement questioned the wisdom of holding another public event to commemorate the June protest. Rumours circulated that security forces had been granted authority to shoot at all future protests. A debate over the efficacy of public gatherings played out among women of both secular and Islamic feminist leanings. According to secular feminist Jelveh Javaheri, Islamic feminists such as Shahla Sherkat said that 'holding public gatherings was futile and furthermore, radical'. Secular feminists countered that even if only a small number of women turned out to commemorate the 22nd Khordad, it was better for the women's movement to maintain a public presence and not back down in the face of state intimidation.

Under the auspices of a handful of secular feminists who, Javaheri admits, felt 'very alone', the 22nd Khordad event went ahead. In a bold move, the protestors called upon the state to re-introduce CEDAW into parliamentary debate. The reaction of the regime was predictable: severe state-sanctioned violence forced the women to disperse. Although this did not come as a complete surprise to secular feminists, the extent of the brutality meted out by security forces, as well as the clandestine procedures that followed, caused perceptible shifts in secular feminist philosophy.

Prominent activist Parvin Ardalan insisted the event made secular feminists 'more determined than ever to overcome the atmosphere of fear', and noted a desire among established feminists to empower women in the wider community, encouraging them to join the struggle for gender equality. At the same time, however, she observed a number of revisions taking place within the secular feminist camp. Given the clear majority of hardliners in parliament, secular feminists decided that to press on with demands for constitutional revision 'seemed out of the question'. This decision held great significance in terms of secular and Islamic women's abilities to work under a common strategic umbrella. Islamic feminists consistently encouraged women's rights activists to maintain a slow pace of reform by exploring the capacities of the existing constitution to accommodate change. Following the brutal crackdown on the 22nd Khordad event in June 2006, secular feminists appeared ready to explore this option. The shift contributed to an emerging resolve among secular feminists to develop a long-term strategy for change – rather than engage in short-term initiatives such as public protests and gatherings. What women needed, they argued, was an ongoing, procedural approach to the issue of gender equality in Iran – a clearly defined modus operandi. Reflecting on the isolation felt during the 22nd Khordad event, secular feminists began to stress the need for collective action. According to Ardalan, 'we learned that in order to achieve nonviolent activism, collaboration with other groups [and] synchronisation of demands and methodologies would strengthen the women's movement'.

This realisation of the need for collective action provided the catalyst for the One Million Signatures Campaign. In late 2006, secular feminists began to explore the potential benefits of activism on a much broader scale than had previously been attempted. In a new round of dialogue with their Islamic counterparts, a general predilection emerged for a framework in which feminists of diverse ideological groundings could work together to call for an end to discrimination against women. Initially, there was no 'solid agreement' as to what this framework would look like. Just as secular women had modified their actions to investigate a more systematic approach to change, they also presented a challenge to the conventions of Islamic feminist methodology by emphasising the need to move away from a heavy focus on women in government. Women had learned from experience, argued Ardalan, that in order to 'have room to manoeuvre in our patriarchal society, we have no choice but to create it ourselves'. One of the first official statements of the One Million Signatures Campaign was in line with Ardalan's sentiments: 'The true path to achieve equality will not be paved though the existing power structure or a dialogue solely with men and women in positions of power'.

According to Sotoudeh, however, religiously-oriented women were initially hesitant to become involved in a project that took the focus away from women's roles in government. Only gradually did Islamic feminists come to a point of collaboration, cooperation, and support. Ardalan attributes this coming-together to a 'minimal commonality' agreed to by secular and Islamic women, namely, that in order for women to enjoy full quality of life in the Islamic state, all civil codes in which women are treated unequally to men would need to be changed. That is, an incremental approach to arguing for changes law by law was not enough. With gender equality as their goal, Iranian feminists started to focus on the overall picture of women's status in the Islamic Republic, and in doing so demanded a comprehensive review of the state's gender ideology. Under the One Million Signatures banner, this review would necessitate bringing all local laws into line with international standards on gender equality.

On the 27th of August 2006 a public seminar was held in Tehran to officially launch the One Million Signatures Campaign. The seminar was publicised throughout the city under the title 'The Effect of Laws on Women's Lives'. Almost immediately, security forces were deployed to stop people from entering the town meeting hall where the seminar was scheduled to take place. But this time the women were ready. With loudspeakers and makeshift lecterns, they held the seminar in the street outside the meeting hall. Shirin Ebadi held the floor in her legal expertise, while other members of the women's movement distributed pamphlets on the campaign. The pamphlets contained information in lay terms about civil laws and the unequal status of women in the Iranian legal code. Providing numerous anecdotes and examples of the disproportionate weight placed on women's shoulders under the existing laws, the pamphlets became prime tools for activism. With the setting-in-motion of the One Million Signatures Campaign, the Iranian women's movement was, by many accounts, 'given new life'.

The primary goal

The One Million Signatures Campaign is characterised by one overarching goal: the removal of all discriminatory laws against women in Iran. Campaign guidelines are clear on what the basis of new laws should be. The petition of the campaign states:

> The Iranian government is a signatory to several international human rights conventions, and accordingly is required to bring its legal code in line with international standards. The most important international human rights standard calls for elimination of discrimination based on gender, ethnicity, [and] religion ... The undersigned ask for the elimination of all forms of legal discrimination against women in Iranian law and ask legislators to review and reform existing laws based on the government's commitments to international human rights conventions.

This excerpt reveals a key strategy of the One Million Signatures Campaign, which emphasises the Iranian government's existing commitments to international human rights treaties. While Iran has rejected the Convention on the Elimination of All Forms of Discrimination against Women on the grounds that it is 'un-Islamic' and 'un-Iranian', the state is already signatory to a number of other human rights documents that precede CEDAW in calling for equality of the sexes. The Universal Declaration of Human Rights is clear on this point: in the preamble, Member States of the United Nations affirm 'faith in fundamental human rights, in the dignity and worth of the human person and in the equal rights of men and women', and Article 2 specifies that 'everyone is entitled to all the rights and freedoms set forth in this Declaration, without distinction of any kind', including sex. The International Covenants on human rights follow suit. Pursuant to Article 3 of both the ICCPR and the ICESCR, as a signatory to these documents, Iran has pledged to 'undertake to ensure the equal right of men and women to the enjoyment of all civil and political rights set forth' in each respective treaty. In addition, Iran was one of the 189 states to unanimously adopt the Beijing Declaration and Platform for Action in 1995, signalling its commitment to 'take all necessary measures to eliminate all forms of discrimination against women and the girl-child and remove all obstacles to gender equality and the advancement and empowerment of women'.

According to Ebadi this shift, from focusing on CEDAW to highlighting the government's existing human rights commitments, was a deliberate strategic move on behalf of the women's movement. Indeed, it is advantageous in a number of ways. Although CEDAW may be more specific and deeper in scope than other human rights documents, it is not the only avenue in the international treaty system available to redress gender inequality and discrimination against women. Within the One Million Signatures Campaign, Iranian feminists focus on the immediacy of their situation, while at the same time maintaining CEDAW as a long-term goal. By calling on the state to live up to its current commitments in the international framework – the UDHR, ICESCR, ICCPR and Beijing Platform for Action – the women behind the campaign are laying the groundwork for future adoption of CEDAW. Furthermore, by highlighting Iran's status as signatory to various human rights documents, Iranian feminists challenge the state's logic that internationally defined women's rights are inapplicable to the Iranian context because of a supposed incompatibility with Islam. What is at issue is not Islam per se, but desires of the conservative elite to maintain societal control via pre-modern patriarchal practices. The Iranian legal code is derived from traditional Islamic jurisprudence. Yet interpretations of shari'a have been debated and challenged for decades, not only by secular-minded Muslims, but also senior Islamic clerics. Both religious and secular members of the campaign have stressed the congruence between the demand to remove all discriminatory laws against women, and principles of the Islamic faith. This sentiment is expressed clearly in the following statement by campaign activist Fatemah Nejati:

> Talking about the Campaign among family and friends resulted in a variety of questions regarding its goals ... Of course, I defended the women's rights movement of my country, as well as the inalienable rights of Muslim women ... Since I believe that Islam is a religion that defends justice and equality ... why should Muslim women be quiet in the face of injustice? Are we less deserving than other women? Since we are Muslims, does this mean we should be without rights?

[...]

Under the One Million Signatures banner, this broadening of feminist outreach has been matched by a broadening of the women's rights agenda. Before the launch of the campaign, Iranian feminists across secular and religious boundaries tended to lobby for the reform of individual laws. The Stop Stoning Forever Campaign is a good example of issue-specific activism. By calling on the state to remove all discrimina-tory laws on women, in line with its existing obligations to international human rights treaties, the One Million Signatures Campaign deals more comprehensively with the status of women in the public and private realms. Addressing the status of women through a human rights paradigm presents a systemic view on gender-based discrimination. Ebadi is clear in describing the campaign as a demand for 'complete equality' between men and women – not limited equality expressed in separate and distinct legal clauses.

42

World Culture in the World Polity

A Century of International Non-Governmental Organization

John Boli and George M. Thomas

For a century and more, the world has constituted a singular polity. By this we mean that the world has been conceptualized as a unitary social system, increasingly integrated by networks of exchange, competition, and cooperation, such that actors have found it "natural" to view the whole world as their arena of action and discourse. Such a conceptualization reifies the world polity implicitly in the often unconscious adoption of this cultural frame by politicians, businesspeople, travelers, and activists, and explicitly in the discourse of intellectuals, policy analysts, and academicians.

Like all polities, the world polity is constituted by a distinct culture – a set of fundamental principles and models, mainly ontological and cognitive in character, defining the nature and purposes of social actors and action. Like all cultures, world culture becomes embedded in social organization, especially in organizations operating at the global level. Because most of these organizations are INGOs, we can identify fundamental principles of world culture by studying structures, purposes, and operations of INGOs. By studying INGOs across social sectors, we can make inferences about the structure of world culture. By studying the promotion of world-cultural principles that INGOs are centrally involved in developing, we can see how INGOs shape the frames that orient other actors, including states. […]

Original publication details: John Boli and George M. Thomas, "World Culture in the World Polity: A Century of International Non-Governmental Organization," in *American Sociological Review*, 1997. pp. 172–3, 174, 179–82, 187–8.

An Historical Overview of the INGO Population

Data

Since 1850 more than 25,000 private, not-for-profit organizations with an international focus have debuted on the world stage. They include the Pan American Association of Ophthalmology, International Exhibitions Bureau, Commission for the Geological Map of the World, International Catholic Child Bureau, International Tin Council, and Tug of War International Federation. Most are highly specialized, drawing members worldwide from a particular occupation, technical field, branch of knowledge, industry, hobby, or sport to promote and regulate their respective areas of concern. Only a few, such as the Scout Movement, International Olympic Committee, International Red Cross, and World Wildlife Fund, are widely known.

We analyze data on 5,983 organizations founded between 1875 and 1988. They constitute the entire population of INGOs classified as genuinely international bodies by the Union of International Associations (UIA) in its *Yearbook of International Organizations*. […]

Data quality and coding issues

The UIA limits INGOs to not-for-profit, non-governmental organizations (TNCs and IGOs are excluded). They vary in size from a few dozen members from only three countries to millions of members from close to 200 countries. About half of the INGOs in our data base have members from at least 25 countries, 20 percent have members from 50 or more countries, and only 11 percent have members from fewer than eight countries. […]

Basic historical patterns

Figure 42.1 presents the number of INGOs founded and dissolved in each year between 1875 and 1973. Not-for-profit international organizing grew rapidly in the latter part of the nineteenth century, with about 10 new organizations emerging each year during the 1890s. The population burgeoned after the turn of the century, reaching a peak of 51 foundings in 1910. The severe collapse after that point led to a low of four foundings in 1915. Swift recovery after World War I yielded a period of fairly steady growth followed by some decline during the 1930s that preceded another steep fall going into World War II.

Following the war, international organizing exploded. By 1947 over 90 organizations a year were being founded, a pace that was maintained and even surpassed through the 1960s. The pattern for dissolved INGOs is similar, indicating a generally steady proportion of INGOs that eventually dissolved, but revealing peaks of fragility among organizations founded just before each of the wars.

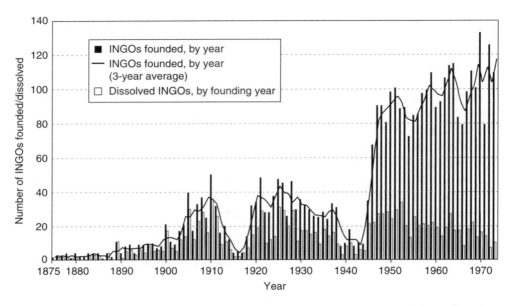

Figure 42.1 International non-governmental organizations: INGOs founded and founding dates of dissolved INGOs, 1875 to 1973.
Source: Yearbook of International Organizations (Brussels: Union of International Associations, 24th edn. 1984–5, 27th edn. 1988–9).

INGO foundings and dissolutions thus match the general "state of the world" rather well, rising in periods of expansion and declining rapidly in times of crisis, with the declines beginning shortly before the outbreaks of the world wars. [...]

World Development, INGOs, and Capitalist and Interstate Systems

Global organizing proceeds in mutually reinforcing tension with the expansion of the nation-state system. INGOs began to proliferate during the heyday of nationalism and European imperialism; bringing the last "unclaimed" regions of the globe into the world economy and under the jurisdiction of states made the notions of "one world" and "one history" structurally compelling.

This dialectic is further evident in the effects of the world wars. The precipitous decline in INGO foundings after 1910 reflects the dominance of states for most of that decade, but the war also strengthened the conception of the world as a single polity and prompted expanded INGO (and IGO) efforts to organize the world polity. After a similar cycle in the 1930s and 1940s, a much broader discursive space for INGOs opened up as global technical and infrastructural resources increased exponentially. World-polity organizing jumped to a higher level than ever before, just as the independent nation-state form was adopted by or imposed on the rest of the world.

The dialectic between world-polity and national-level organization is also evident in the relationship between IGOs and INGOs. Many IGOs were founded as INGOs and later co-opted by states, including such major bodies as the World Meteorological Organization, the International Labor Organization, and the World Tourism Organization. Moreover, INGOs have often been instrumental in founding new IGOs and shaping IGO activities. Thousands of INGOs have consultative status with agencies of the United Nations – over 900 with the Economic and Social Council alone – and most IGOs engage relevant INGOs as providers of information, expertise, and policy alternatives. IGO authority is not relinquished to INGOs, but IGO decisions are heavily influenced by INGO experts and lobbyists. [...]

INGOs as Enactors and Carriers of World Culture

Almost all INGOs originate and persist via voluntary action by individual actors. INGOs have explicit, rationalized goals. They operate under strong norms of open membership and democratic decision-making. They seek, in a general sense, to spread "progress" throughout the world: to encourage safer and more efficient technical systems, more powerful knowledge structures, better care of the body, friendly competition and fair play. To achieve their goals they emphasize communication, knowledge, consensual values and decision-making, and individual commitment. Following are five basic world-cultural principles that underlie INGO ideologies and structures: universalism, individualism, rational voluntaristic authority, human purposes of rationalizing progress, and world citizenship.

Universalism

Humans everywhere have similar needs and desires, can act in accordance with common principles of authority and action, and share common goals. In short, human nature, agency, and purpose are universal, and this universality underlies the many variations in social forms. Most INGOs are explicit about this – any interested person can become an active member, and everyone everywhere is a potential beneficiary of INGO activity.

Universalism is evident also in the breadth of INGOs' claims about what they do. Physics and pharmacology are presumed to be valid everywhere. Techniques for playing better chess are not country-specific. Red Cross aid will alleviate suffering in Africa as well as Asia. Across every sector, the purposes and means of action promoted by INGOs are assumed to be useful and meaningful everywhere.

A world not characterized by universalism does not coalesce as a singular polity; rather, it develops distinct subworld polities (societies, civilizations, empires) across which joint mobilization is unlikely. At the opposite extreme, a world state would thoroughly incorporate and regulate individuals and organizations – universalism would prevail but it would be bureaucratically absorbed.

The present world polity lies between these two extremes. Neither segmental nor ad hoc, neither is it *étatisée;* legal-bureaucratic authority is partitioned among multiple states. The principle of universalism that INGOs embody remains culturally autonomous because INGOs operate in the interstices of this decentralized structure.

Individualism

Most INGOs accept as members only individuals or associations of individuals; the main exceptions are trade and industry bodies, which often have firms as members. Individualism is also evident in their structures: INGOs use democratic, one-person–one-vote decision-making procedures, they assess fees on members individually, and they downplay national and other corporate identities in their conferences and publications. In the world-view embodied by INGOs, individuals are the only "real" actors; collectivities are essentially assemblages of individuals.

The combination of universalism and individualism may undermine traditional collectivities like the family or clan, but it also strengthens the one truly universalistic collectivity – humanity as a whole. INGOs habitually invoke the common good of humanity as a goal. The cultural dynamic at work parallels that characterizing national polities: As cultural constructs, the individual and the nation reinforce one another. In recent times, this centuries-old dynamic has shifted to the global level.

Rational voluntaristic authority

INGOs activate a particular cultural model when they organize globally, debate principles and models, and attempt to influence other actors. This model holds that responsible individuals acting collectively through rational procedures can determine cultural rules that are just, equitable, and efficient, and that no external authority is required for their legitimation. Such "self-authorization" runs counter to Weber's analysis of authority as forms of domination because INGOs cannot dominate in the conventional sense. INGOs have little sanctioning power, yet they act as if they were authorized in the strongest possible terms. They make rules and expect them to be followed; they plead their views with states or transnational corporations and express moral condemnation when their pleas go unheeded.

INGO authority is thus informal – cultural, not organizational. It is the agency presumed to inhere in rational individuals organizing for purposive action. Its basis can only be the diffuse principles of world culture, for INGO authority does not flow from any legal-bureaucratic or supernatural source.

Rational voluntarism is encouraged by the decentralized character of formal authority; at the world level, it is practiced by states and transnational corporations as well. For example, because sovereignty implies that no state has authority over any other, collective actions by states can occur only via rational voluntarism. This is why most IGOs, like INGOs, have resolutely democratic formal structures. It also helps explain why the legal-bureaucratic authority of states is brought into play to enforce INGO conceptions and rules.

Human purposes: Dialectics of rationalizing progress

The rational character of INGOs is evident in their purposive orientation, formalized structures, and attention to procedures. INGOs in science, medicine, technical fields, and infrastructure activities are engaged in purely rationalized and rationalizing activity; almost all other INGOs rely on science, expertise, and professionalization in their operations and programs. What INGOs seek is, in essence, rational progress – not the crude nineteenth-century idea that steam engines and railroads would lead to heaven on earth, but the more diffuse and embedded concept of "development" that now prevails. This concept includes not only economic growth but also individual self-actualization, collective security, and justice.

At all levels, progress is assumed to depend on rationalization. Rational social action is the route to equality, comfort, and the good life. Rational production and distribution achieve all sorts of collective purposes. The scientific method, technique, monetarization, logical analysis – these are the favored *modi operandi*. These instruments of progress may often be criticized, but they are built into worldwide institutions and the ideology of development.

Rationalization, however, has another face. A tension operates between the rational and the irrational that strengthens both. Disenchantment of the world via rationalization endows the agents of disenchantment with increasing substance and sacredness; the apparent failure of actors to behave entirely rationally leads to theorizing about actors' irrational selves or cultures. Rationalized actors are thus culturally constituted as having complex "non-rational" subjectivities that are more primordial than objectified rationality. À la Nietzsche, the irrational becomes the arena of authenticity. Moreover, this face of rationalization launches widespread movements claiming to be anti-science, anti-Western, or postmodern: Western science, capitalism, and bureaucracy are imperialistic, dehumanizing forces against which authentic peoples must struggle to maintain their true, non-rational natures.

The rational/irrational tension thus generates conflict, but the irrational and subjective are continually channeled into rationalized activities and forms (e.g., revolution, UFO cults). Movements of self-exploration and expression, though rhetorically rejecting rationalism, also are rationalized (transcendental meditation becomes a test-improvement technique). Thus we find sports, leisure, spiritual, and psychological INGOs in abundance.

World citizenship

The principles discussed so far come together in the construct of world citizenship. Everyone is an individual endowed with certain rights and subject to certain obligations; everyone is capable of voluntaristic actions that seek rational solutions to social problems; therefore, everyone is a citizen of the world polity. World citizenship rules infuse each individual with the authority to pursue particularistic interests, preferably in organizations, while also authorizing individuals to promote collective goods defined in largely standardized ways.

World citizenship is strongly egalitarian. Individuals vary in their capacities, resources, and industry, but all have the same basic rights and duties. Correspondingly, only fully democratic governance structures are consistent with world citizenship. "Autocratic" tendencies are decried even within some INGOs (e.g., Greenpeace and the International Olympic Committee).

World citizenship is prominently codified in the Universal Declaration of Human Rights, which depicts a global citizen whose rights transcend national boundaries. The Declaration insists that states ensure the rights of their citizens and even that every human has the right to a national citizenship. In the absence of a world state, however, these obligations cannot be imposed on states. Acting as the primary carriers of world culture, INGOs translate the diffuse global identity and authority of world citizenship into specific rights, claims, and prescriptions for state behavior.

Here again we observe that states sometimes act as agents of informal world-polity authority. World citizens must turn to national states for protection of their rights, and INGOs back them up in the process. Increasingly, individuals need not be national citizens to make claims on the state; noncitizen residents of many countries have extensive rights almost equivalent to those of citizens, simply because they are human.

The cultural principles *re*-presented by INGOs are also integral to the world economy and state system, but INGOs push them to extremes. Their discourse is often critical of economic and political structures, stigmatizing "ethnocentric" (non-universalistic) nationalism and "exploitative" (inegalitarian) capitalism. INGOs dramatize violations of world-cultural principles, such as state maltreatment of citizens and corporate disregard for the sacredness of nature. Such examples illustrate the contested nature of these principles; they are widely known but by no means uncontroversial. [...]

Conclusion

INGOs are built on world-cultural principles of universalism, individualism, rational voluntaristic authority, progress, and world citizenship. Individuals and associations construct rationalized structures with defined goals, some diffuse (world peace, international understanding), but most quite specific and functional. Some INGOs, including sports, human rights, and environmental bodies, dramatically reify the world polity; human rights and environmental INGOs are especially prominent because of their conflicts with states over world-cultural principles. But most INGOs unobtrusively foster intellectual, technical, and economic rationalization that is so thoroughly institutionalized that they are hardly seen as actors, despite the enormous effects they have on definitions of reality, material infrastructure, household products, school texts, and much more.

The decentralization of authority among states facilitates transnational organizing (because centralized barriers to rational voluntarism are weak) and forces transnational organizations to focus their attention on states. Contrary to the claims of global neo-realist theories, states are not always leaders of social change; they can also be followers. In mobilizing around and elaborating world-cultural principles, INGOs lobby, criticize, and convince states to act on those principles, at least in some sectors and with respect to some issues.

How extensively this model of global change applies we cannot say. One of the central tasks for world-polity research is the development of a general theory about the conditions under which INGOs are able to take the initiative *vis-à-vis* states. A related task is the study of INGO relationships with the other major sets of reified world-polity actors, IGOs and transnational corporations. The literature contains many case studies touching on these relationships but little systematic analysis.

If a legal-rational world state emerges, much of the INGO population is likely to be co-opted to staff its bureaucracy and advise on policy decisions. To this point, we think of the operation of the world polity only as a world proto-state. A singular authority structure is lacking, states monopolize the legitimated use of violence, and states jealously guard their sovereignty. Nevertheless, the world as a proto-state has shared cultural categories, principles of authority, and universally constructed individuals who, as world proto-citizens, assume the authority to pursue goals that transcend national and local particularisms. More often than is commonly acknowledged, the resulting organizations prove to be effective. If they are absorbed in a formal global authority structure in the future, it may well be said that the road to a world state was paved by the rational voluntarism of INGOs.

43

Closing the Corruption Casino
The Imperatives of a Multilateral Approach

Peter Eigen

It is with very real pleasure that I accepted the invitation of our hosts to speak at this, the opening of Global Forum II, at a time when all the players in the battle against corruption face tremendous challenges.

In facing those challenges, it is imperative that we never forget the victims of corruption, from the plundering and misuse of rich oil resources by Sani Abacha to the wilful abuse of a siege economy by Slobodan Milosevic.

- While the world called for Milosevic to be arrested on war crimes, prosecutors in Serbia arrested him on charges of corruption and abuse of power. More than US $70 million has been located in Swiss bank accounts linked to the Milosevic regime. The people of Serbia have not only lost the lives of many of those closest to them, but have at the same time been swindled by his brutal regime.
- Abacha, who ruled Nigeria until his death in June 1998, stripped Nigeria of at least US $7 billion, a sum vast enough to begin to turn the tide of the HIV AIDS epidemic, a tragedy that is threatening the lives of a new generation in sub-Saharan Africa from the moment each child emerges from a mother's womb.

How can we not act when the proceeds of Abacha's money-laundering remain in the vaults of banks in Britain and Switzerland? This is a challenge we must address in The Hague this week. Another is to ensure that the launch of the Euro does not descend into a carnival of money-laundering.

Original publication details: Peter Eigen, "Closing the Corruption Casino: The Imperatives of a Multilateral Approach," opening address at Global Forum II, The Hague, Netherlands, May 28, 2001. Reproduced with permission from P. Eigen.

To defeat the scourge of money-laundering, we must act together, and I speak from the standpoint of an NGO, Transparency International, which began with two simple beliefs.

First, that corruption – and the struggle against it – was an issue that stands above the divides of party politics, and so one on which all who are concerned for their country's future and the well-being of their people can and should come together.

Second, that the way to progress was through dialogue and involvement rather than the more traditional NGO approach of exposure and confrontation, that we had to raise awareness and build a coalition of all three sectors – government, civil society and the private sector – both at the national and international level.

Today, this coalition approach has taken hold all over the world.

Yet at the outset we were viewed with suspicion from many sides. Despite the fact that many of our founders are from the south, critics in the south accused us of a "developed world agenda", of blaming corruption on the south. Critics in the north liked to imagine that – despite our name, Transparency – we had a hidden agenda and were captives of entrenched interests of one kind or another. Some governments were distinctly nervous at the thought of an NGO coming anywhere near the institutions of which they were members. Within the NGO community, it was said that we were siding with those we should be criticising in the streets. The then leadership of the World Bank wanted nothing whatsoever to do with us. Ours has been a delicate tightrope-walking act.

Our partnership with the government of the Netherlands and the Organising Committee of Global Forum II is further evidence of the way we can all work together effectively and creatively. And I hope to see this partnership given even more coherence in two years' time when the Global Forum and the International Anti-Corruption Conference will be held jointly in Seoul, as I very much hope they will be, rather than being split between different venues, The Hague and Prague (in October), as they are this year.

Looking at your agenda, it is important for all to recognise that there is even more at stake than fighting corruption alone. For the set of instruments we develop and use to combat corruption – accountability, transparency and the involvement of the private sector and civil society – are precisely the instruments that:

- build more efficient, effective and rational government;
- secure the state against infiltration by organised crime;
- protect human rights;
- alleviate poverty through unlocking the development process and access to essential services such as health and education;
- build public belief in the institutions that serve them; and
- forge public confidence in their governments and in the way in which they are governed.

So there is very much more at stake here this week than the essential tasks of containing the petty corruption of junior civil servants and pocket-lining by senior decision-makers. Because corruption is such a broad and cross-cutting issue, confronting corruption is about building a better, fairer and more just world.

And this is why it involves everyone. It is why a strategy built solely on enforcing law and order – important though this is – will never yield the results we all aspire to. No one, I suggest, wants a civil service cowered by fear and nervous about taking initiatives. Civil servants, too, need to feel that they are a part of the creative process.

Back in March, the chief notary of the Russian Federation, Anatoly Tikhenko, was gunned down near his house in Moscow in what was described by Moscow radio station Ekho Moskvy as a "paid killing", a reaction to his efforts to bring increased transparency and accountability to the corruption-ridden notary business. PricewaterhouseCoopers reckons that Russia loses US $10 billion a year in potential foreign investments because of corruption, inadequate accounting procedures, weaknesses in its legal system and lack of reliable financial information. And yet, as recently as March 2, Russia's Interior Minister Vladimir Rushailo denied allegations that 70 per cent of all Russian officials were corrupt with the response that "you should not confuse corruption with bribe taking". Only those with links to organised criminal gangs, he argued, should be regarded as corrupt.

Our movement is not, I repeat not, anti-governments. We do not argue that the problem of corruption rests solely with public servants. Far from it. The private sector, too, shares responsibility by using bribery in its interactions with officials; the public at large is part of the problem, willing to pay bribes or acquiescing in conduct it should not accept. The ethics of the public service reflect in large measure those of society as a whole. So that this is not a struggle of "us" against "them": rather it is a struggle of all of us together to build stronger ethics among society at large.

Nor is countering corruption only a priority for developing countries and for countries in transition. There is a need for continuous improvement in every society as, in a rapidly changing world, events either prove the fallibility of institutions or call into question the reliability of institutional arrangements that may have functioned in the past. Among the country reports TI has prepared for this gathering are two on countries in the north – the Netherlands and Canada – and each points to shortcomings in need of attention.

Responding to the challenge, and working with civil society, the private sector and the governments of Tanzania and Uganda, we developed the concept of the National Integrity System. Available here today is a new, expanded edition of the TI Source Book, which describes this in detail. It is entitled "Confronting Corruption: The Elements of a National Integrity System", and I commend it to each and every one of you.

The approach is an holistic way of looking at the institutions and practices that collectively assure a society of its basic integrity. By looking at these institutions – the executive, the legislature, the judiciary, the watchdog agencies, the mass media, the private sector and civil society – we have a framework within which to study the pluses and minuses in accountability and transparency. It enables us all to diagnose weaknesses and to address them in context and in a co-ordinated way. It provides, if you like, a road map for those who are serious about addressing their country's deficiencies.

This is why TI, with the encouragement and support of the Organising Committee and the countries concerned, has prepared some 19 "country studies" in which the national integrity system has been audited in countries as diverse as Canada and Colombia. Responding to the challenge, the government of Trinidad and Tobago even conducted an audit of its own system. Along with the civil society audits, this too is available here this week.

Let's take the Netherlands where most of the elements of Transparency International's National Integrity System are in place. Even here the country study identifies Dutch blind spots, such as "a broad reluctance concerning managing conflict-of-interest situations and monitoring assets, income, liabilities and business interests of politicians and civil servants as well as political parties". The Netherlands also lacks an adequate system of financial disclosure, and in the private sector there is very limited public involvement to secure integrity. "Business corruption gets no political or judicial attention."

The whole exercise comes together in an overview that draws out the common threads across the country studies, charting successes and shortcomings and setting an agenda for us all to address – all, north, south, east and west.

Why, you may ask, should an NGO like TI undertake such a mission? The answer is that we believe it is incumbent on modern NGOs to join in the search for solutions. Not to be content with identifying problems and calling for remedies, but entering the more challenging area of creative dialogue and doing what we can to assist the search for appropriate responses.

But corruption has no respect for national boundaries. In an increasingly globalised world, corruption seriously distorts economic activity and denies people at large the benefits of their efforts. The scourge of corruption has to be confronted through increased cross-border co-operation.

This is why the OECD Convention outlawing the bribing of foreign public officials to win or retain business is so important. Developing countries never stood a chance of confronting corruption until the exporting countries agreed – albeit for their own reasons – to co-operate to criminalise such conduct and to end the obscenity of granting tax deductions for bribes.

It is why there have to be faster and more effective ways of returning to their rightful owners the contents of national coffers looted by former leaders. And why there is concern that money frozen in European and US bank accounts still lingers there while limitation periods run.

It is why it is unacceptable for countries to grant "safe havens" to their citizens when they are accused of perpetrating serious acts of corruption elsewhere, the more so where that citizen has held a position of high responsibility. And why there is concern that countries that insist on immunity from extradition do not accept the obligation to prosecute such cases in their own courts.

I sincerely hope that the election of the Bush administration does not signal a sea-change in the US stance towards international co-operation against corruption and does not herald a new "unilateral" approach. The recent statement by Paul O'Neill, the US Treasury Secretary, that he has "had cause to re-evaluate the United States' participation in the OECD working group that targets 'harmful tax practices'" has raised alarm bells. I urge the US Government to consult promptly with the other OECD member-states, because US withdrawal from the effort to develop programmes to prevent the misuse of off-shore financial centers would represent a serious blow to effective international co-operation against corruption and money laundering.

Strong multilateral action is required to prevent corrupt officials from hiding their ill-gotten gains in unregulated off-shore accounts. Billions of laundered funds are at stake. Around US$1 trillion of criminal proceeds are laundered through banks world-wide each year, and about half of that is moved through American banks.

More effective international information-sharing regimes and improved mutual legal assistance procedures are required to return that money to its rightful owners in Africa and elsewhere. I would like to remind the Bush Administration that unilateral US efforts to combat corruption through the Foreign Corrupt Practices Act hurt US interests and did not improve the practices of its competitors. It was only when fighting corruption was internationalised in the mid-nineties that progress began to be made. And this was when it was realised that a principal objective was to help developing countries in their efforts to stem the devastation caused – and still being caused – by bribes from the industrial world. It is this concern – for the poor and the marginalised – that is central to the TI coalition.

International money-laundering arrangements are critical, as long as the proceeds of "grand corruption" are spirited away to safe havens. And why there is such concern when French parliamentarians contemplate lifting their anti-money-laundering laws for a period of six months' "grace" during the imminent conversion to the Euro – something that could well trigger the largest money-laundering exercise in the history of the human race.

It is clear that the rush to move dirty money from the Balkans and the CIS from Deutschmarks to US dollars has already begun – and many economists argue that the flood to the dollar of this underworld money accounts for the Euro's continued weakness. The current burst of economic activity in unlikely places across Europe points to a headlong rush to turn dirty money into bricks and mortar – a phenomenon that governments must surely monitor and investigate.

Clearly the proposed United Nations Convention can go some way towards extending the scope and effectiveness of international co-operation. But UN Conventions are less ideal for progressing an anti-corruption campaign. They tend to take years to produce and then only reflect the lowest common denominator. Thereafter they are not monitored and can simply lie in limbo.

This week we hope you will try to ensure that any UN Convention against corruption is limited to areas in which it can be really effective, and is negotiated without delay. Above all, it should not be used as a pretext by governments for failing to take remedial action in the meantime – or to oppose regional initiatives in this field.

The UN Convention could be used as an excuse for inaction. We look to Ministers when they meet on Thursday to recognise this danger and to lock and bolt the door against those who might exploit it.

There has been enough talking about corruption. The need today is for action. This is a government forum. In October, in Prague, the wider anti-corruption movement will come together. And it is not by your rhetoric but by your deeds that your work this week will be judged.

44

Trading Diamonds Responsibly
Institutional Explanations for Corporate Social Responsibility

Franziska Bieri and John Boli

[...]

Conflict or blood diamonds are "rough diamonds used by rebel movements or their allies to finance armed conflict aimed at undermining legitimate governments" (Kimberley Process Secretariat). Conflict diamonds have fueled calamitous civil wars in Angola, Sierra Leone, Liberia, the Democratic Republic of Congo, and Côte D'Ivoire. For most of the 1990s, the conflict diamonds issue went unnoticed. In 1998–1999, however, parallel efforts by a few NGOs and the United Nations catapulted the issue onto the global stage. The result was the Kimberley Process, a series of negotiations involving states, NGOs, and industry but not the United Nations itself. With surprising speed, the KP generated the Kimberley Process Certification Scheme (KPCS) to regulate the diamond trade by certifying that diamonds are conflict-free. "Two and a half years is lightning speed by international negotiating standards" (Smillie). Although the road to success was by no means straight, the conflict diamonds campaign moved unusually quickly from raising concern about the problem to establishing a global mechanism to solve it.

At the heart of the campaign were accusations that De Beers and the Antwerp trading center bore culpability for the brutal civil wars fueled by the diamond trade. NGOs made these powerful actors aware of a new global social problem and redefined long-standing business practices as unacceptable. That they were able to engage the industry and states relatively quickly was a reflection of the growing legitimacy

Original publication details: Franziska Bieri and John Boli, "Trading Diamonds Responsibly: Institutional Explanations for Corporate Social Responsibility", in *Sociological Forum*, 26, 3, September 2011. pp. 510–19. Reproduced with permission from John Wiley & Sons. Note: This text has been edited and all notes and references to third party sources removed. Please refer to the original source text for clarification on what has been omitted.

and value of NGOs as moral guides; industries worldwide were recognizing that it was better to engage with than to fight NGOs.

The campaign efforts were facilitated by the general legitimacy of CSR ideology, which increased greatly in the 1990s. The growth and pervasiveness of CSR ideology in recent times has been documented by various scholars. Vogel gives striking evidence of widespread interest in and acceptance of CSR norms.

> A recent search on Google for "corporate social responsibility" found more than 30,000 sites. More than 15 million pages on the World Wide Web address dimensions of corporate social responsibility, including more than 100,000 pages on corporate websites. Amazon lists 600 books on the subject. More than 1,000 corporations have developed or signed codes of conduct governing dimensions of their social, environmental, and human rights practices, and more than 2,000 firms now issue reports on their CSR practices.

Many global organizations institutionalize CSR principles, such as the UN Global Compact, the International Business Leaders Forum, and Social Accountability International and its SA 8000 standards. In addition, a plethora of surveys have found evidence of growing CSR expectations among consumers. Obviously, opposition to CSR persists, particularly among neoliberal economists; in the early stages of norm construction, contestation is often high, but norms can be powerful even when contested, and their power is normally directly correlated with the prevalence of violations brought to public attention. For CSR norms, violation reporting is increasingly widespread and intense.

In a general sense, growing acceptance of CSR norms is due to economic and cultural forces of globalization. States are deemed increasingly unable to police transnational corporations effectively. At the same time, companies have become more vulnerable to civil-society campaigns, especially those companies that have high-profile global brands. Coupled with the emergence of world citizenship obligations that expand the responsibilities of companies and NGOs, these factors have produced a fertile breeding ground for the global expansion of CSR norms.

Moreover, companies have come to believe that "doing good" can mean "doing well," however dubious that connection may be empirically. According to Vogel, 70% of business executives think that CSR is beneficial to the bottom line, as a result of three processes. First, claims about the virtues of the "triple bottom line" have been widely disseminated in books, popular media treatments, and official documents, such as the European Union's White Paper on CSR. Second, managers who have struggled with conflicting norms regarding profits and philanthropy find that the triple bottom line principle allows them to resolve this conflict. Third, managers have learned that CSR makes sense by observing the success of high-profile companies that have made responsibility a keystone of their operations, such as the Body Shop and Ben and Jerry's.

Apart from these general trends, two specific factors contributed crucially to the positive engagement of the diamond industry with the norms embedded in the KPCS. These factors constitute concrete mechanisms by which the diffuse principles of CSR as world-cultural ideology were "brought home to roost" in the diamond industry. First, social movement organizations in the conflict diamonds campaign defined and pushed the new norms about the responsibilities of the industry, dramatizing their position by publicizing vivid images associating diamonds with destruction. Second, some key industry and state figures were particularly receptive to CSR thinking; as forward-looking leaders, they pulled more reluctant industry and state players into the process.

Global CSR Norms: Opportunities for the Conflict Diamonds Campaign

CSR ideology provided a favorable climate in which the conflict diamonds issue could flourish. Several key developments lead to this conclusion. The first NGO report that sought to put conflict diamonds on the global agenda, *A Rough Trade*, accused De Beers of buying conflict diamonds in violation of UN Security Council Resolution 1173, which had been passed in June 1998. *A Rough Trade* framed Angolan conflict diamonds squarely in terms of unacceptable corporate conduct rather than as an international relations or Angolan peace issue. It portrayed De Beers as irresponsible, nontransparent, and unethical. Global Witness, the tiny, low-budget NGO that prepared the report, exhorted De Beers to heed its own code of conduct, which could readily be interpreted as disallowing the trade in conflict diamonds. De Beers was singled out as the dominant firm and standard-setter in the industry. "It is time that a business which operates in an arcane way, like a family business, re-assesses its opera-tion and accepts that corporate accountability is now an important factor in interna-tional business. The South African-British group De Beers and its Central Selling Organisation (CSO), as the major player in the diamonds trade, must assume significant responsibility for this". The report concludes that "it is encouraging to note that De Beers do have pre-existing corporate statements on ethics and transpar-ency, and so Global Witness challenges De Beers to tackle this complicated and necessary process of change to drag the diamond business into the next century and ensure that key issues of concern such as public scrutiny, accountability and ethical consideration are put in place". Global Witness thus invoked global CSR principles and shamed De Beers for not abiding by them. De Beers was behind the times – it was not keeping up with the world-cultural model of the responsible corporate citizen. Precisely because De Beers had previously portrayed itself as a progressive and responsible leader in the industry and had formally committed itself to CSR prac-tices, it was an obvious target for NGOs pushing new normative concerns.

Meanwhile, the consumer-oriented arm of the campaign developed rapidly. Put together by a coalition of mostly small NGOs under the name Fatal Transactions, the campaign focused on the consumer's "right to know," thus targeting diamond retailers. Fatal Transactions was not the first such effort; previous consumer aware-ness campaigns had targeted furs, the hunting of baby seals, and so on. Consumer awareness campaigns, including boycotts, had become an important political tool, despite uncertainty about the effects of such activism on corporate behavior. Precisely because many consumers were already sensitized to "care," NGOs' efforts to recast the symbolism of the industry were not likely to be ignored. Such symbolic de-legitimation was clearly linked to potential material consequences: declining sales and falling profits. In the conflict diamonds case, however, a boycott was not pursued due to concern about the negative effects on diamond miners. The goal was not to reduce sales but to prompt prospective customers to accept only conflict-free diamonds. Of course, heightened consumer awareness may seem tantamount to a boycott, particularly when no alternative products or brands are available, but most of the NGOs' activities targeted policymakers and industry officials rather than consumers. The primary purpose of the consumer awareness campaigns was to keep governments and industry worried about a potential drop in demand.

The strategy seems to have worked. While the vast majority of consumers remained completely ignorant, De Beers became gravely concerned about the possibility of a boycott. As the company's Head of Public Affairs, Andrew Bone, recalled: "We were concerned that the way the NGOs were putting it at the time was that this was a consumer awareness campaign. Now we knew that with the complexity of the issue, it was too complex for a message to get across to the public in a way that would not alarm them, and therefore instigate a boycott."

That the rupture regarding the symbolic character of diamonds was deep and wide is indicated by the extreme violations of sacred entities (individuals, groups, peoples) publicized by the campaign. The civil wars involved indiscriminate rape, mutilation, and massacre of civilians, particularly women and children, and the forced soldiering of children. Many human rights and principles of law were severely transgressed, and the Fatal Transactions campaign depicted companies and states engaged in the diamond industry as aiding and abetting the transgressors. The Sierra Leone war was especially vicious, magnifying the moral responsibilities of the industry. First-hand observation of the brutal realities of the war prompted some politicians and industry leaders to urge industry action. Martin Rapaport, perhaps the biggest name in US jewelry diamonds, was sufficiently moved by a trip to Sierra Leone to become a key proponent of change. Most telling about Rapaport's reaction is that, in the article he published after that journey, "Guilt Trip", he argued not only that the industry must cooperate fully with states and the United Nations to address the problem, but also that the industry was responsible for ending the war regardless of the cost. Rapaport's trip was prompted by the concerns raised by NGOs and it had the best outcome they could have hoped for: his willing embrace of the industry's social responsibility to end great harm. Winning over Rapaport helped the NGOs greatly in their efforts to bring pressure to bear on more reluctant parties.

Early initial support from proactive state representatives was also crucial to the search for a solution to the conflict diamonds problem. These governmental allies of the NGO campaign, including Canadian Ambassador Bob Fowler at the United Nations, House of Representatives member Tony Hall in the United States, US Special Negotiator for Conflict Diamonds J. D. Bindenagel, and the European Union's Kim Eling, helped create a sense of urgency about conflict diamonds. Numerous other state representatives in the KP were essential to the success of the negotiations, particularly the first two chairmen of the KP, Abbey Chikane of South Africa and Tim Martin of Canada. Notwithstanding the importance of such figures, it appears that governments largely were impelled by nonstate actors to address the issue of conflict diamonds. A key case in point is US involvement. Ian Smillie of the small NGO Partnership Africa Canada, the man who is often described as the "key architect" of the KP, put it this way: "It was really because the American jewelry industry was so scared of what would happen if there wasn't an agreement that they pushed the government to do the right thing. NGOs pushed the industry. Industry pushed the government".

Judging by the response of De Beers, the NGOs, though annoying and potentially harmful, were not seen as illegitimate interlopers imposing misguided morality on the industry. Their cultural authority is further evident in the fact that De Beers decided not to launch a counterattack on the NGOs as being uninformed, incapable, or simply wrong. One of the authors of a report on Sierra Leone, *Heart of the Matter*, later acknowledged that several claims in the report were inaccurate. De Beers had previously sued other groups for disseminating damaging or false information, but it refrained from litigation regarding the conflict diamonds reports and no evidence suggests that it even seriously considered this option. De Beers did dispute some facts, such as the estimate that conflict diamonds were 20% of the trade, but it never tried to vilify or de-legitimate these groups.

Remarkably enough, De Beers perceived the NGOs as potential and credible threats. Consider the paradox: a firm that had tightly controlled the diamond industry for decades felt unable to ignore a handful of small NGOs publishing reports that were not even widely disseminated in the popular media at the time. The consumer awareness campaign, meanwhile, was gaining little traction; customers were not habitually asking jewelers about the link between diamonds and village massacres in Sierra Leone. The threat that they might do so was real enough, however, and the combination of the consumer awareness campaign and the moral exhortation of the NGOs, backed by careful documentation of horrors that could be laid at the door of the diamond industry, impelled positive engagement by the industry. The NGOs were defining a new form of irresponsibility relative to the diamond trade and, thus, a new social responsibility to be met by diamond companies as morally obligated world citizens.

[…]

Translating Norms into Practice: The Kimberley Process

Ever since its inception, the Kimberley Process has been a fully tripartite endeavor, engaging states, NGOs, and the industry. This multistakeholder arrangement is not a façade obscuring behind-the-scenes domination by the industry or major states. NGOs have participated vigorously in all aspects of the KP, including plenary meetings, working groups, and country review visits. Their influence—and often leading role—in the process is well documented by Bieri.

The issue of legitimacy is crucial in explaining the willingness of states and the industry to allow nongovernmental actors to become so heavily engaged in the KP. Practical considerations helped: the NGOs came to be seen as valuable experts in KP working groups, and in many ways they have proven themselves more knowledgeable about the conflict diamonds issue than any other party. But states have also learned that a formal role for NGOs lends the Kimberley Process Certification Scheme greater legitimacy and enhanced moral standing, as a quote from the former KP Chairman illustrates.

> I think it [NGO and industry participation] is essential to the functioning of the Kimberley Process system and I think this is a characteristic of the new diplomacy that we'll see with respect to emerging international challenges .... Something else I would add, and I don't think is always recognized but we see this in the operations of the Kimberley Process, is that Partnership Africa Canada and Global Witness have deep understanding, knowledge, and bring a lot of technical and analytical assets to the Kimberley Process. So it's not a situation where it's, we're being impelled by civil society affecting public opinion—although it does that, and that's healthy—but civil society participates in an integrated, informed, professional, technical way as well.

Even reluctant states understand that the Scheme's reputation as a mechanism that effectively curbs the trade in conflict diamonds is crucial to assure consumers that diamonds are "clean." Obviously, the NGOs' influence in the KP far exceeds their material resources, and their involvement has been not only tolerated but welcomed, not least because they have shown such deep commitment to the success of the KP by devoting themselves so wholeheartedly to it.

NGO strengths include their legitimacy, dense networks, technical expertise, and knowledge of the issues. These strengths can benefit companies and international organizations, like the KP, which associate themselves with NGOs. The legitimacy of NGOs as the "conscience of the world" provides a favorable opportunity for companies faced with global campaigns criticizing their operations; developing partnerships with NGOs holds the promise of achieving a better social responsibility image. Companies can bask in the glow of NGOs' moral legitimacy, which is rooted in world-cultural assumptions about the virtues of NGOs as global champions of the poor, the suffering, and the excluded. Through NGO links, companies can show their commitment to universal rights and the rule of law. In turn, as self-appointed guardians promoting the universal protection of individuals from abuses, NGOs hold companies responsible for their commitments, while at the same time questioning the sincerity of companies' motivations. This legitimacy framework helps explain the striking growth of multistakeholder initiatives.

[...]

The rising legitimacy of CSR as a world-cultural complex also provides opportunities to NGOs. They can latch on to progressive industry leaders to put pressure on less enthusiastic firms by claiming that socially responsible actions make business sense, even if the claim is questionable. Several recent collaborations between companies and NGOs show that dominant industry players (e.g., Nike, Coca-Cola) often feel obliged to match their leading role in the market with leadership on CSR matters, setting the tone for the rest of the industry. However, research on the effects of CSR on profitability yields mixed results: scholars continue to debate whether CSR adds to or harms the financial bottom line of corporations and society at large.

Still, the notion that profits and social responsibility go hand-in-hand aids campaigns in pitching their messages toward wider company audiences. The lack of a clear negative effect of CSR commitments on profits means that, on the one hand, NGOs can argue that they are not asking firms to sacrifice by improving their behavior. On the other hand, the lack of a clear positive effect means that NGOs can avoid engendering criticism from other NGOs for being "too close for comfort" by helping firms improve the bottom line. NGOs can skeptically but honestly present the lack of clear effects of CSR on profitability as a way to bring companies on board while also preserving their legitimacy.

In many cases, companies under fire have had experience with NGOs on previous occasions, which usually makes it easier for NGOs to engage them on new issues. Initial company reactions can be rather dire; they may see NGOs as extremists and imagine worst-case scenarios that threaten their very existence. Once over this hurdle, however, they often find that NGOs are highly professional, knowledgeable, and even constructive in their criticism. In the conflict diamonds case, De Beers and progressive key figures such as Rapaport and Izhakoff relatively early on detected NGO campaign efforts and, despite initial misgivings, soon engaged and pulled the rest of the industry in with them. [...]

45

Poverty Capital

Microfinance and the Making of Development

Ananya Roy

Fall from Grace?

In 2006, Muhammad Yunus and the Grameen Bank were awarded the Nobel Peace Prize. The prize brought new attention to the role of the Grameen Bank as a pioneer of microfinance. Those opposed to the Grameen model of microfinance had to acknowledge its contributions to development. "Yunus was one of the early visionaries who believed in the idea of poor people as viable, worthy, attractive clients for loans," said Elizabeth Littlefield, CEO of CGAP, a donor forum based in the World Bank that advocates a market-based approach to development. And "that simple notion has put in motion a huge range of imitators and innovators who have taken that idea and run with it, improved on it, expanded it". For a moment, the Washington consensus on poverty, anchored by institutions such as CGAP, seemed shaky.

The most elaborate celebrations unfolded at the Microcredit Summit held in Halifax, Canada, in November 2006. From the speeches to the imagery, the summit sought to promote the Grameen Bank's model of microfinance, showcasing an unyielding focus on human development and the role of microfinance in achieving such goals. Each session was inaugurated by a videomontage, the "Faces of Microcredit," usually of a poor woman and how her life has been transformed by microfinance. "We are here because of the women," announced Sam Daley Harris, director of the Microcredit Summit Campaign, at the opening ceremony. Behind him played a song, "Hear Me Now," by the international band, The Green Children, the video featuring Yunus with a

Original publication details: Ananya Roy, *Poverty Capital: Microfinance and the Making of Development*. New York: Routledge, 2010. pp. 89–93, 99–101, 110–11, 116–17, 120. Reproduced with permission from Taylor & Francis Books.

Grameen borrower. Milla Sunde, the lead singer, celebrated the changes in the life of this poor woman: "A smiling face that tells the story of a changing place … a tone in her voice wields the power of choice." Queen Sofia of Spain was on stage in her signature Grameen *gamcha*, the "royal shoulder," as Yunus noted, carrying this 20 cent humble cloth made by poor women as a "symbol of dignity and enterprise." Peter Mackay, now a Cabinet minister in Canada, hailed "microcredit as the vaccine for the pandemic of poverty," one that could address the important issues of "human rights, freedom, democracy, and private sector development." Even in Afghanistan, Mackay noted, microfinance could put "financial power in the hands of poor women."

When Yunus, the Nobel laureate, took the stage, the nearly 2,000 delegates from 100 countries erupted in standing ovations. In a sharply worded speech, Yunus declared victory:

> We are no longer a footnote in the financial system of the world. So those who doubted us, I hope that they will now be with us … The era of showing profits is over. The focus on the poorest is back … We will measure our success not on the rate of return on investment but by the number of people coming out of poverty.

It is thus that John Hatch, founder of Finca International, could insist that microfinance was a "movement, not an industry," and that this summit was the "biggest self-help event in history." "We have created globalization from the bottom up and it is bigger than globalization from top down."

The representatives of the Washington consensus on poverty were also present at the Halifax Summit. They spoke the words of caution, outlining the limits of microfinance, and seeking to temper the eager enthusiasm of the delegates. Kate McKee, formerly head of USAID's microenterprise division and now a senior advisor at CGAP, asked the summit to reflect on the "audacious" nature of the Microcredit Summit's goals and argued that we need to know much more about how microfinance impacts poverty. But the summit was to have little of this. In a bold announcement, Iftikhar Chowdhury, Bangladesh's ambassador to the UN, cited a World Bank report indicating massive improvements in human development in Bangladesh and attributing such achievements to microfinance organizations. Chowdhury went further, arguing that such forms of development also engendered peace and that microcredit thus "drained the marshes of terrorism." The Nobel Prize seems to have reinforced "microfinance evangelism," the "hard-selling" of an "anti-poverty formula" with "destitute women" featured prominently. […]

What followed on the heels of the Nobel Peace Prize was not simply celebration and adulation but equally a sharp critique of microfinance. For example, an essay in *The New Yorker* argued that while "microloans make poor borrowers better off … they often don't do much to make poor countries richer." Rejecting Yunus's argument that the poor are entrepreneurs, the author notes that microloans are more often used to smooth consumption and that they rarely generate new jobs for others. A "missing middle" – small- to medium-sized enterprises – was seen to be the "real engine of macromagic". In a bold articulation of this position, one published the week after the Nobel Prize was granted to Yunus and the Grameen Bank, *New York Times* columnist John Tierney argued that "the Grameen Bank is both an inspiration and a lesson in limits." Wal-Mart, according to Tierney, has done more than any other organization to "alleviate third world poverty," for it provides factory jobs to poor villagers, jobs that may seem to be "sweatshop" jobs but that allow workers to work their way out of poverty. In a similar vein, an essay in the *Wall Street Journal* presented Yunus's ideas as an "ameliorative" rather than "transformative" entrepreneurship. "Can turning more beggars into basket weavers make Bangladesh less of a, well, basket case?" "The poverty of countries like Bangladesh derives from their comprehensive backwardness," the authors concluded. Such critiques frame the Grameen Bank as an outdated native economy, a primitive life form to be soon superseded by forms of economic organization more conducive to global capitalism.

Microfinance's fall from grace had been underway for a while, well prior to the granting of the Nobel Peace Prize to Yunus and the Grameen Bank. As the Washington consensus on poverty sought to remake microfinance into a new financial industry, so the old-type microfinance, focused on poverty, came under attack. In a series of editorials and articles that were published in May 2004, the *New York Times* warned that "no one should be lulled by this microfinance boom into believing that it is a cure-all for global poverty" (*New York Times*, May 5, 2004). Yet, about ten years ago, it was the very same editorial page that had lauded microcredit as a virtual "cure-all," "a much-needed revolution in anti-poverty programs" (*New York Times*, February 16, 1997). […]

This battle of ideas cannot be read as a struggle between a Bangladesh perspective on development and a Washington-centered apparatus of development. For in Bangladesh itself, Yunus has faced severe critique. While the Nobel Prize generated an outpouring of support, Yunus's subsequent decision to run for political office generated controversy. Shortly after the launch of his party, *Nagarik Shakti* (Citizens' Power), in February 2007, a group of Bangladeshi academics publicly challenged Yunus, arguing that microfinance was a tool for the "protection and expansion of capitalism." Microfinance loans, they noted, simply "indebted people" rather than freeing them from poverty (*Daily Star*, February 22 and 25, 2007). In a cruel irony, Yunus's ideas were now equated with the market fundamentalism of Washington-based institutions such as the World Bank and the IMF. In Bangladesh, the critiques of microfinance are not new. The Bangladesh press and academic establishment have often fiercely exposed the power wielded by microfinance organizations in collecting loans. This too seems to be a crucial part of the Bangladesh model: a vigorous auto-critique about development and its instruments. But this time the criticism was explicitly directed at Yunus, a national figure who until now had enjoyed unquestioned moral legitimacy. […]

Homegrown Institutions

The landscape of microfinance in Bangladesh is dominated by a few large players, notably the Grameen Bank, BRAC, and ASA, each of which commands a vast hinterland of clients and also has a global presence. More recently, it is ASA that is often lauded by the microfinance industry as the Bangladesh success story, making it to the top of the "MIX Global 100" lists and Forbes ranking, and hailed by the Asian Development Bank as the "Ford" of microfinance for its "efficiency" and "productivity". In 2008, ASA received the "Banking at the Bottom of the Pyramid" award of the International Finance Corporation and *The Financial Times*. In these global rankings, the Grameen Bank is recognized primarily for its "outreach," in other words for the millions of borrowers that it serves, but it is rarely presented as a model of innovative microfinance. Instead, such praise is reserved for BRAC, whose innovations have been circulated by CGAP and its experts. BRAC's founder Fazle Abed has received substantial global recognition – from the Conrad N. Hilton Foundation Humanitarian Prize to the first Global Citizen Award of the Clinton Global Initiative. In presenting BRAC with the Gates Award for Global Health, Bill Gates noted that "BRAC has done what few others have – they have achieved success on a massive scale, bringing life-saving health programs to millions of the world's poorest people". A recent book on BRAC makes note of its "remarkable success," a message endorsed by the who's who of millennial development: from Bill Clinton to George Soros to James Wolfensohn.

Since its modest inception as a small-scale relief rehabilitation project in 1972, BRAC has grown into one of the world's largest non-profit organizations with over 40,000 full-time staff and over 160,000 para-professionals, 72 percent of whom are women. BRAC's annual budget is over $430 million, 78 percent of which is self-financed. BRAC's microfinance program, with 6 million borrowers, has cumulatively disbursed $4 billion. More than 1.5 million children are currently enrolled in 52,000 BRAC schools and over 3 million have already graduated. BRAC's health program reaches over 100 million people in Bangladesh with basic healthcare services and programs for tuberculosis, malaria, and HIV/AIDS. ASA too is of substantial size, serving 5.7 million borrowers through its microfinance program.

These global rankings and statistics tell us little about how these institutions function and how together they are part of what may be understood as a "Bangladesh consensus on poverty." As development organizations, the Grameen Bank, BRAC, and ASA are indeed impressive in their sheer size and scale serving millions of households. Established in the 1970s, in the wake of Bangladesh's struggle for national independence, these civil society institutions represent an apparatus of development that far outpaces and exceeds the reach of the state. In the skyline of Dhaka, the Grameen and BRAC buildings loom large, as if to declare, as does Abed: "If you want to do significant work, you have to be large. Otherwise we'd be tinkering around on the periphery".

Size and scale are only elements of a distinctive ensemble of development ideas and practices. Led by charismatic men, these are "homegrown institutions" that while different in methodology are united in an ideology of poverty alleviation and institutional practice. I call this ideology the "Bangladesh consensus on poverty." Its hallmark is the non-profit delivery of a wide range of services, including microfinance, to the poor. It is explicitly opposed to the CGAP consensus and its emphasis on market infrastructure, rejecting it as a "commercialization" that distorts "values" and "governance structures." Such critiques emanate not only from the Grameen Bank, but also from ASA. In a set of interviews (July 2004), the program director of ASA insisted that ASA is a "grassroots" organization that serves the poor and that it cannot accept the types of commercialization that are being imposed in top-down fashion by CGAP. This, he argued, has a focus on "profits" rather than poverty; it is a "banking" model rather than a "NGO" model.

[…]

Poverty Truths

Best-practice microfinance, as defined by the Washington consensus on poverty, is meant to be both more and less than the Bangladesh model. On the one hand, the terminology of "microfinance," and now "financial services for the poor," suggests a range of inputs that exceed credit and include services such as savings and insurance. On the other hand, CGAP principles call for a minimalist microfinance, one that draws a clear line between social development and finance and between NGOs and financial institutions. The Bangladesh consensus rejects this idea of minimalist microfinance, instead asserting the norms and values of poverty-focused development. But, while it stubbornly holds on to the term "microcredit," and while the Grameen Bank showcases "credit as a human right," the Bangladesh model in fact provides a range of financial services of which credit is only one among many. These microfinance – rather than microcredit – innovations deserve a closer look.

The Grameen Bank is often associated with a lending orthodoxy: lending groups, weekly meetings, rigid repayment schedules, and joint liability. Yet, nearly a decade ago, the Grameen Bank implemented a lending system that breaks with many elements of this orthodoxy. Known as the Grameen Generalized System, or Grameen II, this recalibration of the Grameen Bank, allows borrowers considerable repayment flexibility with loan rescheduling, customized loans, and even a "flexi-loan detour," a way of "exiting the loan highway" and returning several months later in the case of repayment difficulties. While the lending group is still maintained, Grameen II dismantles the "group fund" and other instruments of joint liability. Instead, it relies on "obligatory savings," a deposit equal to 2.5 percent of the loan value that is deducted from the loan, placed in a special savings account, and that cannot be withdrawn for three years. Another 2.5 percent of the loan value is placed in a personal savings account. For loans over 8,000 taka there is also a mandatory pension deposit. While the Grameen Bank continues to state that it "does not, cannot, and will not accept physical collateral of any kind," the obligatory savings scheme in effect acts as a form of loan security. It is not surprising then that Dowla and Barua title their account of Grameen II with the microfinance cliché: "the poor always pay back."

Grameen II marks an important moment of auto-critique and reflexivity within the Grameen Bank. While the devastating floods of 1998 are often blamed for high default rates in Bangladesh – and thus the formulation of flexible repayment schemes – Yunus himself notes that the floods only revealed long-standing, structural problems with repayment:

> In 1995, a large number of our borrowers stayed away from centre meetings and stopped paying loan installments. Husbands of the borrowers, inspired and supported by local politicians, organized this, demanding a change in Grameen Bank rules to allow withdrawal of "group tax" component of "group fund" at the time of leaving the bank … At the end we resolved the problem by creating some opening in our rules, but Grameen's repayment rate had gone down in the meantime … When the repayment situation did not improve as desired, we thought this would be a good opportunity to be bold, and to dare to design a new Grameen methodology.

Grameen II can be credited for having resolved these issues of repayment and default. But these problems had already garnered the Grameen Bank a certain amount of international notoriety. A 2001 *Wall Street Journal* article presented microcredit as a "great idea with a problem". That problem was the Grameen Bank, its high default rates, increasingly rebellious borrowers, and lack of financial transparency. The article reported:

> In two northern districts of Bangladesh that have been used to highlight Grameen's success, half the loan portfolio is overdue by at least a year, according to monthly figures supplied by Grameen. For the whole bank, 19% of loans are one year overdue.

The article was not sympathetic to the Grameen II overhaul, arguing that since the "bank is converting many overdue loans into new 'flexible' loans ... the situation may be worse than it appears." [...]

The Conditions of Protection

The critics of the Bangladesh model have argued that its "public transcript" of poverty alleviation and gender empowerment is at odds with a "hidden transcript," which is the patriarchal exploitation of poor women. I suggest that a quite different "hidden transcript" is at work. The "public transcript" of microfinance in Bangladesh, especially that advanced by the Grameen Bank has exalted credit, insisting that credit is a human right. It has also exalted the entrepreneurial talents and capacities of the poor, especially poor women. However, a closer look at the Grameen Bank, as well as at BRAC and ASA, suggests a logic of development to which neither credit nor entrepreneurship are key. It is my contention that the poverty truths of the Bangladesh consensus fit much more comfortably in the "social protection" family of programs and policies than in the "micro-enterprises" family. Such forms of social protection are greatly enhanced and deepened by the human development infrastructure and value chains created by these institutions.

[...]

The "hidden transcript" of the Bangladesh model is a far cry from the mythologies of microfinance. It is the story of a unique and ambitious model of development about which we need to learn much more. However, it is the "public transcript" of the Bangladesh model that has come to be globalized, the "hard sell" of "microfinance evangelism". A recent *Financial Times* article thus sought to expose microfinance by showing that "fewer than half of microcredit borrowers invest the money in the grassroots businesses that such loans are intended to foster" and that "microcredit loans are used to buy food". The critique is misplaced, for it is in fact proof of the social protection effects of microfinance that the poor use microfinance loans to smooth dips in consumption and manage vulnerability. This is an effective anti-poverty strategy, not a failure of development. [...]

Part VII Questions

1. How can a social movement be global rather than national? Identify some of the factors that have made it easier since World War II for movements to coordinate their activities and pursue common goals in many countries simultaneously.
2. What international nongovernmental organizations (INGOs) can you name? Do they receive much attention in the media? Why are you more likely to hear about an organization like Amnesty International or the Red Cross than the International Council for Science or the World Federation of Advertisers?
3. The United Nations and its agencies have given consultative status to thousands of INGOs. Would you expect INGOs always to support UN projects and programs? How and why might INGOs be critical of what UN agencies do?
4. For Berkovitch, the women's movement has become more complex and conflictual as Third World women have become more active participants in the movement. Does this mean that the status and role of women are becoming less globalized issues? Does globalization imply consensus, or is it more likely to lead to disagreement and controversy?
5. Boyle argues that women in countries where female genital cutting (FGC) is common were resistant to Western feminists' calls to abolish the practice. Why was this so? How was FGC redefined as a global problem, and how did this redefinition make it more likely that major intergovernmental organizations (IGOs) like the World Health Organization would take steps to address the problem?
6. The Universal Declaration of Human Rights was not simply imposed on the world by the Western powers, according to Barlow. How does she make the case for this claim? How does the women's movement in Iran help support this claim? Why is the engagement of both secular and religious women's groups in the Million Signatures campaign important for our understanding of the women's rights movement in Iran?
7. In the Boli and Thomas selection, five principles that undergird most INGOs are identified. Explain these principles and how they help account for INGOs' ability to influence the behavior of states, IGOs, and corporations. Then identify at least two types of INGOs that are not likely to embrace these principles as fully as most INGOs do.
8. How does Transparency International identify corruption in the countries of the world? Why does it target corruption in states rather than corporations? How does it try to lower the incidence of corruption? What factors make the job of rooting out corruption a difficult one?
9. Who were the three parties to the Kimberley Process that arose to eliminate conflict diamonds from the world market? What role did NGOs play in the Process? How did the idea of corporate social responsibility (CSR) help push the industry to take the conflict diamonds problem seriously? What features of the diamond industry made it especially likely that the NGOs and consumer awareness campaign would succeed in getting a diamond certification scheme in place?
10. Ananya Roy argues that, despite its problems, microfinance can be beneficial to very poor people. How does microfinance work? What problems does Roy discuss? What does she see as the benefits of microfinance, even though it may not do much for economic development?

Part VIII

Globalization and Media

Introduction

Modern media are carriers of globalization. Assisted by the telegraph, nineteenth-century mass newspapers brought information from around the world to the breakfast tables of the Western middle class. From their very beginning, movies were distributed on all continents, creating a common leisure culture among far-flung fans. While radio may have had a mostly domestic reach, broadcast television allowed viewers in many countries to enjoy the same shows, and since the 1960s satellite transmission has further increased that sense of connection by enabling viewers to watch the same events at the same time. Especially with the advent of the World Wide Web in 1991, the internet dramatically increased both connections across space and awareness of those connections by making traditional "content" available and enabling users to communicate with each other in radically new ways. Though none of the modern technologies actually reach everyone in the world – a majority of the world's population does not keep up with the latest Hollywood movies and almost two-thirds have yet to get online – the images, emotions, and information conveyed through the web of mediated connections has tied distant publics far more closely together than ever before.

In this section, we explore questions about the implications of this cultural globalization, focusing on the traditional media of television and film. If more people are exposed to more similar sounds and images, or experience many of the same events at the same time, such mass media may dissolve cultural differences into a dull, colorless homogeneity. Call it "Americanization," call it "Westernization," call it cultural imperialism (and many have, both within and outside the West), critics claim the mass media are driving forces behind the process. Controlled mainly by American and European companies, spreading their ethereal tentacles through the airwaves to the farthest reaches of the globe, the media impose their

The Globalization Reader, Fifth Edition. Edited by Frank J. Lechner and John Boli.
Editorial material and organization © 2015 John Wiley & Sons, Ltd.
Published 2015 by John Wiley & Sons, Ltd.

powerful images, sounds, and advertising on unprepared peoples who succumb meekly to their messages, which are designed to increase the profits of capitalist firms. Such is the kernel of one side of the debate on the role of the media in world society. But contrary voices can also be heard, and changes in the structure of the global news, television, radio, music, and film industries have changed much of the received wisdom about cultural imperialism.

The cultural imperialism debate picked up speed soon after decolonization began to produce dozens of new states in Africa, Asia, and the Pacific. Though colonialism was dead or dying, in its place scholars identified a new form of capitalist subjugation of the Third World (a term that emerged with decolonization), more economic than political, more ideologically than militarily supported: neocolonialism. As the argument goes, because direct politico-military control could no longer be practiced, neocolonialist powers turned to symbolic and psychological means of control, conveniently facilitated by the rapid integration of global telecommunications systems and, especially, by the proliferation of television. Pushing mainly American culture that promoted ideologies of consumption, instant gratification, self-absorption, and the like, the expanded mass media fit neatly with the spread of global capitalism in its struggle with the Communist-dominated "Second World" led by the Soviet Union.

One prominent outcome of the cultural imperialism thesis was the strident call for a "new world information order" (NWIO). Less developed countries pleaded their case against the domination of Western media in UNESCO and other UN forums, arguing that restrictions should be placed on Western cultural propagation and that aid should flow to the former colonies to improve their nascent communications systems. A related issue was the purportedly biased view of the world presented by the major global news organizations, Associated Press (AP) and United Press International (UPI) from the United States, Agence France-Presse (AFP), and British-owned Reuters, which together accounted for the vast majority of stories entering the newsrooms of the world's newspapers and television stations. The NWIO debate led to few concrete actions, in part because the less developed countries lost interest as many new states took direct control of the broadcast media in their countries and turned radio, television, and major newspapers into mouthpieces of official government policy.

While the press wire services (AP, UPI, AFP, and Reuters), all with their roots in the nineteenth century, represent a longstanding form of news globalization, it was only in the 1970s and 1980s that electronic media globalization assumed serious proportions. Mergers and acquisitions by aggressive media companies like Rupert Murdoch's News Corporation yielded massive conglomerates with truly global reach. Ted Turner's upstart Cable News Network (CNN) was taken over by Time Warner after it became a ubiquitous, 24-hour news provider watched by global business and political elites. At the same time, however, a steady process of decentralization of global media industries was under way, as major countries in different world regions became regional production centers: Mexico for Spanish-language television, India for film, Hong Kong for East Asian film and television, and so on. Alongside this development has been the "indigenization" of many television formats and genres that originated in the West. The once hugely popular *Dallas* has given way to local equivalents with local twists – Brazilian soaps,

Mexican *telenovelas*, and many other forms. The net result is an undeniable global increase in the degree to which people's everyday lives are experienced through the media, but the homogenizing effects of media globalization are much less clear than was once supposed.

Summarizing research on the reception of television shows, British cultural analyst John Tomlinson challenges the cultural imperialism argument, conveying his doubts about the degree to which US shows and pharmaceutical advertising in the Third World actually carry US values and improve the profits of US companies. Cultural homogenization is growing in some respects, Tomlinson suggests, but local transformations and interpretations of imported media products imply that cultural diversification is hardly at an end in global society. Daya Kishan Thussu, an Indian-British global communications scholar, expands on this theme in his description of the "multi-vocal, multimedia and multi-directional flows" in the twenty-first-century media landscape while at the same time noting the still-dominant role of "US-led Western media." But even these dominant flows, he suggests, are being localized – or "glocalized" – as standard content is tailored to the tastes and expectations of regionally diverse consumers. "Subaltern flows," neither produced in nor destined for the United States or Western countries, create a transnational culture and audience of their own, though in the end Thussu questions the extent to which they serve as a "contra-flow" challenging American dominance.

Doobo Shim, a Korean media and communications scholar, illustrates Thussu's points with a description of the "Korean wave" of shows, movies, and pop music that became popular in several Asian countries, where things Korean were cool and recognizable without being threatening. To some extent, media liberalization, both in Korea and abroad, fostered that success. As Shim points out, Koreans also tried to "learn from Hollywood." But this learning was no mere imitation: Korean artists appropriated foreign styles to meet a local or regional demand for distinction. Australian media expert Jane Roscoe offers a different variation on the theme in describing how Australian producers "indigenized" the once-popular *Big Brother* reality TV show format to suit Australian tastes. Though the show still followed a formula, it gained a local feel as the participating "mates" gathered for backyard "barbies" (barbecues) at their Aussie house. Roscoe also amplifies Tomlinson's point about the critical role of audiences by showing that as modern media converge, for example through increased use of websites, sophisticated audience involvement and control increase.

Shifting attention to movies, British media analyst Heather Tyrrell's article describes the film industry in India ("Bollywood," centered in Mumbai/Bombay) as a major competitor to the long-term dominance of American Hollywood. She describes Hollywood's difficulties in penetrating the Indian market and the strengths of Indian cinema as an emerging cultural force that explicitly challenges American themes and assumptions about the film-going public. Indian films have become symbols of successful resistance to Western cultural imperialism even while incorporating elements of Hollywood commercialism, illustrating the culture clash and paradoxes of globalization that can also be found in rising film industries in other Third World countries like Mexico, Hong Kong, Brazil, and China. In the final selection, American economist Tyler Cowen discusses Hollywood's dominance from a different vantage point. He first explains why the United States has certain advantages in the production of movies with global appeal. Even in the age of globalization, it turns out, clustering makes economic sense. Like others who are skeptical about the evils of cultural imperialism, Cowen suggests that there is little need to worry about Hollywood's prowess: its movies cater to the demands of world consumers more than they peddle a specifically American message, and global cinema flourishes when creative filmmakers take advantage of particular niches in an open market.

46

Cultural Imperialism

John Tomlinson

"Watching *Dallas*": The Imperialist Text and Audience Research

For many critics, the American TV series *Dallas* had become the byword for cultural imperialism in the 1980s. Ien Ang's study, *Watching Dallas* takes as its central question the tension between the massive international popularity of the Texan soap opera:

> ... in over ninety countries, ranging from Turkey to Australia, from Hong Kong to Great Britain ... with the proverbial empty streets and dramatic drop in water consumption when an episode of the series is going out ...

and the reaction of cultural commentators to this "success":

> *Dallas* was regarded as yet more evidence of the threat posed by American-style commercial culture against authentic national identities. In February 1983 for instance, Jack Lang, the French Minister for Culture ... had even proclaimed *Dallas* as the "symbol of American cultural imperialism".

Ang detects amongst European cultural critics an "ideology of mass culture" by which she means a generalised hostility towards the imported products of the American mass culture industry, which has fixed on *Dallas* as the focus of its contempt.

Original publication details: John Tomlinson, *Cultural Imperialism: A Critical Introduction*. London: Continuum, 1991. pp. 45–50, 108–13.

Ang quotes Michelle Mattelart:

> It is not for nothing that *Dallas* casts its ubiquitous shadow wherever the future of culture is discussed: it has become the perfect hate symbol, the cultural poverty ... against which one struggles.

The evident popularity of *Dallas* juxtaposed with its hostile critical reception amongst "professional intellectuals" and the linked charges of cultural imperialism poses for us nicely the problem of the audience in the discourse of media imperialism. For the cultural critics tend to condemn *Dallas* with scant regard to the way in which the audience may read the text.

Cultural imperialism is once more seen as an ideological property of the text itself. It is seen as inhering in the images of dazzling skyscrapers, expensive clothes and automobiles, lavish settings, the celebration in the narrative of power and wealth and so on. All this is seen to have an obvious ideological manipulative effect on the viewer. As Lealand has put it:

> There is an assumption that American TV imports do have an impact whenever and wherever they are shown, but actual investigation of this seldom occurs. Much of the evidence that is offered is merely anecdotal or circumstantial. Observations of ... Algerian nomads watching *Dallas* in the heat of the desert are offered as sufficient proof.

However, encouraged by developments in British critical media theory, some writers have attempted to probe the audience reception of "imperialist texts" like *Dallas*. Ien Ang's study, although it is not primarily concerned with the issue of media imperialism, is one such.

Ang approaches the *Dallas* audience with the intention of investigating an hypothesis generated from her own experience of watching *Dallas*. She found that her own enjoyment of the show chafed against the awareness she had of its ideological content. Her critical penetration as "an intellectual and a feminist" of this ideology suggested to her that the pleasure she derived from the programme had little connection with, and certainly did not entail, an ideological effect. In reacting to the ideology in the text, she argues, the cultural critics overlook the crucial question in relation to the audience: "For we must accept one thing: *Dallas* is popular because a lot of people somehow *enjoy* watching it."

Ang saw the popularity of the show, which might be read as a sign of its imperialist ideological power, as a complex phenomenon without a single cause, but owing a good deal to the intrinsic pleasure to be derived from its melodramatic narrative structure. The show's ability to connect with "the melodramatic imagination" and the pleasure this provides were, Ang thought, the key to its success, and these had no necessary connection with the power of American culture or the values of consumer capitalism. What the cultural critics overlooked was the capacity of the audience to negotiate the possible contradictions between alien cultural values and the "pleasure of the text".

Ang's study was based on a fairly informal empirical procedure. She placed an advertisement in a Dutch women's magazine asking people to write to her describing what they liked or disliked about *Dallas*. Her correspondents revealed a complex set of reactions, including evidence that some did indeed, like Ang herself, manage to resolve a conflict between their distaste for the ideology of the show and a pleasure in watching it. For example:

> *Dallas*. ... God, don't talk to me about it. I'm hooked on it! But you wouldn't believe the number of people who say to me, "Oh, I thought you were against Capitalism?" I am, but *Dallas* is just so tremendously exaggerated, it has nothing to do with capitalists any more, it's just sheer artistry to make up such nonsense.

Ang found such a high level of disapproval for the cultural values of *Dallas* in some of her correspondents that she speaks of their views being informed by the "ideology of mass culture" of the cultural critics. These viewers, she argues, have internalised what they perceive as the "correct" attitude towards mass-cultural imports – that of the disapproving professional intellectuals. They thus feel the need to justify their enjoyment of the show by, for example, adopting an ironic stance towards it. Alternatively, she suggests, an opposing "anti-intellectual" ideological discourse of "populism" may allow the *Dallas* fan to refuse the ideology of mass culture as elitist and paternalist, and to insist (in such popular maxims as "there's no accounting for taste") on their right to their pleasure without cultural "guilt".

Ang's analysis of the ideological positioning and struggle around the text of *Dallas* is not without its problems. But her empirical work does at the very least suggest how naive and improbable is the simple notion of an immediate ideological effect arising from exposure to the imperialist text. The complex, reflective and self-conscious reactions of her correspondents suggest that cultural critics who assume this sort of effect massively underestimate the audience's active engagement with the text and the critical sophistication of the ordinary viewer/reader.

The same message comes from most recent studies of audience response. Katz and Liebes, for instance, also looked at reactions to *Dallas*, but in a rather more formal empirical study than Ang's. Their work involved a large-scale cross-cultural study of the impact of *Dallas*, comparing different ethnic groups in Israel with a group of American viewers. Katz and Liebes situate themselves within the growing perspective in media research which sees the audience as active and the process of meaning construction as one of "negotiation" with the text in a particular cultural context. They argue that this perspective:

> raises a question about the apparent ease with which American television programmes cross cultural and linguistic frontiers. Indeed, the phenomenon is so taken for granted that hardly any systematic research has been done to explain the reasons why these programmes are so successful. One wonders how such quintessentially American products are understood at all. The often-heard assertion that this phenomenon is part of the process of cultural imperialism presumes, first, that there is an American message in the content and form; second, that this message is somehow perceived by viewers; and, third, that it is perceived in the same way by viewers in different cultures.

Katz and Liebes, like Ang, are generally dubious about the way in which the media imperialism argument has been presented by its adherents:

Since the effects attributed to a TV programme are often inferred from content analysis alone, it is of particular interest to examine the extent to which members of the audience absorb, explicitly or implicitly, the messages which critics and scholars allege they are receiving.

Their study of *Dallas* thus represents perhaps the most ambitious attempt so far to examine the media imperialism argument empirically from the perspective of audience response. In order to do this, they organised fifty "focus groups" consisting of three couples each to watch an episode of *Dallas*. The idea of watching the programme in groups was essential to one of their guiding premises, that the meanings of TV texts are arrived at via a *social* process of viewing and discursive interpretation. They believe, in common with other recent views, that TV viewing is not essentially an isolated individual practice, but one in which social interaction – "conversation with significant others" – is a vital part of the interpretative and evaluative process. This may be even more significant when the programme in question is the product of an alien culture and, thus, potentially more difficult to "decode".

The groups that Katz and Liebes arranged were all from similar class backgrounds – "lower middle class with high school education or less" – and each group was "ethnically homogeneous":

> There were ten groups each of Israeli Arabs, new immigrants to Israel from Russia, first-and second-generation immigrants from Morocco and Kibbutz members. Taking these groups as a microcosm of the worldwide audience of *Dallas*, we are comparing their "readings" of the programme with ten groups of matched Americans in Los Angeles.

The groups followed their viewing of *Dallas* with an hour-long "open structured" discussion and a short individual questionnaire. The discussions were recorded and formed the basic data of the study, what Katz and Liebes refer to as "ethno-semiological data".

The groups were invited to discuss, first, simply what happened in the episode – "the narrative sequence, and the topics, issues and themes with which the programme deals". Even at this basic level Katz and Liebes found examples of divergent readings influenced, they argue, by the cultural background of the groups and reinforced by their interaction. One of the Arabic groups actually "misread" the information of the programme in a way which arguably made it more compatible with their cultural horizon. In the episode viewed, Sue Ellen had taken her baby and run away from her husband JR, moving into the house of her former lover and his father. However, the Arab group confirmed each other in the more conventional reading – in their terms – that she had actually gone to live in her *own* father's house. The implications of this radical translation of the events of the narrative must at least be to undermine the notion that texts cross cultural boundaries intact.

More importantly, perhaps, Katz and Liebes found that different ethnic groups brought their own values to a judgement of the programme's values. They quote a Moroccan Jew's assessment:

Machluf: You see, I'm a Jew who wears a skullcap and I learned from this series to say, "Happy is our lot, goodly is our fate" that we're Jewish. Everything about JR and his baby, who has maybe four or five fathers, who knows? The mother is Sue Ellen, of course, and the brother of Pam left. Maybe he's the father. ... I see that they're almost all bastards.

This sort of response, which seems to be not just a rejection of Western decadence, but an actual reinforcement of the audience's own cultural values, extended from issues of interpersonal and sexual morality to the programme's celebration of wealth: "With all that they have money, my life style is higher than theirs." However, here, at the "real foundations", Katz and Liebes found a more typical response to be an agreement on the importance of money:

MIRIAM: Money will get you anything. That's why people view it. People sit at home and want to see how it looks.
[...]
YOSEF: Everybody wants to be rich. Whatever he has, he wants more.
ZARI: Who doesn't want to be rich? The whole world does.

It scarcely needs saying that responses like these demonstrate no more than agreement with aspects of the perceived message of *Dallas* and cannot be taken as evidence of the programme's ideological effect. All cultures, we must surely assume, will generate their own set of basic attitudes on issues like the relationship between wealth and happiness. *Dallas* represents, perhaps, one very forceful statement of such an attitude, informed by a dominant global culture of capitalism. But it would be absurd to assume that people in any present-day culture do not have developed attitudes to such a central aspect of their lives quite independent of any televisual representations. We clearly cannot assume that simply watching *Dallas* makes people want to be rich! The most we can assume is that agreement here, as with disagreement elsewhere with the programme's message, represents the outcome of people's "negotiations" with the text.

Katz and Liebes are careful not to draw any premature conclusions from this complex data. But they do at least suggest that it supports their belief in the active social process of viewing and demonstrates a high level of sophistication in the discursive interpretations of ordinary people. They also make the interesting suggestion that the social and economic distance between the affluent denizens of the Southfork Range and their spectators around the globe is of less consequence than might be thought: "Unhappiness is the greatest leveller." This thought chimes with Ang's argument that it is the melodramatic nature of the narrative and its appeal to the "tragic structure of feeling", rather than its glimpses of consumer capitalism at its shiny leading edge that scores *Dallas*'s global ratings.

The general message of empirical studies – informal ones like Ang's and more large-scale formal projects like Katz and Liebes's – is that audiences are more active and critical, their responses more complex and reflective, and their cultural values more resistant to manipulation and "invasion" than many critical media theorists have assumed. [...]

Multinational Capitalism and Cultural Homogenisation

Critics of multinational capitalism frequently do complain of its tendency towards cultural convergence and homogenisation. This is the major criticism made in the discourse of cultural imperialism which takes capitalism as its target. A good example is Cees Hamelink's book, *Cultural Autonomy in Global Communications*. Hamelink, who acknowledges the co-operation of both Schiller and Salinas, places the issues of cultural autonomy and cultural homogenisation – or what he refers to as "cultural synchronisation" – at the centre of his analysis. He is broadly correct in identifying the processes of "cultural synchronization" (or homogenisation) as unprecedented in historical terms and in seeing these processes as closely connected to the spread of global capitalism. But he fails to show why cultural synchronisation should be objected to and, specifically, he fails to show that it should be objected to on the grounds of cultural autonomy.

In his opening chapter Hamelink lists a number of personal "experiences of the international scene" to illustrate his thesis. For example:

In a Mexican village the traditional ritual dance precedes a soccer match, but the performance features a gigantic Coca-Cola bottle.

In Singapore, a band dressed in traditional Malay costume offers a heart-breaking imitation of Fats Domino.

In Saudi Arabia, the television station performs only one local cultural function – the call for the Moslem prayer. Five times a day, North American cops and robbers yield to the traditional muezzin.

In its gigantic advertising campaign, IBM assures Navajo Indians that their cultural identity can be effectively protected if they use IBM typewriters equipped with the Navajo alphabet.

The first thing to note about these examples is precisely their significance as *personal* observations – and this is not to make any trivial point about their "subjective" nature. Hamelink expresses the cultural standpoint of the concerned Westerner confronting a perplexing set of global phenomena. We have to accept, at the level of the personal, the sincerity of his concern and also the validity of this personal discourse: it is valid for individuals to express their reaction to global tendencies. But we need to acknowledge that this globe-trotting instancing of cultural imperialism shapes the discourse in a particular way: to say "here is the *sameness* that capitalism brings – and here – and here ..." is to assume, however liberal, radical or critical the intention, the role of the "tourist": the problem of homogenisation is likely to present itself to the Western intellectual who has a sense of the diversity and "richness" of global culture as a particular threat. For the people involved in each discrete instance Hamelink presents, the experience of Western capitalist culture will probably have quite different significance. Only if they can adopt the (privileged) role of the cultural tourist will the sense of the homogenisation of global culture have the same threatening aspect. The Kazakhstani tribesman who has no knowledge of (and, perhaps, no interest in) America or Europe is unlikely to see his cassette player as emblematic of creeping capitalist domination. And we cannot, without irony, argue that the Western intellectual's (informed?) concern is more valid: again much hangs on the question, "who speaks?"

This said, Hamelink does draw from these instances an empirical conclusion which is, I think, fairly uncontroversial:

> One conclusion still seems unanimously shared: the impressive variety of the world's cultural systems is waning due to a process of "cultural synchronisation" that is without historic precedent.

For those in a position to view the world as a cultural totality, it cannot be denied that certain processes of cultural convergence are under way, and that these are new processes. This last is an important point, for Hamelink is careful to acknowledge that cultures have always influenced one another and that this influence has often enriched the interacting communities – "the richest cultural traditions emerged at the actual meeting point of markedly different cultures, such as Sudan, Athens, the Indus Valley, and Mexico". Even where cultural interaction has been in the context of political and economic domination, Hamelink argues, there has been, in most cases a "two-way exchange" or at least a tolerance of cultural diversity. There is a sharp difference for him between these patterns and modern "cultural synchronization":

> In the second half of the twentieth century, a destructive process that differs significantly from the historical examples given above threatens the diversity of cultural systems. Never before has the synchronization with one particular cultural pattern been of such global dimensions and so comprehensive.

Let us be clear about what we are agreeing. It seems to me that Hamelink is right, broadly speaking, to identify cultural synchronisation as an unprecedented feature of global modernity. The evaluative implications of his use of the word "destructive", however, raises larger problems. It is one thing to say that cultural diversity is being destroyed, quite another to lament the fact. The latter position demands reasons which Hamelink cannot convincingly supply. The quotation continues in a way that raises part of the problem: "Never before has the process of cultural influence proceeded so subtly, without any blood being shed and with the receiving culture thinking it had sought such cultural influence." With his last phrase Hamelink slides towards the problematic of false consciousness. As we have seen more than once before, any critique which bases itself in the idea that cultural domination is taking place "behind people's backs" is heading for trouble. To acknowledge that a cultural community might have thought it had sought cultural influence is to acknowledge that such influence has at least *prima facie* attractions.

This thought could lead us to ask if the process of cultural homogenisation itself might not have its attractions. It is not difficult to think of examples of cultural practices which would probably attract a consensus in favour of their universal application: health care; food hygiene; educational provision; various "liberal" cultural attitudes towards honesty, toleration, compassion and so on; democratic public processes etc. This is not to say that any of these are indisputable "goods" under any description whatever, nor that they are all the "gifts" of an expanding capitalist modernity. But it is to say that there are plenty of aspects of "culture", broadly defined, that the severest critic of cultural homogenisation might wish to find the same in any area of the globe. Critics of cultural homogenisation are selective in the things they object to, and there is nothing wrong in this so long as we realise that it undermines the notion that homogenisation is a bad thing *in itself*. But then we enter a quite separate set of arguments – not about the uniformity of capitalist culture, but about the spread of its pernicious features – which require quite different criteria of judgement.

Engaging with the potentially attractive features of homogenisation brings us to see, pretty swiftly, the problems in its use as a critical concept. But there are other ways of approaching the issue, and one of Hamelink's arguments seems on the surface to avoid these problems. He argues that cultural synchronisation is to be deplored on the grounds that it is a threat to cultural autonomy. I would argue against both the notion of autonomy as applied to a "culture" in the holistic sense and against any logical connection between the concept of autonomy and any particular *outcome* of cultural practices. Autonomy, as I understand it, refers to the free and uncoerced choices and actions of agents. But Hamelink uses the notion of autonomy in what strikes me as a curious way, to suggest a feature of cultural practices which is necessary, indeed "critical", for the actual survival of a cultural community.

Hamelink's reasoning appears to be based on the idea that the cultural system of any society is an *adaptive* mechanism which enables the society to exist in its "environment", by which he seems to mean the physical and material features of its global location: "Different climatic conditions, for example, demand different ways of adapting to them (i.e., different types of food, shelter and clothing)." Again, there is nothing particularly controversial about this, except in the obvious sense that we might want to argue that many of the cultural practices of modernity are rather more "distanced" from the function of survival than those of more "primitive" systems. But from this point he argues that the "autonomous" development of cultural systems – the freedom from the processes of "cultural synchronization" – are necessary to the "survival" of societies. Why should this be so? Because "the adequacy of the cultural system can best be decided upon by the members of the society who face directly the problems of survival and adaptation".

There are a number of difficulties arising from this sort of argument. First, what does Hamelink mean by the "survival" of a society? In his reference to very basic adaptations to environmental conditions he seems to trade on the idea that a culture allows for the actual physical survival of its members. At times he explicitly refers to the physical survival of people. For example, he claims that the intensive promotion of milk-powder baby food in the Third World by companies like Nestlé and Cow and Gate is a practice that can have life-threatening consequences:

> Replacing breast-feeding by bottle feeding has had disastrous effects in many Third World countries. An effective, adequate, and cheap method has been exchanged for an expensive, inadequate and dangerous product. ... Many illiterate mothers, unable to prepare the milk powder correctly, have not only used it improperly but have also inadvertently transformed the baby food into a lethal product by using it in unhygienic conditions.

There *are* important issues having to do with the "combined and unequal development" produced by the spread of capitalism of which this is a good example. But the incidence of illness and death Hamelink refers to here, deplorable though it is, will obviously not carry the weight of his argument about cultural synchronisation affecting the physical survival of whole populations in the Third World. He cannot, plausibly, claim that cultural synchronisation with capitalist modernity carries this direct threat. It is probably true that capitalist production has long-term consequences for the global environment, thus for physical survival on a global scale, but this is a separate argument.

At any rate, Hamelink's notion of survival seems to slide from that of physical survival to the *survival of the culture itself*. But this is a very different proposition, which cannot be sustained by the functional view of culture he takes as his premise. For the failure of a culture to "survive" in an "original" form may be taken itself as a process of adaptation to a new "environment" – that of capitalist industrial modernity. A certain circularity is therefore introduced into the argument. Hamelink claims that unique cultures arise as adaptive mechanisms to environments, so he deplores heteronomy since it threatens such adaptation. But what could cultural synchronisation mean if not an "adaptation" to the demands of the social environment of capitalism?

The incoherences of this account arise, I believe, from the attempt to circumvent the problems of autonomy in cultural terms by referring the holistic view to a functional logic of adaptation. Autonomy can only apply to agents, and cultures are not agents. Hamelink seeks to bypass these problems with an argument that reduces the ethical-political content of "autonomy" to make it a mere indicator of social efficiency – the guarantor of the "best" form of social organisation in a particular environment. His argument is incoherent precisely because autonomy cannot be so reduced: in cultural terms, "best" is not to be measured against a simple index of physical survival. Things are far more complicated than this. Cultural autonomy must address the autonomous choices of agents who make up a cultural community; there is no escaping this set of problems by appeal to functionality. Hamelink gives the game away in his reference, cited earlier, to a form of cultural "false consciousness" and elsewhere where he speaks of cultural synchronisation as cultural practices being "persuasively communicated to the receiving countries".

I do not believe the appeal to autonomy grounds Hamelink's critique of cultural synchronisation. Even if it did, this would be an objection to the inhibition of independence by manipulation, not to the resulting "sameness" of global culture. But Hamelink does want to object to "sameness": this is implicit in his constant references to the "rich diversity" of cultures under threat. What are the grounds for such an objection?

Adaptation to physical environments has, historically, produced a diversity in cultural practices across the globe. However, the *preservation* of this diversity – which is what Hamelink wants – seems to draw its justification from the idea that cultural diversity is a good thing in itself. But this depends on the position from which you speak. If the attractions of a uniform capitalist modernity outweigh the charms of diversity, as they well may for those from the outside looking in, it is difficult to insist on the priority of preserving differences. Indeed, the appeal to variety might well be turned back on the critic of capitalism. For it might be argued that individual cultures making up the rich mosaic that Hamelink surveys are lacking in a variety of cultural experience, being tied, as Marx observed, to the narrow demands of the struggle with nature for survival. Cultural synchronisation could in some cases increase variety in cultural experience.

It must be said immediately that arguments exist that the *nature* of such experience in capitalist modernity is in some sense deficient – shallow, "one-dimensional", "commodified", and so on. But this is not a criticism of homogenisation or synchronisation as such: it is a criticism of the sort of culture that synchronisation brings. It is quite different to object to the spread of something bad – uniform badness – than to object to the spread of uniformity itself. This demands quite separate arguments about capitalism as a culture. [...]

47

Mapping Global Media Flow and Contra-Flow

Daya Kishan Thussu

[…]

The global media landscape in the first decade of the twenty-first century represents a complex terrain of multi-vocal, multimedia and multi-directional flows. The proliferation of satellite and cable television, made possible by digital technology, and the growing use of online communication, partly as a result of the deregulation and privatisation of broadcasting and telecommunication networks, have enabled media companies to operate in increasingly transnational rather than national arenas, seeking and creating new consumers worldwide. With the exception of a few powers such as the United States, Britain and France, whose media (particularly broadcasting, both state-run and privately operated) already had an international dimension, most countries have followed a largely domestic media agenda within the borders of a nation-state.

Gradual commercialisation of media systems around the world has created new private networks that are primarily interested in markets and advertising revenues. Nationality scarcely matters in this market-oriented media ecology, as producers view the audience principally as consumers and not as citizens. This shift from a state-centric and national view of media to one defined by consumer interest and transnational markets has been a key factor in the expansion and acceleration of media flows: from North to South, from East to West, and from South to South, though their volume varies according to the size and value of the market.

Original publication details: Daya Kishan Thussu, "Mapping Global Media Flow and Contra-Flow," in *Media on the Move*, ed. Daya Kishan Thussu. Abingdon: Routledge, 2007. pp. 12–13, 20–8. Reproduced with permission from Taylor & Francis.

The US-led Western media, both online and offline, and in various forms – information, infotainment and entertainment – are global in their reach and influence. Given the political and economic power of the United States, its media are available across the globe, if not in English then in dubbed or indigenised versions. As its closest ally, Britain – itself a major presence in global media, particularly in the field of news and current affairs – benefits from the globalisation of Americana. The only non-Western genre with a global presence is Japanese animation (and this would not have been possible without the economic underpinnings of the world's second largest economic power). These represent what might be termed as 'dominant media flows'. Though some peripheral countries have emerged as exporters of television programmes and films, the USA continues to lead the field in the export of audio-visual products. From news and current affairs (CNN, Discovery) through youth programming (MTV), children's television (Disney), feature films (Hollywood), sport (ESPN) to the Internet (Google), the United States is the global behemoth. One result of the privatisation and proliferation of television outlets and the growing glocalisation of US media products is that American film and television exports witnessed nearly a five-fold increase between 1992 and 2004.

The convergence of television and broadband has opened up new opportunities for the flow of media content. As US-led Western media conglomerates have regionalised and localised their content to extend their reach beyond the elites in the world and to create the 'global popular', many Southern media organisations have benefited from synergies emerging from this glocalisation process. Some have skilfully used their position within a media conglomerate, drawing on technological and professional expertise to grow into global operators. In addition, the globalisation of Western or Western-inspired media has contributed to the creation of professional careers in media and cultural industries. The localisation of media content and the outsourcing of digital media for transnational corporations – from Hollywood post-production to animation and digital data management – have provided the impetus for the formation of important global hubs for creative industries: by 2006, for example, India had emerged as a key destination for out-sourcing media content.

A second layer of international media players may include both private as well as state-sponsored flows. The Indian film industry (popularly referred to as Bollywood) and the Latin American telenovelas are the two major examples of transnational global flows that operate in a commercial environment. The South Africa-based, pan-African network M-Net is another example of such transnational and regional communications. Among the state-supported flows we can include Euronews, the 24/7 multilingual news consortium of Europe's public service broadcasters, TV5 and Radio France Internationale, aiming at the francophone market. Other transnational actors may include the Arab news network Al-Jazeera, the pan-Latin American TV channel Televisora del Sur ('Television of the South', Telesur) based in Venezuela, and the round-the-clock English-language global television channel, Russia Today (RTTV), intended to provide news 'from a Russian perspective', launched in 2005. The expansion of CCTV-9, the English language network of China Central Television, reflects the recognition by the Beijing authorities of the importance of the English language as the key to success for global commerce and communication and their strategy to bring Chinese public diplomacy to a global audience. These originators of transnational media flows have a strong regional presence but are also aimed at audiences outside their primary constituency. These can be categorised as representing 'subaltern flows'. As one recent study of Al-Jazeera concluded: 'The information age is upon us and in the decades ahead we can expect only more Al-Jazeeras, adding to an ever greater torrent of information, as regional ideas spread around the world and become global.' [...]

In the era of globalisation, the one-way vertical flow has given way to multiple and horizontal flows, as subaltern media content providers have emerged to service an ever growing geo-cultural market. However, as trade figures demonstrate, the circulation of US media products continues to define the 'global'. But how these products are consumed in a cross-cultural context poses a contested range of responses, made more difficult due to the paucity of well-grounded empirical studies. Some have argued that the global–national–local interaction is producing 'heterogeneous disjunctures' rather than a globally homogenised culture. Others have championed the cause of cultural hybridity, a fusion formed out of adaptation of Western media genres to suit local languages, styles and conventions.

On the other hand, critical theorists have argued that the transnational corporations, with the support of their respective governments, exert indirect control over the developing countries, dominating markets, resources, production and labour. In the process they undermine the cultural autonomy of the countries of the South and create a dependency on both the hardware and software of communication and media: 'transnational corporate cultural domination' is how one prominent scholar defined the phenomenon. Galtung also argued that information flows maintain and reinforce a dependency syndrome: the interests, values and attitudes of the dominant elite in the 'peripheries' of the South coincide with those of the elite in the 'core' – the North. The core–periphery relations create institutional links that serve the interests of the dominant groups, both in the centre and within the periphery. In this analysis of global flows, the audience and media content was largely ignored: that the content can be interpreted differently by different audiences and that the so-called periphery may be able to innovate and improvise on the core was discounted. Theoretical debates have largely been confined to how the rest of the world relates to, adopts, adapts or appropriates Western media genres. There is relatively little work being done on how the 'subaltern flows' create new transnational configurations and how they connect with gradually localising global 'dominant flows'.

Localisation of Global Americana

Glocalisation is central to the acceleration of Western or Westernised media flows across the globe. What seems to be emerging is a glocal media product, conforming to what Sony once characterised as 'global localisation': media content and services being tailored to specific cultural consumers, not so much because of any particular regard for national cultures but as a commercial imperative. Glocalisation strategies exemplify how the global can encompass both the transnational and geo-cultural by co-opting the local in order to maintain the dominant flow. This localisation trend is discernible in the growth of regional or local editions of Western or more specifically American newspapers or magazines; the transmission of television channels in local languages and even producing local programming, as well as having local language websites. [...]

'Subaltern' Contra-Flows: Anti-Hegemonic or Pro-Americana?

In parallel with the globalisation of Americana – whether in its original or hybridised version – new transnational networks have emerged, contributing to what one commentator has called 'Easternisation and South–South flows'. There is evidence that global media traffic is not just one way – from the West (with the USA at its core) to the rest of the world, even though it is disproportionately weighted in favour of the former. These new networks, emanating from such Southern urban creative hubs as Cairo, Hong Kong and Mumbai, and trading in cultural goods represent what could be called 'subaltern flows'. Over the last ten years the media world has witnessed a proliferation of multilingual growth of content emanating from these regional creative centres. The availability of digital technology, privatised and deregulated broadcasting and satellite networks has enabled the increasing flow of content from the global South to the North, for example, the growing international visibility of telenovelas or Korean and Indian films, as well as regional broadcasting, such as the pan-Arabic Middle East Broadcasting Centre (MBC), the pioneering 24/7 news network Al-Jazeera, or the Mandarin language Phoenix channel, which caters to a Chinese diaspora.

Non-Western countries such as China, Japan, South Korea, Brazil and India have become increasingly important in the circulation of cultural products. Japanese animation, film, publishing and music business was worth $140 billion in 2003, with animation, including *manga* (comics), *anime* (animation), films, videos and merchandising products bringing in $26 billion, according to the Digital Content Association of Japan. South Korea has emerged as a major exporter of entertainment – film, television soap operas, popular music and online games – with television dramas such as *Jewel in the Palace* being extremely popular in China, prompting commentators to speak of a Korean wave (the '*Hallyu*') sweeping across east and southeast Asia. [...]

Transnational Telenovelas

Another key example of transnational 'subaltern flow' is the Latin American soap opera, the telenovela, which is increasingly becoming global in its reach. The transnationalisation of telenovelas has been made possible through Televisa in Mexico, Venevisión in Venezuela, and Globo TV in Brazil – the leading producers of the genre. The Brazilian media giant TV Globo (exporting 26,000 hours of programmes annually to 130 countries) and Mexico's Televisa (the world's largest producer of Spanish-language programming, which in 2004 earned $175 million from programming exports, largely from telenovelas), are also the two primary exporters of this popular genre of television across the globe.

By 2005 the telenovela had developed into a $2 billion industry, of which $1.6 billion was earned within the region and $341 million outside, being broadcast in 50 languages and dialects and reaching 100 countries from Latin America to southern and eastern Europe, to Asia, Africa and the Arab world. Apart from being a commercial success, telenovelas can also help in the construction of a transnational 'hispanic' identity, as the Venezuelan scholar Daniel Mato has suggested. The appeal of the genre lies in the melodramatic and often simplistic narrative which can be understood and enjoyed by audiences in a wide variety of cultural contexts. Bielby and Harrington have argued that this reverse flow has influenced soap operas back in the US, leading to 'genre transformation' especially in day-time soaps.

The success of telenovelas outside the 'geo-linguistic market' of Spanish and Portuguese consumers, shows the complexity of media consumption patterns. Such telenovelas as *The Rich Also Cry* were very successful in Russia in the 1990s, while Sony developed its first telenovela in 2003 – *Poor Anastasia* for the Russian network, CTC. The genre has become popular even in Western Europe: a German company has produced their own telenovela, *Bianca: Road to Happiness*, shown in 2004 on the public channel ZDF. In India, Sony has successfully adapted the popular Colombian telenovela *Betty la Fea* into Hindi as *Jassi Jaissi Koi Nahin*, which became one of the most popular programmes on Indian television. The transnationalisation of telenovelas is an indication of contra-flow in television content. As one commentator has noted:

> In all, about two billion people around the world watch *telenovelas*. For better or worse, these programmes have attained a prominent place in the global marketplace of culture, and their success illuminates one of the back channels of globalization. For those who despair that Hollywood or the American television industry dominates and defines globalization, the *telenovela* phenomenon suggests that there is still room for the unexpected.

[…]

Hybridity as Hegemony

These prominent examples of 'subaltern' and 'geo-cultural' media flows may give a false impression that the world communication has become more diverse and democratic. A careful analysis of the reality of global media flows and contra-flows demonstrates a more complex process, however. The imbalance between the 'dominant' and the 'subaltern' and 'geo-cultural' global media flows reflects the 'asymmetries in flows of ideas and goods'. Despite the growing trend towards contra-flow as analysed in this book, the revenues of non-Western media organisations, with the exception of Japanese animation, are relatively small and their global impact is restricted to geo-cultural markets or at best to small pockets of regional transnational consumers. None of the Latin telenovelas has had the international impact comparable with US soaps such as *Dallas* or the cult following of *Friends* or *Sex and the City*, and, despite the growing presence of Indian films outside India, its share in the global film industry valued in 2004 at $200 billion was still less than 0.2 per cent.

At the same time, 'dominant flows' are becoming stronger. It is no coincidence that the world's biggest television network MTV (reaching 418 million households in 2005) is American, as are CNN International (260 million households worldwide) and Discovery Channel (180 million households worldwide). In 2004, out of the world's top five entertainment corporations, according to *Fortune* magazine, four were US-based: Time Warner (2004 revenue: $42.8 billion); Walt Disney (2004 revenue: $30.7 billion); Viacom (2004 revenue: $27.05 billion); and News Corporation (2004 revenue: $20.8 billion). Wal-Mart was for the fourth year running the world's largest corporation, with a revenue in 2004 of nearly $288 billion and profit of $10.2 billion. Not surprisingly, US-based companies – 181 in total – dominated the list (*Fortune*, 2005). Voice of America claims to have 100 million weekly listeners for its 44 languages; AP reaches 8,500 international subscribers in 121 countries, while APTN is a major television news agency. The world's top three largest business newspapers and magazines are American: *The Wall Street Journal* (2005 global circulation 2.3 million), *Business Week* (1.4 million) and *Fortune* (1.1 million). The world's top three magazines too are American: *Reader's Digest* (2005 global circulation, 23 million), *Cosmopolitan* (9.5 million) and *National Geographic* (8.6 million); as are the two major international news magazines: *Time* (2005 global circulation: 5.2 million) and *Newsweek* (4.2 million). The world's top three advertising agencies in 2005 were all based in the US: Young & Rubican (gross worldwide income $9.25 billion), The Ogilvy Group ($6.48 billion) and J. W. Thompson ($5.05 billion).

The question of how contra is contra and against whom also acquires salience. With its slogan 'News from the South', the pan-Latin American 'anti-hegemonic' news network Telesur promises to be an alternative to CNN. 'It's a question of focus, of where we look at our continent from', Jorge Botero, Telesur's news director told the BBC. 'They look at it from the United States. So they give a rose-tinted, flavour-free version of Latin America. We want to look at it from right here.' It has been dubbed as *al-Bolivar* – a combination of Al-Jazeera and the Latin American hero. The French government has announced a 24-hour international TV news network, the French International News Channel (CFII) that aims to be the French-language CNN – 'CNN à la Française'. 'France must ... be on the front line in the global battle of TV pictures' was how President Jacques Chirac justified the network, a joint venture between state-owned broadcaster France Télévisions and commercial television company TF1. These examples, however, are exceptions rather than the rule – both are state-sponsored flows and their impact on global communication is yet to be felt.

In ideological terms, commercial contra-flows champion free-market capitalism, supporting a privatised and commodified media system. One should therefore avoid the temptation to valorise them as counter-hegemonic to the dominant Americana. Subaltern flows are unlikely to have a significant impact on the American hegemony of global media cultures, which, arguably, has strengthened not weakened given the localisation of media content, despite the supposed decentring of global media. This can also bode ill for local cultural sovereignty, as one UN report noted: 'the unequal economic and political powers of countries, industries and corporations cause some cultures to spread, others to wither.' Moreover, as Americana expands and deepens its hegemony, a hybridised and localised media product can provide the more acceptable face of globalisation and therefore effectively legitimise the ideological imperatives of a free-market capitalism. […]

48

Hybridity and the Rise of Korean Popular Culture in Asia

Doobo Shim

Over the past few years, an increasing amount of Korean popular cultural content – including television dramas, movies, pop songs and their associated celebrities – has gained immense popularity in China, Taiwan, Hong Kong and other East and Southeast Asian countries. News media and trade magazines have recognized the rise of Korean popular culture in Asia by dubbing it the 'Korean wave' (*Hallyu* or *Hanryu* in Korean). The Associated Press reported in March 2002: 'Call it "kim chic". All things Korean – from food and music to eyebrow-shaping and shoe styles – are the rage across Asia, where pop culture has long been dominated by Tokyo and Hollywood.' According to *Hollywood Reporter*, 'Korea has transformed itself from an embattled cinematic backwater into the hottest film market in Asia.'

Yet a few years ago Korean popular culture did not have such export capacity, and was not even critically acclaimed by scholars. For example, *The Oxford History of World Cinema*, published in 1996, is alleged to have covered 'every aspect of international film-making' but does not make any reference to Korean cinema, although it pays tribute to Taiwanese, Hong Kong, Chinese and Japanese films. Korean music was also ignored by researchers, as can be seen in the following comment in *World Music: The Rough Guide*, published in 1994: 'The country has developed economically at a staggering pace, but in terms of popular music there is nothing to match the remarkable contemporary sounds of Indonesia, Okinawa, or Japan.' […]

Original publication details: Doobo Shim, "Hybridity and the Rise of Korean Popular Culture in Asia," in *Media, Culture and Society*, 28, 1, 2006. pp. 25, 28–9, 31–3, 35–7, 39–40. Reprinted by permission of SAGE.

What is the Korean Wave?

[…] The Korean wave is indebted to the media liberalization that swept across Asia in the 1990s. The Korean wave seems to have come into existence sometime around 1997, when the national China Central Television Station (CCTV) aired a Korean television drama *What is Love All About?*, which turned out to be a big hit. In response to popular demand, CCTV re-aired the program in 1998 in a prime-time slot, and recorded the second-highest ratings ever in the history of Chinese television. In 1999, *Stars in My Heart*, another Korean television drama serial, became a big hit in China and Taiwan. Since then, Korean television dramas have rapidly taken up airtime on television channels in countries such as Hong Kong, Taiwan, Singapore, Vietnam and Indonesia, which saw media liberalization beginning in the 1990s. In addition, the recent economic crisis in Asia has brought about a situation where Asian buyers prefer the cheaper Korean programming; Korean television dramas were a quarter of the price of Japanese ones, and a tenth of the price of Hong Kong television dramas as of 2000. Korean television programming exports have increased so dramatically that in 2003, they earned $37.5 million, compared with $12.7 million in 1999.

In the late 1990s, a regional music television channel, Channel V, featured Korean pop music videos, creating a huge K-pop fan base in Asia. In particular, the boy band H.O.T. found itself topping the pop charts in China and Taiwan in 1998; the band was so popular that album sales continued to surge, even after the band's break-up in mid-2001. Following H.O.T.'s successful concert in Beijing in February 2000, many K-pop stars such as Ahn Jae-wook (an actor-cum-singer who starred in *Stars in My Heart*), boy bands NRG and Shinhwa, and girl band Baby V.O.X. have held concerts in China, attracting crowds of more than 30,000 Chinese youth for each concert. In 2002, Korean teenage pop sensation BoA's debut album reached the number one spot on the Oricon Weekly Chart, Japan's equivalent of the American Billboard Charts; this firmly established BoA in the Japanese music market. Now, most of Korea's top-notch singers take their concerts to Beijing, Hong Kong and Tokyo and often record their albums in the local languages before marketing their albums in these countries.

In 1999, a Korean blockbuster, *Shiri*, was shown in Japan, Hong Kong, Taiwan and Singapore, receiving critical acclaim and drawing large audiences (for example, it earned $14 million at the Japanese box office). Since then, Korean films have become regular fixtures in cinemas across Asia. For example, among the nine movies screened on 9 August 2003 at the cinema Cathay Cineleisure Orchard, Singapore, three were Korean, including *Conduct Zero, Marriage is a Crazy Thing* and *My Tutor Friend* (sneak preview). When the Korean film *Joint Security Area* opened in Japan on 26 May 2001, it became the first Asian import in the Japanese film market to be shown on as many as 280 screens. The success of Korean cinema in Asia has now spread to North America and Europe, with more and more Korean films attracting theatre-goers in these continents. Major US-based distribution companies such as Fox and Columbia have started to take Korean movies on for their global distribution runs. Furthermore, Hollywood studios are eager to buy remake rights to Korean films. For example, DreamWorks SKG paid $2 million for the remake rights to the Korean horror film, *A Tale of Two Sisters*; that is twice what the studio paid for the Japanese horror movie, *The Ring*, a few years ago.

Against this backdrop, Korean pop stars have become cultural icons in the region. One example is Ahn Jae-wook, who has commanded tremendous popularity in China, as evidenced by his clinching number one spot in a poll of the most popular celebrities in 2001, even surpassing Hollywood actor Leonardo DiCaprio who was then at the apex of his global popularity. Korean stars have had a big impact on consumer culture, including food, fashion, make-up trends and even plastic surgery. It is not uncommon to find Asian youth decorating their backpacks, notebooks and rooms with photographs of Korean stars. In the streets of Hanoi and Beijing, it is common to find young members of the 'Korea Tribe', or Koreanophiles, sporting multiple earrings, baggy hip-hop pants, and the square-toed shoes of Seoul fashion. So popular are Korean actresses Lee Young-ae, Song Hae Gyo, Kim Hee Sun and Jeon Ji-hyun that it has been reported that their wanna-be fans in Taiwan and China request their facial features when going for cosmetic surgery. [...]

Korean Media Liberalization and Development

The period from the late 1980s to the mid-1990s was an important turning point for the Korean media, with the introduction of liberalization in the sector. Until 1987, only domestic film companies were allowed to import and distribute foreign movies in the market. Under US pressure, in 1988 the Korean government allowed Hollywood studios to distribute films directly to local theatres and, by 1994, more than 10 Korean film importers had shut down their businesses. This opening of the market to Hollywood majors affected the vitality of the local film industry in general, such that the number of films produced annually fell from 121 in 1991 to 63 in 1994. In 1994, Hollywood's market share in the local market reached 80 percent, from 53 percent in 1987. Therefore Korean cinema, which was ignored by local audiences, who considered it poorly made, boring and often maudlin, was drawing its last breath.

A rapid increase in foreign television programming as a result of television channel expansion was also a matter of concern. In its first year of cable television services in 1995, Korea imported $42.82 million worth of television programming, marking a sharp increase from the previous year's foreign programming import figure of $19.86 million. Further, the spillover of satellite broadcasting, such as NHK Satellite and Star TV, posed a serious challenge to political sovereignty and cultural integrity.

In this context, two factors awakened Koreans to the importance of culture and its industrial development. In 1993, when the common view was that there was no hope for the revival of the local film industry, the film *Sopyonje* unexpectedly topped the box-office chart with more than a million admissions – the first Korean film ever to attract such a large audience. The film also received unprecedented invitations for screenings in art theatres, and on college campuses in Japan, the United States and some European countries. *Sopyonje* is a film about an itinerant family that earns a living performing *pansori*, the traditional popular musical form of Korea in which a story is sung by a singer, accompanied by a drummer. Although *pansori* was designated as a national cultural treasure by the government, it was neglected once the country was subjected to American culture. The film, which portrayed a declining or 'derelict' traditional folk music genre, and was largely shot in a beautiful rural landscape, revived nostalgia for and public interest in 'our culture'; the family in the film, on the verge of starvation, symbolized the fate of Korean cinema embattled by Hollywood. *Sopyonje* was released when people were beginning to pay attention to leisure, culture and 'self' – aspects they had gone without during the decades of Korean industrialization.

Against this backdrop, a government report awakened the Korean people to the cultural industry's potential contribution to the national economy. In 1994, the Presidential Advisory Board on Science and Technology submitted a report to the president suggesting that the government promote media production as the national strategic industry by taking note of overall revenue (from theatre exhibition, television syndication, licensing, etc.) from the Hollywood blockbuster, *Jurassic Park*, which was worth the foreign sales of 1.5 million Hyundai cars. The comparison of a film to Hyundai cars – which at that time were considered the 'pride of Korea' – was apt enough to awaken the Korean public to the idea of culture as an industry. This revelation became a household topic for quite a long time, in accordance with the globalization-cum-information age discourse. Following the report, the Korean government established the Cultural Industry Bureau within the Ministry of Culture and Sports in 1994, and instituted the Motion Picture Promotion Law in 1995 in order to lure corporate and investment capital into the local film industry.

In their efforts to create a cultural industry, Koreans emulated and appropriated the American media system with the mantra 'Learning from Hollywood'. It was argued that Korea should promote large media companies as well as a more commercial media market. A media policy report submitted to the Korean government in 1995 reads as follows: 'Korea needs to encourage vertically integrated media conglomerates. … While there is a concern for the projected monopoly of information, in order to cope with the large-scale TNCs, we need media conglomerates to match their size and resources.' In this regard, sprawling family-owned, big business groups in Korea, or *chaebol*, such as Samsung, Hyundai and Daewoo, to name a few, expanded into the media sector to include production, import, distribution and exhibition. In the process, the conventional Korean developmental regimen of an export-oriented economy continued, as evidenced by a remark made by a senior manager of the Daewoo group's film division: 'It is our duty and responsibility to export Korean films overseas.' In the context of the public's rising interest in 'our culture' provoked by *Sopyonje*, and the improved film-viewing environment enabled by *chaebol* investment, including expanding film choices and more convenient theatre facilities, Korean cinema gradually began to attract local audiences. [...]

In general, the Korean pop music market was not vibrant before the 1990s. Korean youth preferred American pop songs to local ones; live concerts were not common and, when they were held, they were on a small scale. In fact, the two public television networks, Korea Broadcasting System (KBS) and Munhwa Broadcasting Company (MBC), controlled music distribution and held sway over the direction of music consumption. There was no authoritative record sales chart, except for weekly chart shows on television, which served as the only criteria by which songs and singers were judged popular, and by which audiences decided which albums they should buy. Furthermore, musicians were required to perform with the television networks' in-house studio bands and dancers, which deprived the country of the opportunity for diverse elements of local pop music to grow spontaneously. These conditions influenced musical styles to fit into the specifications of the television medium, such that songs usually had a long instrumental introduction and an extended fade-out, to allow emcees to make some announcements, or a link between one song and another.

Transformation comes from the 'new and unexpected combination of human beings, cultures, ideas, politics, movies, songs' noted by Rushdie, thus changes originating from globalization trends and democratic reforms began to transform the local music market. After Seoul's 1988 lifting of restrictions on foreign travel, the country became more exposed to the outside world. With the sharp rise in disposable income in the early 1990s, many Koreans purchased satellite dishes to pick up Japanese stations and Star TV. Against this backdrop, Korean music fans came to have a better grasp of global music trends, and hungered for new tunes from local musicians. According to Howard: 'Political freedoms were mirrored by musical experimentation, as musicians began to realize that they had to attempt to be distinct if they were to succeed in gaining an audience. ... [M]ore and more musicians appropriated foreign music styles.' In this context, the three-man band Seo Taiji and Boys, composed of underground bassist-singer-songwriter Seo Taiji and two rapper-dancers, released the single 'I Know' in 1992. This was arguably the first rap track in Korea, and it excited local music listeners, who were fed up with the ballads and *ppongjjak* that lacked dynamism and musical experimentation. [...]

Seo Taiji and Boys' popularity was based on innovative hybridization of music. The band creatively mixed genres like rap, soul, rock and roll, techno, punk, hardcore and even *ppongjjak*, and invented a unique musical form which 'employs rap only during the verses, singing choruses in a pop style' with dynamic dance movements. Each of their albums was in itself a musical experimentation. In their first album, they showed how Korean rap would sound. In their second, they experimented with a crossover between 'high and low' music by inviting the traditional Korean percussionist Kim Deoksu and modern jazz saxophonist Lee Jeongsik to play for their album recordings. From their third album, they became 'vocal' in sending out social messages, with an attempt at gangsta rap. Since Seo Taiji, the syncretism of a wide range of musical genres in one album has become commonplace in Korea. What has come into existence is a hybrid but distinctively Korean pop style.

Second, Seo Taiji and Boys not only expanded the scope of K-pop but also the scale of the music market. In the small, dormant market, the group's first album was 'the fastest-selling record since 1982'. During its four years of activity, the band was estimated to have earned more than 10 billion won from record sales (6 million copies of their four albums), music video sales, concerts and other commercial activities. With an endless crop of imitation groups of Seo Taiji and Boys, sales of home-grown pop acts have since outpaced foreign albums by four to one, the Recording Industry Association of Korea reports. As of 2002, Korea is the second largest music market in Asia with $300 million album sales per year. [...]

The factor of 'cultural proximity' is not enough to explain the success of K-pop across the region. According to a Chinese K-pop fan: 'Korean pop culture skillfully blends Western and Asian values to create its own, and the country itself is viewed as a prominent model to follow or catch up, both culturally and economically.' This explanation is most appropriate in Vietnam where 'South Korean TV dramas provide the tightly controlled communist country with an enticing glimpse of the outside world'. As such, the 'vision of modernization' inherent in Korean popular culture plays a part in making it acceptable in some Asian countries.

The development of Korean media industries and their advance into regional markets is clearly a sign of resilience of the subaltern – and of the 'contamination of the imperial', considering the context of decades-long American domination of global cultural industries. However, while Korean cinema is enjoying success, the all-or-nothing blockbuster business has caused concern over a narrowing of diversity. It is reported that, as of early February 2004, *TaeGukGi: The Brotherhood of War* was playing on 110 screens while *Silmido* was being shown on 53 screens, combining to take up nearly 92 percent of Seoul's total 178 screens. Industry observers have begun to say, 'What Korean cinema needs now is not one movie that attracts 10 million viewers, but 10 movies that attract 1 million viewers.' We need to be reminded that, until now, all the outcries against cultural imperialism have been made to protect 'diversity' and the 'coexistence' of cultures. Similarly, the commercial drive of the Korean media is also a cause for concern for the media performance. No longer constrained by the obligation of public service, media companies indulge themselves in pursuing profit maximization by getting their products and services to the largest number of consumers, not only in Korea but also overseas, and this kind of capitalist activity has been justified in the name of national interests. However, it is time for us to ask what constitutes national interests. [...]

49

Watching *Big Brother* at Work
A Production Study of Big Brother *Australia*

Jane Roscoe

This chapter details a production study of *Big Brother* Australia. In doing so, it provides a case study of an innovative multi-platform media event. It is an example of a format that delivers its content across television, the Internet, telephony, print media and radio, in addition to the live events on site at the theme park, *Dreamworld*, where the *Big Brother* house is situated. It also provides an opportunity to examine the indigenisation of an international 'reality TV' format. It also draws on interviews with many of the key creative personnel, textual analyses, as well as on an audience survey conducted on the *Big Brother 2* website. Key issues concerning the development of the format, interactivity and media convergence are analysed and explored. It is also an attempt to move beyond the very tired and simplistic readings of 'reality TV' that seek to position it as evidence of television's 'dumbing down' or as an example of the democratisation of media. Both positions fail to consider the more interesting questions of how these programmes have changed contemporary broadcasting practices, the complexity of the productions and the innovative relationships constructed between the producers, texts and audiences. This chapter thus takes as its starting point the notion that these programmes are not cheap and dumb, but rather they are complex productions that speak to a media-savvy audience who are sophisticated in their understanding and use of the various platforms. It provides an alternative analysis that seeks to move beyond such simplistic readings of the form.

Original publication details: Jane Roscoe, from "Watching Big Brother at Work: A Production Study of Big Brother Australia," in *Big Brother International: Formats, Critics and Publics*, ed. Ernest Mathijs and Janet Jones. London: Wallflower Press, 2004. pp. 181–6, 188–9, 191–2. Reproduced with permission from Columbia University Press.

The Rise of Popular Factual Entertainment

Somewhere along the way television changed.

Reality-based programming, often referred to as 'reality TV' now dominates schedules across the world. A brief look at the TV guide in any number of international locations will probably reveal a week packed with DIY shows, cookery programmes, docu-soap formats such as *Popstars*, and most recently 'reality game shows' such as *Survivor* and *Big Brother*. Certainly in Australia, these shows not only fill the schedules, but also top the highest ratings lists. These are shows that have been able to attract large audiences, thus appearing to satisfy viewers, networks and their advertisers. While initially they were globally cheap to make in comparison with home-produced dramas and documentary (for example, *Funniest Home Videos*, or various emergency style shows) today's programmes are far more sophisticated and expensive to produce. In Australia Network Ten paid $AUS 28 million to secure the second series of *Big Brother* and the first *Celebrity Big Brother*, and is rumoured to have paid about the same for series which aired in April 2003.

James Friedman has argued that 'the proliferation of reality-based programming in the year 2000 does not represent a fundamental shift in televisual programming.' However, I would suggest that in fact there has been a very significant shift in the contemporary television landscape, and that popular factual entertainment is both a symptom and response to those shifts.

There has been a marked swing towards 'light entertainment' in factual programming, and a greater circulation of new television formats. Together this has changed the look of prime-time television. In place of the long-running dramas and current affairs shows are docu-soaps and reality game shows. There is nothing new about formats; soap operas and game shows have been circulating internationally for some time. What is new is the configuration; these formats seem to be at the nexus of the local and the global. That is, they seem to be both reflective of local cultures and adhere to a desire for local content, yet do so within a framework that is clearly designed to be universal and easily sold around the globe much like any other franchise.

There has been considerable debate as to the reasons and consequences of this shift to light entertainment and this reliance on formats. Some critics have argued that popular factual entertainment programmes like *Popstars* and *Big Brother* have directly contributed to the decline in drama production in Australia. Others have argued that such programmes have undermined the documentary project. Both positions see the new television formats as the reason for less local production across factual and fictional programming. What both positions fail to acknowledge is that these new formats are both a consequence of, and a response to, the wider changes in production and policy that have resulted in less drama and documentary.

The contemporary broadcasting landscape has been changed by technological developments, changes in regulation practices and specific changes in production processes. Audiences are more fragmented, sophisticated, knowing, and as a consequence, more demanding. Our relationship to (and with) television has changed; media convergence means that content is now often delivered across a number of different platforms resulting in new relationships between texts and audiences. We might engage with this content simultaneously across different platforms, for example watching the television show while also accessing the website and sending an SMS (short message service delivered via cell or mobile phones) to the show. While this may not yet be the experience of the majority of viewers, recent studies have shown that it is the experience of certain groups of viewers, in particular young people.

Reality formats have changed the broadcasting landscape, but why are they so popular in so many different countries, across so many cultures? Like McDonalds, what they seem to do so well is translate the global product to the local context. Examining the process of 'indigenisation' provides some insight into why a programme like *Big Brother* seems to have done so well.

Making it Aussie: Indigenising an International Format

One of the significant things about *Big Brother* is the way in which it has been translated from an international format into a local phenomenon. Formats are traded around the globe, with the expectation (or assumption) that the local buyer has merely to add the local talent into a pre-determined structure. To a certain extent this is true. Each format comes with a 'Bible' that details every aspect of a show, from the opening graphics, to the number of scenes per episode, to the choice of host. *Big Brother* is no exception. Originally developed by Dutch company Endemol, the Bible lays down details such as how Big Brother should speak to housemates, provides challenges and tasks, and designs for the house. The Bible lays out a blueprint for an international brand. However, it is a misconception that the brand cannot be developed or changed. The Australian *Big Brother* provides a good example of this in that there are a number of ways in which the format has been 'indigenised' and made 'Aussie'.

The house

One of the most obvious ways in which the format is made local is through the design of the actual house. In Australia the *Big Brother* house is set in the grounds of the *Dreamworld* theme park on Queensland's Gold Coast. When series one went to air in 2001, the house looked very different from the images Australian audiences had been offered of the UK and US houses. It was surrounded by bush in a theme park on one of Australia's busiest and most commercial holiday hotspots. A tourist mecca, the Gold Coast embodies the Australian lifestyle – surf, sand and sunshine. The house itself was designed to capture these very qualities and to reflect a sense of 'Australianness'. Tim Clucas (Network Ten executive, and network commissioner of *Big Brother*) remarked, 'we wanted this to be a real Aussie house, that means relaxed lifestyle, sunshine, backyard pool, backyard BBQ, a real Aussie *Big Brother*.'

The house was a far cry from the overseas versions, which looked to Australian audiences like prison compounds. In the second series the comfort was stepped up again, the furnishings supplied by Freedom Furniture (an aspirational furniture store), a spa had been added, and the whole house redecorated. Hanging around the pool and having a 'barbie' (barbeque) are all signifiers of the relaxed Australian life-style, something the show attempted to tap into and represent. It was important then that the house represented the 'local', yet it was also comfortable for other reasons, the house had to be a 'non-issue'. It was suggested by the producers that once you take the house out of the equation, the participants focus on themselves (rather than their surroundings) and the audience are also then able to focus on the participants and their relationships. It seemed to work and perhaps it is not surprising that around the globe *Big Brother* houses were spruced up for the second and third series.

The cast

It is not only the house that represented a certain version of Australian national iden-tity, the housemates also embodied certain characteristics associated with a certain version of national identity. While the producers claim not to be casting particular characters, they acknowledge their desire to reflect Australia in their choices:

> In terms of the casting it was about trying to find, to some extent, Australian types. People who represented the types of people you would meet in the community, and it was useful to think about that without having a shopping list of any specific types.

There was much discussion about the choice of housemates and whether they were representative of Australia. The housemates in the first series seemed to embody the ideals of health, fitness and certain 'outdoorsiness', a central trope of Australianness. The winner, Ben, could be described as the archetypal Aussie male. He is a rugby fan, likes his beer, has a dry sense of humour, calls everyone 'mate' and inhabits what can be called 'good bloke country'. In the second series, Peter (the winner), looked remarkably similar to Ben, and exhibited many of the same 'blokey' characteristics. Marty, the runner-up in series two, was also an archetypal character, a young naïve country boy who embodied 'rural Australia', a land full of drovers (someone who drives cattle, sheep, and so on, to markets, usually over long distances) and farmboys.

In the second series there was an attempt to update the representation of Australia that had been offered in series one. There had been some criticism that the partici-pants in series one had not been a diverse enough group, and not really representative of 'Australia'. However, it should be noted that the producers never made any such claims to represent the nation. This was a discourse drawn on by critics and audi-ences. Certainly in series two there was, on the surface at least, a greater range of identities on offer, from the 'rural young male' (Marty), to the bisexual city girl (Sahra) to the older sporty woman (Shannon) to the mixed heritage social worker (Turkan). All of the participants seemed to be more sophisticated, media savvy, more 'aware' and certainly more 'knowing' about the actual format and so much more aware of being 'on show' at all times. In spite of these surface changes, the same dis-courses seemed to structure the experience of being in the house.

A key discourse is that of 'mateship'. Mateship is central to notions of national identity in Australia. Significantly, it is a discourse that is associated with a certain version of Australian masculinity. It was noted by many people who worked on the show how 'mateship' seemed to be at the centre of the *Big Brother* experience. For example, Dave English, who worked as day-producer on the first series, noted how the housemates reacted to losing tasks. They did not seem to care whether they won or lost; it was more about being in it together: 'It's a cultural thing … They don't seem to give a bugger whether they win or lose.'

In the public discussions of the show, mateship often featured as a key indicator of what the show was about, and it's Australianness. The house activities often focused on activities that might bond the participants together (for example, painting the living room) as well as being a site in which individual housemates were able to exhibit the qualities of mateship (for example, supporting someone through an emotional crisis). [...]

Producing *Big Brother*

The style of the Australian *Big Brother* was also to a certain extent indigenised, with producers responding to the context in which the show was shown. In Australia, the daily show was broadcast at 7pm each night, with a G-rated audience (suitable for all viewers) in mind. It also followed the very successful long-running soap opera, *Neighbours*. It ran on Channel Ten, a commercial broadcaster who has most recently reinvented itself as the 'youth channel' with their target audience being 16 to 39 years old.

Peter Abbott talks about the broader social and cultural factors that impacted on how the show was made, and the relationship between himself and the housemates:

> In terms of how we ultimately made the show, I think it [cultural differences] had most effect upon our structural style and our editing style because classic *Big Brother* has four scenes a show … my sense was – or the sense of a lot of us was – that we should be making something that more closely followed an Australian soap opera model which involved more scenes.
>
> I think the audience is ready for it because they have a literacy in the grammar of soap operas, which means you can come into the scene two-thirds of the way as long as you know what the plot line is. The classic format is not for this time-slot.

The (mostly) non-authoritative relationship between Big Brother (Peter Abbott) and the housemates also owes something to cultural differences:

> It's a very Australian thing. Only in Australia would the housemates, when I come over the loud speaker saying, 'This is Big Brother', say 'Hello Pete'. I said 'stop it' but it's that Australian attitude to authority that goes back to our culture … there is no culture of authoritarianism in Australia and there is no culture of inherited respect.

The relationship also changed between the first and second series. The housemates had seen the first series and, like the audience, knew how the game was played.

Generally more media savvy, the second set of housemates already had a different relationship with Big Brother. This was not just the case in Australia, but in other versions around the globe, as Abbott notes:

> I think from my discussions with other Big Brothers, inevitably one has to become tougher because the housemates become more knowing. They play a tougher game with you and you have to become much tougher with them within limits ... in the second season where everyone understands a bit better what's going on you can start tightening the screws without getting rebellion. [...]

Developing a Fan Base

One of the most significant things about *Big Brother* is the way in which it has been able to mobilise and engage audiences across a number of delivery platforms. *Big Brother* has created an active fan base as well as an audience for the show. The show has rated well with Channel Ten's target audience; in the first and second series they have managed to secure (and retain) over 50 per cent of the 19–39-year-olds. However, it is not just that people are watching but they are participating in a number of ways across the various media platforms.

There are three important ways in which *Big Brother* has allowed for participation on behalf of the audience: through the siting of the House at *Dreamworld* theme park, through *Big Brother Online*, and through telephone voting. These activities and sites are central to the creation of a fan base. Here I am drawing on the work of those who see fans as active in their appropriation of texts, critical in their understandings of them and, importantly, also see the fan as a producer rather than a consumer of texts.

The location of the house, production facilities and the studio set at *Dreamworld* allow for a number of different spin-off events and experiences. It brings together entertainment and education – the location set with the theme park – and is certainly unique in terms of the worldwide *Big Brother* productions. For the fan of the show there are opportunities to go behind the scenes and find out more about how the show is put together. Visitors to the *Big Brother* exhibit are able to view the control room, although they cannot visit the actual house while the series is running. At the end of the series, the house is open to visitors; here they can visit the mock-up Diary Room and have their photograph taken, and share a confession or two. For the fan visitor it is a chance to engage in what Nick Couldry calls a 'shared fiction', that is, the shared experience of being there. He suggests that this experience is not always about memories or nostalgia, but is an 'anticipated act of commemoration', an experience to be remembered in the future when watching the show.

Being on site can enhance the viewing experience and enjoyment of the show because it allows access to the processes of production that are so often hidden. Seeing the banks of TV screens in the control room gives a sense of how much material there is, and how little makes the 7pm show. It erodes the usual distinction between the viewer and the producer by allowing the visitor access to knowledges that are specialised and usually reserved for those working in the industry.

In every *Big Brother* there is always a crowd to greet the week's evictees, but, in Australia, the crowd is managed and regulated in quite a specific way. One of the reasons locating the house at *Dreamworld* was so attractive was the possibility of using the large auditorium to turn the eviction show into a live event. The eviction show has evolved into a forum in which a whole range of fan activities can be performed. The live audience are there to be seen, both by the evictee on arrival in the auditorium, but also by the audience at home. [...]

Big Brother Online

The website is a central component of the event that is *Big Brother* and it provides the audience with a range of activities that allow it to construct different relationships with the text and other viewers.

> We never intended to be just a support site for the TV show. It's actually about something extra ... More depth is what we like to think. Also, it's a direct interface to viewers and users. [...]

The relationship with audience members is potentially extended through the multi-platform experience in a number of ways. Updating the diary section every half-hour was a particularly successful strategy which gave 'fans' of *Big Brother* access to the most up-to-date information/inside gossip (which is the fans' 'currency') and provided a reason to check the website at regular intervals during the day. It also allows a relationship to be built with audience members that is of a different quality. This is where the development of the format is also of keen interest to advertisers. Through a multi-platform delivery, advertisers and broadcasters now have the opportunity to talk to a member of the audience for an extended time each week rather than for the 26 minutes of a specific television show. As noted earlier, the development of new advertising strategies that integrate brands and services across the platforms is a key way in which *Big Brother* has been a leader with continuous innovation over the two series.

The experience of *Big Brother* shows that websites can do more than merely replicate what is represented on a particular television programme. They provide a site for audiences to interact (with the show and each other) and can be used to build loyalty to the product/brand. Far from turning people away from television, the survey results suggest that the website actually drives audiences to the show and to the other platforms. It clearly 'adds value'. It is worth noting that recent studies (in the UK and NZ) looking at young people's use of media shows that many have both TV and computers in their bedrooms, and that they use both media concurrently. Young people will watch TV shows while at the same time have the associated website open (and are probably sending out multiple SMS). Such patterns of usage are not unusual, and are likely to become more commonplace. [...]

Examining the production of *Big Brother* in Australia has provided rich data to explore the changing nature of contemporary popular factual entertainment, particularly the development of reality 'event television'. In particular, greater media convergence, both in terms of technological developments and audience uptake, has meant that there are greater possibilities for the delivery of content. This has been capitalised on by the producers of *Big Brother* who have made good use of the online environment and telephony to allow audiences greater opportunities for interaction, and qualitative advantages for advertisers and brands.

While *Big Brother* is an international format, a brand in itself, it is not an unchanging product. Rather as this case study shows, it has been indigenised and developed for and by the specific cultural and social context of Australia. Here we see the intersection of the local and the global and the negotiation of this terrain. There are indications that the relationship between producers and participants, producers and audiences, and between audiences and texts is constantly changing, which is why the format seems to be able to continue to intrigue audiences and scholars alike. For those who work on the show it also provides an opportunity to make a different type of television. Event television is not the norm, and so provides training and opportunities to both experienced practitioners and emerging producers in Australia.

While many critics (across the world) have been quick to dismiss the format, taking *Big Brother* seriously, as a cultural product and an experiment in multi-platform delivery, allows a different view of the show. Far from being cheap and dumb, it is in fact expensive, complicated and geared to a sophisticated viewer. As digitalisation provides greater access to more channels, as format trade increases and media convergence becomes the mainstream, it will be formats such as *Big Brother* that lead the way. Reality TV is not going away, but it will never be the same.

50

Bollywood versus Hollywood
Battle of the Dream Factories

Heather Tyrrell

Introduction

Theorisation around cinema and globalisation has largely been structured in terms of a basic opposition between Western commercial and culturally imperialist cinema, and Third World non-commercial, indigenous, politicised cinema. Much criticism of Hollywood and much support for alternative cinemas have been based on this under-stood opposition. 'Bollywood', North Indian popular commercial cinema, is an anomalous case which forces us to re-think the global map of cultural consumption and challenge the assumptions generally made concerning world cinema.

While India is not the only non-Western country with a commercial, popular, indigenous cinema – the cinemas of Hong Kong, China, Mexico and Brazil could be similarly described – its film industry is at this time experiencing rapid changes which make it a particularly pertinent subject for examination. '"Bollywood" has become widespread [sic] nomenclature for the Indian movie industry in recent times' and amalgamates two names: 'Hollywood', and 'Bombay' (India's commercial hub, now renamed Mumbai). But is Bollywood named in imitation of Hollywood, or as a challenge to it? For many years commentators have assumed the former, but if Bollywood were simply a substitute for Western film while economic barriers pre-vented the import of the original, once those barriers collapsed it would be expected that Bollywood would collapse too.

Original publication details: Heather Tyrrell, "Bollywood versus Hollywood: Battle of the Dream Factories," in *Culture and Global Change*, ed. Tracey Skelton and Tim Allen. Abingdon: Routledge, 1999. pp. 260–6, 272–3. Reproduced with permission from Taylor & Francis.

However, Indian film culture has not been undermined or devalued by the recent influx of Western product as some expected, and multinational companies have not succeeded in dominating the prized Indian market. The role and the importance of popular Indian cinema culture has been misinterpreted or underestimated by external commentators, perhaps precisely because it does not fit easily into the theoretical model developed around the dichotomy of First World and Third World cinema.

This chapter will begin by situating Bollywood within and against the theories formulated around Third World film known as Third Cinema theory. I will then go on to relate theory to practice by looking at three aspects of the Bollywood film industry: first, the current volatile period of change in India's film and media culture, as the international film industry attempts to enter the Indian market; second, Bollywood itself as an international film industry, in terms of production, distribution and exhibition; and third, oppositions to Bollywood as a dominant cultural force in India. By focusing on these areas I hope to demonstrate why Bollywood is fertile theoretical ground for Development Studies and Cultural Studies alike, and may force us to rethink how Third World popular culture is read.

Bollywood and Third Cinema

'Third Cinema' is a term coined originally by Argentine film-makers Fernando Solanas and Octavio Gettino, and generally applied to the theory of cinemas opposed to imperialism and colonialism. Bollywood, as a commercial popular cinema, has a problematic relationship to theories of Third Cinema, which assume a non-commercial, minority cinema as their subject.

In discussions of world cinema, the mainstream is generally taken to be North American and European cinema, with others as oppositional, marginal, and most significantly, non-commercial. Bollywood, the most prolific film industry in the world, and one with an international commercial market, challenges this assumption. Bollywood films are not solely politically motivated, nor are they entirely devoid of nationalist/anti-colonialist content. They are at once 'escapist' and ideologically loaded.

In *Questions of Third Cinema*, Jim Pines and Paul Willemen (1989) talk about Third World films as 'physical acts of collective self-defence and resistance'. Bollywood can be read both as defending itself and Indian values against the West, and as a dangerous courier of Western values to the Indian audience, and is read in both these ways by the Indian popular film press. A constant process of negotiation between East and West takes place in Bollywood films, operating both in terms of style (narrative continuity, *mise-en-scène*, acting styles), and in terms of content (the values and ideas expressed in the films). Indian cinematic style negotiates the cinematic traditions of Classical Hollywood, while its content addresses the ideological heritage of colonisation; just as, in the 'picturisation' of a single film song, hero and heroine oscillate between Eastern and Western dress in a rapid series of costume swaps as they dance and mime to music which is itself a hybrid of Eastern and Western styles.

But does this negotiation, and its often overt anti-Western agenda, qualify Bollywood as Third Cinema? A cinema does not automatically qualify for the title because it is produced in and for the Third World. Argentine film-makers Fernando Solanas and Octavio Gettino, defined any 'big spectacle cinema' financed by big monopoly capital as First Cinema, 'likely to respond to the aspirations of big capital'. Third Cinema was 'democratic, national, popular cinema'. But both these statements can equally be applied to Bollywood, which, despite its prolific commercial profile, has always been refused industry status by the Indian government, and which, historically, received subsidies from Nehru's government to pursue an explicitly anti-colonial agenda.

Fidel Castro fiercely criticised Hollywood in his closing speech at the 1985 Havana Film Festival:

> They are poisoning the human mind in incredible doses through commercial cinematography, grossly commercial. [Third world cinema must be supported, because] if we do not survive culturally we will not survive economically or politically.

Compare this speech with an article by Shah Rukh Khan, India's top film star, in 1996, defending Bollywood's commercial film industry in an introduction to a feature on 100 years of Indian cinema in *Movie International* magazine.

> I'd like to stress we are part of world cinema and we are making films – films we like, not for film festivals ... Mark my words one day Indian cinema will rule the world. Once we get the technology we are going to kill them.

Khan's military metaphors are directed explicitly against the West, and not only against Hollywood and commercial cinema, but also against the independent, alternative cinema of 'film festivals' – cinema that could, in many cases, be described as 'Third Cinema'.

Bollywood seems both diametrically opposed to, and fiercely aligned to, Third Cinema. This confusion arises because commercialism has been exclusively identified with the West in cultural criticism, without taking into account a non-Western, even anti-Western commercialism. A cinema which is both commercial and concerned with 'decoding ... the deemed superiority of the West' problematises established theoretical oppositions of East and West. Some of the strategies of Third Cinema can be applied to it, but so can some of the criticisms levelled at Hollywood. Vijay Mishra in his essay *The Texts of 'Mother India'* (1989) argues that Bollywood cannot be seen as Third Cinema, despite its 'defiantly subversive' stance, because it is ultimately conforming: 'popular Indian Cinema is so conservative and culture specific as to make a radical post colonial Indian Cinema impossible'.

Third Cinema is commonly perceived as 'serious' cinema, challenging in an aesthetic as well as a political sense. Bollywood films generally include light-hearted song-and-dance numbers, causing Tim Allen to dismiss them from the Third Cinema equation in his dossier on Third Cinema: 'In India serious films are not generally very popular at all. Most cinemas show jolly musicals ...'

However, as Mira Reym Binford says in her essay *Innovation and Imitation in Indian Cinema*:

the obligatory song-and-dance sequences of the Indian mainstream film are a striking example of indigenously based aesthetic principles [with remote antecedents in the traditional Sanskrit drama] shaping the use of imported technology.

These very song-and-dance sequences are a form of opposition to Western cultural imperialism. Also, Bollywood films are not musicals alone; they are an 'Omnibus' or a 'Masala' form, combining melodrama, action, comedy, social commentary and romance, violently juxtaposing intensely tragic scenes with jolly song and dance numbers, jolting the viewer from one extreme of feeling to another (an aesthetic similarly inherited from Sanskrit theatre).

However, if Bollywood has not developed, stylistically, as 'serious' Third Cinema, neither has its style much connection with Hollywood. Indian cinema has developed a film language which has little or nothing in common with the codes of classical Hollywood cinema and, ironically, this has caused some critics to dismiss Bollywood as escapist. Modes of presentation termed escapist according to the classical Hollywood mode, like the song-and-dance number, are, however, used to play on 'deep tensions – between wealth and poverty, old and new, hope and fear' in Indian films. For example, in the 1996 film *Army,* a song-and-dance routine breaks out in a prison compound, and prisoners sing, while cartwheeling about the exercise yard, that poverty is so extreme in Indian society outside the prison walls that they are better off in jail, under a death sentence, because a death sentence hangs over them even outside prison.

Ironically, while, from the outside, Bollywood is popularly viewed as a more escapist cinema than even Western commercial cinema, it has absorbed within it as successful commercial product a number of challenging and 'serious' films that in the West achieved only a small, independent distribution. Shekhar Kapoor's *Bandit Queen* (1995) was among the top ten grossing films of 1996 in India, over a year after its small-scale, independent release in the UK, and made $1 million in its first week of Indian release. The harrowing film is based on the life of outlaw Phoolan Devi, and confronts head-on the abuse of women in Indian society: Bollywood's aesthetic evidently cannot be dismissed as 'frivolous' if a film this 'serious' can achieve such enormous commercial success.

'Hollywood Raises Hell in Bollywood'

Hollywood/Bollywood relations are at a moment of crux, as the lifting of the ban on dubbing foreign films into Hindi in 1992 has left Hollywood free to enter the Indian market. However, audiences have shown little interest in Western imported film product; the barriers against the West are revealed as cultural, not simply economic, and 'Hindi films' have, effectively, 'triumphed over Hollywood in India'. Media coverage taken from the British and American film press, of the attempts of Hollywood to dominate the last remaining world market, chart some of the assumptions made, and broken down, before and during the current surprising impasse for Hollywood in India. In comparison, the discourses around East and West, film and culture, that are used in the Indian press, are just as dismissive, even hostile, towards the West, and believe just as confidently in the greater merit of their own cinema.

The *Guardian's* film critic, Derek Malcolm, warned that 'a giant culture clash [was] looming' in India, as 'Spielberg's *Jurassic Park,* dubbed into Hindi, [had] given a fright to the massive Indian film industry'. An article in *The Sunday Times* in June 1995, 'Hollywood Raises Hell in Bollywood' predicted doom for the Indian film industry following the release of action movies such as Sylvester Stallone's *Cliffhanger* (1993), with its higher production values, and, as Lees quotes Indian sources as saying, 'machine guns instead of rifles'. However, the reception of Stallone's *First Blood* (1982), renamed *Blood* and released in July 1995 in India, was lukewarm. Trade reviews commented that 'the film holds appeal mainly for action film lovers', and judged its publicity and opening 'so so'.

Bollywood vs. Hollywood

The reasons for Bollywood's resistance to colonisation by Hollywood are aesthetic and cultural as well as political. The formula for Bollywood films has been jokingly summarised as 'A star, six songs, three dances', and these Omnibus or Masala films must have the right mix of a diverse range of ingredients to satisfy their audiences. Without them a film 'lacks in entertainment value'.

However rigid this formula, adherence to it does not guarantee a film's success. Only one in ten films makes a profit, and whether a film is a hit or a flop depends on the unquantifiable judgement of the Bombay audience, who either fill or desert cinema houses in a film's first week of release. Films which imitate the formula of previous hits sink without a trace, while others appear from nowhere to become blockbusters. As Subhash K. Jha remarks in *G magazine:* 'The vagaries of the box-office have flummoxed film-makers and trade watchers forever'. If Indian film-makers are unable to guarantee audiences, Western film product is unlikely to do so.

The market for undubbed Western films in India before 1992 was very small, consisting only of an English speaking middle-class élite, and Western films had far shorter runs than Hindi films. Hollywood first attempted to attract Indian audiences after 1992 by dubbing major American hits into Hindi, but so far only a fraction of the films released have been commercially successful with the Hindi-speaking mass market. *Jurassic Park* (1993), *Speed* (1994) and *Dunston Checks In* (1995) – colloquially translated as 'A Monkey in a Hotel' – have been box office successes, but others, such as *Schindler's List* (1993), *The Flintstones* (1994) and *Casper* (1995), have 'bombed'. Even those films which did not 'bomb' achieved only a fraction of the success of domestic Indian films: in the same year that *Jurassic Park* grossed $6 million, *Hum Aapke Hain Koun … !* (1994) grossed $60 million. Hollywood has not yet discerned a pattern as to which films succeed and which 'flop' in India.

One significant factor in films' successes, which may be too culturally specific for Hollywood to duplicate, is their music. 'Popular music in India is synonymous with film music', and the popular film and music industries in India are interdependent. Not only does Indian popular film depend on music, Indian popular music also depends on film. Peter Manuel (1993), in his book *Cassette Culture,* explains the history of this symbiosis in economic terms; before the cassette revolution in the 1970s, the cinema was the most accessible way to hear popular music for many Indians. Film music is also culturally important; as Sanjeev Prakash (1984) notes in his article *La musique, la danse et le film populaire [Music, Dance and Popular Film]*, film music so pervades Indian culture that it is played even at marriages and religious festivals.

The star system too is a formidable force in India, and another factor excluding Western cinema. The earliest Indian films were known as 'mythological', portraying the adventures of Hindu gods such as Krishna, and the equation of actors with gods has remained. Many Indian film stars go on to become politicians and national icons, representing quintessential 'Indianness'. Nargis, 'the woman in white', was the personification of 'Mother India' in the 1950s; Amitabh Bachchan has been India's greatest cinema icon for thirty years, and his face has come to be used as a symbol for India itself (as we shall see later). Western stars cannot compete with such quasi-religious iconography. A recent Hindi film, *Rock Dancer* (1995), starring Samantha Fox, a British glamour model turned pop singer, singing all her own songs in Hindi, received very little press attention and no commercial success. Though the urban middle classes knew her name well enough to merit an aside in one film news column, to the mass Hindi film audience, she was an unknown.

Having largely failed to export Western product to India, Hollywood is now investing in Indian studios – putting money into Bollywood, not attempting to replace it with its own product. The Indian view of this seems to be of a cultural victory; as Shah Rukh Khan (1996) expresses in his piece, 'Soon Hollywood will come to us'; but economically this is no great victory for India over the West, since profits from what appears a quintessentially Indian product will now go back to the West.

The Indian cinema box office was not essentially diminished by the rise of video in the 1970s, but now Bollywood must accommodate satellite and cable expansion. Rupert Murdoch's Star network attempted to sell Western programmes in India, but could only attract élite minority audiences; but when an Indian company set up a Hindi satellite channel, Zee TV, they attracted a far larger market, and were the impetus for a whole industry of Indian satellite and cable channels, which Star have now bought into. As interviews with Zee TV and Star TV spokesmen (they were all men) showed, both Indian and Western companies interpreted this as a victory. The Indian company believed they had beaten Star at their own game and reaped the rewards. Star felt they had finally found a way to infiltrate the Indian market, by using an Indian figurehead company. The successful move of multinational media companies into the Indian market was ultimately demonstrated, however, when the 42nd Annual Filmfare Awards, otherwise known as 'the Indian Oscars', were screened exclusively on Sony Entertainment Television's Hindi Channel in March 1997.

Popular discourses of Hollywood/Bollywood opposition

Both Hollywood and Bollywood have made their direct opposition explicit in India, and their rivalry has passed into popular cultural vocabulary. The promotion poster for Stallone's *Cliffhanger* (1993) reads 'Hollywood challenges Bollywood'; Hollywood's decision to choose *Cliffhanger* as the vehicle for its challenge was perhaps based on a superficial reading of contemporary Indian film as high in action content, without taking into consideration its juxtaposition with other elements of the 'Masala' mix, such as song and emotional melodrama. *Cliffhanger*'s challenge failed. In contrast, as one Indian trade paper commented, a series of Indian music cassettes entitled 'Bollywood vs Hollywood' have been highly commercially successful.

Within Indian popular culture, the commercial success of Indian cinema has become emblematic of India's resistance to the West, and Bollywood stars have become figureheads in what is viewed as a battle against Westernisation. Actress Madhuri Dixit, known as Bollywood's 'queen bee', 'drew herself up and lectured the guy on patriotism' when a fan 'offered her a Canadian dollar for an autograph'. I have already mentioned the nationalist sentiments expressed by actor Shah Rukh Khan in a *Movie* magazine feature. Another instance is an advert for BPL (an Indian electrical hardware company) which appeared in *G magazine,* a leading Indian English-language film magazine, every month from October 1996 to January 1997. The advert combines a photograph of film star Amitabh Bachchan with discourses around national pride. December's advert concludes:

> Who would have guessed a few centuries ago that India would become a poor, Third-World country? And who knows what India will become in the next century? Who knows what may happen if we believe in ourselves?

Hollywood's failure to supersede Bollywood reveals that an existing Third World culture can be a crucial factor in halting Western cultural imperialism, even when political and economic barriers are lifted. Barnouw and Krishnaswamy (1963) describe in *The Indian Film* how Hollywood monopolised the world cinema market during the First World War, while other film producers were handicapped by the loss of resources and labour-power to the war effort, and successfully defined the cinematic experience for the rest of the world according to their product, so that, in effect, politics shaped economics shaped culture. However, Hollywood has not defined what makes a film work in India, where, conversely, cultural disparity, rather than any political or economic factor, has slowed Western commercial expansion. [...]

Conclusion

Bollywood is a wild-card in the globalisation process of the media. Its position is constantly shifting: influenced by its diasporic audiences, by Western moves into India, by newly emerging cultural dialogues between East and West, and by new technologies and their implications. Its relationship with the West has undergone radical changes in the last four years, which will no doubt change its future, although quite probably on its own terms rather than those of the West. Bollywood does not see itself as a minority cinema, but claims the right to be taken seriously as a commercial popular cinema. It demonstrates, finally, that the use of culture as a global force, and as a hegemonic force, is not confined to the West alone.

The existence of another economically imperialist international cinema outside Hollywood is in itself no cause for celebration simply because that cinema opposes Hollywood. Problematic issues around Bollywood and Hindu nationalism, élitism, censorship and corruption should not be glossed over. It has been my intention instead to suggest a reappraisal of current dichotomies of thought between East and West, between commercial and oppositional cinema, by highlighting how unstable these positions look when viewed from an entirely different perspective, a perspective taken, as far as possible, from within India.

A reappraisal of Indian cinema may challenge our assumptions not only about First World and Third World cultural politics, but also our assumptions about what constitutes commercial, and what oppositional, or 'art' cinema, for, as I have discussed, what has in the West been seen as 'difficult' independent cinema fare, has in India been consumed by mass audiences with greater enthusiasm than what we understand as overtly commercial Hollywood films.

I have left the issue of quality out of my discussion of Bollywood, largely because I do not presume to make value judgements on a cultural product designed for consumption by a culture relatively alien to my own experience. Bollywood films have, historically, been dismissed as formulaic and poor quality, and their audience, by inference, as unsophisticated. However, not only can the Bollywood audience watch a film for longer, generally, than a Western audience (Hindi films are uniformly three hours long), it is tolerant of, in fact hungry for, film which in the West is considered too 'challenging' for mainstream, commercial audiences. Which begs the question: which is, in fact, the more truly 'sophisticated' cinema audience? Hollywood's, or Bollywood's?

51

Why Hollywood Rules the World, and Whether We Should Care

Tyler Cowen

Cinema is one of the hard cases for globalization. When we look at world music, the visual arts, or literature, it is readily apparent how trade has brought a more diverse menu of choice *and* helped many regions develop cultural identities. In each of these cultural sectors, the market has room for many producers, in large part because the costs of production are relatively low.

But what about film? In no other cultural area is America's export prowess so strong. Movies are very expensive to make, and in a given year there are far fewer films released than books, CDs, or paintings. These conditions appear to favor dominant producers at the expense of niche markets. So if cross-cultural exchange will look bad anywhere, it is in the realm of cinema.

Moviemaking also is prone to geographic clustering. Many cultural innovations and breakthroughs are spatially concentrated. If a good Italian Renaissance painter was not born in Florence, Venice, or Rome, he usually found it worthwhile to move to one of those locales. An analogous claim is true for Hollywood, which attracts cinematic talent from around the world, strengthening its market position.

The degree of clustering has reached a sufficient extreme, and Hollywood movies have become so publicly visible, as to occasion charges of American cultural imperialism. European movies, in particular, have failed to penetrate global markets and also have lost ground at home. Many individuals claim that when it comes to cinema, global culture is a threat rather than a promise.

Original publication details: Tyler Cowen, "Why Hollywood Rules the World, and Whether We Should Care," in *Creative Destruction*. Princeton: Princeton University Press, 2002. pp. 73–5, 79–80, 83, 87–9, 93–6, 101. Reproduced with permission from Princeton University Press.

What lies behind these charges? To what extent is movie production clustered in Hollywood, and why has such clustering taken place? Why is European cinema so economically moribund? Have other national cinemas fared badly as well? Is cinematic clustering inimical to diversity, and if so, could it be reversed? Most generally, has cross-cultural exchange damaged diversity in the realm of cinema?

Why Clustering in Hollywood?

The current malaise in European cinema is driven by a concatenation of unfavorable forces, involving television, excess subsidies, demographics, language, the size of the American market, and Hollywood's more entrepreneurial environment. While some negative charges can be pinned on globalization, we will see that cross-cultural exchange is not the primary culprit in the story.

The United States has at least one natural advantage in movie making – it has the largest single home-market for cinema in dollar terms (although total attendance is higher in India). The countries that specialize in moviemaking will tend to be those countries where movies are most popular, in this case America and India. Hong Kong has been an exception to this principle, but a large domestic market does give a natural advantage. Home audiences often (though not always) prefer native products, if only for reasons of language and cultural context, and this encourages production to shift to that market.

Aggregate market-size nonetheless remains only a single factor in determining who becomes a market leader. The United States, for instance, has been a large country for a long time, but only recently have European movies held such a low share of their home markets. In the mid-1960s, American films accounted for 35 percent of box office revenues in continental Europe; today the figure ranges between 80 to 90 percent. The greater population of the United States, and the greater American interest in moviegoing, do not themselves account for these changes.

Furthermore, only certain kinds of cinema cluster in Hollywood. In a typical year the Western European nations make more movies than America does. In numeric terms most of the world's movies come from Asia, not from the United States. It is not unusual for India to release between 800 and 900 commercial films a year, compared to about 250 from the United States.

The Hollywood advantage is concentrated in one very particular kind of moviemaking: films that are entertaining, highly visible, and have broad global appeal. The typical European film has about 1 percent of the audience of the typical Hollywood film, and this differential has been growing. American movies have become increasingly popular in international markets, while European movies have become less so. [...]

In the United States, the television and video markets serve as handmaidens for the theatrical market, augmenting its influence over the quality of the product. While some movies succeed on video alone, video success typically depends on the advance publicity generated by the film at the theatrical box office. The same can be said for success on television, or for the sale of television rights. Theatrical revenue thus drives both video revenue and television revenue in the American market. In Europe, in contrast, television revenue is more likely to be a *substitute* for theatrical revenue. European films, which experience major box office successes far less frequently, are more likely to be placed on television as filler.

The roles of television and subsidies are closely linked. Most west European nations have television stations that are owned, controlled, or strictly regulated by their respective governments, which use them to promote a national cultural agenda. Typically the stations face domestic-content restrictions, must spend a certain percentage of revenue on domestic films, must operate a film production subsidiary, or they willfully overpay for films for political reasons. The end result is overpayment for broadcast rights – the most important subsidy that many European moviemakers receive. Audience levels are typically no more than one or two million at the television level, even in the larger countries such as France – too small to justify the sums paid to moviemakers for television rights on economic grounds. [...]

The English language, combined with America's role as world leader, has strengthened Hollywood exports. Cinematic clustering, and the current crisis of European cinema, is rooted partially in the transition from silent film to talkies.

Counterintuitively, the onset of the sound era increased Hollywood's share of world cinematic revenue. At the time of the transition, equipping the theaters with sound and making movies with sound were costly. To recoup these costs, theaters sought out high-quality, high-expenditure productions for large audiences. The small, cheap, quick film became less profitable, given the suddenly higher fixed costs of production and presentation. This shift in emphasis favored Hollywood moviemakers over their foreign competitors.

More generally, the higher the fixed costs of production, the greater the importance of drawing a large audience and the greater the importance of demand forecasting and marketing. Today costly special effects and expensive celebrity stars drive the push for blockbusters in similar fashion, and favor Hollywood production as well.

The talkies, by introducing issues of translation, boosted the dominant world language of English and thus benefited Hollywood. Given the growing importance of English as a world language, and the focal importance of the United States, European countries would sooner import films from Hollywood than from each other. A multiplicity of different cultures or languages often favors the relative position of the dominant one, which becomes established as a common standard of communication. [...]

The Drive towards Clustering

In part, movie production clusters in particular geographic areas simply because there is no reason *not* to have clustering. When the cost of shipping the relevant goods and services are low, clustering makes economic sense.

Consider a more general economic analogy. There is more trade and mobility across the United States of America than across the disparate countries of Western Europe. This trade causes the economic profiles of the American states to diverge.

In economic terms, the countries of Western Europe are more likely to resemble each other than are the American states. Most of the American states have no steel industry, no automobile industry, and no wheat industry; instead they buy the products of these industries from other states or countries. But typically a nation of western Europe has its own steel, automobile, dairy, and agriculture sectors, largely because of subsidies and protectionism. Free trade within the United States allows states and regions to specialize to a high degree and causes their economic profiles to diverge; in a freer economic environment, the economies of western Europe would take the same path.

Trade and specialization thus bring geographic clustering when the basic product is mobile. Most American peanuts are grown in Georgia and Virginia and then shipped to the rest of the country. In contrast, each region of the United States performs its own cement manufacture, as does each country. The costs of trading and transporting cement are too high for clustered production, and subsequent transport, to be feasible. Action movies, however, resemble peanuts more than cement in this regard, especially if the film appeals broadly to many cultural groups.

Some of Hollywood's cinematic clustering is driven by the short-run, dynamic nature of film projects. Studios may dally over projects for years, but once the go-ahead decision has been made, the moviemakers wish to move as quickly as possible, to meet a perceived market demand. They need to assemble a large number of skilled employees on very short notice, and therefore they will "fish" for talent in a common, clustered pool. In similar fashion, the computer industry changes rapidly, many projects are short term, and once a go-ahead decision has been made, large numbers of talented employees must be assembled rapidly. Common forces therefore shape the clusters of Silicon Valley and Hollywood.

It is not always the case that movies can be *filmed* more cheaply in Hollywood than elsewhere. In fact, Hollywood studio hands are worried about how many movies are being outsourced to Canada, Australia, and other non-US locales, to lower production costs. Rather, clustering eases the finding, lining up, and evaluating of the movie's critical assets, such as stars, directors, and screenplays. These tasks are still done in Hollywood rather than in Vancouver or Sydney, regardless of where the movie is filmed.

The Hollywood cluster has a superior ability to evaluate cinematic projects and, in particular, to forecast and meet consumer demand. Hollywood is the geographic center for these kinds of talent. Ironically, it is easier to get a film made in Europe than America. In Hollywood, studios scrutinize projects intensely and refuse to finance projects that do not have a good chance of commercial success. Most European moviemakers do not apply similar filters. Hollywood is a cluster, in part, for the same reasons that New York and London are clustered banking centers. In both cases talents for large-scale project evaluation gravitate towards a single geographic area.

Moviemaking has become more expensive over the last thirty years, due largely to special effects, rising celebrity salaries, and marketing expenditures. All of these features have increased the natural advantage of talents for demand forecasting and project evaluation. They have increased the natural advantage of Hollywood. [...]

American Cultural Imperialism?

When Hollywood penetrates global markets, to what extent is *American* culture being exported? Or is a new global culture being created, above and beyond its specifically American origins? There is no simple answer to this question.

Critics of cultural imperialism make two separate and partially contradictory charges. Some are unhappy with the global spread of the American ethos of commercialism and individualism. Other complaints focus on the strong global-market position of a relatively universal cultural product, rather than local products based on national or particularist inspirations. There is some truth to each complaint, although they point in opposite directions.

If we look at the national identities of the major individuals involved, Hollywood is highly cosmopolitan. Many of the leading Hollywood directors are non-Americans by birth, including Ridley Scott (British) and James Cameron (Canadian), who were among the hottest Hollywood directors circa 2001. Arnold Schwarzenegger, Charlie Chaplin, and Jim Carrey have been among the leading non-American US stars. Most of the major studios are now foreign owned. A typical production will have Sony, a Japanese company, hire a European director to shoot a picture in Canada and then sell the product for global export. Of the world's major entertainment corporations, only Time-Warner is predominantly American in ownership.

For better or worse, Hollywood strives to present the universal to global audiences. As Hollywood markets its films to more non-English speakers, those films become more general. Action films are favored over movies with subtle dialogue. Comedy revolves around slapstick rather than verbal puns. The larger the audience, of course, the more universal the product or celebrity must be. There is relatively little that the world as a whole, or even a select group of fifty million global consumers, can agree on. Greater universality means that the movies are relevant to general features of the human condition, but it also can bring blandness and formulaic treatment. Critics allege that American culture is driving the world, but in reality the two are determined simultaneously, and by the same set of forces.

Non-American movies, when they pursue foreign markets, must strive for universality as well. The Jackie Chan Hong Kong movie *Rumble in the Bronx* was marketed in the United States with success. The producers, however, cut parts of the movie to appeal to American audiences. All of the action sequences were kept, but the relationship of Chan with the co-star was diminished, in part because the woman (Anita Mui) was a star in Asia but not in the United States, and in part because the relationship was based on the "Chinese" values of obligation and loyalty, rather than on a Western sense of erotic romance.

The most successful Canadian cultural export is the Harlequin romance novel. In 1990 Harlequin sold more than 200 million books, accounting for 40 percent (!) of all mass-market paperback sales in the United States. This fact is rarely cited by Canadian critics of American cultural imperialism, largely because this export success does not "count" for them. The Harlequin romance does not reflect a specifically Canadian perspective, whatever that designation might mean, but rather targets a broad circle of female readers.

Despite these powerful universalist forces, the American and national component to Hollywood moviemaking cannot be ignored. Hollywood has always drawn on the national ethos of the United States for cinematic inspiration. The American values of heroism, individualism, and romantic self-fulfillment are well suited for the large screen and for global audiences. It is true that Hollywood will make whatever will sell abroad. Nonetheless, *how well* Hollywood can make movies in various styles will depend on native sources of inspiration. Hollywood has an intrinsic cost-advantage in making movies based upon American values, broadly construed, and thus has an intrinsic advantage in exporting such movies. The clustering of filmmaking in Hollywood cannot help but be based on an partially American ethos.

For this reason, dominant cultures, such as the United States, have an advantage in exporting their values and shaping the preferences of other nations. Consider food markets. Many Third World citizens like to eat at McDonald's, not just because the food tastes good to them, but also because McDonald's is a visible symbol of the West and the United States. When they walk through the doors of a McDonald's, they are entering a different world. The McDonald's corporation, knowing this, designs its Third World interiors to reflect the glamour of Western commerce, much as a shopping mall would. McDonald's shapes its product to meet global demands, but builds on the American roots of the core concept. The McDonald's image and product lines have been refined in the American domestic market and draw heavily on American notions of the relation between food and social life.

The promulgated American ethos will, of course, successfully meld both national and cosmopolitan influences, and will not be purely American in any narrow sense. American cinema, like American cuisine, has been a synthetic, polyglot product from the beginning. Hollywood was developed largely by foreigners – Jewish immigrants from Eastern Europe – and was geared towards entertaining American urban audiences, which were drawn from around the world.

Furthermore, Hollywood's universality has, in part, *become* a central part of American national culture. Commercial forces have led America to adopt "that which can be globally sold" as part of its national culture. Americans have decided to emphasize their international triumphs and their ethnic diversity as part of their national self-image. In doing so, Americans have, to some extent, traded away particularist strands of their culture for success in global markets.

In this regard Hollywood's global-market position is a Faustian bargain. Achieving global dominance requires a sacrifice of a culture's initial perspective to the demands of world consumers. American culture is being exported, but for the most part it is not Amish quilts and Herman Melville. *Jurassic Park*, a movie about dinosaurs, was a huge hit abroad, but *Forrest Gump*, which makes constant reference to American history and national culture, made most of its money at home. […]

In the early silent era, France dominated world cinema markets. Before the First World War, French movies accounted for up to seventy percent of the American market, and even more in Latin America. In a reversal of contemporary trends, American filmmakers charged the French with cultural imperialism and asked Washington for trade protection. It was commonly charged that European movies encouraged lax morals and corrupted American culture. The French responded by noting the openness of their cinematic markets and asking America to compete on equal terms. Like Hollywood today, the French market dominance was achieved without significant subsidies from the French government.

Global cinema is in any case flourishing today, most of all in Asia. As for European cinema, its best hope is to rediscover an economic and cultural dynamic that combines both commercialism and creativity. Such a dynamic will require reliance on international markets and global capital, and is unlikely to flourish in a narrowly protectionist setting. The marketplace never guarantees a favorable result, but excessive insulation from competitive pressures can virtually guarantee an unfavorable result, whether economically or aesthetically.

Part VIII Questions

1. Discuss ways in which media globalization contributes to both homogenization and diversity in the countries of the world.
2. It is common to speak of the "Americanization" of countries influenced by the United States. What evidence do you see of "Japanization," "Africanization," and similar constructs in your culture – the borrowing and adaptation of cultural elements derived from other parts of the world?
3. For Tomlinson, any culture is a mélange of many other cultures. Does this mean that cultural imperialism is a meaningless concept? In responding, consider Tomlinson's emphasis on the survival of cultures as compared to their transformation and adaptation.
4. What does Thussu mean by "contra-flow," and what examples does he provide? How does he assess the strength of this contra-flow? Specifically, does it counter "dominant" flows sufficiently to make the media landscape "multivocal" and "multidirectional"?
5. What is the "Korean wave," as described by Shim? What factors helped to make things Korean "the rage across Asia" by the early 2000s? How might the "development of Korean media industries" serve as a "sign of resilience of the subaltern," as Shim argues?
6. To what extent did Australian producers of Big Brother stick to the global "bible" of instructions that defined the show? What lessons does Roscoe draw from their work? What broader trends emerged in the way the show was marketed and received in Australia in the 2000s?
7. Bollywood is squaring off with Hollywood, according to Tyrrell. What does this article tell us about the capacity of nonwestern countries to resist western culture? Should we expect Hollywood's domination to decline further in the future? Why? What paradoxes about cultural globalization does Tyrrell illustrate through the case of the Indian cinema industry?
8. Why does Cowen call cinema "one of the hard cases for globalization"? Why does the production of certain kinds of movies cluster in Hollywood? Does Hollywood contribute to the Americanization of world culture? Does Cowen worry about that issue?

Part IX

Globalization and Religion

Introduction

Long before the current phase of globalization, religious communities globalized. From northern India, adherents inspired by the Buddha carried his vision of spiritual enlightenment and personal discipline to many parts of Asia, ultimately linking millions of people, from Japan to Afghanistan. Later, followers of Jesus Christ instructed by St Paul carried the Christian gospel of salvation from West Asia to North Africa as well as parts of Europe. Relative latecomers among the world religions, followers of the Prophet Muhammad globalized Islam perhaps even more dramatically in a short period, spreading the Koran and its teachings from the Arabian heartland as far east as what is now Indonesia and as far west as Spain. Each religion had its own kind of mobile messenger, each its own universal message, and each its own impulse to include new adherents. Each created a translocal community among physically distant strangers who nevertheless shared a common identity. To varying degrees and in varied forms, each community also organized its adherents, with the Roman Catholic Church standing out as perhaps the oldest and strongest of the religiously specialized organizations deliberately focused on a global mission. In religion, globalization is nothing new.

Of course, religious globalization did not stop in antiquity. Islam continued to make inroads in southern Europe into the 1600s. Allied with European powers, the Catholic Church spread its influence in the Americas. With less political backing, the Society of Jesus (the Jesuits), itself a transnational religious order, made a classic though ultimately futile attempt to convert the Chinese to Christianity. Upstart Protestant sects followed suit, first moving to North America in search of refuge, later venturing to other continents in ambitious missionary campaigns, planting churches on all continents. Driven less by religious than by worldly motives, recent migration by Hindus and Muslims has created diasporas in Europe and North

The Globalization Reader, Fifth Edition. Edited by Frank J. Lechner and John Boli.
Editorial material and organization © 2015 John Wiley & Sons, Ltd.
Published 2015 by John Wiley & Sons, Ltd.

America, further "deterritorializing" the great religions of old. To some extent, the world religious map still displays the legacy of premodern globalization, and the resilience of that legacy hampers globalization to some extent by the barriers it creates – Christian church planting is prohibited in Saudi Arabia, and Muslim conversion is uncommon in Latin America. But the results of missionary activity and more mundane migration have also complicated that map, as numerous global communities of faith span the continents – we find Buddhists in California, Pentecostals in Papua New Guinea, and Alevi Muslims in Germany. Again, this is not entirely new, but it is fair to say that religious connections have expanded and intensified along with many other types of interconnection. In the twenty-first century, religious globalization is going strong.

This form of globalization matters first and foremost as a global fact in its own right: faith connects billions of people to distant others. Their vision of another world shapes their view of this one. In relation to the world around them, many identify themselves above all as adherents. The religiosity of a majority of the world's people is a dominant feature of world culture. The religions that bind them together have themselves evolved along with the world society of which they are a part, and scholars like Peter Beyer, in his book *Religions in Global Society*, detect a standardizing trend among them, constituting a small set of comparable religious "options." At the same time, the globalization of religions, today perhaps even more than in the past, allows for considerable experimentation: the Americanized version of Hinduism common in the Atlanta suburbs is not quite like that practiced across India, and the fervent Charismatic Renewal that has swept through many Christian churches takes all sorts of "indigenized" forms. In religion, as in other parts of the global cultural economy described by Appadurai in the essay excerpted in the "Explaining Globalization" section, homogenizing trends run into "heterogenizing" ones, creating a varied religious landscape in which many individuals can compose their own mixed identities.

Religious faith, identity, and practice also matter because of the way they intertwine with the affairs of the world. Religious communities command resources and put them to use, for example when American evangelical churches fund social services abroad. Many seek, support, or rely on state power, involving adherents in everyday political and social struggles, most obviously in places like Iran, where an "Islamic Republic" is guided by a cleric as "supreme leader" and maintains close ties with a clerical establishment. By virtue of their specific principles, communities and their spokespersons also address issues of wide public concern, entering areas of moral controversy; opposition to homosexuality among many conservative Christians in the global South is a case in point. Precisely how this plays out varies from community to community and from place to place, of course. But understanding globalization at least requires some grasp of this religious involvement in world society.

The items in this section illustrate a few aspects of that religious involvement, focusing on Islam, evangelical Protestantism, and the Catholic Church. They have some themes in common. For one thing, from their different vantage points, religious actors often adopt a critical view of at least some aspects of the worldly globalization they observe. Though sometimes perceived as marginal in more secularized Western societies, they also attempt, with varying success, to articulate their own vision and exert some influence on a number of issues. In doing so, even actors that rely on a very old tradition, including those trying militantly to restore its greatness, tend to be nimble globalizers, navigating the various channels of communication offered by world society. Sacred texts may be ancient, and ritual practices old, but key players in world religion are often quite up to date.

This point applies to some Muslim groups once called "fundamentalist," now often labeled "Islamist," that aim to restore the rule of Islamic law in an Islamic state. They seek to unify the whole Islamic community and perhaps even transform the world of the unbelievers, the more radical among them advocating violence as a proper means of struggle. To some extent, this brings longstanding intra-Islamic disputes to the global fore, pitting a minority of militants against a moderate majority. But, as American sociologist Charles Kurzman shows, even seemingly "antimodern" Muslims, such as Osama bin Laden, are in fact "thoroughly modern." By contrast with the traditionalist Taliban in Afghanistan, many Islamists attended secular schools, employ modern communications, and do not intend to eliminate the modern state. Kurzman notes that Islamists cannot count on widespread public support but may seek to benefit from the war on terrorism provoked by the attacks of September 11, 2001, on the United States. Olivier Roy, a French political scientist, complements this diagnosis by noting a change among Islamists: in Muslim countries, they increasingly turn to normal politics, while a more radical, rootless wing pursues global jihad through a loose network of militants. In response to globalization, which disconnects religion from territory, they try to formulate a model of Islam that could work beyond any culture, paradoxically fostering a kind of secularization in the process.

Regarding Christianity, Philip Jenkins, a Welsh-American historian, argues that the early twenty-first century is "one of the transforming moments in the history of religion worldwide." As he puts it, "the day of Southern Christianity is dawning." By comparison with their fellow believers in the West, Christians of the global South are poorer, more conservative, strongly supernatural in their thinking, and focused on personal salvation. They therefore change the content and complexion of Christianity, which, if they unite, will have global implications. Joshua J. Yates reinforces Jenkins's points by describing the success of evangelical Protestants even in societies traditionally uncongenial to Christianity, turning this emotional brand of Protestantism into a "thoroughly indigenized global phenomenon." Though seemingly out of sync with some contemporary mores, under the influence of American proselytizers evangelical or charismatic Christians are also at home in the market economy and attuned to the language of multiculturalism, thus unintentionally preaching the "gospel of modernity."

José Casanova, an American sociologist of Spanish origin, describes changes within the Catholic Church that have enabled it to participate in the latest wave of globalization. He shows how the pope, whose position in the church has strengthened since the late nineteenth century, became a key player in global civil society as an advocate for human rights. Even as the Vatican centralized Catholic affairs, it also internationalized the church by greatly expanding in, and recruiting indigenous clergy from, the global South. Casanova thinks this makes it a more truly "universal" church, one that will outlast the modern world system of nation-states. Frank J. Lechner further illustrates this newly vital Catholic involvement in global affairs by showing how, along with other religious groups, the church became deeply involved in the Jubilee movement to reduce the onerous debts of Third World countries and, through the voice of celebrity Pope John Paul II, expressed a nuanced yet critical perspective on secular globalization, arguing ultimately for a "globalization of solidarity." This tendency of the Catholic Church is growing even stronger under Pope Francis, elected in 2013 as the first Latin American pope, who chose his papal name to emphasize his commitment to social justice and concern for poor people of all faiths.

52

Bin Laden and Other Thoroughly Modern Muslims

Charles Kurzman

As the United States wages war on terrorism, media coverage has portrayed the radical Islamism exemplified by Osama bin Laden as medieval, reactionary, and eager to return the Islamic world to its seventh-century roots.

In one sense this is accurate: Islamists, like almost all Muslims, regard the early years of Islam as a golden era, and they aspire to model their behavior after the Prophet Muhammad and his early followers, much as Christians idealize the example of Jesus.

Islamists seek to regain the righteousness of the early years of Islam and implement the rule of *shari'a,* either by using the state to enforce it as the law of the land or by convincing Muslims to abide by these norms of their own accord. Litmus-test issues for Islamists, as for traditional Muslims, include modest dress for women – ranging from headscarves to full veils – abstention from alcohol and other intoxicants and public performance of prayers. However, Islamists have no wish to throw away electricity and other technological inventions. Most have graduated from modern schools, share modern values such as human equality and rule of law, and organize themselves along modern lines, using modern technologies and – some of them – the latest methods of warfare.

Indeed, radical Islamists have much in common with Islamic liberalism, another important movement in the Islamic world. Both Islamic liberals and radical Islamists seek to modernize society and politics, recasting tradition in modern molds. Both Islamist movements maintain that there are multiple ways of being modern, and that

Original publication details: Charles Kurzman, "Bin Laden and Other Thoroughly Modern Muslims," in *Contexts*, Fall–Winter 2002. pp. 13–14, 15–17, 18–19, 19–20. Reprinted by permission of SAGE Publications.

modernity is not limited to Western culture. Islamists may ally themselves on occasion with traditionalist Islamic movements, and they may share certain symbols of piety, but they are quite distinct in sociological terms. Traditionalists such as the Taliban of Afghanistan, by contrast with Islamists such as bin Laden's Al Qaeda network, draw on less educated sectors of society, believe in mystical and personal authority and are skeptical of modern organizational forms. For this reason, traditionalist movements are finding it increasingly difficult to survive in a competitive religious environment and occupy only isolated pockets of Muslim society. Modern movements have taken over the rest.

The Islamists' Roots in Secular Education

Start with bin Laden himself. Though he issued *fatwas* (religious judgments) as though he were a seminary-educated Islamic scholar, his training was in civil engineering. Similarly, many other Islamist leaders have university rather than seminary backgrounds: Hasan Turabi of the Sudan is a lawyer trained in Khartoum, London and Paris; Necmettin Erbakan of Turkey studied mechanical engineering in West Germany; Hasan al-Banna of Egypt, who founded the first mass Islamist group, the Muslim Brotherhood, in the 1920s, was a teacher educated and employed in secular schools.

These leaders railed against seminary-trained scholars, the *'ulama*, for being obscurantist and politically inactive. Bin Laden lambasted the *'ulama* of Saudi Arabia as playing "the most ominous of roles. Regardless of whether they did so intentionally or unintentionally, the harm that resulted from their efforts is no different from the role of the most ardent enemies of the nation." Even Islamist leaders with traditional seminary educations – such as Abu'l-'Ala Maudoodi of Pakistan, Ruhollah Khomeini of Iran, 'Abd al-Hamid Kishk of Egypt – frequently railed against their alma maters for similar reasons. Seminaries were considered so backward in Islamist eyes that for decades Maudoodi hid the fact that he had a seminary degree.

Not only the Islamist leaders but also the rank and file emerge disproportionately from secular universities. [...]

The growth of secular education has led expanding numbers of Muslims to approach religious questions without the skills – or blinders, depending on one's perspective – inculcated in the seminaries. College graduates have turned to the sacred texts and analyzed them in a sort of do-it-yourself theology, developing liberal interpretations in addition to radical ones. In Pakistan, for example, a study group of educated Muslim women met and produced a feminist interpretation, "For Ourselves: Women Reading the Koran" (1997). In North America, a gay convert to Islam produced a Web site called Queer Jihad that espoused tolerance for homosexuality. In Syria, a soil engineer named Muhammad Shahrour decided that traditional scholarship on the Koran was unscientific and that he had a better approach, one that happened to support liberal political positions. According to booksellers interviewed by anthropologist Dale Eickelman, Shahrour's tomes are best-sellers in the Arab world, even where they are banned.

In addition, governments have waded into the religious field throughout the Islamic world. In each country, the state has established its own official religious authorities, which may be pitted against every other state's religious authorities. Many states produce their own schoolbooks to teach Islamic values in the public schools. In Turkish textbooks, these values include secular government; in Saudi textbooks, these values include monarchy; in Palestine National Authority textbooks, according to a review by political scientist Nathan J. Brown, these values include the defense of the Palestinian homeland (though they do not, as often charged, include the destruction of Israel).

The result is a tremendous diversity of Islamic opinion and a corresponding diversity of Islamic authority. There is no universally recognized arbiter to resolve Islamic debates. For most of Islamic history, at least a symbolic arbiter existed: the caliph (*khalifa*), that is, the successor to the Prophet. Caliphs could never impose interpretive uniformity on all Muslims, although some were more inclined than others to try. But since the Turkish Republic abolished the Ottoman caliphate in 1924, even this symbol of authority is gone. Any college graduate in a cave can claim to speak for Islam.

Modern Goals, Modern Methods

Just as the social roots of Islamism are modern, so too are many of its goals. Do not be misled by the language of hostility toward the West. Islamist political platforms share significant planks with Western modernity. Islamists envision overturning tradition in politics, social relations and religious practices. They are hostile to monarchies, such as the Saudi dynasty in Arabia; they favor egalitarian meritocracy, as opposed to inherited social hierarchies; they wish to abolish long-standing religious practices such as the honoring of relics and tombs.

Bin Laden, for example, combined traditional grievances such as injustice, corruption, oppression, and self-defense with contemporary demands such as economic development, human rights and national self-determination. "People are fully occupied with day-to-day survival; everybody talks about the deterioration of the economy, inflation, ever-increasing debts and jails full of prisoners," bin Laden wrote in 1996. "They complain that the value of the [Saudi] *riyal* is greatly and continuously deteriorating against most of the major currencies."

These mundane concerns do not mean that Islamist states look just like Western states, but they are not entirely different, either. The Islamic Republic of Iran, for example, has tried to forge its own path since it replaced the Pahlavi monarchy in 1979. Yet within its first year it copied global norms by writing a new constitution, ratifying it through a referendum with full adult suffrage, holding parliamentary and presidential elections, establishing a cabinet system, and occupying itself with myriad other tasks that the modern world expects of a state, from infrastructure expansion to narcotics interdiction. The 1986 Iranian census conducted by the Islamic Republic was scarcely different from the 1976 census conducted by the monarchy. Similarly in Pakistan and the Sudan, where Islamic laws were introduced in the 1980s, there were changes, but there were also massive continuities. The modern state remained.

Contrast this continuity with the traditionalist Taliban. While most well-educated Islamists disdain relics as verging on idol worship, Taliban leader Mullah Muhammad Omar literally wrapped himself in the cloak of the Prophet – a cherished relic in Qandahar – one April day in 1996. While successful Islamist movements have ensconced themselves in the offices of their predecessors, Omar remained in his home province. The Taliban government reproduced a few of the usual ministries – foreign affairs, for example – but did not bother with most. The Taliban preferred informal and personal administration to the rule-bound bureaucracies favored by modern states.

Western bias tends to lump Khomeini's Iran and the Taliban's Afghanistan in the same category, and indeed both claimed to be building an Islamic state. However, one is a modern state and the other was not. Perhaps the most vivid distinction involved gender. While the Taliban barred girls from attending school, the Islamic Republic of Iran more than doubled girls' education from pre-revolutionary levels. While the Taliban barred women from working at most jobs, Iranian women entered the labor force in unprecedented numbers, as television anchors, parliamentary deputies, government typists and sales clerks – even while dressed in headscarves and long coats. Iranian leaders were as outspoken as Western feminists in condemning Taliban policies on gender and other subjects and felt the Taliban were giving Islam a bad name.

The Taliban reintroduced tradition; Khomeini and other Islamists reinvented it. [...]

Not just in ideology but also in practice, bin Laden and other radical Islamists mirror Western trends. They term their mobilization *jihad*, or sacred struggle, although many Muslims point out that the Prophet called struggle against others the "lesser jihad," with the internal struggle to lead a good life being the "greater jihad." Regardless of the ancient terminology, Al Qaeda and other Islamist groups operate globally like transnational corporations, with affiliates and subsidiaries, strategic partners, commodity chains, standardized training, off-shore financing and other features associated with contemporary global capital. Indeed, insiders often referred to Al Qaeda as the "company."

Documents discovered by *The New York Times* in Afghan training camps after Al Qaeda's departure show a bureaucratic organization with administrative lines of authority and an insistence on budgeting. Islamists use the latest high-tech skills, not just airplane piloting and transponder deactivation, as the world learned tragically on September 11, 2001, but also satellite phones, faxes, wired money orders and the like. Mullah Muhammad Omar was so suspicious of modern technology that he refused to be photographed; bin Laden, by contrast, distributed videotapes of himself to the world's media. [...]

The Radical Minority

A minority of Muslims support Islamist organizations, and not just because they are illegal in many countries. There are only a handful of reputable surveys on the subject, but they show consistently that most Muslims oppose Islamists and their goals. Surveys in 1988 found that 46 and 20 percent of respondents in Kuwait and Egypt, respectively, favored Islamist goals in religion and politics. A 1986 survey in the West Bank and Gaza found 26 percent calling for a state based on *shari'a*, and polls in the same regions showed support for Hamas and other Islamist groups dropping from 23 percent in 1994 to 13 to 18 percent in 1996–97. A 1999 survey in Turkey found 21 percent favoring implementation of *shari'a*, consistent with other surveys in the mid-1990s. In a Gallup poll of nine Muslim societies at the end of 2001, only 15 percent of respondents said they considered the September 11 attacks to be morally justifiable.

When free or partially free elections are held, Islamists rarely fare well. Islamist candidates and parties have won less than 10 percent of the vote in Bangladesh, Egypt, Pakistan and Tajikistan. They have won less than 25 percent of the vote in Egypt, Malaysia, Sudan, Tunisia, Turkey and Yemen. Their best showings have been in Kuwait, where they won 40 percent of seats in 1999, and Jordan, where moderate Islamists won 43 percent of seats in 1989 before dropping to 20 percent in the next election. Virtually the only majority vote that Islamists have ever received was in Algeria in 1991, when the Islamic Salvation Front dominated the first stage of parliamentary elections, winning 81 percent of the seats; it was about to win the second stage of voting when the military annulled the elections and declared martial law.

In the few elections where Islamists fared relatively well, success followed from promises to abide by democratic norms. The Algerian Islamist leader 'Abbasi Madani, who earned a doctorate in education from the University of London, developed a Muslim Democrat position analogous to the Christian Democrat parties of Europe: culturally conservative but committed to democracy. "Pluralism is a guarantee of cultural wealth, and diversity is needed for development. We are Muslims, but we are not Islam itself," Madani said while campaigning. "We do not monopolize religion. Democracy as we understand it means pluralism, choice and freedom." These sentiments may have been insincere, but we will never know. A secular military regime barred Madani from office before he could develop a track record. […]

Sadly, the US-led war on terrorism may inadvertently benefit the Islamists. This is the great debate among scholars of Islamic studies in the months since September 2001. Do the United States and its allies appear hypocritical in supporting autocrats in Muslim-majority countries while claiming to defend human rights and democracy? Will Muslims perceive the war on terrorism as evidence of Western hostility toward Islam? Will military action stoke Islamist radicalism or extinguish it?

In the short run, the war on terrorism has not generated the massive negative reaction among Muslims that some observers expected. Yet there is evidence to suggest that Islamism is gaining in popularity. Gallup polls of nine Muslim societies at the end of 2001 found that a majority considered the United States and the West to be hostile to Islam and Muslims. Since the beginning of 2002, Israel's military operations in Palestinian territories, with Western acquiescence, may have further radicalized Muslim attitudes.

Longer-term approaches to the war on terrorism also face ambivalence. The modernization of Muslim societies, promoted by the United States and its allies as a buffer against traditionalism, may wind up fueling Islamism. Modern schools produce Islamists as well as liberals; modern businesses fund Islamist as well as other causes; modern communications can broadcast Islamist as well as other messages. Western culture, we are learning, is not the only form that modernity may assume.

53

Globalised Islam
The Search for a New Ummah

Olivier Roy

[...] The blurring of the borders between Islam and the West is not just a consequence of immigration. It is linked with a more general phenomenon: deterritorialisation. Islam is less and less ascribed to a specific territory and civilisational area. This is visible also in the slow integration of Eastern Europe into Western Europe, and in Turkey's candidacy for EU membership. The evolution of Eastern Europe has, of course, more to do with the collapse of the communist empire than with the expansion of Islam, but one consequence is that Europe has rediscovered that there are European Muslim countries (Albania, Bosnia and, tomorrow, Kosovo). Contrary to what has been more or less openly advocated by many conservative Europeans, Europe, after some hesitation, chose not to side with 'Christians' against 'Muslims', whatever the real motivations for the strategic choice of supporting the Bosnians and the Kosovars.

The deterritorialisation of Islam is also a result of globalisation and has nothing to do with Islam as such, even if it concerns millions of Muslims. But through the increase in migratory and population flows, more and more Muslims are living in societies that are not Muslim: a third of the world's Muslims now live as members of a minority. While old minorities had time to build their own culture or to share the dominant culture (Tatars, Indian Muslims, China's Hui), Muslims in recently settled minorities have to reinvent what makes them Muslim, in the sense that the common defining factor of this population as Muslim is the mere reference to Islam, with no common cultural or linguistic heritage.

Original publication details: Olivier Roy, *Globalized Islam: The Search for a New Ummah*. New York: Columbia University Press, 2004. pp. 18–25. Reproduced with permission from Columbia University Press and Hurst & Co.

The Globalization Reader, Fifth Edition. Edited by Frank J. Lechner and John Boli.
Editorial material and organization © 2015 John Wiley & Sons, Ltd.
Published 2015 by John Wiley & Sons, Ltd.

Moreover, a Muslim might experience this deterritorialisation without leaving his own country. The sense of belonging to a minority has been exacerbated by the 'westernisation', or at least globalisation, of the traditional Muslim world, to the extent that many practising Muslims consider Islam to have been 'minoritised' in the Muslim world too (in Turkey, for example). While many Muslims live in a demographic minority, many others (including, of course, the more conservative or radical Muslims) feel themselves to be a minority in their own Muslim country. The Muslim *ummah* (or community) no longer has anything to do with a territorial entity. It has to be thought of in abstract or imaginary terms.

The frontier between Islam and the West is no longer geographical, and is less and less civilisational. The process of westernisation of Muslim societies over two centuries has had obvious and permanent effects, even if it has entailed a backlash in the past thirty years, taking the form of 'Islamic revival' at different levels (political with the Iranian revolution, societal with the re-Islamisation of daily life, the increase in the number of veiled women or of references to *sharia* in the law, and so on). This backlash does not mean a return to a 'premodern' society nor to an authenticity that is supposed to have been destroyed by acculturation. It is more an attempt to 'Islamise modernity', as Sheikh Yassin wrote. Academic literature on the 'modernity' of Islamisation is abundant, even if it opposes a popular view among Western media and public opinion. Modernisation and re-Islamisation are, of course, rather problematic concepts. Islamisation might be both a reaction against and a factor of modernization (which is the case with the Islamic revolution in Iran), in the sense that the dominant perception of what modernization meant in the 1960s and 1970s was rather ethnocentric and linear (from religious tradition to secular modernity). But the issue of cultural and social change no longer rests on a dichotomy between tradition and modernity, religion and secularization, or even between liberalism and fundamentalism. We shall see, for example, how neofundamentalism is an agent of acculturation and not a return to a lost authenticity. In short, the confrontation between Islam and the West is cast in Western categories. The illusion held by the Islamic radicals is that they represent tradition, when in fact they express a negative form of westernisation.

At a time when the territorial borders between the great civilisations are fading away, mental borders are being reinvented to give a second life to the ghosts of lost civilisations: multiculturalism, minority groups, clash or dialogue of civilisations, *communautarisation* (communitarisation), and so on. Ethnicity and religion are being marshalled to draw new borders between groups whose identity relies on a performative definition: we are what we say we are, or what others say we are. These new ethnic and religious borders do not correspond to any geographical territory or area. They work in minds, attitudes and discourses. They are more vocal than territorial, but all the more eagerly endorsed and defended because they have to be invented, and because they remain fragile and transitory. Deterritorialisation of Islam leads to a quest for definition, because Islam is no longer embedded in territorial cultures, whatever their diversity – which, incidentally, is always experienced from outside. For example, an Afghan Muslim living in Afghanistan does not understand his religion as being 'Afghan', at least so long he is not challenged by an Arab Wahhabi who blames him for having blended Islam with Afghan traditions. Diversity is not an argument for tolerance whenever it is not experienced as a value.

Such westernisation is not necessarily perceived as a trauma by the 'Muslim in the street'. The challenge of westernisation is clearly understood, but is experienced in practical terms without drama and trauma by the majority of Muslims, either in Muslim countries or in the West. Although there is a long tradition of exegesis and *fatwa* on what a Muslim should or should not do when confronted with a non-Muslim environment and practices, most Muslims find a way to deal with that without contacting fatwa-online.com. We must return to the discourses and practices of the actual actors, without lingering over the theological issues of such cohabitation. Makeshift compromises, personal construction of attitudes, casual use of various levels of self-identity, *ad hoc* quotations from Hadith or the Koran, dogmatic or liberal *post hoc* rationalisation to answer unsolicited inquiries from the non-Muslim colleague or sociologist doing fieldwork – the range of attitudes is very wide and flexible. To be a Muslim in the West is not a schizophrenic experience. Clear-cut categories (like Islamist or neofundamentalist) are useful but cannot pretend to subsume the real life of millions of people, even if these terms are heuristically relevant. [...]

The common point between all fundamentalist and Islamist movements is that they draw a line inside the Muslim world between what is Islamic and what is not. A 'Muslim' society, in the cultural and sociological sense, is not for them an 'Islamic' society *per se* (that is, it is not a society based on the principles of Islam). And the need to formulate what it means to be a Muslim, to define objectively what Islam is – in short, to 'objectify' Islam – is a logical consequence of the end of the social authority of religion, due to westernisation and globalisation.

Re-Islamisation is part of a process of deculturation (that is, of a crisis of pristine cultures giving way to westernisation and reconstructed identities). Of course, I do not believe that such 'pristine' cultures were static and immune from global influence. When speaking of pristine culture, we refer more to what is reconstructed by first-generation immigrants as their own past, and to what is called 'traditional' by most Western actors dealing with immigration, including social workers and anthropologists, but also lawyers when they have to explain specific sociological practices (like arranged marriages) or defend certain customs (like female circumcision or honour crimes) in courts. References to 'tradition' by community leaders in the West or politicians from the country of origin serve as a means of maintaining a link between immigrants and the 'home' country, which could function as a political lever in the host country, as a channel for funds in both directions, or as a basis for business relationships. Youngsters who argue with their parents (or grandparents) about speaking English, wearing Western-style clothes, dating and dancing are confronted with an image of a pristine culture, even if anthropologists know well that such an encapsulated culture never existed (and is actually transformed by the debate). Reference to tradition also has a performative function: tradition is what I call (or, more exactly, what my grandfather calls) tradition.

The relationship between Western Muslims and Muslim countries is no longer diasporic. Syrians or Yemenis in the United States feel above all that they are Arab-Americans. The link is no longer one between a diaspora and a host country, but between immigrants and new sets of identities, most of them being provided by the host country. *Maghrébin* and *beur* in France do not correspond to pristine identities (in North Africa, or the Maghreb, one is first an Algerian or a Tunisian, second an Arab, but never a *maghrébin*). Of course some groups retain longer than others a diasporic dimension, enhanced by arranged and often endogamous marriages with a spouse from the village of origin (for example, Anatolian Turks in Europe, or Sylheti Bengalis in Britain). But among Islamic activists in Europe a trend favours a new sort of Muslim identity detached from pristine cultural links. As we shall see below, a good example of this phenomenon is the growing gap between the Turkish heirs of the Refah Partisi and the Milli Görüs movement, which was initially the European section of the Refah party but has over time become an autonomous religious movement in a purely European context. The quest for authenticity is no longer a quest to maintain a pristine identity, but to go back to and beyond this pristine identity through an ahistorical model of Islam. It is not a matter of nostalgia for a given country, for one's youth or for one's family roots. In this sense westernisation means something other than becoming Western, hence the ambivalent attitude towards it.

How do we reconcile manifesting hatred for the West with the queues for visas outside Western consulates? It is not a contradiction, even if it is often the same people who do both. And we would be mistaken to take the aspiration of Iranian youths for democracy as an invitation for a US military intervention to topple the conservative regime in Tehran. The confrontation with the Western model is a call for another kind of globalisation, expressed in Western terms such as culture, minority rights, Third World and South (developing world). The quest for authenticity is expressed against the culture of origin and Western culture, but by referring indifferently to traditional (*ummah*) or Western (anti-imperialist) categories. There is a constant struggle among many Islamic intellectuals and Third Worldist authors to historicise Western culture in order to debunk its claim to be universal, specifically of course in the field of human rights. But the critique of Western cultural hegemony is not necessarily sustained by a valorisation of existing traditional cultures, but more often by modern reconstructions of new identities, even if they resort to historical themes (for example, Confucian values in China and Singapore). Westernisation, migration and uprooting go hand in hand with the quest for another universality.

Re-Islamisation is part of this process of acculturation, rather than being a reaction against it. It is a way of appropriating this process, of experiencing it in terms of self-affirmation, but also of instrumentalising it to 'purify' Islam. Re-Islamisation means that Muslim identity, self-evident so long as it belonged to an inherited cultural legacy, has to express itself explicitly in a non-Muslim or Western context. The construction of a 'deculturalised' Islam is a means of experiencing a religious identity that is not linked to a given culture and can therefore fit with every culture, or, more precisely, could be defined beyond the very notion of culture. The issue is one not only of recasting an Islamic identity, but also of formulating it in explicit terms. Resorting to an explicit formulation is important, because it obliges one to make choices and to disentangle the different and often contradictory levels of practices and discourses where a religion is embedded in a given culture. Especially in times of political crisis (such as 9 / 11), ordinary Muslims feel compelled (or are explicitly asked) to explain what it means to be a Muslim (by an opinion poll, a neighbour, a news anchorman or spontaneously, because Muslims anticipate the question). The Western press publishes many opinion pieces and other articles, written by 'moderate' or 'liberal' Muslims, stating what Islam is or is not (usually what it is not: radical, violent, fanatical, and so on). This task falls on the shoulders of every Muslim, rather than on legitimate religious authorities, simply because, as we shall see, there are so few or no established Muslim authorities in the West. Each Muslim is accountable for being a Muslim, which offers researchers an interesting opportunity. Instead of trying to penetrate a closed and intimate milieu in order to understand what people think, they are deluged with declarations and statements. To publicly state self-identity has become almost a civic duty for Muslims.

But this objectification of Islam is not only a result of political pressure and events: it is also a mechanical consequence of the delinking of religion and culture. Globalisation has blurred the connection between a religion, a pristine culture, a specific society and a territory. The social authority of religion has disappeared, specifically but not solely, through the experience of being a Muslim in the West. What is nowadays perceived as a pervasive movement of re-Islamisation or Islamic revivalism has been explained in terms of identity protest or as a way to reconcile modernity, self-affirmation and authenticity (as has been said, for example, of the return of the *hijab* among Western-educated women). True enough, but it is also a consequence of the need explicitly to formulate what Islam means for the individual (rather than what it is) when meaning is no longer sustained by social authority. Explicit elaboration also entails a projection into the future, a wish to realise the *ummah* beyond the heterogeneity of societies and cultures.

This leads to the endeavour to define a 'universal' Islam, valid in any cultural context. Of course, by definition Islam is universal, but after the time of the Prophet and his companions (the Salaf) it has always been embedded in given cultures. These cultures seem now a mere product of history and the results of many influences and idiosyncrasies. For fundamentalists (and also for some liberals) there is nothing in these cultures to be proud of, because they have altered the pristine message of Islam. Globalisation is a good opportunity to dissociate Islam from any given culture and to provide a model that could work beyond any culture. [...]

The failure of political Islam means that politics prevail over religion, as is obvious in Iran. The utopian Islamic state has faded away in favour either of practical politics or of another utopia, the *ummah*. Daily politics, political management of issues linked to religion (*sharia*), concrete economic and social challenges, strategic constraints, personal rivalries and corruption, not to mention senseless violence (for example, in Algeria) led to the desacralisation of politics, however Islamic. On the other hand, Islamisation of society led to the Islamisation of secular activities and motivations, which remain secular in essence: business, strategies of social advancement, and entertainment (like the five-star Islamic resorts in Turkey, where the real issue is fun and entertainment, not Islam). When everything has to be Islamic, nothing is.

A final paradox is that the reformulation of Islam as a mere religion is carried out not only by believers who want to secularise their religion (that is, moderate or liberal Muslims), but also by the very ones who deny any delinking of religion, state and society. To be provocative, I would say that the in-depth secularisation of Islam is being achieved by people who are denying the very concept of secularism. 'Secular' Muslims are not the actors of secularisation, because they are not involved in the process of formulating religiosity or shaping the community. The real secularists are the Islamists and neofundamentalists, because they want to bridge the gap between religion and a secularised society by exacerbating the religious dimension, over-stretching it to the extent that it cannot become a habitus by being embedded in a real culture. This overstretching of religion, after a period of paroxysmal parousia (for example, the Islamic revolution of Iran, or any given *jihad*), necessarily leads to a new schism: politics is the ultimate dimension of any religious state, and the death of any *jihad* waged out of a concrete strategy, nation or social fabric. What resurfaces is politics, as in the case of Iran, but also religion as a multifaceted practice, hence the heterogeneous dimension of Islamic revivalism. Redefining Islam as a 'pure' religion turns it into a mere religion and leaves politics to work alone.

Islam is experiencing secularisation, but in the name of fundamentalism. It is a bit confusing for everybody, which is quite logical so far as a religion is concerned and so long as God will let humans speak on His behalf. Secularisation is the unexpected but logical destiny of any mediator of a religious fundamentalism that happens to be taken seriously by a whole nation and society, from Martin Luther to Ruhollah Khomeini. [...]

54

The Christian Revolution

Philip Jenkins

[…] We are currently living through one of the transforming moments in the history of religion worldwide. Over the past five centuries or so, the story of Christianity has been inextricably bound up with that of Europe and European-derived civilizations overseas, above all in North America. Until recently, the overwhelming majority of Christians have lived in White nations, allowing theorists to speak smugly, arrogantly, of "European Christian" civilization. Conversely, radical writers have seen Christianity as an ideological arm of Western imperialism. Many of us share the stereotype of Christianity as the religion of the "West" or, to use another popular metaphor, the global North. It is self-evidently the religion of the haves. To adapt the phrase once applied to the increasingly conservative US electorate of the 1970s, the stereotype holds that Christians are un-Black, un-poor, and un-young. If that is true, then the growing secularization of the West can only mean that Christianity is in its dying days. Globally, the faith of the future must be Islam.

Over the past century, however, the center of gravity in the Christian world has shifted inexorably southward, to Africa, Asia, and Latin America. Already today, the largest Christian communities on the planet are to be found in Africa and Latin America. If we want to visualize a "typical" contemporary Christian, we should think of a woman living in a village in Nigeria or in a Brazilian *favela*. As Kenyan scholar John Mbiti has observed, "the centers of the church's universality [are] no longer in Geneva, Rome, Athens, Paris, London, New York, but Kinshasa, Buenos Aires, Addis Ababa and Manila." Whatever Europeans or North Americans may believe, Christianity is doing very well indeed in the global South – not just surviving but expanding.

Original publication details: Philip Jenkins, *The Next Christendom: The Coming of Global Christianity*. Oxford: Oxford University Press, 2002. pp. 1–3, 7–8, 10–12, 214–15, 217–20. Reproduced with permission from Oxford University Press.

This trend will continue apace in coming years. Many of the fastest-growing countries in the world are either predominantly Christian or else have very sizable Christian minorities. Even if Christians just maintain their present share of the population in countries like Nigeria and Kenya, Mexico and Ethiopia, Brazil and the Philippines, there are soon going to be several hundred million more Christians from those nations alone. Moreover, conversions will swell the Christian share of world population. Meanwhile, historically low birth rates in the traditionally Christian states of Europe mean that these populations are declining or stagnant. In 1950, a list of the world's leading Christian countries would have included Britain, France, Spain, and Italy, but none of these names would be represented in a corresponding list for 2050.

Christianity should enjoy a worldwide boom in the new century, but the vast majority of believers will be neither white nor European, nor Euro-American. According to the respected *World Christian Encyclopedia*, some 2 billion Christians are alive today, about one-third of the planetary total. The largest single bloc, some 560 million people, is still to be found in Europe. Latin America, though, is already close behind with 480 million. Africa has 360 million, and 313 million Asians profess Christianity. North America claims about 260 million believers. If we extrapolate these figures to the year 2025, and assume no great gains or losses through conversion, then there would be around 2.6 billion Christians, of whom 633 million would live in Africa, 640 million in Latin America, and 460 million in Asia. Europe, with 555 million, would have slipped to third place. Africa and Latin America would be in competition for the title of most Christian continent. About this date, too, another significant milestone should occur, namely that these two continents will together account for half the Christians on the planet. By 2050, only about one-fifth of the world's 3 billion Christians will be non-Hispanic Whites. Soon, the phrase "a White Christian" may sound like a curious oxymoron, as mildly surprising as "a Swedish Buddhist." Such people can exist, but a slight eccentricity is implied.

This global perspective should make us think carefully before asserting "what Christians believe" or "how the church is changing." All too often, statements about what "modern Christians accept" or what "Catholics today believe" refer only to what that ever-shrinking remnant of *Western* Christians and Catholics believe. Such assertions are outrageous today, and as time goes by they will become ever further removed from reality. The era of Western Christianity has passed within our lifetimes, and the day of Southern Christianity is dawning. The fact of change itself is undeniable: it has happened, and will continue to happen. So little did we notice this momentous change that it was barely mentioned in all the media hoopla surrounding the end of the second millennium. [...]

But what would [a] new Christian synthesis look like? One obvious fact is that at least for the foreseeable future, members of a Southern-dominated church are likely to be among the poorer people on the planet, in marked contrast to the older Western-dominated world. For this reason, some Western Christians have since the 1960s expected that the religion of their Third World brethren would be fervently liberal, activist, and even revolutionary, the model represented by liberation theology. In this view, the new Christianity would chiefly be concerned with putting down the mighty from their seats, through political action or even armed struggle. All too often, though, these hopes have proved illusory. Frequently, the liberationist voices emanating from the Third World proved to derive from clerics trained in Europe and North America, and their ideas won only limited local appeal. Southern Hemisphere Christians would not avoid political activism, but they would become involved strictly on their own terms.

At present, the most immediately apparent difference between the older and newer churches is that Southern Christians are far more conservative in terms of both beliefs and moral teaching. The denominations that are triumphing all across the global South are stalwartly traditional or even reactionary by the standards of the economically advanced nations. The churches that have made most dramatic progress in the global South have either been Roman Catholic, of a traditionalist and fideistic kind, or radical Protestant sects, evangelical or Pentecostal. Indeed, this conservatism may go far toward explaining the common neglect of Southern Christianity in North America and Europe. Western experts rarely find the ideological tone of the new churches much to their taste.

Southern Christians retain a very strong supernatural orientation, and are by and large far more interested in personal salvation than in radical politics. As Harvey Cox showed in *Fire from Heaven*, Pentecostal expansion across the Southern Hemisphere has been so astonishing as to justify claims of a new reformation. In addition, rapid growth is occurring in non-traditional denominations that adapt Christian belief to local tradition, groups that are categorized by titles like "African indigenous churches." Their exact numbers are none too clear, since they are too busy baptizing newcomers to be counting them very precisely. By most accounts, membership in Pentecostal and independent churches already runs into the hundreds of millions, and congregations are located in precisely the regions of fastest population growth. Within a few decades, such denominations will represent a far larger segment of global Christianity, and just conceivably a majority. These newer churches preach deep personal faith and communal orthodoxy, mysticism and puritanism, all founded on clear scriptural authority. They preach messages that, to a Westerner, appear simplistically charismatic, visionary, and apocalyptic. In this thought-world, prophecy is an everyday reality, while faith-healing, exorcism, and dream-visions are all basic components of religious sensibility. For better or worse, the dominant churches of the future could have much in common with those of medieval or early modern European times. On present evidence, a Southernized Christian future should be distinctly conservative.

The theological coloring of the most successful new churches reminds us once more of the massive gap in most Western listings of the major trends of the past century, which rightly devoted much space to political movements like fascism and communism, but ignored vital religious currents like Pentecostalism. Yet today, Fascists or Nazis are not easy to find, and Communists may be becoming an endangered species, while Pentecostals are flourishing around the globe. Since there were only a handful of Pentecostals in 1900, and several hundred million today, is it not reasonable to identify this as perhaps the most successful social movement of the past century? According to current projections, the number of Pentecostal believers should surpass the one billion mark before 2050. In terms of the global religions, there will by that point be roughly as many Pentecostals as Hindus, and twice as many as there are Buddhists. And that is just taking one of the diverse currents of rising Christianity: there will be even more Catholics than Pentecostals. [...]

The Rise of Christendom

In describing the rising neo-orthodox world, I have spoken of a "new Christendom." The phrase evokes a medieval European age of faith, of passionate spirituality and a pervasive Christian culture. Medieval people spoke readily of "Christendom," the *Res Publica Christiana*, as a true overarching unity and a focus of loyalty transcending mere kingdoms or empires. Kingdoms like Burgundy, Wessex, or Saxony might last for only a century or two before they were replaced by new states and dynasties, but any rational person knew that Christendom simply endured. This perception had political consequences. While the laws of individual nations lasted only as long as the nations themselves, Christendom offered a higher set of standards and mores, which alone could claim to be universal. Although it rarely possessed any potential for common political action, Christendom was a primary form of cultural reference.

Ultimately, Christendom collapsed in the face of the overwhelming power of secular nationalism. Later Christian scholars struggled to live in this new age of "post-Christendom," when one could no longer assume any connection between religion and political order. By the start of the 21st century, however, the whole concept of the nation-state was itself under challenge. Partly, the changes reflected new technologies. According to a report by the US intelligence community, in the coming decades, "governments will have less and less control over flows of information, technology, diseases, migrants, arms, and financial transactions, whether legal or illegal, across their borders. … The very concept of 'belonging' to a particular state will probably erode." To use Benedict Anderson's famous phrase, nation-states are imagined communities of relatively recent date, rather than eternal or inevitable realities. In recent years, many of these communities have begun to reimagine themselves substantially, even to unimagine themselves out of existence. In Europe, loyalties to the nation as such are being replaced by newer forms of adherence, whether to larger entities (Europe itself) or to smaller (regions or ethnic groups). It remains to be seen whether or not the nation-state will outlive the printed book, that other Renaissance invention that may also fade away in the coming decades. If even once unquestioned constructs like Great Britain are under threat, it is not surprising that people are questioning the existence of newer and still more artificial entities in Africa or Asia, with their flimsy national frontiers dreamed up so recently by imperial bureaucrats. As Paul Gifford notes, many Africans live in mere quasi-states: "though they are recognized legal entities, they are not, in a functional sense, states."

For a quarter of a century, social scientists have been analyzing the decline of states in the face of globalization, and have noted parallels with the cosmopolitan world of the Middle Ages. Some scholars have postulated the future emergence of some movement or ideology that could in a sense create something like a new Christendom. This would be what political scientist Hedley Bull called "a modern and secular equivalent of the kind of universal political organization that existed in Western Christendom in the Middle Ages." Might the new ideological force be environmentalism, perhaps with a mystical New Age twist? Yet the more we look at the Southern Hemisphere in particular, the more we see that while universal and supranational ideas are flourishing, they are not secular in the least. The centers of gravest state weakness are often the regions in which political loyalties are secondary to religious beliefs, either Muslim or Christian, and these are the terms in which people define their identities. The new Christian world of the South could find unity in common religious beliefs.

That many Southern societies will develop a powerful Christian identity in culture and politics is beyond doubt. Less obvious is whether, and when, they will aspire to any kind of global unity. In this matter, the Atlantic Ocean initially seems to offer a barrier quite as overwhelming as it was before Columbus. Very soon, the two main centers of Christianity will be Africa and Latin America, and within each region, there is at least some sense of unity. Latin American ecclesiastics meet periodically, scholars treat the region as a whole (albeit a diverse one), and a similar canon of authors is read widely. The same can be said of Africa in its own way. However, next to no common sense of identity currently unites the churches and believers of the two continents. Even in terms of worldwide Christian networks, the two continents belong almost to different planets. For many Protestant Africans, the World Council of Churches offers a major institutional focus of unity, but because the Roman Catholic Church abstains from membership in the Council, this forum is closed to the majority of Latin Americans. When African and Latin American church leaders and scholars do meet, all too often it is at gatherings in Europe or the United States, following agendas conceived in the global North.

The resulting segregation of interests and ideas is remarkable, since the churches in Africa and Latin America share so many common experiences. They are passing through similar phases of growth, and are, independently, developing similar social and theological worldviews. Both also face similar issues, of race, of inculturation, of just how to deal with their respective colonial heritages. All these are common hemispheric issues that fundamentally separate the experiences of Northern and Southern churches. Given the lively scholarly activity and the flourishing spirituality in both Africa and Latin America, a period of mutual discovery is inevitable. When it begins – when, not if – the interaction should launch a revolutionary new era in world religion. Although many see the process of globalization as yet another form of American imperialism, it would be ironic if an early consequence was a growing sense of identity between Southern Christians. Once that axis is established, we really would be speaking of a new Christendom, based in the Southern Hemisphere. [...]

Looking at Southern Christianity gives a surprising new perspective on some other things that might seem to be very familiar. Perhaps the most striking example is how the newer churches can read the Bible in a way that makes that Christianity look like a wholly different religion from the faith of prosperous advanced societies of Europe or North America. We have already seen that Southern churches are quite at home with biblical notions of the supernatural, with ideas like dreams and prophecy. Just as relevant in their eyes are that book's core social and political themes, like martyrdom, oppression, and exile. In the present day, it may be that it is only in the newer churches that the Bible can be read with any authenticity and immediacy, and that the Old Christendom must give priority to Southern voices. If Northern churches cannot help with clergy or missionaries or money, then perhaps they can reinterpret their own religion in light of these experiences.

When we read the New Testament, so many of the basic assumptions seem just as alien in the global North as they do normal and familiar in the South. When

Jesus was not talking about exorcism and healing, his recorded words devoted what today seems like an inordinate amount of attention to issues of persecution and martyrdom. He talked about what believers should do when on trial for the faith, how they should respond when expelled and condemned by families, villages, and Jewish religious authorities. A large proportion of the Bible, both Old and New Testaments, addresses the sufferings of God's people in the face of evil secular authorities.

As an intellectual exercise, modern Westerners can understand the historical circumstances that led to this emphasis on bloodshed and confrontation, but the passages concerned have little current relevance. Nor, for many, do the apocalyptic writings that are so closely linked to the theme of persecution and martyrdom, the visions of a coming world in which God will rule, persecutors will perish, and the righteous be vindicated. In recent decades, some New Testament scholars have tried to undermine the emphasis on martyrdom and apocalyptic in the New Testament by suggesting that these ideas did not come from Jesus' mouth, but were rather attributed to him by later generations. The real Jesus, in this view, was a rational Wisdom teacher much more akin to modern Western tastes, a kind of academic gadfly, rather than the ferocious "Doomsday Jesus" of the Synoptic Gospels. From this perspective, Jesus' authentic views are reflected in mystical texts like the *Gospel of Thomas*. For radical Bible critics like the Jesus Seminar, *Thomas* has a much better claim to be included in a revised New Testament than the book of Revelation, which is seen as a pernicious distortion of Christian truth.

For the average Western audience, New Testament passages about standing firm in the face of pagan persecution have little immediate relevance, about as much perhaps as farmyard images of threshing or vine-grafting. Some fundamentalists imagine that the persecutions described might have some future reality, perhaps during the End Times. But for millions of Southern Christians, there is no such need to dig for arcane meanings. Millions of Christians around the world do in fact live in constant danger of persecution or forced conversion, from either governments or local vigilantes. For modern Christians in Nigeria, Egypt, the Sudan, or Indonesia, it is quite conceivable that they might someday find themselves before a tribunal that would demand that they renounce their faith upon pain of death. In all these varied situations, ordinary believers are forced to understand why they are facing these sufferings, and repeatedly they do so in the familiar language of the Bible and of the earliest Christianity. To quote one Christian in Maluku, recent massacres and expulsions in that region are "according to God's plan. Christians are under purification from the Lord." The church in Sudan, the victim of perhaps the most savage religious repression anywhere in the world, has integrated its sufferings into its liturgy and daily practice, and produced some moving literature in the process ("Death has come to reveal the faith / It has begun with us and it will end with us"). Churches everywhere preach death and resurrection, but nowhere else are these realities such an immediate prospect. As in several other crisis regions, the oppressors in Sudan are Muslim, but elsewhere, they might be Christians of other denominations. In Guatemala or Rwanda, as in the Sudan, martyrdom is not merely a subject for historical research, it is a real prospect. As we move into the new century, the situation is likely to get worse rather than better.

Persecution is not confined to nations in such a state of extreme violence. Even in situations when actual violence might not have occurred for months or years, there is a pervasive sense of threat, a need to be alert and avoid provocations. Hundreds of millions of Christians live in deeply divided societies, constantly needing to be acutely aware of their relationships with Muslim or Hindu neighbors. Unlike in the West, difficulties in interfaith relations in these settings do not just raise the danger of some angry letters to local newspapers, but might well lead to bloodshed and massacre. In these societies, New Testament warnings about humility and discretion are not just laudable Christian virtues, they can make the difference between life and death.

Just as relevant to current concerns is exile, forcible removal from one's homeland, which forms the subject of so much of the Hebrew Bible. About half the refugees in the world today are in Africa, and millions of these are Christian. The wars that have swept over the Congo and Central Africa over the past decade have been devastating in uprooting communities. Often, it is the churches that provide the refugees with cohesion and community, and offer them hope, so that exile and return acquire powerfully religious symbolism. Themes of exile and return also exercise a powerful appeal for those removed voluntarily from their homelands, the tens of millions of migrant workers who have sought better lives in the richer lands.

Read against the background of martyrdom and exile, it is not surprising that so many Christians look for promises that their sufferings are only temporary, and that God will intervene directly to save the situation. In this context, the book of Revelation looks like true prophecy on an epic scale, however unpopular or discredited it may be for most Americans or Europeans. In the South, Revelation simply makes sense, in its description of a world ruled by monstrous demonic powers. These forces might be literal servants of Satan, or symbols for evil social forces, but in either case, they are indisputably real. To quote one Latin American liberation theologian, Néstor Míguez, "The repulsive spirits of violence, racial hatred, mutilation, and exploitation roam the streets of our Babylons in Latin America (and the globe); their presence is clear once one looks behind the glimmering lights of the neon signs."

Making the biblical text sound even more relevant to modern Third World Christians, the evils described in Revelation are distinctively urban. Then as now, evil sets up its throne in cities. Brazilian scholar Gilberto da Silva Gorgulho remarks that "The Book of Revelation is the favorite book of our popular communities. Here they find the encouragement they need in their struggle, and a criterion for the interpretation of official persecution in our society. ... The meaning of the church in history is rooted in the witness of the gospel before the state imperialism that destroys the people's life, looming as an idol and caricature of the Holy Trinity." To a Christian living in a Third World dictatorship, the image of the government as Antichrist is not a bizarre religious fantasy, but a convincing piece of political analysis. Looking at Christianity as a planetary phenomenon, not merely a Western one, makes it impossible to read the New Testament in quite the same way ever again. The Christianity we see through this exercise looks like a very exotic beast indeed, intriguing, exciting, and a little frightening.

Christianity is flourishing wonderfully among the poor and persecuted, while it atrophies among the rich and secure. Using the traditional Marxist view of religion as the opium of the masses, it would be tempting to draw the conclusion that the religion actually does have a connection to underdevelopment and pre-modern cultural ways, and will disappear as society progresses. That conclusion would be fatuous, though, because very enthusiastic kinds of Christianity are also succeeding among professional and highly technologically oriented groups, notably around the Pacific Rim and in the United States. Yet the distribution of modern Christians might well show that the religion does succeed best when it takes very seriously the profound pessimism about the secular world that characterizes the New Testament. If it is not exactly a faith based on the experience of poverty and persecution, then at least it regards these things as normal and expected elements of life. [...]

55

American Evangelicals
The Overlooked Globalizers and Their Unintended Gospel of Modernity

Joshua J. Yates

Introduction

When people talk about the American dimensions of contemporary globalization, they generally speak about the spread of American popular culture, financial markets, multinational corporations, and political ideals. The images they evoke come effortlessly to mind: McDonald's, Nike sneakers, MTV and hip-hop music, Disneyland, Levi's jeans, the New York Stock Exchange, and American-style democracy, to name but a few. More astute observers are quick to note, however, that such examples are simply the more noticeable expressions of a seemingly endless array of other less culturally-identifiable, but no less American "products," including skyscrapers, greeting cards, chewing gum, microwaves, modern passenger airplanes, basketball, snowboards, the ATM, cell phones, computer hackers, and so on. Taken together, these familiar, and often bemoaned, instances of the diffusion of American "goods," "ideas," and "styles" provide a certain warrant for the claim that the US is the primary source and symbol of most of what passes as "globalization" in the planetary popular imagination.

Missing from this typical listing of dominant American cultural diffusions, however, are those emanating from American religion. Indeed, even the more sophisticated academic accounts of the so-called "modern global circumstance" – those charting the "flows" and "networks" of people, images, ideologies, technologies, disease, and the like – often ignore what may be one of the most significant aspects of globalization in the contemporary period: the worldwide spread of a

Original publication details: Joshua J. Yates, "American Evangelicals: The Overlooked Globalizers and Their Unintended Gospel of Modernity," in *Hedgehog Review*, Summer 2002. pp. 66–7, 70–4, 85–9. Reproduced with permission from The Hedgehog Review.

peculiarly American brand (in both origin and form) of Christianity – that is, Evangelical Protestantism. [...]

American Evangelicalism: Vanguard of a Transnational Religious Movement

Of all the instances of religious resurgence, nothing can match the global explosion of Evangelical Protestantism. Not even renascent Islam matches Evangelicalism's spectacular growth: "By 2050," asserts historian Philip Jenkins, "there should be still about three Christians for every two Muslims worldwide." Evangelical Protestantism (especially in its Pentecostal manifestations) is arguably the most consequential religious movement in the world today. Its growth around the world has been nothing short of stunning. In Latin America, for example, Protestants numbered around 15 million in the 1960s; in less than two decades, that number grew to at least 40 million. The growth of Pentecostalism has been particularly noteworthy, growing from only 10,000 in the early 1900s to over 150 million by 2000.

Beyond Latin America, the expansion of Christianity in its Evangelical and Pentecostal forms is as remarkable. The number of Christians on the African continent rose from around 9 million in 1900 to over 330 million by 2000 – over 120 million of whom are Pentecostal. In Asia, the story is no different. In 1900, the number of Christians figured around 20 million; by the year 2000, it had grown to over 300 million – 130 million of whom are Pentecostal. Currently about a third of the world population has some affiliation with Christianity. Estimates of total world population of Evangelicals figure around 700 million, half of whom are charismatic or Pentecostal.

Unlike the upsurge in the number of Muslims worldwide, what makes the growth in Evangelical Christianity even more astounding is that, with the exception of Latin America, a significant amount of the growth has taken place in societies traditionally uncongenial to Christianity in any of its forms. In 1900, 83 percent of the world's Christian population lived in Europe and North America; by the late 1980s, Africa, Asia, Latin America, and the Pacific accounted for 56 percent of Christians worldwide. If current trends hold course, it can be expected that the net effect of this new "Christianization" will revolutionize how the world thinks of Christianity. No longer will it be considered the religion of the North and West, but of the global South (indeed, save perhaps for the US, Ireland, and Poland, practicing Christians number among minorities in nations most associated with Christendom historically). Likewise, it will be increasingly a religion of non-white Africans, Latin Americans, and Asians. "If we want to visualize a 'typical' contemporary Christian," explains Philip Jenkins, "we should think of a woman living in a village in Nigeria or in a Brazilian *favela*."

Although the evidence appears to support the claim that Evangelical Protestantism is a thoroughly indigenized global phenomenon, Western (predominantly American) missionary and para-church organizations, operating in a manner similar to that of multinational, non-governmental organizations and corporations, continue to constitute a primary source of material resources; technical, educational, and professional assistance; as well as evangelistic, ecclesiastical, and theological models to Christians the world over. In this way, the centers of American Evangelicalism, while by no means the center of worldwide Evangelicalism, nevertheless continue to form the backbone of a transnational religious movement. As Steve Brouwer, Paul Gifford, and Susan Rose point out:

> When believers enter a church in Africa, Asia, or Latin America they participate in a form of worship that can be found in Memphis or Portland or New York City. Perhaps it will be Pentecostal, Southern Baptist, or a ubiquitous charismatic product marketed by Bible schools in places like Tulsa and Pasadena.

Organizations such as Campus Crusade for Christ, Youth with a Mission, World Vision, Focus on the Family, Compassion International, the Fuller School of World Mission, and the Christian Broadcasting Network are some of the largest and most visible of the American Evangelical organizations. Campus Crusade for Christ, for instance, employs 20,000 full-time staff, has offices in over 150 countries, and has chapters at nearly 700 universities worldwide. *The Jesus Film*, a project launched by Campus Crusade for Christ, has reportedly been shown in over 236 countries and territories, translated into 745 languages, and presented throughout the world to an estimated 4 billion people – two-thirds of the human race! Youth with a Mission averages a predominantly volunteer staff of 10,000 people in over 650 locations in 130 countries. World Vision, the largest Christian relief and development organization in the world, has an annual budget of $460 million and serves around 73 million people a year in 92 countries. The "global influence for Christ" of Fuller Theological Seminary's School of World Mission (the largest missions school in the world) comes through its vocational training of men and women from all around the globe; its graduates are now ministering in 110 countries as directors of local seminaries, churches, and organizations. The second largest international religious cable network in the world (behind the Trinity Broadcasting Network), the Christian Broadcasting Network airs its *700 Club* in more than 90 countries and in 46 different languages. Likewise, Focus on the Family boasts that its flagship radio program hosted by Dr. James Dobson is heard daily by more than 660 million people in 95 countries. Finally, the total number of American missionaries reportedly at large in the world today ranges from 67,000 to 118,000. With such global reach, it is rather surprising that American Evangelicals are so often overlooked in the popular and scholarly accounts of contemporary global change. [...]

The Language of the Market

Surprisingly, most Evangelical organizations express their mission and work in terms more typical of multinational corporations than religious organizations. One Evangelical leader declares, "We want to do business with the world and in so doing put ourselves out into the market. It's just how it works." All of the American globalizers, including the Evangelicals, describe their operations as taking place in a world characterized by "expanding markets," the need for "competitive advantage," "efficiency," "cost-effectiveness," "maximizing benefits and minimizing costs," "niche markets," "profitability," and the "bottom-line." Nowhere is this view articulated more dramatically among the Evangelicals than when Campus Crusade for Christ's President Bill Bright tells potential investors in a promotional video that for every New Life Training Center established around the world, 100,000 people will hear the gospel and at least 10,000 souls will be saved in the very first year of operation. As he puts it, "I have never heard of an investment with greater spiritual return." With similar dynamism, Paul Crouch, of the Trinity Broadcasting Network, proclaims:

> God promised to give you "EVERY PLACE where you SET YOUR FOOT…" (Josh. 1:3 NIV). With 21 SATELLITES carrying TBN, the WORLD is almost COVERED with your "FOOTPRINTS" spreading the Gospel everywhere! Every SOUL saved through TBN is going to YOUR account in heaven because you GAVE. Praise God, the account is GROWING! [capitalized words in original]

Another component of the market idiom appears in the frequent equation of the believer with consumer. Not surprisingly, this is most explicit among Evangelical broadcasting organizations for which listeners and viewers are, quite literally, consuming their religious media "products." "Not only has your TBN grown to 3,309 stations, and is carried on 21 satellites and thousands of cable systems around the world," exclaims Crouch, "but no matter where you are, day or night, you can watch TBN via the Internet. It is literally available to anyone, anywhere who can access the Internet!" The Christian Broadcasting Network (CBN) is somewhat more strategic in its appeal to religious consumers using the most cutting-edge advertising tactics. Describing the global success of CBN's WorldReach program, one promoter says,

> When the secular world wants to really grab the attention of the consumers of a country, they "four-wall-market" a product. We want nations to know of Jesus' love and His plan for each of us, therefore CBN uses the "four-wall-marketing" concept in the form of media blitzes to spread the Gospel. CBN's creation of the media blitz has proven to be an effective and entertaining outreach tool to share Christian, family-oriented programming using various forms of media: television, radio, videotapes, literature, etc.

The Language of Multiculturalism

Needless to say, this conception of the individual framed by the logic of the market has consequences. In each realm of globalizing activity, it universalizes specific notions of organizational progress and, more generally, human progress. However, the desire to globalize a brand or a message or a service by appeal to these culturally specific, if globally attractive, notions cannot be made without qualification. The elites in the vanguard of globalization are aware of the historical heavy-handedness of American or Western organizations and are eager to temper both the image and reality of their work as a form of cultural imperialism. Balancing the moral appeal to universal rights and needs, then, is a tendency to indigenize their brands, organizational identities, and constituencies. It is here where we see a common recourse to an idiom rooted in multiculturalism, one that focuses on sensitivity to local cultures.

Coca-Cola is paradigmatic in this regard. As the vice president at Coca-Cola puts it, "our business is fundamentally local, our principles are global." To explain he uses the metaphor of architecture:

> Think about the architecture as a blueprint of your house. We operate with a "global brand architecture" in positioning our brands that are essentially the same everywhere. Depending on where we are, the roof shingles might be tile in one place and asphalt in another.

A Vice President for Marketing and Research at MTV articulates the same view of his company, "We're one of the few brands who have nailed the notion of being able to be global and local at the same time." Evangelicals echo the views of Coca-Cola and MTV in this regard. As the Vice President for World Vision explains,

> The business of an NGO is about trust. Local communities won't trust us if we're not local. So we have to be local. Thus, we have a World Vision-New Zealand, World Vision-Taiwan, World Vision-UK, etc. But, on the other hand, if you're truly only local, you may not be trusted by donors and therefore will not be able to get the resources necessary to accomplish your mission.

Similarly, the Vice President for Focus on the Family describes how his organization maintains their global–local structure for radio by contracting with local, indigenous offices that have their own legal status, but "we license the use of the Focus on the Family name." He continues:

> Our local partners have a desire to help families in their regions and we stand behind them. We bring to the table radio expertise as well as resource assistance. However, we do not feel it is our place to control what is aired. We emphasize basic biblical principles; our partners contextualize it so that it will connect and communicate with the local person.

The Campus Crusade for Christ Vice President is as quick to emphasize how most of their international staff are recruited from the societies in which they work: "Most of all our work is directed by nationals. We have only 700 Americans [out of 20,000] serving outside the US." Indeed, nearly all of the Evangelicals claim that they work hand-in-hand with partners from the places they are engaging.

Conclusion: An Unintended Gospel of Modernity

What should be apparent from the foregoing examination of the American Evangelical globalizers is that they do in fact share a family resemblance with their secular counterparts, despite their disagreements. There are important disputes between Evangelicals and their secular counterparts over certain moral issues, representing deeply divided ideological commitments, and these disputes could take on greater global importance if they become politically charged for Evangelicals in other societies. The extent to which such battles are fought abroad is at present, however, limited to the exports of the American globalizers. More significant at present are the commonalities found at the level of institutional and organizational practice. What counts as "success," "progress," "opportunity," and the like is for the American Evangelicals managed according to the same rationalizing techniques as for their secular counterparts and, by and large, accounted for in the same cultural languages. [...]

Thus, it is safe to say that the Evangelical globalizers have endorsed an intensely modern (and modernizing) cultural orientation, if unwitting of its implications for their work and message. Taken individually, there will no doubt be significant differences in the extent to which Evangelical groups reject or embrace the various logics of modernity. Taken as a whole, however, Evangelicals do demonstrate a certain symmetry of engagement at the level of practice both among themselves and with their secular counterparts. Given their access to the most advanced technologies of transportation and communication, moreover, they cannot help but be some of the leading apologists for Western (American) modernity, even if unintentionally. [...]

56

Globalizing Catholicism and the Return to a "Universal" Church

José Casanova

As a religious regime, Catholicism preceded and is likely to outlast the modern world system of nation-states. The transnational character of Catholicism can almost be taken for granted, but historically the nature and manifestations of that transnationalism have changed radically along with changes in the worldly regimes in which Catholicism has been embedded. The very attribute *transnational* only makes sense in relation to the system of sovereign nation-states that emerged in early modernity and eventually replaced the system of medieval Christendom, a system that had been centered on the conflictive interdependent relation between the Roman papacy, or "the political system of the popes," and the Holy Roman Empire. The dynamic synergy of the new world system of sovereign states was such that one after another all the emerging national churches fell under the control of caesaro-papist rulers and the Roman papacy itself became just another, rather marginal and insecure, sovereign territorial state. It is precisely at the point when the Papal States were incorporated into the Kingdom of Italy and the papacy was finally forced to renounce its claims to territorial sovereignty, that the papacy could be reconstituted as the core of a transnational religious regime, this time on a truly Catholic, that is, ecumenical basis.

Ongoing processes of globalization offer a transnational religious regime like Catholicism, which never felt fully at home in a system of sovereign territorial nation-states, unique opportunities to expand, to adapt rapidly to the newly

Original publication details: José Casanova, "Globalizing Catholicism and the Return to a 'Universal' Church," in *Transnational Religion and Fading States*, ed. Susanne Hoeber Rudolph and James Piscatori. Boulder, CO: Westview Press, 1997. pp. 121–2, 130–4, 135–6. Reproduced with permission from Westview Press, a member of Perseus Books Group.

emerging global system, and perhaps even to assume a proactive role in shaping some aspects of the new system. Conversely, an analysis of the contemporary transformation of Catholicism may offer some clues as to the direction of contemporary processes of globalization.

Progressively, from the middle of the nineteenth century to the present, one can trace the reconstruction, reemergence, or reinforcement of all those transnational characteristics of medieval Christendom that had nearly disappeared or been significantly weakened in the early modern era: papal supremacy and the centralization and internationalization of the Church's government; the convocation of ecumenical councils; transnational religious cadres; missionary activity; transnational schools, centers of learning, and intellectual networks; shrines as centers of pilgrimage and international encounters; transnational religious movements. [...]

The definitive assumption by the Church during the papacy of John XXIII of the modern doctrine of universal human rights has altered radically the traditional dynamic of Church-state relations and the role of the Church both nationally and transnationally. It has opened the way for a realignment in the relations between religious and worldly regimes. The cornerstone of the process is the Vatican II Declaration on Religious Freedom, *Dignitatis Humanae*. Significantly, the most eloquent voices in the crucial debate at the floor during the Council came from opposite blocs: from the American bishops, who unanimously defended religious freedom not only on grounds of practical expediency but also on theological grounds provided to them by their *peritus*, the great American theologian John Courtney Murray, and from Cardinal Karol Wojtyla from Kraków, who had learned from the experience of trying to defend the freedom of the Church under communism that the best line of defense, both theoretically and practically, was the defense of the inalienable right of the human person to freedom of conscience. Theologically, this entailed the transference of the principle of *libertas ecclesiae* that the Church had guarded so zealously through the ages to the individual human person – to *libertas personae*.

From now on, the most effective way for the papacy to protect the freedom of the Church worldwide would no longer be to enter into concordats with individual states trying to extract from both friendly and unfriendly regimes the most favorable conditions possible for Catholic subjects but rather to proclaim *urbi et orbi* the sacred right of each and every person to freedom of religion and to remind every government not through discreet diplomatic channels but publicly of their duty to protect this sacred human right. In the process, the pope could be transformed from being the Holy Father of all Catholics to becoming the common father of God's children and the self-appointed spokesman of humanity, the *defensor hominis*. At long last, the papacy could free itself from the postmedieval trappings of territorial sovereignty that historically had hampered so much its freedom of movement. What the papacy and the national churches needed to carry out their spiritual mission was not the protective rule of political overlords who always ended up restricting the Church's freedom of movement but rather a free global civil society.

First Citizen of the Emerging Global Civil Society

Naturally, the pope's voice could only have its effect if three conditions were met: if the voice could infiltrate and cross state boundaries and be heard everywhere; if the papacy could use its transnational resources and the local churches to amplify its voice; and if the pope's voice could actually join and add volume and prestige to the already existing choruses of voices everywhere, until state walls came falling down. The globalization of mass media and the extremely effective use by the papacy of these media have met the first condition. The centralization and homogenization of Catholicism achieved by the Second Vatican Council and by the general process of *aggiornamento* to modernity have met the second condition. The third condition was also met, for, in questioning the principles of state sovereignty and *raison d'état,* the two cornerstones of the modern system of nation-states, the Church was only joining a whole array of local social forces and transnational institutions, organizations, and social movements, working toward the establishment of autonomous civil societies and toward the constitution of one free global civil society.

Particularly in those societies in which the voice of the papacy carried a special weight, this concerted civil effort had dramatic effects. Suddenly, human rights doctrines could be used to put into question simultaneously the national-Catholicism of the Franco regime, the national security doctrines of bureaucratic–authoritarian regimes throughout Latin America, the corrupt oligarchic dictatorship of a cold war caudillo like Ferdinand Marcos, and the official lies of people's democracies in Poland and elsewhere. Those who took the voice of the pope most seriously – priests and nuns, pastoral agents, and engaged laity – were at the forefront of a new worldwide democratic revolution.

Ironically, the diplomatic power of the papacy has also increased as the size of the Vatican state has shrunk and as the Holy See agreed to "remain extraneous to all temporal disputes between nations and to international congresses." The number of countries that have established diplomatic relations with the Vatican has increased continuously: It was four in 1878 at the time of Pius IX's death, fourteen in 1914 when Benedict XV began his papal reign and twenty-five in 1922 at the time of his death; by 1939, on the eve of World War II, the number was thirty-eight, and it reached seventy by 1973. At long last in 1984, overcoming its anti-popish bias, the 1867 US congressional ban on diplomatic relations with the Vatican was lifted and the Reagan administration established full diplomatic relations with the Vatican. The collapse of the Soviet system of states and the disintegration of the Soviet Union have added a significant number of countries to the diplomatic corps at the Vatican. By 1993, 144 countries had established diplomatic relations with the Vatican.

The reason for the growing diplomatic relevance of the Vatican is clearly not that Vatican City is such a powerful sovereign state. Rather, the Catholic Church has become such an important transnational organization in the emerging world system that no state can afford to ignore it. In the open public field of a global civil society the pope's divisions and their allies have appeared to be more effective and to have greater freedom of movement than the riot control units and the mechanized tank divisions amassed by Machiavellian princes and statesmen following the outmoded rules of engagement of realpolitik. In today's world, power does not come solely or even primarily from the barrel of a gun, particularly when states holding onto the monopoly of the means of violence have no legitimacy in civil society and do not have the moral or political resolve to use those guns against unarmed civilians. [...]

To a large extent this process of globalization and the ability of the papacy to exploit the opportunities created by this process, thereby enhancing its role and prestige in the emerging world system, have their origins in World War II and its aftermath. The cold war and the policy of containment of communism offered the Catholic Church, Catholic countries, and Catholic minorities within Protestant countries the possibility to realign themselves and to join the center of the North Atlantic Protestant capitalist system from which they had been alienated or marginalized since the Counter Reformation. The Washington-Rome alliance became one of the key axes in the policy of containment of communism. Catholics became full partners of a Christian Democratic West and of the North Atlantic alliance. Catholics and Christian Democracy led the process of integration of the European Community. The Second Vatican Council had to be called precisely in order to ratify officially the process of *aggiornamento* to modernity that was already well under way in Catholic Western Europe. Once convened, however, the Council created a totally unforeseen dynamic of Catholic transformation and globalization.

The centrality of the papacy in the new global system was even recognized by the Soviets when Nikita Khrushchev welcomed John XXIII's mediation during the Cuban missile crisis and solicited that this mediation for the cause of peace and the sacred values of human life should not be limited to moments of crisis. When the superpowers and the entire world saw themselves at the brink of nuclear war, a higher principle of mediation had to be found. Once it could no longer be taken for granted, the survival of the species had to become a conscious and concerted effort of all of humanity. The security of humanity and of the planet had to have precedence over national and state security. Thereafter, the Vatican's *Ostpolitik* and the United States policy of détente took parallel tracks. Yet the Vatican was careful to cultivate an image of mediation above the superpowers. Indeed, it claims to represent the interests of the international system as a whole. Since Benedict XV's enthusiastic support for the League of Nations, the popes have been consistent advocates of worldwide international bodies, from the World Court to the United Nations, which would limit absolutist state sovereignty, arbitrate international disputes, and represent the interests of the entire family of nations.

The papacy has also assumed eagerly the vacant role of spokesperson for humanity, for the sacred dignity of the human person, for world peace, and for a more fair division of labor and power in the world system. The role comes naturally to the papacy since it is fully in accordance with its traditional claims of universal authority. In a sense the papacy has been trying to re-create the universalistic system of medieval Christendom, but now on a truly global scale. The fundamental difference, however, is that the spiritual sword can no longer seek the protection of the temporal sword to buttress its authority against competing religious regimes in order to gain monopoly of the means of salvation. The official recognition of the principle of religious freedom means that the Church has accepted the challenge to compete in a relatively open global system of religious regimes. Given its highly centralized structure and its imposing transnational network of human, institutional, and material resources, the Church can reasonably assume that it has a competitive advantage.

Considering the fact that for centuries, practically since the early modern era, the papacy has been physically tied to the Vatican and symbolically to Rome, it is striking how eagerly recent popes have tried to globalize their image and become world travelers. Modern mass media and means of communication have given the papacy the opportunity to communicate directly with Catholics, as well as with non-Catholics, all over the world. Particularly, John Paul II has deployed this direct contact with the masses of faithful extremely effectively as a kind of popular plebiscitarian support for his authority and his policies, using it whenever necessary to impress secular leaders, to bypass national hierarchies, or to check dissenting tendencies from Catholic elites.

Even though the Catholic Church has its own network of national and transnational mass media, the impact of the papacy on world public opinion does not derive primarily from Catholic mass media but rather from the prominent and extensive coverage that the pope's words and deeds receive in Western media. Considering that since the late Middle Ages the image of the papacy had been associated, at least in modern hegemonic Protestant cultural areas, with strongly negative symbols, the fact that the very person of the pope has become today a positive media event is in itself an impressive achievement, indicative of the level of prestige and influence reached by the modern papacy. Without discounting the relevance of John Paul II's repeatedly manifest personal charisma, nor the role of a well-orchestrated job of charismatic image management by the Vatican staff, it would seem that the papacy has found a fitting role that meets the expectations of a much wider audience than the Catholic faithful. The pope has learned to play, perhaps more effectively than any competitor, the role of first citizen of a catholic, that is, a global and universal, human society. It just happens that this role is often in tension with his other official role as infallible head and supreme guardian of the particular doctrines, laws, rituals, and traditions of the *Una, Sancta, Catholica*, and *Apostolica* Roman Church. [...]

Simultaneously with this process of Vatican centralization and Romanization of Catholicism, however, there has taken place a parallel process of internationalization of the Roman administrative structures and of globalization of Catholicism as a religious regime. The Roman Catholic Church has ceased being a predominantly Roman and European institution. Along with the demographic increase in Catholic population from 100 million in 1900 to 600 million in 1960 and to close to one billion in 1990, there has been a notable displacement of the Catholic population from the Old to the New World and from North to South. The episcopal and administrative cadres of the Church have changed accordingly. The First Vatican Council was still a predominantly European event, even though the forty-nine prelates from the United States comprised already one-tenth of the gathered bishops. The Second Vatican Council, by contrast, was the first truly ecumenical council. The 2,500 Fathers in attendance came from practically all parts of the world. Europeans no longer formed a majority. The US delegation, with over 200 bishops, was the second largest, though it was already smaller than the combined number of 228 indigenous Asian and African bishops at the end of the Council. The number is significant considering that only under the papacy of Benedict XV did the Vatican begin to promote the recruitment of indigenous clergy and the formation of native hierarchies, thus abandoning the European colonial legacy of considering missions as religious colonies. Even more significant has been the internationalization of the College of Cardinals, and though more slowly, the internationalization of the Curia. Since the time of Julius II (1503) not only the popes but also most of the curials had been Italian. In 1946, Italians still constituted almost two-thirds of all cardinals. That year Pius XII created thirty-two new cardinals, only four of whom were Italians and thirteen were non-European. The College of Cardinals that voted for a non-Italian pope in 1978 already had a much more international and representative composition: 27 Italians, 29 from the rest of Europe, 12 Africans, 13 Asians, 19 Latin Americans, 11 North Americans. The contemporary process of internationalization of Catholicism, moreover, does not have only a radial structure centered in Rome. In the last decades there has been a remarkable increase in transnational Catholic networks and exchanges of all kinds that crisscross nations and world regions, often bypassing Rome.

Interrelated with, yet in tension with this dual process of Romanization of world Catholicism and internationalization of Rome, there has also taken place a process of "nationalization," that is, of centralization of the Catholic churches at the national level. The institutionalization of national conferences of bishops following Vatican II reinforced the dynamics of the process of nationalization that had been carried primarily by different forms of Catholic Action with their shared strategy of mobilization of the Catholic laity to defend and promote the interests of the Catholic Church in what was perceived as a hostile modern secular environment. This political mobilization of Catholicism had been oriented toward the state, its aim being either to resist disestablishment or to counteract state-oriented secularist movements and parties. The final Catholic recognition of the principle of religious freedom, together with the Church's change of attitude toward the modern secular environment, has led to a fundamental transformation of the national Catholic churches. They have ceased being or aspiring to become state compulsory institutions and have become free religious institutions of civil society. In the process, Catholic churches throughout the world have dissociated themselves from and entered into conflict with authoritarian regimes that were predominant in many Catholic countries. This voluntary "disestablishment" of Catholicism has permitted the Church to play a key role in recent transitions to democracy throughout the Catholic world.

The traditional position and attitude of the Catholic Church toward modern political regimes had been that of neutrality toward all "forms" of government. So long as the policies of those governments did not infringe systematically upon the corporate rights of the Church to religious freedom, *libertas ecclesiae,* and to the exercise of its functions as *mater et magistra,* the Church would not question their legitimacy. The assumption of the modern doctrine of human rights entails, however, more than the acceptance of democracy as a legitimate "form" of government. It implies the recognition that modern democracy is not only a form of government but a type of polity based normatively on the universalist principles of individual freedom and individual rights. As national churches transfer the defense of their particularistic privileges to the human person, Catholicism becomes mobilized again, this time to defend the institutionalization of modern universal rights and the very right of a democratic civil society to exist. [...]

57

Religious Rejections of Globalization

Frank J. Lechner

[...]

Religion and Antiglobalization Activism:
The Case of the Debt Movement

On November 6, 2000, President Bill Clinton signed a foreign aid bill fully funding debt relief for poor countries. The Office of Social Development and World Peace of the US Catholic Bishops hailed the occasion by cheering, "We won on debt!" It attributed the "tremendous victory" to a grassroots campaign led by religious groups that had been based "on a quixotic belief that we could turn the Scriptural call of Jubilee into concrete commitments on debt by our government." Describing the range of activities in which Catholics had been involved, the office took some credit for the US Catholic community, which had "played a central role in this victory." Somewhat later, Presbyterians similarly noted their role in advocating debt forgiveness and their participation at all levels of the campaign from the beginning. "Jubilee 2000," commented Rev. Gary Cook, "demonstrated once again the power of scripture to shape what we often call 'secular history.'"

The Clinton signing represented the culmination of an intense global campaign. When third world countries became burdened with debt in the 1980s, a loose group of nongovernmental organizations (NGOs) began to call for restructuring and

Original publication details: Frank J. Lechner, "Religious Rejections of Globalization," in *Religion in Global Civil Society*, ed. Mark Juergensmeyer. New York: Oxford University Press, 2005. pp. 118–20, 122–7. Reproduced with permission from Oxford University Press, USA.

forgiveness of external debt. In the United States, these included shifting and short-lived coalitions, such as the Debt Crisis Network (1985–90); in Europe, Oxfam and the European Network on Debt and Development (1990–) took a leading role, complemented by an African sister organization, AFRODAD, since 1994. But by the mid-1990s, it is fair to say, their actions had produced few tangible results. The effort to resolve the debt crisis only became a global movement when disparate efforts were connected as part of one campaign. Jubilee 2000, formed as a charitable trust in the United Kingdom in 1996, became the spearhead of a transnational advocacy network that used a specifically religious rationale to frame debt as a moral issue, organized the efforts of numerous groups into a single campaign, devised forms of protest drawing attention to their cause, exerted pressure on authorities to take effective action, and helped to turn debt relief into a tool of broader antiglobalization advocacy.

Religious organizations had addressed the debt issue prior to 1996. For example, the Pontifical Commission on Justice and Peace wrote in 1987 that "debt servicing cannot be met at the price of asphyxiation of a country's economy, and no government can morally demand of its people privations incompatible with human dignity." In the United States a 1989 study by the Presbyterian Church–USA entitled *The Third World Debt Dilemma* and a report by US Catholic bishops, *Relieving Third World Debt: A Call for Co-responsibility, Justice and Solidarity*, were similarly critical. Church groups were among the debt activists since the 1980s. But religious involvement changed when a number of people applied the biblical concept of Jubilee to the problem of third world debt. Among the first to do so was the political scientist Martin Dent, who founded a group called Jubilee 2000 at Keele University in 1990, drawing on parallels with the nineteenth-century antislavery movement. After he met Bill Peters, a retired diplomat who headed the United Society for the Propagation of the Gospel, at a seminar in 1993, they joined forces to found Jubilee 2000 as a national organization in 1996. Though they quickly drew in secular groups, such as the UK Debt Crisis Network, the UK coordinator noted that "church groups were the initiators of the campaign and this has allowed it to spread very rapidly." Their impetus came from the biblical injunction in Leviticus (25:10) to "hallow the fiftieth year and proclaim liberty throughout all the land to all the inhabitants thereof: it shall be a jubilee to you; and you shall return every man to his possession, and you shall return every man to his family." As Pope John Paul II interpreted the injunction in a message to a Jubilee 2000 gathering in 1999, the original Jubilee "was a time in which the entire community was called to make efforts to restore to human relations the original harmony which God had given to his creation and which sinfulness had damaged. It was a time to remember that the world we share is not ours but is a gift of God's love. During the Jubilee, the burdens that oppressed and excluded the weakest members of society were to be removed, so that all could share the hope of a new beginning in harmony, according to God's design." Debt forgiveness thus fits divine design.

This new religious impetus behind the antidebt movement proved critical in several ways. By framing a policy issue as one of moral urgency, Jubilee created a new form of symbolic politics. It called upon new symbols and stories to make sense of an otherwise fairly arcane problem for a broad audience in developed countries, thus generating a certain amount of grassroots support. It provided a broad enough rationale to bundle the efforts of numerous groups under one ideological umbrella, thereby breathing new life into the old, loose network. The frame became the movement's primary resource, as it operated on a small budget. The religious factor was a necessary element in the success of the movement on two dimensions conventionally used to judge its success, namely, agenda setting and network building. The religious dimension of the campaign was decisive in very specific ways as well. When rock star Bono lobbied Senator Jesse Helms on behalf of debt relief legislation, his scriptural references were his trump card, moving Helms to unaccustomed tears. Without Helms's support, the Clinton signing might not have occurred. That signing was only one of the movement's tangible results, since the G-7 had already adopted a debt reduction plan in Cologne in 1999. [...]

Religion and Antiglobalization Discourse

On his visit to Cuba in 1998, Pope John Paul II delivered a homily at a mass on José Martí Square in Havana in which he criticized, not surprisingly, systems that "presumed to relegate religion to the merely private sphere" and thereby prevented the expression of faith in the context of public life. Turning to a subject that must have been more congenial to Cuban authorities, he went on to lament "the resurgence of a certain *capitalist neoliberalism* which subordinates the human person to *blind market forces* and conditions the development of peoples on those forces" (emphasis in original). The process was wrong in principle and unjust in practice: "From its centres of power, such neoliberalism often places unbearable burdens upon less favored countries. Hence, at times *unsustainable economic programmes* are imposed on nations as a condition for further assistance. In the international community, we thus see *a small number of countries growing exceedingly rich at the cost of the increasing impoverishment of a great number of other countries*; as a result the wealthy grow ever wealthier, while the poor grow ever poorer." The church, said the pope, has the answer in its "social Gospel," which "*sets before the world a new justice.*" Read against the background of the pope's overall stance toward globalization, his critique of neoliberal market expansion in Havana was hardly intended to placate his hosts. Rather, it was one instance among many in which he applied key tenets of Catholic social ethics to the evils of globalization. As the US bishops have noted, "The Third World debt problem exemplifies a recurring theme of recent Catholic teaching: the meaning and moral implications of increasing global interdependence."

The rejection of ongoing globalization by the Catholic Church under John Paul's leadership has some distinctive features. There is something ironic about the anticapitalist rhetoric of a pope whose opposition to liberation theology was a hallmark of his early tenure. There is also a note of ambivalence in statements about the world economy that recognize ways it can become a force for good. In key respects, however, the pope's message converges with that of other Christian critics. These, in turn, converge with the central thrust of secular globalization critiques.

To describe John Paul II's stance toward globalization as a form of "rejection" at first blush might seem an overstatement. Apart from issues such as celibacy and abortion, church doctrine tends to be formulated in nuanced terms. With regard to globalization, the pope has noted that it is a "complex and rapidly evolving phenomenon," one that is in itself "neither good nor bad." but "basically ambivalent." Its ethical implications "can be positive or negative." Yet his Havana homily reflects a persistent and unmistakably critical diagnosis of globalization. The hallmark of globalization, from the point of view of Catholic social teaching, is that "*the market economy seems to have conquered virtually the entire world*," enshrining "a kind of triumph of the market and its logic" (emphasis in original). But if globalization is "ruled merely by the laws of the market to suit the powerful, the consequences cannot but be negative." Among the negative consequences are "the absolutizing of the economy, unemployment, the reduction and deterioration of public services, the destruction of the environment and natural resources, the growing distance between rich and poor, unfair competition which puts the poor nations in a situation of ever-increasing inferiority."

"Absolutizing" the economy is intrinsically wrong, the pope explained in the encyclical *Centesimus Annus*:

> If economic life is absolutized, if the production and consumption of goods becomes the entire of social life and society's only value, the reason is to be found not so much in the economic system itself as in the fact that the entire socio-cultural system, by ignoring the ethical and religious dimension has been weakened and ends up limiting itself to the production of goods and services alone. ... Economic freedom is only one element of human freedom. When it becomes autonomous, when man is seen more as a producer or consumer of goods than as a subject, who produces and consumes in order to live, then economic freedom loses its necessary relationship to the human person and ends up by alienating and oppressing him.

From the pope's point of view, the consequences are equally worrisome. First, since markets are imperfect, they are bound to leave certain needs unsatisfied – the needs of those without the skills or resources to access the market, collective needs not amenable to market solutions, and immaterial human needs that cannot be left to its mercy. Second, without appropriate regulation by the community, markets do not serve the common good; when commerce knows no borders, the absence of such controls especially risks new forms of exclusion and marginalization. Third, left to their own devices, world markets exacerbate inequality, as the pope noted in Havana; as wealth becomes more concentrated, weaker states lose sovereignty, thereby lagging farther behind. Fourth, "One of the Church's concerns about globalization is that it has quickly become a cultural phenomenon. *The market as an exchange mechanism has become the medium of a new culture*." (emphasis in original).

The Catholic concerns echo in similar statements by the World Council of Churches. Globalization was a key item on the WCC's agenda at its fiftieth anniversary meeting in 1998 in Harare, Zimbabwe. The meeting's official report, *Together on the Way*, treats globalization as a threat. "The vision behind globalization," it says, "includes a competing vision to the Christian commitment to oikoumene." Like the pope, the WCC describes that vision as the "neo-liberal" faith in competitive markets and individual consumption that is bound to produce a "graceless system that renders people surplus and abandons them if they cannot compete with the powerful few."

The consequences of this lamentable "unilateral domination of economic and cultural globalization" are once again dire as well: it contributes to "the erosion of the nation-state, undermines social cohesion, and intensifies the conquest of nature in a merciless attack on the integrity of creation." While new technologies may produce some "potentially positive" consequences, the reality of "unequal distribution of power and wealth, of poverty and exclusion" makes a mockery of neoliberal expectations. "The life of the people is made more vulnerable and insecure than ever before," the WCC declares. Growing interdependence also leads to greater concentration of power, fuels fragmentation of the social fabric of societies, and causes people to lose their cultural identity. "We have compromised our own convictions," a preparatory report concluded. "We acknowledge the temptation we have to strive for our own inclusion in a world which has space for a privileged few." To resist the temptation, *Together on the Way* calls on churches to resist globalization.

After Harare, this became a common theme in the WCC's work. For example, the statement "Economic, Social and Cultural Rights" by a WCC commission to the UN Human Rights Commission laments the way "traditional life styles of self-reliance have been undermined by integrating people into a market culture," opposes the "increasingly dominant role of economic mechanisms" and the concomitant concentration of power in the hands of a global elite, and cites with approval a WCC workshop's definition of the project of globalization as "a link in the chain of series of exploitative actions to appropriate the resources of the countries of the South by the countries of the North – first through slave trade then through colonialism and now through neo-liberalism." Thus, the WCC approach to globalization is even more emphatically negative than the pope's.

What, if anything, does this common Christian critique add to antiglobalization discourse? In many ways, Christian responses resemble their secular counterparts, as exemplified by WSF and other activists' statements and by kindred academic critiques. In both kinds of antiglobalization discourse, globalization is of course subjected to ritual denunciation. Both treat neoliberalism and the "absolutizing" of the world economy as the source of all troubles. Those troubles comprise a highly standardized list: decline of nations, undermining of cultures, ecological devastation, and so on. Inequality of wealth and power is the key shared concern. All sides of the oppositional discourse emphasize advocacy over analysis, attributing assorted problems, from poverty to fragmentation, to vaguely characterized globalization in broad-brush fashion. To be sure, motives differ (few WSF activists claimed to be moved by faith), and so does language (the pope's cautious phrases are mild by WSF standards). But the overall picture is one of convergence: with regard to globalization, the global religious Left and the global secular Left speak with one voice. [...]

Religion and Alternative Visions of Globalization

When the Dalai Lama gave the commencement address at Emory University in 1998, the program quoted him as saying that "compassion can be put into practice if one recognizes the fact that every human being is a member of humanity and the human family regardless of differences in religion, culture, color, and creed. Deep down there is no difference." Like WSF activists, the Dalai Lama obviously believes "another world is possible," but the texture of his vision subtly differs from theirs. Of course, he has different reasons, and therefore justifies his worldview in different terms. His concern is not with any single issue; it is more encompassing. The core value at stake for him is not one that found expression at the WSF.

While the theme of compassion is characteristic of the Dalai Lama, his portrayal of humanity as a single family that strives for universal respect regardless of differences resonates with similar statements from leaders of other traditions. The convergence of religious views on a minimally shared global vision constitutes a distinctive contribution to the way civil society grapples with the implications of globalization. In the evolution of global civil society as a normative order, religious actors stand out in several ways. More explicitly than secular participants in civil society, they focus on the unity of the world, the interests of humanity, and the importance of accommodating cultural difference. Though some traditions show intriguing convergence in the framing of their actual worldviews, there is no full consensus.

One reason the pope described globalization as "ambivalent" is that "for all its risks," it also "offers exceptional and promising opportunities, precisely with a view to enabling humanity to become a single family, built on the values of justice, equity and solidarity." Catholic leaders in fact see the universal church participating in globalization to advance a global moral project. This project starts from "the awareness that humanity, however much marred by sin, hatred and violence, is called by God to be *a single family*" (emphasis in original). While the family metaphor resembles the Dalai Lama's, in the Catholic view the unity of humanity ultimately derives from common dependence on God, which provides a "new model of the unity of the human race" (John Paul II). This conception of unity has moral implications. As the *Catechism* states, "The unity of the human family, embracing people who enjoy equal natural dignity, implies a universal common good. The good calls for an organisation of the community of nations able to provide for the different needs of man." More concretely, "In our linked and limited world, loving our neighbor has global implications ... and continuing participation in the body of Christ call[s] us to action for 'the least among us' without regard for boundaries or borders." The whole church is called to global solidarity and responsibility. "To give positive bearings to developing globalization, a deep commitment to building a 'globalization of solidarity' is needed by means of a new culture, new norms and new institutions at national and international levels" (John Paul II). Central among the new norms, Catholic leaders have repeatedly stressed, must be universal respect for the human person, and here, again, Catholic views resonate with those of Buddhists.

The World Council of Churches, as we have seen, opposes the vision that currently undergirds globalization. It puts forth a competing one: that of the "oikoumene, the unity of humankind and the whole inhabited earth." In *Together on the Way* it said that "the logic of globalization needs to be challenged by an alternative way of life of community in diversity." The "catholicity" of the church may provide a model for the desired plurality within a single ecumenical movement. If the earth is to be treated as "home," then "people in very different situations and contexts" must "practice faith in solidarity and affirm life on earth together." A subsequent WCC consultation in Fiji elaborated the vision of unity. Representatives of Pacific churches offered the "Island of Hope" as a "metaphor for the wholeness of life." In contrast to prevailing features of globalization, that wholeness should be marked by "generosity, reciprocity and the sharing of communal resources." The meeting offered the churches as "places of sharing" on a journey toward "an alternative global family." In this way, the WCC brings to bear its traditional ecumenical commitments on the formulation of alternatives to globalization. [...]

Part IX Questions

1. In what ways are Osama bin Laden and like-minded Muslims "thoroughly modern," according to Kurzman? If they are "modern," what inspires their violent actions? Does Kurzman's analysis suggest any advice for leaders in the war on terrorism?

2. How is "deterritorialisation" changing Islam, according to Roy? Why does he think Islamic radicals "express a negative form of westernisation"? What do they try to achieve? Why are they likely to contribute to "secularisation, but in the name of fundamentalism"?

3. Why is Christianity flourishing in the global South? What impact does Jenkins think this will have on global Christianity? What impact might this have on societies in the South?

4. What makes American evangelicals successful "globalizers," according to Yates, and what makes their cultural orientation "intensely modern"? Is there a contradiction in saying that a certain kind of evangelical Protestantism is a major "American cultural diffusion" and that it also constitutes a "thoroughly indigenized global phenomenon"?

5. What gives Casanova confidence that the Catholic Church will remain durable in this era of globalization? How has the role of the pope in the church changed over the past century or so, and how has this affected the church's role in world society? How does Casanova explain the paradox that the church centralized its affairs in the Vatican while also pursuing a new global strategy?

6. Judging by the examples provided by Lechner, what contribution do religious groups and officials make to initiatives like the antidebt movement or to discourse critical of globalization? Can you think of other examples of direct religious involvement in global causes? Do these examples help to gauge how important religious voices might be compared to secular ones?

Part X

Globalization and Identity

Introduction

As globalization expands human connections, it enables more people to envision or adopt different identities. For example, women from Nepal or India, venturing far from home, may seek to fulfill aspirations unfamiliar to their ancestors. Taking advantage of global resources, African musicians craft a new identity as they mix aesthetic styles. Globalization also offers new arenas for expressing identities – quite literally in the case of international sports tournaments like soccer's World Cup, where national teams represent their countries' special virtues, at least in the eyes of their passionate fans. At the same time, globalization raises uncomfortable questions about identity, notably about where individuals and groups stand in a world that envelops them ever more tightly. For instance, women's participation in "global" practices, as in the case of Indian professionals, may loosen the hold of "local" family culture; national communities seeking to develop new symbols of identity, such as tequila in the case of Mexico, must at the same time contend with transnational business practices. While much of the "identity work" people do in response to globalization consists of variations on older themes, for at least some groups globalization itself can be a new source of identity, in the form of cosmopolitan appreciation of cultural difference or even an explicit commitment to "world citizenship" as a way to promote some universal goals. Our purpose in this section is to illustrate explicitly some of these ways in which globalization affects identity.

The issues addressed here have come up implicitly in several other sections. Exposed to new food, games, or health issues, people experience globalization in ways that may shake settled identities. Global media show the interplay between transnational content and national/local adaptation, often creating tensions in national culture industries. Many religious adherents articulate their faith differently as they grapple with globalization, whether to embrace or oppose it. Many NGO,

The Globalization Reader, Fifth Edition. Edited by Frank J. Lechner and John Boli.
Editorial material and organization © 2015 John Wiley & Sons, Ltd.
Published 2015 by John Wiley & Sons, Ltd.

environmental, or global justice activists in effect derive new identities from their critical involvement in globalization. In short, who-am-I and who-are-we questions often lurk close to the surface of even seemingly mundane and material global processes. By making that point explicit, this section aims to stimulate further thought about the various forms the global redefinition of identity may take.

In drawing attention to the identity issues at stake in globalization, we do not suggest that most people create their identities by being involved in global processes or that globalization inexorably molds all individual or collective identities. Yet as relations across larger distances, backed by transnational power and ideas, create a world society of sorts, comprehending the place of self or community in that wider context becomes a more pressing concern for ever more people. Globalization touches people's self-understanding, at times in very concrete, routine ways, as when teenagers identify with foreign pop stars or soccer fans identify with foreign teams. We cannot fully inventory the forms in which this plays out, but our selections in this section suggest that dualistic effects are evident: in some cases globalization empowers people with new opportunities, while in other instances people confront it as an alien constraint. The identity work that globalization fosters therefore also raises profound questions about the merits of globalization, for example whether we should view it as beneficial or harmful, liberating or intrusive, enriching or unjust.

In the first selection, anthropologist Ernestine McHugh shows how one Nepalese woman, Sumitra, developed a very different sense of self than women of prior generations in her family. Whereas her parents came from a small, tight-knit village with communal houses, Sumitra grew up mainly in a bustling neighborhood in a larger town, in a house with a room of her own. Although aware of many things that proper Nepalese girls still "must not do," Sumitra was allowed to decorate her private space, had a voice in choosing her spouse, gleaned new ideas from foreign movies, and traveled alone to join her husband abroad. Her father's and husband's service in the British army connected her to the wider world, but in a way that enabled her to return comfortably to her family and community in Nepal. McHugh presents Sumitra as empowered rather than burdened by globalization.

Young Indian women who work in the country's information technology (IT) industry, studied by American sociologist Smitha Radhakrishnan, perhaps feel the impact of globalization even more deeply. Speaking for many, one of her interviewees traces many of her attitudes and interests to the fact that "I'm global." "Global" here entails both exposure to things that are non-Indian and immersion in a streamlined corporate culture. Some women IT workers experience that culture as uniform and confining, while others view it as a path to an independent sense of self, sometimes aided by stints abroad. All of them must undertake their "navigations of identity," as Radhakrishnan puts it, to balance their class status, family background, and new gender norms.

In the next selection, ethnomusicologist Timothy D. Taylor describes how one musician has created a new artistic identity through his version of "global pop." Youssou N'Dour, a world music star from Senegal, has brought a mixture of commercialized African music styles to Western audiences while also reaching African audiences as a traditional praise-singer. Musicians like N'Dour, Taylor argues, are not interested in preserving an artificial authenticity expected by outsiders; rather, they strive to be "global citizens" by creatively blending the many sounds they hear.

In many countries, sports play a great role in expressing national identities. The Dutch men's national soccer team, discussed by Frank J. Lechner in the next selection, is a case in point: its successes and failures helped form a collective national memory in the Netherlands, its supposedly special style reflected national virtues in the eyes of passionate fans, and its participation in international tournaments served to define the country's place in the world. In the Netherlands, as in many other places, the quintessential global game also affords new opportunities for national identification, though in Lechner's view that collective identity represents only one layer among others.

In Ulf Hannerz's analysis, globalization has brought about a new world culture that connects diverse local cultures more closely as part of a single whole. In this context, at least some people craft a more "cosmopolitan" identity as they eagerly find their way into other cultures while becoming somewhat detached from their original homes and the "locals" who stayed there. While becoming cosmopolitan takes some skill, Hannerz notes that it is also increasingly difficult to remain purely local, within a culture closed off to the outside. He argues that locals and cosmopolitans need each other, as they play different roles in cultivating the diversity in world culture that they value from different standpoints.

Our final selection in this section is a statement by the World Service Authority, an INGO based in Washington, DC, whose motto is "World Government of World Citizens." Centered on the work and writings of Garry Davis, recently deceased, who as early as 1949 established an "International Registry of World Citizens," the organization seeks to transcend national governments with a global democracy based on human rights and world citizenship. No mere enumeration of universal rights and duties, the document situates the idea of world citizenship in a global historical context. It asserts that, due to the extreme interconnectivity of the contemporary world, and the "tragic contradiction" inherent in national citizenship, only a strong world citizenship institution can carry humanity through its present difficulties "to the future . . . and to the stars."

58

Moral Choices and Global Desires
Feminine Identity in a Transnational Realm

Ernestine McHugh

[…]

This article focuses on the ways in which globalization has influenced the experience of gender and identity in Nepal, attending particularly to one young woman – exceptional in her resourcefulness – and her family. Social change in South Asia has had a much more profound effect on the lives of women than on those of men, as Susan Seymour has made clear in her multigenerational study of women in India. This makes feminine experience particularly valuable as a vehicle for understanding the implications of globalization. By examining the moral perspectives and associated choices of a young woman who has lived through a time of radical change in Nepal, we can ground the much-discussed phenomenon of globalization in lived experience and come to understand it more richly.

Meeting Sumitra

I first met Sumitra in 1978 when she was about four years old. Her hair was in little ponytails, and she wore a red pantsuit that her parents had brought back from Hong Kong when the family returned for a short time to Tebas, a Gurung village of about 500 people, located two days walking distance from the town of Pokhara. I saw her again in 1987, when her family returned to Nepal permanently after her father retired

Original publication details: Ernestine McHugh, "Moral Choices and Global Desires: Feminine Identity in a Transnational Realm," in *Ethos*, 32, 4, December 2004. pp. 575–97. Note: This text has been edited and all notes and references to third party sources removed. Please refer to the original source text for clarification on what has been omitted.

from the British army. They had built a house in Pokhara bazaar – then the second-largest city in Nepal – and Sumitra was a slim schoolgirl, studying at an English-medium school. I stayed with her family that summer, and returned to their home in Pokhara again in 1999 to find Sumitra grown and married. In 2001, I was the guest of Sumitra and her husband at Sandhurst Military Academy in England, where she and her baby daughter accompanied him on his tour of duty as a Gurkha soldier.

I focus on Sumitra and her family in this article because her life has spanned a time of tremendous change in Nepal. During my initial period of research, from 1973 to 1975, national *panchayat* politics, a limited representative system that preserved the power of the king, was just beginning to take hold in a real and transformative way in Tebas village, eroding the power of the *jimwal mukiya*, the village headman, who was Sumitra's grandfather and into whose household I had been adopted. Her mother's generation was the first to move to Pokhara from Tebas, building more Western-style houses and creating neighborhoods as they settled in new areas of the town. She was near 15 when the Nepal *jana andolan,* or People's Movement, agitating for representative multiparty democracy, radically altered the terms of government in the country and facilitated social change through democracy and free speech.

Sumitra's life, and her constructions of gender and identity, are best understood in context. Changing historical, political, and economic conditions in Nepal have profoundly affected her experience and the repertoire of ideas and images in terms of which she understands herself and her life possibilities. These changes have involved processes referred to as "globalization," in that the community that is her reference group goes far beyond the localized region in which her mother and grandmothers grew up. In fact, although she identifies herself in a variety of ways as Gurung, the Gurung village from which her family comes is somewhat peripheral to her as a site of actual interaction and as a basis for self-definition.

[…]

Mapping a Family

I have known Sumitra's family for 31 years. I was adopted by her maternal grandmother as a "dharma-daughter" when I first came to Tebas village in 1973. I got to know her paternal grandmother, who lived on an adjoining terrace, gradually over time. Sumitra's maternal grandfather was the headman of Tebas village and he and his wife lived in a grand house with a large courtyard. Her paternal grandmother, a widow in a more modest lineage, lived nearby.

It is significant that each of their houses consisted of one main room on the ground floor that served the purpose of cooking, eating, visiting, and sleeping. Grain was stored on the floor above that room. In each house there was also a small room, reached from outside, that was used to store fodder or firewood. Newly married couples sometimes occupied such rooms, but usually all the family members slept in the main room of a house. In the daytime people moved through one another's courtyards freely on the way to their fields, on errands, or to visit friends. Although there were brass pots on the kitchen ledges and an incense brazier, water pot, and lamp on the altar, there were no decorations on the walls of either house. The only items I remember seeing in village houses were practical: mats, dishes and cooking implements, and metal boxes in which people kept their clothes. Rarely, there might be a photo or a religious figure. During the first two years I lived in Tebas village (1973–75), several people made the comment that although I came from a rich country and undoubtedly had a lot of money, it made no difference there because there was nothing to buy in the village. Beyond matches and batteries, this seemed to be basically true. "Dhani, garib, kehi pharak chaina" [Rich or poor, it makes no difference], they would say.

Globalization is not a new phenomenon, although its present scale may be unprecedented, and it should not be imagined that Tebas village existed at any time in the 20th century at a great remove from the rest of the world. Sumitra's great-grandfather had served in World War I, and was said to have been one of the first people in the village with cash, which enhanced his hereditary position as headman. About the time that cash entered the village, so did tea, one of the first outside consumer goods to become integrated in village life. Two of this great-grandfather's sons were killed in World War II, and Sumitra's grandfather also fought in that war. Nearly 90 percent of the men in the village had served as Gurkhas, and many spoke movingly of the campaigns in Europe and the suffering they witnessed among the civilians there. Their associations were not then to the West as a site of "progress" or "development" but of human pain, for which they had helped achieve a solution through their courage and skill. Retired soldiers sometimes talked of the surprising physical weakness of the European soldiers, who collapsed going up hills that they themselves could climb with ease. Men in the generations of the two World Wars did not speak of life in Europe as though it represented an ideal to which they aspired, and they returned to the village to live after their army service abroad.

Women in the Village

During the period in which I initially conducted research in Tebas village, 1973–75, feminine identity was framed in terms of land and kinship (so that one was known as a member of a particular village and as kin of a specific lineage and clan), and women's power was increased through traversing villages, developing kin ties in both the marital and natal homes and linking clans through intermarriage. The generation of Sumitra's grandparents was one in which girls married early, many between the ages of 10 to 12. There was no formal schooling in the village. The prestige of the lineage into which a girl was born, and its wealth (these two tended to go together), gave her value, as did her beauty and her character, measured in terms of her adherence to rules of modesty. Cross-cousin marriage was looked on favorably and a girl's mother's brother's son or father's sister's son had the first claim on her for marriage. This meant that women had a network of relations that continued across generations, because the same lineages tended to intermarry. For example, ties between Sumitra's family in Tebas and people in her grandmother's lineage in the large village of Torr were very strong, as there had been intermarriage between them for at least three generations. Women played a crucial role in arranging later marriages, thereby developing and strengthening these ties, and gifts were exchanged each time a woman went back to her place of birth to visit her family, so that goods and kinship were tightly linked.

At this time, women's social and economic well-being depended solely on marriage, and a young woman's potential as a bride was evaluated by neighbors and kin within a clearly defined locality. Thus, we can see that local reputation and geographically bounded ties were very important to a woman's future. Women also felt a personal connection to the land, and those who traveled to visit family members or attend ritual celebrations at other villages noted that they felt safer when they crossed rivers or reached the slopes that marked their home territory. For Sumitra's grandmothers and for many of the women of her mother's generation, territory was not arbitrary and abstract but had emotional power and defined identity in important ways. Thresholds, gateways, and entrances to villages were marked with strings of flowers to keep evil influences out and protect those within the boundaries they marked. A valued woman was meant to move within circumscribed worlds and to remain reserved.

[...]

When I arrived in Pokhara in 1999 after a gap of 12 years, Maili's formerly rustic neighborhood was nearly unrecognizable. There was a bustling market on the corner, with vegetable stands and several shops. All but one or two spaces of open land were filled with houses. Her formerly single-story house was now two stories high, and on the roof was a large satellite dish. She and her husband had rented out the lower floor, and the upper floor consisted of a kitchen, living room with a sofa and chairs, glass cabinets, telephone, and a large television. There were also three bedrooms: one shared by Maili and her husband, another occupied by their son, and the third belonging to Sumitra.

Unlike houses in Tebas village, which were communal and unmarked except for an altar with deities above it, the houses in Pokhara were divided into distinct personal spaces. In Tebas, boys had occasionally commandeered a storage space and made it into a personal room, rather plain and certainly temporary. Girls were never given rooms of their own but, rather, slept in the communal space, bedding down with their sisters, nieces, or mothers. In the town of Pokhara, both boys and girls not only possessed rooms, they marked them with decorations, proclaiming an identity through the display of goods.

Sumitra's room in her family's home was compact but pleasant. Although at the time of my visit she had been married to a soft-spoken young Gurkha soldier for two years, the room she had grown up in was still referred to as "Sumitra's room," and she stayed there on prolonged visits home when he was on duty. There were two beds in the room, a metal wardrobe, and a dressing table. There was a shelf with books and magazines, mainly copies of *Wave*, a youth magazine, and Indian women's magazines, like *Femina*. Above her window was a large poster from her husband with a verse in English, as follows:

> To my wife:
> Just can't say how much I love you,
> Only that I love you more than anybody, anywhere,
> Has ever loved before.

On her dresser was a wedding picture, a photo of Sumitra with some college friends, and a picture of her sitting on a *chautara*, or stone resting place, on the trail to the village, wearing a skirt and blouse with hiking boots. Next to the dressing table, taped to the side of her wardrobe, were photos of Western celebrity couples: Sylvester Stallone with his wife, Tom Cruise and Nicole Kidman, Richard Gere and Cindy Crawford, along with a large picture of a lovely Indian actress. In 1999, Sumitra herself was in London, where she had gone to join her husband, after making a trip on her own to Hong Kong to arrange the papers that would allow her permission to work in Britain.

Articulating Womanhood

What were Sumitra's ideas of feminine identity? The décor of her room provides hints as to what she values, but her words clarify this. When asked what her generation wanted, she emphasized the importance of freedom and exercise of will:

Kids go here and there, like to Hong Kong, and they make their own decisions. When they get big, they have their own opinions. They go places by themselves. They want to be happy. They don't want to act according to someone else's orders. If parents make a child marry someone, they may not be happy with them. They may not get along. People can be happy if they are able to live according to their own ideas. People of my generation want that.

In contrast to young Gurung women who lived in the village of Tebas in the 1970s and 1980s and the urban Newar women described by Parish, all of whom spoke of the value of feminine submissiveness, Sumitra does not see assertiveness as inappropriate for a girl. Her marriage was arranged, but her parents allowed her to correspond with the suitors they selected, to see their photos, and to choose the one that she wished to marry. Boys were regarded by her parents as suitable more in relation to socioeconomic status than kinship status, although restrictions on ethnicity and clan remained strongly in place. As had her mother, but without the social disapproval she endured, Sumitra married a man she cared for and respected, with whom she shared romantic feelings. These were expressed in the affectionate poster on the wall of her room, one whose sentiments the men and women of her mother's generation would have judged immodest. Her display of the poster was tactful, because those who might find it inappropriate were unlikely to be able to read English, and those who could understand it were likely to have been indoctrinated into the ideology of romance that it celebrated. The celebrity photos with happy film star couples holding hands and gazing at the camera embodied that ideology – one that celebrated individual freedom, privacy, and pleasure. Interestingly, the photo of the beautiful woman alone, looking smilingly into the camera, was of an Indian movie star, someone who resembles Sumitra herself. Sumitra saw film and other media as demonstrating life possibilities, especially foreign ones, that viewers might wish to emulate, as she commented: "People learn many things from film. They see other countries and other ways of doing things. Even from ads they can learn many things. I think it is very good." Although she participated in romantic fantasies, as exemplified in her photos and her women's magazines, Sumitra was aware of the pragmatic constraints on women. The restrictions imposed in the village that expressed moral worth and protected a girl from social criticism and male aggression also exist in the town, so that young unmarried women did not go about alone or strike up conversations with unrelated men without incurring criticism and perhaps danger. Although she accepted these limitations, at least when in Nepal, she chafed at them: "What you hear in Nepal is 'Girls must not do this,' and 'Girls must not do that.'"

Synthesizing an Identity

[…]

Sumitra's experience of foreign countries has not alienated her from her Gurung community. Although she traverses a variety of worlds, her cosmopolitan sophistication was gained in the company of her family, and interwoven with trips to the village. Most of her mother's sisters and brothers and their children have shared the experience of living abroad. Those family members who have not are marginalized, both in terms of experience and lifestyle, because money from Gurkha service opens possibilities for acquiring the consumer goods (computers, televisions, furniture, and motorcycles) that now signify honor and status as well as for such lifestyle accoutrements as education, further travel, and residence in fine houses. As formal associations, such as investment clubs, replace village ties, it is the wealthy who can afford to belong and to inhabit positions of influence. Sumitra, with her education and family wealth, can move in and out of the village at will, an enviable position for many Nepalis.

Sumitra's definitions of femininity involved many models and implicated many reference groups: She realized her identity as a woman in reference to her husband and the realm of romantic love, in reference to the West and its media products, in relation to the conditions of her nation, and to the villages in which she spent time as a child. She also spoke of a transcendent role that linked her to all women – motherhood. At the time of this interview (2000), she had recently given birth to her first child. In response to a question I asked about what she would need to have a happy life, she replied:

SUMITRA: I have a happy life. I got to have an education. I got to go to foreign lands. I got to give birth to a child, to have that experience. Just having one child, I got to know that womanly experience. You hear about it in words, but you don't really know it until you have had the experience. I got to have that woman's experience. Now I play a "mom's" role. I'll raise my daughter in a different way from how my mother raised me.

ERNESTINE
McHUGH: How so? What will you do differently?

S: What will I do? Everything is different now from when I was growing up. That is why she will be raised differently…. It is not like when my mother was raising me. The world changes, and that changes the way you raise a child.

[…]

Sumitra's family remains an important part of the relevant public in terms of which she enacts her identity, which provides her with continuity. She has been spared the conflict of those Nepali youth whose parents are unfamiliar with and antagonistic toward the cosmopolitan worlds they wish to inhabit. Unlike those who see the West as the site of success but cannot achieve a "modern" Westernized lifestyle, and can only imagine visiting the West, Sumitra is privileged, in that her financial means and life circumstances have put many of her cosmopolitan aspirations within reach. The status and prestige she accrues through her success in terms of Western values are both understood and appreciated in her community and have precedent in the experience of her well-traveled parents.

Freedom and Possibility: Banishing the Ban Manche

The spatial shifts Sumitra experiences are encompassed in her model of the world as desirable: broadening and enriching, rather than disorienting and threatening. They are felt as an expansion of her world, not as dislocation. Unlike her grandmothers in the village, Sumitra was able to negotiate the terms on which she married and moved away from home, and she has engaged foreign travel in an ordered way, combining the exotic experience of living in England with the familiar one of residing on a military base. Her values are marked by an appreciation of independence and choice, and her circumstances, including an egalitarian marriage to an unusually supportive husband who cooks, participates in child care, and encourages her to work, have allowed her to integrate these values in her daily life. The ideology of modernity works for Sumitra, and it is not surprising that she sees as its symbolic representation the inviting and attractive movie stars that adorn her room.

   [...]

Globalization, Conflict and Self-Definition

Global changes create conditions that erode existing gender relations and require men and women to reconfigure their relationships and reconstitute their identities. In many cases, this deprives them of cultural resources and shatters a sense of continuity and belonging, so that the symbols through which they processed their emotions are rationalized and robbed of their power, although alternative *bikaasi* or modern ways of being – in which exercise of rational choice in service of goals brings success – are far removed from their reach. This kind of alienation and frustration is the lot of many poorer people in contemporary Nepal, making a religion-like ideology such as Maoism, which promises both community and progress, attractive to many.

   Modernity, liberating for Sumitra, presents a conflicting and confusing set of imperatives even for many middle-class women in Nepal. Media images, consumer capitalism, and demands for women to participate in the public sphere are problematic for Nepali women in that they coexist in much of Nepal with the demand that women remain subservient to men and submissive in demeanor. The demand to display modern sophistication through fashion often conflicts with local ideas of appropriately modest feminine attire, public consumption necessary to maintain middle-class status erodes the capital necessary to sustain oneself economically, and presence in the public sphere without companionship makes a woman vulnerable to male harassment. In addition, the limited freedoms that more "modernized" young women enjoy are often abruptly terminated at marriage. Conflicting meaning systems and expectations leave many without a clear basis for self-definition.

This was not true for Sumitra, in part because of the nature of her family and her community. Her parents' own marriage was founded on individual choice, and they invested willingly in Sumitra's education, providing a model for independence and support for female autonomy. The quality of her marriage (like that of her parents, founded on mutual respect and affection), and the comparatively high regard with which women are held in Gurung society (in which they were never confined to the home or barred from participating in public discourse) all contributed to the combination of integration and autonomy that characterizes her life.

It is ironic that the primary vehicle that has loosened the constraints of patriarchy for Sumitra – that allowed her varied experiences within the security of her family, underwrote her education, and provided the prosperity that enabled her to make real choices – is one of the ultimate bearers of masculine values, the British army, within which both her father and husband have served as Gurkhas. This becomes, then, an account of how a young woman from a patriarchal social order was able to craft a life in keeping with her desire for independence and choice, a process in some part facilitated through a deeply patriarchal institution. Life in the Gurkha regiments provided Sumitra a transitional space within which she could integrate the values of her community (collective solidarity) and those of the West (rational self-interest), in which she could actually experience what for most Nepali youth is a place remote and idealized and engaged only through commodities and images. Within the bounded and protected realm of Gurkha bases, which housed a transnational Gurung community and encompassed multiple worldviews, Sumitra could forge an identity that was both relational and independent – locally grounded yet effective in a cosmopolitan context.

[…]

59

Global / Indian

Cultural Politics in the IT Workplace

Smitha Radhakrishnan

I really stress the word global. And not American. Because even if their coworkers are predominantly American … that's changing. So they may work with someone from Poland or China. So the skills that we talk about are going to be useful globally. And that's about being transparent and clear. Because you need that. In virtual teams, you need this kind of communication … And it's a very appealing term. I mean, who doesn't want to work globally? And they [the Indian engineers] love it!

– Luellen Schafer, the founder and director of Global Savvy, a cross-cultural training firm in Silicon Valley

Because I'm global, I tend to be more interested in reading something about the US or whatever. I think a lot of that has got to do with globalization. And even with my television, my news, my movies. My restaurants. When I go out, I eat Italian food, and that makes me curious. So, in that way, I think globalization has really helped me. And, you know, when I was growing up, all this was just "modern" or "Western." I think a lot of that is really going away. I think it's getting to be a part of Indian life … So everything is not just Western and modern, and hence, not so good. Things are changing. Because we have always been aware of the global world, but we have always shut it out. Now, we're letting it in. Always, there's a challenge, right? You have your own way of life and there's another way of life coming in. While it's coming in, while you're creating a new identity for itself, there will be casualties, a bit of confusion. It's okay.

– Malini, a thirty-year-old project leader in Bangalore

Original publication details: Smitha Radhakrishnan, *Appropriately Indian: Gender and Culture in a New Transnational Class*. Durham, NC: Duke University Press, 2011. pp. 53–6, 115–16, 121–7. Reproduced with permission from Duke University Press.

Malini, a longtime employee at a major Indian multinational in Bangalore, has traveled the world and has very specific ideas about what it means to be global. She defends globalization, praises its virtues in India, and does not mind it if the more parochial features of India's society and culture fade away. A few casualties and some confusion, inevitable in the cultural shakeup, are fine with her. For LuEllen Schafer, in contrast, "global" is a keyword meant to describe a particular set of skills that she helps to foster in the IT workplace – an appealing, pragmatic set of skills that is transferable and applicable anywhere. It is Schafer's job to transmit these skills to Indian engineers in a way that does not threaten their sense of Indianness, but rather allows them to maintain what she understands to be their culture. When does the acquired skill of effective global communication become something that defines a person more fundamentally? What are the mechanisms through which this happens? How might Indians working in the IT industry acquire not just the skills to "work globally," but also the personality traits and attitudes that make them feel "global" on a much deeper and more personal level? [...]

Navigating Cultural Terrain at Work: Corporate Perspectives

Indian IT companies do not just produce software products or sell their technical skills to clients abroad; they also produce a new breed of workers. The culture of the IT workplace, and, consequently, the transnational class of Indian IT professionals, is importantly derived from what informants repeatedly called a "global work culture." This culture is defined in myriad ways, the most prominent of which I describe and analyze here. "The global" can indicate a kind of new corporate culture that is separate from either Indian culture or Western culture, although this culture can be very thinly defined, leaving it open to interpretation. A cultivated sense of placelessness and insulation in office interiors, paired with a new awareness of corporate branding, offers little that is distinctive from which to build a new corporate culture. "The global" also refers to certain types of processes, communication styles, and skills, all of which are low context (in that they rely more on words and language than situational or relational cues), standardized, and transferable anywhere in the world. Finally, "the global" refers to a particular kind of organizational and managerial style, indicating flat hierarchies and innovative, empowered employees that emerge from new-age management and globalization discourses. Discourses of personal empowerment have particular resonance for professional women, although in their navigations, the gaps and shortcomings of corporate discourses of empowerment become apparent.

All of these competing meanings of "the global" set the stage for cultural streamlining. In corporate hallways and cross-cultural training sessions, culture becomes something that can be apprehended and absorbed, something transferable and strategically deployable. Corporations are invested in fostering a "global work culture" because it offers the promise of better efficiency and productivity, which improves their bottom line. Individuals, in contrast, are invested in being "global" because it promises a cosmopolitan sensibility that connotes status and refinement outside the workplace, as well as added bonuses within it. Such a strategic approach to culture that begins in the IT workplace, stemming from the capitalist imperative to streamline differences for the sake of efficiency, becomes a way of understanding culture more generally, as corresponding notions of "Indian" take shape alongside competing notions of the "global."

Sometimes, notions of what is "Indian" stand in contradiction to the global, while at other times, they are in concert. The dominant relativist rhetoric of "the global" encourages Indian technologists to maintain an "Indian" core and to adopt a global professional persona purely for the purposes of their own productivity and advancement. In this setting, India is ostensibly being preserved, but it is also being redefined as definitions of "the global" proliferate. This sense of India – at once new and abiding, both informed by discourses transmitted to technologists in the workplace and created by the engineers themselves – reveals itself most clearly in the narratives of professional IT women, whose behaviors within the workplace reflect their commitment to being simultaneously "Indian" and "global," a reconciliation that forms the basis for the cultural navigations that streamline Indian culture into mobile, globalization-friendly appropriate difference.

[...]

In a cozy flat in Bandra, a posh suburb of Mumbai, I am stretched out on a comfortable divan opposite Bharathi, a thoughtful technical writer in her mid-twenties. She sits cross-legged on the floor across from me, her eyebrows knitted together in deep thought as I ask questions. The tiny recorder between us bears witness. To me, Bharathi seems different from the colleagues of hers I have interviewed so far. She is in the IT industry, she is remarkably critical of the culture of IT. It is not completely surprising. A sociology graduate who studied law before realizing that her love for writing would be more lucratively channeled in IT, she has a more formidable set of tools for critical analysis of her social world than do her colleagues who have studied engineering exclusively. Now that I am interviewing her, asking her opinions and thoughts about working in IT, she is even more pensive than usual. In reflecting upon the colleagues she encounters in her field, Bharathi explains,

> And IT, well, I don't know. I think that environment just makes everyone a clone. You start thinking the same way. There's just that much range of a background you will encounter ... It's not like a doctor, when you have patients from all different backgrounds. I will interact with an integrator, a software person, a graphics person. How different would that be? They still speak English, which means they have at least had a certain kind of education. You see them wearing the same jeans and t-shirt ... Had I been a lawyer that would have been different. That empathy [for others unlike me] would have been much more. Now, from an IT field, my interaction with people is very limited.

Despite the popular perception that the experience of IT makes its employees more open-minded, Bharathi argues that the viewpoint of IT professionals is only becoming increasingly narrow. The popular perception of the industry as characterized by openness, communication, and dialogue seems dangerous to her: "IT was supposed to stand for communication – being able to speak another's language. But you are not. You speak the same language. And I mean language in the broadest sense, not just

English … It's a class vocabulary. Even if they come from different places, it's the same class … You can almost rattle off someone's opinion without having to know them." Bharathi observes a uniform class culture surrounding her at work. She feels that this culture has narrowed her outlook on the world. She is frustrated by the complacency of a culture that presumes and produces individuals with similar interests, tastes, aspirations, and even interpretations. This similarity, according to her, trumps class or regional origins because, as she says, "it's the *same* class." Only a very few of my interviewees agreed with Bharathi's sentiments; most argued instead that IT offered them unprecedented "exposure," a term to be explored in the next chapter. Bharathi's claims offer a notion of IT workers as sharing a common culture that few recognize.

Yet, Bharathi's opinions about the culture of the industry are more than keen, albeit unpopular, observations. Her opinions are the basis of a deep-seated fear for herself. She is afraid of how an environment she considers to be suffocating might be affecting her own individual growth and development: "I can interact better with my client in America than I can with the peon who cleans my toilet. Why is that? And I feel that, at some level, is quite debilitating for my personal growth. When I can't carry on a dialogue with another human being, however different that person might be, that's really sad. While this person in Ireland who has something to say about my content, I can talk to him for hours! Which is probably bringing the world closer, but it's still estranging me from my own people." The lifestyle and status that IT offers her fails to fulfill her personal goals, and her criticism hints at far more subtle desires: an individuality she believes she possesses and wishes to develop. For Bharathi, this individuality is made real through independent thought and through the capacity to connect and relate to those outside her own social, economic, and political milieu. This kind of individuality, it seemed to Bharathi, was not encouraged or even recognized as valuable in her industry.

[…]

Shubha, a software engineer I interviewed in Mumbai who first introduced me to the importance of the word "background," comes from a Marwari business family in Mumbai's suburbs. Her parents run a lucrative pharmaceutical business and were dismayed by Shubha's decision to work in IT. A daughter working in this industry was a step down for them, not a step up. After avoiding discussion of her parents for much of the interview, Shubha finally explained, "I do come from a very different family background than most of the people who would work in my company … like, many of them *have* to work … I really didn't have to work for money, I really didn't. My parents could afford to give me anything I wanted … and the amount of money I make [in IT] is nothing compared to the amount I would make if I put the same amount of effort into our business. There's just no comparison … So, it was just crazy for my father. He was like, 'Why are you doing this? You don't have to!'" Shubha was hesitant to explain to me this aspect of her background. She knows that it sets her apart from her peers, and she indicated that she purposely tries not to bring it up around her colleagues. For her, the decision to go into IT stemmed partly from her personal drive and partly from her desire to distance herself from her family:

For me, the major reason was independence, wanting to work on my own. I've been a fairly ambitious person throughout … I was academically very good in school. I was a board rank and my name was in the top ten in the city in my tenth standard. So I've been a very brilliant student. I don't think I'm intelligent; I just work very hard. I am by nature a slogger. So, that sort of fuels you into thinking that you should get ahead …

You see, my mom and my dad and my brother go to the same office. Family business. It was something I never wanted. My father has never been able to understand that … He always takes it that I don't want to be with them, but it's not that. I want to be with people, and at [my] work[place], you're always meeting people your age, and at work there's that fun associated with that. In business, I only meet people my dad's age and you are – well – it's different. I didn't want that and I don't miss that.

In contrast to Bharathi's account of the IT workplace being a place of mind-numbing uniformity and complacence that inhibits individuality, Shubha's narrative describes the IT workplace as a space that can fulfill her individual desires, remove her from the restrictions of her family, and allow her to craft a new independent sense of self, even though it means choosing a less lucrative path than she might have.

Shubha's decision to work in IT opened up opportunities that went far beyond the experience of working in a high-tech Mumbai workplace. When the opportunity to live in the United States temporarily for work arose, Shubha was determined to grab it, despite the very vocal objections of her conservative family. While most of my respondents, even those from otherwise protective and strict families, enjoyed encouragement from their families when the opportunity to go abroad came up, Shubha's parents strongly discouraged her from going to the United States. She fought them and eventually prevailed. Her stay abroad was exuberant for her. "I loved my seven months over there [in Minnesota]," she explained. "For me, it was just amazing. I've been pretty protected with my parents. *Very* protected, actually. So, it was like me spreading my wings and I just had a blast." While in the United States, Shubha lived on her own like most other IT workers, taking care of her own apartment without domestic help, and this distanced her even further from the everyday experience of her class position in India. Shubha explained, "I used to live in my apartment alone for a lot of the time and I had roommates coming and going, which was a big pain, but I used to do everything … My mom would be like, 'Oh, how are you doing this and that, cleaning the toilet?' But you just did it. You don't think, 'Oh my god, I'm cleaning my toilet.' You didn't think of it as a moral issue." Even in the short space of seven months, Shubha assimilated to the norms of suburban life in the United States, an experience that put a hard-won distance between her own sense of what was normal and her family's. When her triumphal stint in Minnesota was over and she returned to India, she agreed to marry, but her reference points for a good mate had changed. After screening and rejecting several potential grooms from business families, who would have expected her to quit her job and join the family business, she reconnected with a man from Mumbai with whom she had worked while living in Minnesota. Also an IT professional, he did not come from the same caste community, nor did he come from a business family, and for Shubha, choosing him also meant opting out of the expectations of business families altogether. Although her parents were initially resistant, they eventually approved of the match.

Once Shubha had married, her parents gave the couple a flat in an expensive part of the city, something they could not have afforded at such a young age from their IT salaries alone. Still, Shubha's everyday professional life has changed the group of people she interacts with, and made her less allied to her family's particular community. Although Shubha's father wanted for her the lifestyle typical of wealthy urban women from business families, who spend their days shopping or at parties, Shubha spends long hours at work in IT. For her, the relative hardships of the industry, and the relatively low compensation she receives, have nonetheless won her independence from her family and the lifestyle that would come along with being part of the family business. Now, most of Shubha's friends work in the IT world, and these social and professional connections help to make Shubha even more closely identified with ideas and pastimes common to other IT workers. Through her interactions with an IT workplace, then, both at home and abroad, Shubha fashions a story of herself that is rooted in striving and individuality, but its unique character is made possible by her preexisting class privilege, which came with both opportunities and obstacles.

[...]

While a drive for individual independence in itself provides a virtuous justification for disavowing economic gain among some informants, another type of narrative coming from those who grew up in wealthy business families underscores the virtue of IT as an industry with the potential to serve the world. Personal development and individualism are important here but are in service of a larger good. Here too, economic motivations are secondary. Rani, a twenty-eight-year-old Silicon Valley engineer moving into product development, works at a powerful company I will call Surge. While Rani's life trajectory took her away from India for the long term, her narrative bears important parallels to Shubha's. Like Shubha, Rani explained her career in IT as one that she pursued for the sake of her own self-actualization. More importantly, Rani explained that she expected to have a major impact on the world through the field of technology. Raised in a wealthy business family, Rani never had the drive to forge a career for herself, or indeed to work at all while growing up. While in college, however, a major Indian multinational identified her as someone with aptitude in the field, and after that she became more and more committed to the notion of a career. Through work, she met and later married her husband and moved to the United States with him in 2000. Since she has been in the United States, her vision for herself and her career has expanded and matured, as she has pursued her career more and more seriously. Rani feels that her work will someday have a major impact on the world, even as it actualizes and transforms her as an individual. "What do you think of cell phones?" she asked me early in our interview. I said I thought they were useful. "No, I mean, do you think it's a great thing? How has it changed your life?" I told her that it had certainly made life more convenient, but that it had downsides too. In response, she explained the scope of her vision and ambition for herself: "I have a different perspective. I feel it is a great technology. The thought of being able to talk to anybody, all my dear ones, even someone who is so far anytime, even if you are hiking or on the road. When I want to make an impact on the society, it is to create an invention, a technology like this, something that would eventually make a difference to all the people in the world." [...]

Like Shubha, Rani outlines a path of self-discovery and actualization through her work, but, importantly, her individuality is deeply tied to her relationship with her family. Her family background did not pose the kinds of obstacles it did for Shubha;

rather, her family supported Rani's decision to pursue a career in IT because it was a respectable career, even if members of her family did not prompt Rani to pursue IT themselves. Indeed, her closeness with her family is quite central to Rani's account of her own drive and success. Her mother's motivation played an especially prominent role in Rani's narrative:

> [When I entered IT] I was not really motivated by technology or any of the latest advancements happening in this field. It was more of my mother's passion to see me leading in whatever I am doing that made me achieve what I have done today. She wanted me to lead everywhere; even if I ever stood second in class she used to be sad. At that time when I had to opt for a career, this was the number one career that I could have gone to, and I felt it was ideal … I never neglected my family. Were it so that I had to make anybody in the family unhappy [in my career pursuits] I would not have stirred out [of the home in the first place]. That is the kind of value I would like to carry on.

Rani asserts her individual development and ambition through a particular discourse of virtue – she aims to contribute to society even as she makes her family proud. Her constant invocation of the family echoes the "family comes first" narratives of most IT women I interviewed, and hints at the ways in which Rani's particular background – her class background, as well as the expectations of her mother – shapes her particular articulation of individuality. In saying that she is not in IT for the money, she relies upon her preexisting class privilege, the moral-support of her family, and her vision to help society through technology in a modified version of knowledge for development discourses.

Although they live in Mumbai and Silicon Valley, respectively, Shubha and Rani invoke notions of individuality that are similarly embedded in the class privilege they were born into, such that the position and feelings of their families profoundly affect the ways in which they imagine and actualize their life trajectories. Although both clearly articulate individualized desires and choices, most obviously in their choices of careers and partners, they also enhance their own symbolic position by disavowing the financial incentives that the IT industry provides because these incentives are actually a step down from lifestyles they were born into. In the way they met their spouses – at work rather than through an arranged process initiated by their families – the examples of Shubha and Rani also hint at the important ways in which their navigations of individuality might be producing new gendered norms, even as these navigations are embedded in the context of class and family dynamics. [...]

60

Strategic Inauthenticity

Timothy D. Taylor

[…]

Youssou N'Dour: "A Modern Griot"

Youssou N'Dour (1959–) is one of a handful but growing number of nonwestern pop stars from the African continent born around or after the independence of their home-land. He is probably the biggest international nonwestern pop star appearing in this book and has been written about extensively by the US music press. N'Dour sings many of the typical stories of those who are trying to be subjects of modernity and not its objects: stories about the dangers of being overrun by tourism, the degradation of the environment, moving from the country to the city, and nostalgia for the ancestors and their wisdom. This modernization, however, in the form of the colonial machine, left N'Dour and his fellow Senegalese few options. The stories of modernization and colonialism/postcolonialism intersect time and again in his music, as, I have been arguing, they do in the "real world."

N'Dour, like Rhoma Irama, expresses the desire to make a new popular music that incorporates elements of indigenous traditional musics and uses the local language. At the same time, N'Dour acknowledges the influence of musics from around the world on him. "It's just a natural process of evolution," N'Dour says. "My style evolves

Original publication details: Timothy D. Taylor, *Global Pop: World Music, World Markets*. New York: Routledge, 1997. pp. 127–8, 129–30, 134–5, 142–3. Reproduced with permission from Taylor & Francis Books.

The Globalization Reader, Fifth Edition. Edited by Frank J. Lechner and John Boli.
Editorial material and organization © 2015 John Wiley & Sons, Ltd.
Published 2015 by John Wiley & Sons, Ltd.

depending on what other musics I've heard." He explains his mix of musics and sounds in explicitly politico-historical terms.

> The process of modernisation began relatively late in Senegambia. Ghana and Nigeria had developed their hi-life and such styles much earlier. The hit sounds in Senegal in the Fifties and Sixties were still the Cuban dance songs of [Orquesta] Aragon and Johnny Pacheco. For those of us who wanted to form a purely Senegalese pop sound, this Cuban music was rhythmically acceptable, but harmonically foreign. And of course there was the problem of language. We wanted to sing in our own Wolof language. The Gambian group, Super Eagles, later called I Fang Bondi, who were pioneering their Afro Manding jazz, and the Senegalese groups, Baobab and Sahel, had already begun to translate local traditional songs and rhythms to the instruments of pop music. Perhaps I had more of what we call in Wolof, *fit*, or courage. When I started with the Star Band, we went even further, developing a dance music which I called mbalax. The dancers at the Miami [a night club in Dakar] were no longer content with the pachanga or the cha cha cha, but followed the tama drum and the other sabars [drums] into their own natural dances.

The traditional stylistic and musical aspects of mbalax, which means "the rhythm of the drum" in Wolof, are mostly concerned with rhythm.

> That drum [mbung mbung], along with others like the talmbeut, ndende, bougarabu, djembe, nder, tunge, gorong and tama, creates the rhythm. When they say in Dakar, '*C'est très mbalax*', they mean it's got a very strong, distinctive rhythm. So the base of mbalax is the drums, collectively known as sabars. There could be up to eight in any traditional line-up. In my group, I gave some of those drum parts to guitars and keyboards. The rhythms can change within songs – that is always a big attraction. This diversity comes from many tribal sources: Toucouleur, Peul, Bambara, Djola, Serer, as well as Wolof. We could make ten songs and they'd all sound different, unusual to people in the West. So I created this modern style, but the Senegalese quickly recognised it as their own popular music, and when it was recorded in France under favourable conditions it made even better sense to them.

The resulting sound brought N'Dour to the attention of western musicians such as Peter Gabriel and Paul Simon (both of whom recorded with him on some of their albums). N'Dour's album *The Guide (Wommat)* of 1994 was nominated for a Grammy (ultimately losing to Ali Farka Toure and Ry Cooder) and features guest appearances by black British American pop star Neneh Cherry and American jazz great Branford Marsalis. "Leaving (Dem)" opens *The Guide* and is the most upbeat song on the album, although the melancholy tale of the lyrics might indicate otherwise. The trajectory of "Leaving" isn't much different from a contemporary US rock song: a brief guitar introduction followed by the rhythm track, then the vocals in N'Dour's amazing voice, supple, grainy, high, muscular. But the guitar sound owes more to South African *mbaqanga* than anything else; it may be *très* mbalax, but it makes use of African popular musics from all over, including soukous, highlife, Afrobeat, reggae, salsa, soul, and disco according to one commentator. Once the rhythm starts, the song inhabits an ecstatic groove, emphasized by N'Dour's conversational yet melodic singing style, and the horns (saxophone, trombones, trumpet). N'Dour further adds to the effect produced by the song by stepping down from it with an improvised, metrically free harmonica solo at the song's conclusion – bringing Stevie Wonder's brand of joyous music to mind – and including applause and whistles, even though this song was recorded in a studio without a live audience. There is also a background chorus that vocalizes along with N'Dour near the end of the song, adding to the celebratory sound. [...]

The lyrics of the song illustrate the kind of movement in the global postmodern that might take those at the traditional metropoles by surprise. Rather than becoming modern and moving, as did so many European moderns from the country to the city, N'Dour instead tells of wanting to move the other direction: he has had enough of modernity, thank you very much. He is interested in cultivating older ways of interaction, through one's friends and family, rather than the faceless, impersonal postcolonial city. "I am a modern man," he says. "I love traditional things, but I think African music must be popular. We have to go forward." So he built a 24-track recording studio in Dakar, naming it Xippi, or "eyes open," also the title of one of his albums.

With songs such as "Leaving," N'Dour's music mounts a different kind of resistance – or different kinds of resistances – than those we have examined so far. *The Guide* does offer songs that rage against the European colonial machine, such as "How you are (No mele)," which incorporates a rap in English. At the same time, however, N'Dour addresses more local concerns, most of which sound familiar to western listeners: "There is a lot of joblessness here [in Senegal]. Many kids here have dreams, but the opportunities are limited."

Although N'Dour is clearly a modern western musician of sorts, he evidently still views himself as a griot, or, a *gawulo,* literally, "the one who is always singing praises," a Tukulor people version of the better-known griot. One of the most revealing statements about him wasn't made by the extremely private musician himself, but by an associate who refused to let *Rolling Stone* use his name.

> Remember, he knows how to use power but not how to give it away. That is a very hard thing for anyone, but especially an African, knowing who to trust and who to give responsibility to. The only people Youssou really trusts are members of his family and the friends he's had since childhood. It's a very insular world. And you also have to remember that first and foremost, he's a griot.
>
> Traditionally, griots are always supported by the king and the country and are paid to sing. The idea that he has to pay someone [to do sound or lights or to produce or accompany him] so that he can sing and perform is very confusing.

N'Dour is a Muslim, though, unlike Rhoma Irama, his music and lyrics have not taken on specifically Islamic issues. But his music is still informed by a strong sense of right and wrong. "You know," he told interviewer Brian Cullman, "when you are walking with a girl, you have to make sure you walk along the right path, that you watch your step. You have a certain responsibility to be very proper." The idea of "propriety" recurs throughout his songs, which exhort youths to behave respectfully toward their parents, caution the west to behave respectfully toward its former colonies, and ask tourists to treat his country well.

Because of his fame, N'Dour realizes the extent to which he, as an international star and local *gawulo,* can help his more provincial listeners understand the events in the larger world. "In my society where there are those who cannot read or write, I was able to tell them in song just what was happening in South Africa. My own mother had seen pictures on TV but she didn't fully understand the situation. I could make a link between the situation in South Africa today and a famous, bloody battle in our own history – the battle of N'Der in the nineteenth century."

The international success N'Dour has achieved leaves him mindful of his roots in the family tradition of musicians and *gawulos.* "Before the radio," he says, "griots gathered the people together and gave them the news, the information from the king. He helped them understand the world, he was their voice. That's what I am, a modern griot." Before that he was a premodern griot, singing for various traditional rituals, including circumcision ceremonies. N'Dour's current duties are thus those of a griot: telling stories, giving admonitions, keeping watch. [...]

N'Dour doesn't use his status just to educate people from the African continent, however; much of his music is aimed at the west. Just as "Leaving" might turn some westerners' ideas about Africa upside down – it is a song about leaving the city for the country, not the other way around – N'Dour is also bent on demonstrating to his growing worldwide listeners that Africa is modern already.

> I'm really defending a cause: the cause of a new image of Africa. For me, the measure of success is more than anything how well I arrive at exposing my music as a representation of not only African music but of African life and the whole image of Africa.
>
> I think Americans are more and more interested in Africa but they have a long way to go. The day that people in the West understand how much we understand about the workings of the rest of the planet will be a happy day for us.

Like so many stars outside the North American/UK rock music circuit, N'Dour was "discovered" by an influential western musician, in this case, Peter Gabriel, resulting in much collaboration since they met in 1984 and leading to other collaborations, such as on Paul Simon's *Graceland,* as well as with Sting, Bruce Springsteen, and Tracy Chapman. By 1990, N'Dour dropped his musicologist manager Verna Gillis for a New York lawyer, Thomas Rome, symbolizing his departure from *mbalax* to pop/ rock. (His latest album, however, lists Gillis as the manager and executive producer, a switch back that has not yet been commented on in the music press.) He lives in London and drives a BMW but hasn't cut ties to Senegal, or his hometown of Dakar, the capital. "I love Dakar, but I am very visible here, I am an example. Everything I do, it's seen."

Now, as a star, N'Dour realizes the role he may be able to play in the globalization of African popular musics such as *mbalax:* "The new generation of African musicians really has a chance to have an impact on American audiences. That has not yet happened, but I think it will, soon." His artistic advisor, Canadian Michael Brook (known for his own syncretic musics), seems to have gotten into the habit of filling in the silences of the taciturn N'Dour.

What's exciting for me is that the band is right on the edge of establishing a personal music. It has traditional African and Senegalese elements in it, and it also has pop elements in it, but it feels like they're going into a new stage of musical maturity, one where the influences become less relevant. They're Africans making music, but you wouldn't necessarily label it African music. It's something altogether new.

As his fame and popularity have grown, N'Dour has had to face criticisms that his music, which was, early on, a conscious attempt to re-Africanize Senegalese music, has become too slick, too commercial, too western. "Well," N'Dour says, "it was first made Senegalese and then opened to show the side of modern Africa, of towns like Dakar and Abidjan. I think my music has really evolved. It's true that it's lost a bit for older people but then it's gained popularity with younger people. That's life. I don't make music for such and such a person; I do it because it's me – what I feel." [...]

N'Dour, in the meantime, continues patiently to explain his position. "In Dakar we hear many different recordings. We are open to these sounds. When people say my music is too Western, they must remember that we, too, hear this music over here. We hear the African music with the modern." [...]

Whose Authenticity?

Given western listeners' concern for authenticity and the desire of musicians from around the world to be stars and make it in the global music industry, N'Dour's and Kidjo's clear lack of concern with authenticity is striking at first. It seems to me there are two reasons for the lack of interest in authenticity by these musicians. One, more prevalent in the west, is aesthetic: these musicians, like Peter Gabriel, are artists, they make art, and in art, anything goes: the aesthetic is by its very nature, voracious. But N'Dour and Kidjo view western demands for authenticity as concomitant with demands that they and their countries remain premodern, or modern, while the rest of the globe moves further toward a postindustrial, late capitalist, postmodern culture. N'Dour and Kidjo are concerned with becoming global citizens and do this by showing that their countries and their continent are neither backward nor pre-modern, that they can make cultural forms as (post)modern as the west's. They hear many sounds – in Kidjo's case, she grew up with lots of sounds, lots of musics – and pull these into their music, to the chagrin of some western critics. [...]

61

Orange Nation

Soccer and National Identity in the Netherlands

Frank J. Lechner

The Aura of 1974

We were the best. Watching the national team advance in the World Cup tournament in 1974, my fellow Dutch soccer fans and I were convinced that "we" played a special kind of soccer. Our style was more fluid, allowing players to switch positions as they kept in constant motion. We were the most creative, always looking for new ways to attack. On this team, individual players showed their genius while everyone sacrificed for the common cause. In the magical phrase of those days, we played "total soccer". As we beat Argentina and Brazil on the way to our first appearance in the final, the nation's confidence grew. Defeating the Germans in Munich would be doubly satisfying. After a hard tackle against Johan Cruyff, our star, earned us a penalty kick in that game before any German player had even touched the ball, victory seemed assured. But, we failed to build on our early lead. The Germans fought back and took advantage of defensive lapses to win the game, 2–1, adding insult to well-remembered injury. The best team had lost, we all felt. The next day, the country nevertheless celebrated as if we had won, treating the team to a tumultuous televised welcome. At a reception with the queen, the otherwise-restrained prime minister danced with the players. The streets of Amsterdam filled with massive crowds. In later years, many in the Netherlands would recall these events as a high point in their lives.

For generations of Dutch fans, 1974 was indeed "our" accomplishment and something "we" experienced. The joy of Dutch soccer brilliance as much as the

Original publication details: Frank J. Lechner, *The Netherlands: Globalization and National Identity*. New York: Routledge, 2008. pp. 1–4, 6–11, 24–7. Reproduced with permission from Taylor & Francis Group.

trauma of eventual loss, broadcast live and in color, created a shared memory. More than ever before, the national team was our team. We identified. Not otherwise given to displays of nationalist sentiment, the country got caught up in the excitement of the tournament and engrossed in the team's exploits, which were reported in unprecedented detail. The experience triggered an "orange craze," with fans using the color of the Dutch monarchy and the team's jerseys to dress in gaudy clothing, create eye-catching paraphernalia, and at times redecorate whole city blocks to express their undying loyalty. After 1974, no tournament would be complete without the ritual of orange legions traveling to the games, singing boisterously from a standard repertoire of songs. [...]

The year 1974 is a shared memory, but it is not really past. Dutch soccer achievements of the early 1970s have inspired a decades-long conversation about what made, and perhaps makes, the Dutch so special. Johan Cruyff himself, often considered the premier European soccer player of the twentieth century, has left his mark on this conversation, arguing over the years in columns, books, and TV commentaries that the Dutch have a distinct style that reflects their innate qualities. Dutch players cannot hold back but must take the initiative, he claims; they are uniquely creative within the constraints of a team. They have the "ideal attitude" for playing top soccer, which they must express in an offensively minded, adventurous style. [...]

Much as they would like to think themselves unique, the Dutch exhibit a familiar pattern. Around the world, nations use sports to "refuel" their popular memory and provide a source of collective identification. If nations consist of imagined ties, then sports constitute an "important aid to national imagining". At times, of course, sports were deliberately used as a tool in the creation of a national identity, notably in the former Soviet sphere. Even if the process is less intentional, as in the Dutch case, sports often serve as a "cultural arena" and a "secular ritual" in which people articulate and strengthen collective identities. Among these identities, national ones remain especially strong. Aided by media coverage of sports that represents the nation as a single "sentient being", soccer, above all, "shapes and cements national identities throughout the world". In the way the Dutch create their soccer self-image they are like many other nations. Claiming a distinct style, focusing on historic events, choosing heroic exemplars, and continually retelling "the" national story are what sporting nations do. The production of difference follows a standard path.

A production it is. However immediate the experience of 1974 seemed, however real the superiority of Dutch performance on the field, the idea of the essential Dutch style emerged afterward. Before long, the unprecedented accomplishments of extraordinary players became the hallmark of typical Dutch play. Their all too ephemeral and unusual success supposedly reflected permanent Dutch qualities. Great team play turned into brilliant orange, modest innovations into total soccer. As in other soccer cultures, then, the Dutch claim to distinction involves more than a little "national mythmaking". It projects a comforting "fantasy image" that satisfies nostalgic longing. Out of a complex reality, it lifts some essential national qualities through a selective process of defining and redefining who "we" are. Clichéd coverage in the media reinforces the process by typically highlighting contrasts among supposedly national styles. Viewed this way, soccer does not simply express something perennially present in the life of the nation; rather, it shows how the nation is a modern myth told for modern purposes. Wallowing in the mythical aura of brilliant orange, the Dutch can set aside the inconsistent national team record and the humdrum quality of domestic league play.

The myth has a point. To the Dutch, 1974 was a statement about who we were in the world – a progressive, free-spirited nation that allows for great individual creativity within the constraints set by the common cause. In the old cliché, it put us on the map. Again, the Dutch were not unique in this regard. All national soccer cultures define themselves in relation to the World Cup – the tournament is a battle of teams and of styles. It is precisely such international competition that excites national passions and triggers national comparisons. Success counts as a national triumph, interpreted as the result of distinct national qualities, as happened when France unexpectedly won the 1998 Cup. For all nations on this global stage, the claim to distinction and the belief in an essential tradition express who "we" are in relation to others and to the universal rules we share with "them". To some extent, this is a defensive reaction to a global challenge. In the global game, in which players, coaches, and ideas circulate widely, affirmations of national difference serve as "ripostes to the juggernaut" of globalization, as a form of resistance that fortifies local identities. Intense globalization, most evident in international soccer competitions, triggers a demand for nostalgia, for a symbolic sense of stability. Against the menacing network of modern soccer, a commercialized game beyond anyone's control that seems to relegate nation-states to insignificance, nations effectively construct "bulwarks" of cultural protection. As academic observers of Dutch soccer put it, the collective focus on the national team is a form of catch-up nationalism that satisfies a "need for feeling of community" and "compensates for the loss" of identity among losers in globalization.

Yet, it is also too simple to follow these themes of academic sportswriting to portray the Dutch soccer experience as a form of defensive, particularist mythmaking, a useful fiction that enables the Dutch to cope with the big bad world outside. In fact, the key ideas in soccer scholarship – that sports have an expressive and unifying role, that they help to construct mythical identities, and that they foster national reactions to a global threat – fit together a bit uneasily insofar as they suggest that patently illusory ties could serve to unite a people against the predations of globalization. In the Dutch case, at any rate, it is not entirely clear what type of nation the soccer exploits of the 1970s helped us to imagine or precisely what national identity was cemented. For a while, certainly, soccer fervor filled a void, creating a virtual orange nation at a time when it was the last remaining form of "acceptable" nationalism in a nation otherwise dismissive of overt national displays. Periodically, major tournaments would revive the national fervor, but in the meantime the orange feeling dissipated. After the games were over, what did the Dutch have in common besides the fact of a common passion? Identifying with their teams did not by itself give the Dutch a new identity. "Reimagining" the nation would take work in the years after.

[...]

That the nation constitutes a beleaguered bulwark against a global menace would have come as surprise to players and fans in 1974. Taking advantage of the global market, Dutch coach Rinus Michels also worked for Barcelona, which he coached in the Spanish competition even during the World Cup. Johan Cruyff, having left Ajax, would soon join him in Spain. Few if any fans accused them of divided loyalties. Cruyff also was a trailblazer for the commercialization of soccer, insisting on wearing his own sponsor's Puma shoes and even stripping the third stripe of national sponsor Adidas off his national team jersey. Far from a threat, the World Cup represented a great opportunity, an enticing challenge. Honing their skills against the best opposition, the Dutch improved their play. The fact that several players became global celebrities only increased the intense satisfaction of Dutch supporters. We learned who we really were by imagining how others must see us now. Of course, no one thought about the game as a form of globalization – a notion that was still on a distant horizon – but that soccer had become a fully global game was simply a fact all took for granted. The year 1974 was an episode in a national conversation that was intertwined with a transnational one, a conversation about the right way to play, about traditions countries represented, about the relative quality of teams, and so on. In this soccer discourse, the Dutch had now gained a voice. As the welcoming celebrations showed, the encounter with "globalization" could prove invigorating.

Dutch soccer does not give any straightforward answer to the question who the Dutch "really" are. The orange nation emerges during major tournaments but enjoys only occasional cohesion, mainly when the national team plays well. Even as they value the myth of distinction, the Dutch also retell it critically, questioning whether they really have a viable national tradition. The global game offers pleasurable opportunity as much as distressing threat, challenging, at times inspiring, the Dutch in different ways. Neither the simple self-description proposed by brilliant orange aficionados nor skeptics' deconstruction of romantic national claims tells the full story of the Dutch soccer experience. The more complex story, only briefly sketched here, gives us hints about how the Dutch think of themselves and relate not only to the global game but also to the world at large. [...]

Globalization consists of many kinds of flows and affects countries in many ways. Even within soccer, globalization involves migration of players and coaches, more extensive broadcasting across national borders, the management of the game by a transnational organization, the exchange of strategies and training methods across the world, and the development of the World Cup as the quintessential global event. The challenge of soccer globalization to national soccer cultures is necessarily complex, so the national response must be as well. Beyond sports, both the overall challenge and the response of nation-states will be that much more complex. Again, this implies that redefining national identity will rarely yield clear-cut answers. In the Dutch case, it is very much a work in progress. Because Dutch identity is in flux, it would be premature to declare what "it" really is. A more promising strategy, which I follow, is to look for a pattern in the identity work, in the process of redefining the nation.

The Dutch attitude toward soccer provides a clue. The global game, I suggested, is not only a threat, but also a fact, an opportunity, a possible source of pleasure. The Dutch see themselves contributing to the game, proving themselves against competition, and earning the respect of connoisseurs worldwide. Although the behavior of orange-clad fans might count against it, they fancy themselves cosmopolitan. The parallel with "the" national identity is not exact, yet if there is a common denominator in Dutch identity efforts, it may be the search for a cosmopolitan brand of nationalism, a way to construe the nation as embodying globally shared values as a distinct part of a wider community. If that sounds more like a convenient formula political philosophers might appreciate than an inspiring vision to bind the nation as an active, self-conscious community, then it may indicate what the Dutch have left to do. To the extent it works, it may point to a new way for nations to be at home in the world. Instead of turning the national "shell" into a bulwark to be preserved at all cost, it would recognize national identity as a flexible part of a larger repertoire of identities. We are who we are to cherish what is ours and to be able to join with others in common causes. That is only a formula, true, but it is one that may prove globally significant.

Much of what the Dutch are doing is not unique. It may hurt their self-image a bit to say so, but in studying globalization and national identity that is an advantage. The resources they use in redefining their national identity resemble those of others, although of course the precise content is theirs. As in most nation-states, their state activity also contributes to reshaping the nation, again with local variations in the actual policies the Dutch adopt. The dilemmas they confront are globally recognizable, whether they concern media, economic competition, or migration. As heirs to a tradition of openness to the world at large, the Dutch may have earned a reputation as unusually liberal, but the overall direction of their responses to globalization need not be the unique adaptation of comfortable northern Europeans. The fact that even the Dutch have embarked on an embattled redefinition of their national identity, after a period in which many leading figures prided themselves on not taking pride in things national, shows that no nation is exempt from the globalization challenge.

[…]

The Dutch case helps to support an argument about the interplay of globalization and national reimagining. It conveys a sense of complexity about the multiple dimensions of globalization. That process is not a single thing or package. It is not an actor or factor. It is not a threat. Its reverberations in any particular place depend on how global challenges are perceived. Of course, at times this may involve high anxiety, but that is only one possible response among many. Real actors, such as those who speak for or act on behalf of nations they claim to represent, do not, in any case, receive the "impact" of globalization as a punch to be taken. Globalization also does not produce an iron cage within which hapless nations struggle to save breathing space. Globalization does not occur "out there;" instead, ostensibly global processes unfold in particular places. For the people involved, it leads to a new layering of identities – local, national, and transnational.

[…]

62

Cosmopolitans and Locals in World Culture

Ulf Hannerz

There is now a world culture, but we had better make sure that we understand what this means. It is marked by an organization of diversity rather than by a replication of uniformity. No total homogenization of systems of meaning and expression has occurred, nor does it appear likely that there will be one any time soon. But the world has become one network of social relationships, and between its different regions there is a flow of meanings as well as of people and goods.

The world culture is created through the increasing interconnectedness of varied local cultures, as well as through the development of cultures without a clear anchorage in any one territory. These are all becoming sub-cultures, as it were, within the wider whole; cultures which are in important ways better understood in the context of their cultural surroundings than in isolation. But to this global interconnected diversity people can relate in different ways. For one thing, there are cosmopolitans, and there are locals.

[…]

The Cosmopolitan Perspective: Orientation and Competence

We often use the term 'cosmopolitan' rather loosely, to describe just about anybody who moves about in the world. But of such people, some would seem more cosmopolitan than others, and others again hardly cosmopolitan at all. I have before me an

Original publication details: Ulf Hannerz, "Cosmopolitans and Locals in World Culture", in *Theory, Culture and Society*, 7, 1990. pp. 237–51. Reprinted by permission of SAGE.

old cutting from the *International Herald Tribune* (16 October 1985) about travel and trade (the latter fairly often illicit) between Lagos and London. The article quotes reports by flight attendants on the route, claiming that Lagos market women board London-bound planes with loose-fitting gowns, which enable them to travel with dried fish tied to their thighs and upper arms. The dried fish is presumably sold to their countrymen in London; on the return trip, the women carry similarly concealed bundles of frozen fish sticks, dried milk, and baby clothes, all of which are in great demand in Lagos. London is a consumer's (or middleman's) paradise for Nigerians. About 1 percent of the passengers on the London-bound flights have excess baggage, and about 30 percent of those travelling in the opposite direction.

Is this cosmopolitanism? In my opinion, no; the shopping trips of Lagosian traders and smugglers hardly go beyond the horizons of urban Nigerian culture, as it now is. The fish sticks and the baby clothes hardly alter structures of meaning more than marginally. And much of that involvement with a wider world which is characteristic of contemporary lives is of this kind, largely a matter of assimilating items of some distant provenience into a fundamentally local culture.

Historically we have been used to think of cultures as distinctive structures of meaning and meaningful form usually closely linked to territories, and of individuals as self-evidently linked to particular such cultures. The underlying assumption here is that culture flows mostly in face-to-face relationships, and that people do not move around much. Such an assumption serves us well enough in delineating the local as an ideal type.

Yet as collective phenomena cultures are by definition linked primarily to interactions and social relationships, and only indirectly and without logical necessity to particular areas in physical space. The less social relationships are confined within territorial boundaries, the less so is also culture; and in our time especially, we can contrast in gross terms those cultures which are territorially defined (in terms of nations, regions, or localities) with those which are carried as collective structures of meaning by networks more extended in space, transnational or even global. This contrast, too – but not it alone – suggests that cultures, rather than being easily separated from one another as the hard-edged pieces in a mosaic, tend to overlap and mingle. While we understand them to be differently located in the social structure of the world, we also realize that the boundaries we draw around them are frequently rather arbitrary.

Anyway, such a view of the present in cultural terms may help us identify the cosmopolitan. The perspective of the cosmopolitan must entail relationships to a plurality of cultures understood as distinctive entities. (And the more the better; cosmopolitans should ideally be foxes rather than hedgehogs.) But furthermore, cosmopolitanism in a stricter sense includes a stance toward diversity itself, toward the coexistence of cultures in the individual experience. A more genuine cosmopolitanism is first of all an orientation, a willingness to engage with the Other. It is an intellectual and aesthetic stance of openness toward divergent cultural experiences, a search for contrasts rather than uniformity. To become acquainted with more cultures is to turn into an *aficionado*, to view them as art works. At the same time, however, cosmopolitanism can be a matter of competence, and competence of both a generalized and a more specialized kind. There is the aspect of a state of readiness, a personal ability to make one's way into other cultures, through listening, looking, intuiting and reflecting. And there is cultural competence in the stricter sense of the term, a built-up skill in manoeuvring more or less expertly with a particular system of meanings and meaningful forms.

In its concern with the Other, cosmopolitanism thus becomes a matter of varieties and levels. Cosmopolitans can be dilettantes as well as connoisseurs, and are often both, at different times. But the willingness to become involved with the Other, and the concern with achieving competence in cultures which are initially alien, relate to considerations of self as well. Cosmopolitanism often has a narcissistic streak; the self is constructed in the space where cultures mirror one another.

Competence with regard to alien cultures itself entails a sense of mastery, as an aspect of the self. One's understandings have expanded, a little more of the world is somehow under control. Yet there is a curious, apparently paradoxical interplay between mastery and surrender here. It may be one kind of cosmopolitanism where the individual picks from other cultures only those pieces which suit himself. In the long term, this is likely to be the way a cosmopolitan constructs his own unique personal perspective out of an idiosyncratic collection of experiences. But such selectivity can operate in the short term, situationally, as well. In another mode, however, the cosmopolitan does not make invidious distinctions among the particular elements of the alien culture in order to admit some of them into his repertoire and refuse others; he does not negotiate with the other culture but accepts it as a package deal. Even this surrender, however, is a part of the sense of mastery. The cosmopolitan's surrender to the alien culture implies personal autonomy vis-à-vis the culture where he originated. He has his obvious competence with regard to it, but he can choose to disengage from it. He possesses it, it does not possess him. Cosmopolitanism becomes proteanism. Some would eat cockroaches to prove the point, others need only eat escargots. [...]

Cosmopolitanism and the Varieties of Mobility

Of course, cosmopolitans are usually somewhat footloose, on the move in the world. Among the several cultures with which they are engaged, at least one is presumably of the territorial kind, a culture encompassing the round of everyday life in a community. The perspective of the cosmopolitan may indeed be composed only from experiences of different cultures of this kind, as his biography includes periods of stays in different places. But he may also be involved with one culture, and possibly but not usually more, of that other kind which is carried by a transnational network rather than by a territory. It is really the growth and proliferation of such cultures and social networks in the present period that generates more cosmopolitans now than there have been at any other time.

But being on the move, I have already argued, is not enough to turn one into a cosmopolitan, and we must not confuse the latter with other kinds of travellers. Are tourists, exiles, and expatriates cosmopolitans, and when not, why not?

In her novel *The Accidental Tourist* (1985), Anne Tyler has a main character who makes his living churning out travel books for anti-cosmopolitans, people (mostly business travellers) who would rather not have left home; people who are locals at heart. These are travel guides for Americans who would want to know what restaurants in Tokyo offer Sweet'n'Low, which hotel in Madrid has king-size Beauty-rest mattresses, and whether there is a Taco Bell in Mexico City.

Another contemporary writer, Paul Theroux, continuously occupied with themes of journeys and the cosmopolitan experience, comments that many people travel for the purpose of 'home plus' – Spain is home plus sunshine, India is home plus servants, Africa is home plus elephants and lions. And for some, of course, travel is ideally home plus more and better business. There is no general openness here to a somewhat unpredictable variety of experiences; the benefits of mobility are strictly regulated. Such travel is not for cosmopolitans, and does little to create cosmopolitans.

Much present-day tourism is of this kind. People engage in it specifically to go to another place, so the cosmopolitanism that could potentially be involved would be that of combinations of territorially based cultures. But the 'plus' often has nothing whatsoever to do with alien systems of meaning, and a lot to do with facts of nature, such as nice beaches. Yet this is not the only reason why cosmopolitans nowadays loathe tourists, and especially loathe being taken for tourists.

Cosmopolitans tend to want to immerse themselves in other cultures, or in any case be free to do so. They want to be participants, or at least do not want to be too readily identifiable within a crowd of participants, that is, of locals in their home territory. They want to be able to sneak backstage rather than being confined to the frontstage areas. Tourists are not participants; tourism is largely a spectator sport. Even if they want to become involved and in that sense have a cosmopolitan orientation, tourists are assumed to be incompetent. They are too likely to make a nuisance of themselves. The local, and the cosmopolitan, can spot them from a mile away. Locals evolve particular ways of handling tourists, keeping a distance from them, not necessarily exploiting them but not admitting them into local reciprocities either. Not least because cosmopolitanism is an uncertain practice, again and again balancing at the edge of competence, the cosmopolitan keeps running the risk of being taken for a tourist by locals whose experience make them apply this label increasingly routinely. And this could ruin many of the pleasures of cosmopolitanism, as well as pose a threat to the cosmopolitan sense of self.

[…]

The Cosmopolitan at Home

[…]

Perhaps real cosmopolitans, after they have taken out membership in that category, are never quite at home again, in the way real locals can be. Home is taken-for-grantedness, but after their perspectives have been irreversibly affected by the experience of the alien and the distant, cosmopolitans may not view either the seasons of the year or the minor rituals of everyday life as absolutely natural, obvious, and necessary. There may be a feeling of detachment, perhaps irritation with those committed to the local common sense and unaware of its arbitrariness. Or perhaps the cosmopolitan makes 'home' as well one of his several sources of personal meaning, not so different from the others which are further away; or he is pleased with his ability both to surrender to and master this one as well.

Or home is really home, but in a special way; a constant reminder of a pre-cosmopolitan past, a privileged site of nostalgia. This is where once things seemed fairly simple and straightforward. Or it is again really home, a comfortable place of familiar faces, where one's competence is undisputed and where one does not have to prove it to either oneself or others, but where for much the same reasons there is some risk of boredom.

At home, for most cosmopolitans, most others are locals. This is true in the great majority of territorially based cultures. Conversely, for most of these locals, the cosmopolitan is someone a little unusual, one of us and yet not quite one of us. Someone to be respected for his experiences, possibly, but equally possibly not somebody to be trusted as a matter of course. Trust tends to be a matter of shared perspectives, of 'I know, and I know that you know, and I know that you know that I know'. And this formula for the social organization of meaning does not necessarily apply to the relationship between local and cosmopolitan.

Some cosmopolitans are more adept at making it apply again. '*Wenn jemand eine Reise tut, dann kann er 'was erzählen*', the saying goes, and there are those who make a speciality out of letting others know what they have come across in distant places. So the cosmopolitan can to some extent be channelled into the local; and precisely because these are on the whole separate spheres the cosmopolitan can become a broker, an entrepreneur who makes a profit. Yet there is a danger that such attempts to make the alien easily accessible only succeeds in trivializing it, and thereby betraying its nature and the character of the real first-hand encounter. So in a way the more purely cosmopolitan attitude may be to let separate things be separate.

Despite all this, home is not necessarily a place where cosmopolitanism is in exile. It is natural that in the contemporary world many local settings are increasingly characterized by cultural diversity. Those of cosmopolitan inclinations may make selective use of their habitats to maintain their expansive orientation toward the wider world. Other cosmopolitans may be there, whether they in their turn are at home or abroad, and strangers of other than cosmopolitan orientations. Apart from the face-to-face encounters, there are the media – both those intended for local consumption, although they speak of what is distant, and those which are really part of other cultures, like foreign books and films. What McLuhan once described as the implosive power of the media may now make just about everybody a little more cosmopolitan. And one may in the end ask whether it is now even possible to become a cosmopolitan without going away at all.

Conclusion: The Dependence of Cosmopolitans on Locals, and their Shared Interests

To repeat, there is now one world culture. All the variously distributed structures of meaning and expression are becoming interrelated, somehow, somewhere. People like the cosmopolitans have a special part in bringing about a degree of coherence, and because they have this part they have received closer attention here. If there were only locals in the world, world culture would be no more than the sum of its separate parts.

As things are now, on the other hand, it is no longer so easy to conform to the ideal type of a local. Some people, like exiles or migrant workers, are indeed taken away from the territorial bases of their local culture, but try to encapsulate themselves within some approximation of it; yet it is a greater number who, even staying home, find their local cultures less pervasive, less to be taken for granted, less clearly bounded toward the outside. If that other kind of world culture were ever to come about, through a terminal process of global homogenization, locals would become extinct; or, seen differently, through the involvement with the one existing culture, everybody would be the same kind of local, at the global level.

Here, however, today's cosmopolitans and locals have common interests in the survival of cultural diversity. For the latter, diversity itself, as a matter of personal access to varied cultures, may be of little intrinsic interest. It just so happens that this is the principle which allows all locals to stick to their respective cultures. For the cosmopolitans, in contrast, there is value in diversity as such, but they are not likely to get it, in anything like the present form, unless other people are allowed to carve out special niches for their cultures, and keep them. Which is to say that there can be no cosmopolitans without locals.

63

World Citizenship Defined

World Service Authority

The world … universally outgoing, conceptually unbounded, the planet dynamically, synergistically and organically one with itself and the cosmos.

Citizenship … the restrictive rights and duties within a given social structure.

The two words together seem paradoxical. "You can educate either the citizen or the man," wrote Thoreau. Yet in their union lies the potential success of the human species; in their non-union lies the demise of a fatally-flawed creature which could not overcome its self-imposed global anarchy.

This is the perennial mystery of the conceptual "joining" the perceptual. How and where does spirit indwell in the body?

World citizenship today implies the joining of the perennial wisdom of humankind with up-to-the-minute geo-political and geo-technical reality.

> The term 'world citizen' can be better understood with a negative definition than with a positive one. If a citizen of a state with political frontiers is expected to pay allegiance to the government of the state to which he or she belongs and is expected to take arms against aliens who might invade the territory of the state, a world citizen recognizes the entire world as one's state and in principle does not recognize any member of one's own species as an alien to the world community to which oneself belongs. Such a person recognizes the earth as one's sustaining mother, the innate inviolable laws of nature as one's protecting father, all sentient beings as one's homes. The world citizen's allegiance is to the foundation of truth, the universality of knowledge and the fundamental ground of all values.
>
> – Guru Nitya Chaitanya Yati, founder/head, East-West University

Original publication details: World Service Authority®, "World Citizenship Defined." Washington, DC: World Service Authority®. http://www.worldservice.org/wcd.html, accessed July 21, 2014. Used with permission from the World Service Authority®.

The Globalization Reader, Fifth Edition. Edited by Frank J. Lechner and John Boli.
Editorial material and organization © 2015 John Wiley & Sons, Ltd.
Published 2015 by John Wiley & Sons, Ltd.

Before the industrial age and the electronic revolution, the identity and functioning boundary of social units was largely determined by the nation-state level and the mechanical barriers of geography. The workings of government and the writings of history were from non-global perspectives. Loyalty to the feudal prince, or later, to the sovereign king was direct, one-dimensional and absolute. Society was aural, its extent determined by the human voice. The development of the printing press and, in 1844, electronic informational transfer, established lines of communication from one relatively isolated social unit to another. A person's thoughts now could be known instantly from a distance. One did not have to know him or her personally. Indirect political representation was born. Inevitably the notion that the governed should have a voice in government became increasingly popular. Democracy, kindled in the context of rising expectations, inflamed revolution after revolution from east to west, north to south.

Yet here was born a tragic paradox: for the essence of democracy is universal participatory decision-making, whereas the essence of national sovereignty, a hangover from the feudalism and the absolute sovereignty of kings, is exclusivity and the non-participation of citizens outside the national boundary. Citizens "belonged" to the nation only while all humans outside that nation were "foreigners," or worse, "aliens."

This tragic contradiction begins to be socially instilled almost at birth. One is not born a human, or politically, a world citizen, but "French," "English," "American," "Russian," "Chinese," or "Iranian." One could add that all labels at birth – "black," "white," "Arab," "Jew," "Catholic," etc. – are essentially false contrasted with the reality of the human emerging from a human womb into the world of humans.

Personal qualities are simplistically attached to national (and other) labels rendering violence and aggression easy to justify by their leaders. We are "good," "noble," "best," etc. because we are "British," or "American," or "Russian." Others are ipso facto "bad," "ignoble," "inferior." Unlike us, they are threats to be feared, even killed.

Those who identified directly with the world of humans were considered starry-eyed idealists, utopians, sentimental humanitarians, impractical moralists, or simply crackpots. The only empirical world "citizens" were the pirates sailing freely on the open seas. They were the forerunners of the multinational corporations, the world "citizens" of the industrial world. The practical world, the world the 17th, 18th and 19th political power, was channeled into a framework based on unreality, the fiction of nationalism.

Then came the 20th century. Speed of transportation increased 100-fold in a few decades. Electricity and electronics linked the global surface eliminating time and distance implosively as barriers between humans leaving only divisive ideas, language and politics, the surrogate of religion. A new "vertical" dimension was added, which, if translated, was the element of reciprocal support, or universality and wholeness.

The world became literally overnight, historically speaking, one community, yet without overall management. The 17th, 18th, and 19th century sovereign state system, imposed by largely reactionary leaders, with notable exceptions, on the 20th century world of four major revolutions: technological, electronic, nuclear and space, proved and is proving daily to be totally inadequate to solve global human problems.

Indeed, the nation-centered way of "solving" problems is the major problem! The nation-state, by insisting on its absolute sovereignty, has become literally suicidal for the entire human species. Today, with virtually no distance and no time between humans, each person is the focus of a global input. Everything happening in the world affects, sooner or later, each individual. With computers and satellites, the input to the individual has become fully supranational. Yet this irrefutable fact and its radical implications is popularly ignored.

A Middle East war raises the price of oil for everyone; an atomic bomb exploding in the South Pacific can mean leukemia for a baby born in Dayton, Ohio; dumping radio-active waste off the coast of Florida can mean radio-active fish caught by fishermen off the coast of Iceland, Great Britain, France or Spain; a shortwave radio placed anywhere on the surface of the globe receives a babble of voices – and ideas – from all corners of the world community.

Everything is happening at once and everything is happening to everybody. This is the most revolutionary fact of any century.

Yet what of the individual's output? Here, the reciprocal truth is, if possible, even less realized. If everything is happening directly to everyone, then every individual should be outputting directly to everything. This means simply that every individual should have the capability of direct democratic effect on the world-at-large. The world's individuals should constitute for themselves a global governing body to represent each individual as an outputting co-trustee of the earth as a whole.

[…]

World citizenship, then, is the only dynamic and imperative political identity capable of relinking the conceptual or moral value of the human being with the social and economic organization of his/her now planetary community. It expresses both the innate and inalienable sovereignty of each human as well as the overall sovereignty of the human species to which he/she belongs, also innately and inalienably. Thus it fulfills at once the criteria for ethical as well as ethnical politics. Also, it connotes a plan of ongoing political action at all levels of social activity, local to global.

If indeed the nation-state has lost its legitimacy as a two-dimensional, horizontal, we-and-they, zero (or negative) sum political entity in a three-dimensional, positive-sum, "We-the-people-of-the-planet-earth" world, then so also has personal commitment to exclusive national citizenship. Just as no one sovereignty or group of sovereignties can directly prevent any other from unleashing a third inter-national war, so also can no amount of commitment to merely national leaders bring the world situation under control.

But just as national citizenship had to be taught, learned and experienced in former centuries, not without great turmoil to the social norms of the period, so world citizenship must now be taught, learned and experienced in these final days of the 20th century.

To think, feel and act globally is almost without precedent in our recorded history. Only rare prophets have managed to do so, but without the aid of modern science and technology. And so they were vilified and put to death. But now, faced with Armageddon, we must all become as prophets, for, as Buckminster Fuller put it, "Either war is obsolete, or (humans) are."

World citizenship is more than merely a political strategy. It "verticalizes" the individual raising him or her above the "left" and "right" of nationalistic politics, to meet and make functional the perennial value systems which heretofore have been only the subject of religious credence. This it complements and fulfills all religious prophecies and integrates at the same time the synergistic worlds of instantaneous communications, energy and ecology with political power systems and institutions.

The "Promised Land" of the Hebrews, the "Peace on earth," and "Thy will be done on earth …" of the Christians, the benevolent social order of the Moslems, the world fraternal order of the Sikhs, the "Middle Way" of the Buddhists, the "universal world order" of the Bah'a'is, all are contained in and can grow out of the multidimensional, human, spiritual/political dispensation of universal world citizenship.

There is no other pathway to the future … and to the stars.

Part X Questions

1. In what way, if any, did globalization spur Sumitra's identity change, as described by McHugh? Are her aspirations "global desires" that emerged in a "transnational realm"? Do you think her experience is likely to be representative of most women of her generation in Nepal?
2. Do the female IT workers in Radhakrishnan's study "navigate" individuality in different ways through their involvement in a global industry? Do their family backgrounds affect their responses to this new way of life? What do they gain and lose by the choices they make?
3. Does Youssou N'Dour's creative mixing of musical styles imply that there can be no "authentic" Senegalese or African identity? Is this type of mixing also characteristic of music in other places? What does it mean to say that artists like N'Dour are "concerned with becoming global citizens"?
4. How do the Dutch use soccer to define a national identity, according to Lechner? Does their experience show that people play up such identities when they feel threatened by the impact of globalization? Can you think of other cases in which people or countries use sports in different ways to foster collective identities?
5. Are "cosmopolitans" in Hannerz's sense more likely than "locals" to become "world citizens" as described by the World Service Authority? Do you see anything in the statement on world citizenship to which both cosmopolitans and locals might object?

Part XI

Global Environmentalism

Introduction

Over the past three decades, thinking of problems as being global in nature has become routine. It seems obvious that environmental degradation, whether as air pollution, tropical deforestation, greenhouse gas emissions, or a thinning ozone layer, affects the entire globe. Hence, it also seems obvious that states and environmentalists would be foolish to adopt anything less than a global approach to such problems. In historical perspective, though, it is difficult to avoid the conclusion that nothing inherent in a given problem, whether related to environmental degradation, human rights violations, inequality, authoritarian political regimes, or the oppression of women, automatically qualifies it as a global concern.

Take air pollution as an example. During the heyday of unregulated industrial capitalism in the nineteenth century, air pollution was far worse in most major cities than it was in the 1960s, when global environmentalism first became a major social movement. The reason the air was so bad is simple: in the days before electric heaters, natural gas furnaces, and centralized delivery of hot water for radiant heat, factories and homes directly burned enormous quantities of coal. Unlike today, however, the smoke belching from factory stacks often evoked not horrified criticism but almost lyrical praise as a sign of the glorious progress that industrialization was bringing to the ever-richer West. Not only was pollution not a global problem; for the most part, it was not a problem at all.

The same analysis applies to human rights violations, inequality, authoritarianism, and women's oppression: though the "problems" have long been widespread and severe, either they have not been interpreted as problems or they have been treated primarily as local or national issues requiring only local or national responses. The sovereign authority of the state to manage its own society meant that critics and activists from outside the country were more likely to be told to mind their own

The Globalization Reader, Fifth Edition. Edited by Frank J. Lechner and John Boli.
Editorial material and organization © 2015 John Wiley & Sons, Ltd.
Published 2015 by John Wiley & Sons, Ltd.

business than to be heeded. Each state was to "put its own house in order," and international cooperation was neither needed nor desired.

By the twenty-first century, of course, much has changed. On the one hand, social conditions that had long been taken for granted are increasingly likely to be interpreted as social problems. No longer can inequality, oppression, or violations of rights be justified as "in the natural order of things" or "divinely ordained," and modern societies are filled with specialists of many stripes who make it their business to identify and publicize new and different problems. On the other hand, the ongoing integration of world society, and the thickening web of international organizations and social movements that cover the globe, have made it increasingly likely that social problems, new or old, will be cast in global terms and lifted up to the global agenda of major IGOs and INGOs. Many INGOs in particular are dedicated to searching out problems and publicizing them so that IGOs, states, transnational corporations, and other INGOs will pay attention to them and begin to work toward global approaches to solving them. To a considerable extent, then, social problems are a core concern of global civil society and the INGOs that are so crucial to global civil action.

In this part, we have chosen readings from a single sector of global social problems, environmentalism. By concentrating on environmentalism, we can illustrate some of the complex issues that arise when a social problem with far-reaching ramifications – for economic development, the quality of life, inequality, foreign investment, and interstate relations – enters the global arena and assumes a prominent place on the agenda of many global organizations. To a large extent, the messages these readings convey are applicable to many other social problems, such as human rights violations, inequality, political repression, and the subordination of women. Important differences will be found across these and other problems, of course, and researchers are busily studying a great many global problems and movements to learn more about the role of global civil society organizations in global governance (some examples are in Part VII).

It is tempting to believe that global civil society groups, most notably INGOs, hold out the promise of considerable progress in solving major social problems. Some successes are striking, such as the ability of two small but highly professional INGOs to win a 50-year moratorium on mineral exploitation in the 1991 revision of the Antarctic Treaty; the international treaty resulting from the International Campaign to Ban Landmines, in which most states have committed themselves to stop using or making antipersonnel mines; and the formation of the International Criminal Court, which was conceived and strongly pushed by a wide array of INGOs. Yet many problems are so large, and so deeply integrated into the structure of global economic and political development, that even modest improvements can come only over a period of decades. One critical issue is whether the global activists who make up the INGOs and NGOs working to ameliorate these stubbornly intractable problems will be able to sustain their efforts long enough to make a substantial difference. An equally critical issue, however, is whether world society will be able to avoid widespread catastrophes and collapses if they do not.

The selections by Paul Wapner and by Margaret E. Keck and Kathryn Sikkink, all three American social scientists, analyze the impact of various nongovernmental groups in creating global concern about, and pressing for action on, the degradation and pollution of the natural world. Wapner discusses Greenpeace, which grew from a small band of activists protesting nuclear bomb tests in Alaska in 1969 to a massive transnational organization that can call on the contributions of millions of supporters to carry out a wide range of attention-grabbing actions all over the globe. Keck and Sikkink emphasize the growth and operation of environmental "advocacy networks" that link local NGOs and global INGOs in the effort to preserve the rain forests. We have chosen their discussion of the campaign in Sarawak, which was able to achieve some success but ultimately could not put an end to logging in this part of Borneo, because of the fine detail they provide about this case.

In the next three selections, we present case studies of particular environmental issues. Sociologist Sanjeev Khagram's concern is the construction of big dams. He traces the emergence of opposition to big dams in local and national movements as far back as the 1940s, with INGOs becoming engaged only much later, in the 1970s. Led by the International Rivers Network, the movement managed to induce the World Bank, a major financer of big dams, to be much more cautious about such projects. With the formation of the World Commission on Dams in 1997, dam construction became subject to a multiparty global governance process in which environmental damage and negative consequences for local populations are crucial concerns in the decision-making process.

The next selection takes up the case of ozone depletion. As political scientists and policy scholars Pamela S. Chasek, David L. Downie, and Janet Welsh Brown show, the depleting effects of chlorofluorocarbons (CFCs, used as propellants in aerosol cans) and other chemicals were identified by the 1970s. Some states began pushing for sharp reductions in the use of these chemicals, but they made little headway until scientists discovered the hole in the ozone layer over Antarctica in the late 1980s. This discovery made the threat of depletion dramatically clear, as ozone protects all forms of life from ultraviolet radiation. Chasek et al. delineate the complicated interstate politics that led to global agreements to reduce the use of the depleting chemicals, and they document the steep decline in the use of CFCs that resulted. This was one of the most successful cases of environmental action to date.

Swedish management professor Kristina Tamm Hallström and sociologist Magnus Boström treat the issue of deforestation and sustainable forestry. Responding to INGO pressure, timber-producing and timber-consuming countries set up the International Tropical Timber Organization (ITTO) in 1986 to encourage more careful forest management. INGOs were far from satisfied; they saw the ITTO as little more than a shield to deflect criticism from the global forest industry. As deforestation continued apace, the INGO-led movement pushed for an independent body that would certify and verify sustainable forest practices. The result was the independent Forest Stewardship Council (FSC), founded in 1993, whose "Principles and Criteria" are built on the triple considerations of environmental impact, economic benefits, and social consequences. The FSC brings together environmental groups, timber companies and professionals, indigenous peoples' groups, and forest product certification organizations in a structure that ensures strong representation from the less developed countries. It does not have sanctioning power, but it is a source of constant pressure on the industry to improve its practices in line with the "Principles and Criteria."

The last selection on environmentalism is a speech to the World Economic Forum in Davos, Switzerland, in 2008, by Rajendra K. Pachauri, the chair of the Intergovernmental Panel on Climate Change (IPCC). The IPCC, which was awarded the Nobel Peace Prize the previous year, is the preeminent global body charged with studying Earth's climate and informing policy about the present and future effects of global warming. Pachauri emphasizes the very strong likelihood that global warming is caused by human action (above all, rising CO_2 levels due to the ever-increasing combustion of fossil fuels) and the urgency of a decisive global program to reduce greenhouse gas emissions. He argues that such a program, which will require cooperation among states, corporations, researchers, and civil society, need not be particularly burdensome economically, though poorer countries will need aid from richer countries in the transition to a "low-carbon" society. The consequences of not taking effective action, however, will be dire indeed, in Pachauri's estimation.

64

Greenpeace and Political Globalism

Paul Wapner

There are forces in the world which work, not in an arithmetical, but in a geometrical ratio of increase. Education, to use the expression of Plato, moves like a wheel with an ever multiplying rapidity. Nor can we say how great may be its influence, when it becomes universal.

Benjamin Jowett

Nonstate-oriented politics is nothing new. Since the dawn of social life, human beings have worked to shape and direct collective affairs independent of formal government. In recent years, however, scholars have begun thinking theoretically about this type of activity and, in so doing, have provided a degree of conceptual clarity to it. In particular, the contributions of social movement theory, post-structuralism, feminism, and critical thought have broadened understandings of power and thus have heightened our sensitivity to how politics takes place in the home, office, and marketplace, as well as in the halls of congresses and parliaments. Politics, in this sense, is much more subtle to notice than the conduct of governments but, according to proponents of these orientations, no less significant for political affairs.

It is with a more comprehensive notion of power that I wish to begin investigating the ways in which transnational environmental groups engage in world civic politics. By suspending judgment about what constitutes real politics, one can focus on diverse forms of agency that actually shape world environmental affairs. In this chapter, I describe the ways in which activists work outside of, around, or at the margins of governmental activity in their efforts to alleviate global environmental problems.

Original publication details: Paul Wapner, "Greenpeace and Political Globalism," in *Environmental Activism and World Civic Politics*. Albany: State University of New York Press, 1996. pp. 41–3, 47–54. Reproduced with permission from State University of New York.

This descriptive element will sensitize readers to genuinely alternative forms of political activism.

In addition to describing forms of nonstate environmental politics, one must still ask the political question about them: namely, do they make a difference? Does all the time, money, and human energy involved actually contribute to addressing and partly alleviating environmental problems? Specifically, in what ways does a non-state-oriented type of political action actually affect world environmental affairs? That activists employ such a politics is, as I will demonstrate, true; but does it really matter in terms of world politics? In this chapter, in addition to describing the work of transnational activists, I furnish evidence to suggest that their efforts actually do matter in world political events. They create conditions that direct the actions of others within a world context.

To begin, I want to draw attention to a level of analysis that has a long history in the study of world politics but which is, at present, still underdeveloped and under-appreciated. This is the level at which norms, values, and discourse operate in the global arena outside the domain of states. It is that dimension of world experience where widespread, shared understandings among people throughout the globe act as determinants for present conditions on the planet. It is part of, for want of a better phrase, the *cultural* school of thought which believes that ideas within societies at large structure human collective life. Working within this tradition, the key argument of this chapter is that transnational environmental groups contribute to addressing global environmental problems by heightening worldwide concern for the environment. They persuade vast numbers of people to care about and take actions to protect the earth's ecosystem. In short, they disseminate what I call an *ecological sensibility*. This serves an important political function in coming to terms with the environmental threat.

A sensibility operates as a political force insofar as it constrains and directs widespread behavior. It works at the ideational level to animate practices and is considered a form of *soft law* in contrast to the *hard law* of government directives, policies, and so forth. Scholars make it a habit of differentiating between hard and soft law insofar as they distinguish legal and cultural factors in their understanding of social change. On the one hand, there are those who claim that governmental action is the key to social change. Laws, policies, and directives drive social norms, and thus as they change, the entire configuration of social life will shift. Those who share this perspective see governmental action as the "base" with cultural and social life being the "superstructure." On the other hand, there are those who claim that social norms are central to social change. Governmental decrees, from this perspective, are not the source of change but merely reflections of it. Laws and policies arise out of, or give authoritative expression to, norms that already enjoy widespread acceptance. Scholars sharing this view see social norms as the "base" and governmental directives as the "superstructure."

Differentiating legal and cultural factors, while analytically helpful, is misguided when it forces a thinker to choose between them. When it comes to such large categories of social analysis, it is a mistake to assume that one dimension of social change is definitively more significant than the other. The obvious response to such differentiation is that both factors are important. Indeed, some argue that they are in dialectical relation to each other. As Christopher Stone writes, "in general, laws and cultural norms are mutually reinforcing. Formal laws arise from cultures, and command obedience in proportion to their coherence with the fundamental beliefs of the culture. Cultures, however, are not static. Law, and especially the activities of law making and legal reform, are among the forces that contribute to cultural evolution."

In this chapter, I do not weigh in on the ideational side and argue for its primacy nor celebrate the dialectical relationship. Rather, I simply emphasize the degree to which widely held conceptualizations animate large-scale practices and use this to show how efforts to disseminate an ecological sensibility have world political significance. What makes such efforts political, it should be clear, is not that they are ultimately codified into law or governmental decree but that they represent the use of power to influence and guide widespread behavior. An ecological sensibility, then, is not itself an answer to global environmental threats nor *the* agent for shifting one state of affairs to another. It is, however, an important part of any genuine response to environmental harm. Put simplistically for the moment, it creates an ideational context which inspires and motivates people to act in the service of environmental well-being and thus constitutes the milieu within which environmentally sound actions can arise and be undertaken. While not solely responsible for the *existence* of this sensibility, transnational environmental groups deserve substantial credit for *spreading* it throughout the world. [...]

Since 1972, Greenpeace has grown from having a single office in Vancouver to staffing offices in over thirty countries and, until recently, a base in Antarctica. Greenpeace has offices in the developed as well as the developing world, including Russia and Eastern Europe. Its eco-navy consists of eight ships, and it owns a helicopter and a hot-air balloon. It employs over 1,000 full-time staff members, plus hundreds of part-timers and thousands of volunteers. As of July 1994, it had over 6 million members worldwide and an estimated income of over $100 million. All money comes from voluntary donations, 90 percent of which is in the form of small contributions from individual members. Additionally, Greenpeace sends hundreds of canvassers out each night to raise funds and educate the general public about current environmental issues. Finally, it has expanded its area of concern. While originally focused on nuclear weapons testing, it is now concerned with all threats to the planetary ecosystem. In short, from 1972 to the present Greenpeace has grown into a full-scale, transnational environmental organization.

Transnational Organizational Structure

Greenpeace sees the bulk of global environmental problems falling into four categories: toxic substances, energy and atmosphere, nuclear issues, and ocean and terrestrial ecology. Greenpeace works for environmental protection by dividing its attention among these four issue areas, also called campaigns. Within each of these, Greenpeace works on numerous subissues. For example, under the rubric of its nuclear campaign, Greenpeace focuses on reprocessing and dumping of nuclear material, sea-based nuclear weapons and nuclear testing. Under the rubric of ocean ecology, Greenpeace concentrates on whales, sea turtles, fisheries, and dolphins.

As a transnational environmental group concerned with threats to the entire planet, Greenpeace undertakes its campaigns and projects worldwide. The problems associated with toxic substances, energy, and atmosphere and so forth are not limited to individual countries. Almost all parts of the world are vulnerable to the environmental consequences involved. Greenpeace is organized to allow it to address these dilemmas on a global scale.

The top tiers of the organization are made up of the Greenpeace Council, an executive board, and regional trustees. The council is made up of representatives from all the countries where Greenpeace has offices and meets once a year to decide on organizational policy. The council is one of the ways Greenpeace coordinates its diverse activities. The council sets guidelines for the general operation of Greenpeace, approves the international budget, and develops long-term goals. Because council members come from around the world, decisions can reflect a sensitivity to differing regional and local aspects of environmental problems. To provide greater efficiency in day-to-day operations, and to emphasize coordination among campaigns and projects, there is an executive board that ratifies all council resolutions and makes significant decisions for Greenpeace throughout the year when the council is not in session. The board consists of both voting and nonvoting members and is elected by the Greenpeace Council.

In addition to the council and the executive board, there are regional trustees that provide the final stamp of approval for Greenpeace's overall operations. Trustees are representatives of the areas of the world where Greenpeace has offices. These include Latin America, the Pacific, North America, and Europe. While the trustees generally approve all decisions put forward by the council and the executive board, it serves as the final arbiter of Greenpeace policies. Because individual trustees represent diverse regions of the world, as a whole the trustees advance a global rather than a national or even regional orientation within Greenpeace.

Aside from the council and executive board, Greenpeace organizes itself worldwide along the lines of its four campaign areas. Heading each campaign is an international coordinator. He or she designs the way specific campaigns play themselves out in different regional and national contexts. For example, the campaign coordinator of toxic substances orchestrates all Greenpeace projects that contribute to achieving the aims of the toxics campaign. She or he provides the global perspective to different projects.

Underneath international campaign coordinators are project directors. Project directors are scattered across the globe and work on subissues of the larger campaigns. For example, there are nine projects currently being undertaken by the toxics campaign. One of these focuses on the pulp and paper industry. The pulp and paper industry is responsible for 50 percent of all organochlorine discharges into the earth's waterways. Organochlorine is dangerous to both humans and the natural environment; it is known to cause sterility and cancer in mammals. The project's aim is to change the production process of the industry away from bleaching procedures that use chlorine. The bulk of the pulp and paper industry is located in a number of countries, and Greenpeace pursues the project in each of them. The project director oversees all these efforts. Project directors, like campaign coordinators, take a global perspective on their respective projects. They make sure that separate Greenpeace activities throughout the world support each other and fit together to advance the cause of their specific project.

Working under the project coordinators are regional and national campaigners. Campaigners devise specific Greenpeace activities. They identify what they take to be the most effective ways to communicate with people and change environmentally destructive practices. For purposes of this chapter, one should think of campaigners as organizers of concrete activities that aim to alter people's perceptions of particular environmental threats. To use the pulp and paper example, there are campaigners in a number of countries including the United States, Canada, Sweden, and Germany. Campaigners focus on the pulp and paper industries in their respective countries, taking into account the governmental, cultural, and industrial attributes of each country to address the problem. Regional and national campaigners are key to Greenpeace's global efforts because they understand the particular contexts within which environmental damage is being caused and fashion appropriate responses. They take the general intentions of projects and overall campaigns and translate them into concrete actions that are tailored for specific geographical and political contexts.

Working with campaigners are a host of assistants and volunteers who help carry out specific activities. There are literally thousands of these people throughout the world. They paint banners, circulate petitions, research issues, organize protests, and take part in direct, nonviolent actions. All levels of activity are designed, at least in theory, to advance the goals of specific campaigns.

Greenpeace's Politics

Key to all Greenpeace's efforts is the insight that people do not damage the ecosystem as a matter of course. Rather, they operate in an ideational context that motivates them to do so. People are not machines; they do not respond directly to situations. In the words of Harry Eckstein, people are moved by "predispositions which pattern behavior." In the language of social science, human behavior is a matter of "oriented action." People process experience into action through general conceptions or interpretations of the world. At the most general level, but also the most important, then, an important step toward protecting the earth is to change the way vast numbers of people understand the world. It involves persuading them to abandon their anti-ecological or non-ecological attitudes and practices, and to be concerned about the environmental well-being of the planet. In short, it requires disseminating an ecological sensibility.

People respond to situations through interpretive categories that reflect a particular understanding of everyday circumstances. Such mediating orientations are cultural in character. They reflect customary, socially transmitted understandings that are embedded in the prevailing values, norms, and modes of discourse. Greenpeace targets and tries to alter these dispositions. It literally attempts to manipulate values, norms, and modes of discourse; it seeks to alter people's conceptions of reality.

Greenpeace hopes that in so doing, people will undertake actions that are more respectful of the ecological integrity of the planet.

Central to Greenpeace's efforts is the practice of "bearing witness." This is a type of political action, originating with the Quakers, which links moral sensitivities with political responsibility. Having observed a morally objectionable act, one cannot turn away in avoidance. One must either take action to prevent further injustice or stand by and attest to its occurrence. While bearing witness often works to stop specific instances of environmental destruction, in general, it aims simply to present ecological injustice to the world. This offers as many people as possible an alternative understanding of contemporary affairs and sets them in motion against such practices. One way Greenpeace does this is by engaging in direct, nonviolent action and advertising it through the media worldwide.

Direct, nonviolent action is a form of political practice that shares much with the passive resistance of Mahatma Gandhi and Martin Luther King. It is a vehicle for confrontation and an outreach to other citizens. For Greenpeace, such action includes climbing aboard whaling ships, parachuting from the top of smokestacks, plugging up industrial discharge pipes, and floating a hot-air balloon into a nuclear test site. Such actions create images that can be broadcasted through the media to spark interest and concern of the largest audience.

Greenpeace is able to capture media attention because its actions are visually spectacular. According to political theorist J. Glenn Gray, human beings have what the New Testament calls "the lust of the eye." This is a primitive urge for visual stimulation; it describes the aesthetic impulse. The urge is lustful because it requires the novel, the unusual, the spectacular. The eye cannot satiate itself on the familiar, the everyday, the normal. Greenpeace actions excite the eye. They portray people taking dangerous risks. These grab attention and thus receive media coverage. By offering spectacular images to the media, Greenpeace invites the public to bear witness; it enables people throughout the world to know about environmental dangers and tries to pique their sense of outrage.

A number of years ago it was difficult to use direct, nonviolent action to change political conditions around the globe. While direct action has always been a political tool for those seeking change, the technology did not exist to publicize specific actions to a global audience. Recent innovations in communication technologies have allowed information to whip around the globe within seconds, linking distant corners of the world. Greenpeace plugs into this planetwide communication system to advertise its direct actions.

For example, in the 1970s Greenpeace ships used Morse code to communicate with their offices on land. Information from sailing expeditions would be translated in a central office and then sent out to other offices and onto the media via the telephone. This was cumbersome and expensive and compromised much of the information that could prove persuasive to public audiences. After weeks at sea, ships would return with still photographs, and these would be the most convincing images Greenpeace could use to communicate about environmental destruction taking place on the high seas.

With the advent of affordable innovations in the field of communications, Greenpeace has been able to update its ability to reach diverse and numerous audiences. Instead of Morse code, Greenpeace ships now use telephones, fax machines, and satellite uplinks to communicate with home offices. This allows for instantaneous information to be communicated and verified. Moreover, Greenpeace uses video cameras to capture its actions. Footage can be taken of whaling expeditions, ocean dumping of nuclear wastes, and discharging of toxic substances into streams and waterways. This documents more accurately actual instances of environmental destruction and the risks that Greenpeace members undertake to protect the environment. Once Greenpeace has footage and photographs of such abuse, it sends them into peoples' homes across the world through the planetwide mass communication system. Greenpeace has its own media facilities and uses these to get its information out to the public. Aside from attracting journalists and television crews to their actions, Greenpeace provides its own photographs to picture editors and has facilities to distribute edited, scripted, and narrated video news spots to television stations in eighty-eight countries within hours.

To see how Greenpeace uses direct, nonviolent action to make the world bear witness, consider its whale campaign. For years, Greenpeace has been trying to preserve whale populations and guard them from extinction. This is part of a larger campaign to generate more awareness and concern for the mass depletion of species currently taking place throughout the world. One technique Greenpeace uses to do this is direct action on the high seas. In one of its early expeditions, for instance, Greenpeace sent a ship to pursue a Russian whaling fleet. One of Greenpeace's first actions was to document the fleet's activities. Greenpeace found that the Russians were killing whales that were smaller than the official allowable size, as designated by the International Whaling Commission. To record this, Greenpeace filmed the killing of an undersized whale and took still photographs of a human being perched over it to demonstrate that it was merely a whale calf. Greenpeace noticed, moreover, that the sheer size and capability of the fleet enabled it to take large catches and thus threaten the sperm whale population in the area. To dramatize this, Greenpeace members boarded inflatable dinghies and positioned themselves between harpoon ships and pods of whales. In essence, they tried to discourage harpooners from firing by threatening to die for the cause. This proved effective as numerous times Russian whalers did not shoot their harpoons for fear of killing Greenpeace members. What turned out to be crucial was that Greenpeace captured this on film. Footage was broadcasted on television stations and still photographs were reproduced in newspapers and magazines worldwide. Greenpeace has engaged in numerous similar actions since then and continues to use such strategies.

A second example of direct action is Greenpeace's campaign to stop ozone depletion. In 1989, Greenpeace members infiltrated a DuPont manufacturing plant in Deepwater, New Jersey. Activists climbed the plant's 180-foot water tower and hung a huge, blue-ribbon banner awarding DuPont a prize for being the world's number-one ozone destroyer. (At the time, DuPont produced half of the chlorofluorocarbons (CFCs) used in the US and 25 percent of world annual production.) The following day, Greenpeace bolted a steel box – with two people inside – onto the plant's railroad tracks and blocked the export of CFCs from the plant. Greenpeace draped the box with a banner that read, "Stop Ozone Destruction Now," with a picture of the earth in the background and used it to stage an 8-hour blockade holding up rail cars carrying 44,000 gallons of CFCs.

What is curious is that, according to Greenpeace, within minutes of removing the blockade, business proceeded as usual. The plant continued to function, producing and sending out substances that are proven to erode the stratospheric ozone layer. Nonetheless, something had happened in those brief 8 hours; something had changed. While DuPont workers continued to manufacture CFCs, they now did so knowing that others knew about and were concerned with the environmental effects. Moreover, because Greenpeace captured its actions on film and distributed video news spots to television stations throughout the world, vast numbers of people were now able to understand the connection between the production of CFCs and ozone depletion. In short, the utility of Greenpeace's activity in this case had less to do with the blocking action and more to do with the message that was conveyed. Greenpeace gave the ozone issue form and used the image of disrupting DuPont's operations to send out a message of concern. As Paul Watson, an early member of Greenpeace put it, "When you do an action it goes through the camera and into the minds of people. The things that were previously out of sight and out of mind now become commonplace. Therefore you use the media as a weapon."

Political Strategies

Greenpeace obviously does more than perform direct actions. It also lobbies government officials, gathers information, organizes protests and boycotts, produces record albums and other educational merchandise, and carries out scientific research. While many of these endeavors, especially lobbying, are directed specifically at states, a large percentage of Greenpeace's work is not meant to change states' policies per se but is aimed at changing the attitudes and behavior of the more general public. It seeks to change prevailing, and at times internationally shared, values, norms, and modes of discourse. It strives to "sting people with an ecological sensibility regardless of occupation, geographical location, or access to government officials. [...]

65

Environmental Advocacy Networks

Margaret E. Keck and Kathryn Sikkink

The Campaign against Deforestation in Sarawak

A case of deforestation that began to receive considerable attention in the late 1980s was the extremely rapid logging of tropical timber in the Malaysian state of Sarawak, on the island of Borneo. Logging had already decimated the forests of neighboring Sabah, but received little public attention. Sarawak was different, for three reasons: (1) a change in the international institutional context for discussion of tropical forestry issues, with establishment of the International Tropical Timber Organization, provided a new campaign focus, following upon a relatively successful effort to target a similar organization on the whaling issue; (2) strong connections between deforestation and native land rights issues brought environmental and indigenous rights campaigners together, especially in Europe, and the actions of Bruno Manser, an amateur anthropologist who had lived with a nomadic people in Sarawak called the Penan, dramatized their plight; and (3) the case was taken up vigorously by a Malaysian organization, Sahabat Alam Malaysia, that was already a member of Friends of the Earth International as well as several other mainly southern, transnational networks.

Original publication details: Margaret E. Keck and Kathryn Sikkink, "Environmental Advocacy Networks," in *Activists beyond Borders: Advocacy Networks in International Politics*, ed. Margaret E. Keck and Kathryn Sikkink. Ithaca, NY: Cornell University Press, 1998. pp. 150–62. Note: This text has been edited and all notes and references to third party sources removed. Please refer to the original source text for clarification on what has been omitted.

Background

Sarawak and Sabah are the two Malaysian states located on the northern coast of Borneo. They enjoy significant autonomy under the country's federal system, with the ability to control customs, civil service, and immigration (Sarawak requires a passport for visitors from peninsular Malaysia). Sarawak also controls the revenues from timber concessions, the result of an agreement at the time of joining the federation that gave peninsular Malaysia, in return, control over oil revenues. As a result of this deal, the federal government in Kuala Lumpur has been able to deny responsibility for logging practices in Sarawak.

With the exception of a severe recession in 1986, Malaysia's GNP has grown at 6–8 percent per annum since the early 1970s. A series of five-year plans have worked toward the goal, articulated in Prime Minister Mahathir Mohamad's "Vision 2020" program, of being a fully industrialized economy by the year 2020. Industry currently represents around 70 percent of the nation's exports. Timber is second to oil as a revenue producer in the primary sector.

The country is a multi-ethnic state. The shadow of ethnic conflict has hung heavily over Malaysia since an explosion of violence in 1969. Although preferential treatment is given to Malays, the benefits of development are very widely distributed. Given the image of rapid modernization which is currently a central component of Malaysia's political identity, the idea that Dayak (indigenous) land rights should be secured in part to preserve traditional lifeways commonly portrayed as backward does not fit with the image of a country racing toward the twenty-first century. Malaysia has been ruled by a large multi-party coalition headed by the UMNO-Baru (United Malays National Organization), a Muslim–Malay party, since independence in 1957, and overtly ethnic politics is seen by dominant groups as potentially destabilizing.

Logging in peninsular Malaysia declined significantly between 1975 and 1985 as a conservationist National Forestry Policy (which does not affect Sarawak and Sabah) came into effect. At the same time, log output in Sarawak increased from 4.4 million cubic meters in 1976 to 12.2 million in 1985. Although in theory logging in Sarawak was tightly controlled from the outset, enforcement has been practically nonexistent; both the geographical constraints of hill logging and the economic incentives for cutting beyond the targets are very strong. Briefly, timber concessions under the control of state politicians are granted (sold) for short-term logging licences to timber companies, whose motivation to log selectively and with care in areas designated for protection is virtually nil.

Logging decimated traditional forms of livelihood, meanwhile accelerating the integration of Dayak communities into the state's cash economy. Although logging brought short-term jobs to native communities, it eroded soils, polluted rivers and reduced fish stocks, eliminated wildlife formerly hunted for food, and increased flooding. Employment benefits ended when the logging companies moved on to the next area. Attempts by Dayak communities to gain the rights to log in their own areas have been unsuccessful, as have most attempts to have areas declared communal forests and thus protected from the loggers. Making land rights effective has been a losing struggle in the state. Logging hit especially hard for the still partially nomadic Penan people of the Baram region, for whom the forest provided food and home.

Dayak resistance came to international attention beginning in March 1987, when the Penan set up barricades on logging roads in the Upper Baram. Use of this tactic quickly spread throughout the region to other Dayak groups (the Kenyah, Kayan, Lambawang, and Kelabit). Activities in at least sixteen logging camps were halted. Although this is not the first time that barricades were used against loggers, it is the first time they were part of a sustained campaign, and the first time the resistance received so much attention.

What elements projected the Sarawak conflicts onto a broader stage in 1987? First, interrelated political crises at the national and state levels amplified their importance. Malaysia had undergone a severe recession in 1986, with per capita income declining by 15.7 percent. Criticism of the government became pervasive both in the governing coalition and the opposition, mainly concerning access to decision-making. Within Sarawak, rising Dayak nationalism since 1983 had spawned the first explicitly ethnic political party in the state (Parti Bansa Dayak Sarawak – PBDS). Prime Minister Mahathir began to fear for his coalition. In addition, by early March 1987 Sarawak was in the midst of its own political crisis, significant for the present story because of revelations about official corruption in granting timber concessions. This multifaceted crisis formed the backdrop for the logging blockades.

Second, tropical forests had become increasingly visible on the international agenda by the mid-1980s. In March 1983 sixty-four countries had agreed to establish an International Tropical Timber Organization (ITTO). Composed of producers and consumers of tropical timber, the new group was given a mandate to consider global resource management issues. Then in 1985, declared the International Year of the Forest, the UN Food and Agriculture Organization, the World Bank, and the UN Development Program, working with the World Resources Institute, produced the Tropical Forestry Action Plan and published "Tropical Forests: A Call for Action." The resulting International Tropical Forest Timber Agreement and Action Plan, passed in June 1986 in Geneva, was to be implemented by the International Tropical Timber Organization, headquartered in Yokohama, Japan. The ITTO council met for the first time in March 1987, at the same time that the blockades of logging roads began to spread throughout the Baram region of Sarawak. […]

The third factor that brought Sarawak logging wide attention was that local protests were linked to international publics through two different network nodes. One was the charismatic (and enigmatic) Bruno Manser, a Swiss national who had lived with the Penan for a number of years and who apparently helped to organize the blockade; and the other was Sahabat Alam Malaysia, one of a set of interrelated organizations based in Penang. Involved in a variety of environmental campaigns in peninsular Malaysia, SAM had an office in Marudi, Sarawak, run by Harrison Ngau, a Kayan from the Baram region. SAM was also the Malaysian member of Friends of the Earth International. SAM provided logistical support for the blockades, and arranged for twelve native representatives to go to Kuala Lumpur, where they met with the acting prime minister and a variety of high government officials. Although Dayak customary rights to land were recognized in law, the state government continued to violate them.

Before the blockades in 1987, forest campaigners had already begun to mount an international campaign involving deforestation in the region. At a meeting of FOE

International in Penang in September 1986, everyone was looking for a way to influence the tropical timber trade, especially with regard to Japan. FOE–UK promoted the view that a campaign needed an institutional lever such as International Tropical Timber Organization. Experience with the International Whaling Commission in the antiwhaling campaign was undoubtedly a factor in that assessment. Others preferred to work for export bans and timber boycotts. Although organizations in the network concentrated on different aspects of the campaign, these were not seen as mutually exclusive. [...]

Despite passages of a forest amendment bill in late 1987 that made interfering with logging operations a criminal act punishable with a heavy fine and imprisonment, the blockades were repeated. From 1988 into the 1990s, they offered a powerful symbol of resistance and a continuing stimulus to network activities though they were of little value in producing concessions from state officials. Although the Penan Association and longhouse organizations continued to try to gain land titles or communal forest designations, the logging went on.

Framing the Sarawak conflict

The Sarawak campaign has different meanings for different groups of proponents. For people influenced by the experiences of Bruno Manser, who emerged from his hiding place in the forest and somehow returned to Europe in 1990, the nomadic Penan tribesmen were the symbolic center of the story. Organizing with the Penan at the center has created powerful images of an exotic and lost people fighting a heroic battle for the forest in the interest, it is implied, of all of us. Not surprisingly, this vision of the conflict has generated the most powerful media images. Filmmakers, journalists, and photographers have in the main placed the Penan at the center of their accounts. Although the Penan are indeed an important part of the Sarawak story, several other frames have produced different kinds of strategies and engaged different constellations of actors.

Some organizations, including the World Rainforest Movement's Forest Peoples' Program, SAM, Survival International, and *The Ecologist*, have placed primary emphasis on indigenous land rights, which is also a central issue in Evelyne Hong's influential book *Natives of Sarawak*. Without secure land title, they argue, the structural inequalities that prevent Dayak populations from resisting timber interests can never be addressed. This cogent vision of the problem is less resonant internationally than the Penan story, and one with which transnational networks have more difficulty organizing. The causal chain is fairly long, and the remedies difficult to devise.

The other main transnational strategy that emerged from the Sarawak case was its embedding in a broader campaign around tropical or rainforest timber (and in some cases temperate and boreal timber as well). This decentralized strategy has allowed space for considerable variation in organizational activities. Its main components have been consumer boycotts, targeting corporations and particular kinds of businesses (Mitsubishi, Do-it-Yourself stores, for example), persuading local or state governments to refrain from using tropical timber in construction projects, pressuring national governments and the European Union for tropical timber bans, pressuring ITTO members to develop sustainability requirements, and, increasingly, "eco-labeling." A large number of organizations have adopted these strategies, shared information, and collaborated on certain activities, though sometimes disagreeing over where to direct energies at particular stages.

This campaign involves a number of loosely connected subcampaigns with different organizational sponsors. A central role, though not always a coordinating one, has belonged to the constellation of organizations headquartered in Penang – SAM, the Asian-Pacific People's Environmental Network, the Third World Network, and the World Rainforest Movement. By the early 1990s the campaign was focused on logging in Papua New Guinea, Guyana, and Brazil (in all of which Sarawak logging companies have expanded their operations). [...]

Campaign strategies around Sarawak's forests

The Sarawak campaign's efforts to set in motion a boomerang strategy had some effect, but fell far short of success. From taking Dayak representatives to meet with officials in Kuala Lumpur and foreign capitals to contesting the information Malaysian representatives presented in international forums, the network mobilized vast quantities of information and testimony. Repeated barricades of logging roads were powerful symbols of resistance. Demanding that the Malaysian federal government intervene to control or block log exports from Sarawak, the network hoped to exert moral leverage. No effective material leverage was available – no World Bank loans in relevant areas, for example, or strategically placed aid programs. However, because Malaysia aspired to leadership in the Southeast Asian region, the idea that it would respond to moral leverage seemed a credible one. Moral leverage proved insufficient, however, to overcome Prime Minister Mahathir's dependence on the votes of Sarawak's political elites to maintain his broad coalition government. Moreover, there is some evidence that Mahathir's willingness to stand up to US and European critics on this issue may even have enhanced his regional prestige.

Beyond the matter of leverage, however, the tropical timber campaign implicitly proposed a different kind of relationship between north and south than existed in the Brazilian case. From the perspective of most of the Sarawak campaigners, the blame for overexploitation of timber in the region belonged even more to importers than it did to the exporter. Without demand, went the argument, there would be no supply. Thus the campaign was framed and focused quite differently from those waged around World Bank projects; instead of focusing the energies of activists in developed countries on a developing country target, it asked them to target their efforts at home.

The reasons for the difference were both ideological and logistical. First, there was no single source of leverage that provided the same purchase over the Sarawak situation that the World Bank seemed to offer in Rondônia. The central government's insistence that it had no authority over timber extraction in Sarawak was not a fiction; the tradeoff between centralizing oil revenues and leaving timber revenues to the states of East Malaysia had been a crucial compromise at the time of federation. For Sarawak's politicians, growing rich from timber concessions, there was simply no incentive – positive or negative – to stop logging. Because of Mahathir's dependence on a very broad coalition, the political costs of attempting to intervene might have been very high. Furthermore, the Malaysian NGOs that provided the bridge between the Dayak populations in Sarawak and the transnational network were not anti-development – though they wanted to see development's fruits distributed more justly – and believed that first-world governments and NGOs should not use the environmental issue as a weapon to prevent third-world countries from developing autonomously. This argument was especially salient in international debates during the preparatory process for the 1992 UN Conference on Environment and Development in Rio de Janeiro. The tropical timber campaign therefore focused attention on the industrialized world, that rabidly consumed Sarawak's tropical hardwoods.

The tropical timber campaign and its effects

Campaigning around tropical timber had the advantage of decentralization, which allowed for a variety of activities and styles – from Rainforest Action Network activists climbing Mitsubishi office buildings to hang boycott banners and parading with huge Godzilla figures to protest Japanese tropical hardwood imports, to WWF's more sober negotiations over sustainability guidelines with corporations.

Organizations in Germany, the United Kingdom, and the Netherlands launched boycotts in 1988. On a motion from a Dutch Green party delegate, the European Parliament voted in 1988 to recommend Malaysian timber bans to European Union (EU) members until its logging became sustainable. The EU Commission subsequently overturned that recommendation, but as a symbol of protest it garnered much publicity. In May 1989 Australia's Rainforest Action Group, which had already called for a boycott, deployed swimmers and kayaks to Malaysian timber-bearing ships. The Rainforest Action Network in the United States declared a boycott of Mitsubishi, and Friends of the Earth did the same in Europe.

In addition to corporate boycotts, environmental organizations organized hundreds of local government boycotts of the use of tropical timber in municipal construction. This strategy was very successful in Europe; by November 1990 local boycotts had so incensed Malaysians and Indonesians that they threatened trade retaliations. In 1993 and 1994 Japanese activists stepped up a similar local campaign.

These protests had little effect on logging. In 1990, timber operators in Sarawak cut a record eighteen million cubic meters of tropical hardwood logs. In early 1990, angry at foreign pressure, the Malaysian government had asked the ITTO to assess the question of sustainability. The ITTO team reported in May 1990 that Sarawak was logging at eight to ten times a sustainable level. The report recommended a reduction in log output by 1.5 million cubic meters a year. In 1992 the Sarawak government claimed it would comply with the recommendation, but regulations continued to be weakly enforced, and illegal logging is common.

But the trade issue had clearly become a serious one. In October 1991 Prime Minister Mahathir gave the keynote address at the meeting of the Association of Southeast Asian Nations (ASEAN) economy ministers, saying that ASEAN countries must speak with one voice against campaigns linking trade and environmental issues, and that the threats these posed to development had reached serious proportions. [...]

Measuring the impact of the tropical timber campaign requires that we define clearly the goals the campaign intended to reach. For those who wanted to preserve the nomadic lifeways of the Penan and the forest in which they lived, the campaign failed. Only a few hundred Penan remain in the forest. The rest live in longhouses, many work in timber camps and others suffer from the chronic unemployment that has beset communities throughout the region as the loggers move on. For those who wanted to fuel a struggle for land rights, the campaign continues. SAM has helped to organize several hundred community associations, for which security of tenure remains the precondition for any kind of community development activity. Although the transnational network does not exert direct leverage over this question, the campaign nonetheless provides some degree of protection to local efforts. For those who wanted to stop tropical timber logging in Sarawak, the campaign also failed. Sarawak will be logged out in five years, and Sarawakian timber companies are now repeating the process in Guyana and Papua New Guinea. The substantive goals of the Sarawak campaign, in other words, were not met.

In some respects, though, the efforts of the NGO networks and activists were remarkably successful. The Malaysian newspaper *Business Times* reported in October 1995, "Malaysia's timber exports to Europe have fallen by half since 1992 due to pressures from environmental groups on local and municipal governments in Europe to boycott or ban tropical timber products." Tropical timber imports into the Netherlands fell by 50 percent between 1990 and 1995, "mainly as a result of an NGO boycott campaign." Everyone seems to agree that the campaign succeeded in reducing consumption of tropical timber in some of the major importing countries.

If we see the tropical timber campaign as pursuing procedural rather than substantive goals, that is, a change in the international timber trading regime, then it has had some limited success. Campaign activities raised the salience of the issue and eventually placed it on the trade agenda. Unlike subsequent environmentalist attempts to use the trade agenda, as in the dispute over the effects of tuna fishing on dolphins, a forum was in place in which the issues could be ajudicated – the ITTO. Within the ITTO, beyond pressuring the institution to send investigative missions to logging areas and holding states accountable to their commitments, activists in the network have forced debates on the social dimensions of logging and on customary and common property arrangements. However, the new international tropical timber agreement negotiated in 1994 was far weaker than expected. [...]

Conclusions

More than other network campaigns, rainforest campaigns are built on the tensions between recognizing structural causes and designing strategies that seek remedies by placing blame on, and influencing the behavior of, particular actors. Furthermore, the struggles they entail over meaning, power, and access to resources highlight the north–south dimension found in many network campaigns. The campaigns include participants whose understandings have been changed by their ongoing conversation with what anthropologist Anna Tsing calls people in out-of-the-way-places. And, since these are stories about the real world, the campaigns include participants whose understandings have not been changed at all.

Environmental advocacy networks have not so much gotten the tropical forest issue onto the agenda – it was already there – as they have changed the tone of the debate. To the frequent consternation of the epistemic community of scientists and policymakers who had succeeded in placing it on the agenda initially, the advocacy networks deliberately politicized the issues. While the epistemic community had sought to design sound policies and tried on the basis of their authoritative knowledge to persuade governments to adopt them, advocacy networks looked for leverage over actors and institutions capable of making the desired changes. Advocacy networks also insisted on different criteria of expertise. Although they did not deny the expertise of the scientists, they demanded equal time for direct testimony about experience. And within the networks they also cultivated the strategic expertise of good organizers. The issue, especially for the multilateral bank campaigners, was not ultimately forests, or dams, or any other particular environmental issue, but leverage over institutions that make a difference.

The advocacy networks helped to broaden the definition of which information and whose knowledge should shape the agenda on tropical forest issues. In the process, they won seats at the bargaining table for new actors. Their campaigns created a new script for sustainable forest management projects, with roles for "local people," "NGOs," and so forth. We must be careful not to exaggerate the power of the individuals and groups that play these roles, relative to that of states, economic actors like corporations, or multilateral organizations (the Planafloro deliberative council is a good example). Nonetheless, once these roles have been legitimized, organizations like the World Bank must address them.

How much change have transnational advocacy networks produced in the tropical forest issue? Because the networks are not the only reform-minded actors engaged, exact attributions of influence are difficult. The multilateral development bank campaign would certainly not have had much success without the collaboration of network members inside the bank. At the levels of both discursive and procedural change the network has been remarkably successful. Multilateral development banks increasingly claim to be addressing environmental objectives in loans, and there is some evidence that they have begun to eliminate high-risk projects much earlier in the project evaluation cycle. Besides having adopted the discourse of sustainable development, the bank has also implemented important procedural changes, including the information policy. Under increased pressure from the United States after the 1989 Pelosi amendment, all of the multilateral banks are taking the environmental assessment process more seriously.

Similarly, though less dramatically, the tropical timber campaign has had considerable success in promoting discursive change and some success with procedural change as well. Malaysia, as well as other tropical forest states, has begun at least to use the discourse of sustainable forestry, whether or not much has changed in practice. Malaysia has also adopted action plans phasing out unsustainable logging, and has begun to encourage local wood processing. The ITTO has adopted somewhat more stringent standards for movement toward demonstrably sustainable forestry practices. Green labeling, about which forest campaign advocates are quite divided, has not yet proved itself; should it change behavior in the ways that its proponents hope, this may stimulate further steps from the ITTO.

Among the people whose testimony generated the sharpest images of the impact of deforestation on lives, signs of success are harder to find. In Sarawak the transnational advocacy campaign has had very little impact. Logging goes on with its ecological and human impacts. [...]

66

Toward Democratic Governance for Sustainable Development
Transnational Civil Society Organizing around Big Dams

Sanjeev Khagram

For proponents, dams symbolize temples of progress and modernity, from a life controlled by nature and tradition to one in which the environment is ruled by technology, and tradition by science. But a growing number of opponents see the same projects as destructive of nature and indigenous cultures, imposing unacceptable costs while rarely delivering on their ostensible benefits.

This chapter tells the story of the conflicts between a powerful set of interests (government agencies, international organizations, multinational corporations, and domestic industrial and agricultural lobbies) that favor dam construction and the affected peoples groups and civil society coalitions that oppose them. It explores what could prove to be an important model for global governance that incorporates all these stakeholders: the World Commission on Dams.

Today, big dams contribute 20 percent of global electricity generation. In sixty-five countries, hydropower produces more than 50 percent of electricity; in twenty-four more than 90 percent. Worldwide, agricultural crops currently get more than 30 percent of their water from irrigation, a lion's share of which comes from big dams. Future increases in agricultural production to meet the needs of a growing global population will require greater numbers of irrigation dams. Moreover, nearly 1 billion people still do not have adequate supplies of drinking water, 2 billion people do not have access to electricity, and the need for better flood management seems undeniable (witness the massive and destructive floods that have engulfed various regions of the world over the past several years).

Original publication details: Sanjeev Khagram, "Toward Democratic Governance for Sustainable Development: Transnational Civil Society Organizing around Big Dams," in *The Third Force*, ed. Ann Florini. Japan Center for International Exchange, 2000. pp. 83–95, 99, 104–5.

Given the seemingly tremendous need for the benefits generated by big dams, and the powerful groups and organizations promoting them, the dramatic decline in the construction of these projects globally over the past twenty-five years is puzzling. The number of big dams built annually grew from virtually zero in 1900 to nearly 250 by midcentury. The rate exploded thereafter and peaked at around 1,000 big dams being finished annually from the mid-1950s to the mid-1970s. But the number fell precipitously to less than 200 by the 1990s – a 75 percent drop in just over a decade.

There are technical, financial, and economic factors behind this trend, but they do not tell the whole story. The technical argument highlights the decreasing availability of sites for big dams. However, as of 1986, 95 percent of big dams were concentrated in 25 countries that had built more than 100, while less than 2 percent were spread over the more than 150 other countries where sites were still available, even plentiful. In other words, sites remain plentiful in many countries. [...]

Over the last two and a half decades, coalescing from a multitude of struggles and campaigns waged all around the world, domestic and transnational civil society organizations have dramatically altered the dynamics of big dam projects. Environmental nongovernmental organizations (NGOs) from the First World and at the international level, along with those working on human rights and the protection of indigenous peoples, increasingly focused on slowing or halting the global spread of big dams. Often independently and before this, directly affected local peoples, social movements, and domestic NGOs in other parts of the world began mobilizing to reform or block the completion of these projects in their own countries. Over time, coalitions were formed between these like-minded domestic and foreign groups. Thus, transnational civil society coalitions were formed from the domestic successes and subsequent internationalization of environmental and human and indigenous rights organizations in the West and the linkages and coalitions forged with people's groups and social movements struggling worldwide against big dam building.

The Rise of Domestic Opposition

Transnational civil society advocacy efforts are often criticized as being more Western than transnational, thus supposedly representing a narrow range of elite values and interests. This may be true for some issues, but it is not true of the historical dynamics around big dams. Domestic opposition has been independently organized in numerous countries outside the West, such as in India, Thailand, Indonesia, Brazil, Chile, Hungary, the former Soviet Union, and South Africa, to name just a few. [...]

In India, for example, domestic opposition began as far back as the 1940s, when authorities initiated one of the most prolific dam-building programs in history. The Hirakud dam, one of independent India's first multipurpose projects, provides a clear demonstration of this opposition. An anti-Hirakud campaign involving the full range of lobbying and pressure tactics was waged immediately after independence. The campaigners were so strident that they disobeyed orders prohibiting further public opposition against the project; 30,000 villagers and townspeople even protested in front of the state governor. Such purely domestic campaigns were generally unsuccessful through the 1960s.

Nevertheless, domestic civil society opposition to big dam building in India mounted during the 1970s and 1980s. The campaign against the Silent Valley hydroelectric project in Kerala, one of the first to eventually draw support from international NGOs, was a harbinger of trends to come. Grassroots mobilization against the project emerged in 1976 when a group of local teachers began assisting villagers who feared the loss of their livelihoods from the destruction of forest resources. At the same time, the World Wildlife Fund for Nature began to highlight internationally the project's negative environmental consequences on the pristine Silent Valley Forests and the endangered lion-tailed monkey. [...]

Cancellation of the Silent Valley project inspired big dam opponents throughout India and all over the world [...] Within India, opposition mounted against such projects as the Tehri, Bodhghat, Subarnarekha, and, most visibly, Sardar Sarovar-Narmada River Valley. By the end of the 1980s, a meeting of over eighty prominent social movement leaders, activists, scholars, and critics representing millions of Indians called for a moratorium on big dam building in an "assertion of collective will against big dams" until domestic decision-making processes became more participatory and the results of projects more socially just and environmentally sustainable. [...]

The two most well-known campaigns in India, the first to reform and the second to halt completely the World Bank-funded Sardar Sarovar-Narmada project, were spearheaded not by foreign or international NGOs, but by local and domestic groups that eventually developed into the powerful social movement known as the Narmada Bachao Andolan (Save the Narmada Movement). Indeed, mobilization against the Sardar Sarovar in the form of rallies, mass protests, letter-writing campaigns, political lobbying, and scientific critiques began as early as the late 1970s, half a decade prior to the active involvement of transnationally linked allies. The degree of opposition, symbolized by the willingness of local people to drown rather than be displaced by the Sardar Sarovar project, was not motivated by outsiders but actually strengthened the organizing efforts of nondomestic supporters (discussed later).

India was not unusual. The campaign of cordilleran peoples in the Philippines against the Chico River project in the mid-1970s became known worldwide for the confrontations between opposition and government. As a result of the sustained and (atypical for antidam movements) violent grassroots opposition, the World Bank eventually withdrew its funding from the project. Similarly, from the 1970s on in Brazil, a nationwide movement of dam-affected peoples grew in size and strength. Combining civil society campaigns against projects in various regions of the country, the movement contributed not only to domestic social and environmental policy reform but also to the broader democratization process in Brazil. [...]

The more successful domestic antidam campaigns in the United States and Western Europe certainly contributed to the subsequent formation of transnational civil society coalitions. During the 1950s, 1960s, and 1970s, civil society groups critical of big dam building emerged in many European countries. New laws requiring public disclosure of information and mandating environmental impact assessments on large projects both resulted from and added to the success of these efforts. These successful campaigns contributed to the broader decline of big dam building in most European countries by the 1970s.

As in Western Europe, the earliest domestic campaigns to reform or halt big dam building in the United States were led primarily by nature conservationists. These early environmentalists, fighting to protect the natural beauty of the American West, achieved major victories by stopping construction of the Echo Park Dam in 1956 and two other big dams proposed for the Grand Canyon in 1967. The struggles against the Grand Canyon dams that began in the mid-1950s heralded the end of the expansion years of big dam building and played a central role in fostering the growth of a national environmental movement in the United States. [...]

The Building of Transnational Linkages

By the 1970s, as civil society groups in the West succeeded in reforming and halting big dams domestically, they realized that similar projects were being formulated and implemented elsewhere. Not surprisingly, big dam proponents moved their activities to countries where demand for these projects was still high, international funding available, criticism of big dam building less organized, and democratic and environmental norms less institutionalized. In fact, more than two-thirds of new big dam starts occurred in the Third World during the 1980s.

In response, European NGOs such as the Ecologist, Survival International, Berne Declaration, Urgewald, and European Rivers Network were formed or shifted their focus to big dam projects in Southern Europe, Eastern Europe, the Soviet Union and its successor states, and the Third World. These indigenous peoples, human rights, environmental, and even sustainable development NGOs consciously built coalitions with allies all over the world. [...]

The transnational coalition received a boost with the initiation of a new campaign that opposed many of the practices of multilateral development banks, including their support for dams. The connection began when Bruce Rich, an attorney with the Natural Resources Defense Council who had been investigating the negative impacts of mega projects funded by the World Bank and other international development organizations, attended the dam fighters' meeting. As the next section describes, the antibank campaign quickly gathered momentum.

Overlapping the initiation of the anti-multilateral development bank campaign was the publication of the first volume of Edward Goldsmith and Nicholas Hildyard's *The Social and Environmental Effects of Large Dams*, which further strengthened emergent transnational connections. The study was the first to systematically integrate the main arguments against big dams and to insist that the problems caused were largely inherent to the technology.

The growing local, national, and transnational civil society organizing around specific dams, the anti–multilateral bank campaign, and the publication of the first Goldsmith and Hildyard volume all contributed to the establishment of the transnational NGO eventually known as the International Rivers Network (IRN). [...]

The IRN organized a conference on the social and environmental effects of big dams in San Francisco in 1988, at which sixty-three civil society activists and scholars from twenty-three countries met. The participants drew up the San Francisco Declaration, demanding an independent assessment of big dam projects and a moratorium on all projects not having the participation of affected persons, free access to project information, environmental impact assessments, comprehensive resettlement plans, and full cost-benefit analyses. They also endorsed a watershed management declaration recommending numerous alternatives to big dams.

The San Francisco Declaration [...] articulated an evolving set of norms on indigenous peoples, human rights, the environment, and democratic governance for sustainable development that were being promoted by civil society organizations working specifically in those areas. The declarations applied the new standards directly to the issues of big dam projects, river basin management, and the provision of water and power services. Groups from very different societies found common ground by developing these norms. They also used these norms strategically, first as guidelines for appropriate policy prescriptions and subsequently as a means of holding authorities accountable when these norms became institutionalized into the procedures and structures of governmental agencies and intergovernmental organizations. [...]

The IRN quickly became a lead NGO in the growing transnational civil society network around big dams and sustainable development, as well as in the continuing anti-multilateral bank campaign. The IRN began publishing another newsletter, *Bankcheck Quarterly*, a precursor to the Fifty Years Is Enough campaign against the World Bank; established an office in Brazil; and significantly expanded its linkages with NGOs and social movements all over the world. [...]

By the 1990s, virtually any big dam being built or proposed in the world became a potential target, a fact that big dam proponents bemoaned. In 1992, the president of the International Commission on Large Dams – the professional association of big dam engineers – warned that the big dam industry faced "a serious general countermovement that has already succeeded in reducing the prestige of dam engineering in the public eye, and it is starting to make work difficult for our profession."

Taking on the World Bank

The World Bank has been the central international organization promoting big dam building around the world since its founding. The Bank's initial loan to fifteen Third World countries was for big dam projects, starting with loans in 1949 and continuing through Lesotho's first loan in 1986. The World Bank's largest borrower through 1993, India, had received $8.38 billion for the construction of 104 big dams, far more than any other country. World Bank technical support is often critical to the initiation and management of big dam projects, and Bank-arranged cofinancing generally increases the funds available for big dam projects between 50 and 70 percent. The Bank has also contributed to the creation of numerous dam-building bureaucratic agencies in the Third World, such as Thailand's Electricity Generating Authority and Colombia's Interconexión Eléctrica SA. [...]

The growing transnational efforts to halt big dam building overlapped with the emergent campaign against the World Bank and other multilateral development banks in the early 1980s. Transnational antidam coalitions linking groups in the West with those elsewhere were critical in broadening and strengthening what was initially conceived as primarily a Western-based conservationists' campaign against multilateral banks. As Paul Nelson suggests, "The agenda of the campaign was initially concerned with protecting river basins, preserving tropical forests and biodiversity, and promoting demand reduction and efficiency in energy lending. However, three related issues have come to equal, and sometimes eclipse, these conservationist themes: involuntary resettlement of communities from dam projects, protection of indigenous peoples' lands, and accountability and transparency at the World Bank." These were among the highest-priority issues for domestic groups from the South fighting big dams.

As part of the broader anti-multilateral development bank campaign, antidam opponents compelled the Bank not only to reduce its involvement in big dam projects but also to adopt new policies and mechanisms for resettlement, environmental management, indigenous peoples, information disclosure, monitoring, and appeals. The cumulative effect of transnationally allied civil society lobbying against World Bank support for dams over the last twenty-five years is most clearly demonstrated by the more than 60 percent decline in Bank funding for these projects – from approximately $11 billion between 1978 and 1982 to an estimated $4 billion between 1993 and 1997. Under sustained pressure, the Bank finally conducted its first comprehensive review of the big dams in which it had been involved after being in the business for forty years. Civil society critiques of the Bank's review, in turn, sparked the creation of an independent World Commission on Dams. [...]

By nearly unanimous agreement, the transnationally allied opposition to India's Sardar Sarovar-Narmada River Valley projects – led by the powerful domestic Save the Narmada movement – produced the most visible change. The World Bank's Operations Evaluation Department (OED) acknowledged this fact in 1995: "The Narmada Projects have had far-reaching influence on the Bank's understanding of the difficulties of achieving lasting development, on its approaches to portfolio management, and on its openness to dialogue on policies and projects. Several of the implications of the Narmada experience resonated with recommendations made by the Bank's Portfolio Management Task Force ... and have been incorporated into the 'Next Steps' action plan that the Bank is now implementing to improve the management of its portfolio." The Bank's subsequent reforms included initiatives in a range of areas, from resettlement and environment to procedural mechanisms that would increase the transparency and accountability of Bank activities. [...]

The Genesis of the World Commission on Dams

[...] At a workshop in Gland, Switzerland, in April 1997, the World Bank and the World Conservation Union brought together thirty-nine representatives of governments, international development agencies, the private sector, and transnational civil society. Representatives of governments and international development agencies participated because they were interested in finding means of achieving the various benefits generated by big dams while avoiding the tremendous social and environmental costs associated with building them. Participants from the private sector attended because of the reputational and financial risks they face from the continuous campaigns. [...]

Representatives of transnational civil society seized the opportunity afforded by the Gland workshop to push for an independent and comprehensive review of big dams, a demand that they had been pursuing for several years and had recently articulated in the Curitiba Declaration. That declaration had been drafted and approved at the historic first International Conference of People Affected by Dams held in Curitiba, Brazil, between March 11 and 14, 1997, and attended by more than 100 dam-affected people and dam critics from seventeen countries. The 1997 Declaration of Curitiba, which affirmed the right to life and livelihood of people affected by dams, built on the norms and goals espoused in the San Francisco Declaration of 1988 and the Manibeli Declaration of 1994. The primary principle espoused was opposition to the construction of any dam that had not been approved by the negatively affected people, especially those to be displaced, through an informed and participatory decision-making process. The declaration demanded the establishment of an independent commission to conduct a comprehensive review of all large dams supported by international agencies, subject to the involvement of representatives of transnational civil society, and similar reviews for each national and regional agency that had supported the building of big dams.

At the Gland workshop, the thirty-nine participants unanimously agreed to this demand, and the World Commission on Dams (WCD) was established shortly thereafter. The WCD is an independent international body composed of twelve commissioners known for their leadership roles in social movements, NGOs, academia, the private sector, and governments directly involved with dam building from all over the world. The unprecedented mandate of the WCD is to (1) conduct a global review of the development effectiveness of dams and assess alternatives for sustainable water resources and energy management, and (2) develop internationally accepted criteria and guidelines for decision making in the planning, design, appraisal, construction, monitoring, operation, and decommissioning of dams. Arguably, the WCD is the most innovative international institutional experiment in the area of democratic governance for sustainable development today, and if it is successful, the WCD could pave the way for a wave of novel multistake-holder global public policy processes in the twenty-first century. [...]

67

Ozone Depletion

Pamela S. Chasek, David L. Downie, and Janet Welsh Brown

Ozone is a pungent, slightly bluish gas composed of three oxygen atoms (O_3). Ninety percent of naturally occurring ozone resides in the **stratosphere**. This "ozone layer" helps to shield the earth from ultraviolet radiation produced by the sun and plays a critical role in absorbing UV-B radiation. Because large increases in UV-B radiation would seriously harm nearly all plants and animals, the ozone layer is considered an essential component of the natural systems that make life on earth possible.

In the 1970s, scientists discovered that certain man-made chemicals, called chlorofluorocarbons (CFCs), posed a serious threat to stratospheric ozone. CFCs release chlorine atoms into the stratosphere that act as a catalyst in the destruction of ozone molecules. Created in the 1920s to replace flammable and noxious refrigerants, CFCs are inert, nonflammable, nontoxic, colorless, odorless, and wonderfully adaptable to a wide variety of profitable uses. By the mid-1970s, CFCs had become the chemical of choice for coolants in air conditioning and refrigerating systems, propellants in aerosol sprays, solvents in the cleaning of electronic components, and the blowing agent for the manufacture of flexible and rigid foam. Scientists later discovered other ozone-depleting compounds, including halons, a tremendous and otherwise safe fire suppressant, carbon tetrachloride, methyl chloroform, and methyl bromide. Each can release ozone-destroying chlorine or bromine atoms into the stratosphere.

The economic importance of these chemicals, especially CFCs, made international controls extremely difficult to establish. The absence of firm scientific consensus on

Original publication details: Pamela S. Chasek, David L. Downie, and Janet Welsh Brown, *Global Environmental Politics*. Boulder, CO: Westview Press, 2006. pp. 106–12, 114–15. Reproduced with permission from Westview Press, a member of Perseus Books Group.

the nature and seriousness of the problem, a strenuous anti-regulatory campaign by corporations producing or using CFCs, concerns for the cost of unilateral regulation, worries by developing countries that restricting access to CFCs would slow economic development, and opposition by the European Community prevented effective action for many years.

The political definition of the ozone depletion issue began in 1977. The fact-finding process lasted many years, however, because scientific estimates of potential depletion fluctuated widely during the late 1970s and early 1980s, and no evidence emerged in nature to confirm the theory. Indeed, when the bargaining process formally began in 1982, the exact nature of the threat was unclear even to proponents of international action.

The United States, which at that time accounted for more than 40 percent of worldwide CFC production, took a lead role in the negotiations in part because it had already banned CFC use in aerosol spray cans, a large percentage of total use at that time, and wanted other states to follow suit. However, for an ozone-protection policy to succeed, it was essential that all states producing and consuming CFCs be part of the regime. Thus, the European Community, which also accounted for more than 40 percent of global CFC production and exported a third of that to developing countries, opposed controls and constituted a potential veto coalition. Germany supported CFC controls, but the EC position was effectively controlled by the other large producing countries – France, Italy, and the United Kingdom – which doubted the science, wanted to preserve their industries' overseas markets, and wished to avoid the costs of adopting substitutes. Japan, a major user of CFCs, supported this position.

Large developing countries, including Brazil, China, India, and Indonesia, formed another veto coalition. Their bargaining leverage stemmed from their potential to produce very large quantities of CFCs in the future – a situation that would eventually eviscerate the effectiveness of any regime. Although most developing countries did not play an active role early in the regime's development, they eventually used this leverage to secure a delayed control schedule and precedent-setting financial and technical assistance.

Although negotiations began with an explicit understanding that only a possible framework convention would be discussed, in 1983, the lead states (the US, Canada and the Nordic states) proposed the adoption of binding restrictions on CFC production. The veto coalition, led by the EC, steadfastly rejected negotiations for regulatory protocols. Thus, the regime's first agreement, the 1985 Vienna Convention for the Protection of the Ozone Layer, affirmed the importance of protecting the ozone layer and included provisions on monitoring, research, and data exchanges, but imposed no specific obligations to reduce the production or use of CFCs. Indeed, it did not even mention CFCs. However, because of a last-minute US initiative, states did agree to resume formal negotiations on a binding protocol if further evidence emerged supporting the potential threat.

Only weeks after nations signed the Vienna Convention, British scientists published the first reports about the Antarctic ozone hole. Although the hole had been forming annually for several years, the possibility of its existence fell so far outside the bounds of existing theory that computers monitoring satellite data on ozone had ignored its presence as a data error. Publication of its existence galvanized proponents of CFC controls, who argued that the hole justified negotiations to strengthen the nascent regime (despite the lack of firm evidence linking the hole to CFCs until 1989). Thus, faced with domestic and international pressure, the veto states returned to the bargaining table in December 1986.

The lead states – a coalition that now included Canada, Finland, Norway, Sweden, Switzerland, and the United States – initially advocated a freeze followed by a 95 percent reduction in production of CFCs over a period of ten to fourteen years. The industrialized-country veto coalition – the EC, Japan, and the Soviet Union – eventually proposed placing a cap on production capacity at current levels. Lead states argued that the capacity cap could lead to actual increases in CFC production (and involve few adjustment costs for veto states) because Europe already possessed significant excess production capacity. Lead states then offered a 50 percent cut as a compromise. As late as April 1987, the EC would not accept more than a 20 percent reduction, but relented in the final days of negotiations. The ten-year evolution of the EC position from rejecting all discussion of control measures to proposing a production cap to accepting a compromise reduction target reflected several factors: disunity within the European Community (West Germany, Denmark, Belgium, and the Netherlands all supported strong regulations); the personal role played by UNEP Executive Director Tolba; diplomatic pressures by the United States; pressure from domestic NGOs; and reluctance by the EC to be seen as the culprit should negotiations fail to produce an agreement.

The 1987 Montreal Protocol on Substances That Deplete the Ozone Layer mandated that industrialized countries reduce their production and use of the five most widely used CFCs by 50 percent. Halon production would be frozen. The expanded regime also included scientific and technological assessment panels, reporting requirements, potential trade sanctions for countries that did not ratify the agreement, and a robust procedure for reviewing the effectiveness of the regime and strengthening controls through amendment and adjustments. To gain the acceptance of the developing country veto coalition, delegates agreed to give developing countries a ten-year grace period, allowing them to increase their use of CFCs before taking on commitments.

Within months of the Montreal accord, there emerged new scientific evidence supporting strengthening the regime. In late 1987, scientists announced that initial studies suggested that CFCs probably were responsible for the ozone hole, which continued to grow larger every year, although natural processes peculiar to Antarctica contributed to its severity. Studies during the next two years confirmed these findings. In March 1988, satellite data revealed that stratospheric ozone above the heavily populated Northern Hemisphere had begun to thin. Finally, the 1989 report of the regime's own Scientific Assessment Panel signaled conclusively that the world's scientific community had reached broad agreement that CFCs had indeed begun to deplete stratospheric ozone.

This period also saw changes in the pattern of economic interests. In 1988, Du Pont announced that they would soon be able to produce CFC substitutes. They were followed the next year by other large chemical manufacturers, including several in Europe. The major producers no longer opposed a CFC phaseout but lobbied instead for extended transition periods and against controls on potential substitutes, particularly hydrochlorofluorocarbons (HCFCs) – a class of CFC substitutes that deplete ozone but at a significantly reduced rate. In response to these scientific and economic changes, and to increased pressure from domestic environmental lobbies, the EC abruptly shifted roles.

At the second Meeting of the Parties to the Montreal Protocol (MOP-2), in London in June 1990, EC states assumed a lead role during difficult negotiations that eventually produced amendments and adjustments that significantly strengthened the regime. Production of the CFCs and halons controlled in 1987, and of carbon tetrachloride and all other CFCs and halons, would now be phased out by 2000, and methyl chloroform by 2005. [...]

In response to evidence of increasing ozone-layer depletion, parties again strengthened the regime at MOP-4 in Copenhagen in 1992. Delegates accelerated the existing phaseouts and added controls on additional chemicals, including [...] HCFCs, which parties agreed to phase out by 2030, all but 0.5 percent being eliminated by 2020. MOP-4 also established an Implementation Committee that examines cases of possible noncompliance and makes recommendations to the MOP aimed at securing compliance.

During this period, the EC and United States completed a near reversal of their respective roles during the regime's development in the 1970s and 1980s. In 1993, the EC argued for the importance of eliminating all threats to the ozone layer as soon as possible when it began the first in a series of attempts to accelerate HCFC controls. Meanwhile, a veto coalition led by the United States and Australia argued that further restrictions on HCFCs would not reduce enough total damage to the ozone layer to justify the extra costs; it would prevent firms that had made significant, and good-faith, investments in HCFC technologies (as substitutes for CFCs) from recouping their investment; a significant proportion of the substitutes for HCFCs would be hydrofluorocarbons (HFCs), which are potent greenhouse gases manufactured almost exclusively by European companies; and other available measures would have a greater impact on the ozone layer. [...]

At MOP-11, held in Beijing in 1999, the EC finally secured US agreement to strengthen controls on HCFCs, albeit modestly. MOP-11 also agreed to phase out the production of bromochloromethane (a recently developed ozone-depleting chemical [...]). The Beijing amendment also bans trade in HCFCs with countries that do not ratify the 1992 Copenhagen amendment, which introduced the HCFC phaseout. [...]

The history of global ozone policy illustrates the role that veto coalitions play in weakening a regime as well as how veto states sometimes shift roles as a result of increasing scientific evidence, domestic political pressures, and changing economic interests. It is also the best example of a global environmental regime that has been continually strengthened in response to new scientific evidence and technological innovations.

Indeed, when one combines all the amendments and adjustments to the Montreal Protocol, the current set of binding controls is impressive. Industrialized countries were required to phase out halons by 1994; CFCs, carbon tetrachloride, methyl chloroform, and HBFCs by 1996; bromochloromethane by 2002, and methyl bromide by 2005 – although various exceptions exist. These parties must still phase

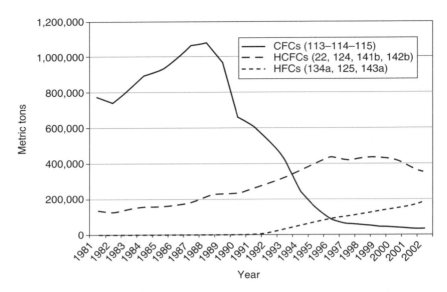

Figure 67.1   Worldwide Production of CFCs, HCFCs, and HFCs.
Data source: Alternative Fluorocarbons Environmental Acceptability Study (AFEAS),
"Production and Sales of Fluorocarbons," (Arlington, VA: RAND Environmental Science &
Policy Center, 2004). http://www.afeas.org/2002/production_2002.html.

out HCFCs by 2030 as well as meet important interim targets. Developing country
parties were required to phase out hydrobromofluorocarbons by 1996 and bromochloromethane by 2002. These parties must still phase out CFCs, halons, and
carbon tetrachloride by 2010; methyl chloroform and methyl bromide by 2015; and
the consumption of HCFCs by 2040.

The ozone regime stands as perhaps the strongest and most effective global environmental regime. The worldwide consumption of CFCs, which was about 1.1 million
tons in 1986, was approximately 100,000 tons in 2003. The Ozone Secretariat calculates
that without the Montreal Protocol, global CFC consumption would have reached
about 3 million tons in 2010 and 8 million tons in 2060, resulting in a 50 percent depletion of the ozone layer by 2035. (See fig. 67.1.) Most parties continue to meet their
commitments to reduce or eliminate production and consumption of ozone depleting
chemicals; as a result, atmospheric concentrations of these chemicals are declining
and, if all the mandated phaseouts are fully achieved (still a big "if"), the ozone layer
could fully recover during the twenty-first century. [...]

68

Forest Stewardship Council

Kristina Tamm Hallström and Magnus Boström

A forest crisis, existing since the late 1970s, served as a background for the market-based initiatives in forest policy during the 1990s. Such threats as tropical deforestation and loss of old-growth forests in temperate and boreal zones, as well as threats to biodiversity, ecological functions, and the land rights of indigenous people, fuelled social movements in their targeting of forest-related industries during the 1980s. Between 1980 and 1995, the planet lost 7% to 8% of the world's total tropical forests, an area roughly the size of Mexico. Intensive and escalating campaigning eventually led to a concerted effort among social and environmental nongovernmental organizations (NGOs), certain actors from forest-related industries, and a few other actors to establish the Forest Stewardship Council (FSC). The FSC was formally established in 1993 as an international nongovernmental association of individuals and organizations with the aim of promoting environmentally appropriate, socially beneficial, and economically viable management of the world's forests. The FSC has established a framework with principles and criteria from which accredited certification bodies can certify forests. Through chain-of-custody certification, the products that come from certified forests can be given the FSC label.

Fifteen years after its establishment, the FSC can report a positive trend in certified forests. By August 2008, FSC certification existed in 81 countries and covered roughly 10% of the world's managed forests. [...]

Original publication details: Kristina Tamm Hallström and Magnus Boström, *Transnational Multi-Stakeholder Standardization: Organizing Fragile Non-State Authority*. Cheltenham: Edward Elgar, 2010. pp. 44–7, 50–3, 56–8.

The Establishment of the FSC

Before forest certification and the establishment of the FSC

In the late 1970s, governments, international governmental organizations (IGOs), and environmental NGOs began to call for action at the international level to conserve forests, and in the 1980s public concern about deforestation increased considerably. In 1983, a first attempt to regulate the issue of deforestation was taken by timber-producing and timber-consuming countries in their International Tropical Timber Agreement, under the auspices of the UN Conference on Trade and Development, which entered into force in 1985. The agreement called for the establishment of an International Tropical Timber Organization (ITTO), which began operation in 1986. The agreement and the organization should, on the one hand, promote expansion of international trade in tropical timber and, on the other hand, encourage implementation of forest management systems that consider measures to conserve tropical forests. The ITTO and other UN units did contribute to a growing awareness of environmental problems, while simultaneously demonstrating an incapacity to solve or deal effectively with the global forest crises.

From the mid-1980s onwards, environmental NGOs sharpened their focus on forest issues in their global campaigning activities. Early on, Friends of the Earth (FoE) took initiatives by linking UK timber companies with tropical deforestation. Indigenous civil society groups in developing countries with tropical forests staged protests, and social movement organizations in northern countries targeted both governments and retailers in the Do-It-Yourself markets. '[T]he anti-DIY demonstrations proved to be highly successful and garnered considerable media and public attention. Customers began to write letters to the retailers and to confront store managers and employees with tough questions about timber sourcing.'

Boycott campaigning led some large private companies to stop using tropical forest products and many municipal governments in the UK, USA, Germany, and the Netherlands to ban the use of tropical forest products in their procurement policies. Yet, the new mobilizations, boycotts, and institution building did not lead to a reduction in deforestation rates. The WWF observed that the boycotting strategy led to a devaluation of the standing timber in tropical forests around the world, which in turn actually caused accelerating deforestation, as forests were cleared for farming, grazing, and building.

Another problem was the one-sided focus on tropical forests. In 1987, Friends of the Earth in the UK (FoE-UK) published the first edition of its *Good Wood Guide* and launched its *Seal of Approval* for dealers and retailers. Although it was one-sided in its total rejection of tropical timber, thereby implying that all other sources, such as temperate timbers, were environmentally benign, 'it set the scene for the next steps, and showed the potential power of the concept of identifying well-managed forests' as explained by Timothy Synnott, first Executive Director of the FSC.

Yet in spite of their best of intentions, environmental NGOs found that their campaign messages were being misinterpreted. 'By focusing on tropical timber, the message the general public understood, was "tropical timber is wrong and non-tropical timber is right".' Companies were being branded as contributing to forest destruction based solely on their use of tropical timber, and as their legitimacy was threatened, business actors began to search for solutions. Manufacturers created labels for their products, claiming sustainability of their forest sources. But as labels began to appear in abundance, confusion spread, and some manufactures and retailers expressed a willingness to learn more about the source of their raw materials.

In the late 1980s, FoE and other actors tried to encourage the ITTO to consider certification and labeling as mechanisms for improving tropical forest management. Although this topic was discussed for some time, no concrete results were produced. Some developing countries responded negatively, fearing that NGOs could introduce labeling as a disguised means of promoting timber boycotts. Others believed that certification was simply not feasible. A number of environmental NGOs concluded that the IGO process had been a failure that would not yield significant improvements in tropical forest management over an acceptable time horizon. Yet, certification and labeling had by now, through the discussions within this IGO, 'entered the consciousness of those interested in shaping global forestry management'.

Timothy Synnott, who also was a key founder of the FSC, summarized his reflections in his notes on the early years. According to him, the tensions within the ITTO showed:

> ... that workable and acceptable solutions would not arise unless representatives of all sectors participate equally in their formulation and design. They also showed how ITTO's abilities were constrained by restricting its mandate to tropical timber, and by its polarizing division into producing and consuming countries. These lessons were learned in the FSC, which was designed from the start to be open and participatory, for application in all forests, worldwide.

Something more sophisticated than the FoE's *Good Wood Guide* was needed, as the experience with this guide showed 'that a single campaigning NGO could not reliably identify sustainable sources, based on its own sources and policies, in an arena as complex as forest management. This demonstrated the need for criteria or standards, and *multi-stakeholder participation*' (our emphasis). [...]

The Standards, Organization, and Governance Structure

Although the FSC was formally established in October 1993, it operated for several months with no funds, staff, or office; and it was still two years away from attaining a legal status. In October 1995, the FSC was legally registered as a Mexican NGO, or Associación Civil (FSC AC). During the first years, 'the FSC framework was laid down: manuals, guidelines, protocols and contracts for certification bodies, National Initiatives and staff, together with the procedures for meetings: formal general assemblies, and less formal annual conferences and working groups.' [...]

The FSC standards, policies, and strategies

People from the FSC's core group wrote seven standard drafts, the sixth of which was broadly discussed during the national consultations. A firm conclusion of the consultations was that forest stewardship must be defined equally by environmental, economic, and social considerations; that the Principles and Criteria must apply equally to boreal, temperate, and tropical forests, defined by global principles but operating locally under ecosystem-specific standards; that these standards should apply equally to plantations and natural forests, and equally to small and large scale operations. And, as Synnott stated, 'the FSC programme has remained consistent with those conclusions ever since'. Indeed, the largest number of controversies did not seem to be on the exact formulation of the FSC standards, but on types of organizational issues we have mentioned previously.

The basic FSC standards are known as the FSC Principles and Criteria. The ten principles are the fundamental rules formulated at a general, abstract level, which are to be worked out in more concrete processes of standard setting and certification at the national or regional level. The criteria should clarify the application of the principles. Each comprises an aspect of a principle, quantitatively or qualitatively formulated. The criteria, as well, require considerable interpretation.

Another main component of the regulatory framework of the FSC is accreditation manuals covering both forest management and chain-of-custody certification, which are used to accredit certifiers. Certification is performed by an accredited certification body (for-profit or not-for-profit) which, in turn, must follow either a national/regional adjusted FSC standard or FSC's Principles and Criteria directly, in case such national- or regional-adjusted FSC standard is not in place.

As can be seen by browsing the FSC website, the FSC has, over time, developed and refined a huge number of associated standards, guidelines, policy documents, and strategies. Several interviewees from the FSC Secretariat maintain that standards and policies are being constantly revised in the light of new experience. It is possible to mention only a few key examples here. In his report, Synnott notes, among other things, the development of policies for percentage-based claims and the use of chemical pesticides (forbidden vs. restricted). It soon also became evident that Principle 9, on the maintenance of natural forests, was unsatisfactorily formulated and required revision, as the criteria provided insufficient guidance on the identification and management of the site, in order to ensure compliance with the principle. The phrase 'high conservation value' was eventually invented in this concretization work. The FSC's tenth principle on plantation, established in 1995, two years later than the other principles, has given rise to controversy, particularly regarding social aspects. And again, in 2004, the FSC launched a two-year Plantations Review process to accommodate increasing criticism raised by NGOs.

One important strategy has been the 'social strategy', launched because the FSC faced extra difficulties in fulfilling its social goals – problems regarding the fragmentation and underrepresentation of members from the social chamber, for instance (see also Chapter 8). Furthermore, the majority of FSC-certified forests appeared in the developed part of the world under the large forest companies, rather than in small family or community-based forestry. This outcome is ironic, as the FSC attempted from the beginning to encourage certification in developing countries and for small-scale operations. Preparing for certification is not without costs, however, and requires some level of administrative, management, and technical skill, as well as access to international market structures. One outcome of the social strategy is the FSC's Small and Low Intensity Management Forest (SLIMF) standards, as applied for example to community-managed forests operations. Although several of our interviewees appreciated this and other measures, most of them maintained that the problems remain, and, as stated in the current FSC global strategy, 'FSC has not made as much impact on small forest owners, community forests, or low intensity managed forests as was initially hoped.' [...]

The FSC's multi-stakeholder organizational form

The FSC was formally established as a membership organization, having both individuals and organizations as members. The FSC is governed by a General Assembly of members divided into three chambers (the environmental, the economic, and the social) – discursively affected by the concept of sustainable development and its three dimensions of social, environmental, and economic sustainability. Each chamber has one-third of the voting power. In addition, the voting power is divided equally between developed (northern) and developing (southern) country members in each of the three chambers. The main aims of the chosen organizational design are to ensure that no group can dominate policy-making and that the north cannot dominate at the expense of the south. The latter goal was deemed necessary because of the strong north-south controversies around tropical deforestation during the late 1980s, which arose again during the Rio summit in 1992. Furthermore, organizations were allotted 90% of the voting power and individuals 10% in each chamber. The General Assembly, which meets every third year (1996, 1999, 2002, 2005, 2008), is the highest decision-making organ. An affirmative vote of two-thirds of the voting power is required to adopt a motion.

The original organizational structure adopted in 1993 involved only two chambers: one with social and environmental interests that was accorded 75% of the votes; and one with economic interests, with 25% of votes. This was a compromise, instituted because some stakeholders at the founding assembly found it difficult to accept any formal decision-making power by economic interests. By 1996, however, the strongest criticism appeared to accumulate from the trade and industry players, which considered themselves underrepresented. The FSC was criticized for being 'anti-industry', and it responded in 1996 with the current tripartite structure. Many industry players, globally and nationally, still think that economic interests should have more than one-third of the voting power, because, at the end of the day, companies have the ultimate responsibility to implement the standards. Such criticism has led to the development of the competing certification schemes discussed later in this chapter.

Individual or organizational members of the FSC are categorized in accordance with the three chambers, and two existing FSC members are required to support applications for membership. FSC has been steadily growing from its inception. By May 2009 it had 827 members, 366 from developed ('northern') countries and 461 from developing ('southern') countries; 328 of the members belonged to the economic chamber, 346 to the environment chamber, and 153 to the social chamber. [...]

The FSC in the Transnational Regulatory Space – Countermoves and Relation to IGOs' Regulatory Frameworks

We have mentioned that the initiation and founding of the FSC gave rise to intensive critiques and controversies, some of which were channeled within the FSC system. According to Kwisthout, who was active from the start, radical environmental groups have been and remain serious critics of FSC. They do not believe in developing a dialogue or engaging in negotiations with large forest companies. Several interviewees mention Simon Counsell, and his NGO Rainforest Foundation in this regard. Counsell was engaged in the FoE and timber boycotting during the 1980s. He participated in the early FSC development, but would later appear primarily as a critic, raising serious concern over dubious FSC certificates. Later, he co-authored the well-known critical report, *Trading in Credibility. The myth and reality of the Forest Stewardship Council*, in which the topic of dubious FSC-certified forestry was discussed with reference to a number of case studies. Counsell is no longer a member of the FSC and eventually formed the FSC-Watch, which is an independent observer of the FSC developed by FSC supporters, members, and nonmembers concerned about what they perceive as 'the constant and serious erosion of the FSC's reliability and thus credibility'. The group critically examines several FSC certifications in a number of countries, and reports their results on its website. Its members argue that the FSC is increasingly captured by vested commercial interests (the economic chamber) and criticize the FSC's inability to address the problem, as well as its tendency to report only success stories.

The FSC initiative has also been controversial for a large number of business actors in the forest sector. Some forest companies have not accepted the invitation to participate in the FSC's tripartite structure, and have initiated competing processes and programs. One early counter-initiative taken by forest industries was to seek forest certification through environmental management systems (ISO 14001). In 1995, the Canadian and Australian standards bodies also proposed to ISO that a guide be prepared for the application of ISO 14001 in the forest sector. Greenpeace and other environmental NGOs opposed such initiatives, however, on the grounds that an environmental management system is an insufficient basis for claims of sustainability, because it lacks performance levels. They also criticized the lack of stakeholder participation in ISO that could allow credible discussions on sustainable forest management. The Canadian/Australian proposal was eventually withdrawn. According to one of our interviewees from an FSC-certified forest company, a new perspective regarding the relationship between ISO 14001 and the FSC, eventually emerged, and it came to be seen that the two standards were compatible rather than competing. In order to establish legitimacy as a global standard setter, it has also become important for the FSC to make certain references to ISO 65.

More challenging for the FSC has been the development of competing programs by forest-industry and forest-landowner associations in Canada, the USA, Europe, and most other countries in which the FSC is active. Such separate initiatives were later merged into the Programme for the Endorsement of Forest Certification (PEFC) schemes. These competing programs mirrored the ISO 14000 family, by emphasizing organizational procedures and discretionary, flexible performance guidelines, in contrast to the FSC's insistence on substantive, nondiscretionary, and fixed performance requirements. Moreover, these competing models were dominated by business interests, in contrast to the equal distribution of voting power among environmental, social, and business interests in the FSC. Their standards were narrower in scope, stressing only forestry management rules and continual improvement, whereas the FSC includes rules on labour and indigenous rights and wide-ranging environmental impact. [...]

69

Speech of the IPCC Chairman, Rajendra K. Pachauri, at the opening session of the World Economic Forum, Davos, Switzerland

Rajendra K. Pachauri

Distinguished Ladies & Gentlemen!

It is a unique privilege for me to speak before this august gathering at [a] time when the world needs to identify and address some formidable new challenges that face us. The year 2007 saw an unprecedented increase in awareness related to global warming and climate change. This explosion of knowledge and awareness resulted from a number of factors, not the least of which is the release of the Fourth Assessment Report of the Intergovernmental Panel on Climate Change (IPCC). The Norwegian Nobel Committee highlighted the threat of climate change to global peace by awarding the 2007 Nobel Peace Prize to the Panel and Mr. Al Gore. But today we also know on the basis of our reports that climate change, if unmitigated, can have serious implications for the economic well-being of human society. It would be convenient to submerge this reality under the financial problems the world is facing this week, but we would indeed be doing so at the peril of ignoring the world's most pressing problems.

The IPCC carries out comprehensive assessments of all aspects of climate change on an inclusive, transparent and objective basis. It accomplishes this by harnessing the best talent from round the globe, following a process of rigorous peer reviews and final acceptance of all reports by governments through a process of consensus.

Why has the latest report made such an impact on the minds of the public and of leaders drawn from different fields of endeavour and different regions of the world? The answer lies in the fact that knowledge and the science related to climate change have progressed substantially in the last six years since the Third Assessment Report

Original publication details: Rajendra K. Pachauri, "Speech of the IPCC Chairman, Rajendra K. Pachauri, at the opening session of the World Economic Forum, Davos, Switzerland," Geneva, Intergovernmental Panel on Climate Change, January 23, 2008.

(TAR) was released. Hence, our findings this time are stronger, the gaps in existing knowledge much narrower and uncertainties substantially lower. Some of the major findings from this report are:

1. "Warming of the climate system is unequivocal, as is now evident from observations of increases in average air and ocean temperatures, widespread melting of snow and ice, and rising average sea level".
2. Also much stronger and sharper is the finding related to the human influence on climate change as conveyed in the statement "Most of the observed increase in temperatures since the mid-20th century is very likely due to the increase in anthropogenic GHG concentrations".

However, despite the global community having agreed to combating anthropogenic climate change through universal acceptance of the UN Framework Convention on Climate Change (UNFCCC) as far back as in 1992, global GHG emissions continue to increase, with a substantial jump of 70% between 1970 and 2004. Within a long-term perspective the atmospheric concentrations of CO_2 and CH_4 in 2005 exceeded by far the natural range over the last 650,000 years. The last time the polar regions were significantly warmer than present for an extended period (about 125,000 years ago), reductions in polar ice volume led to 4 to 6 metres of sea level rise.

Global efforts to address the problem remain weak and inadequate, even as changes in climate become more serious. Eleven of the last twelve years rank among the twelve warmest years in the instrumental record of global surface temperature since 1850. Global average sea level has risen during the 20th century by about 17 cms, while average surface temperature increased by about 0.74 °. Over the 20th century precipitation increased significantly in eastern parts of North and South America, northern Europe and northern and central Asia, but declined in the Sahel, the Mediterranean, southern Africa and parts of southern Asia. It is likely that heat waves have become more frequent over most land areas. The frequency of heavy precipitation events has increased over most areas. There is observational evidence of an increase in intense tropical cyclone activity in the North Atlantic since about 1970.

We now have much stronger evidence of the impacts of climate change in relation to increases in average surface temperature as well as much greater understanding of these impacts across different regions. Water availability is being impacted by climate change such that while even with current levels of temperature increase water availability in the moist tropics and high latitudes will increase, it is likely to decrease in the mid latitudes and semi arid areas, with increase in droughts. Millions of people would be exposed to increased water stress due to climate change.

Anthropogenic warming could lead to some impacts that are abrupt or irreversible, depending upon the rate and magnitude of climate change. Partial loss of ice sheets on polar land and/or the thermal expansion of seawater over very long time scales could imply metres of sea level rise, major changes in coastlines and inundation of low-lying areas, with greatest effects in river deltas and low-lying islands. Particularly vulnerable would be the megadeltas of Asia, which include cities like Shanghai, Dhaka and Kolkata. It is estimated that 20–30% of the species assessed would be at increased risk of extinction if increases in global average temperature exceed 1.5 to

2.5 °C. As global average temperature increase exceeds about 3.5 °C, model projections suggest significant extinctions (40–70% of species assessed) around the globe.

Some of the impacts of climate change are already translating into monetary flows and expenditure as brought out by payments made by the insurance industry. For instance, economic losses attributed to natural disasters have increased from US$75.5 billion in the 1960s to US$659.9 billion in the 1990s. Losses to insurers from natural disasters nearly doubled in 2007 to just below $30 billion globally according to risk records. From 1980 through 2004, the global economic costs of weather-related events totaled $1.4 trillion (inflation-corrected), of which $340 billion was insured.

Far more important than the aggregate impacts of climate change on global economic activity are the consequences for some of the most vulnerable communities across the globe. In Africa, between 75 and 250 million people are projected to be exposed to increased water stress due to climate change by 2020. In the same year, in some countries yields from rainfed agriculture could be reduced by up to 50%. Agricultural production, including access to food, in many African countries would be severely compromised. This would further adversely affect food security and exacerbate malnutrition. Worldwide the health status of millions of people is projected to be affected through, for example, increases in malnutrition; increased deaths, diseases and injury due to extreme weather events; increased burden of diarrhoeal diseases; increased frequency of cardio-respiratory diseases; and other impacts.

The inertia in the climate system is such that even if we were to stabilize the concentration of greenhouse gases (GHGs) in the atmosphere today, climate change would continue for decades. Hence, measures for adapting to the impacts of climate change are urgent and inevitable. However, it is only through appropriate mitigation measures that many impacts can be avoided, reduced or delayed. The IPCC has found that the costs of even stringent mitigation measures would be modest. For achieving a scenario of stabilized temperature increase of 2.0 to 2.4 °C, the cost to the global economy would be around 0.12% per annum, amounting to a loss of less than 3.0% of the GDP by 2030 and less than 5.5% by 2050. Comparing the costs of mitigation with avoided damages would require the reconciliation of welfare impacts on people living in different places and at different points of time into a global aggregate measure of well-being. What other forum would be more suitable for exercising its wisdom, knowledge and enlightenment than this one for defining a strategy for global society to act in response to projected climate change?

Such a strategy must be based on stringent mitigation of emissions of GHGs, through policy measures that lead to development and dissemination of low carbon technologies across the board, paramount among which would be an appropriate price on carbon. The benefits from this go beyond the field of climate change, with substantial benefits in the form of higher levels of energy security, lower pollution at the local level and attendant health benefits. At the same time, the global community has to provide adequate resources for creating capacity and infrastructure for adapting to the impacts of climate change in some of the poorest and most vulnerable communities. Business and industry will, therefore, need to work with governments, civil society and knowledge organizations at an unprecedented level in creating actions and opportunities for themselves and society as a whole. Economic activities will consequently move rapidly towards a low carbon future. Those companies and entities that establish a lead in this endeavour would meet with success in both a business and a societal context. Those that lag behind would suffer the risk of losses in the marketplace and loss of prestige and reputation. The same observation can be applied to nations and governments. There would be dramatic loss of political power and influence for nations that stand unmoved by the growing global consensus for "deep cuts" in emissions of GHGs with a sense of urgency.

If action to tackle the threat of climate change emerges soon, driven by knowledge of where we are heading, as provided by the findings of the IPCC, there would be reason for optimism that other serious challenges facing the world may also evoke similar responses based on rational assessments of problems and knowledge driven solutions. In meeting the threat of climate change we would, therefore, be creating a precedent that would provide the lead in meeting other global challenges that appear prominently on the horizon.

Part XI Questions

1. What makes a social problem global? Discuss features of the contemporary world that make it increasingly likely that problems will be considered global rather than national, regional, or local in character.
2. Given that global civil society organizations lack formal authority and usually have little money or other resources, why do states and intergovernmental organizations (IGOs) pay any attention to them? What is it about international non-governmental organizations (INGOs) and similar bodies that makes them influential with respect to global issues?
3. Are global environmental organizations necessary? How do you think transnational corporations would behave if they were not being constantly scrutinized by groups like EarthAction, Greenpeace, and the World Wildlife Fund? Is there reason to believe that corporations would try to limit the environmental damage they do if there were no environmental INGOs?
4. Wapner says that Greenpeace depends on "visually spectacular" actions to get attention and put environmental problems on the global agenda. Do such actions have any drawbacks? Think about how they may both promote environmentalism and hurt the environmentalist cause.
5. The antilogging campaign in Sarawak was not able to protect the rain forests there, according to Keck and Sikkink. Why? What lessons can you draw from this case about how environmental action can be effective? What else could have been done that might have led to more success for this effort?
6. Outline the process described by Khagram that eventually made big dams an important global issue. Why was the International Rivers Network important in this process? Why did the movement target the World Bank? What effects has the movement had, and how was the creation of the World Commission on Dams important for global governance with respect to dams?
7. In Chasek, Downie, and Brown's description of the ozone depletion issue, what factors made this a global concern? Why did some states initially oppose action

to reduce the use of chlorofluorocarbons (CFCs) and other ozone-depleting chemicals? How and why did the position of some states change over time? How successful has the effort to reduce ozone depletion been?

8. In their discussion of the Forest Stewardship Council (FSC), Tamm Hallström and Boström say that environmentalists were critical of the International Tropical Timber Organization as a solution to the deforestation problem. Why? In what ways does the FSC offer a more satisfactory approach to forest issues, according to environmental INGOs? Given the structure and capabilities of the FSC, is it likely to have beneficial effects? Explain both its strengths and its weaknesses.

9. What are the major findings of the Intergovernmental Panel on Climate Change, as presented by IPCC Chair Rajendra Pachauri? What threats to human life and well-being does he discuss? What measures should be taken to deal with these threats? Would these measures be prohibitively expensive, in his account?

Part XII

Alternative Globalization and the Global Justice Movement

Introduction

After the tumultuous protests in 1999 directed at the World Trade Organization conference in Seattle, meetings of international financial institutions and leaders became the prime targets of people and groups opposed to their policies. Large demonstrations decrying globalization were organized across Europe. In 2001, groups critical of globalization gathered in Porto Alegre, Brazil, for the World Social Forum, which became an annual counterpoint to the elite World Economic Forum held in Davos, Switzerland. Initially, the groups behind these and similar actions were described as the antiglobalization movement, and they signaled an important shift in both popular and scholarly views of globalization. The generally positive, at times even exuberant tone of discussions of globalization in the 1990s was swept aside by a global backlash. Globalization, the critics said, was hardly a panacea for the world's ills; it was in fact the main culprit behind many global problems. For groups engaged in this backlash, globalization has a particular meaning: it is primarily an economic force, emanating from the West, that imposes an unjust, unequal, and environmentally harmful capitalist system on the world to the detriment of local cultures and democratic self-control. This critical view has shaped subsequent global discourse about globalization. To some extent, globalization now is what its critics make of it.

The antiglobalization label turned out to be a poor fit, not least because many features of globalization – including world-spanning communication and transportation systems, the global monetary system, and world science and knowledge dissemination – are crucial to the movement, which itself is decidedly global. As the movement became more coherent and interconnected, the term "alternative globalization" began to displace the original label, reflecting a succinct phrase habitually invoked by the movements' members, "Another world is possible." The core problem was not globalization as such but the kind of globalization

The Globalization Reader, Fifth Edition. Edited by Frank J. Lechner and John Boli.
Editorial material and organization © 2015 John Wiley & Sons, Ltd.
Published 2015 by John Wiley & Sons, Ltd.

promoted by transnational corporations (TNCs), global finance, and elite capitalist classes. This form of globalization was the major source of inequality, exploitation, and oppression in the world, and only a determined global justice movement could begin to ameliorate capitalism's destructive and discriminatory consequences.

The alternative globalization and global justice movement encompasses many groups, from students protesting athletic apparel produced in sweatshops to peasants resisting transnational corporate control of their land and seeds; from indigenous groups defending their forest habitat to religious leaders seeking debt relief for developing countries; from labor unions concerned about the impact of free trade to feminists opposed to trafficking in young women. Transforming globalization can take many forms, and the alternative globalization movement is nothing if not diverse. This diversity reflects the fact that, for many people, "globalization" has become an all-purpose pejorative term. As a result, a wide range of problems are now routinely attributed to globalization and groups pursuing disparate goals increasingly unite behind the alternative globalization banner, making it difficult to articulate a widely supported alternative. But, as the readings in this part confirm, to describe the movement simply as resistance to, or an unthinking rejection of, globalization is to underestimate the global intent they share, which is to remake world society in accordance with principles that often conflict with established institutions.

At least some of those principles, such as equality and justice, derive from a long-standing socialist and social-democratic tradition of opposition to the harsh consequences of modernizing change – including efforts in many countries to reform, or humanize, capitalist development. In many ways, that tradition has been absorbed into the global backlash, which also includes radical nationalist and fundamentalist groups more commonly associated with the political right (whose complaints are, of course, quite different from those of groups on the left). Though the alternative globalization agenda is broader than that of older leftist movements, it has inspired such older groups and their successors to devote considerable resources to the effort. Thus, at the World Social Forum and the regional forums that it has spawned, participants include labor union leaders, peace groups, left-leaning politicians, and women's rights groups, alongside representatives of newer social movements, such as indigenous peoples, farmworkers, environmentalists, gay and lesbian rights advocates, and so on.

Not surprisingly, in light of the readings in Part VII, INGOs are especially prominent in the alternative globalization movement. Much critical energy is generated by these border-transcending voluntary associations that involve experts, activists, and dues-paying members. They attempt to focus public attention on global problems and build support for new policies to resolve them. Though capitalist globalization led by TNCs is a primary target, movement INGOs also aim their fire at states and IGOs. For example, the group Jubilee 2000, illustrated in a reading in Part IX, put pressure on developed countries to forgive the debts of developing countries; the French-based group ATTAC has advocated that countries impose the so-called "Tobin tax" on short-term capital movements across borders; the Seattle protesters in 1999 demanded new rules for international trade from the WTO; and the sweatshop apparel campaign has targeted the labor practices used by corporations such as Nike. These examples further indicate that the alternative globalization movement is hardly limited to rhetorical symbolic politics; its various component groups and supporters have also proposed numerous specific policies. A common denominator in their proposals is the idea that global justice requires global governance, especially greater regulation of global economic activity.

Throughout this book, we have presented examples of scholars, activists, and organizations critical of globalization. For example, Joseph E. Stiglitz's opposition to "market fundamentalism" is a widely shared view. Amartya Sen's concern for a more equitable distribution of resources is a key goal for the overall movement as well. The readings in Part XI on the environment similarly express themes that resonate with alternative globalization activists. In this part, we offer selections that further illustrate the efforts to challenge and restructure globalization.

American sociologist Peter Evans offers a way to think about the resistance to globalization. Its critics challenge the notion that "neoliberal" globalization is a natural, generic process and oppose it by engaging in "counterhegemonic" globalization. He thinks of women's, labor, and environmental movements as three "families" within this joint global effort. The selection briefly illustrates how each tries to blend old themes with new strategies and to achieve global solidarity while holding on to local roots. Over all, Evans thinks the cultural and ideological impact of globalization critics is growing.

Belgian sociologist Geoffrey Pleyers follows with a more detailed history of the global justice movement. After "mobilizations against neoliberalism" in the 1990s, the movement became more organized around 2001, but its early ascendance gave way to what Pleyers calls a hesitant phase after 2005. A common critique of neoliberal economic ideology, and the failure of that ideology's proponents to address poverty and inequality, unifies the movement. In Pleyers's view, it focuses on three tendencies or alternative programs: new advocacy networks, local initiatives, and support for progressive regimes.

One of the best-known alternative globalization figures, Filipino author and activist Walden Bello, presents his views regarding the imperative of "deglobalization" in the next selection. In this interview, Bello sharply critiques the World Trade Organization for policies that he sees as highly detrimental to the "global South." The WTO, he says, is an undemocratic and opaque tool of American and other capitalist interests whose policies benefit only the developed countries. He calls for a decentralized global governance system in which grassroots groups and popular movements have a much larger voice and the "one-policy-fits-all" approach of the current system is abandoned in favor of a more flexible system that allows disadvantaged countries to adopt policies suited to their particular circumstances. He also offers some thoughts on how the alternative globalization movement could reconcile its internal conflicts, not least through the highly inclusive World Social Forum (below).

Vandana Shiva, a prominent Indian author and activist, speaks for many critics when she describes globalization as a normative and political process forced on the weak by the powerful. "Liberalizing" the world economy actually means enhancing state and corporate power. Globalization also leads to a kind of environmental apartheid, as the North relocates pollution-intensive and hazardous-waste industries in the South. But Shiva finds hope in "people's movements" for community rights and biodiversity. Subcommandante Marcos represents one such movement, the Zapatista rebel group in southern Mexico. Addressing a gathering of supporters, he frames his group's struggle as "for humanity and against neoliberalism" – for "plural, different, inclusive" humanity, against the "brutal, universal, complete world war" of neoliberal globalization. He calls for a "network of voices" engaged in rebellion against global power.

One key node in that network of voices is the World Social Forum. An annual gathering of alternative globalization groups of many sorts, its speakers, lecturers, and workshops maintain a steady drumbeat of criticism of neoliberal globalization. The World Social Forum's initial "Call for Mobilisation" attacks "the hegemony of finance, the destruction of cultures, the monopolization of knowledge, mass media and communication, [and] the degradation of nature" brought about by contemporary capitalism. The Forum aims to energize a broad movement that works for global "equity, social justice, democracy and security for everyone" through "participative democratic experiences."[1]

Citing the main slogan of the alternative globalization movement, our final selection, by the International Forum on Globalization, seeks to show more specifically how "another world is possible." Rejecting unbridled liberalization and the commodification of the global commons, it envisions a new form of global economic democracy built on principles of subsidiarity, human rights, common heritage, diversity, and equity.

Note

1.   World Social Forum, "Call for Mobilisation," March 2001, Porto Alegre, Brazil.

70

Counterhegemonic Globalization
Transnational Social Movements in the Contemporary Political Economy

Peter Evans

When people invoke "globalization," they usually mean the prevailing system of transnational domination, which is more accurately called "neoliberal globalization," "corporate globalization," or perhaps "neoliberal, corporate-dominated globalization." Sometimes they are referring to a more generic process – the shrinking of space and increased permeability of borders that result from falling costs of transportation and revolutionary changes in technologies of communication. Often the two are conflated.

Implicit in much of current discourse on globalization is the idea that the particular system of transnational domination that we experience today is the "natural" (indeed inevitable) consequence of exogenously determined generic changes in the means of transportation and communication. A growing body of social science literature and activist argumentation challenges this assumption. Arguing instead that the growth of transnational connections can potentially be harnessed to the construction of more equitable distributions of wealth and power and more socially and ecologically sustainable communities, this literature and argumentation raises the possibility of what I would like to call "counterhegemonic globalization." Activists pursuing this perspective have created a multifaceted set of transnational networks and ideological frames that stand in opposition to contemporary neoliberal globalization. Collectively they are referred to as the "global justice movement." For activists and theorists alike,

Original publication details: Peter Evans, "Counterhegemonic Globalization: Transnational Social Movements in the Contemporary Global Political Economy," in *The Handbook of Political Sociology: States, Civil Societies, and Globalization*, ed. Thomas Janoski, Robert R. Alford, Alexander M. Hicks, and Mildred A. Schwartz. Cambridge: Cambridge University Press, 2005. pp. 655, 658–60, 662–4, 665, 666–7, 668.

these movements have become one of the most promising political antidotes to a system of domination that is increasingly seen as effectual only in its ability to maintain itself in power.

Although the growth of membership and political clout of transnational social movements is hard to measure, the burgeoning of their formal organizational reflections – transnational NGOs – is well-documented. Their numbers have doubled between 1973 and 1983 and doubled again between 1983 and 1993. Perhaps even more important than their quantitative growth has been their ability to seize oppositional imaginations. From the iconic images of Seattle to the universal diffusion of the World Social Forum's vision that "another world is possible," the cultural and ideological impact of these movements has begun to rival that of their corporate adversaries. [...]

The New Organizational Foundations of Counterhegemonic Globalization

Here I will focus on three broad families of transnational social movements aimed at counterhegemonic globalization: labor movements, women's movements, and environmental movements. Each of these movements confronts the dilemmas of using transnational networks to magnify the power of local movements without redefining local interests, of transcending the North–South divide, and of leveraging existing structures of global power without becoming complicit in them. Looking at the three movements together is useful because it highlights the ways in which surmounting these challenges might produce common strategies and possibilities for alliances among them. [...]

It is only a partial caricature to propose that the origins of the World Social Forum, which now arguably represents the largest single agglomeration of South-based organizations and activists, began as a sort of joint venture between ATTAC and the Brazilian Workers Party (Partido dos Trabalhadores or PT). Because the founding vision of the PT's organizers was of a classic Marxist socialist mobilizational party, the party's involvement in the World Social Forum is further confirmation of the extent to which "counterhegemonic globalization" has its roots in both quotidian struggles for dignity and economic security in the workplace and classic agendas of social protection in which the machinery of the nation-state is heavily implicated.

Even unsystematic participant observation of the meetings of the World Social Forum in Porto Alegre, Brazil confirms this hypothesis. The fact that the Workers Party controls the municipal administration of a major city and has (until the 2002 elections) controlled the state government as well has been essential to enabling the infrastructural investments that make a global meeting of thousands of participants and hundreds of oppositional groups from around the globe possible. At the same time, in part because of Workers Party sponsorship, both local and transnational trade unions play a major role in the WSF.

All of this suggests that counterhegemonic globalization is not as "postmodern" as its adherents (and detractors) sometimes argue. To the contrary, rescuing traditional social democratic agendas of social protection, which are otherwise in danger of disappearing below the tide of neoliberal globalization, is a significant part of the agenda of both ATTAC and the World Social Forum. At the same time, it would be a mistake to dismiss counterhegemonic globalization as simply "old wine in new bottles." […]

Labor as a Global Social Movement

Emblematic of the contemporary global neoliberal regime is the effort to reconstruct employment as something closer to a spot market in which labor is bought and sold with only the most minimal expectations regarding a broader employment relationship. Around the globe – from Mumbai to Johannesburg, Shanghai to the Silicon Valley – jobs are being informalized, outsourced, and generally divorced from anything that might be considered a social contract between employer and employee.

Precisely because the attack on the idea of labor as a social contract is generalized across all regions of the world, it creates a powerful basis for generating global labor solidarity. I illustrate the point with two examples: the emerging relations of effective mutual support that join metalworkers in Brazil and Germany and the successful leveraging of transnational solidarity by the International Brotherhood of Teamsters (IBT) in the 1997 UPS strike. In addition to demonstrating again that the "geography of jobs" perspective cannot explain transnational relations among labor movements, these cases also further illustrate how the corporate structures that form the carapace of the global economy contain political opportunities as well as threats.

The long-term collaboration between IG Metal in Germany and the Brazilian Metalworkers affiliated with CUT (Central Unica dos Trabalhadores) provides a good example. In 2001, when IG Metal was starting its spring offensive in Germany, the members of the Brazilian Metalworkers union (CUT) working for Daimler–Chrysler sent their German counterparts a note affirming that they would not accept any increased work designed to replace lost production in Germany. This action grows out of a long-term alliance between the two unions that exploits transnational corporate organizational structures for counterhegemonic purposes and has proven to be of practical value to the Brazilian autoworkers in their struggle to maintain some semblance of a social contract in their employment relations. For example, in the previous year when workers at Volkswagen's biggest factory in Brazil went on strike trying to reverse job cuts, Luiz Marinho, president of CUT VW, was able to go to VW's world headquarters and negotiate directly with management there, bypassing the management of the Brazilian subsidiary, and producing an agreement that restored the jobs.

The successful 1997 UPS strike offers a North–North example of how transnational alliances can be built around the idea of social contract. One element in the victory was a very effective global strategy, one that took advantage of previously underexploited strengths in their own global organization – the International Transport Workers Federation (ITF). Through the ITF, a World Council of UPS unions was created – which decided to mount a "World Action Day" in 150 job actions or demonstrations around the world. A number of European unions took action in support of the US strikers.

Why were the Europeans so willing to take risks for the sake of solidarity with the IBT in the United States? The answer was summarized in one of the ITF's leaflets. "UPS: importing misery from America." UPS was seen as representing the intrusion of the "American Model" of aggressive antiunion behavior, coupled with the expansion of part-time and temporary jobs with low pay and benefits and the use of subcontracting. The Europeans also knew that they had a much better chance of reining in UPS operating in concert with the 185,000 unionized UPS workers in the United States than they would ever have alone. Solidarity made sense and the logic of competition based on the geography of jobs made no sense.

Although defending the idea of the employment relation as a social contract is a project that will draw broad sympathy, the actual organizational efforts remain largely internal to organized labor. Other global social movements may be ideologically supportive, but not likely to be mobilized. Given the fact that those who enjoy the privilege of a formal employment relationship with union representation is a shrinking minority of the global population, the success of labor as a global social movement depends on being able to complement "social contract" and "basic rights" campaigns with other strategies that have the potential of generating broad alliances with a range of other social movements. [...]

Building a feminist movement without borders

While the transnational women's movement also has a long history, global neoliberalism has brought issues of gender to the forefront of transnational social movement organizations in a dramatic way. Until there has been a revolutionary transformation of gender roles, the disadvantages of allocating resources purely on the basis of market logic will fall particularly harshly on women. The UNDP talks of a global "care deficit," pointing out that women spend most of their working hours on unpaid care work and adding that "the market gives almost no rewards for care." Others have pointed out the extent to which "structural adjustment" and other neoliberal strategies for global governance contain a built-in, systematic gender bias. Consequently, it is almost impossible to imagine a movement for counterhegemonic globalization in which a transnational women's movement did not play a leading role.

At first glance, women's organizations have an advantage over transnational labor movements in that they do not have to transcend a zero-sum logic equivalent to that of the "geography of jobs" which would put the gendered interests of women in one region in conflict with those in another region. Perhaps for that reason, the transnational women's movement has been in the vanguard of transnational social movements in the attention that it has devoted to struggles over how to bridge the cultural and political aspects of the North–South divide and how to avoid the potential dangers of difference-erasing universalist agendas.

Like the labor movement, the women's movement's ideological foundations are rooted in a discourse of "human rights," but transnational feminism, much more than in the labor movement, has wrestled with the contradictions of building politics around the universalistic language of rights. Although no one can ignore the ways in which demanding recognition that "women's rights are human rights" has helped empower oppressed and abused women across an incredible gamut of geographic, cultural, and class locations, any earlier naïve assumptions that there was a single "one size fits all" global feminist agenda have been replaced by appreciation that the goal is much more complex.

On the one hand, the adoption of CEDAW (Convention on the Elimination of All Forms of Discrimination Against Women) by the UN might be considered the normative equivalent of the environmental movement's victories in the Montreal Accord to limit CFCs and the Kyoto Accord on global warming. On the other hand, critical feminists have examined UN activities like the 1995 Beijing World Conference on Women and accused them of perpetuating colonialist power relations under the guise of transnational unity. Mohanty summarizes the conundrum nicely: "The challenge is to see how differences allow us to explain the connections and border crossings better and more accurately, how specifying difference allows us to theorize universal concerns more fully." [...]

The numerically predominant situation of women in the global economy is one of precarious participation in the "informal economy" – a vast arena in which the traditional organizational tools of the transnational labor movement are least likely to be effective. Women in the informal sector experience the insecurity and lack of "social contract" that appear to be the neoliberal destiny of all but a small minority of the workforce, regardless of gender. If members of established transnational unions like the metalworkers are to succeed in building general political support for defending the "social contract" aspects of their employment relation, their struggles must be combined with an equally aggressive effort to expand the idea of the social contract into the informal sector. Insofar as the women's movement's campaigns around livelihood issues have focused particularly on the informal sector, it might be considered the vanguard of the labor movement as well as a leading strand in the movement for counterhegemonic globalization more generally.

One response to the challenge of the informal sector has been the diffusion of the "Self-employed Women's Association" (SEWA) as an organizational form, starting in India and spreading to South Africa, Turkey, and other countries in Latin America, Southeast Asia, and Africa, and eventually creating incipient international networks such as "Homenet" and "Streetnet." This is not only a novel form of labor organization. Because the archetypal site of informal sector employment is among the least-privileged women of the global South, it is simultaneously an organizational form that should help build the kind of "feminism without borders" that Mohanty argues is necessary to transcend the contradictions that have divided the international women's movement in the past.

Global and local environmentalism

Environmental stewardship is almost by definition a collective issue and therefore an issue that should lend itself to collective mobilization. Even neoclassical economic theory recognizes that environmental degradation is an externality that markets may not resolve, especially if the externalities are split across national political jurisdictions. Thus, environmental movements have advantages, both relative to mobilization around labor issues, which neoliberal ideology strongly claims must be resolved through market logic if welfare is to be maximized, and relative to women's movements, which are still bedeviled by claims that these issues are "private" and therefore not an appropriate target for collective political action (especially note collective political action that spills across national boundaries).

The obstacles to trying to build a global environmental movement are equally obvious. To begin with, there is the formidable gap that separates the South's "environmentalism of the poor," in which sustainability means above all else sustaining the ability of resource-dependent local communities to extract livelihoods from their natural surroundings, and the "conservationist" agenda of traditional Northern environmental groups, which favors the preservation of fauna and flora without much regard for how this conservation impacts the livelihoods of surrounding communities. The North–South divide in the global environmental movement may be less susceptible to being portrayed as "zero-sum" than in the "geography of jobs" perspective on the labor movement, but the logic of division appears more difficult to surmount than in the case of transnational feminism.

Even aside from the difficulties of superseding North–South divisions, integrating local and global concerns appears more daunting in the environmental arena. Some issues – such as global warming and the ozone layer – seem intrinsically global, whereas the politics of others, such as the health consequences of toxic dumps, can be intensely local. The challenges of building a global organization that effectively integrates locally focused activities with global campaigns would seem particularly challenging in the case of the environmental movement.

Despite the structural challenges it faces, the global environmental movement is usually considered among the most successful of the transnational social movements. How do we explain the relative success of transnational movements with environmental agendas? The first point to be made is how strikingly parallel the political assets of the global environmental movement are to those of the labor and women's movements, despite the obvious differences among them. This is true both of ideological resources and institutional ones. Once again, we see a counterhegemonic movement leveraging the ideas and organizational structures implanted by hegemonic globalization.

As in the case of the labor and women's movements, political clout depends on the global diffusion of a universalistic ideology affirming the value of the movement's agenda. As the labor and women's movements are able to leverage the ideological power of abstract concepts like "human rights" and "democracy," environmentalists can claim an impeccable universal agenda of "saving the planet" and invoke "scientific analysis" as validating their positions. As in the other two cases, these ideological resources are worth little without organizational structures that can exploit them and without complementary mobilization around quotidian interests. Nonetheless, the point is that once again, hegemonic ideological propositions are not simply instruments of domination; they are also a "toolkit" that can be used in potentially powerful ways for "subversive" ends.

The possibility of using governance structures that are part of hegemonic globalization also applies in the case of the environmental movement. Even more than in the case of the women's movement, the UN system has proved an extremely valuable institutional resource. As in the case of the women's movement, global conferences organized by the UN have played a crucial role both in helping to solidify transnational networks and to promote and diffuse discursive positions. [...]

The intensive, widespread, decades-old debate over how to make sure that the women's movement fully reflects the perspectives and interests of its largest constituency (disprivileged women in the global South) rather than its most powerful members (elite women in the global North) appears to have a harder time getting traction in the transnational environmental movement.

The fact that the "scientific analysis" paradigm provides significant advantage to environmentalists in battles against degradation by corporate (and state) polluters may become a disadvantage when it comes to engaging in internal debates over competing visions within the transnational environmental movement, making it easier for Northern activists to assume that the solutions to environmental issues in the South can be "objectively" defined from afar rather than having to emerge out of debate and discussion with those immediately involved. None of this is to suggest that the environmental movement is doomed to go astray or end up fragmented. The point is that just as there is no "natural logic" that dictates the inevitability of a corporate neoliberal trajectory for globalization, even the most successful counter-hegemonic movements have no functionalist guardian angels that will prevent them from undercutting their own potential. [...]

71

The Global Justice Movement

Geoffrey Pleyers

[...]

A Brief History of the Global Justice Movement

The global justice movement has passed through three periods up until now. Local and national mobilizations against neoliberalism occupied the first period, with "water and gas wars" in Bolivia and South Korean workers' movements as well as the Zapatista rebellion in Mexico and the Indian farmers struggle against the WTO. The globality of the movement was readily apparent, particularly during mobilizations organized around global events, the most publicized of which was in Seattle, protesting the third ministerial of the WTO in 1999. Committed intellectuals also played a major role in alerting the public to the social consequences of free trade and challenging the hegemonic Washington Consensus. They initiated civil society networks, which became a feature of the global justice movement, such as ATTAC, Global Trade Watch, the Transnational Institute and Focus on the Global South. Other global coalitions created during this period include the World March of Women, Jubilee South and Via Campiness, which claims to bring together over 100 million small farmers.

Original publication details: Geoffrey Pleyers, "The Global Justice Movement", *Globality Studies Journal* 19, July 1, 2010, pp. 1–14. GSJ is published by the Center for Global & Local History, Stony Brook University. Copyright © GSJ & Author. Reproduced with permission from G. Pleyers. Note: This analysis is developed in Pleyers, G. (2010) *Alter-Globalization. Becoming Actors in the Global Age*, Cambridge, Polity.

These heterogeneous actors gathered at the first World Social Forum (WSF), held in Porto Alegre in January 2001. It marked the beginning of the second phase, as the movement became organized around Social Forums at the local, national, continental, and global level. These meetings were oriented less towards resistance than to bringing together global justice activists from different parts of the world, in some cases with the aim of developing alternative programs. The 2002 European Social Forum in Florence, the 2004 WSF in Mumbai, and the 2005 WSF in Porto Alegre marked three high points of this period of the global justice movement. They were remarkable for their size, their openness to a wide range of civil society sectors and political cultures, and for the active participation of grassroots activists involved in both global justice organization and discussions dealing with thematic issues.

Although many columnists proclaimed the movement dead in the aftermath of September 11, 2001, maintaining that the "War on Terror" had replaced economic globalization as the central issue, this period was a golden age for the global justice movement. From 2000 to 2005, it grew rapidly on every continent. There were 50,000 demonstrators in Seattle in 1999. A year and a half later, 300,000 marched against the G-8 in Genoa in July 2001; the same number in Barcelona in March 2002 at a European summit; a million in Florence in November 2002 at the closing of the first European Social Forum (ESF); and 12 million worldwide against the war in Iraq on 15 February 2003, a global day of action initiated by global justice networks. The number of participants in the yearly World Social Forum climbed from 12,000 in 2001 to 50,000, 100,000, 120,000, and 170,000 successively until 2005. After its success in Brazil, the World Social Forum moved to India in 2004 and the Social Forum evolved to spawn many hundreds of forums at the local, national, and continental levels. While global justice activists opposed the war in Iraq between 2002 and 2004, the struggle against neoliberal ideology remained their top priority. The global justice movement managed to win over public opinion in several countries and, surprisingly, some right-wing politicians and representatives of the World Bank asked to take part in the WSF in Porto Alegre.

After an impressive ascendant phase from 1995 to 2005 – albeit with setbacks and retreats – the global movement, after several unsuccessful events, entered a hesitant phase. The global justice movement has expanded geographically, but at the same time the 2006 "Polycentric" WSF held in Bamako, Caracas, and Karachi and the 2007 WSF in Nairobi were in many respects less successful than previous events. With a reduced audience (15,000 to 50,000 fewer), these forums were also less socially and economically diverse. The integration of grassroots activists diminished, while NGOs and activists who supported formal political actors and regimes became more prominent. Some major global justice organizations disappeared (e.g. the "Movimiento de Resistencia Global" in Barcelona) or were less active (e.g. ATTAC, many social centres in Italy and the Wombles in the UK). Paradoxically, global justice actors had a difficult time adapting to the new skepticism about neoliberalism they had brought about. In addition, the ever-increasing use of the internet led to a decline in the importance of civil society organizations. The movement now mostly relies on loose-knit networks of groups, small organizations, media sources, and individual activists.

The geography of the movement has evolved considerably. New dynamic poles have emerged, while some of the former Western European strongholds have declined. The social forum dynamic has been reinforced in regions that are symbolically or strategically important (North America, the Maghreb, sub-Saharan Africa, South Korea). An enthusiastic acceptance of the global justice ideas and forums has not diminished in Latin America, as is attested by the adoption of anti-neoliberal policies by several heads of state in the region and the participation of 130,000 activists in the WSF held at Belem, Brazil, in January 2009. This forum, held in the Amazon region, also provides an illustration of the growing importance of environmental concerns in the global movement, which have become stronger before and during the World Summit on Climate in Copenhagen and then the "People Summit against Global Warming" in Cochabamba, Bolivia. Twenty-five thousand people from 147 countries joined the conference called by Evo Morales, among which were many indigenous people.

A Movement Against the Neoliberal Ideology

Since the mid-1990s, global justice activists have contested the neoliberal ideology, questioning its axioms and its efficiency. Dominant since the elections of M. Thatcher and R. Reagan, neoliberalism became hegemonic in the Gramscian sense – i.e. able to impose itself as "natural" and "without alternative" – in the early 1990s. It then set forth its view concerning the meaning of globalization, connecting the progressive transition to a global society to the image of a self-regulated global economy, beyond intervention by policy makers. Neoliberalism and its "Washington Consensus agenda" promote free capital movements, monetarism and a minimal state. It favors the implementation of a purely economic rationality, liberated from all obstacles stemming from regulations designed to moderate the economic system.

Global justice activists saw that the battle against neoliberalism plays out primarily in the realm of ideas and that ideological change is the basis for sustainable social transformation. *"From the point of view of development, it is not so much money which counts, as ideas."* Their success in challenging the dominant ideology is based on testing whether neoliberalism has lived up to its own values of democracy and scientific rationality.

Global justice economics moves from a discursive emphasis on poverty and suffering to an analysis of economic inequality, focusing on the logic of social conflict and social agency. Poverty is thus not fatal, but a consequence of the dominant economic model – i.e. capitalism – and the unequal distribution of wealth that "impoverishes" poor and working people around the globe. Global justice activists insist that poverty need not be endemic and suggest relatively inexpensive ways to alleviate or eradicate it. They assert for example that poverty reduction and the implementation of the Millennium Development Goals only depend on political will.

Global justice activists attempt to re-insert social and political questions into issues treated by neoliberal economics as solely involved with the maximization of efficiency. They denounce the imposition of neoliberalism by non-accountable experts and barely democratic institutions. Nobel prize winners Kydland and Prescott indeed argued that experts are more trustworthy than politicians because they act from a long-term perspective, as also did Barro. Following these recommendations, elected officials have handed over a multitude of negotiations and decisions in international trade and economics to independent administrative bodies of experts. Activists reject this position as undemocratic: "It is a matter of re-conquering the spaces lost by democracy to the financial sector". They seek to *create spaces of debate* in many spheres, ranging from economics to new technologies (GMOs, intellectual property, trade etc.). They likewise encourage citizen participation in political discussion and decisions. To build a fairer world, they argue for a notion of active rather than passive citizenship, requiring a public familiar with scientific knowledge and debates, especially in public economics. As major bodies managing the transition to a more global society, the G8, G20, World Bank, IMF, and WTO are the core targets of global justice activists. To their mind, these institutions have come to embody both the *neoliberal ideology* and the *technocratic aspect* of current global governance. The most telling criticisms relate to the technocratic, opaque, and undemocratic way these bodies function: voting is rare, countries are unequal, and World Bank, IMF or WTO delegates are unaccountable to their populations.

[…]

Poverty reduction figures among the essential elements of the World Bank's mandate, notably through its "Poverty Reduction Strategy." Promoters of the free flows of capital have framed their approach as the best way to decrease poverty, claiming that freedom of capital flows means more resources at the disposal of developing countries. Global justice activists argue that economic growth does not necessarily lead to the satisfaction of the needs of the greatest number. Thus the *United Nations Development Report* for 2006 showed that, outside China, poverty has increased in the world, in spite of the economic growth of the 1990s. For global justice advocates, growing poverty results from the rising inequality in three decades of neoliberal policies. Rather than the pursuit of maximal profit or GDP growth, global justice economists define economy as an "instrument" to reduce poverty and satisfy human need. This central idea is expressed in slogans to be found worldwide, like "People, not profits."

Economic and financial stability is the core objective of the IMF. Here too, global justice activists draw up a damning account of the policies that have been pursued. The succession of financial crises throughout the 1990s contradicted the claim that free flows of capital necessarily bring greater financial and economic stability. The founders of ATTAC link its birth to a "diagnosis: the confirmation, in the Asian financial crisis, of the malignancy of markets and of their hegemonic role in neoliberal globalization." To global justice activists, "the market is no longer self-regulating, it amplifies instabilities". The scale of the global crisis in 2008 and 2009 appears to prove them right. Activists consider the crash in 2001–2002 Argentina as another proof of the failure of neoliberal policies. In the 1990s, the country was regularly designated as "IMF's darling" for its careful implementation of the IMF recommendations to open, liberalize and privatize. It eventually led it into an unprecedented economic crisis. The UNDP calculated that the average annual income per resident dropped from US$ 8950 in 1997 to US$ 3194 in March 2002, plunging half of the Argentinean population under the poverty line in 2003. Exports fell from 26.7 billion dollars in 2001 to 10.8 billion dollars in 2003. Global justice economists emphasize how successive economic and financial crises afflicted countries that adopted neoliberal policies, such as Mexico, Turkey, Argentina, as well as the Asian crisis of 1997 and the recent US subprime crisis that resulted in a global financial, economic, and social disaster.

[…]

Three Major Tendencies

Global justice activists now believe that it is time to focus on implementing concrete alternatives. There are three views of how to implement alternative policies and programs.

Citizens' and experts' advocacy networks

One view holds that concrete outcomes may be achieved through efficient single-issue networks like food sovereignty, Third World Debt, or financial speculation and volatility. For example, from an imposition of limits on financial transactions, it is possible to move on to broader question relating to a new world order. Through the issue of water protection, for instance, activists raise the question of global public goods, oppose some activities of global corporations and promote the idea of the long-term efficiency of the public sector. After several years of intense exchanges between citizens and experts focusing on one or another particular issue of this nature, the quality of arguments within these thematic networks has increased considerably and they have become the core of recent social forums. Even without much media attention, these networks have often proved effective. During the autumn of 2008, the European Water Network influenced the City of Paris to re-municipalize its water distribution, which had been managed previously by private corporations. Political commissions in Ecuador have adopted debt cancellation arguments and some of the movement's experts have joined national delegations to major international meetings, including the Geneva WTO negotiations in 2008.

A focus on the local level

Another perspective on how to affect change stresses a less thematic and inclusive approach, namely, participatory, convivial, and sustainable values in daily practices, personal life and local spaces. The Zapatistas and other Latin American indigenous movements focus on community development through local autonomy, participatory self-government, alternative education systems, and improvements in the quality of life. This view finds acceptance in movements in Western countries as well. "Relocalization" movements promote a wide range of local experiments aiming to reduce consumption and increase production, while building community resilience in response to climate change and seeking to preserve and promote local knowledge and culture. Urban activists appreciate the convivial aspect of local initiatives and the fact that they allow the implementation of small but concrete alternatives to corporate globalization and mass consumption. The movement for "convivial de-growth" reflects this tendency and aims for a lifestyle that reduces waste and imposes less strain on natural resources. Other "convivial" urban movements include associations promoting the use of bicycles and local initiatives to strengthen social relations within neighbourhoods.

[...]

Supporting progressive regimes

A third component of the movement believes that broad social change will occur mainly through progressive policies implemented by key actors: national policy makers, governments and institutions. Alter-globalization activists have struggled to strengthen state agency in social, environmental and economic matters. Now that state intervention has regained legitimacy, this more "political" component of the movement believes that the time has come to support progressive political leaders' efforts. These have notably included President Hugo Chavez of Venezuela and President Evo Morales in Bolivia. Alternative programmes and projects are implemented both through national social and economic policies and through international alliances between progressive regimes. New regional projects and institutions have been launched on this basis, like the Bank of the South, which has assumed the main tasks of the IMF in the region. For reasons of history and political culture, Latin American and Indian activists are accustomed to working closely with political parties and leaders. Similar developments have also occurred recently in Western countries. For example, in the United States the impetus produced by the first national Social Forum in 2007 was largely redirected towards the presidential campaign of Senator Obama.

[…]

These three tendencies within the global justice movement are based on distinct conceptions of social change. The different political options they propose have animated countless debates among activists in the last few years. They may be seen as complementary strategies in many respects. Taken together, they offer concrete guidelines for a global and multidimensional approach to social change and poverty reduction that acknowledges simultaneously the key roles to be played by local communities and grassroots social actors, global citizens' activism, international institutions and national political leaders. By debating rarely discussed issues, the global justice movement has undoubtedly contributed to defining a global public space, stronger global consciousness, multiplication of activities on a global scale and more active citizenship at local, national, continental, and global levels.

72

The Global South
The WTO and Deglobalization

Walden Bello

[…]

How would you summarize your own critique of the WTO?

The WTO is an opaque, unrepresentative and undemocratic organization driven by a free-trade ideology which, wherever its recipes – liberalization, privatization, deregulation – have been applied over the past twenty years to re-engineer Third World economies, has generated only greater poverty and inequality. That's the first point: implementation of neoliberal dogmas leads to great suffering. Secondly, the WTO is not an independent body but a representative of American state and corporate interests. Its development has been closely linked to the changing needs of the United States, which has moved from supporting a weak GATT to promoting a muscular WTO as a nominally multilateral order with strong enforcement rules. Neither the EU nor Japan were particular partisans of the WTO when it was founded, at the behest of the Clinton administration. The American state is very flexible in how it pursues its ends – it can be multilateral when it wants to, and unilateral at the same time. The Achilles' heel of the WTO is its secretive, undemocratic, oligarchic decision-making structure. This is where we should take aim.

Original publication details: Walden Bello, "The Global South," in *A Movement of Movements: Is Another World Really Possible?* ed. Tom Mertes. London: Verso, 2004. pp. 59–65.

The Globalization Reader, Fifth Edition. Edited by Frank J. Lechner and John Boli.
Editorial material and organization © 2015 John Wiley & Sons, Ltd.
Published 2015 by John Wiley & Sons, Ltd.

What would you propose as a positive alternative to the WTO regime?

What we call for is deglobalization – hopefully, the term won't contribute to the confusion; I still think it's a useful one. If you have a centralized institution imposing a one-size-fits-all model across the globe, it eliminates the space for developing countries to determine their economic strategies themselves. The use of trade policy for industrialization is now banned by the WTO. Yet if you look at the experience of the newly industrializing countries – of Latin America in the sixties and the seventies, say – the reason they were able to achieve a modicum of capitalist development was precisely because they had that room for manoeuvre. We believe that the WTO and similar bodies need to be weakened, if not eliminated entirely. Other international institutions, such as UNCTAD – the UN Conference on Trade and Development, which was performing reasonably well until the rug was pulled out from under it by the WTO – should be strengthened, as should regional organizations like MERCOSUR, which has the potential for being an effective, locally directed import-substitution bloc. Regional financial institutions need to be created, too. If the Asian Monetary Fund had existed in 1997 and '98 – when it was pushed by all the countries in the region – the course of the Asian financial crisis would have been different. Instead, the idea was killed off by Rubin and Summers, as a challenge to the hegemony of the IMF.

In world terms, then, we call for greater decentralization, greater pluralism, more checks and balances. In a less globalized order, grass-roots groups and popular movements would be in a stronger position to determine economic strategies. At the moment, local elites can always say, 'We have no choice but to follow this course – if we don't, the IMF or WTO will rule our policy protectionist'. Focus on the Global South is not against trade; well managed, an increase in imports and exports could be a good thing. But in the Third World the pendulum has swung so far in the direction of export-oriented production, that it does need to be corrected back towards the domestic market – the balance between the two has been lost in the drive to internationalize our economies. We can only do that if we structure trade not through WTO open-market rules but by practices that are negotiated among different parties, with varying interests. Deglobalization doesn't imply an uncritical acceptance of existing regional organizations. Some of them are merely outposts of the globalized economy, common markets controlled by local technocrats and industrial elites. Others could sustain a genuine regional development programme.

What would deglobalization mean for finance?

The deregulated character of global finance has been responsible for much of the instability that has rocked our economies since the late eighties. We definitely need capital controls, both at regional and local level. In different ways, the experiences of Malaysia, Chile and China have all shown their efficacy. What's required is an Asian monetary mechanism that would not only support countries whose currencies are under attack, but would also begin to furnish a basis for regional control. As to a world monetary authority, I am very sceptical of its viability as a way of controlling global finance, since these centralized structures are now so permeable by the existing market powers, especially the big central banks. I don't think such an institution would provide an effective defence of the interests of Third World countries. I have never believed that access to foreign capital was the strategic factor in development, although it can be a supplementary one. In fact, our local elites – locked as they are into the existing international order – typically have tremendous reserves of capital. The problem is whether governments in the region have the ability to impose capital controls on them. The same goes for tax regimes, which in South-East Asia are very retrograde. Of course, the wealth of these elites should be subject to proper taxation.

Land reform?

The distribution of land remains a central issue. One reason why export-oriented production could be pushed so successfully by the World Bank in the seventies, and had such strong support from local establishments and technocrats, was that the markets in developing countries were so limited, precisely because of highly unequal asset and income distributions. A focus on exports was seen by the elites as a way out of the trap of shrunken local markets – attaching your industrialization to the big market outside. It was a way to dodge the massive land reform needed to create – in Keynesian terms – the local purchasing power that could drive an indigenous process of industrialization. So agrarian reform is a necessity throughout Asia, as well as Latin America, for both social and economic reasons.

From Seattle onwards it's been clear that a critical fault line within the movement runs between those, essentially Northern, activists and organizations who group themselves around a combination of environmental and labour-rights issues – the position you've described as Green protectionism – and those in the South who see development in a much wider sense as the main priority. It would clearly be an illusion to think that these two perspectives could fit together easily. Yet if the movement is to develop, this tension has somehow to be negotiated and resolved.

The fault line is real, though I would point out that there are large areas of agreement between Northern and Southern movements – a shared critique of multinationals and global capital, a common perception that citizens need to play a stronger role in curbing the rules of the market and of trade. The fact that people from both tendencies can come together in coalitions and work on a range of points is testimony to the strength of these overlapping interests. However, I think the labour question has to be worked out. We were very critical of the way that trade unions in the US – and, to a great extent, in Europe, through the ICFTU – argued that the WTO would be strengthened if it took up tariffs and labour rights. In our view they should not be calling for a more powerful WTO. That's a very short-sighted response. Beneath the surface rhetoric about human rights in the South, this is essentially a protectionist movement, aimed at safeguarding Northern jobs. Whenever we raise this in a fraternal way, they get very defensive about it. We say, let's cut out the hypocrisy: of course we should fight for the jobs of workers in the North – but in a way that supports working-class movements everywhere; not so as to protect one section and leave the rest aside. We need to work out long-term strategies to respond to the way that capital is re-stratifying the working class throughout the world – a division in which hundreds of millions of rural workers get the short end of the stick. The dynamics of global capital are creating a vast underclass, with no support from Northern unions. This is where we need to focus our strategy, on a powerful, visionary effort to organize the world working class. So far, the response from the North – especially from the trade unions – has been a very defensive one, hiding behind the mask of human rights. It makes us deeply uneasy when people from our countries, who have been strongly supportive of workers' rights and have actively opposed ecologically damaging development policies, are cast in these polemics as anti-environmentalist and anti-labour.

Market access is not the central problem, but it is *a* problem. There is a tendency in the North – though not all Green organizations fall into this – to use environmental standards as a way of banning goods from developing countries, either on the grounds of the product itself or because of the production methods. The result is a form of discrimination. We need to find a more positive solution to this. We've called for a global Marshall Plan – one in which environmental groups would actively participate – to upgrade production methods in the South and accelerate the transfer of Green technology. The focus should be on supporting indigenous Green organizations in developing countries and this sort of positive technological transfer, rather than on sanctions. Sanctions are so easy – they appeal to defensive, protectionist interests, which even some progressive organizations in the North have taken up. It's very unfortunate that the US labour movement has adopted this hypocritical stance, saying that it's really concerned about people in China, whereas in fact its objectives are quite egotistical. If we can get past this sort of pretence and establish a dialogue at the level of principles, on the interests of the global working class as a whole, we'll be moving forward.

How far do you regard the World Social Forum in Brazil as a representative arena in which these differences can be hammered out?

When the idea of a global forum was first broached, Focus was one of the organizations that immediately gave its full support. What the Brazilians were proposing was a safe space where people in the movement could come together to affirm their solidarity. This was a very important element of the first Social Forum in 2001. There was a strong sense of the need to talk about alternatives, after Seattle. I think there were real efforts to integrate people from Southern movements, both within the organizing structure and on the panels, although this might not have been successful everywhere. Vandana Shiva and others from the South were brought in from the start, not in a paternalistic way but so they could make genuine suggestions about who should be there. It's true that *Le Monde Diplomatique* and ATTAC played an important part in bringing it together, and the support of the PT state government was fairly crucial. But while ATTAC and *Le Monde Diplomatique* were still vital players in the second Forum, they had a much less central role. If anything, it has been the Brazilian NGOs, civil-society groups and the PT that have, not dominated, but been the moving force. One very positive thing they've done since the first Social Forum is to create an international committee, where regional-representation questions can be discussed. Most Third World participants are still Latin Americans, though, and there is a need to bring Africans and Asians into the process. [...]

73

Ecological Balance in an Era of Globalization

Vandana Shiva

In 1992, the Earth Summit in Rio marked the maturing of ecological awareness on a global scale. The world was poised to make a shift to sustainability. However, the Rio process and the sustainability agenda were subverted by the free-trade agenda. In 1993, the Uruguay Round of the General Agreement on Tariffs and Trade (GATT) was completed, in 1995 the World Trade Organization (WTO) was established, and world affairs grew increasingly dictated by trade and commerce. The normative political commitment to sustainability and justice was replaced by the rule of trade and the elevation of exploitation, greed, and profit maximization as the organizing principles of the market, the state, and society. Instead of the state regulating the market for the good of society, global economic powers and commercial forces are now regulating the state and society for the benefit of corporations. Instead of commerce being accountable to state and society, economic globalization is making citizens and their governments accountable to corporations and global economic bodies.

Economic globalization is not merely an economic phenomenon related to reduction of tariff barriers and removal of "protectionist" policies. It is in fact a normative process that reduces all value by commercial value. Free trade is, in reality, the rule of commerce. Both GATT and WTO basically undo the Rio agenda. Five years after Rio, we do not have Rio plus five but Rio minus five.

Original publication details: Vandana Shiva, "Ecological Balance in an Era of Globalization," in *Principled World Politics: The Challenge of Normative International Relations*, ed. Paul Wapner and Lester Edwin J. Ruiz. Lanham, MD: Rowman & Littlefield, 2000. pp. 130–1, 132–3, 135–7, 139–41, 145–7, 148–9. Reproduced with permission from Rowman & Littlefield.

On the one hand, the search for ecological balance in an era of globalization requires an assessment of the social and ecological impact of globalization. On the other hand, it requires an imagination and a realization of an alternative order that puts ecological balance and social and economic justice rather than trade at the center of economic policy.

Globalization is not a natural, evolutionary, or inevitable phenomenon, as is often argued. Globalization is a political process that has been forced on the weak by the powerful. Globalization is not the cross-cultural interaction of diverse societies. It is the imposition of a particular culture on all others. Nor is globalization the search for ecological balance on a planetary scale. It is the predation of one class, one race, and often one gender of a single species on all others. "Global" in the dominant discourse is the political space in which the dominant local seeks control, freeing itself from local, regional, and global sources of accountability arising from the imperatives of ecological sustainability and social justice. "Global" in this sense does not represent the universal human interest; it represents a particular local and parochial interest and culture that has been globalized through its reach and control, irresponsibility, and lack of reciprocity.

The Three Waves of Globalization

Globalization has come in three waves. The first wave was the colonization of the Americas, Africa, Asia, and Australia by European powers over the course of 1,500 years. The second wave was the imposition of the West's idea of "development" on non-Western cultures in the postcolonial era of the past five decades. The third wave of globalization was unleashed approximately five years ago as the era of "free trade," which for some commentators implies an end to history, but for us in the Third World is a repeat of history through recolonization. Each wave of globalization is cumulative in its impact, even while it creates a discontinuity in the dominant metaphors and actors. Each wave of globalization has served Western interests, and each wave has created deeper colonization of other cultures and of the planet's life. [...]

The Community, the State, and the Corporation

Globalization has distorted the relationship between the community, the state, and the economy, or, to use Marc Nerfin's more colorful categories, the relationship between the citizen, the prince, and the merchant. It is privileging the economy and its key actor, the corporation, insofar as the state and the community are increasingly becoming mere instruments of global capital.

The appeal of globalization is usually based on the idea that it implies less red tape, less centralization, and less bureaucratic control. It is celebrated because it implies the erosion of those bureaucratic impediments that drive up the ecological costs of trade and exchange in general.

During the past fifty years, the state has increasingly taken over the functions of the community and the self-organizing capacity of citizens. Through globalization, corporations are taking over the functions of the state and citizens. Food provisioning, health care, education, and social security are all being transformed into corporate projects under the code words of "competitiveness" and "efficiency." People's rights and the public domain are being eroded by exporting the economic label of "protectionism" to cover all domains: ethical, social, and political. The protection of the environment and the protection of people's security are treated as nontariff trade barriers that need to be dismantled.

While the state is being required to step back from the regulation of trade and commerce, it is being increasingly called in to regulate citizens and remove communities that are an "obstruction" to free trade. Thus, the state is becoming leaner in dealing with big business and global industry, and it is becoming meaner in dealing with people.

In the North and in the South, the principle of "eminent domain" is still applied to the state takeover of people's land and resources, which are then handed over to global corporations. For example, in India, under the new infrastructure policies, foreign companies can enjoy up to 100 percent equity participation, but the government will acquire the land, displace people, and deal with "law and order" problems created by displacements.

In the United States, the federal, state, and local governments are appropriating citizens' homes and farms to hand over to large corporations. In Hurst, Texas, a suburb of Fort Worth, the government appropriated the land of more than 100 home owners, handing it over to its largest taxpayer, the Northeast Mall. Additionally, 4,200 residences were destroyed in Detroit, Michigan, so that General Motors could build a new plant. Quite clearly, it is the property of the powerful corporations that is being protected by the state in every part of the world under the new free-trade regimes, while the property of the ordinary citizen has no protection.

Another area in which the role of the state is actually increasing is in intellectual property rights (IPRs). As larger areas are being converted into "intellectual property" through patents – from microbes to mice, from seeds to human cell lines – the state is being increasingly called on to police citizens to prevent them from engaging in everyday activities, such as saving seeds and exchanging knowledge. Our most human acts have been criminalized – in relationship to ourselves, to one another, and to other species through IPR legislation that is being forced on all countries and all people. [...]

Globalization as Environmental Apartheid

"Apartheid" literally means "separate development." However, in practice, apartheid is more appropriately a regime of exclusion. It is based on legislation that protects a privileged minority and that excludes the majority. It is characterized by the appropriation of the resources and wealth of society by a small minority based on privileges of race or class. The majority is then pushed into a marginalized existence without access to resources necessary for well-being and survival.

Erstwhile South Africa is the most dramatic example of a society based on racial apartheid. Globalization has in a deep sense been a globalization of apartheid. This apartheid is especially glaring in the context of the environment. Globalization is restructuring the control over resources in such a way that the natural resources of the poor are systematically taken over by the rich and the pollution of the rich is systematically dumped on the poor.

In the pre-Rio period, it was the North that contributed most to the destruction of the environment. For example, 90 percent of historic carbon dioxide emissions have been by the industrialized countries. The developed countries produce 90 percent of the hazardous wastes produced around the world every year. Global free trade has globalized this environmental destruction in an asymmetric pattern. While the economy is controlled by Northern corporations, they are increasingly exploiting Third World resources for their global activities. It is the South that is disproportionately bearing the environmental burden of the globalized economy. Globalization is thus leading to an environmental apartheid.

The current environmental and social crisis demands that the world economy adjust to ecological limits and the needs of human survival. Instead, global institutions, such as the World Bank and the International Monetary Fund and the WTO, are forcing the costs of adjustment on nature and women and the Third World. Across the Third World, structural adjustment and trade liberalization measures are becoming the most serious threat to the survival of the people.

While the last five decades have been characterized by the "globalization" of maldevelopment and the spread of a nonsustainable Western industrial paradigm in the name of development, the recent trends are toward an environmental apartheid in which, through global policy set by the holy trinity, the Western TNCs, supported by the governments of the economically powerful countries, attempt to maintain the North's economic power and wasteful lifestyles of the rich by exporting the environmental costs to the Third World. Resource- and pollution-intensive industries are being relocated in the South through the economics of free trade.

Lawrence Summers, who was the World Bank's chief economist and was responsible for the *1992 World Development Report*, which was devoted to the economics of the environment, actually suggested that it makes economic sense to shift polluting industries to Third World countries. In a memo dated December 12, 1991, to senior World Bank staff, he wrote, "Just between you and me, shouldn't the World Bank be encouraging more migration of the dirty industries to the LDC?" Summers justified his economic logic of increasing pollution in the Third World on three grounds. First, since wages are low in the Third World, the economic costs of pollution arising from increased illness and death are the least in the poorest countries. According to Summers, "Relocation of pollutants to the lowest wage country is impeccable and we should face up to that." Second, since in large parts of the Third World pollution is still low, it makes economic sense to Summers to introduce pollution: "I've always thought that countries in Africa are vastly under polluted; their air quality is probably vastly inefficiently low compared to Los Angeles or Mexico City." Finally, since the poor are poor, they cannot possibly worry about environmental problems: "The concern over an agent that causes a one in a million change in the odds of prostate cancer is obviously going to be much higher in a country where people survive to get prostate cancer than in a country where under five mortality is 200 per thousand." He recommended the relocation of hazardous and polluting industries to the Third World because, in narrow economic terms, life is cheaper in the poorer countries. The economists' logic might value life differently in the rich North and the poor South. However, all life is precious. It is equally precious to the rich and the poor, to the white and the black, to men and women.

In this context, recent attempts of the North to link trade conditionalities with the environment in platforms such as WTO need to be viewed as an attempt to build on environmental and economic apartheid. The destruction of ecosystems and livelihoods as a result of trade liberalization is a major environmental and social subsidy to global trade and commerce and those who control it. The main mantra of globalization is "international competitiveness." In the context of the environment, this translates into the largest corporations competing for the natural resources that the poor people in the Third World need for their survival. This competition is highly unequal not only because the corporations are powerful and the poor are not but also because the rules of free trade allow corporations to use the machinery of the nation-state to appropriate resources from the people and prevent people from asserting and exercising their rights.

It is often argued that globalization will create more trade, which will create growth, which will remove poverty. What is overlooked in this myth is that globalization and liberalized trade and investment create growth by destroying the environment and local, sustainable livelihoods. They, therefore, create poverty instead of removing it. The new globalization policies have accelerated and expanded environmental destruction and displaced millions of people from their homes and their sustenance base. [...]

Northern Dumping in the South

The United States generates more than 275 million tons of toxic waste every year and is the leading waste-exporting country in the world. The United States is one of the 161 countries that has signed the Basel International Convention but has not ratified it (along with fifty-eight other countries); parties to the convention, such as India, are not allowed to trade in hazardous wastes with nonparties to the convention. However, notwithstanding the convention, the United States continues its long tradition of exporting its toxic wastes, finding loopholes for dumping them on the South. The United States is thus violating international law in sending shipments of its waste, often mislabeled as recyclables, to India.

In the first half of 1996, approximately 1,500 tons of lead wastes were imported to India. Greenpeace findings state that the amount of toxic lead waste imported from industrialized countries into India has doubled since 1995. Imports from the United States, Australia, South Korea, Germany, the Netherlands, France, Japan, and the United Kingdom account for about 67 percent of the total import of lead wastes to India. The Organization of Economic Cooperation and Development (OECD) accounted for 98 percent of the 400 million metric tons of toxic waste generated worldwide.

Toxic waste such as cyanide, mercury, and arsenic is being shipped as "recyclable waste" – a deliberate attempt to mislead and disguise the true nature of the wastes. In reality, there is no such use or demand to recover such toxic chemicals because it is pure waste. The imported waste often ends up in backyard smelting organizations, not the commercial sector as stated by the government. Many of the importing units do not possess the technology or the expertise to process the chemicals they are importing; therefore, they inadvertently cause more harm to the environment and their communities because of their ignorance concerning the chemicals that they are dealing with. Eighty-five hundred such units operate in Maharashtra alone.

Developed countries are offering lucrative prices (in Indian terms) to Indian "recycling" companies to take their material for "processing." India is being used as a dumping ground by the Northern industrialized countries because the cost of treating and disposing waste in a sustainable manner in the North has become highly expensive. Costs have become so high because of stringent laws that ban dumping, burning, and burying waste. Dumping in the developing world therefore becomes justified on grounds of economic efficiency.

The cost of burying one ton of hazardous waste in the United States rose from $15 in 1980 to $350 in 1992. In Germany, it is cheaper, by $2,500, to ship a ton of waste to a developing country than to dispose of it in Europe. Countries such as Germany find it cheaper to export their waste to a landfill than to recycle it themselves. Because India does not charge any landfill costs, the profits made in waste trade has made the industry even more attractive.

In 1966, the Research Foundation for Science, Technology and Ecology (RFSTE) filed public interest litigation seeking a ban on all hazardous and toxic wastes into India. In response, on May 6, 1997, the Supreme Court of India imposed a blanket ban on the import of all kinds of hazardous and toxic wastes into the country. The court also directed state governments to show cause why immediate orders should not be passed for the closure of more than 2,000 unauthorized waste-handling units identified by the central government in various parts of the country. The Supreme Court directed that no import be made or permitted of any hazardous waste that is already banned under the Basel International Convention, or to be banned after the date specified therein by the court.

A court statement established that 2,000 tons of hazardous wastes were being generated every day in India without adequate safe disposal sites. This ban applies to state governments as well as the central government to give authorization for the importation of hazardous wastes.

Today, toxic waste dumping has become a national issue, and several nongovernmental organizations are working specifically on the banning of toxic waste import and dumping and related issues. Srishti, Greenpeace, Toxics Link Exchange, Public Interest Research Group, WWF-India, and the RFSTE are Delhi-based movements that are concerned with hazardous wastes and toxics issues and that, in particular, are opposing the importation of toxic wastes. Furthermore, some of us are involved in creating awareness within India as to the actions of transnational and local industries who often openly defy existing environmental laws regarding importation, treatment, handling, and disposal of hazardous wastes. [...]

People's Movements for the Protection of Biodiversity and Collective Rights

New social and environmental movements are emerging everywhere in response to the widespread destruction of the environment and of the livelihoods that depend on biodiversity and in response to piracy of our indigenous resources and indigenous innovation. In India, the intricate link between people's livelihoods and biodiversity has evolved over centuries. Economic liberalization is threatening to sever this link by treating biodiversity as a raw material for exploitation of life forms as property and of people's livelihoods as an inevitable sacrifice for national economic growth and development. It is also eroding the level of governing control that people have over their lives.

In February 1995, the tribal people from different parts of India were in Delhi on an indefinite fast to force the government to recognize their declaration of "self-rule." The National Front for Tribal Self-Rule, a national organization of organizations of tribal people, has conducted a civil disobedience movement since October 2, 1995, for the establishment of self-rule. As they state,

> We have carried the cross of virtual slavery for much too long in spite of independence. Other rural folks are also in a similar state. Yet, now that everything is clear and there is unanimity in the establishment as also among members of parliament and experts, the change must not be delayed. We will not tolerate this. Even otherwise, on the issue of self-governance we need not be solicitous. It is a natural right. In the hierarchy of democratic institutions gram-sabha is above all, even parliament. This is what Gandhi preached; we will not obey any law which compromises the position of gram-sabha. In any case we resolve to establish self-rule with effect from October 2, 1995. We will have command over our resources and will manage our affairs thereafter.
>
> (Declaration, "Front for Tribal Self-Rule," Delhi, February 1995)

The struggle of the tribal people was successful.

The passing of the Provisions of the Panchayats (Extension to the Scheduled Areas) Act that came into effect in December 1996 represents a landmark piece of legislation as far as acknowledging the legal rights to self-rule of the tribal people are concerned. Section 4(b) and (d) of the act state the following:

- A village shall ordinarily consist of a habitation or a group of habitations, or a hamlet or a group of hamlets comprising a community and managing its affairs in accordance with traditions and customs.
- Each gram-sabha shall be competent to safeguard and preserve the traditions and customs of the people, their cultural identity, community resources and the customary mode of dispute resolution.

The implementation of the Panchayati Raj Act in Scheduled Areas has already set the precedent for the recognition of communities as competent authorities for decision making on resource use, cultural values and traditions, and community rights to common resources as the building block of a decentralized democracy.

More than 100 villages in and around the thick forests of Nagarhole in Karnataka have established self-governments to safeguard their livelihood under the provisions of a law passed by the Parliament that came into effect on December 24, 1996: the Provisions of the Panchayats (Extension to the Scheduled Areas) Act, 1996. However, this law has yet to be passed by the Karnataka Assembly to implement it in that state.

The people have formed gram-sabhas and established task forces to implement the self-rule program. In some of the villages, they have erected gates at the entrance, and only the chief of the tribal community / village has been entrusted with the power to give permission to any outsider to enter their village. The villagers are freely collecting the minor forest produce, and even they are adjudicating the problems themselves rather than going to the police or court.

The Movement for Declaration of Community Rights to Biodiversity: The Case of Pattuvam Panchayat

Nationwide people's movements have succeeded to date in stalling any legislation passing parliament that would promote IPRs over biodiversity. Such opposition signifies the degree of democratic dissent being generated at the grassroots level to laws affecting people's livelihoods and rights over their resources. People's movements against erosion, exploitation, and usurpation of biodiversity are numerous and widespread throughout the country. A small community in southern Kerala has taken a bold step to protect its biodiversity. On April 9, 1997, in a remote part of Kerala, hundreds of local people gathered to declare their local biodiversity as a community-owned resource that they will collectively protect and that they will not allow to be privatized through patents on derived products or varieties.

The community is known as the Pattuvam Panchayat. The Panchayat has set up its own biodiversity register to record all biodiversity of species in the region. It has stated that no individual, TNC, or state or central government can use their biodiversity without the permission of the Pattuvam Panchayat. The people of Pattuvam have taken a pathbreaking step by declaring their biodiversity a community resource over which the community as a whole has rights. This step demonstrates a commitment to rejuvenating and protecting their biodiversity and knowledge systems from the exploitative forces of economic liberalization.

Movements are occurring in other parts of India as well whereby communities are declaring the biodiversity and knowledge as the common heritage of local communities. For example, in Dharward in Karnataka and in Chattisgarh, Madhya Pradesh, declaration ceremonies have been held announcing that biodiversity is a community resource and that privatization of biodiversity and indigenous knowledge through patents is theft. [...]

Navdanya: Seeds of Freedom

I have started a national movement for the recovery of the biological and intellectual commons by saving native seeds from extinction. Seed is the first link in the food chain. It is also the first step toward freedom in food. Globalization is leading to total control over what we eat and what we grow. The tiny seed is becoming an instrument of freedom in this emerging era of total control. Our slogan is, "Native seed – indigenous agriculture – local markets."

Through saving the native seed, we are becoming free of chemicals. By practicing a "free" agriculture, we are saying no to patents on life and to biopiracy. Gandhi called such resistance "Satyagraha": the struggle for truth. Navdanya is a "Seed Satyagraha" in which it is the most marginal and poor peasants who are finding new hope.

A central part of the Seed Satyagraha is to declare the "common intellectual rights" of Third World communities who have gifted the world the knowledge of the rich bounties of nature's diversity. The innovations of Third World communities might differ in process and objectives from the innovations in the commercial world of the West, but they cannot be discounted just because they are different. But we are going beyond just saying no. We are creating alternatives by building community seed banks, strengthening farmers' seed supplies, and searching for sustainable agriculture options that are suitable for different regions.

The seed has become, for us, the site and the symbol of freedom in the age of manipulation and monopoly of its diversity. It plays the role of Gandhi's spinning wheel in this period of recolonization through free trade. The "Charkha" (spinning wheel) became an important symbol of freedom not because it was big and powerful but because it was small and could come alive as a sign of resistance and creativity in the smallest of huts and poorest of families. In smallness lay its power. The seed too is small. It embodies diversity. It embodies the freedom to stay alive. And seed is still the common property of small farmers in India. In the seed, cultural diversity converges with biological diversity. Ecological issues combine with social justice, peace, and democracy.

Conclusion

The dynamics of globalization and their associated violence are posing some of the most severe challenges to ordinary people in India and throughout the world. While this chapter has been pessimistic, outlining the character and strength of globalization and its ability to thwart citizen accountability, I take heart in the resistance movements mentioned in the last few sections. Continuous globalizing efforts may threaten democracy, the vibrancy and diversity of life forms, and ecological well-being in general. However, the human spirit, inspired by justice and environmental protection, can never be fully repressed. Despite the brutal violence of globalization, we have hope because we build alternatives in partnership with nature and people. [...]

74

Tomorrow Begins Today

Subcomandante Marcos

Through my voice speaks the voice of the EZLN.

Brothers and sisters of the whole world
Brothers and sisters of Africa, America, Asia, Europe, and Oceania
Brothers and sisters attending the First Intercontinental Encuentro for Humanity and
against Neoliberalism:

WELCOME TO THE ZAPATISTA LA REALIDAD.
Welcome to this territory in struggle for humanity.
Welcome to this territory in rebellion against neoliberalism. [...]

Welcome, all men, women, children, and elders from the five continents who have responded to the invitation of the Zapatista indigenous to search for hope, for humanity, and to struggle against neoliberalism. [...]

In the world of those who live and kill for Power, there is no room for human beings. There is no space for hope, no place for tomorrow. Slavery or death is the choice that their world offers all worlds. The world of money, their world, governs from the stock exchanges. Today, speculation is the principal source of enrichment, and at the same time the best demonstration of the atrophy of our capacity to work. Work is no longer necessary in order to produce wealth; now all that is needed is speculation.

Original publication details: Subcomandante Marcos, "Tomorrow Begins Today," closing remarks at the First Intercontinental Encuentro for Humanity and against Neoliberalism, August 3, 1996, in *Our Word Is Our Weapon*. New York: Seven Stories Press, 2001. pp. 107–15. Reproduced with permission from Seven Stories Press.

Crimes and wars are carried out so that the global stock exchanges may be pillaged by one or the other.

Meanwhile, millions of women, millions of youths, millions of indigenous, millions of homosexuals, millions of human beings of all races and colors, participate in the financial markets only as a devalued currency, always worth less and less, the currency of their blood turning a profit.

The globalization of markets erases borders for speculation and crime and multiplies them for human beings. Countries are obliged to erase their national borders for money to circulate, but to multiply their internal borders.

Neoliberalism doesn't turn many countries into one country; it turns each country into many countries.

The lie of unipolarity and internationalization turns itself into a nightmare of war, a fragmented war, again and again, so many times that nations are pulverized. In this world, Power globalizes to overcome the obstacles to its war of conquest. National governments are turned into the military underlings of a new world war against humanity.

From the stupid course of nuclear armament – destined to annihilate humanity in one blow – it has turned to the absurd militarization of every aspect in the life of national societies – a militarization destined to annihilate humanity in many blows, in many places, and in many ways. What were formerly known as "national armies" are turning into mere units of a greater army, one that neoliberalism arms to lead against humanity. The end of the so-called Cold War didn't stop the global arms race, it only changed the model for the merchandising of mortality: weapons of all kinds and sizes for all kinds of criminal tastes. More and more, not only are the so-called institutional armies armed, but also the armies' drug-trafficking builds up to ensure its reign. More or less rapidly, national societies are being militarized, and armies – supposedly created to protect their borders from foreign enemies – are turning their cannons and rifles around and aiming them inward.

It is not possible for neoliberalism to become the world's reality without the argument of death served up by institutional and private armies, without the gag served up by prisons, without the blows and assassinations served up by the military and the police. National repression is a necessary premise of the globalization neoliberalism imposes.

The more neoliberalism advances as a global system, the more numerous grow the weapons and the ranks of the armies and national police. The numbers of the imprisoned, the disappeared, and the assassinated in different countries also grows.

A world war:
the most brutal,
the most complete,
the most universal,
the most effective.

Each country,
each city,

each countryside,
each house,
each person,
each is a large or small battleground.

On the one side is neoliberalism, with all its repressive power and all its machinery of death; on the other side is the human being.

There are those who resign themselves to being one more number in the huge exchange of Power. There are those who resign themselves to being slaves. He who is himself master to slaves also cynically walks the slave's horizontal ladder. In exchange for the bad life and crumbs that Power hands out, there are those who sell themselves, resign themselves, surrender themselves.

In any part of the world, there are slaves who say they are happy being slaves. In any part of the world, there are men and women who stop being human and take their place in the gigantic market that trades in dignities.

But there are those who do not resign themselves, there are those who decide not to conform, there are those who do not sell themselves, there are those who do not surrender themselves. Around the world, there are those who resist being annihilated in this war. There are those who decide to fight. In any place in the world, anytime, any man or any woman rebels to the point of tearing off the clothes resignation has woven for them and cynicism has dyed gray. Any man or woman, of whatever color, in whatever tongue, speaks and says to himself or to herself: Enough is enough! – ¡ Ya Basta!

Enough is enough of lies.
Enough is enough of crime.
Enough is enough of death.
Enough is enough of war, says any man or woman.

Any man or woman, in whatever part of any of the five continents, eagerly decides to resist Power and to construct his or her own path that doesn't lead to the loss of dignity and hope.

Any man or woman decides to live and struggle for his or her part in history. No longer does Power dictate his or her steps. No longer does Power administer life and decide death.

Any man or woman responds to death with life, and responds to the nightmare by dreaming and struggling against war, against neoliberalism, for humanity …

For struggling for a better world, all of us are fenced in and threatened with death. The fence is reproduced globally. In every continent, every city, every countryside, every house. Power's fence of war closes in on the rebels, for whom humanity is always grateful.

But fences are broken,
in every house,
in every countryside,
in every city,

in every state,

in every country,

in every continent,

the rebels, whom history repeatedly has given us the length of its long trajectory, struggle and the fence is broken.

The rebels search each other out. They walk toward one another.

They find each other and together break other fences.

In the countryside and cities, in the states, in the nations, on the continents, the rebels begin to recognize each other, to know themselves as equals and different. They continue on their fatiguing walk, walking as it is now necessary to walk, that is to say, struggling … […]

A world made of many worlds found itself these days in the mountains of the Mexican Southeast.

A world made of many worlds opened a space and established its right to exist, raised the banner of being necessary, stuck itself in the middle of the earth's reality to announce a better future.

A world of all the worlds that rebel and resist Power.

A world of all the worlds that inhabit this world, opposing cynicism.

A world that struggles for humanity and against neoliberalism.

This was the world that we lived these days.

This is the world that we found here.

This *encuentro* wasn't to end in La Realidad. Now it must search for a place to carry on.

But what next?

A new number in the useless enumeration of the numerous international orders?

A new scheme for calming and easing the anguish of having no solution?

A global program for world revolution?

A utopian theory so that it can maintain a prudent distance from the reality that anguishes us?

A scheme that assures each of us a position, a task, a title, and no work?

The echo goes, a reflected image of the possible and forgotten: the possibility and necessity of speaking and listening; not an echo that fades away, or a force that decreases after reaching its apogee.

Let it be an echo that breaks barriers and re-echoes.

Let it be an echo of our own smallness, of the local and particular, which reverberates in an echo of our own greatness, the intercontinental and galactic.

An echo that recognizes the existence of the other and does not overpower or attempt to silence it.

An echo that takes its place and speaks its own voice, yet speaks the voice of the other.

An echo that reproduces its own sound, yet opens itself to the sound of the other.

An echo of this rebel voice transforming itself and renewing itself in other voices.

An echo that turns itself into many voices, into a network of voices that, before Power's deafness, opts to speak to itself, knowing itself to be one and many, acknowledging itself to be equal in its desire to listen and be listened to, recognizing itself as diverse in the tones and levels of voices forming it.

Let it be a network of voices that resist the war Power wages on them.

A network of voices that not only speak, but also struggle and resist for humanity and against neoliberalism.

A network of voices that are born resisting, reproducing their resistance in other quiet and solitary voices.

A network that covers the five continents and helps to resist the death that Power promises us.

In the great pocket of voices, sounds continue to search for their place, fitting in with others.

The great pocket, ripped, continues to keep the best of itself, yet opens itself to what is better.

The great pocket continues to mirror voices; it is a world in which sounds may be listened to separately, recognizing their specificity; it is a world in which sounds can include themselves in one great sound.

The multiplication of resistances, the "I am not resigned," the "I am a rebel," continues.

The world, with the many worlds that the world needs, continues.

Humanity, recognizing itself to be plural, different, inclusive, tolerant of itself, full of hope, continues.

The human and rebel voice, consulted on the five continents in order to become a network of voices and resistance, continues.

75

Porto Alegre Call for Mobilization

World Social Forum

Social forces from around the world have gathered here at the World Social Forum in Porto Alegre. Unions and NGOs, movements and organizations, intellectuals and artists, together we are building a great alliance to create a new society, different from the dominant logic wherein the free-market and money are considered the only measure of worth. Davos represents the concentration of wealth, the globalization of poverty and the destruction of our earth. Porto Alegre represents the hope that a new world is possible, where human beings and nature are the center of our concern.

We are part of a movement which has grown since Seattle. We challenge the elite and their undemocratic processes, symbolised by the World Economic Forum in Davos. We came to share our experiences, build our solidarity, and demonstrate our total rejection of the neoliberal policies of globalisation.

We are women and men, farmers, workers, unemployed, professionals, students, blacks and indigenous peoples, coming from the South and from the North, committed to struggle for peoples' rights, freedom, security, employment and education. We are fighting against the hegemony of finance, the destruction of our cultures, the monopolization of knowledge, mass media, and communication, the degradation of nature, and the destruction of the quality of life by multinational corporations and anti-democratic policies. Participative democratic experiences – like that of Porto Alegre – show us that a concrete alternative is possible. We reaffirm the supremacy of human, ecological and social rights over the demands of finance and investors.

At the same time that we strengthen our movements, we resist the global elite and work for equity, social justice, democracy and security for everyone, without

Original publication details: World Social Forum, "Porto Alegre Call for Mobilization," 2001.

distinction. Our methodology and alternatives stand in stark contrast to the destructive policies of neo-liberalism.

Globalisation reinforces a sexist and patriarchal system. It increases the feminisation of poverty and exacerbates all forms of violence against women. Equality between women and men is central to our struggle. Without this, another world will never be possible.

Neoliberal globalization increases racism, continuing the veritable genocide of centuries of slavery and colonialism which destroyed the bases of black African civilizations. We call on all movements to be in solidarity with African peoples in the continent and outside, in defense of their rights to land, citizenship, freedom, peace, and equality, through the reparation of historical and social debts. Slave trade and slavery are crimes against humanity.

We express our special recognition and solidarity with indigenous peoples in their historic struggle against genocide and ethnocide and in defense of their rights, natural resources, culture, autonomy, land, and territory.

Neoliberal globalisation destroys the environment, health and people's living environment. Air, water, land and peoples have become commodities. Life and health must be recognized as fundamental rights which must not be subordinated to economic policies.

The external debt of the countries of the South has been repaid several times over. Illegitimate, unjust and fraudulent, it functions as an instrument of domination, depriving people of their fundamental human rights with the sole aim of increasing international usury. We demand its unconditional cancellation and the reparation of historical, social, and ecological debts, as immediate steps toward a definitive resolution of the crisis this Debt provokes.

Financial markets extract resources and wealth from communities and nations, and subject national economies to the whims of speculators. We call for the closure of tax havens and the introduction of taxes on financial transactions.

Privatisation is a mechanism for transferring public wealth and natural resources to the private sector. We oppose all forms of privatisation of natural resources and public services. We call for the protection of access to resources and public goods necessary for a decent life.

Multinational corporations organise global production with massive unemployment, low wages and unqualified labour and by refusing to recognise the fundamental worker's rights as defined by the ILO. We demand the genuine recognition of the right to organise and negotiate for unions, and new rights for workers to face the globalisation strategy. While goods and money are free to cross borders, the restrictions on the movement of people exacerbate exploitation and repression. We demand an end to such restrictions.

We call for a trading system which guarantees full employment, food security, fair terms of trade and local prosperity. Free trade is anything but free. Global trade rules ensure the accelerated accumulation of wealth and power by multinational corporations and the further marginalisation and impoverishment of small farmers, workers and local enterprises. We demand that governments respect their obligations to the international human rights instruments and multilateral environmental agreements. We call on people everywhere to support the mobilizations against the creation of the Free Trade Area in the Americas, an initiative which means the recolonization of Latin America and the destruction of fundamental social, economic, cultural and environmental human rights.

The IMF, the World Bank and regional banks, the WTO, NATO and other military alliances are some of the multilateral agents of neoliberal globalisation. We call for an end to their interference in national policy. These institutions have no legitimacy in the eyes of the people and we will continue to protest against their measures.

Neoliberal globalization has led to the concentration of land ownership and favored corporate agricultural systems which are environmentally and socially destructive. It is based on export oriented growth backed by large scale infrastructure development, such as dams, which displaces people from their land and destroys their livelihoods. Their loss must be restored. We call for a democratic agrarian reform. Land, water and seeds must be in the hands of the peasants. We promote sustainable agricultural processes. Seeds and genetic stocks are the heritage of humanity. We demand that the use of transgenics and the patenting of life be abolished.

Militarism and corporate globalisation reinforce each other to undermine democracy and peace. We totally refuse war as a way to solve conflicts and we oppose the arms race and the arms trade. We call for an end to the repression and criminalisation of social protest. We condemn foreign military intervention in the internal affairs of our countries. We demand the lifting of embargoes and sanctions used as instruments of aggression, and express our solidarity with those who suffer their consequences. We reject US military intervention in Latin American through the Plan Colombia.

We call for a strengthening of alliances, and the implementation of common actions, on these principal concerns. We will continue to mobilize on them until the next Forum. We recognize that we are now in a better position to undertake the struggle for a different world, a world without misery, hunger, discrimination and violence, with quality of life, equity, respect and peace. [...]

The proposals formulated are part of the alternatives being elaborated by social movements around the world. They are based on the principle that human beings and life are not commodities, and in the commitment to the welfare and human rights of all.

Our involvement in the World Social Forum has enriched understanding of each of our struggles and we have been strengthened. We call on all peoples around the world to join in this struggle to build a better future. The World Social Forum of Porto Alegre is a way to achieve peoples' sovereignty and a just world.

[180 organizations listed as endorsing the Call, from 28 countries]

76

A Better World Is Possible!

International Forum on Globalization

Introduction

A. Global resistance

Society is at a crucial crossroads. A peaceful, equitable and sustainable future depends on the outcome of escalating conflicts between two competing visions: one corporate, one democratic. The schism has been caught by media images and stories accompanying recent meetings of global bureaucracies like the World Trade Organization (WTO), the International Monetary Fund (IMF), the World Bank, the Free Trade Area of the Americas (FTAA), and numerous other gatherings of corporate and economic elites, such as the World Economic Forum at Davos, Switzerland (although in 2002 it will meet in New York City).

Over the past five to ten years, millions of people have taken to the streets in India, the Philippines, Indonesia, Brazil, Bolivia, the United States, Canada, Mexico, Argentina, Venezuela, France, Germany, Italy, the Czech Republic, Spain, Sweden, England, New Zealand, Australia, Kenya, South Africa, Thailand, Malaysia and elsewhere in massive demonstrations against the institutions and policies of corporate globalization. All too often the corporate media have done more to mislead than to inform the public on the issues behind the protests. Thomas Friedman, *The New York Times* foreign affairs columnist, is typical of journalists who characterize the demonstrators as "ignorant protectionists" who offer no alternatives and are unworthy of serious attention.

Original publication details: International Forum on Globalization, "A Better World Is Possible!" Report summary, 2002.

The claim that the protestors have no alternatives is as false as the claims that they are anti-poor, xenophobic, anti-trade, and have no analysis. In addition to countless books, periodicals, conferences, and individual articles and presentations setting forth alternatives, numerous consensus statements have been carefully crafted by civil society groups over the past two decades that set forth a wealth of alternatives with a striking convergence in their beliefs about the underlying values human societies can and should serve. Such consensus statements include a collection of citizen treaties drafted in Rio de Janeiro in 1992 by the 18,000 representatives of global civil society who met in parallel to the official meetings of the United Nations Conference on Environment and Development (UNCED). A subsequent initiative produced The Earth Charter, scheduled for ratification by the UN General Assembly in 2002 – the product of a global process that involved thousands of people. In 2001 and 2002, tens of thousands more gathered in Porto Alegre, Brazil, for the first annual World Social Forum on the theme "Another World Is Possible" to carry forward this process of popular consensus building toward a world that works for all.

B. Different worlds

The corporate globalists who meet in posh gatherings to chart the course of corporate globalization in the name of private profits, and the citizen movements who organize to thwart them in the name of democracy and diversity are separated by deep differences in values, world view, and definitions of progress. At times it seems they must be living in wholly different worlds – which in many respects they are.

Corporate globalists inhabit a world of power and privilege. They see progress everywhere because from their vantage point the drive to privatize public assets and free the market from governmental interference appears to be spreading freedom and prosperity throughout the world, improving the lives of people everywhere, and creating the financial and material wealth necessary to end poverty and protect the environment. They see themselves as champions of an inexorable and beneficial historical process toward erasing the economic and political borders that hinder corporate expansion, eliminating the tyranny of inefficient and meddlesome public bureaucracies, and unleashing the enormous innovation and wealth-creating power of competition and private enterprise.

Citizen movements see a starkly different reality. Focused on people and the environment, they see a world in deepening crisis of such magnitude as to threaten the fabric of civilization and the survival of the species – a world of rapidly growing inequality, erosion of relationships of trust, and failing planetary life support systems. Where corporate globalists see the spread of democracy and vibrant market economies, citizen movements see the power to govern shifting away from people and communities to financial speculators and global corporations dedicated to the pursuit of short-term profit. They see corporations replacing democracies of people with democracies of money, self-organizing markets with centrally planned corporate economies, and diverse ethical cultures with cultures of greed and materialism.

C. Transformational imperative

In a world in which a few enjoy unimaginable wealth, 200 million children under five are underweight due to a lack of food. Fourteen million children die each year from hunger-related disease. A hundred million children are living or working on the streets. Three hundred thousand children were conscripted as soldiers during the 1990s and six million were injured in armed conflicts. Eight hundred million people go to bed hungry each night. Human activity – most particularly fossil fuel combustion is estimated to have increased atmospheric concentrations of carbon dioxide to their highest levels in 20 million years. According to the WorldWatch Institute, natural disasters – including weather related disasters such as storms, floods, and fires – affected more than two billion people and caused in excess of $608 billion in economic losses worldwide during the decade of the 1990s – more than the previous four decades combined.

D. Economic democracy

Humanity has reached the limits of an era of centralized institutional power and control. The global corporation, the WTO, the IMF, and the World Bank are structured to concentrate power in the hands of ruling elites shielded from public accountability. They represent an outmoded, undemocratic, inefficient and ultimately destructive way of organizing human affairs that is as out of step with the needs and values of healthy, sustainable and democratic societies as the institution of monarchy. The current and future well being of humanity depends on transforming the relationships of power within and between human societies toward more democratic and mutually accountable modes of managing human affairs that are self-organizing, power-sharing, and minimize the need for coercive central authority.

E. Global governance

The concern for local self-reliance and self-determination have important implications for global governance. For example, in a self-reliant and localized system the primary authority to set and enforce rules must rest with the national and local governments of the jurisdictions to which they apply. The proper role of global institutions is to facilitate the cooperative coordination of national policies on matters where the interests of nations are inherently intertwined – as with action on global warming.

F. Building momentum

Growing public consciousness of the pervasive abuse of corporate power has fueled the growth of a powerful opposition movement with an increasingly impressive list of achievements. Unified by a deep commitment to universal values of democracy, justice, and respect for life this alliance functions with growing effectiveness without a central organization, charismatic leader, or defining ideology – taking different forms in different settings.

In India, popular movements seek to empower local people through the democratic community control of resources under the banner of a million strong Living Democracy Movement (*Jaiv Panchayat*). In Canada, hundreds of organizations have joined in alliance to articulate a Citizens' Agenda that seeks to wrest control of governmental institutions back away from corporations. In Chile, coalitions of environmental groups have created a powerful Sustainable Chile (*Sustenable Chile*) movement that seeks to reverse Chile's drift toward neoliberalism and re-assert popular democratic control over national priorities and resources. The focus in Brazil is on the rights of the poor and landless. In Bolivia it takes the form of a mass movement of peasants and workers who have successfully blocked the privatization of water. In Mexico, the Mayan people have revived the spirit of Zapata in a movement to confirm the rights of indigenous people to land and resources. Farmers in France have risen up in revolt against trade rules that threaten to destroy small farms. The construction of new highways in England has brought out hundreds of thousands of people who oppose this desecration of the countryside in response to globalization's relentless demand for ever more high speed transport.

These are only a few examples of the popular initiatives and actions in defense of democratic rights that are emerging all around the world. Together these many initiatives are unleashing ever more of the creative energy of humanity toward building cooperative systems of sustainable societies that work for all.

Chapter I   Critique of Economic Globalization

The alternatives offered in this report grow from the widespread damage inflicted by economic globalization over the past five centuries as it passed from colonialism and imperialism through post-colonial, export-led development models. The driving force of economic globalization since World War II has been several hundred large private corporations and banks that have increasingly woven webs of production, consumption, finance, and culture across borders. Indeed, today most of what we eat, drink, wear, drive, and entertain ourselves with is the product of globe-girdling corporations.

A. Key ingredients and general effects

Economic globalization (sometimes referred to as corporate-led globalization), features several key ingredients:

- Corporate deregulation and the unrestricted movement of capital;
- Privatization and commodification of public services, and remaining aspects of the global and community commons, such as bulk water and genetic resources;
- Integration and conversion of national economies (including some that were largely self-reliant) to environmentally and socially harmful export-oriented production;
- Promotion of hyper-growth and unrestricted exploitation of the planet's resources to fuel the growth;
- Dramatically increased corporate concentration;

- Undermining of national social, health and environmental programs;
- Erosion of traditional powers and policies of democratic nation-states and local communities by global corporate bureaucracies;
- Global cultural homogenization, and the intensive promotion of unbridled consumerism.

1. *Pillars of Globalization:* The first tenet of economic globalization, as now designed, is the need to integrate and merge all economic activity of all countries within a single, homogenized model of development; a single centralized system. A second tenet of the globalization design is that primary importance is given to the achievement of ever more rapid, and never ending corporate economic growth – hyper growth – fueled by the constant search for access to natural resources, new and cheaper labor sources, and new markets. A third tenet concerns privatization and commodification of as many traditionally non-commodified nooks and crannies of existence as possible – seeds and genes for example. A fourth important tenet of economic globalization is its strong emphasis on a global conversion to export-oriented production and trade as an economic and social nirvana.
2. *Beneficiaries of Globalization:* The actual beneficiaries of this model have become all too obvious. In the United States, for example, we know that during the period of the most rapid globalization, top corporate executives of the largest global companies have been making salaries and options in the many millions of dollars, often in the hundreds of millions, while real wages of ordinary workers have been declining. The Institute for Policy Studies reports that American CEOs are now paid, on average, 517 times more than production workers, with that rate increasing yearly. The Economic Policy Institute's 1999 report says that median hourly wages are actually down by 10 percent in real wages over the last 25 years. As for lifting the global poor, the U.N. Development Program's 1999 *Human Development Report* indicated that the gap between the wealthy and the poor within and among countries of the world is getting steadily larger, and it named inequities in the global trade system as being one of the key factors.

B. Bureaucratic expressions of globalization

Creating a world that works for all must begin with an effort to undo the enormous damage inflicted by the corporate globalization policies that so badly distort economic relationships among people and countries. The thrust of those policies is perhaps most dramatically revealed in the structural adjustment programs imposed on low and intermediate income countries by the IMF and the World Bank – two institutions that bear responsibility for enormous social and environmental devastation and human suffering. Structural adjustment requires governments to:

- Cut government spending on education, healthcare, the environment, and price subsidies for basic necessities such as food grains, and cooking oils in favor of servicing foreign debt.

- Devalue the national currency and increase exports by accelerating the plunder of natural resources, reducing real wages, and subsidizing export-oriented foreign investments.
- Liberalize financial markets to attract speculative short-term portfolio investments that create enormous financial instability and foreign liabilities while serving little, if any, useful purpose.
- Increase interest rates to attract foreign speculative capital, thereby increasing bankruptcies of domestic businesses and imposing new hardships on indebted individuals.
- Eliminate tariffs, quotas and other controls on imports, thereby increasing the import of consumer goods purchased with borrowed foreign exchange, undermining local industry and agricultural producers unable to compete with cheap imports, which increases the strain on foreign exchange accounts, and deepening external indebtedness.

The World Bank and the IMF, along with the General Agreement on Tariffs and Trade/World Trade Organization (GATT/WTO) are together known as the Bretton Woods institutions – the collective product of agreements reached at an international gathering held in Bretton Woods, New Hampshire, in July, 1944, to create an institutional framework for the post-World War II global economy.

C. Conclusions

The Bretton Woods institutions have a wholly distorted view of economic progress and relationships. Their embrace of unlimited expansion of trade and foreign investment as measures of economic progress suggests that they consider the most advanced state of development to be one in which all productive assets are owned by foreign corporations producing for export; the currency that facilitates day-to-day transactions is borrowed from foreign banks; education and health services are operated by global corporations on a for-profit, fee-for-service basis; and most that people consume is imported. When placed in such stark terms, the absurdity of the "neoliberal" ideology of the Bretton Woods institutions becomes obvious. It also becomes clear who such policies serve. Rather than enhance the life of people and planet, they consolidate and secure the wealth and power of a small corporate elite, the only evident beneficiaries, at the expense of humanity and nature. In the following section, we outline the principles of alternative systems that posit democracy and rights as the means toward sustainable communities, dignified work, and a healthy environment.

Chapter II   Ten Principles for Democratic and Sustainable Societies

The current organizing principles of the institutions that govern the global economy are narrow and serve the few at the expense of the many and the environment. Yet, it is within our collective ability to create healthy, sustainable societies that work for all.

The time has come to make that possibility a reality. Sustainable societies are rooted in certain core principles. The following ten core principles have been put forward in various combinations in citizen programs that are emerging around the world.

A. New democracy

The rallying cry of the amazing diversity of civil society that converged in Seattle in late 1999 was the simple word "democracy." Democracy flourishes when people organize to protect their communities and rights and hold their elected officials accountable. For the past two decades, global corporations and global bureaucracies have grabbed much of the power once held by governments. We advocate a shift from governments serving corporations to governments serving people and communities, a process that is easier at the local level but vital at all levels of government.

B. Subsidiarity

Economic globalization results first, and foremost, in de-localization and disempowerment of communities and local economies. It is therefore necessary to reverse direction and create new rules and structures that consciously favor the local, and follow the principle of subsidiarity, i.e., whatever decisions and activities can be undertaken locally should be. Whatever power can reside at the local level should reside there. Only when additional activity is required that cannot be satisfied locally, should power and activity move to the next higher level: region, nation, and finally the world.

C. Ecological sustainability

Economic activity needs to be ecologically sustainable. It should enable us to meet humans' genuine needs in the present without compromising the ability of future generations to meet theirs, and without diminishing the natural diversity of life on Earth or the viability of the planet's natural life-support systems.

D. Common heritage

There exist common heritage resources that should constitute a collective birthright of the whole species to be shared equitably among all. We assert that there are three categories of such resources. The first consists of the shared natural heritage of the water, land, air, forests, and fisheries on which our lives depend. These physical resources are in finite supply, essential to life, and existed long before any human. A second category includes the heritage of culture and knowledge that is the collective creation of our species. Finally, basic public services relating to health, education, public safety, and social security are "modern" common heritage resources representing the collective efforts of whole societies. They are also as essential to life in modern societies as are air and water. Justice therefore demands that they be readily available to all who need them. Any attempt by persons or corporations to monopolize ownership control of an essential common heritage resource for exclusive private gain to the exclusion of the needs of others is morally unconscionable and politically unacceptable.

E. Human rights

In 1948, governments of the world came together to adopt the United Nations Universal Declaration on Human Rights, which established certain core rights, such as "a standard of living adequate for … health and well-being …, including food, clothing, housing and medical care, and necessary social services, and the right to security in the event of unemployment." Traditionally, most of the human rights debate in the United States and other rich nations has focused on civil and political rights as paramount. We believe that it is the duty of governments to ensure these rights, but also to guarantee the economic, social and cultural rights of all people.

F. Jobs/livelihood/employment

A livelihood is a means of living. The right to a means of livelihood is therefore the most basic of all human rights. Sustainable societies must both protect the rights of workers in the formal sector and address the livelihood needs of the larger share of people who subsist in what has become known as the non-material, or "informal sector" (including small-scale, indigenous, and artisanal activities) as well as those who have no work or are seriously underemployed. Empowering workers to organize for basic rights and fair wages is vital to curb footloose corporations that pit workers against each other in a lose-lose race to the bottom. And, the reversal of globalization policies that displace small farmers from their land and fisherfolk from their coastal ecosystems are central to the goal of a world where all can live and work in dignity.

G. Food security and food safety

Communities and nations are stable and secure when people have enough food, particularly when nations can produce their own food. People also want safe food, a commodity that is increasingly scarce as global agribusiness firms spread chemical- and biotech-intensive agriculture around the world.

H. Equity

Economic globalization, under the current rules, has widened the gap between rich and poor countries and between rich and poor within most countries. The resulting social dislocation and tension are among the greatest threats to peace and security the world over. Greater equity both among nations and within them would reinforce both democracy and sustainable communities. Reducing the growing gap between rich and poor nations requires first and foremost the cancellation of the illegitimate debts of poor countries. And, it requires the replacement of the current institutions of global governance with new ones that include global fairness among their operating principles.

I. Diversity

A few decades ago, it was still possible to leave home and go somewhere else where the architecture was different, the landscape was different, the language, lifestyle, food, dress, and values were different. Today, farmers and filmmakers in France and India, indigenous communities worldwide, and millions of people elsewhere, are protesting to maintain that diversity. Tens of thousands of communities around the world have perfected local resource management systems that work, but they are now being undermined by corporate-led globalization. Cultural, biological, social, and economic diversity are central to a viable, dignified, and healthy life.

J. Precautionary principle

All activity should abide by the precautionary principle. When a practice or product raises potentially significant threats of harm to human health or the environment, precautionary action should be taken to restrict or ban it even if scientific uncertainty remains about whether or how it is actually causing that harm. Because it can take years for scientific proof of harm to be established – during which time undesirable or irreversible effects may continue to be inflicted – the proponents of a practice or product should bear the burden of proving that it is safe, before it is implemented.

Chapter III   Issues on Commodification of the Commons

This section grapples with one of the most pioneering yet difficult arenas in the alternatives dialogue: the question of whether certain goods and services should not be traded or subject to trade agreements, patents or commodification. Lengthy discussions among IFG members have clarified a lot of issues, but discussion is ongoing. The section will lay out the categories of goods and services that the drafters believe should be subject to different kinds of restrictions in global economic commerce: goods that come from the global or local commons, and goods which fulfill basic rights and needs. The section will then offer categories of proposed restrictions.

In a world where many resources have already been over-exploited and seriously depleted, there is constant pressure by global corporations and the public bureaucracies that serve them to privatize and monopolize the full range of common heritage resources from water to genetic codes that have thus far remained off limits to commodification and management as corporate profit centers. Indeed, the more essential the good or service in question to the maintenance of life, the greater its potential for generating monopoly profits and the more attractive its ownership and control becomes to global corporations.

Water, a commonly shared, irreplaceable, and fundamental requirement for the survival of all life, is a leading example. Everywhere around the world, global corporations are seeking to consolidate their ownership and monopoly control of the fresh water resources of rivers, lakes and streams for promotion as an export commodity – like computer memory or car tires. The rules of many new trade agreements directly assist this commodification process.

Another formerly pristine area – one that most human beings had never thought could or ought to be a commodity bought and sold for corporate profits – is the genetic structure of living beings, including humans, which is now falling rapidly within the control of "life science" industries (biotechnology), and coming increasingly under the purview of global trade agreements. A third area concerns indigenous knowledge of plant varieties, seeds, products of the forest, medicinal herbs, and biodiversity itself, which has been vital in successfully sustaining traditional societies for millennia. A fourth area is bioprospecting currently underway by global corporations seeking genetic materials from the skin and other body parts among native peoples. Several of these latter areas, and others, are subject to patenting (monopoly control) by large global corporations, protected under the Trade Related Intellectual Property Rights Agreement (TRIPS) of the WTO and a similar North American Free Trade Agreement (NAFTA) chapter. The net result of these new corporate protections and rights over formerly non-commodified biological materials is to make it costly, difficult or impossible for agricultural or indigenous communities to avail themselves of biological resources that they formerly freely enjoyed.

Parallel to such efforts at privatizing and commodifying areas of the global commons is the tremendous effort to privatize and commodify as many public services that were once taken care of within communities and then performed by local, state and national governments on behalf of all people. These services may address such basic needs as public health and hospital care; public education; public safety and protection; welfare and social security; water delivery and purity; sanitation; public broadcasting, museums and national cultural expressions; food safety systems; and prisons. While these areas may not have been traditionally defined as part of "the commons," in the same way as water, land, air, forests, pasture or other natural expressions of the earth that have been freely shared within communities for millennia, in the modern world these public services have nonetheless been generally understood to fall within the vital fundamental rights and needs of citizens living in any nominally successful, responsible society.

If the corporate globalists have their way in negotiations at the General Agreement on Trade in Services (GATS) of the WTO, or within the FTAA, the way will be cleared for many of these essential services to move directly into the hands of global corporations to be operated as corporate profit centers accountable only to the interests of their shareholders. As with corporatized healthcare in the United States, the rich may be well served, but the vast majority of people will be unsatisfied, overcharged, or abandoned.

In the view of the drafters of this document, this process of privatizing, monopolizing, and commodifying common heritage resources and turning public services into corporate profit centers and the protection of this process within global trade agreements, must be halted at once. There is an appropriate place for private ownership and markets to play in the management, allocation, and delivery of certain common heritage resources, as for example land, within a framework of effective democratically accountable public regulation that guarantees fair pricing, equitable access, quality, and public stewardship. There is no rightful place in any public body, process, or international agreement to facilitate the unaccountable private monopolization of common heritage resources and public services essential to life or to otherwise exclude any person from equitable access to such essential resources and services.

Chapter IV   The Case for Subsidiarity: Bias Away From the Global Toward the Local

It is the major conceit or gamble of the corporate globalists that by removing economic control from the places where it has traditionally resided – in nations, states, sub-regions, communities or indigenous societies – and placing that control into absentee authorities that operate globally via giant corporations and bureaucracies, that all levels of society will benefit. As we have seen, this is not true, and it is a principal reason why so many millions of people are angrily protesting.

The central modus operandi of the globalization model is to delocalize all controls over economic and political activity; a systematic, complete appropriation on the powers, decisions, options and functions that through prior history were fulfilled by the community, region or state. When sovereign powers are finally removed from the local and put into distant bureaucracies, local politics must also be redesigned to conform to the rules and practices of distant bureaucracies. Communities and nations that formerly operated in a relatively self-reliant manner, in the interests of their own peoples, are converted into unwilling subjects of this much larger, undemocratic, unaccountable global structure.

If democracy is based upon the idea that people must participate in the great decisions affecting their lives, then the system we find today of moving basic life decisions to distant venues of centralized, international institutions, which display a disregard for democratic participation, openness, accountability, and transparency, brings the death of democracy. We have reached the end of the road for that process. It's time to change directions.

A. Understanding subsidiarity

As globalization is the intractable problem, then logically a turn toward the local is inevitable; a reinvigoration of the conditions by which local communities regain the powers to determine and control their economic and political paths. Instead of shaping all systems to conform to a global model that emphasizes specialization of production, comparative advantage, export-oriented growth, monoculture, and homogenization of economic, cultural and political forms under the direction of transnational corporate institutions, we must reshape our institutions to favor exactly the opposite.

The operating principle for this turnaround is the concept of subsidiarity, i.e., favoring the local whenever a choice exists. In practice this means that all decisions should be made at the lowest level of governing authority competent to deal with it. Global health crises and global pollution issues often require cooperative international decisions. But most economic, cultural and political decisions should not be international; they should be made at the national, regional or local levels, depending on what they are. Power should be encouraged to evolve downward, not upward. Decisions should constantly move closer to the people most affected by them.

Economic systems should favor local production and markets rather than invariably being designed to serve long distance trade. This means shortening the length of lines for economic activity: fewer food miles; fewer oil supply miles; fewer travel-to-work miles. Technologies should also be chosen that best serve local control, rather than mega-technologies that operate globally.

B. The road to the local

Localization attempts to reverse the trend toward the global by discriminating actively in favor of the local in all policies. Depending on the context, the "local" is defined as a subgrouping within a nation-state; it can also be the nation-state itself or occasionally a regional grouping of nation-states. The overall idea is for power to devolve to the lowest unit appropriate for a particular goal.

Policies that bring about localization are ones that increase democratic control of the economy by communities and/or nation-states, taking it back from global institutions that have appropriated them: bureaucracies and global corporations. These may enable nations, local governments and communities to reclaim their economies; to make them as diverse as possible; and to rebuild stability into community life – to achieve a maximum self-reliance nationally and regionally in a way that ensures sustainable forms of development. [...]

Part XII Questions

1. What is "counterhegemonic" globalization, according to Evans, and what kind of impact has it had? What are the goals and methods of the movements arrayed against neoliberal globalization? What dilemmas do they face?
2. What are the three periods of the global justice movement, as described by Geoffrey Pleyers? What does the movement identify as the primary source of global injustice? What criticisms does the movement level against the World Bank and International Monetary Fund? What "alternative policies and programs"

does the movement support, and what are the prospects of the movement achieving major social change and poverty reduction?

3. Explain Bello's critique of the World Trade Organization. What does he mean by "deglobalization," and why does he think that the deglobalization of trade and finance is necessary? Is deglobalization necessary for the "global South" to develop economically and socially? How well does Bello's argument apply to other major global governance IGOs, such as the International Monetary Fund, the World Health Organization, or the International Postal Union?

4. Why does Shiva describe economic globalization as a "normative" and "political" process? What negative consequences does the latest wave of globalization have, and how does Shiva denounce these? How does native seed become a symbol of freedom for some antiglobalization groups?

5. Why does Marcos believe that neoliberal globalization causes "world war" and turns each country into a "battleground"? What must "rebels" do in their struggle against "the fence [that] is reproduced globally"? Does Marcos propose an alternative kind of globalization? Is his approach likely to draw many supporters?

6. How do both the World Social Forum (WSF) and the International Forum on Globalization (IFG) indict the current form of globalization? What specific demands does the WSF issue? What principles should guide institutions to govern the world economy, according to the IFG? Do the WSF and IFG selections show that a common worldview unites the alternative globalization movement?

Index

The Globalization Reader, Fifth Edition. Edited by Frank J. Lechner and John Boli.
Editorial material and organization © 2015 John Wiley & Sons, Ltd.
Published 2015 by John Wiley & Sons, Ltd.

251, 260, 262, 272, 275–6, 311–12, 317,
337, 421, 446, 545–6, 549–53, 587
movement, 551–3
standards, 247
Lagos, 43, 487
Laos, 204, 240
Latin America, 67, 73, 117, 138–41, 211, 225,
242, 255–7, 273, 275, 380–1, 410, 415,
429–30, 433, 435, 438–9, 445, 505, 552,
557, 562–3, 582
League of Nations, 312, 314, 317, 446
Lebanon, 46, 244, 327
legitimacy, 24, 47, 82–3, 142, 234, 237, 247,
250, 281, 314, 318, 347–8, 351–3, 356,
446, 448, 494, 532, 536, 560, 582
Lehman Brothers, 165, 209, 211–13
liberalism, 45, 47, 278, 418, 424, 453, 581
liberalization, 8, 168, 219–23, 226, 247–9,
252, 257, 268, 278–81, 366, 384–5, 547,
561, 569–70, 572–3
Liberia, 347
liberty, 7, 9, 11, 13–17, 34–5, 38–9, 42, 47,
144, 285, 450
Libya, 46–7, 98
Liebes, Tamar, 368–70
Lilly, Eli, and Company, 157
Lima, 139
Lisbon, 138–9
locals, 84, 138, 145, 457, 460, 486–91, 495
London, 12–13, 43, 64, 86, 97, 112, 114, 138,
146, 242, 295–6, 366, 389, 408, 419, 422,
429, 465, 479, 487, 529, 561
Los Angeles, 13, 17, 120, 129, 171, 181,
369, 569

Macaulay, Thomas Babington, 20
Madras, 97
Madrid, 68, 491
malaria, 203, 269, 301–3, 305, 357
Malawi, 207
Malaysia, 14, 74, 165, 194, 258, 422, 510–12,
514, 516–17, 562, 583
Mali, 323
malnutrition, 204, 306, 540
Manila, 44, 429
Manser, Bruno, 510, 512–13
Marcuse, Herbert, 70
market(s), 2–5, 8–9, 12, 14–15, 23–4, 26–30,
33–5, 37–40, 44, 47, 53, 56–9, 61–2,
64–5, 71–2, 74–5, 83, 98, 100, 107,

110–20, 122–3, 131, 142, 147–8,
157–8, 160, 164, 165–6, 168, 176–84,
186–8, 193–6, 203, 205, 207–13, 215–24,
226, 233–41, 243, 245–7, 249, 260,
262, 264–6, 278, 280, 285, 289,
291, 293, 295, 298–9, 305, 313, 352,
354, 356–7, 361, 364–5, 376–78,
380–8, 392, 398, 400–3, 405–11, 416,
437, 439–40, 451–3, 464, 476, 483, 487,
527, 532, 534, 546, 550–3, 558, 562–4,
566, 574–7, 580–1, 584, 587–8,
593–4
marriage, 35, 324, 384, 463–5, 467–8
Marx, Karl, 3, 11–13, 38, 53, 102, 376
Marxism, 33
Matson, Inc., 293–4
Mauritius, 203
McDonald's, 3, 32, 105, 107, 121–9, 161,
410, 437
McDonaldization, 95
McLuhan, Marshall, 87, 95, 490
McWorld, 3, 7, 9, 32–3, 35–40, 49
media, mass, 3, 5, 30–1, 34, 64, 66, 68–70, 72,
87, 95–6, 98, 100–2, 106, 160, 244, 260,
298–9, 344, 348, 351, 361–4, 367–70,
372, 374, 376–86, 388–90, 392, 394–6,
398, 400, 402–4, 406, 408, 410–11, 418,
421, 424, 430, 440, 445, 447, 458, 465–7,
482, 485, 490, 507–9, 513, 532, 547,
556, 559, 580, 583
media imperialism, 367–9
media policy, 386
mental illness, 160–2, 305
Mercosur, 45, 562
Mexico, 67, 101, 134, 138–9, 193, 225, 258,
260, 284, 288, 316, 327, 363–4, 372, 379,
397, 430, 458, 489, 531, 546, 555, 558,
569, 583, 586
Mexico City, 67, 260, 316, 489, 569
Meyer, John W., 77, 263
microfinance, 309, 313, 354–61
Microsoft, 15, 106
Migdal, Joel, 243
migration, 15, 19, 95, 97, 118, 131–2, 183,
240, 298, 414–15, 426, 484–5, 569
Millennium Development Goals, 202, 557
Milosevic, Slobodan, 342
Mitsubishi Group, 513, 517
mobility, social, 26, 75, 100, 178, 221, 237,
240, 245, 247, 298, 407, 488–9